The Book of a Thousand Poems

THE · BOOK · OF · A
·THOUSAND·
·POEMS·

A Family Treasury

PETER
BEDRICK
BOOKS
NEW YORK

This edition published by
Peter Bedrick Books
125 East 23 Street
New York, NY 10010

Library of Congress Cataloguing in Publication Data

The Book of a Thousand Poems
 Includes Indexes.
 Summary: A collection of poems by writers ranging from Wil-
liam Blake and Henry W. Longfellow to Emily Dickinson and
Robert L. Stevenson, arranged by topics such as "The Seasons,"
"Nursery Rhymes," and "Lullabies and Cradle Songs."

 1. Children's poetry, English.   2. Children's poetry,
American.   1. English poetry—Collections.   2. American
poetry—Collections.
PR1175.3.B66   1986   821'.008'092082   86–7862
ISBN 0–87226–084–4

Manufactured in the United States of America
First American edition September, 1986
10 9 8 7 6 5 4 3 2

Contents

The Anthology

It is hoped that this anthology of verse for young children will be found to be full of interest to the child of today. In addition to favourites chosen from well-known poets, much original verse, on subjects within the child's own experience and environment, has been included from the pages of *Child Education*. To suggest ways in which the anthology may be used may seem superfluous or even unnecessary, but in these unquiet days it is good sometimes to recall—even for ourselves—something of our pre-war ideals and aims (still present with us) when language training, clear speech, understanding of humour and fun, revelation of beauty in thought and appreciation of high values, were—and are—matters worthy of our preoccupation. It will be remembered that the use of poetic ideas in learning to speak and read, trains children in literary appreciation. We may watch idly the sunshine and the rain, but it takes a poet to tell of 'the uncertain glory of an April day'. Poetic study gives a fuller, richer meaning to the reading of word or phrase, the effect of which, if introduced in early years, will continue through life.

Almost parallel with this is the thought that a child need not always comprehend fully all that a poem may mean, but in later years of understanding, to recall such a poem, once learnt, may bring him the greatest happiness. Again—for who can fathom the workings of the human spirit?—a poem seemingly beyond a child's years or comprehension may communicate to him—like the highest teaching—something far beyond mere speech. It may be only a gossamer thread of delicate sparkle, but it can weave and bind; or it may open a window through which he can see to far horizons—'magic casements opening on the foam of perilous seas in faery lands forlorn'. Wonder, in a child, is the beginning of worship. It is we (the upgrown) who often miss 'the many-splendoured thing'.

Some Examples for the Older Children

Again, we know that all children need adventure: it is almost as necessary to them as their sense of security. If it is not abundantly provided in their own lives they get a kind of delicious, fearful joy when they experience it in poem or story. For the older children, therefore, such poems as *The Pedlar's Caravan, The Wraggle Taggle Gipsies, Meg Merrilees, The Jovial Beggar, The Toy Band,* provide this experience, while the longing of *The Old Woman of the Road* touches something of its antithesis—the need of rest and home. *Robin's Song* gives a feeling of thinking backward in time, 'before the Legions came', and so suggests the passing show exemplified in history.

The Wood of Flowers is an example of sheer happiness, while wonder lingers in *The Darkening Garden* and *Who Has Seen the Wind?* A domestic baby ballad is *Little Dame Crump,* whose adventures can be joyously shared round, verse by verse. *The Clothes Line,* with the Flip, Flap, Flop of its fluttering creatures, reveals a hitherto unsuspected source of poetic expression. Lastly, the eternal loveliness of the Christmas story sings its musical way in:

> Winds through the olive trees softly did blow
> Round little Bethlehem, long, long ago.

A Christmas Song

Suggestions for Practical Use
The following further suggestions are offered for the practical use of the anthology:

1 *Rhyme and Rhythm* Images, jingle, pattern, music, repetition— all satisfy an early rhythmic need of the child, and hark back to primitive language days. Two examples which will give delight to the little ones are: *A Cat Came Fiddling out of a Barn,* and (with four little stresses in each line):

> Hów many dáys has my Báby to pláy?
> Sáturday, Súnday, Móndáy,
> Tuésday, Wédnesday, Thúrsday, Fríday,
> Sáturday, Súnday, Móndáy

Incidentally the days of the week are playfully remembered.

Inner rhymes and cross rhythms will later bring delight and interest to the older children.

2 *Speech Purposes* Training in speech, clear articulation and correct pronunciation are obvious aims in the presentation or speaking of verse, as well as modulation of the voice to indicate meaning—surprise, fear, expectation, longing, delight, or mere narration, as in a story poem or ballad.

3 *Natural Punctuation* Much practice can be achieved in natural phrasing before knowledge of comma or full stop. Observation of rhyme-phrases—where each is a complete unit of thought—is

helpful later in 'reading for content', and has its parallel in music where the phrase gives meaning, also in sentence methods of teaching reading.

4 *Verse Speaking* Opportunities here abound in variety for ensemble work, solo and refrain, dialogue, or other antiphonal ways as in question and answer.

5 *Individual Work* A poem may be spoken individually or shared, verse by verse, as in a narrative. This latter allocation to different voices brings out dramatic qualities and varying tone-colour. Moreover, alertness is achieved, and joy in sharing.

6 *Own Choice* In an extensive anthology much individual choice is provided so that the child can, after hearing the verses spoken by the teacher, choose those he wishes to memorise. It is significant that he learns and interprets best where his preference lies.

7 *Memory and Imagination* A poem, like a beautiful piece of music, is mostly a record of an experience—an emotional experience 'recollected in tranquillity'—or sometimes is mere narration of an incident or story. If the experience is a familiar one, memory is drawn upon; if unfamiliar, imagination bodies forth or is nourished by description of the unknown.

8 *Addition to Vocabulary* Poetry or verse is one of the chief channels through which the vocabularly is enriched. New words and phrases should be explained separately, then in their context. Poetic licence, too, might also be anticipated.

9 *Training in Observation* This training will have ample and particular scope in the many nature verses, also animal poems, throughout the anthology, and the children will take delight in verifying facts in their gardening activities and walks farther afield. Here beauty and truth are faithfully sought, and it may be that:

> Truth embodied in a tale
> Shall enter in at lowly doors

1942   J. MURRAY MACBAIN

Nursery Rhymes
and Traditional Verse

Round about in a fair ring-a
Thus we dance and thus we sing-a

Bell horses, bell horses,
What time of day?
One o'clock, two o'clock,
Three and away.

Round about in a fair ring-a,
Thus we dance and thus we sing-a;
Trip and go, to and fro,
Over this green-a;
All about, in and out,
Over this green-a.

Here we come a-piping,
In Springtime and in May;
Green fruit a-ripening,
And Winter fled away.
The Queen she sits upon the strand,
Fair as a lily, white as wand;
Seven billows on the sea,
Horses riding fast and free,
And bells beyond the sand.

Here we go up, up, up,
And here we go down, down, downy,
And here we go backwards and forwards,
And here we go round, round, roundy.

On Mayday we dance,
On Mayday we sing,
For this is the day
We welcome the Spring.

2

Full early in the morning
Awakes the summer sun,
The month of June arriving,
The cold and night are done;
The cuckoo is a fine bird,
She whistles as she flies,
And as she whistles "cuckoo,"
The bluer grow the skies.

As I went up the garden
I found a little farthing;
I gave it to my mother,
To buy a little brother;
My brother was a sailor,
He sailed across the sea,
And all the fish that he could catch
Were one, two, three.

Bless you, bless you, bonnie bee:
Say, when will your wedding be?
If it be to-morrow day,
Take your wings and fly away.

How many miles to Barley Bridge?
Fourscore miles and ten!
Shall we be there by candlelight?
Yes, and back again:
If your heels are nimble and light,
You may get there by candlelight.
Open the doors as wide as wide,
And let King George go thro' with his bride!
A curtsy to you, and curtsy to you,
If you please, will you let the king's horses go through?

3

Monday's child is fair of face,
Tuesday's child is full of grace,
Wednesday's child is full of woe,
Thursday's child has far to go,
Friday's child is loving and giving,
Saturday's child works hard for a living,
But the child that is born on the Sabbath day
Is bonny, and blithe, and good, and gay.

A cat came fiddling out of a barn,
With a pair of bagpipes under her arm,
She could sing nothing but "Fiddle-de-de.
The mouse has married the bumble bee."
Pipe, cat—dance, mouse—
We'll have a wedding at our good house.

Cock Robin got up early
    At the break of day,
And went to Jenny's window
    To sing a roundelay,
He sang Cock Robin's love
    To the little Jenny Wren,
And when he got unto the end,
    Then he began again.

The lion and the unicorn
    Were fighting for the crown;
The lion beat the unicorn
    All round the town.
Some gave them white bread,
    And some gave them brown;
Some gave them plum cake,
    And sent them out of town.

Dame, get up and bake your pies,
Bake your pies,
Bake your pies,
Dame, get up and bake your pies,
On Christmas Day in the morning.

Dame Trot and her cat
Sat down for to chat;
The Dame sat on this side,
And Puss sat on that.

"Puss," says the Dame,
"Can you catch a rat,
Or a mouse in the dark?"
"Purr," says the cat.

On the wind of January
Down flits the snow,
Travelling from the frozen north
As cold as it can blow.

If all the seas were one sea,
What a great sea that would be!
If all the trees were one tree,
What a great tree that would be!
And if all the axes were one axe,
What a great axe that would be!
And if all the men were one man,
What a great man that would be!
And if the great man took the great axe
And cut down the great tree,
And let it fall into the great sea,
What a splish-splash that would be!

"Little girl, little girl,
    Where have you been?"
"Gathering roses
    To give to the Queen."
"Little girl, little girl,
    What gave she you?"
"She gave me a diamond
    As big as my shoe."

Diddle, diddle, dumpling,
My son John
Went to bed
With his stockings on:
One shoe off,
And the other shoe on:
Diddle, diddle, dumpling,
My son John.

Draw a pail of water
For my lady's daughter;
My father's a king, and my mother's a queen,
My two little sisters are dressed in green,
    Stamping grass and parsley,
    Marigold leaves and daisies.
    One rush, two rush,
Prithee, fine lady, come under my bush.

In the month of February,
    When green leaves begin to spring,
Little lambs do skip like fairies,
    Birds do couple, build, and sing.

Girls and boys come out to play,
The moon doth shine as bright as day;
Leave your supper and leave your sleep,
And come with your playfellows in the street,
Come with a whoop and come with a call.
Come with a goodwill or not at all.
Up the ladder and down the wall,
A halfpenny roll will serve us all.
You find milk and I'll find flour,
And we'll make a pudding in half an hour.

Where are you going,
My little kittens?

We are going to town
To get us some mittens.

What! mittens for kittens!
Do kittens wear mittens?
Who ever saw little kittens with mittens?

Once I saw a little bird going hop, hop, hop.
So I cried, "Little bird, will you stop, stop, stop?"
And was going to the window to say "How do you do?"
When he shook his little tail and away he flew.

One misty moisty morning
    When cloudy was the weather,
There I met an old man
    Clothèd all in leather;

Clothèd all in leather,
    With cap under his chin,—
How do you do. and how do you do,
    And how do you do again?

7

The first of April, some do say,
Is set apart for All Fools' Day,
But why the people call it so
Nor I nor they themselves do know.

Go to bed early wake up with joy;
Go to bed late—cross girl or boy.
Go to bed early—ready for play;
Go to bed late—moping all day.
Go to bed early—no pains or ills;
Go to bed late—doctors and pills.
Go to bed early—grow very tall;
Go to bed late—stay very small.

The grand old Duke of York,
  He had ten thousand men;
He marched them up to the top of the hill
  And he marched them down again!
And when they were up, they were up,
  And when they were down, they were down,
And when they were neither down nor up,
  They were neither up nor down.

Willie boy, Willie boy, where are you going?
  I will go with you, if I may.
I'm going to the meadows to see them mowing,
  I'm going to see them make the hay.

Hey diddle, dinkety, poppety pet,
The merchants of London they wear scarlet;
Silk in the collar and gold in the hem,
So merrily march with the merchantmen.

The dove says Coo,
What shall I do?
I can hardly maintain my two.
Pooh, says the wren,
Why, I've got ten
And keep them all like gentlemen!

Hickety, pickety,
My black hen,
She lays eggs
For gentlemen;
Sometimes nine,
And sometimes ten.
Hickety, pickety,
My black hen!

Hot-cross buns! Hot-cross buns!
One a penny, two a penny,
Hot-cross buns!
If you have no daughters,
Give them to your sons,
One a penny, two a penny,
Hot-cross buns!
But if you have none of these little elves,
Then you may eat them all yourselves.

I had a little hobby-horse,
And it was dapple grey;
Its head was made of peastraw,
Its tail was made of hay.

I sold it to an old woman
For a copper groat;
And I'll not sing my song again
Without a new coat.

I had a little pony,
　　His name was Dapple-gray,
I lent him to a lady,
　　To ride a mile away;
She whipped him, she slashed him,
　　She rode him through the mire;
I would not lend my pony now
　　For all the lady's hire.

Pitty Patty Polt!
Shoe the wild colt,
Here a nail,
There a nail,
Pitty Patty Polt!

Here's to the poor widow from Babylon
With six poor children all alone:
One can bake and one can brew,
One can shape and one can sew,
One can sit at the fire and spin,
One can bake a cake for the king.
Come choose you east, come choose you west,
Come choose you the one that you love the best.

I had a little nut-tree, nothing would it bear
But a silver nutmeg and a golden pear;
The King of Spain's daughter came to visit me,
And all was because of my little nut-tree.
I skipped over water, I dancèd over sea,
And all the birds in the air couldn't catch me.

Little Boy Blue, come, blow up your horn,
The sheep's in the meadow, the cow's in the corn;
But where is the boy that looks after the sheep?
He is under the haystack, fast asleep.
Will you wake him? No, not I;
For if I do, he'll be sure to cry.

Juniper, Juniper,
    Green in the snow;
Sweetly you smell
    And prickly you grow.

Juniper, Juniper,
    Blue in the fall:
Give me some berries,
    Prickles and all.

Said a frog on a log,
    "Listen, little Bunny.
Will you ride by my side?
    Wouldn't that be funny!"

Jeanie, come tie my,
    Jeanie, come tie my,
Jeanie, come tie my bonny cravat;
    I've tied it behind,
    I've tied it before,
And I've tied it so often, I'll tie it no more.

I had a little hen, the prettiest ever seen,
She washed me the dishes and kept the house clean.

She went to the mill to fetch me some flour,
She brought it home in less than an hour.

She baked me my bread, she brewed me my ale,
She sat by the fire and told many a fine tale.

Peter and Michael were two little menikin,
They kept a cock and a fat little henikin;
Instead of an egg, it laid a gold penikin,
Oh, how they wish it would do it againikin!

I had a little husband,
  No bigger than my thumb;
I put him in a pint pot,
  And there bade him drum.

I bought a little horse
  That galloped up and down;
I bridled him, and saddled him,
  And sent him out of town.

Little Robin Redbreast
Sat upon a tree,
He sang merrily,
As merrily as could be.
He nodded with his head,
And his tail waggled he,
As little Robin Redbreast
Sat upon a tree.

Welcome, little Robin,
  With your scarlet breast,
In this winter weather
  Cold must be your nest.
Hopping on the carpet,
  Picking up the crumbs,
Robin knows the children
  Love him when he comes.

A little cock sparrow sat on a tree,
Looking as happy as happy could be,
Till a boy came by with his bow and arrow,
Says he, "I will shoot the little cock sparrow.

"His body will make me a nice little stew,
And his giblets will make me a little pie too."
Says the little cock sparrow, "I'll be shot if I stay,'
So he clapped his wings and flew away.

Where are you going,
My little cat?

I am going to town,
To get me a hat.

What! a hat for a cat!
A cat get a hat!
Who ever saw a cat with a hat?

A man went a-hunting at Reigate;
He wished to jump over a high gate.
Said the owner, "Go round,
With your gun and your hound,
For you never shall jump over my gate."

Rock-a-bye, baby, thy cradle is green;
Father's a nobleman, mother's a queen;
And Betty's a lady, and wears a gold ring;
And Johnny's a drummer, and drums for the king.

"Who's that ringing at the front door bell?"
Miau! Miau! Miau!
"I'm a little Pussy Cat and I'm not very well!"
Miau! Miau! Miau!
"Then rub your nose in a bit of mutton fat."
Miau! Miau! Miau!
"For that's the way to cure a little Pussy Cat."
Miau! Miau! Miau!

Pussy Cat, Pussy Cat. where have you been?
I've been to London to look at the Queen.

Pussy Cat, Pussy Cat, what did you there?
I frightened a little mouse under the chair.

From house to house he goes,
    A messenger small and slight;
And whether it rains or snows,
    He sleeps outside in the night.

Answer: A Lane.

Robin sang sweetly
    In the Autumn days,
"There are fruits for every one.
    Let all give praise!"

Poor old Robinson Crusoe!
Poor old Robinson Crusoe!
    They made him a coat
    From an old nanny goat,
I wonder how they could do so!
    With a ring-a-ting tang,
    And a ring-a-ting tang,
Poor old Robinson Crusoe!

Ride a-cock horse to Banbury Cross,
    To see a fine lady upon a white horse;
Rings on her fingers and bells on her toes,
    She shall have music wherever she goes.

"Which is the way to London Town,
To see the King in his golden crown?"
"One foot up and one foot down,
That's the way to London Town."
"Which is the way to London Town,
To see the Queen in her silken gown?"
"Left! Right! Left! Right! up and down,
Soon you'll be in London Town!"

14

Lilies are white,
    Rosemary's green;
When you are king,
    I will be queen.

Roses are red,
    Lavender's blue;
If you will have me,
    I will have you.

To market, to market, to buy a fat pig;
Home again, home again, jiggety jig.
To market, to market, to buy a fine hog;
Home again, home again, joggety jog.

Six little mice sat down to spin,
Pussy passed by, and she peeped in.
"What are you at, my little men?"
"Making coats for gentlemen."
"Shall I come in and bite off your threads?"
"No, no, Miss Pussy, you'll snip off our heads."
"Oh, no, I'll not, I'll help you to spin."
"That may be so, but you don't come in!"

There was a crooked man, and he went a crooked mile,
He found a crooked sixpence against a crooked stile:
He bought a crooked cat, which caught a crooked mouse,
And they all lived together in a little crooked house.

The doggies went to the mill,
This way and that way;
They took a lick out of this one's sack,
They took a lick out of that one's sack,
And a leap in the stream, and a dip in the dam,
And went walloping, walloping, walloping home!

High in the pine-tree
The little Turtle-dove
Made a little nursery,
To please her little love.
"Coo," said the Turtle-dove,
"Coo," said she;
In the long shady branches
Of the dark pine-tree.

Cock a doodle doo!
My dame has lost her shoe;
My master's lost his fiddling stick,
And don't know what to do.

Cock a doodle doo!
What is my dame to do?
Till master finds his fiddling stick,
She'll dance without her shoe.

Cock a doodle doo!
My dame has found her shoe,
And master's found his fiddling stick,
Sing doodle doodle doo!

Cock a doodle doo!
My dame will dance with you,
While master fiddles his fiddling stick,
For dame and doodle doo.

There was a little dog, and he had a little tail,
And he used to wag, wag, wag it.
But whenever he was sad because he had been bad,
On the ground he would drag, drag, drag it.

He had a little nose, as of course you would suppose,
And on it was a muz-muz-muzzle,
And to get it off he'd try till a tear stood in his eye,
But he found it a puz-puz-puzzle.

Robin and Richard
  Were two little men,
They did not awake
  Till the clock struck ten:

Then up starts Robin,
  And looks at the sky:
"Oh! Brother Richard,
  The sun's very high!"

They both were ashamed
  On such a fine day,
When they were wanted
  To make new hay.

Do you go before,
  With bottle and bag,
I will come after
  On little jack nag.

When I was a little boy
  I lived by myself,
And all the bread and cheese I got
  I put upon the shelf.

The rats and the mice,
  They led me such a life,
I was forced to go to London
  To get myself a wife.

The roads were so bad,
  And the lanes were so narrow.
I could not get my wife home
  In a wheelbarrow.

The wheelbarrow broke,
  And my wife had a fall;
Down came the wheelbarrow,
  Wife and all.

Robin Hood, Robin Hood,
In the mickle wood!
Little John, Little John,
He to the town has gone.

Robin Hood, Robin Hood,
Is telling his beads
All in the green wood,
Among the green weeds.

Little John, Little John,
If he comes no more,
Robin Hood, Robin Hood,
He will fret full sore!

This is the Key of the Kingdom:
In that Kingdom is a city;
In that city is a town;
In that town is a street;
In that street there winds a lane;
In that lane there is a yard;
In that yard there is a house;
In that house there waits a room
In that room an empty bed;
And on that bed a basket—
A Basket of Sweet Flowers:
Of Flowers, of Flowers;
A basket of Sweet Flowers.

Flowers in a Basket;
Basket on the bed;
Bed in the chamber;
Chamber in the house;
House in the weedy yard;
Yard in the winding lane;
Lane in the broad street;
Street in the high town;
Town in the city;
City in the Kingdom—
This is the Key of the Kingdom.
Of the Kingdom this is the Key.

A knight and a lady
  Went riding one day
Far into the forest,
  Away, away.

"Fair knight," said the lady,
  "I pray, have a care.
This forest is evil;
  Beware, beware."

A fiery red dragon
  They spied on the grass;
The lady wept sorely,
  Alas! Alas!

The knight slew the dragon,
  The lady was gay,
They rode on together,
  Away, away.

Little Jenny Wren,
  Fell sick upon a time;
In came Robin Redbreast,
  And brought her bread and wine.

"Eat of my cake, Jenny,
  And drink of my wine";
"Thank you, Robin, kindly,
  You shall be mine."

Jenny she got well,
  And stood upon her feet,
And told Robin plainly,
  "I love you not a bit."

Robin he was angry,
  And hopped upon a twig,
"Out upon you, fie upon you,
  Bold-faced jig!"

A dis, a dis, a green grass
A dis, a dis, a dis;
Come, all you pretty fair maids
And dance along with us.

For we are going roving,
A roving in this land;
We take this pretty fair maid,
We take her by the hand.

She shall get a duke, my dear,
As duck do get a drake;
And she shall have a young prince,
For her own fair sake.

And if this young prince chance to die,
She shall get another;
The bells will ring, and the birds will sing,
And we clap hands together.

A farmer went trotting on his grey mare,
Bumpety, bumpety, bump!
With his daughter behind him so rosy and fair,
Lumpety, lumpety, lump!

A raven cried "Crook" and they all tumbled down,
Bumpety, bumpety, bump!
The mare broke her knees, and the farmer his crown,
Lumpety, lumpety, lump!

The mischievous raven flew laughing away,
Bumpety, bumpety, bump!
And said he would serve them the same the next day,
Lumpety, lumpety, lump!

Down by the meadows, chasing butterflies,
Two little folk were taken by surprise,
When a tiny gallant came, with a bow and a smile,
And begged them to be seated, in his mushroom house awhile

Spring is coming, spring is coming,
  Birdies, build your nest;
Weave together straw and feather,
  Doing each your best.

Spring is coming, spring is coming,
  Flowers are coming too;
Pansies, lilies, daffodillies,
  Now are coming through.

Spring is coming, spring is coming,
  All around is fair;
Shimmer and quiver on the river,
  Joy is everywhere.
We wish you a happy May.

Which is the way to London Town?
Over the hills, across the down:
Over the ridges and over the bridges,
That is the way to London Town.

And what shall I see in London Town?
Many a building old and brown,
Many a real, old-fashioned street
You'll be sure to see in London Town.

What else shall I see in London Town?
Many a maiden in silken gown;
Pretty pink faces, tied up in laces,
You'll certainly see in London Town.

Then onward I hurried to London Town,
Over the hills and across the down,
Over the ridges and over the bridges,
Until I found me in London Town.

Whether the weather be fine, or whether the weather be not,
Whether the weather be cold, or whether the weather be hot,
We'll weather the weather, whatever the weather,
  Whether we like it or not.

21

Three Riddles

The man in the wilderness asked of me
How many strawberries grew in the sea.
I answered him, as I thought good,
As many red herrings as grew in the wood.

In Spring I look gay
Deck'd in comely array,
In Summer more clothing I wear;
When colder it grows
I fling off my clothes,
And in Winter quite naked appear.

Answer: A Tree

I have a little sister, they call her Peep, Peep,
She wades the water so deep, deep, deep;
She climbs the mountains, high, high, high;
Poor little creature, she has but one eye.

Answer: A Star

One, two,
    Buckle my shoe;
Three four,
    Knock at the door;
Five, six,
    Pick up sticks;
Seven, eight,
    Lay them straight;
Nine, ten,
    A good fat hen.
Eleven, twelve,
    Dig and delve;
Thirteen, fourteen,
    Maids a-courting;
Fifteen, sixteen,
    Maids in the kitchen;
Seventeen, eighteen,
    Maids a-waiting;
Nineteen, twenty,
    My plate's empty.

Once there lived a little man
  Where a little river ran,
And he had a little farm and a little dairy O!
  And he had a little plough,
  And a little dappled cow,
Which he often called his pretty little fairy O!

And his dog he called Fidèle,
  For he loved his master well,
And he had a little pony for his pleasure O!
  In a sty, not very big,
  He'd a frisky little pig
Which he often called his little piggy treasure O!

Simple Simon

Simple Simon met a pieman
  Going to the fair;
Says Simple Simon to the pieman,
  "Let me taste your ware."

Says the pieman unto Simon,
  "Show me first your penny";
Says Simple Simon to the pieman,
  "Indeed I have not any."

Simple Simon went a-fishing
  For to catch a whale;
All the water he had got
  Was in his mother's pail.

Simple Simon went to look
  If plums grew on a thistle;
He pricked his fingers very much
  Which made poor Simon whistle.

When the wind is in the east,
'Tis good for neither man nor beast;
When the wind is in the north,
The skilful fisher goes not forth;
When the wind is in the south,
It blows the bait in the fishes' mouth
When the wind is in the west,
Then 'tis at the very best.

My mother said that I never should
Play with the gipsies in the wood;
The wood was dark, the grass was green,
In came Sally with a tambourine.

I went to the sea — no ships to get across,
I paid ten shillings for a blind white horse.
I jumped on his back, and was off in a crack;
Sally, tell your mother I shall never come back.

There was a little Rabbit sprig,
Which being little was not big;
He always walked upon his feet,
And never fasted when he eat.
When from a place he did run away,
He never at that place did stay;
And when he ran, as I am told,
He ne'er stood still for young or old
Tho' ne'er instructed by a cat,
He knew a mouse was not a rat;
One day, as I am certified,
He took a whim and fairly died:
And, as I'm told, by men of sense,
He never has been walking since.

Little Dame Crump

Little Dame Crump, with her little hair broom,
One morning was sweeping her little bedroom,
When, casting her little grey eyes on the ground,
In a sly little corner a penny she found.

"Ods bobs!" cried the Dame, while she stared with surprise.
"How lucky I am! bless my heart, what a prize!
To market I'll go, and a pig I will buy,
And little John Gubbins shall make him a stye."

So she washed her face clean, and put on her gown,
And locked up the house, and set off for the town;
When to market she went, and a purchase she made
Of a little white pig, and a penny she paid.

When she'd purchased the pig, she was puzzled to know
How they both should get home, if the pig would not go;
So fearing lest piggie should play her a trick,
She drove him along with a little crab stick.

Piggie ran till they came to the foot of a hill,
Where a little bridge stood o'er the stream of a mill;
Piggie grunted and squeaked, but no farther would go;
Oh, fie! Piggie, fie! to serve little Dame so.

She went to the mill, and she borrowed a sack
To put the pig in, and took him on her back;
Piggie squeaked to get out, but the little Dame said,
"If you won't go by fair means, why, you must be made."

At last to the end of her journey she came,
And was mightily glad when she got the pig hame;
She carried him straight to his nice little stye,
And gave him some hay and clean straw nice and dry.

With a handful of peas then Piggie she fed,
And put on her night-cap and got into bed;
Having first said her prayers, she extinguished the light
And being quite tired, we'll wish her good night.

An Old Rhyme

I went to market and bought me a Cat.
Cat had four legs, I had but two.
'Tis almost midnight, what shall I do?

I went a little further and found me a Dog.
Dog wouldn't carry the cat; Cat wouldn't goo.
'Tis almost midnight; what shall I do?

I went a little further and found me a Boy.
Boy wouldn't carry the dog;
Dog wouldn't carry the cat; Cat wouldn't goo.
'Tis almost midnight; what shall I do?

I went a little further and found me a Stick.
Stick wouldn't beat the boy;
Boy wouldn't carry the dog;
Dog wouldn't carry the cat; Cat wouldn't goo.
'Tis almost midnight; what shall I do?

I went a little further and found me a Fire.
Fire wouldn't burn the stick;
Stick wouldn't beat the boy;
Boy wouldn't carry the dog;
                    Repeat as before

I went a little further and found me some Water.
Water wouldn't quench the fire;
Fire wouldn't burn the stick;
                    Repeat as before

I went a little further and found me an Ox.
Ox wouldn't drink the water;
Water wouldn't quench the fire;
                    Repeat as before

I went a little further and found me a Butcher.
Butcher wouldn't kill the ox;
Ox wouldn't drink the water;
                    Repeat as before

I went a little further and found me a Rope.
Rope wouldn't hang the butcher;
  Repeat as before

I went a little further and found me some Grease.
Grease wouldn't grease the rope;
  Repeat as before

I went a little further and found me a Rat.
Rat began to eat the grease; Grease began to grease the rope,
Rope began to hang the butcher; Butcher began to kill the ox;
Ox began to drink the water; Water began to quench the fire;
Fire began to burn the stick; Stick began to beat the boy;
Boy began to carry the dog; Dog began to carry the cat;
Cat began to goo,
So now it's all over and I am happy.

Thoughts for a Cold Day

A little bit of blowing,
  A little bit of snow,
A little bit of growing,
  And crocuses will show;
On every twig that's lonely
  A new green leaf will spring;
On every patient tree-top
  A thrush will stop and sing.

Scaring Crows

O all you little blackey tops,
Pray, don't you eat my father's crops,
While I lie down to take a nap.
  Shua-O! Shua-O!

If father he perchance should come,
With his cocked hat and his long gun,
Then you must fly and I must run.
  Shua-O! Shua-O!

When good King Arthur ruled this land,
  He was a goodly king;
He stole three pecks of barley meal,
  To make a bag-pudding.

A bag-pudding the queen did make,
  And stuffed it well with plums:
And in it put great lumps of fat,
  As big as my two thumbs.

The king and queen did eat thereof,
  And noblemen beside;
And what they could not eat that night,
  The queen next morning fried.

The Mouse, The Frog and The Little Red Hen

Once a Mouse, a Frog, and a Little Red Hen,
  Together kept a house;
The Frog was the laziest of frogs,
  And lazier still was the Mouse.

The work all fell on the Little Red Hen,
  Who had to get the wood,
And build the fires, and scrub, and cook,
  And sometimes hunt the food.

One day, as she went scratching round,
  She found a bag of rye;
Said she, "Now who will make some bread?"
  Said the lazy Mouse, "Not I."

"Nor I," croaked the Frog as he drowsed in the shade,
  Red Hen made no reply,
But flew around with bowl and spoon,
  And mixed and stirred the rye.

"Who'll make the fire to bake the bread?"
  Said the Mouse again, "Not I,"
And, scarcely op'ning his sleepy eyes,
  Frog made the same reply.

The Little Red Hen said never a word,
  But a roaring fire she made;
And while the bread was baking brown,
  "Who'll set the table?" she said.

"Not I," said the sleepy Frog with a yawn;
  "Nor I," said the Mouse again.
So the table she set and the bread put on,
  "Who'll eat this bread?" said the Hen.

"I will!" cried the Frog. "And I!" squeaked the Mouse,
  As they near the table drew:
"Oh, no, you won't!" said the Little Red Hen,
  And away with the loaf she flew.

Old Mother Hubbard

Old Mother Hubbard
Went to the cupboard
To get her poor dog a bone;
But when she got there,
The cupboard was bare,
And so the poor dog got none.

She went to the baker's
To buy him some bread;
But when she got back
The poor dog was dead.

She went to the joiner's
To buy him a coffin;
But when she got back
The doggie was laughing.

She took a clean dish
    To get him some tripe;
But when she came back
    He was smoking his pipe.

She went to the fishmonger's
    To buy him some fish;
And when she came back.
    He was licking the dish.

She went to the tavern
    For white wine and red;
But when she came back
    The dog stood on his head.

She went to the hatter's
    To buy him a hat;
But when she came back
    He was feeding the cat.

She went to the cobbler's
    To buy him some shoes;
But when she came back
    He was reading the news.

The Dame made a curtsey,
    The dog made a bow;
The Dame said, "Your servant,"
    The dog said, "Bow-wow."

This wonderful dog
    Was Dame Hubbard's delight;
He could sing, he could dance,
    He could read, he could write.

She gave him rich dainties
    Whenever he fed,
And erected a monument
    When he was dead.

A Party Song

Merry have we met
And merry have we been;
Merry let us part,
And merry meet again.

With a merry sing-song,
Happy, gay and free,
With a merry ding-dong
Again we'll happy be.

The Squirrel

The winds they did blow,
　The leaves they did wag;
Along came a beggar boy
　And put me in his bag.
He took me to London;
　A lady did me buy,
And put me in a silver cage,
　And hung me up on high;
With apples by the fire,
　And hazel nuts to crack,
Besides a little feather bed
　To rest my tiny back.

The Cuckoo

In April
Come he will,
In flow'ry May
He sings all day,
In leafy June
He changes his tune,
In bright July
He's ready to fly,
In August
Go he must.

The House that Jack Built

This is the house that Jack built.

This is the malt
That lay in the house that Jack built.

This is the rat
That ate the malt
That lay in the house that Jack built.

This is the cat
That killed the rat
That ate the malt
That lay in the house that Jack built.

This is the dog
That worried the cat
That killed the rat
That ate the malt
That lay in the house that Jack built.

This is the cow with the crumpled horn
That tossed the dog
That worried the cat
That killed the rat
That ate the malt
That lay in the house that Jack built.

This is the maiden all forlorn
That milked the cow with the crumpled horn
That tossed the dog
That worried the cat
That killed the rat
That ate the malt
That lay in the house that Jack built.

That is the man all tattered and torn
That kissed the maiden all forlorn
That milked the cow with the crumpled horn
That tossed the dog
That worried the cat

That killed the rat
That ate the malt
That lay in the house that Jack built.

This is the priest all shaven and shorn
That married the man all tattered and torn
That kissed the maiden all forlorn
That milked the cow with the crumpled horn
That tossed the dog
That worried the cat
That killed the rat
That ate the malt
That lay in the house that Jack built.

This is the cock that crowed in the morn
That waked the priest all shaven and shorn
That married the man all tattered and torn
That kissed the maiden all forlorn
That milked the cow with the crumpled horn
That tossed the dog
That worried the cat
That killed the rat
That ate the malt
That lay in the house that Jack built.

Sing Ivy

My father left me three acres of land,
Sing ivy, sing ivy;
My father left me three acres of land,
Sing holly, go whistle, and ivy!

I ploughed it with a ram's horn,
Sing ivy, sing ivy;
And sowed it all over with one peppercorn,
Sing holly, go whistle, and ivy!

I harrowed it with a bramble bush,
Sing ivy, sing ivy;
And reaped it with my little penknife,
Sing holly, go whistle, and ivy.

Poems for the Very Young

Now rocking horse, rocking horse, where shall we go?
The world's such a very wide place, you must know

Merry Birds

Merrily, merrily,
All the spring,
Merrily, merrily
Small birds sing.
All through April,
All through May,
Small birds merrily
Carol all day.

Rodney Bennett

Seven Little Pigs

Seven little pigs went to market,
One of them fell down;
One of them, he ran away,
And five got to town.

Shower and Sunshine

Shower and sunshine,
Sunshine and shower,
Green are the tree tops
And blooming the flower,
Nesting are wild birds,
Air full of song;
Hark! now the cuckoo—
He does not stay long.

Maud Morin

A Rhyme for Washing Hands

Wash, hands, wash,
Daddy's gone to plough.
Splash, hands, splash,
They're all washed now.

Writing Letters

Every time I write a letter,
   If I do not write too fast,
It is sure to be a better,
   Neater letter than the last.

Rodney Bennett

The Queen Bee

When I was in the garden,
   I saw a great Queen Bee;
She was the very largest one
   That I did ever see.
She wore a shiny helmet
   And a lovely velvet gown,
But I was rather sad, because
   She didn't wear a crown.

Mary K. Robinson

Action Rhyme

The policeman walks with heavy tread,
   Left, right, left, right,
Swings his arms, holds up his head.
   Left, right, left, right.

E. H. Adams

A E I O U

We are very little creatures,
All of different voice and features;
One of us in glass is set,
One of us you'll find in jet.
T'other you may see in tin,
And the fourth a box within.
If the fifth you should pursue,
It can never fly from you.

Jonathan Swift

The Rain

Rain on the green grass,
And rain on the tree,
And rain on the house-top.
But not upon me!

Little Clotilda

Little Clotilda,
Well and hearty,
Thought she'd like
To give a party.

But as her friends
Were shy and wary,
Nobody came
But her own canary.

The Pancake

Mix a pancake,
Stir a pancake,
Pop it in the pan.

Fry the pancake,
Toss the pancake,
Catch it if you can.

Christina Rossetti

Daffodils

We make both mead and garden gay,
We spend the sweet spring hours in play,
And dance like sunbeams gone astray.

P. A. Ropes

Out of Doors

Birds and bees and butterflies,
Bobbing all about!
What a jolly world it is,
Sing and laugh and shout!

E. North

A Baby Verse

Tit-tat-toe,
My first go,
Three jolly butcher boys
All in a row;
Stick one up,
Stick one down,
Stick one in the old man's crown.

White Sheep

White sheep, white sheep
On a blue hill,
When the wind stops
You all stand still.
You all run away
When the winds blow;
White sheep, white sheep,
Where do you go?

W. H. Davies

Two Little Blackbirds

Two little blackbirds singing in the sun,
One flew away and then there was one;
One little blackbird, very black and tall,
He flew away and then there was the wall.
One little brick wall lonely in the rain,
Waiting for the blackbirds to come and sing again.

39

A Chill

What can lambkins do
All the keen night through?
Nestle by their woolly mother,
The careful ewe.

What can nestlings do
In the nightly dew?
Sleep beneath their mother's wing
Till day breaks anew.

If in field or tree
There might only be
Such a warm, soft sleeping-place
Found for me.

Christina Rossetti

Buttercups

Buttercups golden and gay,
Sway in the wind all day.
They tickle the nose of the cow as she goes,
And they call to the bees, "Come away."

"Banbury Fair"

"Where have you been,
 Miss Marjorie Keen?"
"To Banbury Fair,
 In a carriage and pair."
"And what could there be
 That was funny to see?"
'A dame in a wig
 A-dancing a jig."
'And what did you get
 For six pennies, my pet?"
"A pink sugar mouse
 And a gingerbread house."

Edith G. Millard

The Donkey

My donkey has a bridle
Hung with silver bells,
He feeds upon the thistles
Growing on the fells.

The bells keep chiming, chiming
A little silver song;
If ever I should lose him
It would not be for long.

Rose Fyleman

Boots and Shoes

My Wellington boots go
Thump-thump, thump-thump,
My leather shoes go
Pit-pat, pit-pat,
But my rubber sandals
Make no noise at all.

1. *Children beat loudly on the floor with their feet.*
2. *They beat softly with their feet.*
3. *They beat with their feet making no noise at all.*

Lilian McCrea

Rain

Pitter-patter, hear it raining?
Slow at first, then faster, faster.
Put on your raincoat,
Hold up your umbrella,
Pull on your Wellingtons
And splash in the puddles.

1. *Children clap hands slowly and lightly, gradually getting faster and louder.*
2. *They pretend to button up raincoats, open umbrellas and pull on Wellington boots.*
3. *They stamp their feet on the ground.*

Lilian McCrea

Who has seen the Wind?

Who has seen the wind?
Neither I nor you:
But when the leaves hang trembling
The wind is passing through.

Who has seen the wind?
Neither you nor I:
But when the trees bow down their heads
The wind is passing by.

Christina Rossetti

What the Weather Does

The rooks are alive
On the tops of the trees;
They look like a hive
Of jolly black bees;
They all squawk together,
And loud is their squawking—
It must be the weather
That sets them a-talking.

What Does the Bee Do?

What does the bee do?
Bring home honey.
What does father do?
Bring home money.
And what does mother do?
Lay out the money.
And what does baby do?
Eat up the honey.

Christina Rossetti

Summer Breeze

Summer breeze, so softly blowing,
In my garden pinks are growing.
If you'll go and send the showers,
You may come and smell my flowers.

A Tug-of-War

Three little chickens
And one little worm,
Oh what a tug-of-war!
And each little chick
Thinks he knows very well
What fat little worms are for.

M. M. Hutchinson

The Dandelion Puff

The dandelion puff
Is a very queer clock,
It doesn't say tick,
And it doesn't say tock,
It hasn't a cuckoo,
It hasn't a chime,
And I really don't think
It can tell me the time!

Mary K. Robinson

Finger Folk

Putting on gloves

Finger Folk, Finger Folk,
Four Fairy Finger Folk;
Wearing suits of leather,
All of them together—
Funny Finger Folk!

Finger Folk and Thumb-man,
Short, sturdy Thumb-man:
Just as quaintly dressed
In a leather vest—
Funny Thumb-man!

H. M. Tharp

43

Daisies and Grasses

Daisies so bright,
Grasses so green,
Tell me, I pray,
How you keep clean?

Summertime showers,
Summertime rain,
Wash dusty flowers
All clean again.

"Good Night," Says the Owl

"Tu-whitt, Tu-whitt, Tu-whoo, Tu-whoo,
Good night to me, good night to you."
'Tis the old white owl in the ivy tree,
But I can't see him, and he can't see me!

Lady Erskine Crum

Three Plum Buns

Three plum buns
To eat here at the stile
In the clover meadow,
For we have walked a mile.

One for you, and one for me,
And one left over:
Give it to the boy who shouts
To scare sheep from the clover.

Christina Rossetti

Bachelors' Buttons

Bill the Bachelor lived by himself,
He'd little of comfort in cupboard or shelf,
But skill with his needle he ever did show
With Bachelors' Buttons sewed on in a row.

Maud Morin

I Spy

One, round the candytuft,
Two, round the tree,
Three, round the hollyhock,
Then find me.

Candytuft! Hollyhock!
Where can you be?
I've looked in front, I'll look behind,
One—two—THREE!

N. E. Hussey

Finger Play

Each finger is touched in turn

This little bunny said, "Let's play,"
This little bunny said, "In the hay."
This one saw a man with his gun.
This one said, "This isn't fun."
This one said, "I'm off for a run."
　　"Bang" went the gun,
　　　They ran away
And didn't come back for a year and a day.

Kind Deeds

Little drops of water,
　Little grains of sand,
Make the mighty ocean,
　And the pleasant land.

This the little minutes,
　Humble though they be,
Make the mighty ages
　Of eternity.

Little deeds of kindness,
　Little words of love,
Make this earth an Eden
　Like the heaven above.

Isaac Watts

45

The Disappointed Shrimper

My net
Is heavy with weed.
My net
Is heavy indeed
With wet,
Wet weed.

For an hour I tried,
For two, for three,
I fished,
I kept looking inside
My net to see
Some shrimps for tea.
I wished
For shrimps for tea.

And the day is done,
And I haven't one
Shrimp
         for
              tea.

P. A. Ropes

Getting Up

When I get up in the morning
I'll tell you what I do,
I wash my hands and I wash my face,
Splishity-splash, splishity-splash.
I clean my teeth till they're shining white,
Scrubbity-scrub, scrubbity-scrub,
Then I put on my clothes and brush my hair,
And runnity-run, I run downstairs.

*Children dramatise all the actions as they say the story. For
the last line they raise both arms and lower them quickly, making
running movements with their fingers.*

Lilian McCrea

Conversation

Mousie, mousie,
Where is your little wee housie?
  Here is the door,
  Under the floor,
    Said mousie, mousie.

Mousie, mousie,
May I come into your housie?
  You can't get in,
  You have to be thin,
    Said mousie, mousie

Mousie, mousie,
Won't you come out of your housie?
  I'm sorry to say
  I'm busy all day,
    Said mousie, mousie.

Rose Fyleman

Robin Hood

I've got a bow and arrow,
And I take them to the wood,
And don't the rabbits scuttle
For they think I'm Robin Hood!

Rachel MacAndrew

Billy Boy

Billy Boy, Billy Boy, what will you bring for me?
Riding Old Dobbin to Banbury Fair.
Billy Boy, Billy Boy, shall you be long away?
Just twice as long as it takes to get there.

Billy Boy, Billy Boy, what will you bring for me?
One golden fiddle to play a fine tune,
Two magic wishes and three fairy fishes,
And four rainbow ropes to climb up to the moon.

Dorothy King

47

A Frisky Lamb

A frisky lamb
And a frisky child
Playing their pranks
In a cowslip meadow:
The sky all blue
And the air all mild
And the fields all sun
And the lanes half shadow.

Christina Rossetti

.

Four Scarlet Berries

Four scarlet berries
Left upon the tree,
"Thanks," cried the blackbird,
"These will do for me."
He ate numbers one and two,
Then ate number three,
When he'd eaten number four,
There was none to see!

Mary Vivian

Eggs For Breakfast

Get up at once, now, Margaret May!
There are eggs in the kitchen for breakfast to-day;
    We have porridge on Mondays,
    On Wednesdays and Sundays,
But we've brown eggs for breakfast to-day.

Get up at once, now, Margaret May!
Our white porridge bowls are all put away;
    We have them on Mondays,
    On Wednesdays and Sundays,
But we've little blue egg-cups to-day.

Irene F. Pawsey

Bed-Time

Robin Friend has gone to bed,
Little wing to hide his head.
Mother's bird must slumber, too—
Just as baby robins do.
When the stars begin to rise
Birds and Babies close their eyes.

L. Alma Tadema

The Blackbird

1st Child:
Out in the garden,
Up in a tree,
There is a blackbird
Singing to me.

2nd Child:
What is he singing
Up in the tree?
What is he piping
So merrily?

1st Child:
Come out in the garden,
Come out and hear!
Stand still and listen
(But not too near).

Blackbird:
I love the wind, and the stars, and the moon.
I love the sun when it shines at noon;
I love the trees, but I love best
My little brown wife in our cosy nest!

1st Child:
That is the song
He's singing to me,
That's what he's piping
So merrily!

Phyllis Drayson

Baby-Land

"Which is the way to Baby-land?"
"Anyone can tell;
    Up one flight,
    To your right;
Please ring the bell."

"What can you see in Baby-land?"
"Little folks in white—
    Downy heads,
    Cradle-beds,
Faces pure and bright!"

"What do they do in Baby-land?"
"Dream and wake and play,
    Laugh and crow,
    Shout and grow;
Jolly times have they!"

"What do they say in Baby-land?"
"Why, the oddest things;
    Might as well
    Try to tell
What a birdie sings!"

"Who is the Queen of Baby-land?"
"Mother kind and sweet;
    And her love,
    Born above,
Guides the little feet."

George Cooper

My Toys

My red engine goes chuff-chuff-choo! chuff-chuff-choo!
My shiny drum goes rum-tum-tum, rum-tum-tum.
My teddy bear goes grr . . . grrr . . . grrr . . .
And my wooden bricks go clitter-clatter, clitter-clatter,
    rattle-bang—BUMP!

Lilian McCrea

When We Are Men

Jim says a sailor man
  He means to be;
He'll sail a splendid ship
  Out on the sea.

Dick wants to buy a farm
  When he's a man
He'll get some cows and sheep
  Soon as he can

Tom says he'll keep a shop;
  Nice things to eat,
Two windows full of cakes,
  Down in the street.

I'd hate a stuffy shop—
  When I'm a man
I'll buy a trotting horse
  And caravan.

E. Stella Mead

My Doggie

I have a dog,
  His name is Jack,
His coat is white
  With spots of black.

I take him out,
  Most every day,
Such fun we have,
  We run and play.

Such clever tricks
  My dog can do,
I love my Jack,
  He loves me too.

C. Nurton

A Giant's Cake

Each year I have a birthday,
    When people buy me toys,
And mother gives a party
    To lots of girls and boys.

I have a cake with candles,
    And icing, pink and white,
With rosy candles lighted,
    It makes a lovely sight.

Each year the cake grows larger,
    Another light to take,
So if I grow much older
    I'll need a giant's cake.

Evelina San Garde

The Bells of London

Gay go up and gay go down,
To ring the bells of London town.
    Halfpence and farthings,
        Say the bells of St. Martin's.
        Oranges and lemons,
            Say the bells of St. Clement's.
        Pancakes and fritters,
            Say the bells of St. Peter's.
            Two sticks and an apple,
                Say the bells of Whitechapel.

Kettles and pans,
Say the bells of St. Ann's.
    You owe me ten shillings,
        Say the bells of St. Helen's.
        When will you pay me?
            Say the bells of Old Bailey.
    When I grow rich,
        Say the bells of Shoreditch.
Pray when will that be?
Say the bells of Stepney.
    I am sure I don't know,
        Says the great bell of Bow.

Here We Come A-haying

Here we come a-haying,
   A-haying, a-haying,
Here we come a-haying,
   Among the leaves so green.

Up and down the mower goes
   All the long field over,
Cutting down the long green grass,
   And the purple clover.

Toss the hay and turn it,
   Laid in rows so neatly,
Summer sun a-shining down,
   Makes it smell so sweetly.

Rake it into tidy piles
   Now the farmer's ready,
Load it on the old hay cart,
   Drawn by faithful Neddy.

Down the lane the last load goes,
   Hear the swallows calling.
Now at last our work is done,
   Night is softly falling.

Eunice Close

Hide and Seek

Baby loves to play with me,
Peek-a-boo! Peek-a-boo!
She goes and hides behind a tree,
I see you! I see you!

Baby is so very wee,
Hiding's easy as can be!

Phyllis Drayson

The Balloon Man

This is a little "action poem" for the littlest ones, in which five children may take part. It includes some useful "colour training".

Characters:	Properties:
Balloon man	Coloured balloons
Mother	
Three children	

Balloon Man:
> I stand here every afternoon,
> Waiting for someone to buy a balloon.
> Look at the colours bright and gay.
> Just one penny is all you pay.
> Plenty for all who come, have I,
> Come and buy! Come and buy!

First Child:
> I have a penny, Mother said,
> So I think I'd like one of red.

Second Child:
> I would like that one of green.
> It is the prettiest that I've seen.

Third Child:
> Lucky am I, please give me two,
> One of yellow, and one of blue.

Balloon Man:
> Now with your balloons just run and play,
> I like to see you happy and gay.
> *(Children play with balloons.)*

Mother:
> Children! Children! Come home to tea!

First Child:
> That is my Mother calling me.

All Together :
All Together :
      Balloon man, don't go away,
      We'll come and see you another day.
      (Children run out saying "Good-bye!")

                                          E. Herbert

To Let

      Two little beaks went tap! tap! tap!
      Two little shells went crack! crack! crack!
      Two fluffy chicks peeped out, and oh,
      They liked the look of the big world so,
      That they left their houses without a fret
      And two little shells are not to LET.

                                          D. Newey-Johnson

Little Blue Apron

      "Little Blue Apron,
            How do you do?
         Never a stocking
         And never a shoe!"

      Little Blue Apron
            She answered me,
         "You don't wear stockings
         And shoes by the sea."

      "Little Blue Apron—
            Never a hat?
         How do you manage
         To go out like that?"

      "Why, what is the use
            Of a hat?" said she,
         "You never wear hats
         When you're by the sea."

      "Why, little Blue Apron, it seems to me
      Very delightful to live by the sea;
      But what would hatters and shoemakers do
      If everyone lived by the sea like you?"

                                    From an Old Story Book

The Furry Home

If I were a mouse
And wanted a house,
I think I would choose
My new red shoes.
Furry edges,
Fur inside,
What a lovely
Place to hide!
I'd not travel,
I'd not roam—
Just sit in
My furry home.

J. M. Westrup

The Mouse

There's such a tiny little mouse
Living safely in my house.

Out at night he'll softly creep,
When everyone is fast asleep.

But always in the light of day
He softly, softly creeps away.

Thirza Wakley

Five Sisters

Five little sisters walking in a row;
Now, isn't that the best way for little girls to go?
Each had a round hat, each had a muff,
And each had a new pelisse of soft green stuff.

Five little marigolds standing in a row;
Now, isn't that the best way for marigolds to grow?
Each with a green stalk, and all five had got
A bright yellow flower, and a new red pot.

Kate Greenaway

High June

Fiddle-de-dee!
Grasshoppers three,
Rollicking over the meadow;
Scarcely the grass,
Bends as they pass,
So fairy-light is their tread, O!

Said Grasshopper One,
"The summer's begun,
This sunshine is driving me crazy!"
Said Grasshopper Two,
"I feel just like you!"
And leapt to the top of a daisy.

"Please wait for me!"
Cried Grasshopper Three,
"My legs are ready for hopping!"
So grasshoppers three,
Fiddle-de-dee,
Raced all the day without stopping.

C. A. Morin

My New Umbrella

I have a new umbrella,
A bright red new umbrella,
A new red silk umbrella,
I wish that it would rain,

And then I could go walking,
Just like a lady walking,
A grown-up lady walking
Away 'way down the lane.

I could not step in puddles,
The shiny tempting puddles,
No lady walks in puddles,
Then turn, and home again.

M. M. Hutchinson

57

The Holiday Train

Tall children or boys are arranged in double file to form train.
Other children as passengers enter train after first verse.
Train proceeds to rhythm of voices.

Here is the train!
Here is the train!
Let us get in!
Let us get in!

Where shall we sit?
Where shall we sit?
When will it go?
When will it go?

What does it say?
What does it say?
"Let us get on!"
"Let us get on!"

Look at the trees!
Look at the trees!
See all the cows!
See all the cows!

Isn't it fun?
Isn't it fun?
Going along!
Going along!

Hurrying on!
Hurrying on!
Nearly there!
Nearly there!

Look at the sea!
Look at the sea!
See all the ships!
See all the ships!

Here we are!
Here we are!
Out we get!
Out we get!

Irene Thompson

Jack Tar

Jack Tar, Sailor Man,
   Can you tell me
How much water
   Is in the sea?

Yes, Miss, Yes, Miss,
   Certainly!
There's just as much
   As there ought to be.

Emile Jacot

The Pony

I've got a pony
All of my own;
So has Tony,
But his is roan
Mine is a black one,
With such a long mane;
"Let's have a gallop
Right down the lane!"

Rachel MacAndrew

Honey Bear

There was a big bear
Who lived in a cave;
His greatest love
Was honey.
He had twopence a week
Which he never could save,
So he never had
Any money.
I bought him a money box
Red and round,
In which to put
His money.
He saved and saved
Till he got a pound,
Then spent it all
On honey.

Elizabeth Lang

The Robin

When father takes his spade to dig,
    Then Robin comes along;
He sits upon a little twig
    And sings a little song.

Or, if the trees are rather far,
    He does not stay alone,
But comes up close to where we are
    And bobs upon a stone.

L. Alma Tadema

The Bus

There is a painted bus
With twenty painted seats.
It carries painted people
Along the painted streets.
They pull the painted bell,
The painted driver stops,
And they all get out together
At the little painted shops.

"Peter"

The Ferryman

"Ferry me across the water,
    Do, boatman, do."
"If you've a penny in your purse
    I'll ferry you."

"I have a penny in my purse,
    And my eyes are blue;
So ferry me across the water,
    Do, boatman, do."

"Step into my ferry-boat,
    Be they black or blue,
And for the penny in your purse
    I'll ferry you."

Christina Rossetti

Yesterday

Where have you gone to, Yesterday,
   And why did you have to go?
I've been wondering all the day,
   And nobody seems to know.

Say, is it true that you've journeyed far,
   Over the hills to Spain,
And no one to see which road you took
   Nor call you back again?

Hugh Chesterman

The Woodpecker

Last night I heard him in the woods,
   When everything was still,
Tappity-tap on the dreaming trees
   Under the fairy hill.

I wonder if he lost his way,
   As I did long before.
So had to tap and tap until
   He found the fairies' door.

Joyce Sambrook

Fish and Bird

How happy to be a fish,
To dive and skim,
To dart and float and swim
And play.

How happy to be a bird,
To fly and sing,
To glide on feathered wing
All day.

Rosemary Brinckman

61

The Snowman

Come in the garden
And play in the snow,
A snowman we'll make,
See how quickly he'll grow!
Give him hat, stick, and pipe,
And make him look gay,
Such a fine game
For a cold winter day!

E. M. Adams

The Wind

What can be the matter
    With Mr. Wind to-day?
He calls for me so loudly,
    Through the key-hole, "Come and play."

I'll put my warm red jacket on
    And pull my hat on tight,
He'll never get it off, although
    He tries with all his might.

I'll stand so firm upon my legs,
    I'm strong, what do I care?
Now, Mr. Wind, just come along
    And blow me if you dare.

Dorothy Gradon

The Frog

A little green frog once lived in a pool,
The sun was hot but the water was cool;
He sat in the pool the whole day long,
And sang a queer little, dear little song.

"Quaggery do, quaggery dee,
No one was ever so happy as me."
He sang this song to his little green brother,
And if you don't like it then make me another.

Rose Fyleman

Doves

High on the dove-cot
In the sunny weather,
The doves nod and bow,
Crooning together:

"Oh, how do you do?
How do you do?"
Nodding and crooning
"How do you do?"

E. J. Falconer

The Dustman

Every Thursday morning
Before we're quite awake,
Without the slightest warning
The house begins to shake
With a Biff! Bang!
Biff! Bang! Biff!
It's the Dustman, who begins
(BANG! CRASH!)
To empty all the bins
Of their rubbish and their ash
With a Biff! Bang!
Biff! Bang! Bash!

Clive Sansom

The Dragon

What do you think? Last night I saw
A fiery dragon pass!
He blazed with light from head to tail,
As though his sides were glass.

But when my Mummie came to look
Out through the window-pane,
She laughed, and said: "You silly boy—
It's an electric train!"

Mary Mullineaux

63

Calendar Rhyme

January falls the snow,
February cold winds blow,
In March peep out the early flowers,
And April comes with sunny showers.
In May the roses bloom so gay,
In June the farmer mows his hay,
In July brightly shines the sun,
In August harvest is begun.
September turns the green leaves brown,
October winds then shake them down,
November fills with bleak and smear,
December comes and ends the year.

Flora Willis Watson

Sing-Song Rhyme

One! two! three!
Outside the school,
Three small ducks splash in a pool.

Quack! quack! quack!
That door is wide.
Say the ducks: "Let's peep inside."

Flip! flap! flip!
A waddling row,
Right into the school they go.

Oh! oh! oh!
'Tis fun to see
These new scholars—one! two! three!

Look! look! look!
The children shout:
'Teacher, shall we drive them out?"
(Teacher) "Yes"—sh! sh! sh!

64

Feet

Big feet,
Black feet,
Going up and down the street;
Dull and shiny
Father's feet,
Walk by me!

Nice feet,
Brown feet,
Going up and down the street;
Pretty, dainty,
Ladies' feet,
Trip by me!

Small feet,
Light feet,
Going up and down the street;
Little children's
Happy feet,
Run by me!

Suggestions for rhythmic action:
Children are arranged in three groups:
(1) Tall children or boys, slow walking step;
(2) Girls, quick walking or tripping;
(3) Smallest children, running.
Each Group interprets movements of verses as indicated by
words. The verses are spoken by one child or in Choric Speech
by several children.   Irene Thompson

An Egg for Easter

I want an egg for Easter,
A browny egg for Easter;
I want an egg for Easter,
So I'll tell my browny hen.
    I'll take her corn and water,
    And show her what I've brought her,
    And she'll lay my egg for Easter,
    Inside her little pen.
                              Irene F. Pawsey

65

Wash-Day

This is the way we wash our clothes,
Rub-a-dub-dub, rub-a-dub-dub!
Watch them getting clean and white,
Rub-a-dub-dub, rub-a-dub-dub!

This is the way we mangle them,
Rumble-de-dee, rumble-de-dee!
Round and round the handle goes,
Rumble-de-dee, rumble-de-dee!

This is the way we hang them out,
Flippity-flap, flippity-flap!
See them blowing in the wind,
Flippity-flap, flippity-flap!

This is the way we iron them
Smooth as smooth can be!
Soon our wash-day will be done,
Then we'll all have tea.

Lilian McCrea

Wishes

Said the first little chicken,
    With a queer little squirm,
"I wish I could find
    A fat little worm."

Said the next little chicken,
    With a sharp little squeal,
"I wish I could find
    Some nice yellow meal."

Said the third little chicken,
    With a small sigh of grief,
"I wish I could find
    A little green leaf."

"See here," said the mother,
    From the green garden patch,
"If you want any breakfast,
    Just come here and scratch."

Best Of All

I've got a lovely home,
With every single thing—
A mother and a father,
And a front-door bell to ring.
A dining-room and kitchen,
Some bedrooms and a hall,
But the baby in the cradle
Is the nicest thing of all.

J. M. Westrup

Lucy Lavender

Little Lucy Lavender,
Aged just three,
Dances over the water,
Dances over the sea,
Dances by the streamlet,
Dances on the hill—
Little Lucy Lavender
She can't stand still!

Little Lucy Lavender,
Aged just three,
Sang as she clambered
Up the apple tree;
Sang in her bath-tub,
Sang in her bed,
For—"I can't stay quiet,"
Little Lucy said.

Ivy O. Eastwick

To The Bat

Little bat, little bat,
Pray, when you speak,
Speak a bit louder,
You've such a high squeak,
That only those people
With quite a good ear,
Who know all about you,
Can possibly hear.

Edith King

Wishes

I wish I were an Emperor,
　　With subjects of my own,
And sat in royal robes upon
　　A splendid golden throne.

I wish I were a Muffin Man,
　　And rang a muffin bell,
And every day for tea I'd have
　　The ones I didn't sell.

I wish I were a Pirate Chief,
　　And sailed the stormy sea,
With lace and earrings and a sword
　　As fine as I could be.

I wish I were a Railway Guard,
　　With bright green flag to wave,
Watching the people catch their train
　　By such a narrow shave!

I wish I were a Drummer Boy,
　　And beat upon a drum,
And heard the crowd all shouting out:
　　"Look, here the soldiers come!"

I wish I were Aladdin, or
　　I knew some magic way
To make my wishes all come true
　　And not be only play.

F. Rogers

Dancing on the Shore

Ten in circle. Queen in centre.
　　Ten little children
　　Dancing on the shore;
　　The queen waved a royal wand
　　And out went four.

Four step outside circle.
>Six little children
>Dancing merrily;
>The queen waved a royal wand
>And out went three.

Three step out and join hands with four, making an outside circle around the smaller one.
>Three little children
>Danced as children do;
>The queen waved a royal wand
>And out went two.

Two join larger circle.
>One little maiden,
>Dancing just for fun;
>The queen waved a royal wand
>And out went one.

>>*M. M. Hutchinson*

Three Mice

Three little mice walked into town,
Their coats were grey, and their eyes were brown.

Three little mice went down the street,
With woolwork slippers upon their feet.

Three little mice sat down to dine
On curranty bread and gooseberry wine.

Three little mice ate on and on,
Till every crumb of the bread was gone.

Three little mice, when the feast was done,
Crept home quietly one by one.

Three little mice went straight to bed,
And dreamt of crumbly, curranty bread.

>>*Charlotte Druitt Cole*

69

Things I Like

I like blowing bubbles, and swinging on a swing;
I love to take a country walk and hear the birdies sing.

I like little kittens, and I love puppies too;
And calves and little squealing pigs and baby ducks, don't
you?

I like picking daisies, I love my Teddy bear;
I like to look at picture books in Daddy's big armchair.

Marjorie H. Greenfield

Twinkle, Twinkle, Little Star

Twinkle, twinkle little star,
How I wonder what you are!
Up above the world so high
Like a diamond in the sky.

When the blazing sun is gone,
When he nothing shines upon,
Then you show your little light,
Twinkle, twinkle, all the night.

Then the traveller in the dark
Thanks you for your tiny spark!
He could not see which way to go,
If you did not twinkle so.

In the dark blue sky you keep,
And often through my curtains peep,
For you never shut your eye
Till the sun is in the sky.

As your bright and tiny spark
Lights the traveller in the dark,
Though I know not what you are,
Twinkle, twinkle, little star.

Jane Taylor

Primrose Hill

On Primrose Hill in the early spring
The soft winds blow and sweet birds sing
And the little brown thrush is king—is king.

On Primrose Hill in the sunny weather
The children dance on the grass together
And the larch's bough has a bright green feather.

Rose Fyleman

My New Rabbit

We brought him home, I was so pleased,
   We made a rabbit-hutch,
I give him oats, I talk to him,
   I love him very much.

Now when I talk to Rover dog,
   He answers me "Bow-wow!"
And when I speak to Pussy-cat,
   She purrs and says "Mee-ow!"

But Bunny never says a word,
   Just twinkles with his nose,
And what that rabbit thinks about,
   Why! no one ever knows.

My Mother says the fairies must
   Have put on him a spell,
They told him all their secrets, then
   They whispered, "Pray don't tell."

So Bunny sits there looking wise,
   And twinkling with his nose,
And never, never, never tells
   A single thing he knows.

Elizabeth Gould

71

Topsy-Turvy Land

Will you come to Turvy Land,
To Tipsy-Topsy-Turvy Land,
And see the fishes growing, like the apples on the tree?
The houses are of silk there,
And the sea is made of milk there,
And the rain comes down in strawberries for Mother and
     for me.

Phyllis M. Stone

Jenny and Johnny

Jenny gay and Johnny grim,
In your house so green, so trim,
Tell me truly, tell me, pray,
What's the weather for to-day?
Jenny's standing at her door,
So dull days are surely o'er . . .
Ah, but John's popped out again
Just to say, "It's going to rain."

Dorothy King

Jeremy Hobbler

Sing a song of cobbler!
Jeremiah Hobbler
Mended boots and shoes
By ones and by twos.
His room had a floor and a ceiling
And he did soling and heeling.
But oh, he was so funny!
He always expected his money;
And—oh, would anybody believe it?
He generally used to receive it
When the boots and shoes were mended.
And now the song is ended—
The song of Jeremy Hobbler
Who followed the trade of cobbler.

Whisky Frisky

Whisky Frisky,
Hipperty hop,
Up he goes
To the tree top!

Whirly, twirly,
Round and round,
Down he scampers
To the ground.

Furly, curly,
What a tail,
Tall as a feather,
Broad as a sail.

Where's his supper?
In the shell.
Snappy, cracky,
Out it fell.

A Watering Rhyme

Early in the morning,
    Or the evening hour,
Are the times to water
    Every kind of flower.
Watering at noonday,
    When the sun is high,
Doesn't help the flowers,
    Only makes them die.

Also, when you water,
    Water at the roots;
Flowers keep their mouths where
    We should wear our boots.
Soak the earth around them,
    Then through all the heat
The flowers will have water
    For their thirsty "feet"!

P. A. Ropes

73

The Postman

Rat-a-tat-tat, Rat-a-tat-tat,
  Rat-a-tat-tat tattoo!
That's the way the Postman goes,
  Rat-a-tat-tat tattoo!
Every morning at half-past eight
You hear a bang at the garden gate,
And Rat-a-tat-tat, Rat-a-tat-tat,
  Rat-a-tat-tat tattoo!

Clive Sansom

If

If I were oh, so very small,
  I'd hide myself away,
And creep into a p eony cup
  To spend the summer's day.

If I were oh, so very tall,
  I'd walk among the trees,
And bend to pick the topmost leaf
  As easy as you please.

P. A. Ropes

Timid Bunnies

See the bunnies sitting there,
Let us give them all a scare,
Clap your hands, ha, ha! they flop
Each beneath a turnip top;
Clap again, see how they run,
White tails bobbing in the sun;
Fathers, sons, and big, big brothers,
Little babies and their mothers;
Helter-skelter, off they go,
To their burrows down below.

Jeannie Kirby

Johnny's Farm

Johnny had a little dove;
 Coo, coo, coo.
Johnny had a little mill;
 Clack, clack, clack.
Johnny had a little cow;
 Moo, moo, moo.
Johnny had a little duck;
 Quack, quack, quack.
Coo, coo; clack, clack; moo, moo; quack, quack;
Down on Johnny's little farm.

Johnny had a little hen;
 Cluck, cluck, cluck.
Johnny had a little crow;
 Caw, caw, caw.
Johnny had a little pig;
 Chook, chook, chook.
Johnny had a little donkey;
 Haw, haw, haw.
Coo, coo; clack, clack; moo, moo; quack, quack;
Cluck, cluck; caw, caw; chook, chook; haw, haw;
Down on Johnny's little farm.

Johnny had a little dog,
 Bow, wow, wow;
Johnny had a little lamb,
 Baa, baa, baa;
Johnny had a little son,
 Now, now, now!
Johnny had a little wife,
 Ha! ha!! ha!!!
Coo, coo; clack, clack; moo, moo; quack, quack;
Cluck, cluck; caw, caw; chook, chook; haw, haw;
Bow-wow; baa, baa; now, now; ha! ha!!
Down on Johnny's little farm.

H. M. Adams

75

I Saw a Ship A-Sailing

I saw a ship a-sailing,
A-sailing on the sea;
And, oh! it was laden
With pretty things for me.

There were comfits in the cabin,
And apples in the hold;
The sails were made of silk,
And the masts were made of gold.

The four-and-twenty sailors
That stood between the decks,
Were four-and-twenty white mice,
With chains about their necks.

The Captain was a duck,
With a packet on his back,
And when the ship began to move,
The Captain said, "Quack quack!"

If

If I take an acorn
    That's fallen from its cup,
And plant it in the garden
    And never dig it up;
The sun and rain will change it
    To a great big tree,
With lots of acorns on it
    Growing all for me.

I'll plant an orange pippin,
    And see what that will do;
I hope an orange tree will grow,
    I think it will, don't you?
If oranges should really grow,
    And if there should be many,
I'll put them in a basket
    And sell them two a penny.

Alice Todd

Mr. Brown

Mr. Brown
Goes up and down,
And round and round,
And round the town;
Up and down,
Round and round,
Up and down
And round the town.

Rodney Bennett

Little Betty Blue

Little Betty Blue
Has a button on her shoe;
But she's too fat to button it,
So what can Betty do?

She can ask her brother Paul
Who is rather thin and small;
Then he will come and button it
Without a fuss at all!

Agnes Grozier Herbertson

A Little Bird's Song

Sometimes I've seen,
Sometimes I've heard,
Up in the tree
A little bird,
Singing a song,
A song to me,
A little brown bird
Up in the tree.
Sometimes he stays,
Sometimes he sings,
Then to the wind
He spreads his wings,
Flying away,
Away from me,
A little brown bird
Up in the tree.

Margaret Rose

Pussy-Cat and Puppy-Dog

Mee-ow, mee-ow,
Here's a little pussy-cat
With furry, furry fur,
Stroke her very gently
And she'll purr, purr, purr.

Bow-wow, bow-wow,
Here's a little puppy-dog
With a wiggly-waggly tail,
Pat him and he'll wag it
With a wiggy-wag-wag
And a waggy-wag-wag.

Lilian McCrea

My Party

I'm giving a party to-morrow at three,
And these are the people I'm asking to tea.

I'm sure you will know them—they're old friends, not new;
Bo-peep and Jack Horner and Little Boy Blue.

And Little Miss Muffet, and Jack and his Jill
(Please don't mention spiders—nor having a spill).

And Little Red Riding-Hood—Goldilocks too
(When sitting beside them, don't talk of the Zoo).

And sweet Cinderella, and also her Prince
(They're married—and happy they've lived ever since!)

And Polly, and Sukey; who happily settle
On each side the hearth, to look after the kettle.

All these are the people I'm asking to tea;
So please come and meet them to-morrow at three.

Queenie Scott-Hopper

Just Like Me

I went up one pair of stairs
        Just like me.
I went up two pairs of stairs
        Just like me.
I went into a room
        Just like me,
I looked out of a window
        Just like me,
And there I saw a monkey
        Just like me.

Our Mother

Hundreds of stars in the pretty sky,
Hundreds of shells on the shore together,
Hundreds of birds that go singing by,
Hundreds of birds in the sunny weather.

Hundreds of dewdrops to greet the dawn,
Hundreds of bees in the purple clover,
Hundreds of butterflies on the lawn,
But only one mother the wide world over.

There Are Big Waves

There are big waves and little waves,
    Green waves and blue,
Waves you can jump over,
    Waves you dive thro',
Waves that rise up
    Like a great water wall,
Waves that swell softly
    And don't break at all,
Waves that can whisper,
    Waves that can roar,
And tiny waves that run at you
    Running on the shore.

Eleanor Farjeon

79

Just Like This

Action Rhyme

The trees are waving to and fro,
Just like this; just like this;
Branches swaying high and low,
Just like this; just like this.

The waves are tossing up and down,
Just like this; just like this;
On the sand lies seaweed brown,
Just like this; just like this.

The birds are always on the wing,
Just like this; just like this;
Bees are humming in the ling,
Just like this; just like this.

The gnats are darting through the air,
Just like this; just like this;
Dragon-flies flit here and there,
Just like this; just like this.

Squirrels are racing up the trees,
Just like this; just like this;
Rabbits scurry o'er the leas,
Just like this; just like this.

Forest ponies frisk and prance,
Just like this; just like this;
Little children play and dance,
Just like this; just like this.

D. A. Olney

A Finger Play for a Snowy Day

I

This is how snowflakes play about,
Up in cloudland they dance in and out.

II

This is how they whirl down the street,
Powdering everybody they meet.

III

This is how they come fluttering down,
Whitening the roads, the fields, and the town.

IV

This is how snowflakes cover the trees,
Each branch and twig bends in the breeze.

V

This is how snowflakes blow in a heap,
Looking just like fleecy sheep.

VI

This is how they cover the ground,
Cover it thickly, with never a sound.

VII

This is how people shiver and shake
On a snowy morning when first they wake.

VIII

This is how snowflakes melt away
When the sun sends out his beams to play.

The Butterfly

I know a little butterfly with tiny golden wings,
He plays among the summer flowers and up and down he
    swings,
He dances on their honey cups so happy all the day,
And then he spreads his tiny wings—and softly flies away.

Margaret Rose

The Washing-up Song

Sing a song of washing-up,
Water hot as hot,
Cups and saucers, plates and spoons,
Dishes such a lot!
Work the dish-mop round and round,
Wash them clean as clean,
Polish with a dry white cloth,
How busy we have been!

Elizabeth Gould

The Clucking Hen

"Will you take a walk with me,
    My little wife, to-day?
There's barley in the barley-field,
    And hay-seed in the hay."

"Thank you," said the clucking hen;
    "I've something else to do;
I'm busy sitting on my eggs,
    I cannot walk with you."

"Cluck, cluck, cluck, cluck,"
    Said the clucking hen;
"My little chicks will soon be hatched,
    I'll think about it then."

The clucking hen sat on her nest,
    She made it in the hay;
And warm and snug beneath her breast
    A dozen white eggs lay.

Crack, crack, went all the eggs,
    Out dropt the chickens small!
"Cluck," said the clucking hen,
    "Now I have you all.

"Come along, my little chicks,
    I'll take a walk with you";
"Hello!" said the barn-door cock,
    "Cock-a-doodle-do!"

82

Laughter

No one in the garden
Up the mossy path,
Yet I almost certainly
Heard a little laugh.

Light as fluffy thistledown,
Fresh as dew at morning,
Happy as a bird's song
When the day is dawning.

No one in the rockery
As I tiptoe round,
Listening for another laugh,
But scarce a *single sound.*

Nothing but the sound of grass
Rippling in the breeze.
No one in the garden
But the flowers and trees.

Olive Enoch

Over the Fields

*Children walk in single file or with partners, reciting poem and
keeping time to the rhythm of the verses.*

Over the fields where the cornflowers grow,
Over the fields where the poppies blow,
Over the stile there's a way we know—
    Down to a rustling wood!

Over the fields where the daisies grow,
Over the bank where the willows blow,
Over the bridge there's a way we know—
    Down to a rippling brook!

Over the hills where the rainbows go,
Where golden gorse and brambles grow,
Over the hills there's a way we know—
    Down to a rolling sea!

Adeline White

83

In My Garden

A Poem for Dramatisation

In my little garden
By the apple tree,
Daffodils are dancing—
One—two—three!

In my little garden
By the kitchen door,
Daisies red are smiling—
Two—three—four!

In my little garden
By the winding drive,
Roses bright are climbing—
Three—four—five!

In my little garden
By the pile of bricks,
Hollyhocks are growing—
Four—five—six!

In my little garden
Down in sunny Devon,
Violets are hiding—
Five—six—seven!

In my little garden
By the cottage gate,
Pansies gay are shining—
Six—seven—eight!

Daffodils in golden gowns,
Daisies all in red,
Hollyhocks so very tall
By the garden shed,
Roses in the sunshine,
Violets dewy bright,
Pansies smiling gaily—
What a lovely sight!

Gipsy Man

Gipsy man, O gipsy man,
In your yellow caravan,
Up and down the world you go—
Tell me all the things you know!

Sun and moon and stars are bright,
Summer's green and winter's white,
And I'm the gayest gipsy man
That rides inside a caravan.

Dorothy King

A Happy Child

My house is red—a little house,
    A happy child am I,
I laugh and play the livelong day,
    I hardly ever cry.

I have a tree, a green, green tree,
    To shade me from the sun;
And under it I often sit,
    When all my work is done.

My little basket I will take,
    And trip into the town;
When next I'm there I'll buy some cake,
    And spend my bright half-crown.

Kate Greenaway

Haymaking

The farmer is busy, so busy, to-day,
Trying to gather in all his hay,
So off to the hayfield hurry away
And see what you can do.
Will you rake, and toss, and turn the hay?
Will you ride in the cart which takes it away?
Or pile up the rick as high as you may?
Or—will-you-only-*play*?

E. M. Adams

If I Were an Apple

If I were an apple
  And grew upon a tree,
I think I'd fall down
  On a nice boy like me.

I wouldn't stay there,
  Giving nobody joy;
I'd fall down at once,
  And say, "Eat me, my boy."

The King of China's Daughter

The King of China's daughter,
  So beautiful to see
With her face like yellow water, left
  Her nutmeg tree.
Her little rope for skipping
  She kissed and gave it me—
Made of painted notes of singing-birds
  Among the fields of tea.
I skipped across the nutmeg grove,
  I skipped across the sea;
But neither sun nor moon, my dear,
  Has yet caught me.

Edith Sitwell

Haymaking

This is the way we make our hay;
Men cut the grass, then lad and lass,
We take it and shake it, and shake it,
Then into heaps we rake it,
And leave it to the sun to bake it;
And when it is brown we pull it down,
And again we take it and shake it,
And again with our rakes we rake it;
And when we have done, with dance and fun,
Home in our carts we take it.

A. P. Graves

My Little Dog

I helped a little lame dog
  Over such a stile,
He followed me with gratitude
  Many a weary mile.
I shoo-ed at him and chased him,
  But he stuck there, close behind;
(I'm sure his bark was saying,
  "I know that you'll be kind!")
He came into my housie,
  And he wouldn't go away,
So I'll keep my little lame dog
  To myself, if I may.

                              Pearl Forbes MacEwen

Who's that A-knocking?

Who's that a-knocking,
  A-knocking at the door—
One knock!—two knocks!
  Three knocks!—four!
He's come to the window,
  He's taking a peep
To find out whether
  Baby's asleep.

                              Emile Jacot

Little Robin Redbreast

Little Robin Redbreast sat upon a tree,
Up went Pussy-cat, and down went he;
Down came Pussy-cat, and away Robin ran;
Says little Robin Redbreast, "Catch me if you can!"

Little Robin Redbreast jumped upon a wall,
Pussy-cat jumped after him, and almost got a fall;
Little Robin chirped and sang, and what did Pussy say?
Pussy-cat said, "Mew!" and Robin jumped away.

87

How Many Days Has My Baby To Play?

How many days has my baby to play?
Saturday, Sunday, Monday,
Tuesday, Wednesday, Thursday, Friday,
Saturday, Sunday, Monday.

The Wolf and the Lambs

A verse-speaking piece suitable for acting

Wolf:
Little young lambs, oh! why do you stay
Up in the bleak hills amid the snow?
I know a place where the fields are gay,
Where sweet-stalked clovers and daisies grow!
Follow me, little lambs! Follow me, do!
And pleasant pastures I'll show to you!

Lambs:
Oh, Mr. Wolf, how kind you are
To offer us lambs such splendid things!
But, tell us, please, is it very far?
We are lambs, not birds, for we have no wings,
And little legs tire, indeed they do!
So perhaps we had better not go with you!

Wolf:
Little young lambs, it is very near!
Only a dozen steps away!
How cold it is and dreary here,
But there it is sunshine all the day!
Follow me, little lambs! Follow me, do!
And pleasant pastures I'll show to you!

Lambs:
Oh, Mr. Wolf, how kind you are,
But our mother has told us not to go!
She says that such pastures may be too far,
She says there are far worse things than snow!
In fact, Mr. Wolf—we tell you true!—
She says there is nothing worse than you!

Ivy O. Eastwick

Boats Sail on the Rivers

Boats sail on the rivers,
　And ships sail on the seas;
But clouds that sail across the sky
　Are prettier far than these.

There are bridges on the rivers,
　As pretty as you please;
But the bow that bridges heaven,
　And overtops the trees,
And builds a road from earth to sky,
　Is prettier far than these.

Christina Rossetti

Five Little Brothers

Five little brothers set out together
　To journey the live-long day,
In an odd little carriage, all made of leather,
　They hurried away, away—
One big brother and three quite small,
And one wee fellow, no size at all.

The carriage was dark and none too roomy,
　And they could not move about;
The five little brothers grew very gloomy,
　And the wee one began to pout;
Till the biggest one whispered: "What do you say?
Let's leave the carriage and run away."

So out they scampered, the five together,
　And off and away they sped.
When somebody found the carriage of leather,
　Oh, my! how she shook her head!
'Twas her little boy's shoe, as everyone knows,
And the five little brothers were five little toes!

Ella Wheeler Wilcox

89

We Thank You!

Bus driver,
Tram driver,
Driver of a train:
They take us out,
And bring us back again.
Tram conductor,
Bus conductor,
Train guard too:
They look after us,
Tell us what to do.
Bus men, train men,
Tram men, and motor men:
For all you do for us
WE THANK YOU!

L. E. Cox

The Little Piggies

Child: Where are you going, you little pig?
1st Pig: I'm leaving my mother, I'm growing so big!

Child: So big, young pig!
      So young, so big!
What, leaving your mother, you foolish young pig!
Where are you going, you little pig?

2nd Pig: I've got a new spade, and I'm going to dig.

Child: To dig, little pig!
      A little pig dig!
Well, I never saw a pig with a spade that could dig!
Where are you going, you little pig?

3rd Pig: Why, I'm going to have a nice ride in a gig.

Child: In a gig, little pig!
      What, a pig in a gig!
Well, I never saw a pig ride in a gig!
Where are you going, little pig?

4th Pig: I'm going to the barber's to buy a wig.

Child: A wig, little pig!
              A pig in a wig!
     Why, whoever before saw a pig in a wig?
     Where are you going, you little pig?

5th Pig: Why, I'm going to the ball to dance a fine jig.

Child: A jig, little pig!
              A pig dance a jig!
     Well, I never before saw a pig dance a jig!

Thomas Hood

Through Nurseryland

Now, rocking horse! rocking horse! where shall we go?
The world's such a very big place, you must know,
That to see all its wonders, the wiseacres say,
'Twould take us together a year and a day.

Suppose we first gallop to Banbury Cross,
To visit that lady upon a white horse,
And see if it's true that her fingers and toes
Make beautiful music, wherever she goes.

Then knock at the door of the Old Woman's Shoe,
And ask if her wonderful house is on view,
And peep at the children, all tucked up in bed,
And beg for a taste of the broth without bread.

On poor Humpty-Dumpty we'll certainly call,
Perhaps we might help him to get back on his wall;
Spare two or three minutes to comfort the Kits
Who've been kept without pie, just for losing their mits.

A rush to Jack Horner's, then down a steep hill,
Not over and over, like poor Jack and Jill!
So, rocking horse! rocking horse! scamper away,
Or we'll never get back in a year and a day.

My Little House

I have a little house
   With windows and a door,
Two chimneys on the top,
   And a plot of grass before.

I have a little house,
   With curtains and a blind,
Two chimneys on the top,
   And a plot of grass behind.

I have a little house,
   Where I go in and out,
Two chimneys on the top,
   And a garden all about.

J. M. Westrup

Trouble at the Farm

Help! Help!
What's to do?
Dobbin the horse
Has cast a shoe!

Help! Help!
What is the matter?
Porkie the pig
Has eaten the platter!

Help! Help!
What is it now?
Sammie the sheep-dog
Is chasing the cow!

Oh! dear!
What a to-do!
Such muddles and troubles
I never knew!

Ivy O. Eastwick

Off we go to Market

1. We feed the chickens every day,

Action of feeding chickens.

    Singing as we go.

Partners take hands and swing across to opposite positions.

We gather up the eggs they lay,

Action of picking up eggs.

    Singing as we go.

Partners take hands and swing back to places.

    Then off we go to market,
    Off we go to market,
    Off we go to market,
    Singing as we go.

Still with hands across, all follow the first couple down the room and back to place.

2. We plant the turnips in the ground,
    Singing as we go,
We pull them when they're large and round,
    Singing as we go.
Then off we go to market,
Off we go to market,
Off we go to market,
    Singing as we go.

3. We gather cherries ripe and red,
    Singing as we go.
We put them in a basket bed,
    Singing as we go,
Then off we go to market,
Off we go to market,
Off we go to market,
    Singing as we go.

Gwen A. Smith

93

O Sailor, Come Ashore

O sailor, come ashore,
   What have you brought for me?
Red coral, white coral,
   Coral from the sea.

I did not dig it from the ground,
   Nor pluck it from a tree;
Feeble insects made it,
   In the stormy sea.

Christina Rossetti

Oh! Look at the Moon

Oh! look at the moon,
She is shining up there;
Oh! Mother, she looks
Like a lamp in the air.

Last week she was smaller,
And shaped like a bow;
But now she's grown bigger,
And round as an O.

Pretty moon, pretty moon,
How you shine on the door,
And make it all bright
On my nursery floor!

You shine on my playthings,
And show me their place,
And I love to look up
At your pretty bright face.

And there is the star
Close by you, and maybe
That small, twinkling star
Is your little baby.

Eliza Lee Follen

Three Dogs

I know a dog called Isaac,
  Who begs for cake at tea;
He's fat and white and most polite,
  And belongs to Timothy.

I know a dog who carries
  His master's walking-stick:
He's old and slow, and his name is Joe,
  And *he* belongs to Dick.

I know a dog called Jacob,
  The best of all the three,
Sedate and wise, with nice brown eyes,
  And *he* belongs to Me.

                    E. C. Brereton

Making Tens

How many ways can you bring me ten?
Now think fast, my merry little men.

Glad to be first, see Jack's eyes shine,
As he quickly comes to me with one and—

Right on his heels his usual mate
Robert follows with two and—

Next to come is Dick from Devon,
And he has written three and—

Then follows quickly Harold Hicks,
I see he makes it four and—

Last of all comes Mortimer Clive,
But first to think of five and—

                    M. M. Hutchinson

O Dandelion

"O dandelion, yellow as gold,
What do you do all day?"

"I just wait here in the tall green grass
Till the children come to play."

"O dandelion, yellow as gold,
What do you do all night?"

"I wait and wait till the cool dews fall
And my hair grows long and white."

"And what do you do when your hair is white
And the children come to play?"

"They take me up in their dimpled hands
And blow my hair away!"

Old Mother Goose

Old Mother Goose when
    She wanted to wander,
Would ride through the air
    On a very fine gander.

Mother Goose had a house,
    'Twas built in a wood,
Where an owl at the door
    For sentinel stood.

She had a son Jack,
    A plain-looking lad,
He was not very good,
    Nor yet very bad.

She sent him to market,
    A live goose he bought;
"Here, Mother," says he,
    "It will not go for nought."

Jack's goose and her gander
   Grew very fond,
They'd both eat together,
   Or swim in one pond.

Jack found one morning,
   As I have been told,
His goose had laid him
   An egg of pure gold.

Jack rode to his mother,
   The news for to tell;
She call'd him a good boy,
   And said it was well.

A rogue got the goose,
   Which he vow'd he would kill,
Resolving at once
   His pockets to fill.

Jack's mother came in
   And caught the goose soon,
And mounting its back,
   Flew up to the moon.

A-Hunting

The queen is gone a-hunting in the royal wood,
Between ourselves, at hunting she is not much good—
She will not catch the things she hunts, she doesn't think
   it right,
But in her scarlet hunting robes, she's such a pretty sight.
   Hey ho! derry, derry, in the woods so green
   That's how I'd go hunting if I were a queen.

The king is gone a-hunting in the palace pond,
Of hunting little tadpoles he is very fond.
His robes are wet as anything, his crown is all awry,
He's taken off his shoes and socks and hung them out to
   dry.
   Fee fo! fiddle daddle, let him have his fling,
   That's how I'd go hunting if I were a king.
                       Jennie Dunbar

97

Who Likes the Rain?

"I," said the duck. "I call it fun,
For I have my pretty red rubbers on;
They make a little three-toed track
In the soft, cool mud—quack! quack!"

"I," cried the dandelion, "I,
My roots are thirsty, my buds are dry,"
And she lifted a tousled yellow head
Out of her green and grassy bed.

Sang the brook: "I welcome every drop,
Come down, dear raindrops; never stop
Until a broad river you make of me,
And then I will carry you to the sea."

"I," shouted Ted, "for I can run,
With my high-top boots and raincoat on,
Through every puddle and runlet and pool
I find on the road to school."

Mrs. Indiarubber Duck

Mrs. Indiarubber Duck,
I like to see you float
Round and round my bath-tub
Like a tiny sailing boat.

Mrs. Indiarubber Duck,
I like to see you sip
The lovely soapy water
When you take your morning dip.

Mrs. Indiarubber Duck,
I stroke your shining back,
But oh! how splendid it would be
If only you could quack.

D. Carter

98

Marketing

I am going to market
  To buy a loaf of bread;
But if the buns are shiny ones
  I'll buy some buns instead.

I am going to market
  To buy a Cheddar cheese,
And I shall tell the men who sell,
  "A fresh one, if you please."

I am going to market
  To buy some juicy plums,
The men will say, "They're fresh to-day,"
  To everyone that comes.

I am going to market
  To see what I can see;
I'll look around and spend a pound,
  And come back home for tea.

E. J. Falconer

Little Trotty Wagtail

Little Trotty Wagtail, he went in the rain,
And twittering, tottering sideways he ne'er got straight
    again.
He stooped to get a worm, and looked up to get a fly,
And then he flew away ere his feathers they were dry.

Little Trotty Wagtail, he waddled in the mud,
And left his little footmarks, trample where he would.
He waddled in the water-pudge, and waggle went his tail,
And chirrupt up his wings to dry upon the garden rail.

Little Trotty Wagtail, you nimble all about,
And in the dimpling water-pudge you waddle in and out;
Your home is nigh at hand, and in the warm pig-stye,
So, little Master Wagtail, I'll bid you a good-bye.

John Clare

Baby Beds

Little lambs, little lambs,
Where do you sleep?
"In the green meadow,
With mother sheep."

Little birds, little birds,
Where do you rest?
"Close to our mother,
In a warm nest."

Baby dear, Baby dear,
Where do you lie?
"In my warm bed,
With Mother close by."

The Pigeons

Out in the garden,
    Out in the sun,
Two pigeons were talking.
    I listened. Said One:
"I do think it's fine
For the time of the year.
    Don't yo-ou? Don't yo-o-ou?"
And Two, from the branch
Of another tree near,
    Said, "I do-o. I do-o-o."

Number One called:
    "Do come and look,
I've found in this thorn-tree
    The cosiest nook.
I do think a thorn
Is a snug sort of tree.
    Don't you-ou? Don't yo-o-ou?"
And Two, as she flew
Through the garden to see,
    Said, "I do-o. I do-o-o."

Number One said:
  "I've found a twig,
It isn't too little,
  It isn't too big.
I think it is time
We were building a nest.
  Don't you-ou? Don't yo-o-ou?"
And Two said: "My dear,
If you think it is best,
  Yes, I do-o. I do-o-o."

Out in the garden,
  Out in the sun,
They're talking this morning.
  Hush! Listen to One:
"I think that's the finest egg
Ever was laid.
  Don't yo-ou? Don't yo-o-ou?"
And Two, sitting snug
  In the nest they have made,
  Says, "I do-o. They're two-o-o!"

Rodney Bennett

The Muffin-Man's Bell

"Tinkle, tinkle, tinkle": 'tis the muffin-man you see:
  "Tinkle, tinkle," says the muffin-man's bell;
"Any crumpets, any muffins, any cakes for your tea:
  There are plenty here to sell."

"Tinkle," says the little bell, clear and bright:
  "Tinkle, tinkle," says the muffin-man's bell;
We have had bread and milk for supper to-night,
  And some nice plum-cake as well.

"Tinkle, tinkle, tinkle," says the little bell again,
  But it sounds quite far away;
"If you don't buy my muffins and my cakes, it is plain
  I must take them home to-day."

Ann Hawkshawe

101

Mr. Beetle

With a very big yawn
Mr. Beetle awoke.
"Oh dear, oh dear,
I do feel queer!
My neck is stiff,
My legs are as if
I'd slept in a pig-and-a-poke."

He ran to the sunlight,
He bathed in the dew,
He cleaned his teeth
With a grassy sheath,
He shaved and behaved
As gentlemen beetles do.

He lived all alone—
Maria did too,
But he wanted some stitches
In jacket and breeches,
So he called at her house
And made her his spouse.
And they lived, they did,
Under the yew.

Emily Hover

The Moonlight

The moonlight is a gentle thing,
    Through the window it gleams
Upon the snowy pillow where
    The happy infant dreams.

It shines upon the fisher's boat,
    Out on the lovely sea;
Or where the little lambkins lie
    Beneath the old oak tree.

Ann Hawkshawe

Twice

Twice one are two,
And twice two are four,
Say it over carefully
At least once more.

Twice two are four,
And twice three are six,
Say it over carefully
Until it sticks.

Twice three are six,
And twice four are eight,
Write it down on paper, pad,
Or on your slate.

Twice four are eight,
And twice five are ten,
Write it down with pencil
Or with chalk or pen.

Twice five are ten,
And twice six are twelve,
In the number garden
You must delve, delve, delve.

M. M. Hutchinson

Come Here, Little Robin

Come here, little Robin, and don't be afraid,
    I would not hurt even a feather;
Come here, little Robin, and pick up some bread,
    To feed you this very cold weather.

The winter has come, but it will not stay long,
    And summer we soon shall be greeting;
Then remember, dear Robin, to sing me a song
    In return for the breakfast you're eating.

What Piggy-Wig Found

Piggy-wig found he had four little feet,
    And said to his mother one day,
"Mother, I find I have four little feet,
    What shall I do with them, pray?"

"Run about, run about, Piggy-wig-wig,
    Run on your four little feet and grow big!"

Piggy-wig found he had two little eyes,
    And said to his mother one day,
"Mother, I find I have two little eyes,
    What shall I do with them, pray?"

"Look about, look about, Piggy-wig-wig,
    Look with your two little eyes, and grow big!"

Piggy-wig found he had one little nose,
    And said to his mother one day,
"Mother, I find I have one little nose,
    What shall I do with it, pray?"

"Sniff about, sniff about, Piggy-wig-wig,
    Sniff with your one little nose and grow big!"

Piggy-wig found he had one little mouth,
    And said to his mother one day,
"Mother, I find I have one little mouth,
    What shall I do with it, pray?"

"Eat with it, eat with it, Piggy-wig-wig,
    Eat with your one little mouth and grow big!"

So Piggy-wig ran on his four little toes,
    And looked with his two little eyes,
And ate with his mouth, and sniffed with his nose,
    And soon he grew BIG and WISE!

Enid Blyton

My Garden

I picked fresh mint
For Mary Quint,
Who made it, of course,
Into Canterbury sauce.
She said: "Thank you, Poppet,
And here's for your pains
Gooseberry bushes
And Raspberry canes."

I borrowed a spade
With a speedy blade,
And dug at the soil
With desperate toil;
Then I put them in,
And I hope that it rains
On my Gooseberry bushes
And Raspberry canes.

Time will tell
If I planted well,
But if every shoot
Should be hung with fruit,
And Mary calls
About mid-July,
There'll be Gooseberry pudding
And Raspberry pie!

Norah Hussey

The Weathercock

The moon is like a lamp,
    The sun is like a fire,
The weathercock can see them both;
    He sits upon the spire.

He sits upon the spire
    High above the ground—
I'd like to be a weathercock
    Turning round and round.

Rose Fyleman

Strange Talk

A little green frog lived under a log,
  And every time he spoke.
Instead of saying, "Good morning,"
  He only said, "Croak—croak."

A duck lived by the waterside,
  And little did he lack,
But when we asked, "How do you do,"
  He only said, "Quack-quack."

A rook lived in an elm tree,
  And all the world he saw,
But when he tried to make a speech
  It sounded like, "Caw-caw."

A little pig lived in a sty,
  As fat as he could be,
And when he asked for dinner
  He cried aloud, "Wee-wee."

Three pups lived in a kennel,
  And loved to make a row,
And when they meant, "May we go out?"
  They said, "Bow-wow! Bow-wow!"

If all these animals talked as much
  As little girls and boys,
And all of them tried to speak at once,
  Wouldn't it make a noise?

L. E. Yates

The Muffin Man

The muffin man walked down our street,
And whom do you think he happened to meet?
John and Ann were standing there,
Both with pennies to spend at the fair.
But when they thought about our tea
They bought muffins for you and me!

Ann Croasdell

Three Little Men in a Boat

Three little men,
On a lake afloat,
Three little men
With a leaf for a boat.
One moon shines on them
High overhead,
One shines up
From the lake's deep bed.

Between two moons,
Among lilies afloat,
The little men sail
In their aspen boat,
Till the moons grow pale,
And the stars, and then
Three little men
Sail homeward again.

Rodney Bennett

Who?

Who will feed the dicky-birds on the garden wall?
Winter-time is very big—they are very small!

Who will feed the dicky-birds on the frozen trees?
Every little twitter means, "Feed us, if you please!"

Who will feed the dicky-birds in the frost and snow?
See them on the chimney pot—cuddled in a row!

Who will feed the dicky-birds till the days of spring?
Think of what they do for you and the songs they sing!

I will feed the dicky-birds, and when springtime comes,
Every little song will mean, "Thank you for the crumbs!"

Florence Hoatson

Trains

Our garden's very near the trains;
    I think it's jolly fine
That I have just to climb the fence
    To watch the railway line!

I love to see the train that takes
    A minute to the mile;
The engine-man, as he goes past,
    Has only time to smile!

Then comes a train with empty trucks,
    That never goes so fast;
Its driver-man has always time
    To wave as he goes past!

The man who drives the luggage train,
    That passes here at three,
Not only smiles and waves his hand,
    But whistles once for me!

Hope Shepherd

Minnie and Mattie

Minnie and Mattie,
    And fat little May,
Out in the country,
    Spending a day.

Such a bright day,
    With the sun glowing,
And the trees half in leaf,
    And the grass growing.

Pinky white pigling
    Squeals through his snout,
Woolly white lambkin
    Frisks all about.

Cluck! cluck! the nursing hen
    Summons her folk,
Ducklings all downy soft,
    Yellow as yolk.

Cluck! cluck! the mother hen
  Summons her chickens
To peck the dainty bits
  Found in her pickings.

Minnie and Mattie
  And May carry posies,
Half of sweet violets,
  Half of primroses.

Give the sun time enough,
  Glowing and glowing,
He'll rouse the roses
  And bring them blowing.

Don't wait for roses
  Losing to-day,
O Minnie, Mattie,
  And wise little May.

Violets and primroses,
  Blossoms to-day
For Minnie and Mattie
  And fat little May.

Christina Rossetti

Mincemeat

Sing a song of mincemeat,
Currants, raisins, spice,
Apples, sugar, nutmeg,
Everything that's nice,
Stir it with a ladle,
Wish a lovely wish,
Drop it in the middle
Of your well-filled dish,
Stir again for good luck,
Pack it all away
Tied in little jars and pots,
Until Christmas Day.

Elizabeth Gould

Two Little Kittens

Two little kittens,
One stormy night,
Began to quarrel,
And then to fight.

One had a mouse
And the other had none;
And that was the way
The quarrel begun.

"I'll have that mouse,"
Said the bigger cat.
"You'll have that mouse?
We'll see about that!"

"I will have that mouse,"
Said the tortoise-shell;
And, spitting and scratching,
On her sister she fell.

I've told you before
'Twas a stormy night,
When these two kittens
Began to fight.

The old woman took
The sweeping broom,
And swept them both
Right out of the room.

The ground was covered
With frost and snow,
They had lost the mouse,
And had nowhere to go.

So they lay and shivered
Beside the door,
Till the old woman finished
Sweeping the floor.

And then they crept in
As quiet as mice,
All wet with snow
And as cold as ice.

They found it much better
That stormy night,
To lie by the fire,
Than to quarrel and fight.

Jane Taylor

Ten Little Indian Boys

One little Indian boy making a canoe,
Another came to help him and then there were two.

Two little Indian boys climbing up a tree,
They spied another one and then there were three.

Three little Indian boys playing on the shore,
They called another one and then there were four.

Four little Indian boys learning how to dive,
An older one taught them and then there were five.

Five making arrows then from slender shining sticks,
One came to lend a bow and then there were six.

Six little Indian boys wishing for eleven,
One only could they find and then there were seven.

Seven little Indian boys marched along in state,
One joined the growing line and then there were eight.

Eight little Indian boys camping near the pine,
One came with bait for fish and then there were nine.

Nine little Indian boys growing to be men,
Captured another brave and then there were ten.

M. M. Hutchinson

Toad The Tailor

Toad the Tailor lived in a well,
 Croak! Croak! Croak! he would sing.
Instead of a knocker his door had a bell.
 Croak! C-C-C-Croak!

The bell, it was hung with the greatest of care,
 Croak! Croak! Croak! he would sing.
At the top of the steps leading down to him there,
 Croak! C-C-C-Croak!

By the light or a lantern his customers came,
 Croak! Croak! he would sing.
He measured them all by the length of their name.
 Croak! C-C-C-Croak!

But nobody grumbled a bit about that,
 Croak! Croak! Croak! he would sing.
It suited the thin and it suited the fat,
 Croak! C-C-C-Croak!

In time the old Toad grew as rich as could be,
 Croak! Croak! Croak! he would sing.
So he hung out a notice, "All Tailoring Free."
 Croak! C-C-C-Croak!

N. E. Hussey

Little Lucy Lester

Little Lucy Lester was a funny little lady;
Up the grassy meadow she would run with all her might;
When she reached the other end, she'd scamper back so
 gaily,
Right into her little house where lived her cat so white.
"Why for do you run so fast?" said Farmer Giles in
 passing,
"Are you going to catch a train, or is your white cat ill?"
"Neither, thank you kindly," said that little Lucy
 Lester—
"You see, I go by clock-work, and I can't stand still."

M. Steel

The Little Old Lady

That little grey-haired lady
   Is as old as old can be,
Yet once she was a little girl,
   A little girl like me.

She liked to skip instead of walk,
   She wore her hair in curls;
She went to school at nine, and played
   With other little girls.

I wonder if, in years and years,
   Some little girl at play,
Who's very like what I am now,
   Will stop to look my way,

And think: "That grey-haired lady
   Is as old as old can be,
Yet once she was a little girl,
   A little girl like me."

Rodney Bennett

Mice

I think mice
Are rather nice.

Their tails are long,
Their faces small,
They haven't any
Chins at all.
Their ears are pink,
Their teeth are white,
They run about
The house at night.
They nibble things
They shouldn't touch
And no one seems
To like them much.

But I think mice
Are nice.

Rose Fyleman

113

Little Brown Seed

Little brown seed, round and sound,
Here I put you in the ground.

You can sleep a week or two,
Then—I'll tell you what to do:

You must grow some downward roots,
Then some tiny upward shoots.

From those green shoots' folded sheaves
Soon must come some healthy leaves.

When the leaves have time to grow,
Next a bunch of buds must show.

Last of all, the buds must spread
Into blossoms white or red.

There, Seed! I've done my best.
Please to grow and do the rest.

Rodney Bennett

What Is It?

Here's a guessing story,
    Listen and you'll hear,
We have something in our house,
    Very, very queer.

It hasn't any teeth,
It hasn't any hair,
It cannot walk,
It cannot talk,
And yet it's always there.

Here's a guessing story,
Will you give it up?
It's just a little-little-little
Tiny, baby pup!

H. E. Wilkinson

114

The March Wind

The merry March wind is a boisterous fellow,
He tosses the trees; and the daffodils yellow
Dance and sway, as he blows by
To hurry the clouds across the sky.

He plays such pranks with the weather vane,
Turning it round, then back again.
But the game he enjoys the best of all,
Is blowing my bonnet right over a wall.

E. H. Henderson

A Little Finger Game

Here is a house with a pointed door,
"Pointed door." Index fingers and thumbs together.
Windows tall, and a fine flat floor.
*"Windows tall." Fingers of both hands joined at the tips
and stretched apart. "Fine flat floor." Hands held
flat, palms down, side by side on floor or desk.*
Three good people live in the house,
*"Three good people." Three middle fingers of one hand
standing up under shelter of the other.*
One fat cat, and one thin mouse.
*"One fat cat." Right-hand thumb stands up. "One thin
mouse." Right-hand little finger stands up.*
Out of his hole the mousie peeps,
*"Out of his hole." Right-hand little finger peeps through
left hand folded into a fist.*
Out of his corner the pussie-cat leaps!
*"Out of his corner." Right-hand thumb jumps over upon
left-hand fist.*
Three good people say "Oh! oh! oh!"
"Three good people." Fingers stand up as before.
Mousie inside says "No! no! no!"
*"Mousie inside." Little finger draws back inside left-hand
fist.*

E. J. Falconer

115

The Postman

Bring me a letter, postman!
Bring me a letter, do!
To-morrow at the garden gate
I will wait for you.

Bring one from a fairy
Who says she'll come to tea,
Then I'll put on my party frock,
How lovely that will be.

And please, oh Mr. Postman,
If fairies you know none,
Write me a letter from yourself,
And bring it, just for fun.

Alice Todd

Mrs. Jenny Wren

Mrs. Jenny Wren!
    I have never, never heard
Such a very big voice
    For a very tiny bird.
You sit on a post
    And you sing and you sing,
You're a very bold bird
    For such a tiny little thing,
Jenny Wren.

If I had a voice
    For my size as big as yours,
I should never dare sing
    Without shutting all the doors.
I'd sing very softly
    For fear they should hear,
Or they'd hurry away
    And put a finger in each ear,
Jenny Wren.

Rodney Bennett

Mistress Comfort

Little Mistress Comfort got up early one fine day,
She swept her little porch, and cleaned
The knocker on her door,
She gave her little cat some milk,
Her little cow some hay,
She fed her little cocks and hens,
Then swept her little floor.

She filled a little platter with some porridge, nice and hot,
She ate her little breakfast,
Then she climbed her little stair;
She shook her little pillows up,
She made her little cot
And all her little house so clean
And shining everywhere.

She sat down by her spinning-wheel and spun a little thread,
She made a little loaf for tea.
She mended her red cloak.
As busy as a bee she was,
And ere she went to bed
She set a little crock of cream
For chance-come Fairy Folk.

Then tired Mistress Comfort sweetly slept
The whole night through,
In the morning, when she woke, she found a
SIXPENCE IN HER SHOE.

Elizabeth Gould

Mr. Pennycomequick

There was an old party called Pennycomequick,
Who rode off to town on the back of a stick;
His house was a teapot without any spout,
He just lifted the lid when he wished to look out.

P. M. Stone

117

Noises in the Night

When I'm in bed at night,
All tucked up warm and tight,
All kinds of noises
Go in at my two ears.
Brr . . . go the motor cars
Out on the street.
Whirr . . . sings the wind
As it blows round the house.
Ting-a-ling-ling
Ring the bicycle bells.
And ding-dong, ding-dong,
Sings the Grandfather Clock downstairs.
Then I hear nothing—nothing at all,
Because I'm asleep, sound asleep.

1. *Children pretend to cuddle down in bed.*
2. *They listen to the noises as the teacher tells the story.*
3. *They close their eyes and go fast asleep as the teacher very quietly and slowly says the last two lines.*

Lilian McCrea

Miller, Miller

Miller, Miller,
Meet the farmer
When the weather
Has turned warmer!

Buy his wheat
And stack it till
You shall take it
To the mill.

Windmill, Windmill,
Turn a round!
Never stop
Till the wheat is ground!

Baker, Baker,
Hurry and go
To the bakehouse
And bake your dough!

Oven, Oven,
Cook the bread,
Or else the children
Cannot be fed!

Oven, Oven,
See that you bake
An icy, spicy,
Sugary cake!

A sugary cake
And a loaf of bread,
And so the children
Shall all be fed!

Ivy O. Eastwick

The Little Maid and the Cowslips

"Where art thou wandering, little child?"
    I said to one I met to-day—
She push'd her bonnet up and smil'd,
    "I'm going upon the green to play:
Folks tell me that the May's in flower,
    That Cowslip-peeps are fit to pull,
And I've got leave to spend an hour
    To get this little basket full."

John Clare

Pretty Lady

The prettiest lady that ever I've seen
Came dancing, dancing, over the green.
She wore a hat with a curly feather,
Her dear little shoes were of scarlet leather.

With the tips of her fingers she held up her gown;
She didn't look up, she didn't look down,
She didn't look left, she didn't look right,
Her curls flew out in a stream of light.
My mother called and I looked away—
I never have seen her since that day.

Rose Fyleman

119

In the Mirror

In the mirror
On the wall,
There's a face
I always see;
Round and pink,
And rather small,
Looking back again
At me.

It is very
Rude to stare,
But she never
Thinks of that,
For her eyes are
Always there;
What can she be
Looking at?

Elizabeth Fleming

The Three Little Kittens

Three little kittens lost their mittens,
And they began to cry:
"Oh, Mother dear,
We very much fear
That we have lost our mittens!"

"Lost your mittens!
You naughty kittens!
Then you shall have no pie!"
"Mee-ow, mee-ow, mee-ow."
"No, you shall have no pie."
"Mee-ow, mee-ow, mee-ow!"

The three little kittens found their mittens,
And they began to cry:
"Oh, Mother dear,
See here — see here!
See, we have found our mittens!"

"Put on your mitte
You silly kittens,
And you may have some pie."
"Purr, purr, purr,
Oh, let us taste the pie!
Purr, purr, purr."

The three little kittens put on their mittens,
And soon ate up the pie;
"Oh, Mother dear,
We greatly fear
That we have soiled our mittens!"

"Soiled your mittens!
You naughty kittens!"
Then they began to sigh:
"Mee-ow, mee-ow, mee-ow!"
Then they began to sigh:
"Mee-ow, mee-ow, mee-ow!"

The three little kittens washed their mittens
And hung them out to dry;
"Oh, Mother dear,
Do you not hear
That we have washed our mittens?"

"Washed your mittens!
Then you're good kittens;
But I smell a rat close by!"
"Hush, hush! Mee-ow, mee-ow!
We smell a rat close by!
Mee-ow, mee-ow, mee-ow!"

The Milkman

Clink, clink, clinkety-clink,
The milkman's on his rounds, I think.
Crunch, crunch, come the milkman's feet
Closer and closer along the street—
Then clink, clink, clinkety-clink,
He's left our bottles of milk to drink.

Clive Sansom

Little Tommy Tiddler

Little Tommy Tiddler
Is going to be a fiddler;
They've given him a fiddle,
And they've given him a bow.
Play, play, play, Tommy Tiddler!
Say, say, say, Tommy Tiddler,
Play a little twiddle
On the middle of your fiddle,
Or we'll go, we'll go, we'll go, go, go,
And take away your fiddle and your bow.

Paul Edmonds

A Summer Shower

"Hurry!" said the leaves;
"Hurry, birds, hurry!
See how the tall trees
Are all in a flurry!"

"Come under, quick,
Grasshoppers, cricket!"
Said the leafy vines
Down in the thicket.

"Come here," said the rose
To bee and spider;
"Ant, here's a place!
Fly, sit beside her!"

"Rest, butterfly,
Here in the bushes,
Close by the robin,
While the rain rushes!"

"Why, there is the sun!
And the birds are singing:
Good-bye, dear leaves,
We'll all be winging."

"Bee," said the rose,
"Thank you for calling.
Come in again
When the rain is falling."

Dicky-Birds

Two little dicky-birds
Sitting on a twig,
Both very plump
And neither very big.

"Tweet!" said the first one,
"Cheep!" said his brother—
Wasn't that a funny way
To talk to one another?

Down flew one bird
And picked up a crust;
Off went the other
To a little heap of dust;

Plunged into a dust-bath,
All puffed out and fat,
Wouldn't it be very strange
To have a bath like that?

Both little brown birds
At the set of sun
Flew into a big tree
Because the day was done.

Cuddled in a warm nest,
Cosy as could be,
Mustn't it be lovely
Sleeping in a tree?

Natalie Joan

123

Ten Little Dicky-Birds

Addition in Ones to Ten

1. One little dicky-bird
   Hopped on my shoe;
   Along came another one,
   And that made two.

Chorus:
   Fly to the tree-tops;
   Fly to the ground;
   Fly, little dicky-birds,
   Round and round.

2. Two little dicky-birds,
   Singing in a tree;
   Along came another one,
   And that made three.

   Chorus

3. Three little dicky-birds,
   Came to my door;
   Along came another one,
   And that made four.

   Chorus

4. Four little dicky-birds
   Perched on a hive;
   Along came another one,
   And that made five.

   Chorus

5. Five little dicky-birds
   Nesting in the ricks;
   Along came another one,
   And that made six.

   Chorus

6. Six little dicky-birds
   Flying up to heaven;
   Along came another one,
   And that made seven.

   Chorus

7. Seven little dicky-birds ·
   Sat upon a gate;
   Along came another one,
   And that made eight.

   Chorus

8. Eight little dicky-birds
   Swinging on a line;
   Along came another one,
   And that made nine.

   Chorus

9. Nine little dicky-birds
   Looking at a hen;
   Along came another one,
   And that made ten.

   Chorus

Actions:
Fingers are erected one by one from closed fists, to re-
present the birds. During the chorus, actions are as follows:
Line 1. "Birds" are held up high.
Line 2. "Birds" are held down low.
Lines 3 and 4. "Birds" are circled round and round.

A. W. I. Baldwin

Love Me—I Love You

Love me—I love you,
Love me, my baby;
Sing it high, sing it low,
Sing it as may be.

Mother's arms under you;
Her eyes above you;
Sing it high, sing it low,
Love me—I love you.

Christina Rossetti

125

Thank You, Pretty Cow

Thank you, pretty cow, that made
Pleasant milk to soak my bread,
Every day and every night
Warm, and fresh, and sweet, and white.

Do not chew the hemlock rank,
Growing on the weedy bank,
But the yellow cowslip eat,
That will make it very sweet.

Where the purple violet grows,
Where the bubbling water flows,
Where the grass is fresh and fine,
Pretty cow, go there and dine.

Jane Taylor

The Dormouse

The Dormouse felt so sleepy
  Nid-nodding went his head,
He said "Good night" to everyone,
  And cuddled up in bed.

Down fell the icy raindrops,
  The cold wind whistled round;
The Dormouse in his snuggly bed,
  Lay sleeping safe and sound.

There he was found one morning
  By Jeremy and Jane;
They whispered low, then on tip-toe,
  They crept away again.

They filled a bag with acorns,
  And hid it in the brakes,
So that the little Dormouse,
  May find it when he wakes.

Charlotte Druitt Cole

Song for a Ball-Game

Bounce ball! Bounce ball!
　One—two—three.
Underneath my right leg
　And round about my knee.
Bounce ball! Bounce ball!
　Bird—or—bee
Flying from the rose-bud
　Up into the tree.

Bounce ball! Bounce ball!
　Fast—you—go
Underneath my left leg
　And round about my toe.
Bounce ball! Bounce ball!
　Butt—er—fly
Flying from the rosebud
　Up in the sky.

Bounce ball! Bounce ball!
　You—can't—stop.
Right leg and left leg
　Round them both you hop.
Bounce ball! Bounce ball!
　Shy—white—dove,
Tell me how to find him,
　My own true love.

Wilfred Thorley

The Farmyard

One black horse standing by the gate,
Two plump cats eating from a plate;
Three big goats kicking up their heels,
Four pink pigs full of grunts and squeals;
Five white cows coming slowly home,
Six small chicks starting off to roam;
Seven fine doves perched upon the shed,
Eight grey geese eager to be fed;
Nine young lambs full of frisky fun,
Ten brown bees buzzing in the sun.

A. A. Attwood

Ding-Dong!

Ding-dong! Ding-dong!
  All the bells are ringing,
Ding-dong! Ding-dong!
  'Tis a holiday.

Ding-dong! Ding-dong!
  All the birds are singing,
Ding-dong! Ding-dong!
  Let's go out and play.

Kitty

Once there was a little Kitty
  Whiter than snow;
In a barn she used to frolic,
  Long time ago.

In the barn a little mousie
  Ran to and fro;
For she heard the Kitty coming,
  Long time ago.

Two eyes had little Kitty,
  Black as a sloe;
And they spied the little mousie,
  Long time ago.

Four paws had little Kitty,
  Paws soft as dough,
And they caught the little mousie,
  Long time ago.

Nine teeth had little Kitty,
  All in a row;
And they bit the little mousie,
  Long time ago.

When the teeth bit little mousie,
  Little mouse cried "Oh!"
But she got away from Kitty,
  Long time ago.

A Penny Wish

I wish I had an aeroplane
To fetch my oranges from Spain.

I wish I had a motor car
To ride in when I go too far.

I wish I had a little train
To go to town and home again.

And if I had a sailing boat
I'd use it with my sailor coat.

But what's the good of wanting any
When all I have is just a penny!

Irene Thompson

The Pigeon's Story

Where do you think I've been to-day?
  Rooketty coo! rooketty coo!
Off to the town in the farmer's dray,
  Rooketty, rooketty coo!

What do you think I did to-day?
  Rooketty coo! rooketty coo!
Out of the cage I hopped away,
  Rooketty, rooketty coo!

What happened next? I hear you say,
  Rooketty coo! rooketty coo!
Spreading my wings I flew away,
  Rooketty, rooketty coo!

Back to my mate I found my way,
  Rooketty coo! rooketty coo!
Now I am home with you to play,
  Rooketty, rooketty coo!

Jeannie Kirby

129

The Song of the Engine

Slowly

With snort and pant the engine dragged
  Its heavy train uphill,
And puffed these words the while she puffed
  And laboured with a will:

Very slowly

"I think—I can—I think—I can,
  I've got—to reach—the top,
I'm sure—I can—I will—get there,
  I sim—ply must—not stop!"

More quickly

At last the top was reached and passed,
  And then—how changed the song!
The wheels all joined in the engine's joy,
  As quickly she tore along!

Very fast

"I knew I could do it, I knew I could win,
  Oh, rickety rackety rack!
And now for a roaring rushing race
  On my smooth and shining track!"

H. Worsley-Benison

The Paddling Pool

If you find a paddling pool,
Dabble your toes to make them cool.
  Splash! Splash! Splash!
Kick up your feet and scatter the spray,
Oh what fun for a bright sunny day!
  Splash! Splash! Splash!

E. M. Adams

130

Wandering Jack

Listen to the song
   Of Wandering Jack.
He carries a bundle
   On his back.
What is inside it?
   Shall I tell?
He carries inside it
   Dreams to sell.
Some cost a penny,
   Some cost a pound.
But some cost nothing,
   I'll be bound.

Emile Jacot

A Growing Rhyme

A farmer once planted some little brown seeds
With a pit-a-pit, pit-a-pat, pit-a-pat, pat.
He watered them often and pulled up the weeds,
With a tug-tug at this and a tug-tug at that.
The little seeds grew tall and green in the sun,
With a push-push up here, and a push-push up there,
And a beautiful plant grew from every one,
With a hey diddle, holding their heads in the air.

J. M. Westrup

Good Morning

Good morning to you and good morning to you;
Come pull on your stocking and put on your shoe;
There are bees, there are birds, there are flowers in the
   sun—

Good morning to you and good morning to you;
Come out of your beds, there is plenty to do.
Come out with a shout and a laugh and a run—
Good morning, good morning to every one.

Rose Fyleman

131

The Two Families

One summer I stayed
On a farm, and I saw
A quaint little sight
I had not seen before.

A cat and her kittens,
And a sow and her troup
Of little pink pigs,
In one family group.

The mother cat came
To be petted by me,
While I looked at her kittens,
So sooty and wee!

Like tiny black smuts,
The two little dears
Contentedly slept
Beside the sow's ears.

Till one kitten woke,
And started to roam
On Mrs. Pig's back
As if quite at home.

And there it sat down
To gaze at its friends,
The little pink pigs
With their queer curly ends!

And old Mother Pig
Snored loudly and deep,
Nor noticed the kittens,
Awake or asleep!

Joyce L. Brisley

The Birdies' Breakfast

Two little birdies, one wintry day,
Began to wonder, and then to say,
"How about breakfast, this wintry day?"

Two little maidens, that wintry day,
Into the garden soon took their way,
Where the snow lay deep, that wintry day.

One with her broom swept the snow away;
One scattered crumbs, then went to play;
So the birdies had breakfast that wintry day.

Pretty Maid Marion

Pretty Maid Marion, where have you been?
Gathering buttercups down on the green.

Pretty Maid Marion, what did you see?
A skylark, a grasshopper-green, and a bee.

Pretty Maid Marion, what did you hear?
A little lark singing high up in the air!

Pretty Maid Marion, what did you do?
I screwed up my mouth—so!—and I whistled too!

Ivy O. Eastwick

Fantasy and Fairyland

We want to go to Fairyland
To dance by the light of the moon

I'd Love to be a Fairy's Child

Children born of fairy stock
Never need for shirt or frock,
Never want for food or fire,
Always get their heart's desire:
Jingle pockets full of gold,
Marry when they're seven years old,
Every fairy child may keep
Two strong ponies and ten sheep;
All have houses, each his own,
Built of brick or granite stone;
They live on cherries, they run wild—
I'd love to be a fairy's child.

Robert Graves

The Fairy Flute

My brother has a little flute
    Of gold and ivory,
He found it on a summer night
    Within a hollow tree,
He plays it every morning
    And every afternoon,
And all the little singing-birds
    Listen to the tune.
He plays it in the meadows,
    And everywhere he walks
The flowers start a-nodding
    And dancing on their stalks.
He plays it in the village,
    And all along the street
The people stop to listen,
    The music is so sweet.
And none but he can play it
    And none can understand,
Because it is a fairy flute
    And comes from Fairyland.

Rose Fyleman

The Faerie Fair

The fairies hold a fair, they say,
Beyond the hills when skies are grey
And daylight things are laid away.

And very strange their marketing,
If we could see them on the wing
With all the fairy ware they bring.

Long strings they sell, of berries bright,
And wet wind-fallen apples light
Blown from the trees some starry night.

Gay patches, too, for tattered wings,
Gold bubbles blown by goblin things,
And mushrooms for the fairy rings.

Fine flutes are there, of magic reed,
Whose piping sets the elves indeed
A-dancing down the dewy mead.

These barter they for bats and moles,
For beaten silver bells and bowls
Bright from the caverns of the Trolls.

And so they show, and sell and buy,
With song and dance right merrily,
Until the morning gilds the sky.

Florence Harrison

Where The Bee Sucks

Where the bee sucks, there suck I:
In a cowslip's bell I lie;
There I couch when owls do cry.
On the bat's back I do fly
After summer merrily.
Merrily, merrily shall I live now
Under the blossom that hangs on the bough.

Shakespeare

137

Hob the Elf

Perhaps, if you
  Are very good,
You'll see a cottage
  In the wood,
Where lies in comfort
  Hob, the elf,
All in the cottage
  By himself.
The cottage small
  Is made of bark.
Inside it is
  So very dark,
That when night comes
  Our little elf
Puts a bright lantern
  On the shelf,
And there he sits
  With glasses round,
Reading his book
  Without a sound.

Norman M. Johnson

Fairy Feet

Nobody lives in the cottage now,
  But birds build under the thatch,
And a trailing rose half hides the door
  And twines itself round the latch.

Nobody walks up the cobble path,
  Where the grass peeps in between,
But fairy feet tread the cobble stones
  And keep them wonderfully clean.

Nobody knows that the raindrops bright
  Which fall on the grey old stones
Are the feet of the fairies dancing for joy
  On the path that nobody owns.

Phyllis L. Garlick

138

The Little Elf-Man

I met a little elf-man once
Down where the lilies blow.
I asked him why he was so small,
And why he didn't grow.

He slightly frowned, and with his eye
He looked me through and through—
"I'm just as big for me," said he,
"As you are big for you!"

J. K. Bangs

About the Fairies

Pray, where are the little bluebells gone,
    That lately blossomed in the wood?
Why, the little fairies have each taken one,
    And put it on for a hood.

And where are the pretty grass-stalks gone,
    That waved in the summer breeze?
Oh, the fairies have taken them, every one,
    To plant in their gardens like trees.

And where are the great big blue-bottles gone,
    That buzzed in their busy pride?
Oh, the fairies have caught them, every one,
    And have broken them in, to ride.

And they've taken the glow-worms to light their halls,
    And the cricket to sing them a song;
And the great red rose leaves to paper their walls,
    And they're feasting the whole night long.

And when Spring comes back, with its soft mild ray,
    And the ripple of gentle rain,
The fairies bring what they've taken away,
    And give it us all again.

Jean Ingelow

Bramble Jam

A little old woman,
As old as could be,
Picked the ripe berries
From bush and tree.

Then in a clearing
She made a fire,
Piling the dry sticks
Higher and higher;
And at the top
Of the crackling pile,
She put her gallipot
On to boil,
Sugar and fruit
She boiled for hours,
Till the juice set red
As peony-flowers;
And all the next morning
The Little Folks ran
With pursefuls of money
To buy pots of jam.

Irene F. Pawsey

The Elfin People Fill the Tubes

"I know a solemn secret to keep between ourselves—
I heard it from a sparrow who heard it from the elves—
That always after 2 a.m., before the first cock-crow,
The elfin people fill the Tubes just full to overflow.

"The grown-ups do not know it; they put the trains to bed
And never guess that magic will drive them in their stead;
All day the goblin drivers were hiding in the dark
(If mortals catch a fairy's eye they take it for a spark).

"Elves patter down the subways; they crowd the moving
        stairs;
From purses full of tiddly-winks they pay the clerk their
        fares;
A Brownie checks the tickets and says the proper things:
'Come, pass along the car there!' 'Now, ladies, mind your
        wings!'

140

"They're never dull like mortals who read and dream and
    doze;
The fairies hang head downwards, strap-hanging by their
    toes;
When Puck is the conductor he also acts as host
And sets them playing Leapfrog or Coach or General Post.

"I'd love to travel with them! The sparrow says he thinks
I'd get from here to Golders Green for three red
    tiddly-winks;
Two yellows pay to Euston, four whites to Waterloo;
Perhaps I'll go some moonlight night; the question is—
    will *you*?"

Winifred Letts

Picnics

If you go a-picnicking and throw your scraps about,
You'll never see the little folk go running in and out;
And if you leave your orange-peel all littered on the grass,
You'll never go to Fairy Land or see the fairies pass.
    For empty tins and tangled strings
    And paper bags are not the things
    To scatter where a linnet sings.

So if you go a-picnicking remember you're a guest
Of all the tiny people, and you'll really find it best
To leave their ballroom tidy and to clear away the mess,
And perhaps you'll see a fairy in her newest dancing dress.
    But paper bags and broken combs
    Will really wreck the pixie homes
    And frighten all the tiny gnomes.

But if you go a-picnicking and you are elfin wise,
You'll maybe hear with fairy ears and see with goblin eyes;
The little folk will welcome you, and they will open wide
The hidden doors of Fairy Land, and you will pass inside,
    And maybe see a baby fay
    White cradled in a cherry spray,
    Although it is Bank Holiday.

From "Punch"

141

The Way to Fairyland

Which is the way to Fairyland,
  To Fairyland, to Fairyland?
We want to go to Fairyland,
  To dance by the light of the moon.

Up the hill and down the lane,
  Down the lane, down the lane,
Up te hill and down the lane,
  You'll get there very soon.

Across the common and through the gate,
  Through the gate, through the gate,
Across the common and through the gate,
  You'll get there very soon.

Over the stile and into the wood,
  Into the wood, into the wood,
Over the stile and into the wood,
  You'll get there very soon.

Here we are in Fairyland,
  In Fairyland, in Fairyland,
Here we are in Fairyland,
  We'll dance by the light of the moon.

Eunice Close

Who'll Help a Fairy?

"Oh! what shall I do?" sobbed a tiny mole,
"A Fairy has tumbled into my hole;
It is full of water and crawling things,
And she can't get out, for she's hurt her wings.

"I did my best to catch hold of her hair,
But my arms are short, and she's still in there.
Oh! help her, white rabbit, your arms are long;
You say you're good, and I know you're strong."

"Don't bother me," the white rabbit said—
She shut up her eyes, and her ears grew red—
"There's lots of mud, and it's sure to stick
On my beautiful fur, so white and thick."

"Oh dear! oh dear!" sobbed the poor little mole,
"Who'll help the Fairy out of the hole?"
A little brown rabbit popped up from the gorse,
"I'm not very strong, but I'll try, of course."

His little tail bobbed as he waddled in,
The muddy water came up to his chin;
But he caught the Fairy tight by the hand,
And helped her to get to Fairyland.

But she kissed him first on his muddy nose,
She kissed his face and his little wet toes;
And when the day dawned in the early light,
The common brown rabbit was silvery white.

The Light-Hearted Fairy

Oh, what is so merry, so merry, heigh-ho!
As the light-hearted fairy? Heigh-ho, heigh-ho!
    He dances and sings
    To the sound of his wings
With a hey and a heigh and a ho!

Oh, who is so merry, so airy, heigh-ho!
As the light-headed fairy? Heigh-ho, heigh-ho!
    His nectar he sips
    From the primroses' lips,
With a hey and a heigh and a ho!

Oh, who is so merry, so merry, heigh-ho!
As the light-footed fairy? Heigh-ho, heigh-ho!
    The night is his noon
    And his sun is the moon
With a hey and a heigh and a ho!

The Yellow Fairy

There lived in a laburnum tree
  A little fairy fellow,
He wore a feather in his cap,
  And he was dressed in yellow.

He sang a song the whole day long
  So merry and so clever,
But when I climbed to peep at him,
  He flew away for ever.

Charlotte Druitt Cole

The Kind Mousie

There once was a cobbler,
  And he was so wee
That he lived in a hole
  In a very big tree.
He had a good neighbour,
  And she was a mouse—
She did his wee washing
  And tidied his house.

Each morning at seven
  He heard a wee tap,
And in came the mouse
  In her apron and cap.
She lighted his fire
  And she fetched a wee broom,
And she swept and she polished
  His little Tree-room.

To take any wages
  She'd always refuse,
So the cobbler said, "Thank you!"
  And mended her shoes;
And the owl didn't eat her,
  And even the cat
Said, "I *never* would catch
  A kind mousie like that!"

Natalie Joan

144

Bubbles

Out in the garden
When school was done
I blew bubbles
In the sun.

I blew a bubble
Huge as could be!
It hung in the air
For all to see.

Into my bubble
I looked and found
A chining land
That was rainbow round.

It looked like a world
Meant for no one but fairies.
They'd keep little farms there
With cows, chicks, and dairies.
Woods where the pixies
Could picnic for pleasure,
And hide near the rainbows
Their crocks of strange treasure.

Countries were marked there
Plain as could be;
Green for the country,
Blue for the sea.
Purple for heather,
Sunshine like gold,
Bubble-land weather
Could never be cold.

And then came a bee
All furry and fat.
Before I could think
What he would be at
My beautiful bubble
He brushed with his wing,
And all that was left
Was a little damp ring.

L. Nicholson

145

The Magic Whistle

On my little magic whistle I will play to you all day;
I will play you songs of Summer and the hilltops far away;
I will play you songs of Spring-time when the daffodillies
   bloom
And the wild March horses scamper by across the golden
   broom.

I will play you sweetest music of the silver fluttering trees,
When the raindrops gently falling touch the quivering
   autumn leaves;
I will play to you of castles 'neath a fairy sky of blue;
On my little magic whistle, oh! I'd play it all to you.

Margaret Rose

You Spotted Snakes

You spotted snakes, with double tongue,
   Thorny hedgehogs, be not seen;
Newts and blind-worms, do no wrong;
   Come not near our fairy queen;

   Philomel, with melody,
   Sing in our sweet lullaby;
Lulla, lulla, lullaby; lulla, lulla, lullaby!
   Never harm,
   Nor spell nor charm,
   Come our lovely lady nigh;
   So, good night, with lullaby.

Weaving spiders, come not here;
   Hence, you long-legg'd spinners, hence;
Beetles black, approach not near;
   Worm nor snail, do no offence.

   Philomel, with melody,
   Sing in our sweet lullaby;
Lulla, lulla, lullaby; lulla, lulla, lullaby!
   Never harm,
   Nor spell nor charm,
   Come our lovely lady nigh;
   So, good night, with lullaby.

Shakespeare

Puk-Wudjies

They live 'neath the curtain
Of fir woods and heather,
And never take hurt in
The wildest of weather,
But best they love Autumn—she's brown as—themselves—
And they are the brownest of all the brown elves;
When loud sings the West Wind,
The bravest and best wind,
And puddles are shining in all the cart ruts,
They turn up the dead leaves,
The russet and red leaves,
Where squirrels have taught them to look out for nuts.

The hedge-cutters hear them
Where berries are glowing,
The scythe circles near them
At time of the mowing,
But most they love woodlands when Autumn winds pipe.
And all through the cover the beechnuts are ripe.
And great spiky chestnuts,
The biggest and best nuts
Blown down in the ditches, fair windfalls lie cast,
And no tree begrudges
The little Puk-Wudjies
A pocket of acorns, or handful of mast.

So should you be roaming,
When branches are sighing,
When up in the gloaming
The moon-wrack is flying,
And hear through the darkness, again and again,
What's neither the wind nor the spatter of rain—
A flurry, a flurry,
A scuffle, a scurry,
A bump like the rabbits that bump on the ground,
A patter, a bustle,
Of small things that rustle,
You'll know the Puk-Wudjies are somewhere around.

Patrick R. Chalmers

Jock O' Dreams

When the sun goes down and the world is still,
Then Jock o' Dreams comes over the hill;
Over the hill he quietly slips,
Holding his finger to his lips.

His golden hair is pale as the moon,
He has two bright stars on his velvet shoon;
Soft his step as an elfin dance,
His sea-blue eyes have an elfin glance.

The dreams he carries are light as air,
He tosses them here, he tosses them there,
In at the windows, under the doors,
All the way up to the attic floors.

Through the silent streets he goes walking about
Till the moon drops down and the stars go out;
Then lightly swinging his empty sack,
Softly, softly, he wanders back.

A cold little wind runs over the ground,
A sleepy bird makes a tiny sound,
The sky in the East grows rosily red,
The children murmur and turn in bed.
Over the world the sunlight streams—
But what has become of Jock o' Dreams?

Rose Fyleman

The Dream Ship

I want to go aboard my ship, and sail and sail away—
To see the whales a-spouting and the porpoises at play;
To meet Atlantic rollers with their wild and mighty
    sweep—
I want to know the dangers and the wonders of the deep.

I want to see tall icebergs, all a-sparkle, drifting by
With surf about their buttresses, their spires against the
    sky,
To make my voyage northwards till we're fast amid the floe
Where the white bear prowls around us, hunting seals
    across the snow.

I want to land on coral isles, far in the ocean blue,
To battle round the dreadful Horn as all stout seamen do.
But since I'm not quite old enough I sometimes dream
  instead,
And make myself adventures though they're only in my
  head.

W. K. Holmes

Romance

I saw a ship a-sailing,
    A-sailing on the sea;
Her masts were of the shining gold,
    Her deck of ivory;
And sails of silk, as soft as milk,
    And silvern shrouds had she.

And round about her sailing
    The sea was sparkling white,
The waves all clapped their hands and sang
    To see so fair a sight;
They kissed her twice, they kissed her thrice,
    And murmured with delight.

Then came the gallant captain
    And stood upon the deck,
In velvet coat and ruffles white,
    Without a spot or speck,
And diamond rings and triple strings
    Of pearls about his neck.

And four and twenty sailors
    Were round him bowing low,
On every jacket three times three
    Gold buttons in a row,
And cutlasses down to their knees;
    They made a goodly show.

And then the ship went sailing,
    A-sailing o'er the sea;
She dived beneath the setting sun,
    But never back came she,
For she found the lands of the golden sands,
    Where the pearls and diamonds be.

Gabriel Setoun

149

Fairy Music

I found a little fairy flute
    Beneath a harebell blue;
I sat me down upon the moss
    And blew a note or two.

And as I blew the rabbits came
    Around me in the sun,
And little mice and velvet moles
    Came creeping, one by one.

A swallow perched upon my head,
    A robin on my thumb,
The thrushes sang in tune with me,
    The bees began to hum.

I loved to see them all around
    And wished they'd always stay,
When down a little fairy flew
    And snatched my flute away!

And then the swallow fluttered off,
    And gone were all the bees,
The rabbits ran, and I was left
    Alone among the trees!

Enid Blyton

Friday

This is the day when the fairy kind
Sit weeping alone for their hopeless lot,
And the wood-maiden sighs to the sighing wind,
And the mermaiden weeps in her crystal grot;
For this is a day that the deed was wrought,
In which we have neither part nor share,
For the children of clay was salvation bought,
But not for the forms of sea or air!
And ever the mortal is most forlorn,
Who meeteth our race on the Friday morn.

Sir Walter Scott

150

Merry Little Men

Down in the grassy hollow
Live merry little men,
On moonlight nights they frolic—but
They don't come out till ten.

And I'm in bed by seven,
And so I don't know when
I'll go and play with them—because
They don't come out till ten!

Kathleen M. Chaplin

The Rock-a-by Lady

The Rock-a-by Lady from Hush-a-by Street
Comes stealing; comes creeping;
The poppies they hang from her head to her feet,
And each hath a dream that is tiny and fleet—
She bringeth her poppies to you, my sweet,
When she findeth you sleeping!

There is one little dream of a beautiful drum—
"Rub-a-dub!" it goeth:
There is one little dream of a big sugar-plum,
And lo! thick and fast the other dreams come,
Of popguns that bang, and tin tops that hum,
And a trumpet that bloweth.

And dollies peep out of these wee little drums
With laughter and singing;
And boats go a-floating on silvery streams,
And the stars peek-a-boo with their own misty gleams.
And up, up, and up, where the mother Moon beams,
The fairies go winging.

Would you dream of these dreams that are tiny and fleet?
They'll come to you sleeping:
So shut the two eyes that are weary, my sweet,
For the Rock-a-by Lady from Hush-a-by Street,
With poppies that hang from her head to her feet,
Comes stealing; comes creeping.

Eugene Field

151

A Fairy Dream

Two little elves
Were lost one night.
"Where can they be?" said the Queen.
The fairies searched
Till morning light,
But never a trace was seen.

When the sun was up
And the sky was clear,
The wee elves laughed with joy,
They'd whispered a fairy
Dream in the ear
Of the newest baby boy.

Dorothy Gradon

The Dream Fairy

A little fairy comes at night,
Her eyes are blue, her hair is brown,
With silver spots upon her wings,
And from the moon she flutters down.

She has a little silver wand,
And when a good child goes to bed
She waves her wand from right to left
And makes a circle round her head.

And then it dreams of pleasant things,
Of fountains filled with fairy fish,
And trees that bear delicious fruit,
And bow their branches at a wish;

Of arbours filled with dainty scents
From lovely flowers that never fade,
Bright flies that glitter in the sun,
And glow-worms shining in the shade;

And talking birds with gifted tongues
For singing songs and telling tales,
And pretty dwarfs to show the way
Through fairy hills and fairy dales.

Thomas Hood

152

A Child's Thought

At seven, when I go to bed,
I find such pictures in my head:
Castles with dragons prowling round,
Gardens where magic fruits are found;
Fair ladies prisoned in a tower,
Or lost in an enchanted bower;
While gallant horsemen ride by streams
That border all this land of dreams
I find, so clearly in my head
At seven, when I go to bed.

At seven, when I wake again,
The magic land I seek in vain;
A chair stands where the castle frowned,
The carpet hides the garden ground,
No fairies trip across the floor,
Boots, and not horsemen, flank the door,
And where the blue streams rippling ran
Is now a bath and water-can;
I seek the magic land in vain
At seven, when I wake again.

Robert Louis Stevenson

A Wish

I'd love to give a party
　To all the fairy folk,
With scarlet autumn leaves for plates,
　Oh! it would be a joke!
And every little lady fay
　Should have her acorn cup,
To hold her fragrant rose-leaf tea,
　Until she drank it up;
And every little elf should have
　His acorn pipe to smoke;
I'd love to give a party
　Beneath this grand old oak.

Elizabeth Gould

153

The Little Men

Would you see the little men
Coming down a moonlit glen?—
Gnome and elf and woodland sprite,
Clad in brown and green and white,
Skipping, hopping, never stopping,
Stumbling, grumbling, tumbling, mumbling,
Dancing, prancing, singing, swinging—
Coats of red and coats of brown,
Put on straight or upside down,
Outside in or inside out,
Some with sleeves and some without,
Rustling, bustling, stomping, romping,
Strumming, humming, hear them coming—
You will see the Little Men
If it be a Fairy glen.

Flora Fearne

The Fairies

Come, follow, follow me,
You fairy elves that be
Which circle on the green,
Come, follow Mab, your queen,
Hand in hand let's dance around,
For this place is fairy ground.

When mortals are at rest,
And snoring in their rest,
Unheard and unespied
Through keyholes we do glide;
Over tables, stools and shelves,
We trip it with our fairy elves.

Upon a mushroom's head
Our table-cloth we spread;
A grain of rye or wheat
Is manchet, which we eat;
Pearly drops of dew we drink
In acorn-cups fill'd to the brink.

The grasshopper, gnat and fly,
Serve for our minstrelsy;
Grace said, we dance awhile,
And so the time beguile;
And if the moon doth hide her head,
The glow-worm lights us home to bed.

On tops of dewy grass
So nimbly do we pass,
The young and tender stalk
Ne'er bends when we do walk;
Yet in the morning may be seen
Where we the night before have been.

Mrs. Brown

As soon as I'm in bed at night
    And snugly settled down,
The little girl I am by day
Goes very suddenly away,
    And then I'm Mrs. Brown.

I have a family of six,
    And all of them have names,
The girls are Joyce and Nancy Maud,
The boys are Marmaduke and Claude
    And Percival and James.

We have a house with twenty rooms
    A mile away from town;
I think it's good for girls and boys
To be allowed to make a noise,
    And so does Mr. Brown.

We do the most exciting things,
    Enough to make you creep,
And on and on and on we go,
I sometimes wonder if I know
    When I have gone to sleep.

Rose Fyleman

155

The Fairy Cobbler

What do you think I saw to-day
When I walked forth to take the air?
I saw a little house of hay,
All in a pasture fair.

And just within the green grass door
I saw a little cobbler sit:
He sat crossed-legged upon the floor,
And tapped, tip-tit, tip-tit!

"What are you making there so neat?"
"Gaiters for glow-worms," he made reply,
"And thistledown slippers for fairy feet,
And garden boots for a butterfly."

"What do they pay you, my busy mite?"
"Some bring me honey and some bring dew
And the glow-worms visit me every night
And light my chamber through."

A. Neil Lyons

Child's Song

I know the sky will fall one day,
The great green trees will topple down,
The spires will wither far away
Upon the battlemented town;
When winds and waves forget to flow
And the wild song-birds cease from calling,
Then shall I take my shoes and go
To tell the King the sky is falling.

There's lots of things I've never done,
And lots of things I'll never see;
The nearest rainbow ever spun
Is much too far away from me;
But when the dark air's lost in snow
And the long quiet strikes appalling,
I learn how it will feel to go
To tell the King the sky is falling.

Gerald Gould

156

The Fairy Ring

Let us dance and let us sing,
Dancing in a merry ring;
We'll be fairies on the green,
Sporting round the Fairy Queen.

Like the seasons of the year,
Round we circle in a sphere;
I'll be Summer, you'll be Spring;
Dancing in a fairy ring.

Spring and summer glide away,
Autumn comes with tresses gray,
Winter hand in hand with Spring,
Dancing in a fairy ring.

Faster, faster, round we go,
While our cheeks with roses glow,
Free as birds upon the wing,
Dancing in a fairy ring.

An Elfin Knight

He put his acorn helmet on;
It was plumed of the silk of the thistle down;
The corselet plate that guarded his breast
Was once the wild bee's golden vest;
His cloak, of a thousand mingled dyes,
Was formed of the wings of butterflies;
His shield was the shell of a ladybird green,
Studs of gold on a ground of green;
And the quivering lance which he brandished bright,
Was the sting of a wasp he had slain in fight.

Swift he bestrode his firefly steed;
He bared his blade of the bent-grass blue;
He drove his spurs of the cockle-seed,
And away like a glance of thought he flew,
To skim the heavens, and follow far
The fiery trail of the rocket star.

John Rodman Drake

157

The Rainbow Fairies

Two little clouds, one summer's day,
    Went flying through the sky;
They went so fast they bumped their heads,
    And both began to cry.

Old Father Sun looked out and said:
    "Oh, never mind, my dears,
I'll send my little fairy folk
    To dry your falling tears."

One fairy came in violet,
    And one wore indigo;
In blue, green, yellow, orange, red,
    They made a pretty row.

They wiped the cloud-tears all away,
    And then from out the sky,
Upon a line the sunbeams made,
    They hung their gowns to dry.

Little Kings and Queens of the May

Little Kings and Queens of the May,
Listen to me,
If you want to be
Every one of you very good
In that beautiful, beautiful, beautiful wood,
Where the little birds' heads get so turned with delight
That some of them sing all night,
Whatever you pluck,
Leave some for good luck,
Picked from the stalk, or pulled by the root,
From overhead or from underfoot,
Water wonders of ponds or brook,
Wherever you look
And whatever you find,
Leave something behind;
Some for the Naiads,
Some for the Dryads,
And a bit for the Nixies and the Pixies.

Juliana Horatia Ewing

Sea Fairies

They're hiding by the pebbles,
   They're running round the rocks.
Each of them, and all of them
   In dazzling sea-green frocks.

They're gathering strips of sea-weed,
   The ribands fair that lie
Along the winding water mark
   The tide has left so high.

They're flying with the sand,
   They're singing in the caves,
And dancing in the white foam
   They toss from off the waves.

But if you try to catch them
   They're always out of reach—
Not everywhere and anywhere,
   But somewhere on the beach.

Eileen Mathias

Rufty and Tufty

Rufty and Tufty were two little elves
   Who lived in a hollow oak tree.
They did all the cooking and cleaning themselves
   And often asked friends in to tea.

Rufty wore blue, and Tufty wore red,
   And each had a hat with a feather.
Their best Sunday shoes they kept under the bed—
   They were made of magic green leather.

Rufty was clever and kept the accounts,
   But Tufty preferred to do cooking.
He could make a fine cake without weighing amounts—
   And eat it when no one was looking!

Isabell Hempseed

The Fairy Sleep and Little Bo-Peep

Little Bo-Peep,
Had lost her sheep,
And didn't know where to find them,
All tired she sank
On a grassy bank,
And left the birds to mind them.

Then the fairy, Sleep,
Took little Bo-Peep,
In a spell of dreams he bound her,
And silently brought
The flock she sought,
Like summer clouds around her.

When little Bo-Peep—
In her slumber deep—
Saw lambs and sheep together,
All fleecy and white,
And soft and light,
As clouds in July weather;

Then little Bo-Peep
Awoke from her sleep,
And laughed with glee to find them
Coming home once more,
The old sheep before,
And the little lambs behind them.

A Fairy Went A-Marketing

A fairy went a-marketing—
She bought a little fish;
She put it in a crystal bowl
Upon a golden dish.
An hour she sat in wonderment
And watched its silver gleam,
And then she gently took it up
And slipped it in a stream.

A fairy went a-marketing—
  She bought a coloured bird;
It sang the sweetest, shrillest song
  That ever she had heard,
She sat beside its painted cage
  And listened half the day,
And then she opened wide the door
  And let it fly away.

A fairy went a-marketing—
  She bought a winter gown
All stitched about with gossamer
  And lined with thistledown.
She wore it all the afternoon
  With prancing and delight,
Then gave it to a little frog
  To keep him warm at night.

A fairy went a-marketing—
  She bought a gentle mouse
To take her tiny messages,
  To keep her little house.
All day she kept its busy feet
  Pit-patting to and fro,
And then she kissed its silken ears,
  Thanked it, and let it go.

Rose Fyleman

If You See a Fairy Ring

If you see a fairy ring
  In a field of grass,
Very lightly step around,
  Tiptoe as you pass;
Last night fairies frolicked there,
And they're sleeping somewhere near.

If you see a tiny fay
  Lying fast asleep,
Shut your eyes and run away,
  Do not stay to peep;
And be sure you never tell,
Or you'll break a fairy spell.

A Fairy Song

Over hill, over dale,
    Thorough bush, thorough brier,
Over park, over pale,
    Thorough flood, thorough fire!
I do wander everywhere,
Swifter than the moon's sphere;
And I serve the fairy queen,
To dew her orbs upon the green;
The cowslips tall her pensioners be;
In their gold coats spots you see;
Those be rubies, fairy favours,
In those freckles live their savours:
I must go seek some dewdrops here,
And hang a pearl in every cowslip's ear.

Shakespeare

Pigwiggen

Pigwiggen arms him for the field,
A little cockle-shell his shield,
Which he could very bravely wield,
    Yet could it not be piercèd.
His spear abent both stiff and strong,
And well-near of two inches long;
The pile was of a horse-fly's tongue,
    Whose sharpness nought reversèd.

And puts him on a coat of mail,
Which was of a fish's scale,
That when his foe should him assail,
    No point should be prevailing.
His rapier was a hornet's sting;
It was a very dangerous thing,
For if he chanc'd to hurt the king
    It would be long in healing.

His helmet was a beetle's head,
Most horrible and full of dread,
That able was to strike one dead,
    Yet it did well become him;
And for a plume a horse's hair
Which, being tossèd with the air,
Had force to strike his foe with fear,
    And turn his weapon from him.

Himself he on an earwig set,
Yet scarce be on his back could get,
So oft and high he did curvet
 Ere he himself could settle.
He made him turn, and stop, and bound,
To gallop and to trot the round;
He scarce could stand on any ground,
 He was so full of mettle.

Michael Drayton

The Urchin's Dance

By the moon we sport and play,
With the night begins our day:
As we dance the dew doth fall:
Trip it, little urchins all!
Lightly as the little bee,
Two by two, and three by three,
And about go we, and about go we!

John Lyly

The Goblin

A goblin lives in our house, in our house, in our house,
A goblin lives in our house all the year round.

He bumps
And he jumps
And he thumps
And he stumps.
He knocks
And he rocks
And he rattles at the locks.

A goblin lives in our house, in our house, in our house,
A goblin lives in our house all the year round.

Rose Fyleman

163

Found in the Woods

I found a little brown purse
The fairies left for me,
It was stitch'd with green and yellow,
As pretty as could be.
It was full of fairy-money,
As full as it could be,
So I bought a pot of honey,
And had it for my tea.

Irene F. Pawsey

From The Merman

Who would be
A merman bold,
Sitting alone,
Singing alone
Under the sea,
With a crown of gold,
On a throne?

I would be a merman bold,
I would sit and sing the whole of the day;
I would fill the sea-halls with a voice of power;
But at night I would roam abroad and play
With the mermaids in and out of the rocks,
Dressing their hair with the white sea-flower;
And holding them back by their flowing locks
I would kiss them often under the sea,
And kiss them again till they kiss'd me
    Laughingly, laughingly;
And then we would wander away, away
To the pale-green sea-groves straight and high,
    Chasing each other merrily.

Lord Tennyson

From The Mermaid

Who would be
A mermaid fair,
Singing alone,
Combing her hair
Under the sea,
In a golden curl
With a comb of pearl,
On a throne?

I would be a mermaid fair;
I would sing to myself the whole of the day;
With a comb of pearl I would comb my hair;
And still as I comb'd I would sing and say,
"Who is it loves me? who loves not me?"
I would comb my hair till my ringlets would fall.

Lord Tennyson

Toadstools

It's not a bit windy,
    It's not a bit wet,
The sky is as sunny
    As summer, and yet
Little umbrellas are
    Everywhere spread,
Pink ones, and brown ones,
    And orange, and red.

I can't see the folks
    Who are hidden below;
I've peeped, and I've peeped
    Round the edges, but no!
They hold their umbrellas
    So tight and so close
That nothing shows under,
    Not even a nose!

Elizabeth Fleming

165

The Fairy Shoemaker

Tiny shoes so trim and neat,
Fairy shoes for dancing feet;
See the elfin cobbler's shelves
Filled with shoes for tiny elves.

And sitting there he hammers,
And hammering he sings. . . .

"This small shoe of silver,
This small shoe of gold,
This small shoe of diamonds bright—
Will none of them grow old.

"This small shoe will hurry,
This small shoe will skip,
This small shoe will dance all night,
Tipperty, tip, tip, tip.

"This small shoe will twinkle,
This small shoe will shine,
This small shoe will bring me home,
For I shall make it mine."

And sitting there he hammers,
And hammering he dreams. . . .

Tiny shoes so trim and neat,
Fairy shoes for dancing feet,
See the elfin cobbler smile
As he sits and rests awhile.

Phyllis Garlick

The Elfin Pedlar

Lady and gentlemen fays, come buy!
No pedlar has such a rich packet as I.

Who wants a gown
Of purple fold,
Embroidered down
The seams with gold?

See here!—A Tulip richly laced
To please a royal fairy's taste!

Who wants a cap
Of crimson grand?
By great good hap
I've one on hand;
Look, sir!—a Cockscomb, flowering red,
'Tis just the thing, sir, for your head!

Who wants a frock
Of vestal hue?
Or snowy smock?—
Fair maid, do you?
O me!—a Ladysmock so white!
Your bosom's self is not more bright!

Who wants to sport
A slender limb?
I've every sort
Of hose for him:
Both scarlet, striped, and yellow ones,
This Woodbine makes such pantaloons.

Who wants—(hush! hush!)
A box of paint?
'Twill give a blush
Yet leave no taint:
This Rose with natural rouge is fill'd,
From its own dewy leaves distill'd.

Then, lady and gentlemen, come buy!
You never will meet such a merchant as I!

George Darley

The Seasons

Therefore all seasons shall be sweet to thee

Slow Spring

O Year, grow slowly. Exquisite, holy,
    The days go on.
With almonds showing, the pink stars blowing,
    And birds in the dawn.

Grow slowly, year, like a child that is dear,
    Or a lamb that is mild,
By little steps, and by little skips,
    Like a lamb or a child.

Katharine Tynan

Round the Year

The Crocus, while the days are dark,
    Unfolds its saffron sheen;
At April's touch, the crudest bark
    Discovers germs of green.

Then sleep the seasons, full of might;
    While swells the pod
And rounds the peach, and in the night
    The mushroom bursts the sod.

The winter falls; the frozen rut
    Is bound with silver bars,
The snowdrift heaps against the hut
    And night is pierced with stars.

Coventry Patmore

Winter and Spring

But a little while ago
All the ground was white with snow;
Trees and shrubs were dry and bare,
Not a sign of life was there;
Now the buds and leaves are seen,
Now the fields are fresh and green,
Pretty birds are on the wing,
With a merry song they sing!
There's new life in everything!
How I love the pleasant spring!

A Chanted Calendar

First came the primrose,
On the bank high,
Like a maiden looking forth
From the window of a tower
When the battle rolls below,
So look'd she,
And saw the storms go by.

Then came the wind-flower
In the valley left behind,
As a wounded maiden, pale
With purple streaks of woe,
When the battle has roll'd by
Wanders to and fro,
So totter'd she,
Dishevell'd in the wind.

Then came the daisies,
On the first of May,
Like a banner'd show's advance
While the crowd runs by the way,
With ten thousand flowers about them they came
      trooping through the fields,
As a happy people come,
So came they,
As a happy people come
When the war has roll'd away,
With dance and tabor, pipe and drum,
And all make holiday.

Then came the cowslip,
Like a dancer in the fair,
She spread her little mat of green,
And on it danced she.
With a fillet bound about her brow,
A fillet round her happy brow,
A golden fillet round her brow,
And rubies in her hair.

Sydney Dobell

171

Before Spring

Jonquils and violets smelling sweet
In this grey, unblossoming street—
These to our midwinter bring
The first frail beauty of the Spring.

Sixpence—sixpence for the Spring—
For south wind and bird on wing—
Pennies for a priceless thing!

Glory of flower cups, flower eyes,
Wild, soft grace under iron skies,
Deathless in the gift they bring,
Though they die at evening.

Sixpence—sixpence for the Spring!

P. A. Ropes

February

To-day, I saw the catkins blow,
Altho' the hills are white with snow

White throstles sang "The sun is good";
They waved their banners in the wood.

They come to greet the lurking Spring
As messengers from Winter's King.

And thus they wave while Winter reigns,
While his cold grip still holds the plains.

Oh, tho' the hills are white with snow,
To-day I saw the catkins blow.

Dorothy Una Ratcliffe

A Change in the Year

It is the first mild day of March:
  Each minute sweeter than before,
The redbreast sings from the tall larch
  That stands beside our door.

There is a blessing in the air,
  Which seems a sense of joy to yield
To the bare trees, and mountains bare;
  And grass in the green field.

William Wordsworth

First Spring Morning

Look! look! the spring is come:
  O feel the gentle air,
That wanders thro' the boughs to burst
  The thick buds everywhere!
  The birds are glad to see
  The high unclouded sun:
Winter is fled away, they sing,
  The gay time is begun.

Adown the meadows green
  Let us go dance and play,
And look for violets in the lane,
  And ramble far away
  To gather primroses,
  That in the woodland grow,
And hunt for oxlips, or if yet
  The blades of bluebells show.

There the old woodman gruff
  Hath half the coppice cut,
And weaves the hurdles all day long
  Beside his willow hut.
  We'll steal on him, and then
  Startle him, all with glee
Singing our song of winter fled
  And summer soon to be.

Robert Bridges

173

Welcome to Spring

I have heard a mother bird
  Singing in the rain—
Telling all her little ones
  Spring has come again!

I have seen a wave of green
  Down a lovely lane—
Making all the hedges glad
  Spring has come again!

I have found a patch of ground
  Golden in the sun;
Crocuses are calling out
  Spring has just begun!

Irene Thompson

Spring Has Come

Hark! the tiny cowslip bell
  In the breeze is ringing;
Birds in every woodland dell
  Songs of joy are singing.
Winter is o'er, Spring once more
  Spreads abroad her golden store;
Hark! the tiny cowslip bell
  In the breeze is ringing.

Spring has come to make us glad,
  Let us give her greeting;
Winter days were cold and sad,
  Winter's reign is fleeting;
Hearts are gay, blithe as May,
  Dance and sport the livelong day;
Spring has come to make us glad,
  Let us give her greeting.

A Seventeenth-century Song

Now that the Winter's Gone

Now that the winter's gone, the earth hath lost
Her snow-white robes; and no more the frost
Candies the grass, or casts an icy cream
Upon the silver lake or crystal stream;
But the warm sun thaws the benumbed earth,
And makes it tender; gives a sacred birth
To the dead swallow; wakes in hollow tree
The drowsy cuckoo and the bumble-bee.
Now do a choir of chirping minstrels bring
In triumph to the world, the youthful Spring:
The valleys, hills and woods, in rich array,
Welcome the coming of the long'd-for May.

Thomas Carew

To Spring

O thou, with dewy locks who lookest down
Thro' the clear windows of the morning, turn
Thine angel eyes upon our western isle,
Which in full choir hails thy approach, O Spring!

William Blake

Spring, the Travelling Man

Spring, the Travelling Man, has been here,
Here in the glen;
He must have passed by in the grey of the dawn,
When only the robin and wren
Were awake,
Watching out with their bright little eyes
In the midst of the brake.
The rabbits, maybe, heard him pass,
Stepping light on the grass,
Whistling careless and gay at the break o' the day.
Then the blackthorn to give him delight
Put on raiment of white;
And, all for his sake,
The gorse on the hill, where he rested an hour,
Grew bright with a splendour of flower.

Winifred M. Letts

175

In Springtime

All Nature seems at work. Slugs leave their lair—
The bees are stirring—birds are on the wing—
And Winter, slumbering in the open air,
Wears on his smiling face a dream of Spring!

S. T. Coleridge

The Barrel Organ

Go down to Kew in lilac-time, in lilac-time, in lilac-time,
Go down to Kew in lilac-time (it isn't far from London!);
And you shall wander hand in hand with love in summer's
wonderland;
Go down to Kew in lilac-time (it isn't far from London!).

The cherry trees are seas of bloom and soft perfume and
sweet perfume,
The cherry trees are seas of bloom (and oh! so near to
London!);
And there they say, when dawn is high, and all the world's
a blaze of sky,
The cuckoo, though he's very shy, will sing a song for
London.

The nightingale is rather rare and yet they say you'll
hear him there,
At Kew, at Kew, in lilac-time (and oh! so near to
London!);
The linnet and the throstle, too, and after dark the long
halloo,
And golden-eyed tu-whit, tu-whoo of owls that ogle
London.

For Noah hardly knew a bird of any kind that isn't heard
At Kew, at Kew, in lilac-time (and oh! so near to
London!);
And when the rose begins to pout, and all the chestnut
spires are out,
You'll hear the rest without a doubt, all chorusing for
London:

Come down to Kew in lilac-time, in lilac-time, in lilac-time,
Come down to Kew in lilac-time (it isn't far from
    London!);
And you shall wander hand in hand with love in summer's
    wonderland;
Come down to Kew in lilac-time (it isn't far from
    London!).

Alfred Noyes

Spring Morning

Now the moisty wood discloses
Wrinkled leaves of primèroses,
While the birds, they flute and sing:
Build your nests, for here is Spring.

All about the open hills
Daisies shew their peasant frills,
Washed and white and newly spun
For a festival of sun.

Like a blossom from the sky,
Drops a yellow butterfly,
Dancing down the hedges grey
Snow-bestrewn till yesterday.

Squirrels skipping up the trees
Smell how Spring is in the breeze,
While the birds, they flute and sing:
Build your nests, for here is Spring.

Frances Cornford

Spring Work at the Farm

What does the farmer in the spring?
He sows the seed that harvests bring;
But first he wakes the earth from sleep
By ploughing it well and harrowing it deep.

And busy must be the farmer's boy!
To care for the lambs that leap for joy.
To feed the calves so tender and young
He rises as soon as the day's begun.

And then the farmer's wife so kind,
Food for the ducklings and chicks will find.
And hark! what the queer little piggy-wigs say,
"Don't forget me, I'm hungry to-day."

Thirza Wakley

Spring Goeth All in White

Spring goeth all in white,
  Crowned with milk-white may:
In fleecy flocks of light
  O'er heaven the white clouds stray:

White butterflies in the air;
  White daisies prank the ground:
The cherry and hoary pear
  Scatter their snow around.

Robert Bridges

The Green Lady

A lovely Green Lady
  Embroiders and stitches
Sweet flowers in the meadows,
  On banks and in ditches.

All day she is sewing,
  Embroidering all night;
For she works in the darkness
  As well as the light.

She makes no mistake in
  The silks which she uses,
And all her gay colours
  She carefully chooses.

She fills nooks and corners
  With blossoms so small,
Where none but the fairies
  Will see them at all.

She sews them so quickly,
    She trims them so neatly,
Though much of her broidery
    Is hidden completely.

She scatters her tapestry
    Scented and sweet,
In the loneliest places,
    Or 'neath careless feet;
For bee, or for bird folk,
    For children like me,
But the lovely Green Lady,
    No mortal may see.

Charlotte Druitt Cole

Spring

Sound the flute!
Now 'tis mute;
Birds delight
Day and night
Nightingale
In the dale;
Lark in the sky
Merrily,
Merrily, merrily to welcome in the year.

Little boy,
Full of joy;
Little girl,
Sweet and small;
Cock docs crow,
So do you;
Merry voice
Infant noise;
Merrily, merrily to welcome in the year.

Little lamb,
Here I am;
Come and lick
My white neck;
Let me pull
Your soft wool;
Let me kiss
Your soft face;
Merrily, merrily we welcome in the year.

William Blake

My Lady Spring

My Lady Spring is dressed in green,
　　She wears a primrose crown,
And little baby buds and twigs
　　Are clinging to her gown;
The sun shines if she laughs at all,
But if she weeps the raindrops fall.

Spring Quiet

Gone were but the Winter,
　　Come were but the Spring,
I would go to a covert
　　Where the birds sing.

Where in the whitethorn
　　Singeth a thrush,
And a robin sings
　　In the holly-bush.

Full of fresh scents
　　Are the budding boughs
Arching high over
　　A cool green house:

Full of sweet scents,
　　And whispering air
Which sayeth softly:
　　"We spread no snare;

"Here dwell in safety,
　　Here dwell alone,
With a clear stream
　　And a mossy stone.

"Here the sun shineth
　　Most shadily;
Here is heard an echo
　　Of the far sea,
　　Though far off it be."

Christina Rossetti

The Magic Piper

There piped a piper in the wood
 Strange music—soft and sweet—
And all the little wild things
 Came hurrying to his feet.

They sat around him on the grass,
 Enchanted, unafraid,
And listened, as with shining eyes
 Sweet melodies he made.

The wood grew green, and flowers sprang up,
 The birds began to sing;
For the music it was magic,
 And the piper's name was—Spring!

E. L. Marsh

Promise

There's a black fog hiding London
 And every tree looks dead,
But I've seen a purple crocus and a jonquil's golden head.
 The shallow ponds are frozen
 And there's snow upon the hills,
But they're selling scarlet tulips now and yellow daffodils.

A bitter wind is blowing,
 The rivers are abrim,
But I toss my head at Winter, I am not afraid of him.
 Although the sun is shrouded
 Spring is just across the sea,
For I've seen a spray of lilac and a red anemone.

Florence Lacey

Spring

Now daisies pied, and violets blue,
 And lady-smocks all silver white,
And cuckoo-buds of yellow hue
 Do paint the meadows with delight,
The cuckoo now on every tree
 Sings cuckoo, cuckoo.

Shakespeare

181

Slumber in Spring

Grey pussy-willows
For fairy pillows,
So soft for fairy's head;
Cherry-petals sweet
For a cool, clean sheet,
Green moss for a fairy bed.
Fragrant violet for a coverlet.
And hush! down the hill's green sweep,
Comes the wind's soft sigh
For a lullaby;
Sound, sound will a fairy sleep.

Elizabeth Gould

Written in March

The cock is crowing,
The stream is flowing,
The small birds twitter,
The lake doth glitter,
The green field sleeps in the sun;

The oldest and youngest
Are at work with the strongest,
The cattle are grazing,
Their heads never raising;
There are forty feeding like one!

Like an army defeated
The snow hath retreated,
And now doth fare ill
On the top of the bare hill;
The plough-boy is whooping—anon—anon;

There's joy in the mountains;
There's life in the fountains;
Small clouds are sailing,
Blue sky prevailing;
The rain is over and gone.

William Wordsworth

In February

The frozen ground is broken
  Where snowdrops raise their heads,
And nod their tiny greeting
  In glades and garden beds.

The frozen stream is melted,
  The white brook turns to brown,
And foaming through the coppice
  Flows helter skelter down.

The frozen air is golden
  With February sun,
The winter days are over,
  Oh, has the Spring begun?

P. A. Ropes

A Spring Song

See the yellow catkins cover
All the slender willows over;
And on mossy banks so green
Star-like primroses are seen;
And their clustering leaves below,
White and purple violets grow.

Hark! the little lambs are bleating,
And the cawing rooks are meeting
In the elms—a noisy crowd;
And all birds are singing loud,
There, the first white butterfly
In the sun goes flitting by.

Mary Howitt

Spring Prayer

For flowers that bloom about our feet;
For tender grass, so fresh, so sweet;
For song of bird, and hum of bee;
For all things fair we hear or see,
Father in heaven, we thank Thee!

183

For blue of stream and blue of sky;
For pleasant shade of branches high;
For fragrant air and cooling breeze;
For beauty of the blooming trees,
Father in heaven, we thank Thee!

Ralph W. Emerson

Snowflakes

I heard the snowflakes whisper in the still dark night,
And when I peeped at bedtime, all the roofs were white.
Although the pussy willows their mittened buds unfold,
Although the hazel catkins are waving tails of gold,
Although the buds are bursting on the chestnuts by
    the gate,
And spring is in the countryside—the snow came late.

I saw it in the twilight, and I looked for it at dawn,
But all I found were thrushes on the smooth green lawn,
All the roofs were twinkling and sparkling in the sun,
And myriad buds were waking and opening one by one,
And all that could remind me of snowflakes on the beds
Were clusterings of snowdrops, with whitely drooping
    heads.

Ruth M. Arthur

A Walk in Spring

What could be nicer than the spring,
When little birds begin to sing?
When for my daily walk I go
Through fields that once were white with snow?
When in the green and open spaces
Lie baby lambs with sweet black faces?
What could be finer than to shout
That all the buds are bursting out—
And oh, at last beneath the hill,
To pick a yellow daffodil?

K. C. Lart

184

Night of Spring

Slow, horses, slow,
As through the wood we go—
We would count the stars in heaven,
Hear the grasses grow:

Watch the cloudlets few
Dappling the deep blue.
In our open palms outspread
Catch the blessed dew.

Slow, horses, slow,
As through the wood we go—
All the beauty of the night
We would learn and know!

Thomas Westwood

April

April, April,
Laugh thy girlish laughter;
Then, the moment after,
Weep thy girlish tears!
April, that mine ears
Like a lover greetest,
If I tell thee, sweetest,
All my hopes and fears,
April, April,
Laugh thy golden laughter,
But, the moment after,
Weep thy golden tears.

Sir William Watson

In the April Rain

Listen! In the April rain,
Brother Robin's here again;
Songs, like showers, come and go;
He's house-building, that I know.

185

Though he finds the old pine tree
Is not where it used to be,
And the nest he made last year
Torn and scattered far and near,

He has neither grief nor care,
Building sites are everywhere;
If one nest is blown away,
Fields are full of sticks and hay.

Listen! In the April rain,
Brother Robin sings again,
Sings so full of joy and glee,
He's house-building, don't you see?

Mary Anderson

April Rain

It isn't raining rain to me,
　It's raining daffodils;
In every dimpled drop I see
　Wild flowers on the hills.
The clouds of grey engulf the day
　And overwhelm the town—
It isn't raining rain to me,
　It's raining roses down.

It isn't raining rain to me,
　But fields of clover bloom
Where any buccaneering bee
　May find a bed and room.
A health unto the happy,
　A fig for him who frets—
It isn't raining rain to me,
　It's raining violets.

Robert Loveman

Old May Song

All in this pleasant evening, together come are we,
For the summer springs so fresh, green, and gay;
We tell you of a blossoming and buds on every tree,
Drawing near unto the merry month of May.

May

I feel a newer life in every gale;
  The winds, that fan the flowers,
And with their welcome breathings fill the sail,
  Tell of serener hours—
    Of hours that glide unfelt away
    Beneath the sky of May.

The spirit of the gentle south-wind calls
  From his blue throne of air,
And where his whispering voice in music falls,
  Beauty is budding there;
    The bright ones of the valley break
    Their slumbers, and awake.

The waving verdure rolls along the plain,
  And the wide forest weaves,
To welcome back its playful mates again,
  A canopy of leaves;
    And from its darkening shadows floats
    A gush of trembling notes.

Fairer and brighter spreads the reign of May;
  The tresses of the woods
With the light dallying of the west-wind play;
  And the full-brimming floods,
    As gladly to their goal they run,
    Hail the returning sun.

J. G. Percival

187

May-Time

There is but one May in the year,
　And sometimes May is wet and cold;
There is but one May in the year,
　But before the year grows old.

Yet, though it be the chilliest May
　With least of sun, and most of showers,
Its wind and dew, its night and day,
　Bring up the flowers.

In May

In May I go a-walking to hear the linnet sing,
The blackbird and the throstle, a-praising God the King;
It cheers the heart to hear them, to see the leaves unfold,
And the meadows scattered over with buttercups of gold.

Summer is Nigh

Summer is nigh!
How do I know?
Why, this very day
A robin sat
On a tilting spray,
And merrily sang
A song of May.
Jack Frost has fled
From the rippling brook;
And a trout peeped out
From his shady nook.
A butterfly too
Flew lazily by,
And the willow catkins
Shook from on high
Their yellow dust
As I passed by:
And so I know
That summer is nigh.

June

Month of leaves,
Month of roses;
Gardens full
Of dainty posies;
   Skies of blue,
   Hedgerows gay,
   Meadows sweet
   With the new-mown hay.

Flowery banks,
A-drone with bees,
Dreaming cattle
Under trees:
   Song-birds pipe
   A merry tune—
   This is summer,
   This is June.

Irene F. Pawsey

A Summer Day

Not by the city bells that chime the hours
   I'll tell this day,
But by the bloom and fall of things in flowers
   And the slow way
Of cloud shadows, and swathing sunshine wrapping
   The gorse-gilt plain;
And little lifted leaves, and water lapping,
   And maybe rain.

A shaken bough, a circle on the water,
   A rose a-blush,
A yellow iris crowned like a king's daughter,
   A piping thrush.
Swift fiery dragon-flies, and brown bees humming,
   And tiny things
Making strange music, and the twilight coming
   On measureless wings.

Florence Harrison

189

Midsummer Night

The sun goes down,
  The stars peep out,
And long slim shadows
  Flit about.

In velvet shoes
  The quiet dark
Comes stepping soft
  O'er wood and park.

And now the world
  Is fast asleep;
And fays and elves
  Their revels keep.

They fly on the backs of the grey-winged moths,
  They skim on the dragon-flies green and gold.
On shimmering dew-wet grass they alight,
  Tiny petal-skirts whirl, gauzy wings unfold.

The fairies are dancing beneath the moon.
Hush! See the shimmer of their twinkling shoon!
                                    Elizabeth Gould

Hay-Time

Come out, come out, this sunny day,
The fields are sweet with new-mown hay,
The birds are singing loud and clear,
For summer-time once more is here;
So bring your rakes and come and play,
And toss and tumble in the hay.
The sweet wild roses softly blow,
All pink and white the roses grow;
The nodding daisies in the grass,
Lift up their heads to hear you pass
Upon this happy, sunny day,
When you come out to make the hay.
                                    C. M. Lowe

Haytime

It's Midsummer Day
And they're cutting the hay
Down in the meadow just over the way,
The children all run
For a frolic, and fun—
For haytime is playtime out in the sun.

It's Midsummer Day,
And they're making the hay
Down in the meadow all golden and gay,
They're tossing it high
Beneath the June sky,
And the hay rakes are spreading it out to dry.

Irene F. Pawsey

Summer Evening

Crows crowd croaking overhead,
Hastening to the woods to bed.
Cooing sits the lonely dove,
Calling home her absent love.
With "Kirchup! Kirchup!" 'mong the wheats
Partridge distant partridge greets.

Bats fly by in hood and cowl; .
Through the barn-hole pops the owl;
From the hedge, in drowsy hum,
Heedless buzzing beetles hum,
Haunting every bushy place,
Flopping in the labourer's face.

Flowers now sleep within their hoods;
Daisies button into buds;
From soiling dew the buttercup
Shuts his golden jewels up;
And the rose and woodbine they
Wait again the smiles of day.

John Clare

191

A Night in June

The sun has long been set,
   The stars are out by twos and threes,
The little birds are piping yet
   Among the bushes and the trees;
There's a cuckoo, and one or two thrushes,
And a far-off wind that rushes,
And a sound of water that gushes,
And the cuckoo's sovereign cry
Fills all the hollow of the sky.

William Wordsworth

June

The greenest of grass in the long meadow grows;
   And the stream, how the stream is dancing!
How cool is its kiss on the little brown toes
   That find it a playmate entrancing!
      Forgotten the bad days—
      The weary and sad days,
      Or time all unheeding
      That bright hours are speeding,
Forgotten is "bed" by the children in June.

Jane G. Stewart

Lanes in Summer

I love the little winding lanes,
In the sweet days when summer reigns;
The eglantine and hawkweed's plume;
The dog-rose and the bramble bloom,
Like stars from heaven gone astray;
The fragrant scent of new-mown hay;
The poppies in the green-aisled wheat;
The bees that find that clover sweet;
The last song of the wren and thrush
Breaking through the drowsy hush—
If kindly peace be anywhere
'Tis surely there, 'tis surely there.

Malcolm Hemphrey

In the Fair Forest

In Summer when the woods are green
And leaves are large and long,
Full merry it is in the fair forest
To hear the small birds' song.

To see the red deer seek the dale
And leave the hills so high,
To shade themselves among the glades
Under the greenwood tree.

Old Ballad

Song of Summer Days

Sing a song of hollow logs,
Chirp of cricket, croak of frogs,
Cry of wild bird, hum of bees,
Dancing leaves and whisp'ring trees;
Legs all bare, and dusty toes,
Ruddy cheeks and freckled nose,
Splash of brook and swish of line,
Where the song that's half so fine?

Sing a song of summer days,
Leafy nooks and shady ways,
Nodding roses, apples red,
Clover like a carpet spread;
Sing a song of running brooks,
Cans of bait and fishing hooks,
Dewy hollows, yellow moons,
Birds a-pipe with merry tunes.

Sing a song of skies of blue,
Eden's garden made anew,
Scarlet hedges, leafy lanes,
Vine-embowered sills and panes;
Stretch of meadows, splash'd with dew,
Silver clouds with sunlight through,
Call of thrush and pipe of wren,
Sing and call it home again.

J. W. Foley

The Four Sweet Months

First, April, she with mellow showers
Opens the way for early flowers;
Then after her comes smiling May,
In a more sweet and rich array;
Next enters June, and brings us more
Gems than those two that went before:
Then, lastly, July comes, and she
More wealth brings in than all those three.

Robert Herrick

August

The wind sang to the cornfields
　　A happy little song,
And this is what he whispered.
　　"The harvest won't be long."

The wind sang to the windmill
　　A merry little tune.
The windmill answered gaily,
　　"The harvest's coming soon."

The whispering of the poppies
　　Through the cornfields steals along,
They are joining with the fairies
　　Singing harvest's merry song.

Eunice Fallon

Harvest Song

The boughs do shake and the bells do ring,
So merrily comes our harvest in,
Our harvest in, our harvest in,
So merrily comes our harvest in.

We have ploughed, we have sowed,
We have reaped, we have mowed,
We have brought home every load,
Hip, hip, hip, harvest home!

The Harvest

The silver rain, the shining sun,
The fields where scarlet poppies run,
And all the ripples of the wheat
Are in the bread that I do eat.

So when I sit for every meal
And say a grace, I always feel
That I am eating rain and sun,
And fields where scarlet poppies run.

Alice C. Henderson

Harvest

I saw the farmer plough the field,
And row on row
The furrows grow.
I saw the farmer plough the field,
And hungry furrows grow.

I saw the farmer sow the wheat,
The golden grain,
In sun and rain.
I saw the farmer sow the wheat,
In shining sun and rain.

I saw at first a silvery sheen,
Then line on line
Of living green.
I saw at first a silvery sheen,
Then lines of living green.

The living green then turned to gold,
In thirty—fifty—
Hundred fold.
The living green then turned to gold
In mercies manifold.

M. M. Hutchinson

195

Story of the Corn

The grains of corn were planted
  Where plough and rake had been,
And soon, through brown earth pushing
  The young green shoots were seen.

Cleared of weeds by harrow,
  And watered by the rain,
Aided by the sunshine,
  Appears the ripening grain.

The fields of bearded barley,
  The graceful hanging oats,
And ears of wheat packed closely,
  The cheerful reaper notes.

He sees the cornfields waving,
  Yellow and ripe and strong,
And so, his heart rejoicing,
  He sings his harvest song.

K. Fisher

Autumn

I love the fitful gust that shakes
  The casement all the day,
And from the glossy elm tree takes
  The faded leaves away,
Twirling them by the window pane
With thousand others down the lane.

I love to see the shaking twig
  Dance till shut of eve,
The sparrow on the cottage rig,
  Whose chirp would make believe
That Spring was just now flirting by
In Summer's lap with flowers to lie.

I love to see the cottage smoke
  Curl upwards through the trees;
The pigeons nestled round the cote
  On November days like these;
The cock upon the dunghill crowing,
The mill sails on the heath a-going.

John Clare

Autumn

Yellow the bracken,
  Golden the sheaves,
Rosy the apples,
  Crimson the leaves;
Mist on the hillside,
  Clouds grey and white.
Autumn, good morning!
  Summer, good night!

Florence Hoatson

Red in Autumn

Tipperty-toes, the smallest elf,
Sat on a mushroom by himself,
Playing a little tinkling tune
Under the big round harvest moon;
And this is the song that Tipperty made
To sing to the little tune he played.

"Red are the hips, red are the haws,
Red and gold are the leaves that fall,
Red are the poppies in the corn,
Red berries on the rowan tall;
Red is the big round harvest moon,
And red are my new little dancing shoon."

Elizabeth Gould

197

September

There are twelve months throughout the year,
    From January to December—
And the primest month of all the twelve
    Is the merry month of September!
        Then apples so red
        Hang overhead,
        And nuts ripe-brown
        Come showering down
    In the bountiful days of September!

There are flowers enough in the summer-time,
    More flowers than I can remember—
But none with the purple, gold, and red
    That dye the flowers of September!
    The gorgeous flowers of September!
        And the sun looks through
        A clearer blue,
        And the moon at night
        Sheds a clearer light
    On the beautiful flowers of September!

The poor too often go scant and bare,
    But it glads my soul to remember
That 'tis harvest-time throughout the land
    In the bountiful month of September!
    Oh! the good, kind month of September!
        It giveth the poor
        The growth of the moor;
        And young and old
        'Mong sheaves of gold
    Go gleaning in rich September!

Mary Howitt

October

I love to wander through the woodlands hoary,
    In the soft light of an autumnal day,
When summer gathers up her robes of glory,
    And, like a dream of beauty, glides away.

S. W. Whitman

198

An Autumn Morning

It seems like a dream
  In the garden to-day;
The trees, once so green,
  With rich colours are gay.

The oak is aglow
  With a warm, crimson blush;
The maple leaves show
  A deep purple flush.

The elm tree with bold
  Yellow patches is bright,
And with pale gleaming gold
  The beech seems alight.

And the creeper leaves flare
  Like red flame on the wall;
Their dazzle and glare
  Is the brightest of all.

The big chestnut trees
  Are all russet and brown,
And everywhere leaves
  One by one flutter down.

And all the leaves seem
  To be dressed up so gay,
That it seems like a dream
  In the garden to-day.

Autumn Morning

The south-west wind is blowing,
  A red fox hurries by;
A lake of silver water
  Reflects a rainbow sky!

The morning sun is shining
Upon the golden corn;
An early blackbird wakens
And sings to greet the dawn!

Adeline White

Autumn Song

October is a piper,
    Piping down the dell—
Sad sweet songs of sunshine—
    Summer's last farewell,
He pipes till grey November
    Comes in the mist and rain,
And then he puts his pipe away
    Till Autumn comes again.

Margaret Rose

Colour

The world is full of colour!
    'Tis Autumn once again
And leaves of gold and crimson
    Are lying in the lane.

There are brown and yellow acorns,
    Berries and scarlet haws,
Amber gorse and heather
    Purple across the moors!

Green apples in the orchard,
    Flushed by a glowing sun;
Mellow pears and brambles
    Where coloured pheasants run!

Yellow, blue and orange,
    Russet, rose and red—
A gaily-coloured pageant—
    An Autumn flower bed.

Beauty of light and shadow,
　Glory of wheat and rye,
Colour of shining water
　Under a sunset sky!

Adeline White

October's Party

October gave a party,
　The leaves by hundreds came—
The Chestnuts, Oaks and Maples,
　And leaves of every name.
The sunshine spread a carpet,
　And everything was grand,
Miss Weather led the dancing,
　Professor Wind the band.

The Chestnuts came in yellow,
　The Oaks in crimson dressed;
The lovely Misses Maple
　In scarlet looked their best;
All balanced to their partners,
　And gaily fluttered by;
The sight was like a rainbow
　New fallen from the sky.

Then, in the rustic hollow,
　At hide-and-seek they played,
The party closed at sundown,
　And everybody stayed.
Professor Wind played louder;
　They flew along the ground;
And then the party ended
　In jolly "hands around."

George Cooper
201

To Autumn

Season of mists and mellow fruitfulness!
  Close bosom-friend of the maturing sun;
Conspiring with him how to load and bless
  With fruit the vines that round the thatch-eaves run;
To bend with apples the moss'd cottage-trees,
  And fill all fruit with ripeness to the core;
    To swell the gourd, and plump the hazel shells
  With a sweet kernel; to set budding more,
And still more, later flowers for the bees,
Until they think warm days will never cease,
    For Summer has o'er-brimmed their clammy cells.

Who hath not seen thee oft amid thy store?
  Sometimes whoever seeks abroad may find
Thee sitting careless on a granary floor,
  Thy hair soft-lifted by the winnowing wind;
Or on a half-reap'd furrow sound asleep,
  Drowsed with the fumes of poppies, while thy hook
    Spares the next swath and all its twinèd flowers;
And sometime like a gleaner thou dost keep
  Steady thy laden head across a brook;
  Or by a cider-press, with patient look,
    Thou watchest the last oozings, hours by hours.

Where are the songs of Spring? Ay, where are they?
  Think not of them, thou hast thy music too–
While barred clouds bloom the soft-dying day,
  And touch the stubble-plains with rosy hue:
Then in a wailful choir, the small gnats mourn
  Among the river sallows, borne aloft
    Or sinking as the light wind lives or dies;
And full-grown lambs loud bleat from hilly bourn;
  Hedge-crickets sing; and now with treble soft
  The redbreast whistles from a garden-croft,
    And gathering swallows twitter in the skies.

J. Keats

October

I've brought you nuts and hops;
And when the leaf drops, why, the walnut drops.
Crack your first nut and light your first fire,
Roast your first chestnut crisp on the bar;
Make the logs sparkle, stir the blaze higher,
Logs are as cheery as sun or as star,
Logs we can find wherever we are.
Spring one soft day will open the leaves,
Spring one bright day will lure back the flowers;
Never fancy my whistling wind grieves,
Never fancy I've tears in my showers:
Dance, night and days! and dance on, my hours!

Christina Rossetti

Rich Days

Welcome to you, rich Autumn days,
Ere comes the cold, leaf-picking wind;
When golden stocks are seen in fields,
All standing arm-in-arm entwined;
And gallons of sweet cider seen
On trees in apples red and green.

With mellow pears that cheat our teeth,
Which melt that tongues may suck them in,
With blue-black damsons, yellow plums,
And woodnuts rich, to make us go
Into the loneliest lanes we know.

W. H. Davies

November

November is a spinner
Spinning in the mist,
Weaving such a lovely web
Of gold and amethyst.
In among the shadows
She spins till close of day,
Then quietly she folds her hands
And puts her work away.

Margaret Rose

In the Wood

Cold winter's in the wood,
　I saw him pass
Crinkling up fallen leaves
　Along the grass.

Bleak winter's in the wood,
　The birds have flown
Leaving the naked trees
　Shivering alone.

King Winter's in the wood,
　I saw him go
Crowned with a coronet
　Of crystal snow.

Eileen Mathias

A Greenland Winter

Such a wide, still landscape, all cold and white!
And the stars look down through the endless night;
And it's ever so lonely over there,
Where the white bear sleeps in his hidden lair!
There is never the sound of a sea-bird's cry,
No murmuring waters go rippling by,
No breakers roll up to the rocky beach;
There is ice as far as the eye can reach—
A desolate waste, where the foxes roam,
And the seal and the walrus have their home.
If anyone strange came wandering here,
Would they ever guess that our homes are near?
So sheltered and hidden the igloos lie,
Like hillocks of snow 'neath the Arctic sky.

Lucy Diamond

Winter's Song

Drop down, drop down, white snowflakes!
We shall hide ourselves in fur coats
And when the blizzard comes
We shall put on fur caps,
We shall harness our golden sleighs,
We shall drive down from our hillside
And if we fall into a snowdrift
We hope that the wind will not cover us,
So that we can drive back quickly
For the fairy tales which grandfather will tell us.

Translation from the Bohemian

White Fields

In winter-time we go
Walking in the fields of snow;

Where there is no grass at all;
Where the top of every wall,

Every fence, and every tree,
Is as white as white can be.

Pointing out the way we came—
Every one of them the same—

All across the fields there be
Prints in silver filigree;

And our mothers always know,
By the footprints in the snow,

Where it is the children go.

James Stephens

Winter

O Winter's a beautiful time of the year.
  There's frost on the hills,
    There's snow in the air.
  The buds are all still,
    The boughs are all bare.

This little maid of long ago
Is warmly dressed from top to toe.
Her hands are hidden in her muff,
I wonder if she's warm enough!

Enid Blyton

Winter

Sweet blackbird is silenced with chaffinch and thrush,
Only waistcoated robin still chirps in the bush:
Soft sun-loving swallows have mustered in force,
And winged to the spice-teeming southlands their course.

Plump housekeeper dormouse has tucked himself neat,
Just a brown ball in moss with a morsel to eat:
Armed hedgehog has huddled him into the hedge,
While frogs scarce miss freezing deep down in the sedge.

Soft swallows have left us alone in the lurch,
But robin sits whistling to us from his perch:
If I were red robin, I'd pipe you a tune,
Would make you despise all the beauties of June.

But, since that cannot be, let us draw round the fire,
Munch chestnuts, tell stories, and stir the blaze higher:
We'll comfort pinched robin with crumbs, little man,
Till he'll sing us the very best song that he can.

Christina Rossetti

Jack Frost

The door was shut, as doors should be,
   Before you went to bed last night;
But Jack Frost has got in, you see,
   And left your window silver white.

He must have waited till you slept;
   And not a single word he spoke,
But pencilled o'er the panes and crept
   Away again before you woke.

And now you cannot see the hills
   Nor fields that stretch beyond the lane
But there are fairer things than these
   His fingers traced on every pane.

Rocks and castles towering high;
   Hills and dales and streams and fields;
And knights in armour riding by,
   With nodding plumes and shining shields.

And here are little boats, and there
   Big ships with sails spread to the breeze;
And yonder, palm trees waving fair
   On islands set in silver seas.

And butterflies with gauzy wings;
   And herds of cows and flocks of sheep
And fruit and flowers and all the things
   You see when you are sound asleep.

For creeping softly underneath
   The door, when all the lights are out,
Jack Frost takes every breath you breathe
   And knows the things you think about.

He paints them on the window pane,
   In fairy lines with frozen steam;
And when you wake you see again
   The lovely things you saw in dream.

Gabriel Setoun

Jack Frost in the Garden

Jack Frost was in the garden;
I saw him there at dawn;
He was dancing round the bushes
And prancing on the lawn.
He had a cloak of silver,
A hat all shimm'ring white,
A wand of glittering star-dust,
And shoes of sunbeam light.

Jack Frost was in the garden,
When I went out to play
He nipped my toes and fingers
And quickly ran away.
I chased him round the wood-shed,
But, oh! I'm sad to say
That though I chased him everywhere
He simply wouldn't stay.

Jack Frost was in the garden:
But now I'd like to know
Where I can find him hiding;
I've hunted high and low—
I've lost his cloak of silver,
His hat all shimm'ring white,
His wand of glittering star-dust,
His shoes of sunbeam light.

John P. Smeeton

Snow

Out of the bosom of the air,
Out of the cloudfolds of her garment shaken,
Over the woodlands, brown and bare,
Over the harvest-fields forsaken,
Silent, and soft, and slow
Descends the snow.

H. W. Longfellow

The Snow

The snow, in bitter cold,
 Fell all the night;
And we awoke to see
 The garden white.

And still the silvery flakes
 Go whirling by,
White feathers fluttering
 From a grey sky.

Beyond the gate, soft feet
 In silence go,
Beyond the frosted pane
 White shines the snow.

F. Ann Elliott

Outside

King Winter sat in his Hall one day,
 And he said to himself, said he,
"I must admit I've had some fun,
I've chilled the Earth and cooled the Sun,
 And not a flower or tree
But wishes that my reign were done,
And as long as Time and Tide shall run,
I'll go on making everyone
 As cold as cold can be."

There came a knock at the outer door:
 "Who's there?" King Winter cried;
"Open your Palace Gate," said Spring
"For you can reign no more as King,
 Nor longer here abide;
This message from the Sun I bring,
'The trees are green, the birds do sing;
The hills with joy are echoing':
 So pray, Sir—step outside!"

Hugh Chesterman

209

There's Snow on the Fields

There's snow on the fields,
And cold in the cottage,
While I sit in the chimney nook
Supping hot pottage.

My clothes are soft and warm,
Fold upon fold,
But I'm so sorry for the poor
Out in the cold.

Christina Rossetti

The North Wind

The north wind doth blow,
And we shall have snow,
And what will poor robin do then, poor thing?
O, he'll go to the barn,
And to keep himself warm
He'll hide his head under his wing, poor thing.

The north wind doth blow,
And we shall have snow,
And what will the swallow do then, poor thing?
O, do you not know,
He's gone long ago
To a country much warmer than ours, poor thing?

The north wind doth blow,
And we shall have snow,
And what will the dormouse do then, poor thing?
Rolled up in a ball,
In his nest snug and small,
He'll sleep till the winter is past, poor thing.

The north wind doth blow,
And we shall have snow,
And what will the children do then, poor things?
O, when lessons are done,
They'll jump, skip, and run,
And play till they make themselves warm, poor things.

Winter Joys

White stars falling gently,
  Softly down to earth,
Red fires burning brightly
  In the warm and cosy hearth.

White trees changed to elfin-land,
  By red sun's dazzling glow,
Little robin redbreasts
  Hopping in the snow.

Happy children's voices,
  Shouting loud with glee,
Oh! the joys of winter
  Are wonderful to me.

Dorothy Gradon

Jack Frost

Look out! look out!
Jack Frost is about!
He's after our fingers and toes;
  And, all through the night,
  The gay little sprite
Is working where nobody knows.

  He'll climb each tree,
  So nimble is he,
His silvery powder he'll shake;
  To windows he'll creep,
  And while we're asleep,
Such wonderful pictures he'll make.

  Across the grass
  He'll merrily pass,
And change all its greenness to white;
  Then home he will go,
  And laugh, "Ho! ho! ho!
What fun I have had in the night!"

Cecily E. Pike

The North Wind

The Snow Queen comes on dazzling feet
And brings the sparkling snows,
The clouds fly fast with icy sleet,
And the North Wind blows.

Robin is singing a brave little song,
The sweetest song he knows,
But winter nights are dark and long
And the North Wind blows.

Squirrels are sleeping in hollow tree:
Seeds are asleep below;
Baby is cosy as cosy can be;
Let the North Wind blow!

Dorothy Gradon

New Year's Days

The New Year's days are white with snow,
The winds are laughing as they blow.
Across the ponds and lakes we glide,
And o'er the drifting snow we ride,
And down the hills we gaily slide,
For it is winter weather.

Each rushing stream is warmly dress'd,
An icy coat upon its breast,
And on each branch of every tree,
Packed in as close as close can be,
The next year's leaflets we can see,
All nestled close together.

Celia Standish

Winter

Summer has doft his latest green,
And Autumn ranged the barley-mows.
So long away when have you been?
And are you coming back to close
The year? It sadly wants repose.

W. D. Landor

All Seasons Shall Be Sweet

Therefore all seasons shall be sweet to thee,
Whether the summer clothe the general earth
With greenness, or redbreast sit and sing
Betwixt the tufts of snow on the bare branch
Of mossy apple-tree, while the nigh thatch
Smokes in the sun-thaw; whether the eve-drops fall
Heard only in the trances of the blast,
Or if the secret ministry of frost
Shall hang them up in silent icicles,
Quietly shining to the quiet moon.

S. T. Coleridge

Flowers and Trees

There is nothing I know of to compare
With apple blossoms falling through the air

The Aconite

Earth has borne a little son,
He is a very little one,
He wears a bib all frilled with green
Around his neck to keep him clean.
Though before another Spring
A thousand children Earth may bring
Forth to bud and blossoming—
Lily daughters, cool and slender,
Roses, passionate and tender,
Tulip sons as brave as swords,
Hollyhocks, like laughing lords,
Yet she'll never love them quite
As much as she loves Aconite:
Aconite, the first of all,
Who is so very, very small,
Who is so golden-haired and good,
And wears a bib, as babies should.

A. M. Graham

Apple Blossoms

Is there anything in Spring so fair
As apple blossoms falling through the air?

When from a hill there comes a sudden breeze
That blows freshly through all the orchard trees.

The petals drop in clouds of pink and white,
Noiseless like snow and shining in the light.

Making beautiful an old stone wall,
Scattering a rich fragrance as they fall.

There is nothing I know of to compare
With apple blossoms falling through the air.

Helen Adams Parker

216

Pink Almond

So delicate, so airy,
    The almond on the tree,
Pink stars that some good fairy
    Has made for you and me.

A little cloud of roses,
    All in a world of grey,
The almond flower uncloses
    Upon the wild March day.

A mist of roses blowing
    The way of fog and sleet,
A dust of roses showing
    For grey dust in the street.

Pink snow upon the branches,
    Pink snowflakes falling down
In rosy avalanches,
    Upon the dreary town.

A rain, a shower of roses,
    All in a roseless day,
The almond tree uncloses
    Her roses on the grey.

Katharine Tynan

Roses

You love the roses—so do I. I wish
The sky would rain down roses, as they rain
From off the shaken bush. Why will it not?
Then all the valley would be pink and white
And soft to tread on. They would fall as light
As feathers, smelling sweet: and it would be
Like sleeping and yet waking, all at once.

George Eliot

Marigolds

Do you like marigolds?
  If you do
Then my garden is
  Gay for you!

I've been cutting their
  Fragrant stalks
Where they lean on
  The garden walks.

The head's too heavy for
  The brittle stem,
A careless touch and
  You've broken them

Each one shines like a
  Separate star
Set in some heaven where
  Gardens are.

My hands smell of the
  Herb-like scent,
Telling what garden
  Way I went.

Pungent, vivid and
  Strong, they stay
Long after Summer has
  Gone away.

Do you like marigolds?
  Here's a pledge
To meet the frost with
  A golden edge—

To go as far as
  A weak thing may
Linking to-morrow with
  Yesterday.

Louise Driscoll

Larch Wood Secrets

In Larch Wood
Is a little grey pool;
I go there
When the day is cool.
And when I see the sea-gulls
Come flying down the sky,
Then I know that Winter
And the cold days are nigh.

In Larch Wood
There are growing seven larches,
One green hazel
And two silver birches;
And when I hear the squirrel
Chitter-chattering to the sky,
Then I know that Maytime
And the warm days are nigh.

Ivy O. Eastwick

The Stately Lady

I saw a stately lady
In a green gown,
When the moon was shooting
Silver arrows down.
And the stately lady
In her gown of green
Made the sweetest curtsy
I have ever seen.

"Little lovely lady,
You must be a queen,
In your yellow satin
And your gown of green."
But the stately lady
Bowed her gracious head;
"I was made a tulip,
Not a Queen," she said.

Flora Sandstrom

Wild Flower's Song

As I wandered in the forest
The green leaves among,
I heard a wild flower
Singing a song.

I slept on the earth
In the silent night:
I murmured my thought,
And I felt delight.

In the morning I went,
As rosy as morn,
To seek for fresh joy
But I met with scorn.

William Blake

Child's Song in Spring

The silver birch is a dainty lady,
　　She wears a satin gown;
The elm-tree makes the churchyard shady,
　　She will not live in town.

The English oak is a sturdy fellow;
　　He gets his green coat late;
The willow is smart in a suit of yellow,
　　While brown the beech trees wait.

Such a gay green gown God gives the larches—
　　As green as He is good!
The hazels hold up their arms for arches
　　When Spring rides through the wood.

The chestnut's proud, and the lilac's pretty,
　　The poplar's gentle and tall,
But the plane tree's kind to the poor dull city—
　　I love him best of all!

E. Nesbit

Bluebells

In the bluebell forest
    There is scarce a sound,
Only bluebells growing
    Everywhere around.

I can't see a blackbird
    Or a thrush to sing,
I think I can almost
    Hear the bluebells ring.

Ah! there is a bunny,
    And he's listening too,
Or perhaps he's thinking—
    What a sea of blue!

O. Enoch

Snowdrops

Little ladies, white and green,
    With your spears about you,
Will you tell us where you've been
    Since we lived without you?

You are sweet, and fresh, and clean,
    With your pearly faces;
In the dark earth where you've been
    There are wondrous places:

Yet you come again, serene,
    When the leaves are hidden;
Bringing joy from where you've been
    You return unbidden—

Little ladies, white and green,
    Are you glad to cheer us?
Hunger not for where you've been,
    Stay till Spring be near us!

L. Alma Tadema

221

Cherry Tree

The Chaffinch flies fast
To the red cherry tree,
And sings as he goes:
"All for me! All for me!"

The Speckled Brown Thrush
Upon fluttering wing
Goes flying and scolds:
"Greedy thing! Greedy thing!"

The chattering Starling
He visits there, too,
And cries as he flies:
"Leave a few! Leave a few!"

But the Blackbird retreats
As the others advance,
And calls to them, laughing:
"Not a chance! Not a chance!"

Ivy O. Eastwick

The Poppies in the Garden

The poppies in the garden, they all wear frocks of silk,
Some are purple, some are pink, and others white as milk,
Light, light, for dancing in, for dancing when the breeze
Plays a little two-step for the blossoms and the bees.
Fine, fine, for dancing in, all frilly at the hem,
Oh, when I watch the poppies dance I long to dance
    like them!

The poppies in the garden have let their silk frocks fall
All about the border paths, but where are they at all?
Here a frill and there a flounce—a rag of silky red,
But not a poppy-girl is left—I think they've gone to bed.
Gone to bed and gone to sleep; and weary they must be,
For each has left her box of dreams upon the stem for me.

ffrida Wolfe

222

Crocuses

A kind voice calls, "Come, little ones,
'Tis time to wake from sleeping!"
And out of bed without a word
The drowsy folk come creeping,
And soon above the chilly earth
Their tiny heads are peeping.

They bravely face the wind of March,
Its bite and bluster scorning
Like little soldiers—till, oh joy!
With scarce a word of warning
The crocuses slip off their caps
And give us gay good morning.

Anna M. Platt

Violets

Under the green hedges, after the snow,
There do the dear little violets grow;
Hiding their modest and beautiful heads
Under the hawthorn in soft mossy beds.

Sweet as the roses and blue as the sky,
Down there do the dear little violets lie;
Hiding their heads where they scarce may be seen,
By the leaves you may know where the violet hath been.

John Moultrie

The Beanfield

A beanfield in blossom smells as sweet
As araby, or groves of orange flowers;
Black-eyed and white, and feathered to one's feet,
How sweet they smell in morning's dewy hours.
When soothing night is left upon the flowers,
Another morn's sun shines brightly o'er the field,
And bean bloom glitters in the gems of showers,
And sweet the fragrance which the union yields
To battered footpaths crossing o'er the fields.

John Clare

223

From The Daisy

There is a flower, a little flower,
    With silver crest and golden eye,
That welcomes every changing hour,
    And weathers every sky.

It smiles upon the lap of May,
    To sultry August spreads its charms,
Lights pale October on his way,
    And twines December's arms.

But this bold flowerlet climbs the hill,
    Hides in the forest, haunts the glen,
Plays on the margin of the rill,
    Peeps round the fox's den.

On waste and woodland, rock and plain,
    Its humble buds unheeded rise;
The Rose has but a summer reign,
    The Daisy never dies.

James Montgomery

A Buttercup

A little yellow buttercup
    Stood laughing in the sun;
The grass all green around it,
    The summer just begun;
Its saucy little head abrim
    With happiness and fun.

Near by—grown old, and gone to seed—
    A dandelion grew;
To right and left with every breeze
    His snowy tresses flew.
He shook his hoary head, and said:
    "I've some advice for you.

"Don't think because you're yellow now
   That golden days will last;
I was as gay as you are once,
   But now my youth is past.
This day will be my last to bloom;
   The hours are going fast.

"Perhaps your fun may last a week,
   But then you'll have to die."
The dandelion ceased to speak —
   A breeze that capered by
Snatched all the white hairs from his head
   And wafted them on high.

His yellow neighbour first looked sad,
   Then, cheering up, he said:
"If one's to live in fear of death,
   One might as well be dead."
The little buttercup laughed on,
   And waved his golden head.

Buttercups and Daisies

Buttercups and daisies,
   Oh, the pretty flowers;
Coming ere the spring-time,
   To tell of sunny hours,
While the trees are leafless,
   While the fields are bare,
Buttercups and daisies
   Spring up here and there.

Ere the snowdrop peepeth,
   Ere the crocus bold,
Ere the early primrose
   Opes its paly gold —
Somewhere on the sunny bank
   Buttercups are bright;
Somewhere 'mong the frozen grass
   Peeps the daisy white.

                              Mary Howitt
                              225

Bluebells

The breeze is on the bluebells,
　　The wind is on the lea;
Stay out! Stay out! my little lad,
　　And chase the wind with me.
If you will give yourself to me
　　Within the fairy ring,
　　　　At dead midnight,
　　　　When stars are bright,
Y ou'll hear the bluebells sing.

Juliana Horatia Ewing

The Dandelions

Some young and saucy dandelions
　　Stood laughing in the sun;
They were brimming full of happiness,
　　And running o'er with fun.

They stretched their necks so slender
　　To stare up to the sky;
They frolicked with the bumble-bee,
　　And teased the butterfly.

At length they saw beside them
　　A dandelion old;
His form was bent and withered,
　　Gone were his looks of gold.

"Oh, oh!" they cried, "just see him;
　　"Old greybeard, how d'ye do?
We'd hide our heads in the grasses,
　　If we were as bald as you."

So they mocked the poor old fellow,
　　Till night came on apace;
Then a cunning little green night-cap
　　Hid each tiny little face.

But lo! when dawned the morning,
  Up rose each tiny head,
Decked not with golden tresses,
  But long grey locks instead.

The Jungle Trees

The golden trees of England
  They dance on every hill.
The giants of the jungle
  Are terrible and still.

The trees that live in England
  They wave their arms about,
And little paths of greeting
  Run gaily in and out.

But trees that make the jungle
  Are fortified and great;
And he shall find no welcome
  Who enters by their gate.

And I have seen them watching,
  And I have heard them say,
"Our beasts are fierce and hungry,
  And tangled is the way;

"And when behind our branches
  Burns out the sunset flame,
No wanderer who ventures
  Returns the way he came.

"Go back where softer sunlight
  Its sprinkled shadow spills—
Where elm and fir are holding
  High welcome on the hills."

Marjorie Wilson

Poppies

The strange, bright dancers
Are in the garden.
The wind of summer
Is a soft music.
Scarlet and orange,
Flaming and golden,
The strange, bright dancers
Move to the music.
And some are whiter
Than snow in winter,
And float like snowflakes
Drifting the garden.
Oh, have you seen them,
The strange, bright dancers,
Nodding and swaying
To the wind's music?

P. A. Ropes

I Wandered Lonely

I wandered lonely as a cloud
That floats on high o'er vales and hills,
When all at once I saw a crowd,
A host of golden daffodils;
Beside the lake, beneath the trees,
Fluttering and dancing in the breeze.

Continuous as the stars that shine
And twinkle on the milky way,
They stretched in never-ending line
Along the margin of a bay:
Ten thousand saw I at a glance,
Tossing their heads in sprightly dance.

The waves beside them danced; but they
Out-did the sparkling waves in glee.
A poet could not be but gay,
In such a jocund company:
I gazed—and gazed—but little thought
What wealth the show to me had brought:

For oft, when on my couch I lie
In vacant or in pensive mood,
They flash upon that inward eye
Which is the bliss of solitude;
And then my heart with pleasure fills,
And dances with the daffodils.

William Wordsworth

The Apple Rhyme

In my garden grows a tree
Of apple-blossom, where for me
A blackbird perches every day,
Sings his song and flies away.
So since fairies make for birds
Music out of fairy words,
I have learned from it a rhyme
For folk to sing at apple-time,
Which (if you live where apples grow)
You'll find a useful thing to know.

*The rhyme to be sung very slowly under an apple-tree
(in August or September).*

Apples ripe and apples red,
Grow they high above my head.
Alack-a-day! for I am small
And apple-trees are mostly tall;
Dreary me! But what is sadder,
Nobody can find a ladder.
Call a pixy, green or brown,
And bid him throw the apples down.
Pixy, throw them down as quick
Or quicker than my hands could pick!
One, two, three and now another
Each one bigger than the other.
Pixies green and pixies brown,
Throw the big red apples down.

Madeleine Nightingale

The Tree

Oh, like a tree
Let me grow up to Thee!
And like a tree
Send down my roots to Thee.

Let my leaves stir
In each sigh of the air,
My branches be
Lively and glad in Thee;

Each leaf a prayer,
And green fire everywhere . . .
And all from Thee
The sap within the tree.

And let Thy rain
Fall—or as joy and pain,
So that I be
Yet unforgot of Thee.

Then shall I sing
The new song of Thy Spring,
Every leaf of me
Whispering Love in Thee.

John Freeman

Sowing Seeds

I've dug up all my garden
And got the watering pan,
And packets full of seeds I mean to sow;
I'll have marigolds and pansies,
And Canterbury bells,
And asters all set neatly in a row.
I'll have mignonette and stocks,
And some tall red hollyhocks,
If sun and rain will come to help them grow.

Ursula Cornwall

Flower Chorus

O such a commotion under the ground,
    When March called, "Ho, there! ho!"
Such spreading of rootlets far and wide,
    Such whisperings to and fro!
"Are you ready?" the Snowdrop asked,
    "'Tis time to start, you know."
"Almost, my dear!" the Scilla replied,
    "I'll follow as soon as you go."
Then "Ha! ha! ha!" a chorus came
    Of laughter sweet and slow,
From millions of flowers under the ground,
    Yes, millions beginning to grow.

"I'll promise my blossoms," the Crocus said,
    "When I hear the blackbird sing."
And straight thereafter Narcissus cried,
    "My silver and gold I'll bring."
"And ere they are dulled," another spoke,
    "The Hyacinth bells shall ring."
But the Violet only murmured, "I'm here,"
    And sweet grew the air of Spring.
Then "Ha! ha! ha!" a chorus came
    Of laughter sweet and low,
From millions of flowers under the ground,
    Yes, millions beginning to grow.

O the pretty brave things, thro' the coldest days
    Imprisoned in walls of brown,
They never lost heart tho' the blast shrieked loud,
    And the sleet and the hail came down;
But patiently each wrought her wonderful dress,
    Or fashioned her beautiful crown,
And now they are coming to lighten the world
    Still shadowed by winter's frown.
And well may they cheerily laugh "Ha! ha!"
    In laughter sweet and low,
The millions of flowers under the ground,
    Yes, millions beginning to grow.

Ralph W. Emerson

The Lamp Flower

The campion white
Above the grass
Her lamps doth light
Where fairies pass.

Softly they show
The secret way,
Unflickering glow
For elf and fay.

My little thought
Hath donned her shoe,
And all untaught
Gone dancing too.

Sadly I peer
Among the grass
And seem to hear
The fairies pass.

But where they go
I cannot see,
Too faintly glow
The lamps for me.

My thought is gone
With fay and elf,
We mope alone,
I and myself.

Margaret Cecilia Furse

Bluebells

Throughout the day our sweet bells chime
The hours of the fairy time.
At night with music soft and deep,
We lull a drowsy world to sleep.

P. A. Ropes

Fluttering Leaves

In the the Spring, on the trees
Green leaves flutter in the breeze,
Flutter, flutter, flutter, flutter,
Flutter, flutter in the breeze.

Later on, when they're brown,
Leaves go drifting slowly down,
Flutter, flutter, flutter, flutter,
Flutter, flutter slowly down.

Rodney Bennett

Trees

The Oak is called the King of Trees,
The Aspen quivers in the breeze,
The Poplar grows up straight and tall,
The Pear tree spreads along the wall,
The Sycamore gives pleasant shade,
The Willow droops in watery glade,
The Fir tree useful timber gives,
The Beech amid the forest lives.

S. Coleridge

The Forget-Me-Not

When to the flowers so beautiful
    The Father gave a name,
Back came a little blue-eyed one
    (All timidly it came);
And standing at its Father's feet,
    And gazing in His face,
It said in low and trembling tones,
    "Dear God, the name Thou gavest me,
    Alas! I have forgot."
Then kindly looked the Father down,
    And said, "Forget Me Not."

233

Song of Spring

And O and O,
The daisies blow,
And the primroses are wakened;
And the violets white
Sit in silver light,
And in the green buds are long in the spike end.

J. Keats

Snowdrops

I like to think
That, long ago,
There fell to earth
Some flakes of snow
Which loved this cold,
Grey world of ours
So much, they stayed
As snowdrop flowers.

Mary Vivian

London Trees

These trees that fling their leafy boughs aloft
In city squares
So little know of ocean-scented winds
And country airs—

And yet so green they are,
So deep a shade they swing,
And from their topmost heights
So sweet the blackbirds sing!

Here, in the city's heart,
'Neath smoke-hazed skies,
Green trees do their glad part
To lighten country-weary eyes.

Beryl Netherclift

Violets

Modestly we violets cower,
Each within a little bower,
   Cool and green.
Each contented with the hour,
Welcoming both sun and shower,
   In our leafy home unseen.

P. A. Ropes

I'd Choose to be a Daisy

I'd choose to be a daisy,
   If I might be a flower;
Closing my petals softly
   At twilight's quiet hour;
And waking in the morning,
   When falls the early dew,
To welcome Heaven's bright sunshine,
   And Heaven's bright tear-drops too.

I'd choose to be a skylark,
   If I might be a bird;
My song should be the loudest
   The sun has ever heard;
I'd wander through the cloudland,
   Far, far above the moon,
And reach right up to heaven,
   Where it is always noon.

And yet I think I'd rather
   Be changed into a lamb,
And in the fields spend pleasant days
   A-playing by my dam.
But then, you see, I cannot be
   A flower, or bird or lamb.
And why? Because I'm made to be
   The little child I am!

235

Heigh Ho!

Heigh ho! daisies and buttercups,
Fair yellow daffodils, stately and tall!
When the wind wakes how they rock in the grasses,
And dance with the cuckoo-buds, slender and small!
Here's two bonny boys, and here's mother's own lasses,
Eager to gather them all.

Heigh ho! daisies and buttercups:
Mother shall thread them a daisy chain;
Sing them a song of the pretty hedge-sparrow,
That loved her brown little ones, loved them full fain;
Sing, "Heart, thou art wide, though the house be but
        narrow"—
Sing once, and sing it again.

Heigh ho! daisies and buttercups,
Sweet wagging cowslips they bend and they bow;
A ship sails afar over warm ocean waters,
And haply one musing doth stand at her prow.
O bonny brown sons, and O sweet little daughters,
Maybe he thinks on you now!

Heigh ho! daisies and buttercups,
Fair yellow daffodils stately and tall;
A sunshiny world full of laughter and leisure,
And fresh hearts unconscious of sorrow and thrall;
Send down on their pleasure smiles passing its measure—
God, that is over us all.

Jean Ingelow

Pimpernel

I'm the pert little pimpernel,
Who ever so cleverly weather foretells;
If I open my eye,
There's a cloudless sky;
If I shut it again,
Then it's sure to rain.

Charlotte Druitt Cole

Shady Woods

When the sun is shining overhead
'Tis nice to make a leafy bed
　　Deep in the shady wood;
To lie and gaze towards the sky
Peeping through the leaves on high,
　　Above the shady wood.

E. M. Adams

Tall Trees

With their feet in the earth
　And their heads in the sky
The tall trees watch
　The clouds go by.

When the dusk sends quickly
　The birds to rest,
The tall trees shelter them
　Safe in a nest.

And then in the night
　With the tall trees peeping,
The moon shines down
　On a world that's sleeping.

Eileen Mathias

The Five-Fingered Maple

"Green leaves, what are you doing
Up there on the tree so high?"
"We are shaking hands with the breezes,
As they go singing by."

"What, green leaves! Have you fingers?"
Then the Maple laughed with glee:
"Yes, just as many as you have;
Count us, and you will see!"

Kate Louise Brown

237

Violets

I know, blue modest violets
  Gleaming with dew at morn—
I know the place you come from
  And the way that you are born!

When God cut holes in heaven—
  The holes the stars look through—
He let the scraps fall down to earth;
  The little scraps are you!

The Field Daisy

I'm a pretty little thing,
Always coming with the Spring;
In the meadows green I'm found,
Peeping just above the ground;
And my stalk is covered flat
With a white and yellow hat.

Little Mary, when you pass
Lightly o'er the tender grass,
Skip about, but do not tread
On my bright but lowly head;
For I always seem to say,
"Surely Winter's gone away."

Jane Taylor

Foxgloves

The foxglove bells, with lolling tongue,
Will not reveal what peals were rung
In Faery, in Faery,
A thousand ages gone.
All the golden clappers hang
As if but now the changes rang;
Only from the mottled throat
Never any echoes float.
Quite forgotten, in the wood,
Pale, crowded steeples rise;

All the time that they have stood
None has heard their melodies,
Deep, deep in wizardry
All the foxglove belfries stand.
Should they startle over the land,
None would know what bells they be.
Never any wind can ring them,
Nor the great black bees that swing them—
Every crimson bell, down-slanted,
Is so utterly enchanted.

Mary Webb

The Thief

Autumn wind came stealing
  Through the woods one day,
And, creeping round the tree, he stole
  Their beauty all away.

He tore their russet dresses,
  Combed off their golden hair;
He blew away the tattered bits—
  And left them brown and bare.

Irene F. Pawsey

Waking Up

Pretty little crocus, in your cosy bed,
Mr. Sun is calling you, won't you show your head?
Mother Earth has sheltered you all the winter through,
Now warm winds are blowing and the skies are blue.

Little baby crocus, in his earthy bed,
With the warm sun drawing him, popped out his tiny head;
Just as he was stirring underneath the ground,
Other little crocuses were looking all around.

Further down the garden, by a running brook,
Two little snowdrops thought they'd have a look;
Saw the sun was shining and the world was gay,
For into the garden Spring had come that day!

239

Poplars

Seven lovely poplars
  Swaying in the breeze,
Seven softly sighing
  Tall and slender trees.

Silver'd by the moonlight,
  Pointing to the sky:
Look! like leafy spears, they
  Hold the stars on high.

Helen Leuty

Snowdrop

Close to the sod
There can be seen
A thought of God
In white and green.
Unmarred, unsoiled,
It cleft the clay;
Serene, unspoiled,
It views the day.

It is so holy
And yet so lowly,
Would you enjoy
Its grace and dower
And not destroy
The living flower?
Then you must, please,
Fall on your knees.

Anna Bunston de Bary

Among the Nuts

A wee little nut lay deep in its nest
Of satin and down, the softest and best;
And slept and grew, while its cradle rocked,
As it hung in the boughs that interlocked.

Now the house was small where the cradle lay,
As it swung in the wind by night and day;
For a thicket of underbush fenced it round,
This little lone cot by the great sun browned.

The little nut grew, and ere long it found
There was work outside on the soft green ground;
It must do its part so the world might know
It had tried one little seed to sow.

And soon the house that had kept it warm
Was tossed about by the winter's storm;
The stem was cracked, the old house fell
And the chestnut burr was an empty shell,

But the little seed, as it waiting lay,
Dreamed a wonderful dream from day to day,
Of how it should break its coat of brown,
And live as a tree to grow up and down.

The Leaves

The leaves had a wonderful frolic,
  They danced to the wind's loud song,
They whirled, and they floated, and scampered,
  They circled and flew along.

The moon saw the little leaves dancing,
  Each looked like a small brown bird.
The man in the moon smiled and listened,
  And this is the song he heard:

The North Wind is calling, is calling,
  And we must whirl round and round,
And then when our dancing is ended
  We'll make a warm quilt for the ground.

Proud Little Spruce Fir

On a cold winter day the snow came down
    To cover the leafless trees,
Very glad they were of a snow-white gown,
    To keep out the chilly breeze.

But a little spruce fir, all gaily dressed
    In tiny sharp leaves of green,
Was drooping beneath the load on its breast,
    And not a leaf could be seen.

"I'm an evergreen tree," he proudly thought,
    "And really they ought to know
That I'm looking my best, and care not a jot
    How bitter the wind may blow."

Jeannie Kirby

The Acorn

In small green cup an acorn grew
    On tall and stately oak;
The spreading leaves the secret knew,
    And hid it like a cloak.
The breezes rocked it tenderly,
    The sunbeams whispered low,
"Some day the smallest acorn here
    Will make an oak, you know."

The little acorn heard it all,
    And thought it quite a joke;
How could he dream an acorn small
    Would ever be an oak?
He laughed so much that presently
    He tumbled from his cup,
And rolled a long way from the tree,
    Where no one picked him up.

Close by him was a rabbit hole,
　And when the wind blew high,
Down went the acorn with a roll
　For weeks in gloom to lie.
But, one bright day, a shoot of green
　Broke from his body dry,
And pushed its way with longing keen
　To see the glorious sky.

It grew, and grew, with all its might,
　As weeks and months rolled on:
The sunbeam's words were proving right.
　For, ere a year had gone,
The shoot became a sturdy plant,
　While now the country folk
Can sit beneath the spreading leaves
　Of a mighty forest oak.

Leaves

Myriads and myriads plumed their glittering wings,
As fine as any bird that soars and sings,
As bright as fireflies or the dragon-flies
Or birds of paradise.

Myriads and myriads waved their sheeny fans,
Soft as the dove's breast, or the pelican's;
And some were gold, and some were green, and some
Pink-lipped, like apple-bloom.

A low wind tossed the plumage all one way,
Rippled the gold feathers, and green and gray—
A low wind that in moving sang one song
All day and all night long.

Some trees hung lanterns out, and some had stars
Silver as Hesper, and rose-red as Mars;
A low wind flung the lanterns low and high—
A low wind like a sigh.

Katharine Tynan

Apple Harvest

O down in the orchard
'Tis harvesting time,
And up the tall ladders
The fruit pickers climb.

Among the green branches
That sway overhead
The apples are hanging
All rosy and red.

Just ripe for the picking,
All juicy and sweet!
So pretty to look at
And lovely to eat!

Helen Leuty

Chestnut Buds

I have a mackintosh shiny brown,
To keep me warm when the rain pours down,
And the baby buds on the chestnut tree
Have shiny brown coverings, just like me.
For they've waited all through the frost and snow
For the Spring to come and the Winter to go;
That's why they've wrapped up so cosily,
Those little brown buds on the chestnut tree.

Evelyn M. Williams

Leaves

Leaves are always beautiful, I think.
At first they part their baby lips to drink
The rain in Spring, then open wider still,
Hungry for sweet winds and the sun, until
They lift their faces to the Summer rain,
Whose heavy drops pit-patter loud and plain.
The Autumn comes upon them and they change,
Decked out in glorious colours, rich and strange.
Then in the Winter they come flying down
Light as a breath, and crisp, and brown.
They fly before the wind like little elves,
And oh, I know they must enjoy themselves.

J. M. Westrup

244

The Lavender Bush

At her doorway Mrs. Mayle
Grows a bush of lavender,
Large, and round, and silver-pale,
Where the blooms, a misty blur,
Lift their purple spikes on high,
Loved of butterflies and moths,
And on these, to bleach and dry,
Mrs. Mayle spreads little cloths.

Tray cloths, mats of cobweb-weave,
All of them too fairy-fine
For a careful soul to leave
Dangling on a washing-line,
Mrs. Mayle lays softly there
Till she brings them in once more,
Sweet with blossom-scented air,
From the bush beside the door.

Elizabeth Fleming

The Secret Joy

Face to face with the sunflower,
Cheek to cheek with the rose,
We follow a secret highway
Hardly a traveller knows.
The gold that lies in the folded bloom
Is all our wealth;
We eat of the heart of the forest
With innocent stealth.
We know the ancient roads
In the leaf of a nettle,
And bathe in the blue profound
Of a speedwell petal.

Mary Webb

Out and About

It is good to be out on the road, and going one knows not where

Leisure

What is this life if, full of care,
We have no time to stand and stare?

No time to stand beneath the boughs
And stare as long as sheep or cows.

No time to see, when woods we pass,
Where squirrels hide their nuts in grass.

No time to see, in broad daylight,
Streams full of stars, like skies at night.

No time to turn at Beauty's glance,
And watch her feet, how they can dance.

No time to wait till her mouth can
Enrich that smile her eyes began.

A poor life this if, full of care,
We have no time to stand and stare.

W. H. Davies

The Song of a Traveller

I will make you brooches and toys for your delight
Of bird-song at morning and star-shine at night.
I will make a palace fit for you and me
Of green days in forests and blue days at sea.

I will make my kitchen, and you shall keep your room,
Where white flows the river and bright blows the broom,
And you shall wash your linen and keep your body white
In rainfall at morning and dewfall at night.

And this shall be for music when no one else is near,
The fine song for singing, the rare song to hear!
That only I remember, that only you admire,
Of the broad road that stretches and the roadside fire.

Robert Louis Stevenson

Puppy and I

I met a Man as I went walking;
We got talking,
Man and I.
"Where are you going to, Man?" I said
  (I said to the Man as he went by).
"Down to the village, to get some bread.
  Will you come with me?" "No, not I."

I met a Horse as I went walking;
We got talking,
Horse and I.
"Where are you going to, Horse, to-day?"
  (I said to the Horse as he went by).
"Down to the village to get some hay.
  Will you come with me?" "No, not I."

I met a Woman, as I went walking;
We got talking,
Woman and I.
"Where are you going to, Woman, so early?"
  (I said to the Woman as she went by).
"Down to the village to get some barley.
  Will you come with me?" "No, not I."

I met some Rabbits as I went walking;
We got talking,
Rabbits and I.
"Where are you going in your brown fur coats?"
  (I said to the Rabbits as they went by).
"Down to the village to get some oats.
  Will you come with us?" "No, not I."

I met a Puppy as I went walking;
We got talking,
Puppy and I.
"Where are you going this nice fine day?"
  (I said to the Puppy as he went by).
"Up in the hills to roll and play."
  "I'll come with you, Puppy," said I.

A. A. Milne

When Mary Goes Walking

When Mary goes walking
  The autumn winds blow,
The poplars they curtsey,
  The larches bend low;
The oaks and the beeches
  Their gold they fling down,
To make her a carpet,
  To make her a crown.

Patrick R. Chalmers

Tewkesbury Road

It is good to be out on the road, and going one knows not
    where,
  Going through meadow and village, one knows not
    whither nor why;
Through the grey light drift of the dust, in the keen cool
    rush of the air.
  Under the flying white clouds, and the broad blue lift of
    the sky.

And to halt at the chattering brook, in the tall green fern
    at the brink
  Where the harebell grows, and the gorse, and the
    foxgloves purple and white;
Where the shy-eyed delicate deer come down in a troop
    to drink
  When the stars are mellow and large at the coming on
    of the night.

O, to feel the beat of the rain, and the homely smell of the
    earth,
  Is a tune for the blood to jig to, a joy past power of
    words;
And the blessed green comely meadows are all a-ripple
    with mirth
  At the noise of the lambs at play and the dear wild cry
    of the birds.

John Masefield

Pedlar Jim

A dusty road is mine to tread,
From grey of dawn to sunset red,
    And slow my pace because, alack!
    I've all my wealth upon my back.

'Tis honest toil for homely fare,
A penny here, a sixpence there,
    Or maybe, on my lucky days,
    A seat beside the good wife's blaze.

With fairy tales and legends gay
I cheer the lasses when I may,
    And oft the little children cry,
    "Be sure to call as you pass by."
Florence Hoare

Weathers

This is the weather the cuckoo likes,
    And so do I:
When showers betumble the chestnut spikes,
    And nestlings fly;
And the little brown nightingale bills his best,
And they sit outside at "The Travellers' Rest,"
And maids come forth sprig-muslin drest,
And citizens dream of the south and west,
    And so do I.

This is the weather the shepherd shuns,
    And so do I;
When beeches drip in browns and duns,
    And thresh, and ply;
And hill-hid tides throb, throe on throe,
And meadows rivulets overflow,
And drops on gate-bars hang in a row,
And rooks in families homeward go,
    And so do I.

Thomas Hardy

The Night

In a scented wood
  An owl is calling;
O'er the resting land
  The night is falling;
The air is sweet
  With the scent of may;
The birds are asleep,
  They are waiting for day.

In the purple night
  No light is showing;
O'er the silent land
  A breeze is blowing,
It rustles the leaves
  With a soft little sigh;
The owl is so still,
  Then gives, softly, a cry.

Helen Leuty

The Road to Town

The road to town goes up and down,
  The road to the sea is winding,
With a follow me Jack, and a follow me Jill,
And jiggetty, joggetty over the hill,
  And a follow me over the down, O!

The road to town is easily found,
  The other takes some finding,
With a follow me Jack, and a follow me Jill,
And jiggetty, joggetty over the hill,
  And a follow me over the down, O!

The road to town is broad and fair,
  The road to the sea is shady,
With a follow me Jack, and a follow me Jill,
And jiggetty, joggetty over the hill,
  And a follow me over the down, O!

H. M. Sarson

Sunset

The summer sun is sinking low;
Only the tree-tops redden and glow;
Only the weather-cock on the spire
Of the village church is a flame of fire;
All is in shadow below.

H. W. Longfellow

Evening

She sweeps with many-coloured brooms,
And leaves the shreds behind;
Oh, housewife in the evening west,
Come back, and dust the pond!

You dropped a purple ravelling in,
You dropped an amber thread;
And now you've littered all the East
With duds of emerald!

And still she plies her spotted brooms,
And still the aprons fly,
Till brooms fade softly into stars—
And then I come away.

Emily Dickinson

The Silver Road

Last night I saw a Silver Road
Go straight across the Sea;
And quick as I raced along the Shore,
That quick Road followed me.

It followed me all round the Bay,
Where small Waves danced in tune;
And at the end of the Silver Road
There hung a Silver Moon.

A large round Moon on a pale green Sky,
With a Pathway bright and broad;
Some night I shall bring that Silver Moon
Across that Silver Road!

Hamish Hendry

253

The Early Morning

The moon on the one hand, the dawn on the other:
The moon is my sister, the dawn is my brother.
The moon on my left and the dawn on my right.
My brother, good morning: my sister, good night.

H. Belloc

To Senaca Lake

On thy fair bosom, silver lake,
    The wild swan spreads his snowy sail,
And round his breast the ripples break,
    As down he bears before the gale.

On thy fair bosom, waveless stream,
    The dippling paddle echoes far,
And flashes in the moonlight gleam,
    And bright reflects the polar star.

The waves along thy pebble shore,
    As blows the north-wind, heave their foam,
And curl around the dashing oar,
    As late the boatman hies him home.

How sweet, at set of sun, to view
    Thy golden mirror spreading wide,
And see the mist of mantling blue
    Float round the distant mountain's side.

At midnight hour, as shines the moon,
    A sheet of silver spreads below,
And swift she cuts, at highest noon,
    Light clouds, like wreaths of purest snow.

On thy fair bosom, silver lake!
    O, I could ever sweep the oar,
When early birds at morning wake,
    And evening tells us toil is o'er.

J. G. Percival

Night

The sun descending in the west,
  The evening star does shine,
The birds are silent in their nest,
  And I must seek for mine.
    The moon, like a flower,
    In heaven's high bower,
    With silent delight
    Sits and smiles on the night.

William Blake

The Moon

The moon was but a chin of gold
  A night or two ago,
And now she turns her perfect face
  Upon the world below.

Her forehead is of amplest blond;
  Her cheek like beryl stone;
Her eye unto the summer dew
  The likest I have known.

Her lips of amber never part;
  But what must be the smile
Upon her friend she could bestow
  Were such her silver will!

And what a privilege to be
  But the remotest star!
For certainly her way might pass
  Beside your twinkling door.

Her bonnet is the firmament,
  The universe her shoe,
The stars the trinkets at her belt,
  Her dimities of blue.

Emily Dickinson

255

Travellers

Come, let us go a-roaming!
  The world is all our own,
And half its paths are still untrod,
  And half its joys unknown.

The way that leads to winter
  Will lead to summer too,
For all roads end in other roads
  Where we may start anew.

Arthur St. John Adcock

The Traveller's Return

Sweet to the morning traveller
  The song amid the sky,
Where, twinkling in the dewy light,
  The skylark soars on high.

And cheering to the traveller
  The gales that round him play,
When faint and heavily he drags
  Along his noontide way.

And when beneath the unclouded sun
  Full wearily toils he,
The flowing water makes to him
  A soothing melody.

And when the evening light decays.
  And all is calm around,
There is sweet music to the ear
  In the distant sheep-bell's sound.

But, oh! of all delightful sounds
  Of evening or of morn,
The sweetest is the voice of Love
  That welcomes his return.

Sweet Surprises

A dance of blue-bells in the shady places;
A crimson flush of sunset in the west;
The cobwebs, delicate as fairy laces:
The sudden finding of a wood-bird's nest.

S. Doudney

Roadways

One road leads to London,
One road runs to Wales,
My road leads me seawards
To the white dipping sails.

One road leads to the river,
As it goes singing slow;
My road leads to shipping,
Where the bronzed sailors go.

Leads me, lures me, calls me
To salt, green, tossing sea;
A road without earth's road-dust
Is the right road for me.

A wet road, heaving, shining,
And wild with seagulls' cries,
A mad salt sea-wind blowing
The salt spray in my eyes.

My road calls me, lures me
West, east, south, and north;
Most roads lead men homewards,
My road leads me forth.

To add more miles to the tally
Of grey miles left behind,
In quest of that one beauty
God put me here to find.

John Masefield

The Fountain

Into the sunshine, full of light,
Leaping and flashing from morn till night;
Into the moonlight, whiter than snow,
Waving so flower-like when the winds blow.
Into the starlight, rushing in spray,
Happy at midnight, happy by day;
Ever in motion, blithesome and cheery,
Still climbing heavenwards, never aweary.
Glad of all weathers, still seeming best,
Upward or downward motion thy rest;
Ceaseless aspiring, ceaseless content,
Darkness or sunshine thy element;
Full of nature nothing can tame,
Changed every moment, ever the same:
Glorious fountain! let my heart be
Fresh, changeful, constant, upward, like thee!

James Russell Lowell

The Rain

I hear leaves drinking Rain;
  I hear rich leaves on top
Giving the poor beneath
  Drop after drop;
'Tis a sweet noise to hear
These green leaves drinking near.

And when the Sun comes out,
  After this Rain shall stop,
A wondrous Light will fill
  Each dark, round drop;
I hope the Sun shines bright:
'Twill be a lovely sight.

W. H. Davies

There—

If I could climb the garden wall
I'd see an elm tree green and tall.
If I could climb the green elm tree,
A grand and grassy hill I'd see.
If I could climb the grassy hill,
I'd see a mountain larger still.
If I could climb the mountain steep,
I'd see the ocean broad and deep
With great ships sailing from the bay
To foreign countries far away.

Rodney Bennett

And Back

Then, when I'd seen them leave the bay
For those strange countries far away,
If on the sea I turned my back
And faced the dizzy mountain track,
I'd see a rather little hill,
And then an elm tree smaller still,
And last, and furthest off of all,
A tiny speck—the garden wall.

Rodney Bennett

It Is a Pleasant Day

Everything is laughing, singing,
All the pretty flowers are springing;
See the kitten, full of fun,
Sporting in the brilliant sun;
Children too may sport and play.
For it is a pleasant day.

Bring the hoop, and bring the ball,
Come with happy faces all;
Let us make a merry ring,
Talk and laugh and dance and sing.
Quickly, quickly, come away,
For it is a pleasant day.

259

The Wood of Flowers

I went to the Wood of Flowers,
  (No one was with me)
I was there alone for hours;
  I was as happy as could be
In the Wood of Flowers.

There was grass on the ground,
  There were buds on the tree,
And the wind had a sound
  Of such gaiety,
That I was as happy,
  As happy could be,
In the Wood of Flowers.

James Stephens

Day and Night

When the bright eyes of the day
  Open on the dusk, to see
Mist and shadow fade away
  And the sun shine merrily,
Then I leave my bed and run
Out to frolic in the sun.

Through the sunny hours I play
  Where the stream is wandering,
Plucking daisies by the way;
  And I laugh and dance and sing,
While the birds fly here and there
Singing on the sunny air.

When the night comes, cold and slow,
  And the sad moon walks the sky;
When the whispering wind says "Boh,
  Little boy!" and makes me cry,
By my mother I am led
Home again and put to bed.

James Stephens

The Upper Skies

The upper skies are palest blue,
    Mottled with pearl and fretted snow:
With tattered fleece of inky hue
    Close overhead the storm-clouds go.

Their shadows fly along the hill
    And o'er the crest mount one by one,
The whitened planking of the mill
    Is now in shade and now in sun.

Robert Bridges

The Pedlar's Caravan

I wish I lived in a caravan,
With a horse to drive, like a pedlar-man!
Where he comes from nobody knows,
Nor where he goes to, but on he goes.

His caravan has windows two,
With a chimney of tin that the smoke comes through,
He has a wife, and a baby brown,
And they go riding from town to town.

Chairs to mend and delf to sell—
He clashes the basins like a bell.
Tea-trays, baskets, ranged in order,
Plates, with the alphabet round the border.

The roads are brown, and the sea is green,
But his house is just like a bathing-machine.
The world is round, but he can ride,
Rumble, and splash to the other side.

With the pedlar-man I should like to roam,
And write a book when I come home.
All the people would read my book,
Just like the Travels of Captain Cook.

W. B. Rands

261

Go Out

Go out
When the wind's about;
Let him buffet you
Inside out.

Go out
In a rainy drizzle;
Never sit by the fire
To sizzle.

Go out
When the snowflakes play;
Toss them about
On the white highway.

Go out
And stay till night;
When the sun is shedding
Its golden light.

Eileen Mathias

Pine Music

Last night, within my dreaming,
There somehow came to me
The faint and fairy music
Of the far-off, singing sea.

This morning, 'neath the pine tree,
I heard that song once more;
And I seemed to see the billows,
As they broke against the shore.

O wandering summer breezes!
The pine harps touch again
For the child who loves the ocean,
And longs for it in vain.

Kate Louise Brown

262

Madrigal

Sister, awake, close not your eyes,
   The day her light discloses;
And the bright morning doth arise
   Out of her bed of roses.

See, the dear sun, the world's bright eye
   In at our windows peeping;
Lo! how he blushes to espy
   Us idle wenches, sleeping.

Therefore awake, make haste, I say,
   And let us without staying,
All in our gowns of green so gay,
   Into the park a-maying.

Lady Moon

Lady Moon, Lady Moon, where are you roving?
      Over the sea.
Lady Moon, Lady Moon, whom are you loving?
      All that love me.

Are you not tired with rolling, and never
      Resting to sleep?
Why look so pale and sad, as forever
      Wishing to weep?

Ask me not this, little child, if you love me:
      You are too bold;
I must obey my dear Father above me,
      And do as I'm told.

Lady Moon, Lady Moon, where are you roving?
      Over the sea.
Lady Moon, Lady Moon, whom are you loving?
      All that love me.

Lord Houghton

263

Half Holiday

What shall I do this afternoon?
Shall I go down to the river soon?
Or to the field where kingcups grow?
Or sail my kite if the breezes blow?

What shall I do that's best of all?
And shall I take my ship or ball?
For there are plenty of things to do,
The sunbeams dance and skies are blue.

P'r'aps I might hear the cuckoo sing,
Or find a new-grown fairy ring,
I saw a squirrel once over the hill,
P'r'aps he'd come out if I sat still.

What shall I do? Where shall I go?
See how the yellow gorse is a-glow,
All things are lovely that I see,
I'll follow this happy bumble-bee.

Olive Enoch

Up, Up! Ye Dames and Lasses Gay

Up, up! ye dames and lasses gay!
To the meadows trip away.
'Tis you must tend the flocks this morn,
And scare the small birds from the corn,
  Not a soul at home must stay:
  For the shepherds must go
  With lance and bow
To hunt the wolf in the woods to-day.

Leave the hearth and leave the house
To the cricket and the mouse;
Find grannam out a sunny seat,
With babe and lambkin at her feet.
  Not a soul at home may stay:
  For the shepherds must go
  With lance and bow
To hunt the wolf in the woods to-day.

Samuel Taylor Coleridge

I Must Away

I know the hedge in Briar Lane
Is white with hawthorn snow again,
And scented in the summer rain.

I know that at this very hour
The lovely lilac is in flower;
Laburnum, too, a golden shower.

The Days pass—each a precious link
In summer's chain; and oh, to think
Of orchards dressed in white and pink.

The little lambs are out to play,
The countryside keeps holiday,
The birds have never been so gay.

Because the town is smoked and grey—
Good-bye! I cannot stay.

May Sarson

The Meadows

We'll go to the meadows, where cowslips do grow,
    And buttercups, looking as yellow as gold;
And daisies and violets beginning to blow;
    For it is a most beautiful sight to behold.

The little bee humming about them is seen,
    The butterfly merrily dances along;
The grasshopper chirps in the hedges so green,
    And the linnet is singing his liveliest song.

The birds and the insects are happy and gay,
    The beasts of the field they are glad and rejoice,
And we will be thankful to God every day,
    And praise His great name in a loftier voice.

He made the green meadows, He planted the flowers.
    He sent His bright sun in the heavens to blaze;
He created these wonderful bodies of ours,
    And as long as we live we will sing of His praise.

Jane and Ann Taylor

265

I Wonder

I wonder why the grass is green,
And why the wind is never seen?

Who taught the birds to build a nest,
And told the trees to take a rest?

O, when the moon is not quite round,
Where can the missing bit be found?

Who lights the stars, when they blow out,
And makes the lightning flash about?

Who paints the rainbow in the sky,
And hangs the fluffy clouds so high?

Why is it now, do you suppose,
That Dad won't tell me, if he knows?

Jeannie Kirby

Such a Blustery Day!

A merry wind danced over the hill,
    A madcap wind,
He shook the daffodil's golden crown,
And ruffled the clover's creamy gown;
Then off he sped, with a laughing shout,
To blow the hurrying clouds about,
And bustling back to earth again
He blew my bonnet all down the lane;

Then he hid behind a tree,
And pounced on me,

He blew me behind,
He blew me before,
He blew me right through the schoolroom door.

Elizabeth Gould

266

A Sussex Legend

Above the place where children play
A window opens, far away,
For God to hear the happy noise
Made by His little girls and boys.

Charles Dalmon

Madrigal

Come let's begin to revel 't out,
And tread the hills and dales about,
That hills and dales and woods may sound
An echo to this warbling sound:
Fa la la la.

Lads merry be with music sweet,
And Fairies trip it with your feet,
Pan's pipe is dull; a better strain
Doth stretch itself to please your vein:
Fa la la la.

South Wind

Where have you been, South Wind, this May-day morning?
With larks aloft, or skimming with the swallow,
Or with blackbirds in a green sun-glinted thicket?

O, I heard you like a tyrant in the valley,
Your ruffian haste shook the young-blossoming orchards;
You clapped rude hands, hallooing round the chimney
And white your pennons streamed along the river.

You have robbed the bee, South Wind, in your adventure,
Blustering with gentle flowers; but I forgave you
When you stole to me shyly with scent of hawthorn.

Siegfried Sassoon

267

The Wind In The Grass

The green grass is bowing,
The morning wind is in it,
'Tis a tune worth thy knowing,
Though it change every minute.

Ralph W. Emerson

Morning

The little red lark
Arises with dawn,
And soars to the skies
From her nest on the lawn.

But the little brown thrush,
When morning is red,
He flies to our casement,
And pops in his head.

"Get up, lazy bones!
Here's your shift! There's your smock!
Get up now. Get up,
For it's past eight o'clock!"

Ivy O. Eastwick

Come Unto These Yellow Sands

Come unto these yellow sands,
And then take hands:
Curtsied when you have, and kiss'd,
The wild waves whist,
Foot it neatly here and there;
And, sweet sprites, the burthen bear.
Hark, hark!
Bow, wow,
The watch-dogs bark;
Bow, wow,
Hark, hark! I hear
The strain of strutting chanticleer
Cry, Cock-a-diddle-dow!

Shakespeare

There Isn't Time

There isn't time, there isn't time
    To do the things I want to do—
With all the mountain tops to climb
    And all the woods to wander through
And all the seas to sail upon,
    And everywhere there is to go,
And all the people, every one,
    Who live upon the earth to know.
There's only time, there's only time
    To know a few, and do a few,
And then sit down and make a rhyme
    About the rest I want to do.

Eleanor Farjeon

In The Woods

Oh where have you been all the day
That you have been so long away?
Oh, I have been a woodland child,
And walked alone in places wild,
Bright eyes peered at me everywhere,
And voices filled the evening air;
All sounds of furred and feathered things,
The footfall soft, the whirr of wings.
Oh, I have seen grey squirrels play
At hide-and-seek the live-long day;
And baby rabbits full of fun
Poked out their noses in the sun,
And, unafraid, played there with me
In that still place of greenery.
A thousand secrets I have heard
From every lovely feathered bird;
The little red and yellow leaves
Danced round me in the autumn breeze,
In merry frolic to and fro,
As if they would not let me go.
How can I stay in this full town,
When those far woods are green and brown?

Dorothy Baker

269

O Wind, Where Have you Been?

O wind, where have you been,
That you blow so sweet?
Among the violets
Which blossom at your feet.

The honeysuckle waits
For Summer and for heat;
But violets in the chilly Spring
Make the turf so sweet.

Christina Rossetti

Sun and Moon

The moon shines clear as silver,
The sun shines bright like gold,
And both are very lovely,
And very, very old.

God hung them up as lanterns,
For all beneath the sky;
And nobody can blow them out,
For they are up too high.

Charlotte Druitt Cole

Laughing Song

When the green woods laugh with the voice of joy,
And the dimpling stream runs laughing by;
When the air does laugh with our merry wit,
And the green hill laughs with the noise of it;

When the meadows laugh with lively green,
And the grasshopper laughs in the merry scene;
When Mary, and Susan, and Emily
With their sweet round mouths sing, "Ha, ha, he!"

When the painted birds laugh in the shade,
When our table with cherries and nuts is spread:
Come live, and be merry, and join with me,
To sing the sweet chorus of "Ha, ha, he!"

William Blake

Wild Thyme

On the high hill pastures
　　The west wind blows,
And little ones are dancing
　　Where wild thyme grows.

Children and fairies
　　Have dreams to keep,
Where wild thyme blossoms
　　And old folk sleep.

Joyce Sambrook

Pebbles

Pebbles, pebbles, pebbles,
　　For miles and miles and miles:
A sloping bank of pebbles
　　Round all the British Isles.

Grinding, grinding, grinding,
　　Where the heavy billows pound,
Till they are smooth as marbles,
　　And often just as round.

White ones, grey ones, brown ones,
　　Lime and slate and quartz;
Yellow ones and pink ones,
　　Pebbles of all sorts.

Tinkle, tinkle, tinkle,
　　How strange it is to think
That after all these ages
　　In my tin pail they clink.

Jewels, jewels, jewels
　　For every child like me.
Oh, how I love the pebbles,
　　Beside the sounding sea.

Edith King

The Sound of the Wind

The wind has such a rainy sound
Moaning through the town,
The sea has such a windy sound—
Will the ships go down?

The apples in the orchard
Tumble from the tree.
Oh, will the ships go down, go down,
In the windy sea?

Christina Rossetti

The Night Sky

All day long
    The sun shines bright.
The moon and stars
    Come out by night.
From twilight time
    They line the skies
And watch the world
    With quiet eyes.

The Wind

I saw you toss the kites on high
And blow the birds about the sky;
And all around I heard you pass,
Like ladies' skirts across the grass—
    O wind, a-blowing all day long,
    O wind, that sings so loud a song!

I saw the different things you did,
But always you yourself you hid.
I felt you push, I heard you call,
I could not see yourself at all—
    O wind, a-blowing all day long,
    O wind, that sings so loud a song!

O you that are so strong and cold,
O blower, are you young or old?
Are you a beast of field and tree,
Or just a stronger child than me?
  O wind, a-blowing all day long,
  O wind, that sings so loud a song!

Robert Louis Stevenson

Hay Harvest

I met a man mowing
  A meadow of hay;
So smoothly and flowing
  His swathes fell away,
    At break of the day
    Up Hambleden way;
A yellow-eyed collie
  Was guarding his coat—
Loose-limbed and lob-lolly,
  But wise and remote.

The morning came leaping—
  'Twas five o' the clock,
The world was still sleeping
  At Hambleden Lock—
    As sound as a rock
    Slept village and Lock;
"Fine morning!" the man says,
  And I says: "Fine day!"
Then I to my fancies
  And he to his hay!

And lovely and quiet
  And lonely and chill,
Lay river and eyot,
  And meadow and mill;
    I think of them still—
    Mead, river, and mill;
For wasn't it jolly
  With only us three—
The yellow-eyed collie,
  The mower and me?

Patrick R. Chalmers
273

The Brook

I come from haunts of coot and hern,
   I make a sudden sally,
And sparkle out among the fern,
   To bicker down a valley.

By thirty hills I hurry down,
   Or slip between the ridges,
By twenty thorps, a little town,
   And half a hundred bridges.

I chatter over stony ways,
   In little sharps and trebles,
I bubble into eddying bays,
   I babble on the pebbles.

With many a curve my banks I fret
   By many a field and fallow,
And many a fairy foreland set
   With willow-weed and mallow.

I chatter, chatter, as I flow
   To join the brimming river,
For men may come and men may go,
   But I go on for ever.

I wind about, and in and out,
   With here a blossom sailing,
And here and there a lusty trout,
   And here and there a grayling.

And here and there a foamy flake
   Upon me, as I travel
With many a silvery waterbreak
   Above the golden gravel,

And draw them all along, and flow
   To join the brimming river,
For men may come and men may go,
   But I go on for ever.

I slip, I slide, I gloom, I glance,
  Among my skimming swallows;
I make the netted sunbeam dance
  Against my sandy shallows.

I murmur under moon and stars
  In brambly wildernesses;
I linger by my shingly bars;
  I loiter round my cresses;

And out again I curve and flow
  To join the brimming river,
For men may come and men may go,
  But I go on for ever.

Lord Tennyson

Day

"I am busy," said the sea.
"I am busy. Think of me,
Making continents to be.
I am busy," said the sea.

"I am busy," said the rain.
"When I fall, it's not in vain;
Wait and you will see the grain.
I am busy," said the rain.

"I am busy," said the air.
"Blowing here and blowing there,
Up and down and everywhere.
I am busy," said the air.

"I am busy," said the sun,
"All my planets, every one,
Know my work is never done.
I am busy," said the sun.

Sea and rain and air and sun,
Here's a fellow toiler:—one
Whose task will soon be done.

Sir Cecil Spring-Rice

275

On a Dark Road

Her eyes the glow-worm lend thee,
The shooting stars attend thee,
    And the elves also,
    Whose little eyes glow
Like the sparks of fire, befriend thee.

No will-o'-the-wisp mislight thee,
Nor snake or slow-worm bite thee;
    But on, on thy way,
    Not making a stay
Since ghost there's none to affright thee.

Let not the dark thee cumber
What though the moon does slumber!
    The stars of the night
    Will lend thee their light
Like tapers clear, without number.

Robert Herrick

Night

The sun that shines all day so bright,
I wonder where he goes at night.
He sinks behind a distant hill
And all the world grows dark and still,
And then I go to bed and sleep
Until the day begins to peep.
And when my eyes unclose, I see
The sun is shining down on me.

While we are fast asleep in bed
The sun must go, I've heard it said,
To other countries far away,
To make them warm and bright and gay.
I do not know—but hope the sun,
When all his nightly work is done,
Will not forget to come again
And wake me through the window-pane.

Pippa's Song

The year's at the spring;
The day's at the morn;
Morning's at seven;
The hill-side's dew-pearled;
The lark's on the wing;
The snail's on the thorn;
God's in His heaven—
All's right with the world!

Robert Browning

The Song of the Grass

Here I come creeping, creeping everywhere;
    By the dusty road-side,
    On the sunny hill-side,
    Close by the noisy brook,
    In every shady nook,
I come creeping, creeping everywhere.

Here I come creeping, creeping everywhere;
    All around the open door,
    Where sit the aged poor,
    Here where the children play,
    In the bright and merry May,
I come creeping, creeping everywhere.

Here I come creeping, creeping everywhere;
    You cannot see me coming,
    Nor hear my low, sweet humming;
    For in the starry night,
    And the glad morning light,
I come quietly creeping everywhere.

Here I come creeping, creeping everywhere;
    More welcome than the flowers,
    In Summer's pleasant hours;
    The gentle cow is glad,
    And the merry bird not sad,
To see me creeping, creeping everywhere.

Leigh Hunt

Song

A sunny shaft did I behold,
  From sky to earth it slanted;
And poised therein a bird so bold—
  Sweet bird, thou wert enchanted!

He sank, he rose, he twinkled, he trolled
  Within that shaft of sunny mist;
His eyes of fire, his beak of gold,
  All else of amethyst!

S. T. Coleridge

Rain in Summer

How beautiful is the rain!
After the dust and heat,
In the broad and fiery street,
In the narrow lane,
How beautiful is the rain!

How it clatters along the roofs,
Like the tramp of hoofs!
How it gushes and struggles out
From the throat of the overflowing spout!
Across the window pane
It pours and pours;
And swift and wide,
With a muddy tide,
Like a river down the gutter roars
The rain, the welcome rain!

H. W. Longfellow

The City Child

Dainty little maiden, whither would you wander?
  Whither from this pretty home, the home where mother
    dwells?
"Far and far away," said the dainty little maiden,
  "All among the gardens, auriculas, anemones,
    Roses and lilies and Canterbury-bells."

Dainty little maiden, whither would you wander?
  Whither from this pretty house, this city-house of ours?
"Far and far away," said the dainty little maiden,
  "All among the meadows, the clover and the clematis,
  Daisies and kingcups and honeysuckle-flowers."

Lord Tennyson

The Scarecrow

A scarecrow stood in a field one day,
    Stuffed with straw,
    Stuffed with hay;
He watched the folk on the king's highway,
    But never a word said he.

Much he saw, but naught did heed,
    Knowing not night,
    Knowing not day,
For, having nought, did nothing need,
    And never a word said he.

A little grey mouse had made its nest,
    Oh so wee,
    Oh so grey,
In a sleeve of a coat that was poor Tom's best,
    But the scarecrow naught said he.

His hat was the home of a small jenny wren,
    Ever so sweet,
    Ever so gay,
A squirrel had put by his fear of men,
    And kissed him, but naught heeded he.

Ragged old man, I loved him well,
    Stuffed with straw,
    Stuffed with hay,
Many's the tale that he could tell,
    But never a word says he.

Michael Franklin

The Rivals

I heard a bird at dawn
   Singing sweetly on a tree,
That the dew was on the lawn,
   And the wind was on the lea;
But I didn't listen to him,
   For he didn't sing to me!

I didn't listen to him,
   For he didn't sing to me
That the dew was on the lawn,
   And the wind was on the lea!
I was singing at the time,
   Just as prettily as he!

I was singing all the time,
   Just as prettily as he,
About the dew upon the lawn,
   And the wind upon the lea!
So I didn't listen to him,
   As he sang upon a tree!

James Stephens

Silver

Slowly, silently, now the moon
Walks the night in her silver shoon;
This way, and that, she peers, and sees
Silver fruit upon silver trees;
One by one the casements catch
Her beams beneath the silvery thatch;
Couched in his kennel, like a log,
With paws of silver sleeps the dog;
From their shadowy cote the white breasts peep
Of doves in a silver-feathered sleep;
A harvest mouse goes scampering by,
With silver claws, and silver eye;
And moveless fish in the water gleam,
By silver reeds in a silver stream.

Walter de la Mare

Is the Moon Tired?

Is the moon tired? She looks so pale
Within her misty veil;
She scales the sky from east to west,
And takes no rest.

Before the coming of the night
The moon shows papery white;
Before the dawning of the day,
She fades away.

Christina Rossetti

The Aeroplane

Look at the aeroplane
    Up in the sky,
Seems like a giant lark
    Soaring on high.

See! on its outspread wing
    Flashes the light;
There sits the pilot brave,
    Guiding its flight.

Hark! what a whirring song
    Comes from its throat,
Purr, purr of the engine,
    Its only note.

Now! high and higher yet,
    Upward it goes,
Till but a tiny speck
    'Gainst heaven it shows.

Oh! here it is again,
    Big as before,
Gracefully gliding down
    To earth once more.

Jeannie Kirby

The Little Moon

The night is come, but not too soon,
And sinking silently,
All silently, the little moon
Drops down behind the sky.

H. W. Longfellow

Swinging

Slowly, slowly, swinging low,
Let me see how far I go!
Slowly, slowly, keeping low,
I see where the wild flowers grow!

(Getting quicker):
Quicker, quicker,
Swinging higher,
I can see
A shining spire!
Quicker, quicker,
Swinging higher,
I can see
The sunset's fire!

Faster, faster,
Through the air,
I see almost
Everywhere.
Woods and hills,
And sheep that stare—
And things I never
Knew were there!

(Getting slower):
Slower, slower, now I go,
Swinging, dreaming, getting low;
Slowly, slowly, down I go—
Till I touch the grass below.

Irene Thompson

Under the Greenwood Tree

Under the greenwood tree
Who loves to lie with me,
And tune his merry note
Unto the sweet bird's throat,
Come hither, come hither, come hither;
Here shall he see
No enemy
But Winter and rough weather.

Who doth ambition shun
And loves to live i' the sun,
Seeking the food he eats,
And pleas'd with what he gets,
Come hither, come hither, come hither;
Here shall he see
No enemy
But Winter and rough weather.

Shakespeare

Midsummer Moon

When the woods are green again
With summer suns and gentle rain,
When birds do pipe their sweet refrain
With bees in chorus droning,
When the heat of day is o'er,
And human voice is heard no more,
The evening sounds begin to soar,
An echo sweet intoning.

When upon the hush of night,
There beams a lamp of silver light,
And earth is bathed in radiance bright,
New loveliness revealing;
Then the waking woods resound
With elfin laughter all around,
And from each bush and wooded mound
Is elfin music stealing.

E. M. G. R.

Windy Nights

Whenever the moon and stars are set,
  Whenever the wind is high,
All night long in the dark and wet,
  A man goes riding by.
Late in the night when the fires are out,
Why does he gallop and gallop about?

Whenever the trees are crying aloud,
  And ships are tossed at sea,
By, on the highway, low and loud,
  By at the gallop goes he:
By at the gallop he goes, and then
By he comes back at the gallop again.

Robert Louis Stevenson

The Darkening Garden

Where have all the colours gone?

Red of roses, green of grass,
Brown of tree-trunk, gold of cowslip,
Pink of poppy, blue of cornflower,
Who among you saw them pass?

They have gone to make the sunset

Broidered on the western sky,
All the colours of our garden,
Woven into a lovely curtain,
O'er the bed where Day doth lie.

Wind and the Leaves

"Come, little Leaves," said the Wind one day,
"Come o'er the meadows with me, and play;
Put on your dresses of red and gold;
Summer is gone, and the days grow cold."

Soon as the Leaves heard the Wind's loud call,
Down they came fluttering, one and all;
Over the fields they danced and flew,
Singing the soft little songs they knew.

Dancing and whirling the little Leaves went;
Winter had called them, and they were content.
Soon, fast asleep in their earthy beds,
The snow laid a coverlet over their heads.

A Fine Day

Clear had the day been from the dawn,
    All chequer'd was the sky,
Thin clouds like scarfs of cobweb lawn
    Veiled heaven's most glorious eye.
The Wind had no more strength than this,
    That leisurely it blew,
To make one leaf the next to kiss
    That closely by it grew.

Michael Drayton

The Silver House

There's a silver house in the lovely sky,
    As round as a silver crown;
It takes two weeks to build it up,
    And two to pull it down.
There's a man who lives in the silver house,
    In a lonely sort of way;
But what his name is no one knows,
    Or no one likes to say.

Yet when you go to bed to-night,
    Just draw the window blind,
And peep out at the silver moon,
    This lonely man to find.
But if his house is taken down,
    And all the sky is bare,
Then go to bed, because, of course,
    The poor man won't be there.

John Lea

Chillingham

Through the sunny garden
　The humming bees are still;
The fir climbs the heather,
　The heather climbs the hill.

The low clouds have riven
　The little rift through.
The hill climbs to heaven,
　Far away and blue.

Mary E. Coleridge

A Day at the Farm

Hurrah! for a day with the farmer
　Away in the country so sweet.
Just peep in his beautiful orchard
　And take a nice apple to eat.

Now come to the farmyard so noisy
　And hunt for fresh eggs in the hay,
We'll see the fat turkeys and chickens
　All crackling so loudly to-day.

We'll peep at the pigs and the horses,
　Then off to the meadow we'll run
To play in the grass in the sunshine
　And tumble and roll, Oh! what fun!

Oh, look at kind Betty the milkmaid,
　She's off to the cowshed, I see.
She will take the new milk to the dairy:
　I think there's a glassful for me.

How lovely and sweet is the country!
　How happy the farmer must be!
We all love to pay him a visit,
　His wonderful farmyard to see.

L. J.

The Far-Farers

The broad sun,
    The bright day,
White sails
    On the blue bay:
The far-farers
    Draw away.

Light the fires
    And close the door.
To the old homes,
    To the loved shore,
The far-farers
    Return no more.

Robert Louis Stevenson

Farewell to the Farm

The coach is at the door at last;
The eager children, mounting fast
And kissing hands, in chorus sing:
"Good-bye, good-bye, to everything!

"To house and garden, field and lawn,
The meadow-gates we swang upon,
To pump and stable, tree and swing,
Good-bye, good-bye, to everything!

"And fare you well for evermore,
O ladder at the hayloft door,
O hayloft where the cobwebs cling,
Good-bye, good-bye, to everything!"

Crack goes the whip, and off we go;
The trees and houses smaller grow;
Last, round the woody turn we swing:
"Good-bye, good-bye, to everything!"

Robert Louis Stevenson

Gipsy Jane

She had cornflowers in her ear,
  As she came up the lane;
"What may be your name, my dear?"
  "Oh, sir, Gipsy Jane."

"You are berry-brown, my dear" —
  "That, sir, well may be;
For I live, more than half the year,
  Under tent or tree."

Shine, Sun, blow, Wind!
  Fall gently, Rain!
The year's declined; be soft and kind,
  Kind to Gipsy Jane.

W. B. Rands

The Fiddle

When I was young, I had no sense,
I bought a fiddle for eighteenpence,
And the only tune that I could play
Was "Over the Hills and Far Away."

To learn another I had no care,
For oh, it was a wondrous air,
And all the wee things of the glen
Came out and gathered round me then.

The furry folk that dwelt in wood
Quitted their hushed green solitude,
Sat round about me, unafraid,
And skipped to the music that I made.

Birds of the moor, birds of the tree,
Took up the tune with fiddle and me,
Happy were we on that summer day
With "Over the Hills and Far Away."

Neil Munro

Joys

We may shut our eyes,
But we cannot help knowing
That skies are clear
And grass is growing;
The breeze comes whispering in our ear,
That dandelions are blossoming near,
That corn has sprouted,
That streams are flowing,
That the river is bluer than the sky,
That the robin is plastering his home hard by.

J. R. Lowell

Foreign Lands

Up into the cherry tree
Who should climb but little me?
I held the trunk with both my hands
And looked abroad on foreign lands.

I saw the next-door garden lie,
Adorned with flowers, before my eye,
And many pleasant places more
That I had never seen before.

I saw the dimpling river pass
And be the sun's blue looking-glass,
The dusty roads go up and down
With people tramping into town.

If I could find a higher tree,
Farther and farther I should see,
To where the grown-up river slips
Into the sun among the ships.

To where the roads on either hand
Lead onward into fairy-land,
Where all the children dine at five,
And all the playthings come alive.

Robert Louis Stevenson

289

Mr. Scarecrow

There's a ragged old man in the garden to-day,
And Gardener, laughing, says there he can stay;
His coat is in tatters, he wears an old hat,
And the birds do not like him, I'm quite sure of that.

They chatter, chit-chatter up there in the tree,
And aren't half as friendly as they used to be;
But Gardener says: "That's a good job, indeed!
If it weren't for that old man, they'd have all my seed!"

Sheila Braine

The Bells of Youth

The Bells of Youth are ringing in the gateways of the South;
    The bannerets of green are now unfurled;
Spring has risen with a laugh, a wild-rose in her mouth,
    And is singing, singing, singing thro' the world.

The Bells of Youth are ringing in the silent places,
    The primrose and the celandine are out:
Children run a-laughing with joy upon their faces,
    The west wind follows after with a shout.

The Bells of Youth are ringing from the forests to the moun-
        tains,
    From the meadows to the moorlands, hark their ringing!
Ten thousand thousand splashing rills and fern-dappled
        fountains
        Are flinging wide the Song of Youth, and onward flowing
        singing.

The Bells of Youth are ringing in the gateways of the South;
    The bannerets of green are now unfurled;
Spring has risen with a laugh, a wild-rose in her mouth,
    And is singing, singing, singing thro' the world.

"Fiona Macleod" (William Sharp)

The Cliff-Top

The cliff-top has a carpet
Of lilac, gold and green:
The blue sky bounds the ocean,
The white clouds scud between.

A flock of gulls are wheeling
And wailing round my seat;
Above my head the heaven,
The sea beneath my feet.

Robert Bridges

The Boy's Song

Where the pools are bright and deep,
Where the grey trout lies asleep,
Up the river and o'er the lea—
That's the way for Billy and me.

Where the blackbird sings the latest,
Where the hawthorn blooms the sweetest,
Where the nestlings chirp and flee—
That's the way for Billy and me.

Where the mowers mow the cleanest,
Where the hay lies thick and greenest,
There to trace the homeward bee—
That's the way for Billy and me.

Where the hazel bank is steepest,
Where the shadow falls the deepest,
Where the clustering nuts fall free—
That's the way for Billy and me.

There let us walk, there let us play,
Through the meadows, among the hay,
Up the water, and o'er the lea—
That's the way for Billy and me.

James Hogg

291

Frolic

The children were shouting together
And racing along the sands,
A glimmer of dancing shadows,
A dove-like flutter of hands.

The stars were shouting in heaven,
The sun was chasing the moon,
The game was the same as the children's,
They danced to the self-same tune.

The whole of the world was merry,
One joy from the vale to the height,
Where the blue woods of twilight encircled
The lovely lawns of the light.

A. E.

The Day Before April

The day before April
Alone, alone,
I walked in the woods
And I sat on a stone.

I sat on a broad stone
And sang to the birds,
The tune was God's making,
But I made the words.

May Carolyn Davies

Rainy Nights

I like the town on rainy nights
When everything is wet—
When all the town has magic lights
And streets of shining jet!

When all the rain about the town
Is like a looking-glass,
And all the lights are upside down
Below me as I pass.

In all the pools are velvet skies,
  And down the dazzling street
A fairy city gleams and lies
  In beauty at my feet.

Irene Thompson

Glow-Worms

With a yellow lantern
  I take the road at night,
And chase the flying shadows
  By its cheerful light.

From the banks and hedgerows
  Other lanterns shine,
Tiny elfin glimmers,
  Not so bright as mine.

Those are glow-worm lanterns,
  Coloured green and blue,
Orange, red and purple,
  Gaily winking through.

See the glow-worms hurry!
  See them climb and crawl!
They go to light the dancers
  At the fairy ball.

P. A. Ropes

Dawn

A thrush is tapping a stone
  With a snail-shell in its beak;
A small bird hangs from a cherry
  Until the stem shall break.
No waking song has begun,
And yet birds chatter and hurry
And throng in the elm's gloom,
Because an owl goes home.

Gordon Bottomley
293

Cobwebs

Between me and the rising sun,
This way and that the cobwebs run;
Their myriad wavering lines of light
Dance up the hill and out of sight.

There is no land possesses half
So many lines of telegraph
As those the spider-elves have spun
Between me and the rising sun.

E. L. M. King

The Piper

A piper in the streets to-day
Set up and tuned, and started to play,
And away, away, away on the tide
Of his music we started; on every side
Doors and windows were opened wide,
And men left their work and came,
And women with petticoats coloured like flame,
And little bare feet that were blue with cold,
Went dancing back to the age of gold,
And all the world went gay, went gay,
For half an hour in the street to-day.

Seumas O'Sullivan

Hie Away!

Hie away! hie away!
Over bank and over brae,
Where the copsewood is the greenest,
Where the fountains glisten sheenest,
Where the lady-fern grows strongest,
Where the morning dew lies longest,
Where the black-cock sweetest sips it,
Where the fairy latest trips it;
Hie to haunts right seldom seen,
Lovely, lonesome, cool and green:
Over bank and over brae
Hie away! hie away!

Sir Walter Scott

Castles in the Sand

I've built a castle in the sand
  In less than half an hour,
With grim portcullis, and a moat,
  And battlements and tower.

The seaweed banners wave, and when
  I let the drawbridge down,
The knights come riding two by two
  In armour rusty brown.

And ladies lean from turrets high,
  And watch them as they pass,
And wave their floating silken scarves,
  As light and green as grass.

But see! across the shining sand,
  That enemy the sea
Creeps slowly to my castle walls,
  Advancing stealthily.

No bugles sound a wild alarm,
  No warders close the gate;
The knights and ladies disappear,
  And all alone I wait.

For where my fairy fortress stood
  And glistened in the sun,
There lies a heap of ruins now,
  My work is all undone.

Dorothy Baker

The Wind

What way does the Wind come? What way does he go?
He rides over the water, and over the snow,
Through wood and through vale: and o'er rocky height
Which goat cannot climb, takes his sounding flight.
He tosses about in every bare tree,
As, if you look up, you plainly may see;
But how he will come, and whither he goes,
There's never a scholar in England knows.

Dorothy Wordsworth

295

The Caravan

If I could be a gipsy-boy
  And have a caravan
I'd travel all the world, I would,
  Before I was a man;
We'd drive beyond the far blue hills—
  We two, my horse and me—
And on and on and on and on
  Until we reached the sea.

And there I'd wash his legs quite clean
  And bid him come inside,
Whilst I would stand upon the roof
  And scan the flowing tide,
And he and I would sail away
  And scour the Spanish main,
And when we'd swept the Spaniards out
  We'd p'raps sail home again.

Or if my horse was very tired
  Of ships and being good,
And wanted most to stretch his legs
  (As many horses would),
We'd call a whale to tow us
  To a desert island beach,
And there we'd search for coconuts
  And have a whole one each.

If I could be a gipsy-boy
  I wouldn't bring a load
Of pots and pans and chairs and things
  And sell them in the road.
Oh, if I was a gipsy-boy
  And had a caravan,
I'd see the whole wide world, I would,
  Before I was a man.

Madeline Nightingale

Freedom

Out in the garden, sunny and still,
    Nothing to do till tea,
Let's go up to the top of the hill!
    Come along, puppy, with me.

Up on the hill-top, sunny and tall,
    Nothing to do till tea,
Let's go down to the old stone wall!
    Come along, puppy, with me.

Down by the old wall, sunny and grey,
    Nothing do to till tea,
Let's go out to the meadow to play!
    Come along, puppy, with me!

Out in the meadow, sunny and wide,
    Come along, puppy, with me.
Let's go right to the other side!
    And then go home to tea.

Joan Agnew

Afternoon on a Hill

I will be the gladdest thing
    Under the sun!
I will touch a hundred flowers
    And not pick one.

I will look at cliffs and clouds
    With quiet eyes,
Watch the wind bow down the grass
    And the grass rise.

And when the lights begin to show
    Up from the town,
I will mark which must be mine,
    And then start down!

Edna St. Vincent Millay

The Swing

Now so high,
Now so low,
Up in the air,
Then down I go.
Up to the sky,
Down to the grass,
I watch birds fly,
I see worms pass.

With feet in front,
And hair behind,
I race the birds,
I race the wind,
Over the world,
Under the tree,
Nobody knows
What things I see.
Wonderful lands
Where children play
From early morn
All thro' the day.

Mary I. Osborn

The Night

The night was creeping on the ground;
She crept and did not make a sound
Until she reached the tree, and then
She covered it, and stole again
Along the grass beside the wall.

I heard the rustle of her shawl
As she threw blackness everywhere
Upon the sky and ground and air,
And in the room where I was hid:
But no matter what she did
To everything that was without,
She could not put my candle out.

So I stared at the night, and she
Stared back solemnly at me.

James Stephens

The Lighthouse

Burning upon some hidden shore
    Across the sea one night
("A little reef," the Captain said),
    We saw a shining light.

He said there was a lighthouse there
    Where, lonely in the sea,
Men lived to guard that moving light,
    And trim the lamp for me.

For me, for him, for every ship
    That passes by that way.
I thought it must be strange and quiet
    To be there every day.

They have no shops, no fields, no streets;
    No whispering sound of trees,
But always shouting at their feet
    The great voice of the seas.

And when we sleep at night they wake,
    And over every wave
They send that straight strong arm of light
    Stretched like a rope to save.

Marjorie Wilson

Daybreak in a Garden

I heard the farm cocks crowing loud, and faint, and thin,
When hooded night was going and one clear planet winked;
I heard shrill notes begin down the spired wood distant
When cloudy shoals were chinked and gilt with fires of day.
White-misted was the weald; the lawns were silver-grey;
The lark his lonely field for heaven had forsaken;
And the wind upon the way whispered the boughs of may
And touched the nodding peony-flowers to bid them waken.

Siegfried Sassoon

The Playhouse Key

This is the key to the playhouse,
  In the woods by the pebbly shore,
It's winter now; I wonder if
  There's snow about the door?

I wonder if the fir trees tap
  Green fingers on the pane,
If sea gulls cry and the roof is wet
  And tinkle-y with rain?

I wonder if the flower-sprigged cups
  And plates sit on their shelf,
And if my little painted chair
  Is rocking by itself?

Rachel Field

The Lady Moon

The Lady Moon is sailing,
High up in heaven she rides;
I see her shining silver car,
Attended by full many a star,
  Keeping the tides.

Oh, Lady Moon! so shining,
Your face is sweet and mild;
I long with you, dear moon, to be
Afloat upon that silver sea,
  A happy child.

Oh, Lady Moon! still sailing,
A constant watch you keep;
From east to west you steer your car;
I feel your smile, dear moon, afar,
  Guarding my sleep.

Kate Louise Brown

Colour

Colour is a lovely thing.
Given to soothe our sight,
Blue for sky, green for grass,
And brown for roads where wee folks pass;
Golden sun that shines o'er head,
Silver for moon, for sunset red,
Soft cool black for night!

Flying

I saw the moon,
One windy night,
Flying so fast—
All silvery white—
Over the sky
Like a toy balloon
Loose from its string—
A runaway moon.
The frosty stars
Went racing past,
Chasing her on
Ever so fast.
Then everyone said,
"It's the clouds that fly,
And the stars and moon
Stand still in the sky."
But I don't mind—
I saw the moon
Sailing away
Like a toy
Balloon.

J. M. Westrup

301

From a Walking Song

Here we go a-walking, so softly, so softly,
  Down the world, round the world, back to London town,
To see the waters and the whales, the emus and the mandarins,
  To see the Chinese mandarins, each in a silken gown.

Here we go a-walking, so softly, so softly,
  Through the vast Atlantic waves, back to London town,
To see the ships made whole again that sank below the tempest,
  The Trojan and Phoenician ships that long ago went down.
And there are sailors keeping watch on many a Roman galley,
  And silver bars and golden bars and mighty treasure hid,
And splendid Spanish gentlemen majestically walking
  And waiting on their Admiral as once in far Madrid.

Here we go a-walking, so softly, so softly,
  Down and under to New York, back to London town,
To see the face of Liberty that smiles upon all children,
  But when too soon they come of age she answers with a
    frown.

Here we go a-walking, so softly, so softly,
  O'er the wide Tibetan plains, back to London town,
To see the Youthful Emperor among his seventy princes,
  Who bears the magic sceptre, who wears the magic crown.

Here we go a-walking, so softly, so softly,
  Through the jungles African, back to London town,
To see the shining rivers and the drinking place by moonlight,
  And the lions and hyenas and the zebras coming down:
To see bright birds and butterflies, the monstrous hippopotami,
  The silent secret crocodiles that keep their ancient guile,
The white road of the caravans that stretches o'er Sahara,
  And the Pharaoh in his litter at the fording of the Nile.

Here we go a-walking, so softly, so softly,
  Up the hills of Hampstead, back to London town,
And the garden gate stands open and the house door swings
    before us,
  And the candles twinkle happily as we lie down.

302

For here the noble lady is who meets us from our wanderings,
   Here are all the sensible and very needful things,
Here are blankets, here is milk, here are rest and slumber,
   And the courteous prince of angels with the fire about his
      wings.

Charles Williams

The Echoing Green

The Sun doth arise,
And make happy the skies;
The merry bells ring
To welcome the Spring;
The skylark and thrush,
The birds of the bush
Sing louder around
To the bells' cheerful sound,
While our sports shall be seen
On the Echoing Green.

Old John, with white hair,
Does laugh away care,
Sitting under the oak,
Among the old folk;
They laugh at our play,
And soon they all say:
"Such, such were the joys
When we all, girls and boys,
In our youth time were seen
On the Echoing Green."

Till the little ones, weary,
No more can be merry;
The sun does descend,
And our sports have an end.
Round the laps of their mothers
Many sisters and brothers,
Like birds in their nest,
Are ready for rest,
And sport no more seen
On the darkening Green.

William Blake

303

The King's Wood

The King is out a-hunting,
A-hunting in the King's Wood;
Hang the house with bunting,
    The King is riding by.

With him the Queen is riding,
A-riding to the King's Wood;
Oh, who'd be idly biding,
    When the King and Queen go by?

Come lords and ladies prancing,
A-prancing to the King's Wood;
And eager eyes are glancing,
    As stately they go by.

With morn they're quickly pacing,
A-pacing to the King's Wood;
The tall red deer a-chasing,
    They let the day go by.

Then home they come returning,
Returning to the King's Wood;
And gallant hearts are burning
    As beauty passes by.

C. S. Holder

The Sea

Take your bucket, and take your spade,
    And come to the sea with me,
Building castles upon the sand
    Is the game for you and me!
Races run with the tumbling waves,
Then rest awhile in the cool, dark caves.
Oh, the greatest joy in the summer time
    Is the sea, the sparkling sea!

E. M. Adams

The Tree in the Garden

There's a tree out in our garden which is very nice to climb,
And I often go and climb it when it's fine in summer time,
And when I've climbed right up it I pretend it's not a tree
But a ship in which I'm sailing, far away across the sea.

Its branches are the rigging and the grass so far below
I make believe's the ocean over which my ship must go;
And when the wind is blowing then I really seem to be
A-sailing, sailing, sailing, far away across the sea.

Then I hunt for desert islands and I very often find
A chest stuffed full of treasure which some pirate's left
behind—
My good ship's hold is filled with gold—it all belongs to me—
For I've found it when I'm sailing far away across the sea.

It's a lovely game to play at—though the tree trunk's rather
green,
Still, when I'm in my bath at night I always come quite clean.
And so through all the summer, in my good ship Treasure-
Tree,
I shall often go a-sailing far away across the sea.

Christine Chaundler

Youth

Oh, the wild joy of living; the leaping from rock to rock,
The strong rending of boughs from the fir-trees, the cool
silver shock
Of the plunge in the pool's living water, the hunt of the bear,
And the sultriness showing the lion is couch'd in his lair.
And the meal, the rich dates yellow'd over with gold-dust
divine,
And the locust fresh steeped in the pitcher, the full draught of
wine,
And the sleep in the dried river-channel where bulrushes tell
That the water was wont to go warbling so softly and well.
How good is man's life, the mere living! how fit to employ
All the heart and the soul and the senses for ever in joy!

Robert Browning

305

A Rune of Riches

I have a golden ball,
   A big, bright shining one,
Pure gold; and it is all
   Mine. It is the sun.

I have a silver ball,
   A white and glistering stone
That other people call
   The moon—my very own!

The jewel things that prick
   My cushion's soft blue cover
Are mine—my stars, thick, thick,
   Scattered the sky over.

And everything that's mine
   Is yours, and yours, and yours—
The shimmer and the shine!—
   Let's lock our wealth out-doors!

Florence Converse

Where Lies the Land?

Where lies the land to which the ship would go?
Far, far ahead is all her seamen know.
And where the land she travels from? Away,
Far, far behind, is all that they can say.

On sunny noons upon the deck's smooth face,
Linked arm in arm, how pleasant here to pace!
Or, o'er the stern reclining, watch below
The foaming wake far-widening as we go.

On stormy nights when wild north-westerns rave,
How proud a thing to fight with wind and wave!
The dripping sailor on the reeling mast
Exults to bear, and scorns to wish it past.

Where lies the land to which the ship would go?
Far, far ahead is all her seamen know.
And where the land she travels from? Away,
Far, far behind is all that they can say.

Arthur Hugh Clough

Daybreak

A wind came up out of the sea,
And said, "O mists, make room for me."

It hailed the ships, and cried, "Sail on,
Ye mariners, the night is gone."

And hurried landward far away,
Crying, "Awake! it is the day."

It said unto the forest, "Shout!
Hang all your leafy banners out!"

It touched the wood-bird's folded wing,
And said, "O bird, awake and sing."

And o'er the farms, "O chanticleer,
Your clarion blow; the day is near."

It whispered to the fields of corn,
"Bow down, and hail the coming morn."

It shouted through the belfry tower,
"Awake, O bell! proclaim the hour."

It crossed the churchyard with a sigh,
And said, "Not yet! in quiet lie."

H. W. Longfellow

The Lights

I know the ships that pass by day:
I guess their business, grave or gay,
   And spy their flags, and learn their names,
      And whence they come and where they go—
      But in the night I only know
   Some little starry flames.

And yet I think these jewelled lights
Have meanings full as noonday sights:
   For every emerald signs to me
      That ship and souls are harbour near,
      And every ruby rich and clear
   Proclaims them bound for sea.

And all the yellow diamonds set
On mast and deck and hull in jet
   Have meanings real as day can show:
      They tell of care, of watchful eyes,
      Of labour, slumber, hopes, and sighs—
   Of human joy and woe.

O ships that come and go by night,
God's blessing be on every light!

J. J. Bell

Sherwood

Sherwood in the twilight, is Robin Hood awake?
Grey and ghostly shadows are gliding through the brake;
Shadows of the dappled deer, dreaming of the morn,
Dreaming of a shadowy man that winds a shadowy horn.

Robin Hood is here again; all his merry thieves
Hear a ghostly bugle-note, shivering through the leaves,
Calling as he used to call, faint and far away,
In Sherwood, in Sherwood, about the break of day.

Merry, merry England has kissed the lips of June;
All the wings of fairyland are here beneath the moon;
Like a flight of rose-leaves fluttering in a mist
Of opal and ruby and pearl and amethyst.

Merry, merry England is waking as of old,
With eyes of blither hazel and hair of brighter gold:
For Robin Hood is here again beneath the bursting spray
In Sherwood, in Sherwood, about the break of day.

Love is in the greenwood building him a house
Of wild rose and hawthorn and honeysuckle boughs;
Love is in the greenwood: dawn is in the skies;
And Marian is waiting with a glory in her eyes.

Hark! the dazzled laverock climbs the golden steep:
Marian is waiting: is Robin Hood asleep?
Round the fairy grass-rings frolic elf and fay,
In Sherwood, in Sherwood, about the break of day.

Oberon, Oberon, rake away the gold,
Rake away the red leaves, roll away the mould,
Rake away the gold leaves, roll away the red,
And wake Will Scarlett from his leafy forest bed.

Friar Tuck and Little John are riding down together
With quarter-staff and drinking-can and grey goose-feather
The dead are coming back again; the years are rolled away
In Sherwood, in Sherwood, about the break of day.

Softly over Sherwood the South wind blows;
All the heart of England hid in every rose
Hears across the greenwood the sunny whisper leap,
Sherwood in the red dawn, is Robin Hood asleep?

Hark, the voice of England wakes him as of old
And, shattering the silence with a cry of brighter gold,
Bugles in the greenwood echo from the steep,
Sherwood in the red dawn, is Robin Hood asleep?

Where the deer are gliding down the shadowy glen
All across the glades of fern he calls his merry men;
Doublets of the Lincoln green glancing through the May
In Sherwood, in Sherwood, about the break of day;

Call them and they answer; from aisles of oak and ash
Rings the *Follow! Follow!* and the boughs begin to crash;
The ferns begin to flutter and the flowers begin to fly;
And through the crimson dawning the robber band goes by.

Robin! Robin! Robin! all his merry thieves
Answer as the bugle-note shivers through the leaves;
Calling as he used to call, faint and far away,
In Sherwood, in Sherwood, about the break of day.

A. Noyes

The Windmill

If you should bid me make a choice
   'Twixt wind- and water-mill,
In spite of all the mill-pond's charms
I'd take those gleaming, sweeping arms
   High on a windy hill.

The miller stands before his door
   And whistles for a breeze;
And, when it comes, his sails go round
With such a mighty rushing sound
   You think of heavy seas.

And if the wind declines to blow
   The miller takes a nap
(Although he'd better spend an hour
In brushing at the dust and flour
   That line his coat and cap).

Now, if a water-mill were his,
   Such rest he'd never know,
For round and round his crashing wheel,
His dashing, splashing, plashing wheel,
   Unceasingly would go.

310

So, if you'd bid me take a choice
   'Twixt wind- and water-mill,
In spite of all a mill-pond's charms,
I'd take those gleaming, sweeping arms
   High on a windy hill.

E. V. Lucas

White Horses

Far out at sea
   There are horses to ride,
Little white horses
   That race with the tide.

Their tossing manes
   Are the white sea-foam,
And the lashing winds
   Are driving them home—

To shadowy stables
   Fast they must flee,
To the great green caverns
   Down under the sea.

Irene F. Pawsey

The Gallant Ship

Upon the gale she stooped her side,
And bounded o'er the swelling tide,
   As she were dancing home;
The merry seamen laughed to see
Their gallant ship so lustily
   Furrow the sea-green foam.

Sir Walter Scott

311

All Creatures Great and Small

Little children, never give
Pain to things that feel and live

The Browny Hen

A browny hen sat on her nest
  With a hey-ho for the springtime!
Seven brown eggs 'neath her downy breast,
  With a hey-ho for the springtime!

A brown hen clucks all day from dawn,
  With a hey-ho for the springtime!
She's seven wee chicks as yellow as corn,
  With a hey-ho for the springtime!

Irene F. Fawsey

Duck's Ditty

All along the backwater,
  Through the rushes tall,
Ducks are a-dabbling,
  Up tails all!

Duck's tails, drakes' tails,
  Yellow feet a-quiver,
Yellow bills all out of sight
  Busy in the river!

Slushy green undergrowth
  Where the roach swim,
Here we keep our larder
  Cool and full and dim!

Every one for what he likes!
  We like to be
Heads down, tails up,
  Dabbling free!

High in the blue above
  Swifts whirl and call—
We are down a-dabbling,
  Up tails all!

Kenneth Grahame,

Michael's Song

Because I set no snare
But leave them flying free,
All the birds of the air
Belong to me.

From the blue-tit on the sloe
To the eagle on the height,
Uncaged they come and go
For my delight.

And so the sunward way
I soar on the eagle's wings,
And in my heart all day
The blue-tit sings.

Wilfrid Gibson

The Grasshopper and the Cricket

The poetry of earth is never dead:
When all the birds are faint with the hot sun,
And hide in cooling trees, a voice will run
From hedge to hedge about the new-mown mead:
This is the grasshopper's—he takes the lead
In summer luxury—he has never done
With his delights, for when tired out with fun,
He rests at ease beneath some pleasant weed.
The poetry of earth is ceasing never:
On a lone winter evening, when the frost
Has wrought a silence, from the stove there shrills,
The Cricket's song, in warmth increasing ever,
And seems to one in drowsiness half lost,
The grasshopper's among the grassy hills.

J. Keats

The Eagle

He clasps the crag with crooked hands;
Close to the sun in lonely lands,
Ringed with the azure world, he stands.

The wrinkled sea beneath him crawls;
He watches from his mountain walls,
And like a thunderbolt he falls.

Lord Tennyson

Gay Robin is seen no More

Gay Robin is seen no more:
    He is gone with the snow,
    For winter is o'er
    And Robin will go.
In need he was fed, and now he is fled
    Away to his secret nest.
    No more will he stand
    Begging for crumbs,
    No longer he comes
    Beseeching our hand
    And showing his breast
    At window and door: —
Gay Robin is seen no more.

Blithe Robin is heard no more:
    He gave us his song
    When summer was o'er
    And winter was long:
    Beseeching our hand
He sang for his bread, and now he is fled
    Away to his secret nest,
    And there in the green
    Early and late
    Alone to his mate
    He pipeth unseen
    And swelleth his breast;
    For us it is o'er: —
Blithe Robin is heard no more.

Robert Bridges

L'Oiseau Bleu

(The Blue Bird)

The lake blue below the hill.
O'er it, as I looked, there flew
Across the waters, cold and still,
A bird whose wings were palest blue.

The sky above was blue at last,
The sky beneath me blue in blue.
A moment, ere the bird had passed,
It caught his image as he flew.

Mary E. Coleridge

The Birds on the School Windowsill

Robin: I'm hungry, oh so hungry!
               I'd love a piece of bread!
Sparrow: I've looked for nice cold water,
               But found hard ice instead.
Birds: Please, please, do give us food and drink!
               You boys and girls are kind, I think.

Alec: Here's piece of crust.
Betty: Here's another, too.
Charles: Don't be frightened, pretty birds,
               We love you, yes, we do.
Dorothy: Here's a drink of water
               In a little dish:
               Help yourselves, poor thirsty birds;
               There's still more if you wish.

Children: Come again, Cock Sparrow;
               Robin Redbreast, too,
               Please come every morning—
               There's always food for you.
Birds: Thank you, thank you, children,
               And now we'll fly away
               To bring our hungry friends to share
               The feast we've found to-day.

Evelyn Dainty

The Tadpole

Underneath the water-weeds
    Small and black, I wriggle,
And life is most surprising!
    Wiggle! waggle! wiggle!
There's every now and then a most
    Exciting change in me,
I wonder, wiggle! waggle!
    What I *shall* turn out to be!

E. E. Gould

The Brown Thrush

There's a merry brown thrush sitting up in the tree,
"He's singing to me! He's singing to me!"
And what does he say, little girl, little boy?
"Oh, the world's running over with joy!
Don't you hear? don't you see?
Hush! Look! In my tree
I'm as happy as happy can be!"

And the brown thrush keeps singing, "A nest do you see,
And five eggs, hid by me in the juniper-tree?
Don't meddle! don't touch! little girl, little boy,
Or the world will lose some of its joy!
Now I'm glad! now I'm free!
And I always shall be,
If you never bring sorrow to me."

So the merry brown thrush sings away in the tree,
To you and to me, to you and to me;
And he sings all the day, little girl, little boy,
"Oh, the world's running over with joy!
But long it won't be,
Don't you know? don't you see?
Unless we are as good as can be!"

Lucy Larcom

318

The Curliest Thing

The squirrel is the curliest thing
   I think I ever saw;
He curls his back, he curls his tail,
   He curls each little paw,
He curls his little vest so white,
   His little coat so grey—
He is the most curled-up wee soul
   Out in the woods at play!

Zoo Manners

Be careful what
   You say or do
When you visit the animals
   At the Zoo.

Don't make fun
   Of the Camel's hump
He's very proud
   Of his noble bump.

Don't laugh too much
   At the Chimpanzee
He thinks he's as wise
   As you or me.

And the Penguins
   Strutting round the lake
Can understand
   Remarks you make.

Treat them as well
   As they do you,
And you'll always be welcome
   At the Zoo.

Eileen Mathias.

319

The Poor Snail

The snail says, "Alas!"
And the snail says, "Alack!
Why must I carry
My house on my back?
You have a home
To go in and out,
Why must mine always be
Carried about?
Not any tables,
Not any chairs,
Not any windows,
Not any stairs,
Pity my misery,
Pity my wail—
For I must always be
Just a poor snail."
But he's terribly slow,
So perhaps it's as well
That his shell is his home,
And his home is his shell.

J. M. Westrup

The Fifteen Acres

I cling and swing
On a branch, or sing
Through the cool, clear hush of Morning, O!
Or fling my wing
On the air, and bring
To sleepier birds a warning, O!
That the night's in flight,
And the sun's in sight,
And the dew is the grass adorning, O!
And the green leaves swing

As I sing, sing, sing,
Up by the river,
Down the dell,
To the little wee nest,
Where the big tree fell,
So early in the morning, O!

I flit and twit
In the sun for a bit
When his light so bright is shining, O!
Or sit and fit
My plumes, or knit
Straw plaits for the nest's nice lining, O!
And she with glee
Shows unto me
Underneath her wings reclining, O!
And I sing that Peg
Has an egg, egg, egg,
Up by the oat-field
Round the mill,
Past the meadow,
Down by the hill,
So early in the morning, O!

I stoop and swoop
On the air, or loop
Through the trees, and then go soaring, O!
To group with a troop
On the gusty poop
While the wind behind is roaring, O!
I skim and swim
By a cloud's red rim
And up to the azure flooring, O!
And my wide wings drip
As I slip, slip, slip
Down through the rain-drops,
Back where Peg
Broods in the nest
On the little white egg,
So early in the morning, O!

James Stephens

The Elephant

When people call this beast to mind,
They marvel more and more
At such a little tail behind
So *large* a trunk before.

Hilaire Belloc

321

Lambs at Play

On the grassy banks
Lambkins at their pranks;
Woolly sisters, woolly brothers,
Jumping off their feet
While their woolly mothers
Watch by them and bleat.

Christina Rossetti

Michael Met a Duck

Michael met a white duck
  Walking on the green.
"How are you?" said Michael.
  "How fine the weather's been!
Blue sky and sunshine,
  All thro'out the day;
Not a single raindrop
  Came to spoil our play."

But the sad white duck said,
  "I myself want rain.
I'd like to see the brooklets
  And the streams fill up again.
Now I can't go swimming,
  It really makes me cry
To see the little duckponds
  Look so very dry."

But behold, next morning,
  The clouds are looking black:
Down the rain came pouncing,
  Said the duck, "Quack, quack.
Ponds are full of water,
  Ducks are full of joy."
But someone else is not pleased,
  And that's the little boy.

J. Dupuy

The Duck

If I were in a fairy tale,
  And it were my good luck
To have to wish, I'd choose to be
  A lovely snow-white duck.

When she puts off into the pond
  And leaves me on the brink,
She wags her stumpy tail at me,
  And gives a saucy wink

Which says as plain as words could say,
  I'm safe as safe can be,
Stay there, or you will drown yourself,
  This pond was made for me.

She goes a-sailing to and fro,
  Just like a fishing-boat,
And steers and paddles all herself,
  And never wets her coat.

Then in the water, upside down,
  I've often see her stand,
More neatly than the little boys
  Who do it on the land.

And best of all, her children are
  The ducklings, bright as gold,
Who swim about the pond with her
  And do as they are told.

Edith King

The Brown Frog

To-day as I went out to play
I saw a brown frog in the way,
I know that frogs are smooth and green,
But this was brown—what could it mean?
I asked a lady in the road;
She said it was a spotted toad!

Mary K. Robinson

323

Milk for the Cat

When the tea is brought at five o'clock,
And all the neat curtains are drawn with care,
The little black cat with bright green eyes
Is suddenly purring there.

At first she pretends, having nothing to do,
She has come in merely to blink by the grate;
But, though tea may be late or the milk may be sour,
She is never late.

And presently her agate eyes
Take a soft large milky haze,
And her independent casual glance
Becomes a stiff hard gaze.

Then she stamps her claws or lifts her ears,
Or twists her tail and begins to stir,
Till suddenly all her lithe body becomes
One breathing trembling purr.

The children eat and wriggle and laugh;
The two old ladies stroke their silk:
But the cat is grown small and thin with desire,
Transformed to a creeping lust for milk.

The white saucer like some full moon descends
At last from the clouds of the table above;
She sighs and dreams and thrills and glows,
Transfigured with love.

She nestles over the shining rim,
Buries her chin in the creamy sea;
Her tail hangs loose; each drowsy paw
Is doubled under each bending knee.

A long dim ecstasy holds her life;
Her world is an infinite shapeless white,
Till her tongue has curled the last holy drop,
Then she sinks back into the night.

Draws and dips her body to heap
Her sleepy nerves in the great arm-chair,
Lies defeated and buried deep
Three or four hours unconscious there.

Harold Monro

Prayer for Gentleness to all Creatures

To all the humble beasts there be,
To all the birds on land and sea,
Great Spirit, sweet protection give
That free and happy they may live!

And to our hearts the rapture bring
Of love for every living thing;
Make us all one kin, and bless
Our ways with Christ's own gentleness!

John Galsworthy

The Woodman's Dog

Shaggy, and lean, and shrewd, with pointed ears,
And tail cropp'd short, half lurcher and half cur —
His dog attends him. Close behind his heel
Now creeps he slow; and now, with many a frisk
Wide-scampering, snatches up the drifted snow
With ivory teeth, or ploughs it with his snout;
Then shakes his powder'd coat, and barks for joy.

William Cowper

325

The Mouse

I heard a mouse
Bitterly complaining
In a crack of moonlight
Aslant on the floor.

"Little I ask
And that little is not granted.
There are very few crumbs
In the world any more.

"The bread box is tin
And I cannot get in.

"The jam's in a jar
My teeth cannot mar.

"The cheese sits by itself
On the pantry shelf.

"All night I run
Searching and seeking,
All night I run
About on the floor.

"Moonlight is there
And a bare place for dancing,
But no little feast
Is spread any more."

Elizabeth Coatsworth

The Autumn Robin

Sweet little bird in russet coat,
    The livery of the closing year,
I love thy lonely plaintive note
    And tiny whispering song to hear,
While on the stile or garden seat
    I sit to watch the falling leaves,
The song thy little joys repeat
    My loneliness relieves.

John Clare

326

Browny Bee

Little Mr. Browny Bee,
Gather honey for my tea;
Come into my garden, do,
I've every kind of flower for you.

There's blossom on my tiny tree,
And daisies in the grass you'll see;
There's lavender, and scented stocks,
And rows of frilly hollyhocks

I've marigolds, and pansies too,
And Canterbury-bells of blue;
There's rosemary, and scented thyme,
And foxglove heads you'll love to climb.

I've gilly-flowers, and roses red,
All waiting in my garden bed;
Seek honey where my flowers are
To fill my little honey-jar.

Irene F. Pawsey

At Breakfast

When I sit up to bread and milk
I feel a head as soft as silk
Against my knee. And on my sock
A gentle paw. It is my "Jock,"
The dearest doggie ever seen,
My knowing, faithful Aberdeen.
And then two eyes say, "Little Master,
I think these legs would run much faster
And p'raps would grow a little longer,
And certainly would grow much stronger,
If only they were fed more often."
And then, as if my heart to soften,
He wags his tail. And then he begs
Upon his stumpy, short, hind legs.
Of course I give him some. Who would
Refuse to feed him if they could?
And when he looks up in my face
I feel quite sure he's saying Grace.

I. M. Mills

327

The Caterpillar

Brown and furry
Caterpillar in a hurry,
Take your walk
To the shady leaf, or stalk,
Or what not,
Which may be the chosen spot.
No toad to spy you,
Hovering bird of prey pass by you;
Spin and die,
To live again a butterfly.

Christina Rossetti

The Elephant

Here comes the elephant
Swaying along
With his cargo of children
All singing a song:
To the tinkle of laughter
He goes on his way,
And his cargo of children
Have crowned him with May.
His legs are in leather
And padded his toes;
He can root up an oak
With a whisk of his nose:
With a wave of his trunk
And a turn of his chin
He can pull down a house,
Or pick up a pin.
Beneath his grey forehead
A little eye peers!
Of what is he thinking
Between those wide ears?
Of what does he think?
If he wished to tease,
He could twirl his keeper
Over the trees:

If he were not kind,
He could play cup and ball
With Robert and Helen
And Uncle Paul:
But that grey forehead,
Those crinkled ears,
Have learned to be kind
In a hundred years!
And so with the children
He goes on his way
To the tinkle of laughter
And crowned with the May.

Herbert Asquith

The Field-Mouse

I live among the grasses,
    And watch them growing high,
And as the summer passes
    They seem to touch the sky.

The Spiders are my neighbours,
    Busy people they,
I watch them at their labours,
    Spinning day by day.

The Earwig comes a-calling,
    The Ladybird as well,
And snails go slowly crawling,
    And Slugs, without a shell.

The Bumble, fat and furry,
    A flying visit pays,
And Caterpillars hurry
    Adown the grassy ways.

I am your little brother,
    A Mouse in brown and grey,
So if we meet each other,
    Please let me run away!

Enid Blyton

329

A Friend in the Garden

He is not John, the gardener,
  And yet the whole day long
Employs himself most usefully,
  The flower-beds among.

He is not Tom, the pussy-cat,
  And yet the other day,
With stealthy stride and glistening eye,
  He crept upon his prey.

He is not Dash, the dear old dog,
  And yet, perhaps, if you
Took pains with him and petted him,
  You'd come to love him too.

He's not a Blackbird, though he chirps,
  And though he once was black;
And now he wears a loose grey coat,
  All wrinkled on the back.

He's got a very dirty face,
  And very shining eyes!
He sometimes comes and sits indoors;
  He looks—and p'r'aps is—wise.

But in a sunny flower-bed
  He has his fixed abode;
He eats the things that eat my plants—
  He is a friendly *Toad*.

Juliana Horatia Ewing

Ducks

As I went down the village green,
    Quack-quack! Quack-quack!
Such a sight as never was seen,
    On a fine wet day in the morning.

Three ducks came swimming down the stream,
Quack-quack! Quack-quack!
(I was awake: it was no dream)
On a gay grey day in the morning.

Yet when they saw me standing by,
Quack-quack! Quack-quack!
They stood on their heads with their tails to the sky,
On a mild wild day in the morning.

And when they had done just what I say,
Quack-quack! Quack-quack!
They shook their tails and sailed away,
On a fine wet day in the morning.

Norman Ault

What the Thrush Says

"Come and see! Come and see!"
The thrush pipes out of the hawthorn tree:
And I and Dicky on tiptoe go
To see what treasures he wants to show.
His call is clear as a call can be—
And "Come and see!" he says:
    "Come and see!"

"Come and see! Come and see!"
His house is there in the hawthorn-tree:
The neatest house that ever you saw,
Built all of mosses and twigs and straw:
The folk who built were his wife and he—
And "Come and see!" he says:
    "Come and see!"

"Come and see! Come and see!"
Within this house there are treasures three:
So warm and snug in its curve they lie—
Like three bright bits out of Spring's blue sky.
We would not hurt them, he knows: not we!
So "Come and see!" he says:
    "Come and see!"

Queenie Scott-Hopper

Robin's Song

Robins sang in England,
  Frost or rain or snow,
All the long December days
  Endless years ago.

Robins sang in England
  Before the Legions came,
Before our English fields were tilled
  Or England was a name.

Robins sang in England
  When forests dark and wild
Stretched across from sea to sea
  And Jesus was a child.

Listen! in the frosty dawn
  From his leafless bough
The same brave song he ever sang
  A robin's singing now.

Rodney Bennett

The Owl

When cats run home and light is come,
  And dew is cold upon the ground,
And the far-off stream is dumb,
  And the whirring sail goes round,
  And the whirring sail goes round;
    Alone and warming his five wits,
    The white owl in the belfry sits.

When merry milkmaids click the latch,
  And rarely smells the new-mown hay,
And the cock hath sung beneath the thatch
  Twice or thrice his roundelay,
  Twice or thrice his roundelay;
    Alone and warming his five wits,
    The white owl in the belfry sits.

Lord Tennyson

Mother Duck

Old Mother Duck has hatched a brood
  Of ducklings, small and callow;
Their little wings are short, their down
  Is mottled, grey and yellow.

There is a quiet little stream
  That runs into the moat,
Where tall green sedges spread their leaves,
  And water-lilies float.

Close by the margin of the brook
  The old duck made her nest,
Of straw, and leaves, and withered grass,
  And down from her own breast.

And there she sat for four long weeks,
  In rainy days and fine,
Until the ducklings all came out—
  Four, five, six, seven, eight, nine.

One peeped out from beneath her wing,
  One scrambled on her back;
"That's very rude," said Old Dame Duck,
  "Get off! quack, quack, quack, quack!"

Aunt Effie's Rhymes

The Blackbird

A slender young Blackbird built in a thorn-tree:
A spruce little fellow as ever could be;
His bill was so yellow, his feathers so black,
So long was his tail, and so glossy his back,
That his good little wife, who sat hatching her eggs,
And only just left them to stretch her poor legs,
And pick for a minute the worm she preferred,
Thought there never was seen such a beautiful bird.

D. M. Mulock

333

The Rabbit

Brown bunny sits inside his burrow
    Till everything is still,
Then out he slips along the furrow,
    Or up the grassy hill.

He nibbles all about the bushes
    Or sits to wash his face,
But at a sound he stamps, and rushes
    At a surprising pace.

You see some little streaks and flashes,
    A last sharp twink of white,
As down his hidey-hole he dashes
    And disappears from sight.

Edith King

The Hedgehog

The hedgehog is a little beast
    Who likes a quiet wood,
Where he can feed his family
    On proper hedgehog food.

He has a funny little snout
    That's rather like a pig's,
With which he smells, like us, of course,
    But also runts and digs.

He wears the queerest prickle coat,
    Instead of hair or fur,
And only has to curl himself
    To bristle like a burr.

He does not need to battle with
    Or run away from foes,
His coat does all the work for him,
    It pricks them on the nose.

Edith King

The Birds

Do you ask what the birds say?
   The sparrow, the dove,
The linnet, and thrush say:
   I love and I love.

In the Winter they're silent,
   The wind is so strong;
What it says I don't know,
   But it sings a loud song.

But green leaves and blossoms,
   And sunny, warm weather,
And singing and loving,
   All come back together.

Then the lark is so brimful
   Of gladness and love,
The green fields below him,
   The blue sky above,

That he sings and he sings,
   And for ever sings he:
I love my love,
   And my love loves me.

S. T. Coleridge

If I were a Pig

If I were a pig and lived under a thatch
With nothing to do but gobble and scratch,
How nice it would be to look out now and then
And see the great winds blowing over the fen.

For pigs, though so greedy and ugly, are wise,
And see quite a lot with their funny slit-eyes—
Little soft breezes that shimmer and shine,
And winds like green oceans, all misty and fine.

Elizabeth Fleming

335

The Bird Bath

There is a bird bath on our grass,
I wait to watch it as I pass,
And see the little sparrow things
Stand on the edge with flapping wings.
They give each eye a merry wink
And stoop to take a little drink,
And then, before I'm fairly gone,
They bath with all their clothing on!

Florence Hoatson

Skippets, the Bad One

High upon the hillside where the shadows play
 Lives gentle Mrs. Rabbit with her family of three,
And Spillikins and Spottikins, it's only right to say,
 Are the dearest little rabbits you can ever hope to see.

But Skippets is the bad one,
 The mad one,
 The saucy one,
Skippets is the lazy one who won't wash his face.
 Skippets is the naughty one,
 The haughty one,
 The pushing one,
Skippets is the forward one who doesn't know his place.

Spillikins and Spottikins will never stay out late,
 And wander in the gloomy woods as many rabbits do.
Why, even in the summer-time, they're always in by eight—
 In case they catch a cold, you see, by sitting in the dew.

But Skippets is the frisky one,
 The risky one,
 The roving one,
Skippets is the wilful one whose ways are hard to trace.
 Skippets is the careless one,
 The won't-come-home-at-bedtime one—
Skippets is the wicked one who's always in disgrace!

Christine E. Bradley

336

Birds' Nests

"Caw," said the rook,
"My nest is here. Look!
At the top of a tree
Is the best place for me."

"Coo," called the dove
From her nest above;
"In the fork of a beech
I am quite out of reach."

"Hark!" carolled a lark,
"I sing until dark,
My nest on the ground
Is not easily found."

"Hush!" sang a thrush,
"In this holly bush
I am safe from all harm
With my blue eggs so warm."

But Robin Redbreast
From her mossy nest
Said never a word,
What a wise little bird!

Millicent Seager

The Song of the Bird

"The rivers rush into the sea,
  By castle and town they go;
The winds behind them merrily
  Their noisy trumpets blow.

"The clouds are passing far and high,
  We little birds in them play;
And everything that can sing and fly
  Goes with us, and far away."

H. W. Longfellow

337

The Robin

Some folk like the Chaffinch,
    Others fancy Tits,
But I prefer the Robin
    That near my window sits.

The Tits they love bright colours;
    Their coats are yellow-green.
That they fancy fine, gay clothing
    Is plainly to be seen.

The Robin dresses simply—
    A brown cap on his head,
Brown coat with soft grey breeches,
    And waistcoat orange-red.

He comes into my kitchen;
    Some crumbs to him I give;
And he shall have my friendship
    As long as he shall live.

O. M. Bent

One Blackbird

The stars must make an awful noise
    In whirling round the sky;
Yet somehow I can't even hear
    Their loudest song or sigh.

So it is wonderful to think
    One blackbird can outsing
The voice of all the swarming stars
    On any day in spring.

Harold Monro

The Crow

Old Crow, upon the tall tree-top
I see you sitting at your ease,
You hang upon the highest bough
And balance in the breeze.

How many miles you've been to-day
Upon your wing so strong and black,
And steered across the dark grey sky
Without a guide or track;

Above the city wrapped in smoke,
Green fields and rivers flowing clear;
Now tell me, as you passed them o'er,
What did you see and hear?

The old crow shakes his sooty wing
And answers hoarsely, "Caw, caw, caw,"
And that is all the crow can tell
Of what he heard and saw.

Mrs. Alexander

To a Cricket

Voice of summer, keen and shrill,
Chirping round the winter fire,
Of thy song I never tire,
Weary others as they will,
For thy song with summer's filled—
Filled with sunshine, filled with June;
Firelight echo of that noon
Heard in fields when all is still
In the golden light of May,
Bringing scents of new-mown hay,
Bees, and birds, and flowers away,
Prithee, haunt my fireside still,
Voice of summer, keen and shrill.

William Cox Bennett

Grasshopper Green

Grasshopper Green is a comical chap;
    He lives on the best of fare.
Bright little trousers, jacket and cap,
    These are his summer wear.
Out in the meadow he loves to go,
    Playing away in the sun;
It's hopperty, skipperty, high and low—
    Summer's the time for fun.

Grasshopper Green has a quaint little house;
    It's under the hedgerow gay.
Grandmother Spider, as still as a mouse,
    Watches him over the way.
Gladly he's calling the children, I know,
    Out in the beautiful sun;
It's hopperty, skipperty, high and low—
    Summer's the time for fun.

"Four-Paws"

Four-Paws, the kitten from the farm,
    Is come to live with Betsy Jane,
Leaving the stack-yard for the warm
    Flower-compassed cottage in the lane,
To wash his idle face and play
Among chintz cushions all the day.

Under the shadow of her hair
    He lies, who loves him, nor desists
To praise his whiskers and compare
    The tabby bracelets on his wrists—
Omelet at lunch, and milk at tea
Suits Betsy Jane, and so fares he.

Happy beneath her golden hand
    He purrs contentedly, nor hears
His Mother mourning through the land
    The old grey cat with tattered ears
And humble tail and heavy paw
Who brought him up among the straw.

Never by day she ventures nigh,
    But when the dusk grows dim and deep,
And moths flit out of the strange sky
    And Betsy has been long asleep—
Out of the dark she comes and brings
Her dark maternal offerings;

Some field-mouse or throstle caught
    Near netted fruit or in the corn,
Or rat, for this her darling sought
    In the old barn where he was born;
And all lest on his dainty bed
Four-Paws were faint or underfed.

Only between the midnight hours,
    Under the window-panes she walks,
Shrewdly among the scented flowers
    Nor snaps the soft nasturtium stalks,
Uttering still her plaintive cries,
And Four-Paws, from the house, replies,

Leaps from his cushion to the floor,
    Down the brick passage scantly lit,
Waits wailing at the outer door
    Till one arise and open it—
Then, from the swinging lantern's light
Runs to his Mother in the night.

                                    H. Parry Eden

The Wasp

When the ripe pears droop heavily,
The yellow wasp hums loud and long
His hot and drowsy autumn song.
A yellow flame he seems to be,
When darting suddenly from high
He lights where fallen peaches lie.

Yellow and black—this tiny thing's
A tiger-soul on elfin wings.

                                    William Sharp

A Green Cornfield

The earth was green, the sky was blue:
I saw and heard one sunny morn
A skylark hang between the two,
   A singing speck above the corn;

A stage below, in gay accord,
   White butterflies danced on the wing,
And still the singing skylark soared,
   And silent sank and soared to sing.

The cornfield stretched a tender green
   To right and left beside my walks;
I knew he had a nest unseen
   Somewhere among the million stalks.

And as I paused to hear his song
   While swift the sunny moments slid,
Perhaps his mate sat listening long,
   And listened longer than I did.

Christina Rossetti

Bunny Rabbit

Bunny creeps out and caresses his nose,
Combs out his ears with his fluttering toes,
   Blinks at the sun
   And commences to run
   With a skip and a hop
   And a flippety-flop,
Nibbling the clover wherever he goes;
But only when he is quite easy in mind
Does he button his little white tail down behind.

Bunny stops dead and stiffens each hair,
And his eyelids freeze in a terrified stare,
   And he pricks up his ears,
   For the sound that he hears
   Is a low muffled beat
   And a drumming of feet
And an ominous rub-a-dub-dubbing—but where?
He's off like the wind! He's off like the wind!
And his little white tail is unbuttoned behind.

Old Shellover

"Come!" said Old Shellover.
"What?" says Creep.
"The horny old Gardener's fast asleep;
    The fat cock Thrush
    To his nest has gone,
    And the dew shines bright
    In the rising Moon;
Old Sallie Worm from her hole doth peep;
"Come!" says old Shellover.
"Ay!" said Creep.

Walter de la Mare

The Kitten at Play

See the kitten on the wall,
Sporting with the leaves that fall,
Withered leaves, one, two and three,
Falling from the elder-tree;
Through the calm and frosty air
Of the morning bright and fair.

See the kitten, how she starts,
Crouches, stretches, paws and darts;
With a tiger-leap half way
Now she meets her coming prey.
Lets it go as fast as then
Has it in her power again.

Now she works with three and four,
Like an Indian conjurer;
Quick as he in feats of art,
Gracefully she plays her part;
Yet were gazing thousands there,
What would little Tabby care?

William Wordsworth

The City Mouse and the Garden Mouse

The city mouse lives in a house;
　The garden mouse lives in a bower,
He's friendly with the frogs and toads,
　And sees the pretty plants in flower.

The city mouse eats bread and cheese;
　The garden mouse eats what he can;
We will not grudge him seeds and stocks,
　Poor little timid furry man.

Christina Rossetti

Nicholas Nye

Thistle and darnel and dock grew there,
　And a bush, in the corner, of may,
On the orchard wall I used to sprawl
　In the blazing heat of the day;
Half asleep and half awake,
　While the birds went twittering by,
And nobody there my lone to share
　But Nicholas Nye.

Nicholas Nye was lean and grey,
　Lame of a leg and old,
More than a score of donkey's years
　He had seen since he was foaled;
He munched the thistles, purple and spiked,
　Would sometimes stoop and sigh,
And turn to his head, as if he said,
　"Poor Nicholas Nye!"

Alone with his shadow he'd drowse in the meadow,
　Lazily swinging his tail,
At break of day he used to bray—
　Not much too hearty and hale;
But a wonderful gumption was under his skin,
　And a clean calm light in his eye,
And once in a while, he'd smile—
　Would Nicholas Nye.

Seem to be smiling at me, he would,
　From his bush, in the corner, of may—
Bony and ownerless, widowed and worn,
　Knobble-kneed, lonely and grey;
And over the grass would seem to pass
　'Neath the deep dark blue of the sky,
Something much better than words between me
　And Nicholas Nye.

But dusk would come in the apple boughs,
　The green of the glow-worm shine,
The birds in nest would crouch to rest,
　And home I'd trudge to mine;
And there, in the moonlight, dark with dew,
　Asking not wherefore nor why,
Would brood like a ghost, and still as a post,
　Old Nicholas Nye.

W. de la Mare

Grey Brother

The grey goat grazed on the hill,
　The grey hare grazed by his side,
And never a word they said
　From morning till eventide,
And never a word they said,
　Though each understood the other,
For the wind that played on the hill
　Whispered, "My dear grey brother."

The grey goat went home at dusk,
　Down to the cottage door,
The grey hare scuttled away
　To his burrow across the moor.
And never a word they said,
　Though each understood the other,
For the wind that slept on the hill
　Murmured, "Good night, grey brother."

U. M. Montgomery

Birds' Nests

The skylark's nest among the grass
   And waving corn is found;
The robin's on a shady bank,
   With oak leaves strewn around.

The wren builds in an ivied thorn,
   Or old and ruined wall;
The mossy nest, so covered in,
   You scarce can see at all.

The martins build their nests of clay,
   In rows beneath the eaves;
While silvery lichens, moss and hair,
   The chaffinch interweaves.

The cuckoo makes no nest at all,
   But through the wood she strays
Until she finds one snug and warm,
   And there her egg she lays.

The sparrow has a nest of hay,
   With feathers warmly lined;
The ring-dove's careless nest of sticks
   On lofty trees we find.

Rooks build together in a wood,
   And often disagree;
The owl will build inside a barn
   Or in a hollow tree.

The blackbird's nest of grass and mud
   In brush and bank is found;
The lapwing's darkly spotted eggs
   Are laid upon the ground.

The magpie's nest is girt with thorns
   In leafless trees or hedge;
The wild duck and the water-hen
   Build by the water's edge.

Birds build their nests from year to year,
   According to their kind,
Some very neat and beautiful,
   Some easily designed.

The habits of each little bird,
   And all its patient skill,
Are surely taught by God Himself
And ordered by His will.

The Pig's Tail

A furry coat has the bear to wear,
   The tortoise a coat of mail,
The yak has more than his share of hair,
   But—the pig has the curly tail.

The elephant's tusks are sold for gold,
   The slug leaves a silver trail,
The parrot is never too old to scold,
   But—the pig has the curly tail.

The lion can either roar or snore,
   The cow gives milk in a pail,
The dog can guard a door, and more,
   But—the pig has the curly tail.

The monkey makes you smile a while,
   The tiger makes you quail,
The fox has many a wile of guile,
   But—the pig has the curly tail.

For the rest of the beasts that prey or play,
   From tiny mouse to the whale,
There's much that I could say to-day,
   But—the pig has the curly tail.

Norman Ault

Secret Places

Nests well hidden,
   Secret treasure—
Bird's black eyes are
   Bright with pleasure.

Woods have many
   Secret spaces;
Violet-scented,
   Silent places.

Buds are cradles;
   Leaves and flowers
Wake when called
   By sun and showers.

Bees know where
   The blossoms keep
Their sweetest secrets
   Hidden deep.

After flying,
   After roaming,
Swallows know
   The way back—homing!

Irene Thompson

The Blackbird

In the far corner,
close by the swings,
every morning
a blackbird sings.

His bill's so yellow,
his coat's so black,
that he makes a fellow
whistle back.

Ann, my daughter,
thinks that he
sings for us two
especially.

Humbert Wolfe

Hark! Hark! The Lark

Hark! hark! the lark at heaven's gate sings,
    And Phoebus 'gins arise,
His steeds to water at those springs
    On chalic'd flowers that lies;
And winking Mary-buds begin
    To ope their golden eyes:
With everything that pretty bin,
    My lady sweet, arise!

Shakespeare

Vespers

O Blackbird, what a boy you are!
How do you go it!
Blowing your bugle to that one sweet star—
How do you blow it!
And does she hear you, blackbird boy, so far?
Or is it wasted breath?
"Good Lord. She is so bright
To-night!"
The Blackbird saith.

T. E. Brown

The Bells of Heaven

'Twould ring the bells of Heaven
    The wildest peal for years,
If Parson lost his senses
    And people came to theirs,
And he and they together
    Knelt down with angry prayers
For tamed and shabby tigers,
    And dancing dogs and bears,
And wretched, blind pit-ponies,
    And little hunted hares.

Ralph Hodgson

The Silent Snake

The birds go fluttering in the air,
   The rabbits run and skip,
Brown squirrels race along the bough,
   The May-flies rise and dip;
But, whilst these creatures play and leap,
The silent snake goes creepy-creep!

The birdies sing and whistle loud,
   The busy insects hum,
The squirrels chat, the frogs say "croak!"
   But the snake is always dumb.
With not a sound through grasses deep
The silent snake goes creepy-creep!

The Snail

To grass, or leaf, or fruit, or wall,
The Snail sticks close, nor fears to fall,
As if he grew there, house and all
           Together.

Within that house secure he hides,
When danger imminent betides
Of storms, or other harm besides,
           Of weather.

Give but his horns the slightest touch,
His self-collecting power is such,
He shrinks into his house with much
           Displeasure.

Where'er he dwells, he dwells alone,
Except himself has chattels none,
Well satisfied to be his own
           Whole treasure.

Thus hermit-like, his life he leads,
Nor partner of his Banquet needs,
And if he meets one, only feeds
        The faster.

Who seeks him must be worse than blind
(He and his house are so combined)
If, finding it, he fails to find
        Its master.

William Cowper

My Dog, Spot

I have a white dog
   Whose name is Spot,
And he's sometimes white
   And he's sometimes not.
But whether he's white
   Or whether he's not,
There's a patch on his ear
   That makes him Spot.

He has a tongue
   That is long and pink,
And he lolls it out
   When he wants to think,
He seems to think most
   When the weather is hot.
He's a wise sort of dog,
   Is my dog, Spot.

He likes a bone
   And he likes a ball,
But he doesn't care
   For a cat at all.
He waggles his tail
   And he knows what's what,
So I'm glad that he's my dog,
   My dog, Spot.

Rodney Bennett

The Secret

Jenny Wren's got a house
　　Very cosy and round,
In a nook of green boughs
　　Not too far from the ground.
And she sits very still
　　In case people should know
Of the little warm eggs
　　She is hiding, below.

Jenny Wren's little nest
　　Has a secret to-day;
It's one that I guessed
　　When I passed by that way.
For small Jenny Wren
　　Was so busy about
I knew in a moment
　　Her eggs had hatched out!

Elizabeth Fleming

The Greedy Little Pig

A little pig lived in a sty,
　　He fed on meals three times a day,
He drank sweet milk from a shining trough
　　And slept at night on a bed of hay.

This little pig once left his sty
　　And roam'd three fields or more away,
He found the slope where the oak trees grew
　　And where the plump brown acorns lay.
　　And he ate, and he ate,
　　　　As little pigs do;
　　He ate and he ate,
　　　　The whole day through.
Then he came back home to his bed of hay,
Grunt-grunt-grunting all the way.

Irene F. Pawsey

352

Sheep and Lambs

All in the April evening,
 April airs were abroad;
The sheep with their little lambs
 Pass'd me by on the road.

The sheep with their little lambs
 Pass'd me by on the road;
All in the April evening
 I thought on the Lamb of God.

Up in the blue, blue mountains
 Dewy pastures are sweet:
Rest for the little bodies,
 Rest for the little feet.

All in the April evening,
 April airs were abroad;
I saw the sheep with their lambs,
 And thought on the Lamb of God.

Katharine Tynan

Mr Squirrel

I saw a brown squirrel to-day in the wood,
He ran here and there just as fast as he could;
I think he was looking for nuts for his store,
He'd found quite a lot, but he still wanted more.

He can't find much food once the winter is here,
He hides all his nuts in a hole somewhere near,
Then settles himself for a long winter sleep,
Coming out now and then for a nut and a peep.

His long bushy tail keeps him cosy and warm,
His nest's far away from the wind and the storm.
But when Springtime comes back, I think that, maybe,
He'll be waiting again in the woodland for me.

V. M. Julian

353

The Snare

I hear a sudden cry of pain!
   There is a rabbit in a snare;
Now I hear the cry again,
   But I cannot tell from where.

But I cannot tell from where
   He is calling out for aid;
Crying on the frightened air,
   Making everything afraid.

Making everything afraid,
   Wrinkling up his little face,
As he cries again for aid;
   And I cannot find the place!

And I cannot find the place
   Where his paw is in the snare;
Little one! Oh, little one!
   I am searching everywhere.

James Stephens

Whale

Wouldn't you like to be a whale
And sail serenely by—
An eighty-foot whale from the tip of your tail
And a tiny, briny eye?
Wouldn't you like to wallow
Where nobody says "Come out!"?
Wouldn't you *love* to swallow
And blow all the brine about?
Wouldn't you like to be always clean
But never to have to wash, I mean,
And wouldn't you love to spout—
   O yes, just think—
A feather of spray as you sail away,
And rise and sink and rise and sink,
And blow all the brine about?

Geoffrey Dearmer

354

The Old Brown Horse

The old brown horse looks over the fence
   In a weary sort of way;
He seems to be saying to all who pass:
   "Well, folks, I've had my day—
I'm simply watching the world go by,
   And nobody seems to mind,
As they're dashing past in their motor-cars,
   A horse who is lame and half-blind."

The old brown horse has a shaggy coat,
   But once he was young and trim,
And he used to trot through the woods and lanes
   With the man who was fond of him.
But his master rides in a motor-car,
   And it makes him feel quite sad
When he thinks of the days that used to be,
   And of all the times they had.

Sometimes a friendly soul will stop
   Near the fence, where the tired old head
Rests wearily on the topmost bar,
   And a friendly word is said.
Then the old brown horse gives a little sigh
   As he feels the kindly touch
Of a hand on his mane or his shaggy coat,
   And he doesn't mind so much.

So if you pass by the field one day,
   Just stop for a word or two
With the old brown horse who was once as young
   And as full of life as you.
He'll love the touch of your soft young hand,
   And I know he'll seem to say—
"Oh, thank you, friend, for the kindly thought
   For a horse who has had his day."

W. F. Holmes

Just Jumbo

A big grey elephant
        Lives in the Zoo,
And what does that big
        Grey elephant do?

He spends all day long
        Going back and fore,
Carrying children
        By the score.

Little Richard
        And Robin and Claude,
Angela Jane
        And her sister Maude.

Big grey elephant—
        He never tires,
In the hottest sunshine
        He never perspires.

Patient and quiet
        He walks to-day
And waves his trunk
        With a gentle sway.

Eileen Mathias

From Ducks

Yes, ducks are valiant things
On nests of twigs and straws,
And ducks are soothy things
And lovely on the lake
When that the sunlight draws
Thereon their pictures dim
In colours cool.
And when beneath the pool
They dabble, and when they swim
And make their rippling rings,
O ducks are beautiful things!

But ducks are comical things—
As comical as you.
Quack!
They waddle round, they do.
They eat all sorts of things,
And then they quack.
By barn and stable and stack
They wander at their will,
But if you go too near
They look at you through black
Small topaz-glinted eyes
And wish you ill.
Triangular and clear
They leave their curious track
In mud at the water's edge,
And there amid the sedge
And slime they gobble and peer
Saying "Quack! quack!"

F. W. Harvey

The Girl and her Fawn

With sweetest milk and sugar first
I it at my own fingers nursed;
And as it grew, so every day
It wax'd more white and sweet than they—
It had so sweet a breath! and oft
I blush'd to see its foot more soft
And white—shall I say?—than my hand,
Nay, any lady's of the land!

It is a wondrous thing how fleet
'Twas on those little silver feet:
With what a pretty skipping grace
It oft would challenge me the race:—
And when't had left me far away
'Twould stay, and run again, and stay:
For it was nimbler much than hinds,
And trod as if on the four winds.

A. Marvell
357

The Thrush's Nest

Within a thick and spreading hawthorn bush
    That overhung a molehill large and round,
I heard from morn to morn a merry thrush
    Sing hymns to sunrise, and I drank the sound
With joy; and often, an intruding guest,
    I watched her secret toil from day to day.
How true she warped the moss, to form a nest,
    And modelled it within with wood and clay;
And by and by, like heath bells gilt with dew,
    There lay her shining eggs, as bright as flowers,
Ink-spotted over shells of greeny blue;
    And there I witnessed in the sunny hours
A brood of Nature's minstrels chirp and fly,
Glad as the sunshine and the laughing sky.

John Clare

The Cow and the Ass

Beside a green meadow a stream used to flow,
So clear, you might see the white pebbles below;
To this cooling brook, the warm cattle would stray,
To stand in the shade on a hot summer's day.

A cow quite oppressed by the heat of the sun,
Came here to refresh as she often had done;
And, standing quite still, stooping over the stream
Was musing, perhaps—or perhaps she might dream.

But soon a brown ass of respectable look
Came trotting up also to taste of the brook,
And to nibble a few of the daisies and grass.
"How d'ye do?" said the cow. "How d'ye do?" said the
    ass.

"Take a seat!" said the cow, gently waving her hand.
"By no means, dear madam," said he, "while you stand!"
Then, stooping to drink, with a very low bow,
"Ma'am, your health!" said the ass.
"Thank you, sir," said the cow.

Ann and Jane Taylor

Hiawatha's Childhood

At the door on summer evenings
Sat the little Hiawatha;
Heard the whispering of the pine-trees,
Heard the lapping of the water,
Sounds of music, words of wonder;
"Minne-wawa!" said the pine-trees,
"Mudway-aushka!" said the water.
Saw the fire-fly, Wah-wah-taysee,
Flitting through the dusk of evening,
With the twinkle of its candle
Lighting up the brakes and bushes,
And he sang the song of children,
Sang the song Nokomis taught him:
"Wah-wah-taysee, little firefly,
Little, flitting, white-fire insect,
Little, dancing, white-fire creature,
Light me with your little candle,
Ere upon my bed I lay me,
Ere in sleep I close my eyelids!"

Henry Wadsworth Longfellow

Hiawatha's Brothers

Then the little Hiawatha
Learned of every bird its language,
Learned their names and all their secrets,
How they built their nest in summer,
Where they hid themselves in winter,
Talked with them whene'er he met them,
Called them "Hiawatha's chickens."
Of all beasts he learned the language,
Learned their names and all their secrets,
How the beavers built their lodges,
Where the squirrels hid their acorns,
How the reindeer ran so swiftly,
Why the rabbit was so timid,
Talked with them whene'er he met them,
Called them "Hiawatha's brothers."

Henry Wadsworth Longfellow

359

Pensioners

My pensioners who daily
　　Come here to beg their fare,
For all their need dress gaily,
　　And have a jaunty air.
With "Tira-lira-lira—
　　Now of your charity,
Pray help the little brethern
　　Of noble poverty."

One shines in glossy sable,
　　One wears a russet coat,
And one who seeks a table
　　Has red about his throat.
With "Tira-lira-lira"—
　　Gay waistcoat, speckled vest,
Black cap and fine blue bonnet,
　　They come so bravely dressed.

To all I gladly scatter
　　In this their time of need,
Heap bread upon their platter
　　And ask not for my meed,
But in their jocund spring-time
　　Their songs give back to me
A thousandfold, my brethern,
　　Of noble poverty.

W. M. Letts

The Hedgehog and His Coat

The owls have feathers lined with down
　　To keep them nice and warm;
The rats have top-coats soft and brown
　　To wrap in from the storm;
And nearly every bird and beast
　　Has cosy suits to wear,
But Mr Hedgehog has the least
　　Of any for his share.

His back is stuck with prickly pins
  That breezes whistle through,
And when the winter-time begins
  The only thing to do
Is just to find a leafy spot,
  And curl up from the rain,
Until the Spring comes, bright and hot,
  To waken him again.

The owls and rats and all their folk
  Are soft and smooth to touch,
But hedgehogs are not nice to stroke,
  Their prickles hurt so much.
So, though it looks a little queer,
  His coat is best of all;
For nobody could interfere
  With such a bristly ball!

Elizabeth Fleming

The Lamb

      Little lamb, who made thee?
      Dost thou know who made thee,
    Gave thee life, and bade thee feed
    By the stream and o'er the mead.
    Gave thee clothing of delight,
    Softest clothing, woolly, bright;
    Gave thee such a tender voice,
    Making all the vales rejoice?
      Little lamb, who made thee?
      Dost thou know who made thee?

      Little lamb, I'll tell thee;
      Little lamb, I'll tell thee:
    He is called by thy name,
    For He calls Himself a Lamb;
    He is meek, and He is mild,
    He became a little child.
    I a child, and thou a lamb,
    We are called by His name.
      Little lamb, God bless thee!
      Little lamb, God bless thee!

William Blake

The Tyger

Tyger! Tyger! burning bright
In the forests of the night,
What immortal hand or eye
Could frame thy fearful symmetry?

In what distant deeps or skies
Burnt the fire of thine eyes?
On what wings dare he aspire?
What the hand dare seize the fire?

And what shoulder, and what art,
Could twist the sinews of thy heart?
And when thy heart began to beat,
What dread hand? and what dread feet?

What the hammer? what the chain?
In what furnace was thy brain?
What the anvil? what dread grasp
Dare its deadly terrors clasp?

When the stars threw down their spears,
And watered Heaven with their tears,
Did he smile his work to see?
Did He who made the Lamb make thee?

Tyger! Tyger! burning bright
In the forests of the night,
What immortal hand or eye,
Dare frame thy fearful symmetry?

William Blake

Fan, the Filly

Bumpety, bumpety, bump.
The horses run down the green hill.
There's Fan the wild filly again at her tricks!
She rears at the fence and she knocks down the sticks
To get at the hay at the base of the ricks.
Bumpety, bumpety, bump.

Bumpety, bumpety, bump.
The horses run down the green hill.
They're all of them wanting a share of the hay,
The Roan and the Dapple, the Black and the Bay;
They follow the filly and gallop away.
Bumpety, bumpety, bump.

Bumpety, bumpety, bump.
The horses run up the green hill.
For old Farmer Brown has come out with his man
To halter the mischievous filly called Fan,
And sell her for gold at the Fair if he can.
Bumpety, bumpety, bump.

Bumpety, bumpety, bump.
The horses run up the green hill.
But where there were five there are now only four,
For Fan the wild filly will gallop no more;
She stands in the shafts at a gentleman's door.
Bumpety, bumpety, bump.

Wilfred Thorley

The Badgers

Brocks snuffle from their holt within
A writhen root of black thorn old,
And moonlight streaks the gashes bold
Of lemon fur from ear to chin.
They stretch and snort and snuff the air,
Then sit, to plan the night's affair.

The neighbours, fox and owl, they heed
And many whispering scents and sounds
Familiar on their secret rounds,
Then silently make sudden speed,
Paddling away in single file
Adown the eagle fern's dim aisle.

Eden Philpotts

The Nightingale

The speckled bird sings in the tree
　　When all the stars are silver-pale.
Come, children, walk the night with me,
　　And we shall hear the nightingale.

The nightingale is a shy bird,
　　He flits before you through the night.
And now the sleepy vale is stirred
　　Through all its green and gold and white.

The moon leans from her place to hear,
　　The stars shed golden star-dust down,
For now comes in the sweet o' the year,
　　The country's gotten the greenest gown.

The blackbird turns upon his bed,
　　The thrush has oped a sleeping eye,
Quiet each downy sleepy-head;
　　But who goes singing up the sky?

It is, it is the nightingale,
　　In the tall tree upon the hill.
To moonlight and the dewy vale
　　The nightingale will sing his fill.

He's but a homely, speckled bird,
　　But he has gotten a golden flute,
And when his wondrous song is heard,
　　Blackbird and thrush and lark are mute.

Troop, children dear, out to the night,
　　Clad in the moonlight silver-pale,
And in the world of green and white
　　'Tis you shall hear the nightingale.

Katharine Tynan

The Squirrel

The pretty red Squirrel lives up in a tree,
A little blithe creature as ever can be;
He dwells in the boughs where the stock-dove broods,
Far in the shades of the green summer woods,
His food is the young juicy cones of the pine,
And the milky beech-nut is his bread and his wine.
In the joy of his nature he frisks with a bound
To the topmost twigs, and then down to the ground,
Then up again like a wingèd thing,
And from tree to tree with a vaulting spring;
Then he sits up aloft, and looks waggish and queer,
As if he would say, "Ay, follow me here!"
And then he grows pettish, and stamps his foot;
And then independently cracks his nut!
And thus he lives the long summer through,
Without a care or a thought of sorrow,
But, small as he is, he knows he may want
In the bleak winter weather, when food is scant:
So he finds a hole in an old tree's core,
And there makes his nest and lays up his store;
Then when cold winter comes and the trees are bare,
When the white snow is falling and keen is the air,
He heeds it not, as he sits by himself
In his warm little nest, with his nuts on his shelf.
O wise little squirrel! no wonder that he,
In the green summer woods, is as blithe as can be!

Mary Howitt

Valentine's Day

Oh! I wish I were a tiny brown bird from out the south,
    Settled among the alder holts, and twittering by the stream;
I would put my tiny tail down, and put up my tiny mouth,
    And sing my tiny life away in one melodious dream.

I would sing about the blossoms, and the sunshine and the sky
    And the tiny wife I mean to have in such a cosy nest;
And if someone came and shot me dead, why then I could but die,
    With my tiny life and tiny song just ended at their best.

Charles Kingsley

The Sea-Gull

Oh, the white Sea-gull, the wild Sea-gull,
  A joyful bird is he,
As he lies like a cradled thing at rest
  In the arms of a sunny sea!
The little waves rock to and fro,
  And the white Gull lies asleep,
As the fisher's bark, with breeze and tide,
  Goes merrily over the deep.
The ship, with her fair sails set, goes by,
  And her people stand to note
How the Sea-gull sits on the rocking waves,
  As if in an anchored boat.

The sea is fresh, the sea is fair,
  And the sky calm overhead,
And the Sea-gull lies on the deep, deep sea,
  Like a king in his royal bed!
Oh, the white Sea-gull, the bold Sea-gull,
  A joyful bird is he,
Throned like a king, in calm repose
  On the breast of the heaving sea!

The waves leap up, the wild wind blows,
  And the Gulls together crowd,
And wheel about, and madly scream
  To the deep sea roaring loud.
And let the sea roar ever so loud,
  And the wind pipe ever so high,
With a wilder joy the bold Sea-gull
  Sends forth a wilder cry.

For the Sea-gull, he is a daring bird,
  And he loves with the storm to sail;
To ride in the strength of the billowy sea,
  And to breast the driving gale!
The little boat, she is tossed about,
  Like a sea-weed, to and fro;
The tall ship reels like a drunken man,
  As the gusty tempests blow.

But the Sea-gull laughs at the fear of man,
    And sails in a wild delight
On the torn-up breast of the night-black sea,
    Like a foam cloud, calm and white.
The waves may rage and the winds may roar,
    But he fears not wreck nor need;
For he rides the sea, in its stormy strength,
    As a strong man rides his steed.

Oh, the white Sea-gull, the bold Sea-gull!
    He makes on the shore his nest,
And he tries what the inland fields may be;
    But he loveth the sea the best!
And away from land a thousand leagues,
    He goes 'mid surging foam;
What matter to him is land or shore,
    For the sea is his truest home!

Mary Howitt

Kindness to Animals

Little children, never give
Pain to things that feel and live:
Let the gentle robin come
For the crumbs you save at home,
As his meat you throw along
He'll repay you with a song;
Never hurt the timid hare
Peeping from her green grass lair,
Let her come and sport and play
On the lawn at close of day;
The little lark goes soaring high
To the bright windows of the sky,
Singing as if 'twere always spring,
And fluttering on an untired wing,—
Oh! let him sing his happy song,
Nor do these gentle creatures wrong.

367

The Plaint of the Camel

Canary-birds feed on sugar and seed,
    Parrots have crackers to crunch;
And as for the poodles, they tell me the noodles
    Have chicken and cream for their lunch.
But there's never a question
About MY digestion,
    ANYTHING does for me.

Cats, you're aware, can repose in a chair,
    Chickens can roost upon rails;
Puppies are able to sleep in a stable,
    And oysters can slumber in pails.
But no one supposes
A poor Camel dozes.
    ANY PLACE does for me.

Lambs are enclosed where it's never exposed,
    Coops are constructed for hens;
Kittens are treated to houses well heated,
    And pigs are protected by pens.
But a Camel comes handy
Wherever it's sandy,
    ANYWHERE does for me.

People would laugh if you rode a giraffe,
    Or mounted the back of an ox;
It's nobody's habit to ride on a rabbit,
    Or try to bestraddle a fox.
But as for a Camel, he's
Ridden by families—
    ANY LOAD does for me.

A snake is as round as a hole in the ground;
    Weasels are wavy and sleek;
And no alligator could ever be straighter
    Than lizards that live in a creek.
But a camel's all lumpy,
And bumpy, and humpy,
    ANY SHAPE does for me.

Charles Edward Carryl

The Elephant

The Elephant is like a wall,
He is broad and very tall.
Upon his back we have a ride,
And swing and sway from side to side.

E. J. Falconer

The Bird at Dawn

What I saw was just one eye
In the dawn as I was going:
A bird can carry all the sky
In that little button glowing.

Never in my life I went
So deep into a firmament.

He was standing on a tree,
All in blossom overflowing;
And purposely looked hard at me,
At first, as if to question merrily:
"Where are you going?"
But next some far more serious thing to say:
I could not answer, could not look away.

Oh, that hard, round, and so distracting eye:
Little mirror of all sky!—
And then the after-song another tree
Held, and sent radiating back on me.

If no man had invented human word,
And a bird-song had been
The only way to utter what we mean,
What would we men have heard,
What understood, what seen,
Between the trills and pauses, in between
The singing and the silence of a bird?

Harold Monro

369

Familiar Friends

The horses, the pigs,
And the chickens,
The turkeys, the ducks,
And the sheep!
I can see all my friends
From my window
As soon as I waken
From sleep.

The cat on the fence
Is out walking.
The geese have gone down
For a swim.
The pony comes trotting
Right up to the gate;
He knows I have candy
For him.

The cows in the pasture
Are switching
Their long tails
To keep off the flies.
And old mother dog
Has come out in the yard
With five pups, to give me
A surprise.

James S. Tippett

To the Cuckoo

O blithe new-comer, I have heard,
I hear thee, and rejoice:
O Cuckoo! shall I call thee bird
Or but a wandering voice?

While I am lying on the grass,
The two-fold shout I hear;
From hill to hill it seems to pass,
At once far off and near.

Though babbling only to the vale
   Of sunshine and of flowers,
Thou bringest unto me a tale
   Of visionary hours.

Thrice, welcome, darling of the Spring!
   Even yet thou art to me
No bird, but an invisible thing,
   A voice, a mystery.

W. Wordsworth

The Sheep

Lazy sheep, pray tell me why
In the grassy fields you lie,
Eating grass and daisies white,
From the morning till the night?
Everything can something do,
But what kind of use are you?

Nay, my little master, nay,
Do not serve me so, I pray;
Don't you see the wool that grows
On my back to make you clothes?
Cold, and very cold you'd get,
If I did not give you it.

Sure it seems a pleasant thing
To nip the daisies in the spring,
But many chilly nights I pass
On the cold and dewy grass,
Or pick a scanty dinner where
All the common's brown and bare.

Then the farmer comes at last,
When the merry spring is past,
And cuts my woolly coat away
To warm you in the winter's day;
Little master, this is why
In the grassy fields I lie.

Ann Taylor

A Number of Things

I love all beauteous things,
I seek and adore them

Mrs. MacQueen
(OR The Lollie-Shop)

With glass like a bull's eye,
And shutters of green,
Down on the cobbles
Lives Mrs. MacQueen.

At six she rises;
At nine you see
Her candle shine out
In the linden tree;

And at half-past nine
Not a sound is nigh,
But the bright moon's creeping
Across the sky;

Or a far dog baying;
Or a twittering bird
In its drowsy nest,
In the darkness stirred;

Or like the roar
Of a distant sea
A long-drawn S-s-sh!
In the linden tree.

Walter de la Mare

The Lace Pedlar

Who'll buy my laces? I've laces to sell!
Long laces, strong laces, short laces as well.
Laces of cotton, of silk and mohair,
Laces of leather, a penny a pair;
A lace for your body, a lace for your shoe;
Black laces, white laces, scarlet and blue,
Here is leather for schoolboys, and silk for a girl;
But a queen must have silver with taggles of pearl.

Catherine A. Morin

Everyday Things

Millionaires, presidents—even kings
Can't get along without everyday things.

Were you president, king or millionaire,
You'd use a comb to comb your hair.

If you wished to be clean—and you would, I hope—
You'd take a bath with water and soap.

And you'd have to eat—if you wanted to eat—
Bread and vegetables, fish and meat;

While your drink for breakfast would probably be
Milk or chocolate, coffee or tea.

You'd have to wear—you could hardly refuse—
Under clothes, outer clothes, stockings and shoes.

If you wished to make a reminding note,
You'd take a pencil out of your coat;

And you couldn't sign a letter, I think,
With anything better than pen and ink.

If you wanted to read, you'd be sure to look
At newspaper, magazine, or book;

And if it happened that you were ill,
You'd down some oil or choke on a pill.

If you had a cold I can only suppose
You'd use a handkerchief for your nose.

When you wanted to rest your weary head,
Like other folks, you'd hop into bed.

Millionaires, presidents—even kings
Can't get along without everyday things.

Jean Ayer

In the Train

As we rush, as we rush in the train,
  The trees and the houses go wheeling back,
But the starry heavens above the plain
  Come flying on our track.

All the beautiful stars of the sky,
  The silver doves of the forest of night,
Over the dull earth swarm and fly,
  Companions of our flight.

We will rush ever on without fear;
  Let the goal be far, the flight be fleet!
For we carry the heavens with us, dear,
  While the earth slips from under our feet!

James Thomson ("B.V.")

The Balloon Man

He always comes on market days,
  And holds balloons—a lovely bunch—
And in the market square he stays,
  And never seems to think of lunch.

They're red and purple, blue and green,
  And when it is a sunny day
Tho' carts and people get between
  You see them shining far away.

And some are big and some are small,
  All tied together with a string,
And if there is a wind at all
  They tug and tug like anything.

Some day perhaps he'll let them go
  And we shall see them sailing high,
And stand and watch them from below—
  They *would* look pretty in the sky!

Rose Fyleman

I Love All Beauteous Things

I love all beauteous things,
    I seek and adore them;
God hath no better praise,
And man in his hasty days
    Is honoured for them.

I too will something make
    And joy in the making;
Although tomorrow it seem
Like the empty words of a dream
    Remembered on waking.

Robert Bridges

Snow In Town

Nothing is quite so quiet and clean
    As snow that falls in the night;
And isn't it jolly to jump from bed
    And find the whole world white?

It lies on the window ledges,
    It lies on the boughs of the trees,
While sparrows crowd at the kitchen door,
    With a pitiful "If you please?"

It lies on the arm of the lamp-post,
    Where the lighter's ladder goes
And the policeman under it beats his arms,
    And stamps to feel his toes;

No sound there is in the snowy road
    From the horse's cautious feet,
And all is hushed but the postman's knocks
    Rat-tatting down the street.

Till men come round with shovels
    To clear the snow away, —
What a pity it is that when it falls
    They never let it stay!

Rickman Mark

377

My Playmate

I often wonder how it is
   That on a rainy day,
A little boy, just like myself,
   Comes out with me to play.

And we step in all the puddles
   When walking into town,
But though I stand the right way up,
   He's always upside down.

I have to tread upon his feet,
   Which is a sorry sight,
With my right foot on his left foot,
   My left foot on his right.

I really wish he'd talk to me,
   He seems so very kind
For when I look and smile at him
   He does the same, I find.

But I never hear him speaking,
   So surely he must be
In some strange land the other side,
   Just opposite to me.

Mary I. Osborn

Street Scene

In the placid summer midnight,
   Under the drowsy sky,
I seem to hear in the stillness
   The moths go glimmering by.

One by one from the windows
   The lights have all been sped,
Never a blind looks conscious—
   The street is asleep in bed!

W. E. Henley

Postman's Knock

Rattat! Rattat!
  There's the postman at the door,
He always knocks like that,
  No matter who it's for.
It may be a letter
  And it might be a box,
So I'm always very glad
  When the postman knocks.

Rattat! Rattat!
  Shall I run along to see
If he is on the mat
  With something meant for me?
It may be just a postcard,
  But it might be a box,
So I always run to look
  When the postman knocks.

Rodney Bennett

Mr Coggs

A watch will tell the time of day,
Or tell it nearly, any way,
Excepting when it's overwound,
Or when you drop it on the ground.

If any of our watches stop,
We haste to Mr Cogg's shop,
For though to scold he pretends
He's quite among our special friends.

He fits a dice-box in his eye,
And takes a long and thoughtful spy,
And prods the wheels, and says, "Dear, dear!
More carelessness I greatly fear!"

And then he lays his dice-box down
And frowns a most prodigious frown;
But if we ask him what's the time,
He'll make his gold repeater chime.

E. V. Lucas

Blacksmith

All the night
And all day long
I hark to the sound
Of the blacksmith's song.

Red his fire—
The bright sparks fly
To dance with stars
In the joyous sky.

B. K. Pyke

The Engine Driver

Onward flies the rushing train,
Now in sunshine, now in rain;
Now through pleasant banks we ride,
Now o'er fenland stretching wide.

Now it is a forest nook.
Now a village by a brook,
Now a tunnel, black as night,
Shutting all things from the sight.

Now through meadows green we sweep,
Now below a wooded steep,
Now by smoky hives of men,
Now through quiet fields again.

Still the fiery steeds obey,
Still we rattle on our way;
Now beneath the placid moon,
Silvering the woods of June.

Now beneath a wilder sky,
Where the moon rides fast and high;
Now through snowflakes on the blast,
To the lights of home at last.

Who is he that drives the train,
In the sunshine and the rain;
Weather-beaten, bluff and strong,
Hero worthy of a song?

Who more earnest, brave and true,
In the work he has to do?
First in danger, first in blame,
No man earns a nobler name.

G.S.O.

The Journey

We are going on a journey,
   We are going all the way,
A-riding in a wagon
   On soft sweet-scented hay:
The Wagoner is waiting
   (A jolly coachman he)
To take us on our journey
   To a farm-house by the sea.
Our great big friends the horses
   Are joining in the fun,
A knowing look they're wearing
   While waiting in the sun;
It's such a jolly farm-house
   In the valley by the sea,
And the farmer's just as jolly
   As any man could be.
There isn't any hurry,
   The ride is spendid sport,
A wood, a windy common,
   Then a little sleepy port.
The farmer's wife is waiting,
   With strawberries for tea,
And cream and smiles of welcome,
   In the farm-house by the sea.
And when the day is over,
   All tired with sheer delight,
We'll climb up to our bedroom
   To sleep away the night
Where linen smells of lavender;
   Then waking full of glee,
We'll hear the farmer calling,
   And murmur of the sea.

Aidan Clarke

A Bit of Colour

Grey was the morn, all things were grey,
　'Twas winter more than spring;
A bleak east wind swept o'er the land,
　And sobered everything.

Grey was the sky, the fields were grey,
　The hills, the woods, the trees —
Distance and foreground — all the scene
　Was grey in the grey breeze.

Grey cushions, and a grey skin rug,
　A dark grey wicker trap,
Grey were the ladies' hats and cloaks,
　And grey my coat and cap.

A narrow, lonely, grey old lane;
　And lo, on a grey gate,
Just by the side of a grey wood,
　A sooty sweep there sat!

With grimy chin 'twixt grimy hands
　He sat and whistled shrill;
And in his sooty cap he wore
　A yellow daffodil.

And often when the days are dull,
　I seem to see him still —
The jaunty air, the sooty face —
　And the yellow daffodil.

Horace Smith

Gypsies

Last night the gypsies came —
　Nobody knows from where.
Where they've gone to nobody knows,
　And nobody seems to care!

Between the trees on the old swamp road
  I saw them round their fire:
Tattered children and dogs that barked
  As the flames leaped high and higher;
There were black-eyed girls in scarlet shawls,
  Old folk wrinkled with years,
Men with handkerchiefs round their throats
  And silver loops in their ears.
Ragged and red like maple leaves
  When frost comes in the fall,
The gypsies stayed but a single night;
  In the morning gone were all—
Never a shaggy gypsy dog,
  Never a gypsy child;
Only a burnt-out gypsy fire
  Where danced that band so wild.

All gone and away,
  Who knows where?
Only the wind that sweeps
  Maple branches bare.

Rachel Field

The Idlers

The gipsies lit their fires by the chalk-pit anew,
And the hoppled horses supped in the further dusk and dew,
The gnats flocked round the smoke like idlers as they were
And through the grass and bushes the owls began to churr.

An ell above the woods the last of sunset glowed
With a dusky gold that filled the pond beside the road;
The cricketers had done, the leas all silent lay,
And the carrier's clattering wheels went past and died away.

The gipsies lolled and gossipped, and ate their stolen swedes,
Made merry with mouth-organs, worked toys with piths of
    reeds:
The old wives puffed their pipes, nigh as black as their hair,
And not one of them all seemed to know the name of care.

Edmund Blunden

The Deserted House

There's no smoke in the chimney,
　And the rain beats on the floor;
There's no glass in the window,
　There's no wood in the door;
The heather grows behind the house,
　And the sand lies before.

No hand hath trained the ivy,
　The walls are grey and bare;
The boats upon the sea sail by,
　Nor never tarry there.
No beast of the field comes nigh,
　Nor any bird of the air.

Mary E. Coleridge

In Days Gone By

I feel that in the days gone by
　I did not live with walls and roofs.
Long years ago in deserts dry
I lived beneath the open sky
　And heard the roar of thudding hoofs,
　　And I was racing madly,
　　My head bent to the wind,
　　And fifty thousand horsemen
　　　Galloping behind!

I feel that in that long ago
　I must have been a Nomad child
Feeling the desert sun's fierce glow,
And then, in saddle, head bent low,
　Heading a horde of Bedouins wild.
　　I shut my eyes an instant
　　And see them in my mind,
　　These fifty thousand horsemen
　　　Galloping, galloping,
　　Fifty thousand horsemen
　　　Galloping behind!

Ida M. Mills

The Watchmaker's Shop

A street in our town
Has a queer little shop
With tumble-down walls
And a thatch on the top;
And all the wee windows
With crookedy panes
Are shining and winking
With watches and chains.

(All sorts and all sizes
In silver and gold,
And brass ones and tin ones
And the new ones and old;
And clocks for the kitchen
And clocks for the hall,
High ones and low ones
And wag-at-the-wall.)

The watchmaker sits
On a long-leggèd seat
And bids you the time
Of the day when you meet;
And round and about him
There's ticketty-tock
From the tiniest watch
To the grandfather clock.

I wonder he doesn't
Get tired of the chime
And all the clocks ticking
And telling the time;
But there he goes winding
Lest any should stop,
This queer little man
In the watchmaker's shop.

Caravans

I've seen caravans
Going to the fair!
   Come along,
   Come along,
Let's go there!

Hurrah! roundabouts
Lovely little swings,
   Coconuts,
   Coconuts,
Heaps of things!

See all the animals
Waiting for the show;
   Elephants,
   Elephants,
Let's all go!

Look! There's a tiger
Watching baby bears;
   Come away,
   Come away,
How he stares!

Hark! how the music plays
Ready for the fun!
   Come along,
   Come along,
Let's all run.

Irene Thompson

A Kayak Song

Over the dark water
   See the kayak steal;
Father's going searching
   For the fish and seal.

Will he have good hunting
    Out beyond the floe?
He may see a bear there
    'Mid the ice and snow.

If he gets a walrus,
    There will be for me
Thongs and reins for sledges,
    Whips of ivory.

Over the dark water
    See the kayak steal
Softly— lest it frighten
    Hidden fish and seal.

                        Lucy Diamond

Through the Porthole

(At Night)

When I went to bed at night,
    Then my porthole was a frame:
If I watched a little while,
    I would find that pictures came.

Once I saw the mast-head light
    Of a far-off passing ship:
On the rolling, splashing sea
    I could see it rise and dip.

In the great dark sky above
    Stars were scattered everywhere,
Ships, I thought, were just like stars
    As I lay and watched them there.

For a world is every star
    In a heaven of its own:
Every ship a little world
    Out upon the sea alone.

                        Marjorie Wilson
                        387

The Train

A green eye—and a red—in the dark,
Thunder—smoke—and a spark.

It is there—it is here—flashed by.
Whither will the wild thing fly?

It is rushing, tearing through the night,
Rending her gloom in its flight.

It shatters her silence with shrieks.
What is it the wild thing seeks?

Alas! for it hurries away
Them that are fain to stay.

Hurrah! for it carries home
Lovers and friends that roam.

Mary E. Coleridge

The Window Cleaner

A window cleaner's life is grand!
  Hurrying up his ladder-stair,
He sets himself with mop in hand
  To let in sunshine everywhere;
It makes me feel I'd like to be
  A window cleaner too, like him,
Taking my ladder round with me
  To get at windows dark and dim.

Having my polisher and mop
  On every dull and grimy pane,
I'd rub, and rub, and never stop
  Until I made them bright again;
I'd do the same by high and low,
  Making their glass so shiny-clean
That all who looked through it would know
  At once—the window-man had been!

Elizabeth Fleming

Fires

The kitchen fire that wakes so soon
And has to work so hard,
Would rather be the fire that burns
Behind the nursery guard.

The nursery fire that burns all day,
And keeps alive so late,
Would rather be the pretty fire
Within the parlour grate.

The parlour fire, so swept and fine,
Would rather be, I know,
The gipsy fire that sparks away
With all the winds that blow.

The gipsy fire burns out-of-doors
In places wild and free;
I'd rather be a gipsy fire
Than any fire, says she!

Elizabeth Fleming

The Flower-Seller

The Flower-seller's fat, and she wears a big shawl!
She sits on the kerb with her basket and all;
The wares that she sells us are not very dear
And are always the loveliest things of the year.
        Daffodils in April,
            Purple flags in May,
        Sweet peas like butterflies
            Upon a summer day,
        Brown leaves in autumn,
            Green leaves in spring,
        And berries in the winter
            When the carol-singers sing.
The Flower-seller sits with her hands in her lap,
When she's not crying Roses, she's taking a nap;
Her bonnet is queer, and she calls you My dear,
And sells you the loveliest things of the year.

Eleanor Farjeon

389

The Upside-Down World

I know a place that holds the Sky
A place where little white clouds lie;

The edge is all green as Grass,
The middle is as smooth as Glass;

And there the round sun makes his Bed;
And there a Tree stands on its Head;

Sometimes a Bird sits on that Tree;
Sometimes it sings a Song to me;

And always in that shining place
I see a little smiling Face;

She nods and smiles; but all the same
The Girl down there won't tell her name!

Hamish Hendry

The Scissor-Man

Sing a song of Scissor-men,
  "Mend a broken plate,
Bring your knives and garden shears,
  I'll do them while you wait.
Buzz-a-wuzz! Buzz-a-wuzz!
  Fast the wheel or slow,
Ticker Tacker! Ticker Tack!
  Rivets in a row."

Sing a song of Scissor-men,
  Sitting in the sun,
Sing it when the day begins,
  Sing it when it's done.
Be it hard or be it soft,
  Here's a jolly plan;
Sing to make the work go well,
  Like the Scissor-man.

Madeleine Nightingale

Shining Things

I love all shining things—
        the lovely moon,
The silver stars at night,
        gold sun at noon.
A glowing rainbow in
        a stormy sky,
Or bright clouds hurrying
        when wind goes by.

I love the glow-worm's elf-light
        in the lane,
And leaves a-shine with glistening
        drops of rain,
The glinting wings of bees,
        and butterflies,
My purring pussy's green
        and shining eyes.

I love the street-lamps shining
        through the gloom,
Tall candles lighted in
        a shadowy room,
New-tumbled chestnuts from
        the chestnut tree,
And gleaming fairy bubbles
        blown by me.

I love the shining buttons
        on my coat,
I love the bright beads round
        my mother's throat.
I love the coppery flames
        of red and gold,
That cheer and comfort me,
        when I'm a-cold.

The beauty of all shining things
        is yours and mine,
It was a *lovely* thought of God
        to make things shine.

Elizabeth Gould

The Shepherd Boy

The shepherd boy a kingdom rules,
   An emerald hill his throne;
Crown'd with golden sunshine,
   He reigneth there alone.

His goats, court-players are;
   Each wears a tinkling bell,
And the bird's sweet pipings,
   A royal concert tell.

And the piping and the bells,
   With the brook's soft rhymes,
Lull the drowsy king to sleep,
   While gently nod the pines.

Heinrich Heine

Topsy-Turvy Land

The people walk upon their heads,
   The sea is made of sand,
The children go to school by night,
   In Topsy-Turvy Land.

The front-door step is at the back,
   You're walking when you stand,
You wear your hat upon your feet,
   In Topsy-Turvy Land.

And 'buses on the sea you'll meet,
   While pleasure boats are planned
To travel up and down the streets
   Of Topsy-Turvy Land.

You pay for what you never get,
   I think it must be grand,
For when you go you're coming back,
   In Topsy-Turvy Land.

H. E. Wilkinson

The Ships

For many a year I've watched the ships a-sailing to and fro,
The mighty ships, the little ships, the speedy and the slow;
And many a time I've told myself that some day I would go
    Around the world that is so full of wonders.

The swift and stately liners, how they run without a rest!
The great three-masters, they have touched the East and told
    the West!
The monster burden-bearers—oh, they all have plunged and
    pressed
    Around the world that is so full of wonders!

The cruiser and the battleship that loom as dark as doubt,
The devilish destroyer and the hateful, hideous scout—
These deathly things may also rush, with roar and snarl and
    shout,
    Around the world that is so full of wonders!

The shabby tramp that like a wedge is hammered through the
    seas,
The little brown sailed brigantine that traps the lightest
    breeze—
Oh, I'd be well content to fare aboard the least of these
    Around the world that is so full of wonders.

The things I've heard, the things I've read, the things I've
    dreamed might be,
The boyish tales, the old men's yarns—they will not pass
    from me.
I've heard, I've read, I've dreamed—but all the time I've
    longed to *see*
    Around the world that is so full of wonders.

So year by year I watch the ships a-sailing to and fro,
The ships that come as strangers and the ships I've learned to
    know—
Folk smile to hear an old man say that *some* day he will go
    Around the world that is so full of wonders.

J. J. Bell

Dream Pedlary

If there were dreams to sell,
    What would you buy?
Some cost a passing bell;
    Some a light sigh,
That shakes from Life's fresh crown
Only a rose-leaf down.
If there were dreams to sell,
Merry and sad to tell,
And the crier rang the bell,
    What would you buy?

A cottage lone and still,
    With bowers nigh,
Shadowy, my woes to still,
    Until I die.
Such pearl from Life's fresh crown
Fain would I shake me down,
Were dreams to have at will,
This would best heal my ill,
    This would I buy.

Thomas Lovell Beddoes

The Old Kitchen Clock

Listen to the Kitchen Clock,
To itself it ever talks,
From its place it never walks;
"Tick-tock—tick-tock,"
Tell me what it says.

"I'm a very patient clock,
Never moved by hope or fear,
Though I've stood for many a year;
Tick-tock—tick-tock,"
That is what it says.

"I'm a very truthful clock;
People say, about the place,
Truth is written on my face;
Tick-tock—tick-tock,"
That is what it says.

"I'm a very active clock,
For I go while you're asleep.
Though you never take a peep.
Tick-tock—tick-tock,"
That is what it says.

"I'm a most obliging clock;
If you wish to hear me strike,
You may do it when you like;
Tick-tock—tick-tock,"
That is what it says.

What a talkative old clock!
Let us see what it will do
When the pointer reaches two.
"Ding-ding—tick-tock."
That is what it says.

Ann Hawkshawe

My Hut

I built a hut in a little wood;
Nobody came there   nobody could;
Only a bird and a rabbit perhaps—
Only the wind with three small taps.

You'll never find my hut in the wood;
If I can't find it, nobody could.
For the wind one day, crazy with play,
Carried my little hut away.

He didn't come with three small taps,
He banged on the door with thunderous raps.
Then he carried my lonely house away,
And I've searched for it now for a year and a day.

E. Mathias

395

New Sights

I like to see a thing I know
   Has not been seen before,
That's why I cut my apple through
   To look into the core.

It's nice to think, though many an eye
   Has seen the ruddy skin,
Mine is the very first to spy
   The five brown pips within.

Old Morgan

Old Morgan had a lovely harp,
   But he was no musician.
One day a man called at his door
   Upon a curious mission.

"I'm very hungry," said the man,
   "Just hear my tummy rumble."
"Come in," said Morgan, "take a seat,
   I'm not the man to grumble."

"I've eaten nothing," said the man,
   "I'm as empty as a drum."
"Sit down," said Morgan, "rest yourself,
   And please don't suck your thumb.

"Here's bread and cheese and butter,
   And the kettle singing sweetly.
We'll make a cup of tea," said he,
   As he spread the cloth on neatly.

And so the stranger ate his fill,
   And Morgan he ate with him,
"Play me a tune," said the stranger,
   And Morgan groaned within him.

Then sitting down beside his harp
   He made his sad confession.
"I love my lovely harp," he said,
   "But I am no musician.

"My music isn't fit to hear,
    The noise I make's outrageous,
My fingers won't do what I want,
    My thumbs are most rampageous."

"What is your dearest wish, sir?"
    Said the stranger most benignly.
"To play my harp," said Morgan,
    "I'd like to play divinely."

"I must be off," said the stranger,
    "I really cannot linger.
You've been most kind to me," said he,
    And he touched the harp with his finger.

And then the stranger vanished quite,
    He vanished in a twinkling.
Old Morgan rubbed his wond'ring eyes,
    And then he fell a-thinking.

But when his fingers touched the strings
    The liquid notes came dancing,
And all the neighbours crowded in—
    The music was entrancing.

                                        G. D. Roberts

Shell Secrets

Tell me your secrets, pretty shell,
I will promise not to tell!

Humming, humming, soft and low—
All about the sea, I know.

You are murmuring, I think,
Of the sea-weeds, green and pink,

Of the tiny baby shells
Where the mother mermaid dwells.

Pretty shell, I'm waiting here,
Come, and whisper in my ear.

397

Pictures

I can see a picture.
 Tell me what you see—
Blue-bells in a beech wood.
 And green leaves on a tree.

I can see a picture.
 Tell me what you see—
A fleet, a fleet of fishing boats
And sunshine on the sea.

I can see a picture.
 Tell me what you see—
Apples on the bending bough,
 As rosy as can be.

I can see a picture.
 Tell me what you see—
A choir of children carolling
 Around a Christmas Tree.

F. Ann Elliott

The Balloon Seller

I'd like to peddle toy balloons;
With globes like jolly suns and moons
Bobbing and bouncing there, I'd stay
Holding them high the live-long day.

I'd make them dance like anything,
All fastened to a bit of string,
Their golds and greens, and blues and reds
Glimmering over people's heads.

And all the folks would turn and stare,
And long to free them on the air.

Elizabeth Fleming

Playgrounds

In summer I am very glad
  We children are so small,
For we can see a thousand things
  That men can't see at all.

They don't know much about the moss
  And all the stones they pass:
They never lie and play among
  The forests in the grass:

They walk about a long way off:
  And, when we're at the sea,
Let father stoop as best he can
  He can't find things like me.

But, when the snow is on the ground
  And all the puddles freeze,
I wish that I were very tall,
  High up above the trees.

L. Alma Tadema

The Clothes-Line

Hand in hand they dance in a row,
Hither and thither, and to and fro,
Flip! Flap! Flop! and away they go—
Flutt'ring creatures as white as snow,
Like restive horses they caper and prance;
Like fairy-tale witches they wildly dance;
Rounded in front, but hollow behind,
They shiver and skip in the merry March wind.
One I saw dancing excitedly,
Struggling so wildly till she was free,
Then, leaving pegs and clothes-line behind her,
She flew like a bird, and no one can find her.
I saw her gleam, like a sail, in the sun,
Flipping and flapping and flopping for fun.
Nobody knows where she now can be,
Hid in a ditch, or drowned in the sea.
She was my handkerchief not long ago,
But she'll never come back to my pocket, I know.

Charlotte Druitt Cole

399

The Children's Bells

Where are your Oranges?
　　Where are your Lemons?
What, are you silent now,
　　Bells of St. Clement's?
You, of all bells that rang
　　Once in old London,
You, of all bells that sang,
　　Utterly undone?
You whom all children know
　　Ere they know letters,
Making Big Ben himself
　　Call you his betters?
Where are your lovely tones
　　Fruitful and mellow,
Full-flavoured orange-gold,
　　Clear lemon-yellow?
Ring again, sing again,
　　Bells of St. Clement's!
Call as you swing again,
　　"Oranges! Lemons!"
Fatherless children
　　Are listening near you—
Sing for the children,
　　The fathers will hear you.

Eleanor Farjeon

Tall Nettles

Tall nettles cover up, as they have done
　　These many springs, the rusty harrow, the plough
Long worn out, and the roller made of stone;
　　Only the elm butt tops the nettles now.

This corner of the farmyard I like most:
　　As well as any bloom upon a flower
I like the dust on the nettles, never lost
　　Except to prove the sweetness of a shower.

Edward Thomas

The Merry Heart

Jog on, jog on, the footpath way,
And merrily hent the stile-a;
A merry heart goes all the day,
Your sad tires in a mile-a.

Shakespeare

Beautiful Meals

How nice it is to eat!
All creatures love it so,
That they who first did spread,
Ere breaking bread,
A cloth like level snow,
Were right, I know.

And they were wise and sweet
Who, glad that meats taste good,
Used speech in an arch style,
And oft would smile
To raise the cheerful mood,
While at their food.

And those who first, so neat,
Placed fork and knife quite straight,
The glass on the right hand;
And all, as planned,
Each day set round the plate, —
Be their praise great!

For then, their hearts being light,
They plucked hedge-posies bright—
Flowers who, their scent being sweet,
Give nose and eye a treat:
'Twas they, my heart can tell,
Not eating fast but well,
Who wove the spell
Which finds me every day,
And makes each meal-time gay;
I know 'twas they.

T. Sturge Moore

Bread

"Farmer, is the harvest ready
  For we must have bread?"
"Go and look at all my fields,"
  Is what the farmer said.

So we ran and saw the wheat
  Standing straight and tall.
"There's your bread," the farmer said,
  "Have no fear at all."

"Miller, is the flour ready
  For we must have bread?"
"Go and look in all my sacks,"
  Is what the miller said.

So we ran and saw the flour,
  Soft and white as snow.
"There's your flour," the miller said,
  As we turned to go.

"Mother, is the oven ready
  For we must have bread?"
"Go and open wide the door,"
  Is what our mother said.

So we ran and saw the loaves
  Crisp and brown to see.
"There's your bread," our mother said,
  "Ready for your tea."

H. E. Wilkinson

Wireless

By the wireless I can hear
Voices sounding loud and clear,
Some alone and some in choirs,
Coming over with no wires,
Floating out upon the air,
From one small room to everywhere.

Rodney Bennett

402

Amy Elizabeth Ermyntrude Annie

Amy Elizabeth Ermyntrude Annie
Went to the country to visit her Grannie;

Learnt to churn butter and learnt to make cheese,
Learnt to milk cows and take honey from bees;

Learnt to spice roseleaves and learnt to cure ham,
Learnt to make cider and black-currant jam.

When she came home she could not settle down,
Said there was nothing to do in the town.

Nothing to do there and nothing to see:
Life was all shopping and afternoon tea!

Amy Elizabeth Ermyntrude Annie
Ran away back to the country and Grannie!

Queenie Scott-Hopper

The Little Things That Happen

The Little Things That Happen
    Are tucked into your mind,
And come again to greet you
    (Or most of them, you'll find).

Through many little doorways,
    Of which you keep the keys,
They crowd into your thinking—
    We call them Memories.

But some of them are rovers
    And wander off and get
So lost, the keys grow rusty,
    And that means—you forget.

But some stay ever near you;
    You'll find they never rove—
The keys are always shining—
Those are the things you love.

Marjorie Wilson

403

The Town Child

I live in the town
　　In a street;
It is crowded with traffic
　　And feet;
There are buses and motors
　　And trams;
I wish there were meadows
　　And lambs.

The houses all wait
　　In a row,
There is smoke everywhere
　　That I go.
I don't like the noises
　　I hear —
I wish there were woods
　　Very near.

There is only one thing
　　That I love,
And that is the sky
　　Far above,
There is plenty of room
　　In the blue
For castles of clouds
　　And me, too!

Irene Thompson

The Country Child

My home is a house
　　Near a wood
(I'd live in a street
　　If I could!).
The lanes are so quiet,
　　Oh, dear!
I do wish that someone
　　Lived near.

There is no one to play with
    At all,
The trees are so high
    And so tall;
And I should be lonely
    For hours,
Were it not for the birds
    And the flowers.

I wish that I lived
    In a town—
To see all the trams
    Going down
A twinkling street
    That is bright
With wonderful colours,
    At night!

Irene Thompson

From a Railway Carriage

Faster than fairies, faster than witches,
Bridges and houses, hedges and ditches;
And charging along like troops in a battle,
All through the meadows the horses and cattle;
All of the sights of the hill and the plain
Fly as thick as driving rain;
And ever again, in the wink of an eye,
Painted stations whistle by.

Here is a child who clambers and scrambles,
All by himself and gathering brambles;
Here is a tramp who stands and gazes;
And there is the green for stringing the daisies!
Here is a cart run away in the road
Lumping along with man and load;
And here is a mill, and there is a river:
Each a glimpse and gone for ever!

Robert Louis Stevenson

The Last Gate

I know a garden with three strange gates
  Of silver, of gold, and glass,
At every gate, in a deep, soft voice,
  A sentinel murmurs, "Pass."

At night I passed through the silver gate,
  An ivory moon rode high;
I heard the song of the silver stars
  That swung in the silver sky.

I walked at dawn through the gate of gold,
  And came to a golden sea,
Seven mermaids rose from the golden waves
  And fluttered white hands to me.

At last I came to the other gate,
  The sentinel murmured, "Pass!"
I never will tell what lovely things
  I saw through that gate of glass.

Stella Mead

Meg Merrilees

Old Meg she was a gipsy,
  And lived upon the moors;
Her bed it was the brown heath turf,
  And her house was out of doors,
Her apples were swart blackberries,
  Her currants, pods o' broom;
Her wine was dew of the wild white rose,
  Her book a churchyard tomb.

Her brothers were the craggy hills,
  Her sisters larchen trees;
Alone with her great family
  She lived as she did please.
No breakfast had she many a morn,
  No dinner many a noon,
And, 'stead of supper, she would stare
  Full hard against the moon.

But every morn, of woodbine fresh,
    She made her garlanding,
And, every night, the dark glen yew
    She wove, and she would sing.
And with her fingers, old and brown,
    She plaited mats of rushes,
And gave them to the cottagers
    She met among the bushes.

Old Meg was brave as Margaret Queen,
    And tall as Amazon;
An old red blanket cloak she wore,
    A chip-hat had she on:
God rest her aged bones somewhere!
    She died full long agone!

J. Keats

Danny Murphy

He was as old as old could be,
His little eye could scarcely see,
His mouth was sunken in between
His nose and chin, and he was lean
And twisted up and withered quite,
So that he couldn't walk aright.

His pipe was always going out,
And then he'd have to search about
In all his pockets, and he'd mow—
O deary me! and, musha now!
And then he'd light his pipe, and then
He'd let it go clean out again.

He couldn't dance or jump or run,
Or ever have a bit of fun
Like me and Susan, when we shout
And jump and throw ourselves about—
But when he laughed, then you could see
He was as young as young could be!

James Stephens

407

"Sooeep!"

Black as a chimney is his face,
　And ivory white his teeth,
And in his brass-bound cart he rides,
　The chestnut blooms beneath.

"Sooeep, Sooeep!" he cries, and brightly peers
　This way and that to see
With his two light-blue shining eyes
　What custom there may be.

And once inside the house, he'll squat,
　And drive his rods on high,
Till twirls his sudden sooty brush
　Against the morning sky.

Then 'mid his bulging bags of soot,
　With half the world asleep,
His small cart wheels him off again,
　Still hoarsely bawling, "Sooeep!"

Walter de la Mare

Street Lanterns

Country roads are yellow and brown.
We mend the roads in London town.

Never a hansom dare come nigh,
Never a cart goes rolling by.

An unwonted silence steals
In between the turning wheels.

Quickly ends the autumn day,
And the workman goes his way.

Leaving, midst the traffic rude,
One small isle of solitude.

Lit, throughout the lengthy night,
By the little lantern's light.

Jewels of the dark have we,
Brighter than the rustic's be.

Over the dull earth are thrown
Topaz, and the ruby stone.

Mary E. Coleridge

An Eskimo Baby

If you were an Eskimo baby
You'd live in a bag all day.
   Right up from your toes
   To the tip of your nose,
All in thick cosy furs tucked away.

And if you went out for an airing
In mother's warm hood you would go,
   Tied close to her back,
   Like a soft, furry pack,
You could laugh at the cold and the snow.

But if they brought water at bedtime —
As people at home always do —
   You'd cough and you'd sneeze,
   And perhaps you would freeze,
You would certainly turn very blue!

An Eskimo mummy would rub you
With oil from your heels to your head.
   And then you'd be rolled
   (For it's terribly cold)
In warm furs, and put safely to bed.

No nice creamy milk for your supper,
But bits of raw blubber and fat!
   Would you like to go
   To the land of the snow,
Where they have such a bedtime as that?

Lucy Diamond

409

Foreign Children

Little Indian, Sioux, or Crow,
Little frosty Eskimo,
Little Turk or Japanee,
O! don't you wish that you were me?

You have seen the scarlet trees,
And the lions overseas;
You have eaten ostrich eggs,
And turned the turtles off their legs.

Such a life is very fine,
But it's not so nice as mine;
You must often, as you trod,
Have wearied not to be abroad.

You have curious things to eat,
I am fed on proper meat;
You must dwell beyond the foam,
But I am safe and live at home.

Little Indian, Sioux, or Crow,
Little frosty Eskimo,
Little Turk or Japanee,
O! don't you wish that you were me?

Robert Louis Stevenson

No Thoroughfare

In a dear little home of tarpaulin and boards,
  Where the wood-blocks are ``up'' in our street,
Lives a little old man dressed in sacking and cords,
  Crouching snug on a low wooden seat.

There's a brazier of charcoal that flickers and glows
  Where the wigwam's front door ought to be;
As the little old man toasts his fingers and nose
  How I wish he had room there for me!

I could hang out the lanterns on trestles and poles,
   Like big rubies all shining and red,
And to guard a wide street full of wood-blocks and holes
   Is far nicer than going to bed.

I could stay all night long by the little old man
   Keeping watch o'er each pickaxe and spade,
Frying sausages too, in a battered old pan,
   For the dark would not make me afraid.

And the little old man might drop off in a doze
   Till the sky turned to orange and pink,
But the street would be safe from all brigands and foes
   For *I* should not have slumbered a wink.

Ruth Holmes

The Shiny Little House

I wish, how I wish that I had a little house,
With a mat for the cat and a hole for a mouse,
And a clock going "tock" in a corner of the room,
And a kettle, and a cupboard, and a big birch broom.

To school in the morning the children off would run,
And I'd give them a kiss and a penny and a bun,
But directly they had gone from this little house of mine,
I'd clap my hands and snatch a cloth, and shine, shine, shine.

I'd shine all the knives, all the windows, and the floors,
All the grates, all the plates, all the handles on the doors,
Every fork, every spoon, every lid, and every tin,
Till everything was shining like a new bright pin.

At night, by the fire, when the children were in bed,
I'd sit and I'd knit, with a cap upon my head,
And the kettles and the saucepans they would shine, shine,
      shine,
In this tweeny little, cosy little house of mine!

Nancy M. Hayes

411

Sea Shell

Sea Shell, Sea Shell,
    Sing me a song, O please!
A song of ships, and sailor men,
    And parrots, and tropical trees,
Of islands lost in the Spanish Main
Which no man ever may find again,
Of fishes and corals under the waves,
And sea-horses stabled in great green caves.
Sea Shell, Sea Shell,
Sing of the things you know so well.

Amy Lowell

The Shell

See what a lovely shell,
Small and pure as a pearl,
Lying close to my foot,
Frail, but a work divine,
Made so fairly well
With delicate spire and whorl,
How exquisitely minute,
A miracle of design!

What is it? a learnèd man
Could give it a clumsy name.
Let him name it who can,
The beauty would be the same.

The tiny cell is forlorn,
Void of the little living will
That made it stir on the shore.
Did he stand at the diamond door
Of his house in a rainbow frill?
Did he push, when he was uncurl'd,
A golden foot or fairy horn
Thro' his dim water-world?

Slight, to be crush'd with a tap
Of my finger-nail on the sand;
Small, but a work divine,
Frail, but of force to withstand,
Year upon year, the shock
Of cataract seas that snap
The three-decker's oaken spine
Athwart the ledges of rock,
Here on the Breton strand!

Lord Tennyson

The Shell

And then I pressed the shell
  Close to my ear
And listened well,
And straightway like a bell
  Came low and clear
The slow, sad murmur of far distant seas,
Whipped by an icy breeze
Upon a shore
Wind-swept and desolate.
It was a sunless strand that never bore
The footprint of a man,
Nor felt the weight
Since time began
Of any human quality or stir
Save what the dreary winds and waves incur.
And in the hush of waters was the sound
Of pebbles rolling round,
For ever rolling with a hollow sound.
And bubbling sea-weeds as the waters go
Swish to and fro
Their long, cold tentacles of shiny grey.
There was no day,
Nor ever came a night
Setting the stars alight
To wonder at the moon:
Was twilight only and the frightened croon,
Smitten to whimpers, of the dreary wind
And waves that journeyed blind—
And then I loosed my ear—O, it was sweet
To hear a cart go jolting down the street.

James Stephens

413

A Widow Bird

A widow bird sate mourning for her love
Upon a wintry bough;
The frozen wind crept on above,
The freezing stream below.

There was no leaf upon the forest bare,
No flower upon the ground,
And little motion in the air
Except the mill-wheel's sound.

P. Bysshe Shelley

Wishing

Ring-ting! I wish I were a primrose,
A bright yellow primrose blowing in the spring!
The stooping boughs above me,
The wandering bee to love me,
The fern and moss to creep across,
And the elm-tree for our king!

Nay, stay! I wish I were an elm-tree,
A great lofty elm-tree, with green leaves gay!
The winds would set them dancing,
The sun and moonshine glance in,
And birds would house among the boughs,
And sweetly sing!

Oh—no! I wish I were a robin,
A robin or a little wren, everywhere to go;
Through forest, field or garden,
And ask no leave or pardon,
Till winter comes with icy thumbs
To ruffle up our wing.

Well—tell! Where should I fly to,
Where go to sleep in the dark wood or dell?
Before a day was over,
Home comes the rover,
For mother's kiss—sweeter this
Than any other thing!

W. Allingham

Dust

The grey dust runs on the ground like a mouse,
Over the doorstep and into the house,
Under the bedsteads and tables and chairs,
Up to the rooms at the top of the stairs,
Down to the cellar, across the brick floor—
There! It is off again by the back door!
Never a mousetrap can catch the grey mouse
Who keeps the brooms busy all over the house!

P. A. Ropes

On the Banisters

Sliding down the banisters,
  The day it rained all day,
We played at flying fairies
  Coming down a rainbow ray.
I slit my frock a little bit,
  And Billy tore the mat—
But fairies aren't particular
  About such things as that.

Sliding down the banisters
  The day it rained all day,
We played at sailing aeroplanes
  To countries miles away.
I hurt my hand a little bit,
  And Billy bumped his nose,
But airmen take no notice,
  Of such little things as those.

Sliding down the banisters
  The day it rained all day,
We played at swings and switchbacks
  Like they have Olympia way.
Then folks came in, all wet and cross,
  And made us stop our play.
But oh, we did enjoy ourselves
  The day it rained all day.

Margaret E. Gibbs

415

Gold

Evening is tawny on the old
　Deep-windowed farm,
And the great elm-trees fold on fold
　Are golden-warm.

And a fountain-basin drips its gold
　'Mid gleaming lawns
Where mellow statue-bases hold
　Their gilded fawns.

Martin Armstrong

Overheard on a Saltmarsh

Nymph, nymph, what are your beads?
Green glass, goblin. Why do you stare at them?
Give them me.
　　　　No.
Give them me. Give them me.
　　　　　　No.
Then I will howl all night in the reeds,
Lie in the mud and howl for them.

Goblin, why do you love them so?

They are better than stars or water,
Better than voices of winds that sing,
Better than any man's fair daughter,
Your green glass beads on a silver ring.

Hush, I stole them out of the moon.

Give me your beads, I want them.
　　　　　　No.

I will howl in a deep lagoon
For your green glass beads, I love them so.
Give them me. Give them me.
　　　　　No.

Harold Monro

416

The Shepherd

How sweet is the shepherd's sweet lot!
From the morn to the evening he strays;
He shall follow his sheep all the day,
And his tongue shall be filled with praise.

For he hears the lambs' innocent call,
And he hears the ewes' tender reply;
He is watchful while they are in peace,
For they know when their shepherd is nigh.

William Blake

The Little Herd-Boy's Song

Where the buttercups so sweet
Dust with gold my naked feet,
Where the grass grows green and long,
Sit I here and sing my song,
And the brown bird cries "Cuckoo!"
Under skies for ever blue!

Now and then, while I sing loud,
Flits a little fleecy cloud,
And uplooking I behold
How it turns to rain of gold,
Falling lightly, while around
Comes the stir of its soft sound!

Bright above and dim below
Is the many colour'd Bow;
'Tis the only light I mark,
Till the mountain tops grow dark,
And uplooking I espy
Shining glow-worms in the sky.

Then I hear the runlet's call,
And the voice of the waterfall
Growing louder, and 'tis cold
As I guide my flocks to fold;
But no City, great or small,
Have I ever seen at all.

Robert Buchanan

Little Things

From a little seed
A flower grows.
From a little flower
A fragrance blows—
A little fragrance
That's wafted to me
As I lie in the shade
Of the chestnut tree.

Eileen Mathias

A Rhyme Sheet of Other Lands

The Japanese have funny things
For dinner, so they say;
The tails of fish and dragon's wings
Are eaten every day.

Of all the men who search for gold,
Some find as much of it
As both their restless hands can hold,
And others ne'er a bit.

I think this picture here shall be
The famous river Nile
And, lying near the bank, you see
The curious crocodile.

The Greeks of old were wise and skilled,
What wonders they could do!
What towns and temples they could build,
And stately houses, too!

Now every child in China knows
The way to spell and write with speed;
From right to left the writing goes—
It must be very hard indeed!

I'd love to go to Switzerland,
Although the air is colder:
There's little doubt that it's a land
I'll go to when I'm older.

Hugh Chesterman

Chimes

Brief, on a flying night,
   From the shaken tower,
A flock of bells take flight,
   And go with the hour.

Like birds from the cote to the gales,
   Abrupt--O hark!
A fleet of bells sets sails,
   And go to the dark.

Sudden the cold airs swing.
   Alone, aloud,
A verse of bells takes wing
   And flies with the cloud.

Alice Meynell

"Littles"

From "A Ternarie of Littles"

A little Saint best fits a little Shrine,
A little Prop best fits a little Vine,
As my small Cruse best fits my little Wine.

A little Seed best fits a little Soil,
A little Trade best fits a little Toil,
As my small Jar best fits my little Oil.

A little Bin best fits a little Bread,
A little Garland fits a little Head,
As my small Stuff best fits my little Shed.

A little Hearth best fits a little Fire,
A little Chapel fits a little Choir,
As my small Bell best fits my little Spire.

A little Stream best fits a little Boat,
A little Lead best fits a little Float,
As my small Pipe best fits my little Note.

Robert Herrick

The World

Great, wide, beautiful, wonderful world,
With the wonderful water round you curled,
And the wonderful grass upon your breast—
World, you are beautifully drest.

The wonderful air is over me,
And the wonderful wind is shaking the tree,
It walks on the water, and whirls the mills,
And talks to itself on the tops of the hills.

You friendly Earth! how far you go,
With wheat-fields that nod, and the rivers that flow,
With cities and gardens, and cliffs and isles,
And people upon you for thousands of miles!

Ah! you are so great, and I am so small,
I tremble to think of you, World, at all;
And yet, when I said my prayers to-day,
A whisper inside me seemed to say,
"You are more than the Earth, though you are such a dot:
You can love and think, and the Earth cannot!"

W. B. Rands

A Town Window

Beyond my window in the night
    Is but a drab inglorious street,
Yet there the frost and clean starlight
    As over Warwick woods are sweet.

Under the grey drift of the town
    The crocus works among the mould
As eagerly as those that crown
    The Warwick spring in flame and gold.

420

And when the tramway down the hill
  Across the cobbles moans and rings,
There is about my window-sill
  The tumult of a thousand wings.

John Drinkwater

The Hurdy-Gurdy Man

There's lots of things I'd like to be,
A sailor sailing on the sea;
A soldier standing stiff and straight
Beside King George's palace gate;
A baker kneading mounds of dough;
The man who shovels up the snow;
The pilot of an aeroplane;
The engine driver on a train;
A gipsy in a caravan,
Or else a hurdy-gurdy man.

There are so many things to choose—
A blacksmith making horses' shoes;
The man who works a windmill sails;
A writer writing fairy-tales;
The man with toy balloons to sell;
The muffin man who rings a bell;
The Lord Mayor in the Lord Mayor's Show—
I'd like to be them all, but oh!
I'm going to manage, if I can,
To be a hurdy-gurdy man!

A hurdy-gurdy is so gay,
I'd like to go with one all day,
And turn the handle round and round
And listen to the jolly sound;
I'd see the people peering out,
And watch the children crowd about,
And tap their feet in time and sing—
Oh, what a lot of fun I'd bring
If I could carry out my plan,
And be a hurdy-gurdy man!

Elizabeth Fleming

Song for a Little House

I'm glad our house is a little house,
  Not too tall nor too wide;
I'm glad the hovering butterflies
  Feel free to come inside.

Our little house is a friendly house,
  It is not shy or vain;
It gossips with the talking trees
  And makes friends with the rain.

And quick leaves cast a shimmer of green
  Against our whited walls,
And in the phlox, the courteous bees
  Are paying duty calls.

Christopher Morley

The Song of the Bath

Bring the biggest bath you've seen,
Water hot and towels clean,
Bring the soap that smells so sweetly;
Bring the nighties, folded neatly—
Bath time! Bath time! Hip hooray!
Jolliest time of all the day!

Bring the funny rubber toys,
Bring the little girls and boys;
Sticky fingers, grubby knees,
Rub them, scrub them, if you please.
Bath time! Bath time! Work away—
Busiest time of all the day.

Bring the grumbles and complainings,
Bring the little aches and painings,
All the frowns and all the tears,
Drown them in the bath, my dears.
Bath time! Bath time! Kiss, and say,
Happiest time of all the day!

Margaret Gibbs

Marching Song

Bring the comb and play upon it!
  Marching, here we come!
Willie cocks his Highland bonnet,
  Johnnie beats the drum.

Mary Jane commands the party,
  Peter leads the rear;
Feet in time, alert and hearty,
  Each a Grenadier!

All in the most martial manner
  Marching double-quick;
While the napkin like a banner
  Waves upon the stick!

Here's enough of fame and pillage,
  Great commander Jane!
Now that we've been round the village
  Let's go home again.

Robert Louis Stevenson

The Saint Wears a Halo

The saint wears a halo;
  The king wears a crown;
The milkmaid a bonnet
  To match her white gown;
The toadstool a hat
  And the foxgloves a hood;
A canopy covers
  The trees in the wood.

The elf has a cap
  That fits close to his head;
The witch stole a steeple
  (The storybook said).
But when I go running,
  I leave my head bare
To feel the warm sun
  And the wind in my hair!

"Peter"

Someone

Someone came knocking
    At my wee, small door;
Someone came knocking,
    I'm sure—sure—sure;
I listened, I opened,
    I looked to left and right,
But nought there was a-stirring
    In the still dark night.
Only the busy beetle
    Tap-tapping in the wall,
Only from the forest
    The screech-owl's call,
Only the cricket whistling
    While the dewdrops fall,
So I know not who came knocking,
    At all, at all, at all.

Walter de la Mare

The Scarf

Old Mrs. Tressider
Over at Winches
Is knitting a scarf
Of many gay inches,
An inch of scarlet,
Another of blue,
An inch of green
(The apple'y hue),
Another, bright
As a sunlit meadow,
And yet a third
Like a tree in shadow;
Crimson like sunset,
Rosy like dawn,
Purple like twilight
Over a lawn;
Noonday blue
And rain-cloud grey,
And an inch of white
As flowers-o'-May.

So she purls
And plains them together—
All the moods
Of the world and weather—
Into a scarf
Of many gay inches—
Old Mrs. Tressider
Over at Winches.

Ivy O. Eastwick

My Early Home

Here sparrows build upon the trees,
    And stockdove hides her nest;
The leaves are winnowed by the breeze
    Into a calmer rest;
The blackcap's song was very sweet,
    That used the rose to kiss;
It made the Paradise complete:
    My early home was this.

The red-breast from the sweet briar bush
    Drop't down to pick the worm;
On the horse-chestnut sang the thrush,
    O'er the house where I was born;
The moonlight, like a shower of pearls,
    Fell o'er this "bower of bliss,"
And on the bench sat boys and girls:
    My early home was this.

The old house stooped just like a cave,
    Thatched o'er with mosses green;
Winter around the walls would rave,
    But all was calm within;
The trees are here all green agen,
    Here bees the flowers still kiss,
But flowers and trees seemed sweeter then:
    My early home was this.

John Clare
425

The Trains

A Child's Fancy

> Every morning at break of day
> I can hear (so far away,
> They sound like voices in a dream!)
> The trains in the station whistle and scream.
>
> Every morning in the week
> I can hear them whistle and shriek,
> But who are the people that go away
> Into the country at break of day?

Seumas O'Sullivan

The Old Woman of the Roads

> O, to have a little house!
>   To own the hearth and stool and all!
> The heaped-up sods upon the fire,
>   The pile of turf against the wall!
>
> To have a clock with weights and chains
>   And pendulum swinging up and down!
> A dresser filled with shining delph,
>   Speckled and white and blue and brown!
>
> I could be busy all the day
>   Clearing and sweeping hearth and floor,
> And fixing on their shelf again
>   My white and blue and speckled store!
>
> I could be quiet there at night,
>   Beside the fire and by myself,
> Sure of a bed; and loth to leave
>   The ticking clock and the shining delph!
>
> Oh! but I'm weary of mist and dark,
>   And roads where there's never a house or bush,
> And tired I am of the bog, and the road,
>   And the crying wind and the lonesome hush!

426

And I am praying to God on high,
  And I am praying Him night and day,
For a little house—a house of my own—
  Out of the wind's and the rain's way.

Padraic Column

Who's In?

    "The door is shut fast
        And everyone's out."
    But people don't know
        What they're talking about!
    Say the fly on the wall,
    And the flame on the coals,
    And the dog on his rug,
    And the mice in their holes,
    And the kitten curled up,
    And the spiders that spin—
    "What, everyone out?
        Why, everyone's in!"

Elizabeth Fleming

The Little Dancers

A London Vision

Lonely, save for a few faint stars, the sky
Dreams; and lonely, below, the little street
Into its gloom retires, secluded and shy.
Scarcely the dumb roar enters this soft retreat;
And all is dark, save where come flooding rays
From a tavern window: there to the brisk measure
Of an organ that down in an alley merrily plays,
Two children, all alone and no one by,
Holding their tatter'd frocks, through an airy maze
Of motion, lightly threaded with nimble feet,
Dance sedately; face to face they gaze,
Their eyes shining, grave with a perfect pleasure.

Laurence Binyon

Vacation Time

Good-bye, little desk at school, good-bye,
We're off to the fields and the open sky.
The bells of the brooks and the woodland bells
Are ringing us out to the vales and dells,
To meadow-ways fair, and to hilltops cool,
Good-bye, little desk at school.

Good-bye, little desk at school, good-bye,
We've other brave lessons and tasks to try;
But we shall come back in the fall, you know,
And as gay to come as we are to go,
With ever a laugh and never a sigh—
Good-bye, little desk, good-bye!

Frank Hutt

Chimney-Tops

Ah! the morning is grey;
And what kind of day
Is it likely to be?
You must look up and see
What the chimney-tops say.

If the smoke from the mouth
Of the chimney goes south,
'Tis the north wind that blows
From the country of snows;
Look out for rough weather.
The cold and the north wind
Are always together.

If the smoke pouring forth
From the chimney goes north,
A mild day it will be,
A warm time we shall see;
The south wind is blowing
From lands where the orange
And fig trees are growing.

Every Day

There are so many things to do to-day
  In city, field and street,
And people are going everywhere,
  With quickly hurrying feet.

Some are ploughing and sowing the seed,
  And some are reaping the grain;
And some, who worked the whole night through,
  Are coming home again.

Over the hills the shepherd goes,
  While in the busy town
People and carts and motor cars
  Are running up and down;

And everywhere they come and go
  In sun and rain and sleet,
That we may have warm clothes to wear,
  And food enough to eat.

Mary Osborn

The Speed Track

The Hour-hand and the Minute-hand upon a polished dial
A meeting planned at twelve o'clock to walk and talk awhile.
The Hour-hand with the Minute-hand could never keep
  apace.
"The speed at which you move," he said, "is really a dis-
  grace!"

Then laughed the Minute-hand and sang, "The way that I
  must go
Is marked with milestones all along, and there are twelve,
  you know.
And I must call at each of these before my journey's done,
While you are creeping like a snail from twelve o'clock to
  one.
So now, farewell! But we shall meet again, good sir,"
  said he,
"The road that we are following is circular, you see!"

"Peter"

429

Old Mrs. Jarvis

Old Mrs. Jarvis, she sits on a cart,
Her pony is quicker to stop than to start,
But always she ambles on fine easy rambles
From village to village, to fair and to mart.

The pony is fat and a-glitter with brass,
The cart it is green as the greenest of grass,
And rabbit skins dangle and old bottles jangle,
And she sits in the midst, and she bows as you pass.

Her eyes are like blackberries shining with dew,
She wears a red kerchief and a jacket of blue;
And a hat with a feather, a-nodding together,
A-nodding, a-nodding, a-nodding at you!

How splendid to sit up so lofty and lone,
To go any whither, a leaf that is blown;
To wander and wander up here and down yonder,
With a pony and trap and a trade all your own!

Elizabeth Fleming

Time, You Old Gipsy Man

Time, you old gipsy man,
    Will you not stay,
Put up your caravan,
    Just for one day?

All things I'll give you
    Will you be my guest;
Bells for your jennet
    Of silver the best.
Goldsmiths shall beat you
    A great golden ring,
Peacocks shall bow to you,
    Little boys sing,
Oh, and sweet girls will
    Festoon you with may;
Time, you old gipsy,
    Why hasten away?

Last week in Babylon,
    Last night in Rome,
Morning, and in the crush
    Under Paul's dome;
Under Paul's dial
    You tighten your rein—
Only a moment,
    And off once again;
Off to some city
    Now blind in the womb,
Off to another
    Ere that's in the tomb.

Time, you old gipsy man,
    Will you not stay,
Put up your caravan,
    Just for one day?

                              Ralph Hodgson

The Patchwork Quilt

She mixes blue and mauve and green,
    Purple and orange, white and red,
And all the colours in between
    To patch a cover for her bed.

Oblong, triangle, star and square,
    Oval, and round, she makes them fit
Into a wondrous medley there,
    Colour by colour, bit by bit.

Over her knee it swiftly flows,
    And round her feet, a bright cascade,
While at her touch it grows and grows,
    Until at last the quilt is made.

And then across the bed it lies,
    A thing of gorgeous crazy bloom,
As if a rainbow from the skies
    Had shattered in her little room.

                              Elizabeth Fleming

Open Sesame

Oh, for a book and a shady nook
    Either in-a-door or out,
With the green leaves whispering overhead
    Or the street cry all about,
Where I may read all at my ease,
    Both of the new and old;
For a jolly good book whereon to look
    Is better to me than gold.

The Cobbler

Wandering up and down one day,
    I peeped into a window over the way;
And putting his needle through and through,
There sat a cobbler making a shoe:
For the world he cares never the whisk of a broom—
All he wants is elbow-room.
    Rap-a-tap-tap, tick-a-tack-too,
    That is the way he makes a shoe!

Over laths of wood his bits of leather
He stretches and fits, then sews together;
He puts his wax ends through and through;
And still as he stitches, his body goes too:
For the world he cares never the whisk of a broom—
All he wants is elbow-room.
    Rap-a-tap-tap, tick-a-tack-too,
    This is the way he makes a shoe!

With his little sharp awl he makes a hole
Right through the upper and through the sole;
He puts in one peg, and he puts in two,
And chuckles and laughs as he hammers them through:
For the world he cares never the whisk of a broom—
All he wants is elbow-room.
    Rap-a-tap-tap, tick-a-tack-too,
    This is the way to make a shoe!

Pack, Clouds, Away

Pack, clouds, away! and welcome, day!
  With night we banish sorrow:
Sweet air, blow soft! mount, lark, aloft!
  To give my Love good-morrow;
Wings from the wind, to please her mind,
  Notes from the lark I'll borrow.
Bird, prune thy wing! nightingale, sing!
  To give my Love good-morrow.
  To give my Love good-morrow,
  Notes from them I'll borrow.

Wake from thy nest, robin redbreast!
  Sing, birds, in every furrow!
And from each hill let music shrill
  Give my fair Love good-morrow.
Blackbird and thrush, in every bush—
  Stare, linnet, and cock-sparrow,
You pretty-elves—amongst yourselves
  Sing my fair Love good-morrow!
  To give my Love good-morrow,
  Sing, birds, in every furrow.

Thomas Heywood

The Kite

I wonder what my kite can see,
So high above the world and me;
And if the birds are friends to him,
As I am friends with Jack and Jim,
And are the clouds just really rain,
That melts and pours all down again?
O! he must know a thousand things,
As much as schoolmasters, and kings;
But will he breathe a word to me?
No, he's as quiet as quiet can be.

Pearl Forbes MacEwen

433

Ragged Robin

Rags and tatters,
   Tatters and rags,
A split in my coat
   And a patch on my bags—
My vest is torn
   And outside in.
Can anyone lend me
   A safety pin?

Rags and tatters,
   Darns and tears,
I'm all to pieces
   And nobody cares—
My hat blew away
   In yesterday's wind,
My braces are broken,
   No shoe can I find.

Rags and tatters,
   Tatters and rags,
Bootlaces, buttonhooks,
   Tapes, and tags
Might keep me together
   For one more day—
If they can't be found,
   You must throw me away.

Elizabeth Godley

The Unknown Wind

When the day darkens,
When dusk grows light,
When the dew is falling
   When silence dreams.
I hear a wind
Calling, calling
By day and by night.

What is the wind
That I hear calling
By day and by night,
    The crying of wind?
When the day darkens,
When dusk grows light,
When the dew is falling.

Fiona Macleod

The Wind

Why does the wind so want to be
Here in my little room with me?
He's all the world to blow about,
But just because I keep him out
He cannot be a moment still,
But frets upon my window sill,
And sometimes brings a noisy rain
To help him batter at the pane.

Upon my door he comes to knock.
He rattles, rattles at the lock
And lifts the latch and stirs the key—
Then waits a moment breathlessly,
And soon, more fiercely than before,
He shakes my little trembling door,
And though "Come in, come in!" I say,
He neither comes nor goes away.

Barefoot across the chilly floor
I run and open wide the door;
He rushes in, and back again
He goes to batter door and pane,
Pleased to have blown my candle out.
He's all the world to blow about,
Why does he want so much to be
Here in my little room with me?

Elizabeth Rendall

Travelling

I like to ride in a tramcar
  On a fine and sunny day,
And hear it going clang! clang!
  When someone's in the way.

I like to ride in a railway train
  Through tunnels dark and wide,
Over the bridges crossing the river,
  I feel so safe inside.

Motor cars are jolly too,
  They go so very fast,
Whitewashed houses and fields of cows
  And sheep go flying past.

But an aeroplane is best of all,
  It climbs so very high
That people look like tiny dots,
  And clouds go sailing by.

Dorothy Gradon

From the Train

In England from the train you see
  Green fields and peaceful cows and sheep,
And lazy farmsteads racing by
  In smoke-blue valleys quiet with sleep;

And primroses and meadow sweet,
  And daisies white about the way;
And you can trace the paths that wind
  To where the trees are snowed with may.

In India from the stifling train
  You see great rocky hills go by;
Brown miles of parched, unhappy grass,
  And hot blue tracts of cloudless sky.

And slow, indifferent bullocks, too,
  Well laden on the dusty roads—
And then a station where you stop,
  With brightly-coloured chattering crowds.

And rows and rows of tiny huts,
  And young green rice, or sugar-cane,
And little dark-skinned boys and girls
  Who wonder at the rumbling train.

And many scorching miles you go,
  And sometimes weary days you spend
Gazing across that burning land
  And dreaming of your journey's end.

Marjorie Wilson

Moonlit Apples

At the top of the house the apples are laid in rows,
And the skylight lets the moonlight in, and those
Apples are deep-sea apples of green. There goes
  A cloud on the moon in the autumn night.

A mouse in the wainscot scratches, and scratches, and then
There is no sound at the top of the house of men
Or mice; and the cloud is blown, and the moon again
  Dapples the apples with deep-sea light.

They are lying in rows there, under the gloomy beams;
On the sagging floor; they gather the silver streams
Out of the moon, those moonlit apples of dreams,
  And quiet is the steep stair under.

In the corridors under there is nothing but sleep.
And stiller than ever on orchard boughs they keep
Tryst with the moon, and deep is the silence, deep
  On moon-washed apples of wonder.

John Drinkwater

437

The Night Will Never Stay

The night will never stay,
The night will still go by,
Though with a million stars
You pin it to the sky,
Though you bind it with the blowing wind
And buckle it with the moon,
The night will slip away
Like sorrow or a tune.

Eleanor Farjeon

Little Rain-Drops

Oh, where do you come from,
You little drops of rain,
Pitter, patter, pitter, patter,
Down the window pane?

They won't let me walk,
And they won't let me play,
And they won't let me go
Out of doors at all to-day.

They put away my playthings
Because I broke them all,
And then they locked up all my bricks,
And took away my ball.

Tell me, little rain-drops,
Is that the way you play,
Pitter, patter, pitter, patter,
All the rainy day?

They say I'm very naughty,
But I've nothing else to do
But sit here at the window:
I should like to play with you.

But "Pitter, patter, pat,"
The little rain-drops cannot speak,
But "Pitter, patter, pat,"
Means "We can play on *this* side,
Why can't you play on *that*?"

Ann Hawkshawe

Good Night and Good Morning

A fair little girl sat under a tree,
Sewing as long as her eyes could see;
Then smoothed her work, and folded it right,
And said, 'Dear work, Good Night! Good Night!"

Such a number of rooks came over her head,
Crying, "Caw! caw!" on their way to bed;
She said, as she watched their curious flight,
"Little black things, Good Night! Good Night!"

The horses neighed, and the oxen lowed;
The sheep's "Bleat! bleat!" came over the road;
All seeming to say with a quiet delight,
"Good little girl, Good Night! Good Night!"

She did not say to the sun, "Good Night!"
Though she saw him there like a ball of light;
For she knew he had God's time to keep
All over the world, and never could sleep.

The tall pink fox-glove bowed his head—
The violets curtsied and went to bed;
And good little Lucy tied up her hair,
And said, on her knees, her favourite prayer.

And while on her pillow she softly lay
She knew nothing more till again it was day:
And all things said to the beautiful sun,
"Good Morning! Good Morning! our work is begun!"

Lord Houghton

From A Blessing for the Blessed

When the sun has left the hill-top,
  And the daisy-fringe is furled,
When the birds from wood and meadow
  In their hidden nests are curled,
Then I think of all the babies
  That are sleeping in the world.

There are babies in the high lands
  And babies in the low,
There are pale ones wrapped in furry-skins
  On the margin of the snow,
And brown ones naked in the isles
  Where all the spices grow.

L. Alma Tadema

A Sea Song from the Shore

Hail! Ho!
  Sail! Ho!
Ahoy! Ahoy! Ahoy
  Who calls to me
  So far at sea?
Only a little boy.

Sail! Ho!
  Hail! Ho!
The sailor he sails the sea:
  I wish he would capture
  A little sea-horse
And send him home to me.

I wish as he sails
Through the tropical gales,
He would catch me a sea bird, too,
  With its silver wings
  And the song it sings,
And its breast of down and dew!

I wish he would catch me
  A little mermaid,
Some island where he lands,
  With her dripping curls,
  And her crown of pearls,
And the looking-glass in her hands!

Hail! Ho!
  Sail! Ho!
Sail far o'er the fabulous main!
  And if I were a sailor
  I'd sail with you,
Though I never sailed back again.

James Whitcomb Riley

Four and Eight

The Foxglove by the cottage door
Looks down on Joe, and Joe is four.

The Foxglove by the garden gate
Looks down on Joan, and Joan is eight.

"I'm glad we're small," said Joan, "I love
To see inside the fox's glove,
Where taller people cannot see,
And all is ready for the bee;
The door is wide, the feast is spread,
The walls are dotted rosy red."
"And only little people know
How nice it looks in there," said Joe.
Said Joan, "The upper rooms are locked;
A bee went buzzing up—he knocked,
But no one let him in, so then
He bumbled gaily down again."
"Oh dear!" sighed Joe, "if only we
Could grow as little as that bee,
We too might room by room explore
The Foxglove by the cottage door."

The Foxglove by the garden gate
Looked down and smiled on Four and Eight.

ffrida Wolfe

The Witch

I saw her plucking cowslips,
  And marked her where she stood:
She never knew I watched her
  While hiding in the wood.

Her skirt was brightest crimson,
  And black her steeple hat,
Her broomstick lay beside her—
  I'm positive of that.

Her chin was sharp and pointed,
  Her eyes were—I don't know—
For, when she turned towards me—
  I thought it best—to go!

Percy H. Ilott

A Wish

Mine be a cot beside a hill;
A beehive's hum shall soothe my ear;
A willowy brook that turns a mill
With many a fall, shall linger near.

The swallow oft, beneath my thatch,
Shall twitter from her clay-built nest;
Oft shall the pilgrim lift the latch,
And share my meal, a welcome guest.

Around my ivied porch shall spring,
Each fragrant flower that drinks the dew;
And Lucy, at her wheel, shall sing
In russet gown and apron blue.

The village-church among the trees,
Where first our marriage vows were given,
With merry peals shall swell the breeze
And point with taper spire to Heaven.

Samuel Rogers

If I Had But Two Little Wings

If I had but two little wings
And were a little feathery bird,
    To you I'd fly, my dear!
But thoughts like these are idle things
    And I stay here.

But in my sleep to you I fly:
I'm always with you in my sleep!
    The world is all one's own.
But then one wakes, and where am I?
    All, all alone.

Sleep stays not, though a monarch bids:
So I love to wake ere break of day:
    For though my sleep be gone,
Yet while 'tis dark, one shuts one's lids,
    And still dreams on.

                        Samuel Taylor Coleridge

When all the World is Young

When all the world is young, lad,
    And all the trees are green;
And every goose a swan, lad,
    And every lass a queen;
Then hey for boot and horse, lad,
    And round the world away;
Young blood must have its course, lad,
    And every dog his day.

When all the world is old, lad,
    And all the trees are brown;
And all the sport is stale, lad,
    And all the wheels run down:
Creep home, and take your place there,
    The spent and maimed among:
God grant you find one face there
    You loved when all was young.

                        Charles Kingsley

The Piper

Piping down the valleys wild,
   Piping songs of pleasant glee,
On a cloud I saw a child,
   And he laughing said to me:

"Pipe a song about a Lamb!"
   So I piped with merry cheer.
"Piper, pipe that song again";
   So I piped: he wept to hear.

"Drop thy pipe, thy happy pipe;
   Sing thy songs of happy cheer":
So I sang the same again,
   While he wept with joy to hear.

"Piper, sit thee down and write
   In a book, that all may read."
So he vanish'd from my sight,
   And I pluck'd a hollow reed.

And I made a rural pen,
   And I stain'd the water clear,
And I wrote my happy songs
   Every child may joy to hear.

William Blake

A Feather for my Cap

Seagull flying from the sea,
Drop a feather here for me!
Drop it down into my lap—
I need a feather for my cap!

My satin gown's as white as milk,
My stockings are the finest silk,
My shoes are made of Spanish leather,
But oh! my cap! it lacks a feather!

My girdle is of precious gold,
A bouquet in my hands I hold
Of wild rose buds and lucky heather —
But oh! my cap! it lacks a feather!

What use a gown of satin fine?
What use a grand bouquet — like mine?
What use are shoes of Spanish leather
If caps, or hats, do lack a feather?

Ivy O. Eastwick

The Growing River

At first the river's very small,
And can't float anything at all;
But later, as it journeys on,
It's large enough to float a swan.

It grows till it can safely float
A slim canoe and then a boat;
And later still, as like as not,
It manages to float a yacht.

And presently, when really large,
It takes a steamer, then a barge.
And last it passes busy quays
And floats great ships to foreign seas.

Rodney Bennett

Happy Thought

The world is so full of a number of things,
I'm sure we should all be as happy as kings.

Robert Louis Stevenson

Water

Water has no taste at all,
  Water has no smell;
Water's in the waterfall,
  In pump, and tap, and well.

Water's everywhere about;
  Water's in the rain,
In the bath, the pond, and out
  At sea it's there again.

Water comes into my eyes
  And down my cheek in tears,
· When mother cries, "Go back and try
  To wash behind those ears."

                                    John R. Crossland

Goldenhair

Lean out of the window,
  Goldenhair,
I heard you singing
  A merry air.

My book is closed;
  I read no more,
Watching the fire dance
  On the floor.

I have left my book;
  I have left my room,
For I heard you singing
  Through the gloom.

Singing and singing
  A merry air,
Lean out of the window,
  Goldenhair.

                                    James Joyce

446

A Farewell, To C.E.G.

My fairest child, I have no song to sing thee;
No lark could pipe in skies so dull and grey;
Yet, if thou wilt, one lesson I will give thee
For every day.

Be good, sweet maid, and let who will be clever;
Do noble things, not dream them, all day long;
And so make Life, Death, and that vast For Ever
One grand, sweet song.

Charles Kingsley

Song

For Mercy, Courage, Kindness, Mirth
There is no measure upon earth.
Nay, they wither, root and stem,
If an end be set to them.

Overbrim and overflow
If your own heart you would know;
For the spirit born to bless
Lives but in its own excess.

Laurence Binyon

Fables and Stories—
Grave and Gay

Such wondrous tales as childhood loves to hear

The New Duckling

"I want to be new," said the duckling.
"O, ho!" said the wise old owl,
While the guinea-pig cluttered off chuckling
To tell all the rest of the fowl.

"I should like a more elegant figure,"
That child of a duck went on.
"I should like to grow bigger and bigger,
Until I could swallow a swan.

"I won't be the bond-slave of habit,
I won't have those webs on my toes,
I want to run round as a rabbit,
A rabbit as red as a rose.

"I don't want to waddle like mother,
Or quack like my silly old dad.
I want to be utterly other,
And frightfully modern and mad."

"Do you know," said the turkey, "you're quacking!
There's a fox creeping up thro' the rye:
And, if you're not utterly lacking,
You'll make for that duck-pond. Good-bye!"

But the duckling was perky as perky.
"Take care of your stuffing!" he called.
(This was horribly rude to a turkey!)
"But you aren't a real turkey," he bawled.

"You're an early Victorian sparrow!
A fox is more fun than a sheep!
I shall show that my mind is not narrow
And give him my feathers—to keep."

Now the curious end of this fable,
So far as the rest ascertained,
Though they searched from the barn to the stable,
Was that only his feathers remained.

So he wasn't the bond-slave of habit,
  And he didn't have webs on his toes;
And perhaps he runs round like a rabbit,
  A rabbit as red as a rose.

Alfred Noyes

The Pilgrim Fathers

The breaking waves dashed high
  On a stern and rock-bound coast,
And the woods against a stormy sky
  Their giant branches tossed;

And the heavy night hung dark
  The hills and waters o'er,
When a band of exiles moored their bark
  On the wild New England shore.

Not as the conqueror comes,
  They, the true-hearted, came;
Not with the roll of stirring drums,
  And the trumpet that sings of fame;

Not as the flying come,
  In silence and in fear;
They shook the depths of the desert gloom
  With their hymns of lofty cheer.

Amidst the storm they sang,
  And the stars heard and the sea;
And the sounding aisles of the dim woods rang
  To the anthem of the free!

The ocean eagle soared
  From his nest by the white wave's foam;
And the rocking pines of the forest roared—
  This was their welcome home!

451

There were men with hoary hair
   Amidst that pilgrim band;
Why had they come to wither there,
   Away from their childhood's land?

There was woman's fearless eye,
   Lit by her deep love's truth;
There was manhood's brow serenely high,
   And the fiery heart of youth.

What sought they thus afar?
   Bright jewels of the mine?
The wealth of seas, the spoils of war?
   They sought a faith's pure shrine!

Ay, call it holy ground,
   The soil where first they trod.
They have left unstained what there they found—
   Freedom to worship God.

Felicia Hemans

The Frog and the Bird

By a quiet little stream on an old mossy log,
Looking very forlorn, sat a little green frog;
He'd a sleek speckled back, and two bright yellow eyes,
And when dining, selected the choicest of flies.

The sun was so hot he scarce opened his eyes,
Far too lazy to stir, let alone watch for flies,
He was nodding, and nodding, and almost asleep,
When a voice in the branches chirped: "Froggie, cheep,
   cheep!"

"You'd better take care," piped the bird to the frog,
"In the water you'll be if you fall off that log.
Can't you see that the streamlet is up to the brim?"
Croaked the froggie: "What odds! You forget I can·swim!"

Then the froggie looked up at the bird perched so high
On a bough that to him seemed to reach to the sky;
So he croaked to the bird: "If you fall, you will die!"
Chirped the birdie: "What odds! You forget I can fly!"

Vera Hessey

Lord Ullin's Daughter

A Chieftain to the Highlands bound
   Cries "Boatman, do not tarry!
And I'll give thee a silver pound
   To row us o'er the ferry!

"Now who would be ye, would cross Lochgyle
   This dark and stormy water?"
"O I'm the chief of Ulva's isle,
   And this, Lord Ullin's daughter

"And fast before her father's men
   Three days we've fled together,
For should he find us in the glen,
   My blood would stain the heather.

"His horsemen hard behind us ride—
   Should they our steps discover,
Then who would cheer my bonny bride
   When they have slain her lover?"

Out spake the hardy Highland wight,
   "I'll go, my chief, I'm ready:
It is not for your silver bright,
   But for your winsome lady:—

"And by my word! the bonny bird
   In danger shall not tarry;
So though the waves are raging white
   I'll row you o'er the ferry."

By this the storm grew loud apace,
   The water-wraith was shrieking;
And in the scowl of heaven each face
   Grew dark as they were speaking.

But still as wilder blew the wind
   And as the night grew drearer,
Adown the glen rode armèd men,
   Their trampling sounded nearer.

"O haste thee, haste!" the lady cries,
  "Though tempests round us gather;
I'll meet the raging of the skies,
  But not an angry father."

The boat has left a stormy land,
  A stormy sea before her,—
When, oh! too strong for human hand
  The tempest gather'd o'er her.

And still they row'd amidst the roar
  Of waters still prevailing:
Lord Ullin reached that fatal shore,—
  His wrath was changed to wailing.

For, sore dismay'd, through storm and shade
  His child he did discover:—
One lovely hand she stretch'd for aid,
  And one was round her lover.

"Come back! come back!" he cried in grief,
  "Across this stormy water:
And I'll forgive your Highland chief,
  My daughter!—O my daughter!"

'Twas vain: the loud waves lash'd the shore,
  Return or aid preventing:
The waters wild went o'er his child,
  And he was left lamenting.

                                    Thomas Campbell

Sir Nicketty Nox

Sir Nicketty Nox was an ancient knight,
So old was he that he'd lost his sight.
Blind as a mole, and slim as a fox,
And dry as a stick was Sir Nicketty Nox.

His sword and buckler were old and cracked,
So was his charger and that's a fact.
Thin as a rake from head to hocks,
Was this rickety nag of Sir Nicketty Nox.

A wife he had and daughters three,
And all were as old, as old could be.
They mended the shirts and darned the socks
Of that old Antiquity, Nicketty Nox.

Sir Nicketty Nox would fly in a rage
If anyone tried to guess his age.
He'd mouth and mutter and tear his locks,
This very pernickety Nicketty Nox.

Hugh Chesterman

A Tragic Story

There lived a sage in days of yore,
And he a handsome pigtail wore:
But wondered much and sorrowed more
    Because it hung behind him.

He mused upon this curious case,
And swore he'd change the pigtail's place,
And have it hanging at his face,
    Not dangling there behind him.

Says he, "The mystery I've found—
I'll turn me round"—he turned him round;
    But still it hung behind him.

Then round, and round, and out and in,
All day the puzzled sage did spin;
In vain—it mattered not a pin—
    The pigtail hung behind him.

And right and left, and round about,
And up and down, and in and out,
He turned; but still the pigtail stout
    Hung steadily behind him.

And though his efforts never slack,
And though he twist, and twirl, and tack,
Alas! still faithful to his back,
    The pigtail hangs behind him.

W. M. Thackeray

From The Piped Piper of Hamelin

Into the street the Piper stept,
  Smiling first a little smile,
As if he knew what magic slept
  In his quiet pipe the while;
Then, like a musical adept,
To blow the pipe his lips he wrinkled,
And green and blue his sharp-eyes twinkled,
Lik a candle-flame where salt is sprinkled;
And ere three shrill notes the pipe uttered,
You heard as if an army muttered;
And the muttering grew to a grumbling;
And the grumbling grew to a mighty rumbling;
And out of the houses the rats came tumbling;
Great rats, small rats, lean rats, brawny rats,
Brown rats, black rats, grey rats, tawny rats,
Grave old plodders, gay young friskers,
  Fathers, mothers, uncles, cousins,
Cocking tails, and pricking whiskers,
  Families by tens and dozens;
Brothers, sisters, husbands, wives—
Followed the piper for their lives.
From street to street he piped, advancing,
And step for step they followed dancing.

Robert Browning

Lochinvar

O, young Lochinvar is come out of the west,
Through all the wide Border his steed was the best;
And save his good broadsword he weapons had none,
He rode all unarm'd, and he rode all alone.
So faithful in love, and so dauntless in war,
There never was knight like the young Lochinvar.

He staid not for brake, and he stopped not for stone,
He swam the Esk river where ford there was none;
But ere he alighted at Netherby gate,
The bride had consented, the gallant came late:
For a laggard in love, and a dastard in war,
Was to wed the fair Ellen of brave Lochinvar.

So boldly he enter'd the Netherby Hall,
Among bride's-men, and kinsmen and brothers, and all:
Then spoke the bride's father, his hand on his sword,
(For the craven bridegroom said never a word),
"O come ye in peace here, or come ye in war,
Or to dance at our bridal, young Lord Lochinvar?"

"I long woo'd your daughter, my suit you denied;—
Love swells like the Solway, but ebbs like its tide—
And now I am come, with this lost love of mine,
To lead but one measure, drink one cup of wine.
There are maidens in Scotland more lovely by far,
That would gladly be bride to young Lochinvar."

The bride kiss'd the goblet: the knight took it up,
He quaff'd of the wine, and he threw down the cup.
She look'd down to blush, and she look's up to sigh,
With a smile on her lips, and a tear in her eye.
He took the soft hand, ere her mother could bar,
"Now tread we a measure!" said young Lochinvar.

So stately his form, and so lovely her face,
That never a hall such a' galliard did grace;
While her mother did fret, and her father did fume,
And the bridegroom stood dangling his bonnet and plume,
And the bride-maidens whisper'd, " 'Twere better by far,
To have match'd our fair cousin with young Lochinvar."

One touch of her hand, and one word in her ear,
When they reached the hall-door and the charger stood near;
So light to the croupe the fair lady he swung,
So light to the saddle before her he sprung!
"She is won! we are gone, over bank, bush and scaur;
They'll have fleet steeds that follow," quoth young
    Lochinvar.

There was mounting 'mong Graemes of the Netherby clan;
Forsters, Fenwicks, and Musgraves, they rode and they ran:
There was racing, and chasing, on Cannobie Lee,
 But the lost bride of Netherby ne'er did they see.
 So daring in love, and so dauntless in war,
 Have ye e'er heard of gallant like young Lochinvar?

Walter Scott

Jack O' the Inkpot

I dance on your paper,
  I hide in your pen,
I make in your ink-stand
  My little black den;
And when you're not looking
  I hop on your nose,
And leave on your forehead
  The marks of my toes.

When you're trying to finish
  Your "i" with a dot,
I slip down your finger
  And make it a blot;
And when you're so busy
  To cross a bit "t,"
I make on the paper
  A little Black Sea.

I drink blotting-paper,
  Eat penwiper pie,
You never can catch me,
  You never need try!
I leap any distance,
  I use any ink,
I'm on to your fingers
  Before you can wink.

Algernon Blackwood

Stalky Jack

I knew a boy who took long walks,
Who lived on beans and ate the stalks;
To the Giant's Country he lost his way;
They kept him there for a year and a day,
But he has not been the same boy since;
An alteration he did evince;
For you may suppose that he underwent
A change in his notions of extent!

He looks with contempt on a nice high door,
And tries to walk in at the second floor;
He stares with surprise at a basin of soup,
He fancies a bowl as big as a hoop;
He calls the people minniken mites;
He calls a sirloin a couple of bites!
Things having come to these pretty passes,
They bought him some magnifying glasses.

He put on the goggles, and said, "My eyes!
The world has come to its proper size!"
But all the boys cry, "Stalky John!
There you go with your goggles on."
What girl would marry him—and *quite* right—
To be taken for three times her proper height?
So this comes of taking extravagant walks,
And living on beans and eating the stalks.

W. B. Rands

The Wonderful Derby Ram

As I was going to Derby, all on a market day,
I met the finest ram, sir, that ever was fed upon hay,
    Upon hay, upon hay, upon hay;
I met the finest ram, sir, that ever was fed upon hay.

This ram was fat behind, sir, this ram was fat before,
This ram was ten yards round, sir, indeed he was no more,
    No more, no more, no more;
This ram was ten yards round, sir, indeed he was no more.

The horns that grew on his head, sir, they were so wondrous
    high,
As I've been plainly told, sir, they reached up to the sky,
    The sky, the sky, the sky;
As I've been plainly told, sir, they reached up to the sky.

The tail that grew from his back, sir, was six yards and an ell,
And it was sent to Derby to toll the market bell,
    The bell, the bell, the bell,
And it was sent to Derby to toll the market bell.

From A Song About Myself

There was a naughty boy,
A naughty boy was he,
He would not stop at home,
He could not quiet be—
He took
In his knapsack
A Book
Full of vowels,
And a shirt
With some towels—
A slight cap
For night cap—
A hair brush,
Comb ditto,
New stockings,
For old ones
Would split O!
This knapsack
Tight at 'a back
He riveted close
And followed his nose
To the North,
To the North,
And followed his nose
To the North.

There was a naughty boy,
And a naughty boy was he,
For nothing would he do
But scribble poetry—
He took
An inkstand
In his hand
And a Pen
Big as ten
In the other,
And away
In a pother
He ran
To the mountains
And fountains

And ghostes
And witches
And ditches
And wrote
In his coat
When the weather
Was cool
Fearing gout,
And without
When the weather
Was warm—
O the charm
When we choose
To follow one's nose
To the North,
To the North,
To follow one's nose
To the North!

These delightful nonsense verses were written by John Keats to amuse his little sister. Playing with words is a game which amuses many children and some may like to write their own nonsense verses after hearing these.

Just Like a Man

He sat at the dinner table
  With a discontented frown,
The potatoes and steak were underdone
  And the bread was baked too brown;
The pie was too sour and the pudding too sweet,
  And the roast was much too fat;
The soup so greasy, too, and salt,
  'Twas hardly fit for the cat.

"I wish you could eat the bread and pie
  I've seen my mother make,
They are something like, and 'twould do you good
  Just to look at a loaf of her cake."
Said the smiling wife, "I'll improve with age—
  Just now I'm but a beginner;
But your mother has come to visit us,
  And to-day she cooked the dinner."

461

Yussouf

A stranger came one night to Yussouf's tent,
Saying—"Behold one outcast and in dread,
Against whose life the bow of Power is bent,
Who flies, and hath not where to lay his head.
I come to thee for shelter and for food:
To Yussouf, call'd through all our tribes the Good."

"This tent is mine," said Yussouf—"but no more
Than it is God's: come in and be at peace;
Freely shalt thou partake of all my store,
As I of His who buildeth over these
Our tents his glorious roof of night and day,
And at whose door none ever yet heard Nay."

So Yussouf entertain'd his guest that night;
And waking him ere day, said—"Here is gold;
My swiftest horse is saddled for thy flight,—
Depart before the prying day grow bold!"
As one lamp lights another, nor grows less,
So nobleness enkindleth nobleness.

That inward light the stranger's face made grand
Which shines from all self-conquest; kneeling low,
He bow'd his forehead upon Yussouf's hand,
Sobbing—"O Sheikh! I cannot leave thee so.—
I will repay thee,—all this thou has done
Unto that Ibrahim who slew thy son!"

"Take thrice the gold!" said Yussouf,—"for with thee
Into the desert, never to return,
My one black thought shall ride away from me.
First-born, for whom by day and night I yearn,
Balanced and just are all of God's decrees;
Thou art avenged, my First-born! sleep in peace!"

J. R. Lowell

The Owl and the Pussy-Cat

The Owl and the Pussy-Cat went to sea
    In a beautiful pea-green boat.
They took some honey, and plenty of money,
    Wrapped up in a five-pound note.

The Owl looked up to the stars above,
  And sang to a small guitar,
"O lovely Pussy! O Pussy, my love,
  What a beautiful Pussy you are,
     You are!
  What a beautiful Pussy you are!"

Pussy said to the Owl, "You elegant fowl!
  How charmingly sweet you sing!
O let us be married! too long we have tarried:
  But what shall we do for a ring?"
They sailed away for a year and a day,
  To the land where the Bong-tree grows,
And there in a wood a Piggy-wig stood,
  With a ring at the end of his nose,
     His nose,
  With a ring at the end of his nose.

"Dear Pig, are you willing to sell for one shilling
  Your ring?" Said the Piggy, "I will."
So they took it away, and were married next day
  By the Turkey who lives on the hill.
They dined on mince, and slices of quince,
  Which they ate with a runcible spoon;
And hand in hand, on the edge of the sand,
  They danced by the light of the moon.

Edward Lear

The Lobster Quadrille

"Will you walk a little faster?" said a whiting to a snail,
"There's a porpoise close behind us, and he's treading on my
  tail.
See how eagerly the lobsters and the turtles all advance!
They are waiting on the shingle—will you come and join the
  dance?
  Will you, won't you, will you, won't you, will you join the
    dance?
  Will you, won't you, will you, won't you, won't you join
    the dance?

"You can really have no notion how delightful it will be,
When they take us up and throw us, with the lobsters, out to
    sea!"
But the snail replied, "Too far, too far!" and gave a look
    askance,
Said he thanked the whiting kindly, but he would not join the
    dance,
    Would not, could not, would not, could not, would not
    join the dance,
    Would not, could not, would not, could not, could not
    join the dance.

"What matters it how far we go?" his scaly friend replied.
"There is another shore, you know, upon the other side.
The further off from England the nearer is to France—
Then turn not pale, beloved snail, but come and join the
    dance?
Will you, won't you, will you, won't you, will you join the
    dance?
Will you, won't you, will you, won't you, won't you join
    the dance?"

Lewis Carroll

What Became of Them?

He was a rat, and she was a rat,
    And down in one hole they did dwell,
And both were as black as a witch's cat,
    And they loved one another well.

He had a tail, and she had a tail,
    Both long and curling and fine;
And each said, "Yours is the finest tail
    In the world, excepting mine."

He smelt the cheese, and she smelt the cheese,
    And they both pronounced it good;
And both remarked it would greatly add
    To the charms of their daily food.

So he ventured out, and she ventured out,
    And I saw them go with pain;
For what befell them I never can tell,
    For they never came back again.

Godfrey Gordon Gustavus Gore

Godfrey Gordon Gustavus Gore—
No doubt you have heard that name before—
Was a boy who never would shut a door!

The wind might whistle, the wind might roar,
And teeth be aching and throats be sore,
But still he never would shut the door.

His father would beg, his mother implore,
"Godfrey Gordon Gustavus Gore,
We really do wish you would shut the door!"

Their hands they wrung, their hair they tore;
But Godfrey Gordon Gustavus Gore
Was as deaf as the buoy out at the Nore.

When he walked forth the folks would roar,
"Godfrey Gordon Gustavus Gore,
Why don't you think to shut the door?"

They rigged out a shutter with sail and oar,
And threatened to pack off Gustavus Gore
On a voyage of penance to Singapore.

But he begged for mercy, and said, "No more!
Pray do not send me to Singapore
On a shutter, and then I will shut the door!"

The Wraggle Taggle Gipsies

There were three gipsies a-come to my door,
  And down-stairs ran this lady, O!
One sang high, and another sang low,
  And the other sang, Bonny, bonny, Biscay, O!

Then she pulled off her silk finished gown
  And put on hose of leather, O!
The ragged, ragged rags about our door—
  She's gone with the wraggle taggle gipsies, O!

It was late last night, when my lord came home,
Enquiring for his a-lady, O!
The servants said on every hand:
"She's gone with the wraggle taggle gipsies, O!"

"O saddle to me my milk-white steed,
Go and fetch me my pony, O!
That I may ride and seek my bride,
Who is gone with the wraggle taggle gipsies, O!"

O he rode high and he rode low,
He rode through woods and copses too,
Until he came to an open field,
And there he espied his a-lady, O!

"What makes you leave your house and land?
What makes you leave your money, O?
What makes you leave your new-wedded lord;
To go with the wraggle taggle gipsies, O?"

"What care I for my house and my land?
What care I for my money, O?
What care I for my new-wedded lord?
I'm off with the wraggle taggle gipsies, O!"

"Last night you slept on a goose-feather bed,
With the sheet turned down so bravely, O!
And to-night you'll sleep in a cold open field,
Along with the wraggle taggle gipsies, O!"

"What care I for a goose-feather bed,
With the sheet turned down so bravely, O!
For to-night I shall sleep in a cold open field,
Along with the wraggle taggle gipsies, O!"

The Three Little Pigs

A jolly old sow once lived in a sty,
And three little piggies had she;
And she waddled about saying, "Umph! umph! umph!"
While the little ones said, "Wee! wee!"

"My dear little brothers," said one of the brats,
  "My dear little piggies," said he,
"Let us all for the future say, 'Umph! umph! umph!'
  'Tis so childish to say, 'Wee! wee!' "

Then these three little pigs grew skinny and lean,
  And lean they might very well be;
For somehow they couldn't say, "Umph! umph! umph!"
  And they wouldn't say, "Wee! wee! wee!"

So after a time these little pigs died,
  They all died of felo-de-se,
From trying too hard to say, "Umph! umph! umph!"
  When they only could say, "Wee! wee!"

MORAL:

A moral there is to this little song,
  A moral that's easy to see;
Don't try while yet young to say, "Umph! umph! umph!"
  For you only can say, "Wee! wee!"

                              Sir Alfred A. Scott-Gatty

Betty at the Party

        "When I was at the party,"
          Said Betty, aged just four,
        "A little girl fell off her chair
          Right down upon the floor;
        And all the other little girls
          Began to laugh, but me —
        I didn't laugh a single bit,"
          Said Betty seriously.

        "Why not?" her mother asked her,
          Full of delight to find
        That Betty—bless her little heart!—
          Had been so sweetly kind.
        "Why didn't you laugh, my darling?
          Or don't you like to tell?"
        "I didn't laugh," said Betty,
          " 'Cause it was me that fell."

467

Sons of the King

A little Prince of long ago
  The day that he was six
Put away his birthday toys,
  His soldiers, trains and bricks.

And stealing down the golden stair,
  His slippers in his hand,
He from the shady courtyard stepped
  Into a sunlit land.

And sitting there beside the wall
  He buttoned up his shoes
And wondered—looking up and down
  Which highway should he choose.

When by there rode a gipsy boy,
  His pony dark as he,
Who smiled upon the little Prince
  So golden-fair to see.

"Where are you riding, gipsy boy,
  This lovely summer day?"
"Over the hills and through the woods
  To the land of Far-Away."

"Who is your father, gipsy boy?
  For mine, you know, is king,
And I shall be like him one day
  And wear his crown and ring."

"My father," said the gipsy boy,
  "He also is a king.
Although he sits upon no throne
  And wears no crown or ring.

"He's king of all the gipsy-folk
  Twixt here and Far-Away,
And I, who am his eldest son,
  Shall be a king some day."

"May I go with you, gipsy boy,
    To ride your little horse,
To see your tents and caravans
    Between the golden gorse?

"There I could run without my shoes
    And climb your forest trees,
I seem to smell your smoky fires
    Of crackling twigs and leaves."

Within the Palace voices call,
    The gates are opened wide,
The kindly watchmen see the Prince
    And beckon him inside.

The gipsy smiles and shakes his head,
    He jerks the pony's rein;
"When you and I are kings," he says,
    "Then we shall meet again."

Joan Agnew

Mr. Nobody

I know a funny little man,
    As quiet as a mouse,
Who does the mischief that is done
    In everybody's house!
There's no one ever sees his face,
    And yet we all agree
That every plate we break was cracked
    By Mr. Nobody.

'Tis he who always tears our books,
    Who leaves the door ajar,
He pulls the buttons from our shirts,
    And scatters pins afar;
That squeaking door will always squeak,
    For, prithee, don't you see,
We leave the oiling to be done
    By Mr. Nobody.

469

He puts damp wood upon the fire,
    That kettles cannot boil;
His are the feet that bring in the mud,
    And all the carpets soil.
The papers always are mislaid,
    Who had them last but he?
There's not one tosses them about
    But Mr. Nobody.

The finger-marks upon the door
    By none of us are made;
We never leave the blinds unclosed,
    To let the curtains fade;
The ink we never spill; the boots
    That lying round you see
Are not our boots; they all belong
    To Mr. Nobody.

The Pirates' Tea-party

We'd ever so many kinds of cake
    And at least three sorts of jam.
Doughnuts and cucumber sandwiches,
    Some made with chicken and ham,
Scones and parkin and honey had we
The day that the pirates came to tea.

The oldest, he had twinkly eyes,
    A deep sword-slash on his cheek,
A stubbly beard that was nearly red,
    He hadn't washed for a week.
He showed me his cutlass sharp and bright,
He slept with it 'tween his teeth at night.

The second, he was thin and fair,
    He blushed when they yelled at him;
Tho' young he had killed a dozen Turks,
    They called him "Terrible Tim."
He wore a handkerchief round his head,
Purple and yellow with spots of red.

The third of the crew was extra tall,
   He knew many foreign parts,
He knew some wonderful swearing words,
   He understood all the charts,
But he only whispered one—when he found
His toast with the buttery side on the ground.

The fourth was merely a boy from a school,
   And altho' he wore a belt,
A pistol in it and high sea-boots,
   And a frightful hat of felt,
He is just pretending that he is one
With his "Yo, ho, ho," and "Son of a gun!"

If he is a pirate, I'm one too;
   Says he, "Then be one quick;
Remember whatever the weather's like
   A pirate's never sea-sick."
When the pirates came I wished that we
Had not asked that hateful boy to tea.

                              Dorothy Una Ratcliffe

When Polly Buys a Hat

When Father goes to town with me to buy my Sunday hat,
We can't afford to waste much time in doing things like
      that;
We walk into the nearest shop, and Father tells them then,
"Just bring a hat you think will fit a little girl of ten!"

It may be plain, it may be fine with lace and flowers too;
If it just "feels right" on my head we think that it will do;
It may be red or brown or blue, with ribbons light or dark;
We put it on—and take the car that goes to Central Park.

When Mother buys a hat for me, we choose the shape
      with care;
We ask if it's the best they have, and if they're sure 'twill
      wear;
And when the trimming's rather fine, why, Mother shakes
      her head
And says, "Please take the feathers off—we'd like a bow
instead!"

But oh, when Sister buys my hats, you really do not know
The hurry and the worry that we have to undergo!
How many times I've heard her say—and shivered where I
  sat—
"I think I'll go to town to-day, and buy that child a hat!"

They bring great hats with curving brims, but I'm too tall
  for those;
And hats that have no brim at all, which do not suit my
  nose;
I walk about, and turn around, and struggle not to frown:
I wish I had long curly hair like Angelina Brown.

Till when at last the daylight goes, and I'm so tired then,
I hope I'll never, never need another hat again,
And when I've quite made up my mind that shopping is
  the worst
Of all my tasks—then Sister buys the hat that we saw first

And so we take it home with us as quickly as we may,
And Sister lifts it from the box and wonders what they'll
  say;
And I—I peep into the glass, and (promise not to tell!)
I smile, because I really think it suits me very well.

Then slip into the library as quiet as can be,
And this is what my Brother says when first he looks at
  me:
"Upon—my—word! I never saw a queerer sight than that!
Don't tell me this outrageous thing is Polly's Sunday hat!"

E. Hill

Tired Tim

Poor tired Tim! It's sad for him.
He lags the long bright morning through,
Ever so tired of nothing to do;
He moons and mopes the livelong day,
Nothing to think about, nothing to say
Up to bed with his candle to creep,
Too tired to yawn; too tired to sleep;
Poor tired Tim! It's sad for him.

Walter de la Mare.

The Jovial Beggar

There was a jovial beggar,
  He had a wooden leg,
Lame from his cradle,
  And forced for to beg.
And a-begging we will go, will go, will go
And a-begging we will go!

A bag for his oatmeal,
  Another for his salt,
And a pair of crutches,
  To show that he can halt.
And a-begging we will go—

A bag for his wheat,
  Another for his rye,
A little bottle by his side,
  To drink when he's a-dry,
And a-begging we will go—

"Seven years I begged
  For my old Master Wild,
He taught me to beg
  When I was but a child,
And a-begging we will go—

"I begged for my master
  And got him store of pelf;
But, now, Jove be praised!
  I'm begging for myself;
And a-begging we will go—

"In a hollow tree
  I live and pay no rent.
Providence provides for me,
  And I am well content;
And a-begging we will go—

"Of all the occupations
  A beggar's life is best,
For whenever he's a-weary
  He'll lay him down and rest;
And a-begging we will go—

"I fear no plots against me,
  I live in open cell;
Then who would be a king,
  When beggars live so well?
Then a-begging we will go, will go, will go,
  And a-begging we will go!"

The Priest and the Mulberry Tree

Did you hear of the curate who mounted his mare,
And merrily trotted along to the fair?
Of creature more tractable none ever heard:
In the height of her speed she would stop at a word;
But again with a word, when the curate said "Hey,"
She put forth her mettle and gallop'd away.

As near to the gates of the city he rode,
While the sun of September all brilliantly glow'd,
The good priest discover'd, with eyes of desire,
A mulberry tree in a hedge of wild brier;
On boughs long and lofty, in many a green shoot,
Hung, large, black, and glossy, the beautiful fruit.

The curate was hungry and thirsty to boot;
He shrank from the thorns, though he longed for the fruit;
With a word he arrested his courser's keen speed,
And he stood up erect on the back of his steed;
On the saddle he stood while the creature stood still,
And he gather'd the fruit till he took his good fill.

"Sure never," he thought, "was a creature so rare,
So docile, so true, as my excellent mare;
Lo, here now I stand," and he gazed all around,
"As safe and as steady as if on the ground;
Yet how had it been, if some traveller this way,
Had, dreaming no mischief, but chanced to cry 'Hey'?"

He stood with his head in the mulberry tree,
And he spoke out aloud in his fond revery;
At the sound of the word the good mare made a push,
And down went the priest in the wild-brier bush.
He remember'd too late, on his thorny green bed,
Much that well may be thought cannot wisely be said.

Thomas Love Peacock

Barbara Frietchie

Up from the meadows rich with corn,
Clear in the cool September morn,

The clustered spires of Frederick stand
Green-walled by the hills of Maryland.

Round about them orchards sweep,
Apple and peach tree fruited deep,

Fair as the garden of the Lord
To the eyes of the famished rebel horde,

On that pleasant morn of the early fall
When Lee marched over the mountain wall;

Over the mountains winding down,
Horse and foot, into Frederick town.

Forty flags with their silver stars,
Forty flags with their crimson bars,

Flapped in the morning wind: the sun
Of noon looked down, and saw not one.

Up rose old Barbara Frietchie then,
Bowed with her fourscore years and ten;

475

Bravest of all in Frederick town,
She took up the flag the men hauled down

In her attic window the staff she set,
To show one heart was loyal yet.

Up the street came the rebel tread,
Stonewall Jackson riding ahead.

Under his slouched hat left and right
He glanced; the old flag met his sight.

"Halt!"—the dust-brown ranks stood fast.
"Fire!"—out blazed the rifle-blast.

It shivered the window, pane and sash;
It rent the banner with seam and gash.

Quick, as it fell, from the broken staff
Dame Barbara snatched the silken scarf.

She leaned far out on the window-sill,
And shook it forth with a royal will.

"Shoot, if you must, this old grey head,
But spare your country's flag," she said.

A shade of sadness, a blush of shame,
Over the face of the leader came;

The nobler nature within him stirred
To life at that woman's deed and word;

"Who touches a hair of yon grey head
Dies like a dog. March on!" he said.

All day long through Frederick street
Sounded the tramp of marching feet:

All day long that free flag tost
Over the heads of the rebel host.

Ever its torn folds rose and fell
On the loyal winds that loved it well;

And through the hill-gaps sunset light
Shone over it with a warm good-night.

Barbara Frietchie's work is o'er,
And the rebel rides on his raids no more.

Honour to her, and let a tear
Fall, for her sake, on Stonewall's bier.

Over Barbara Frietchie's grave,
Flag of Freedom and Union, wave:

Peace and order and beauty draw
Round the symbol of light and law;

And ever the stars above look down
On thy stars below in Frederick town!

John Greenleaf Whittier

Mountain and the Squirrel

The Mountain and the Squirrel
Had a quarrel,
And the former call'd the latter "Little Prig";
Bun replied,
"You are doubtless very big,
But all sorts of things and weather
Must be taken in together
To make up a year
And a sphere.
And I think it no disgrace
To occupy my place.
If I'm not so large as you,
You are not so small as I,
And not half so spry;
I'll not deny you make
A very pretty squirrel-track;
Talents differ; all is well and wisely put;
If I cannot carry forests on my back,
Neither can you crack a nut."

R. W. Emerson

477

King John and the Abbot of Canterbury

An ancient story I'll tell you anon
Of a notable prince that was called King John;
And he ruled England with main and with might,
For he did great wrong, and maintained little right.

And I'll tell you a story, a story so merrie,
Concerning the Abbot of Canterbury;
How for his housekeeping and high renown,
They rode post for him to fair London town.

An hundred men, the king did hear say,
The abbot kept in his house every day;
And fifty gold chains without any doubt,
In velvet coats waited the abbot about.

"How now, father abbot, I hear it of thee,
Thou keepest a far better house than me;
And for thy housekeeping and high renown,
I fear thou work'st treason against my crown."

"My liege," quo' the abbot, "I would it were known
I never spend nothing, but what is my own;
And I trust your grace will do me no deere,
For spending of my own true-gotten gear."

"Yes, yes, father abbot, thy fault is high,
And now for the same thou needst must die;
For except thou canst answer me questions three,
Thy head shall be smitten from thy bodie.

"And first," quo' the king, "when I'm in this stead,
With my crown of gold so fair on my head,
Among all my liege-men so noble of birth,
Thou must tell me to one penny what I am worth.

"Secondlie, tell me, without any doubt,
How soon I may ride the whole world about;
And at the third question thou must not shrink,
But tell me here truly what I do think."

"Oh, these are hard questions for my shallow wit,
Nor I cannot answer your grace as yet:
But if you will give me but three weeks' space,
I'll do my endeavour to answer your grace."

"Now three weeks' space to thee will I give,
And that is the longest time thou hast to live;
For if thou dost not answer my questions three,
Thy lands and thy livings are forfeit to me."

Away rode the abbot all sad at that word,
And he rode to Cambridge and Oxenford,
But never a doctor there so wise,
That could with his learning an answer devise.

Then home rode the abbot of comfort so cold,
And he met his shepherd a-going to fold;
"How now, my lord abbot, you are welcome home;
What news do you bring us from good King John?"

"Sad news, sad news, shepherd, I must give,
That I have but three days more to live;
For if I do not answer him questions three,
My head will be smitten from my bodie.

"The first is to tell him there in that stead
With his crown of gold so fair on his head,
Among all his liege-men so noble of birth,
To within one penny of what he is worth.

"The second to tell him, without any doubt,
How soon he may ride the whole world about:
And at the third question I must not shrink,
But tell him there truly what he does think."

"Now cheer up, sir abbot, did you never hear yet,
That a fool he may learn a wise man wit?
Lend me your horse and serving men, and your apparel,
And I'll ride to London to answer your quarrel.

"Nay, frown not, if it hath been told unto me,
I am like your lordship as ever may be;
And if you will but lend me your gown,
There is none shall know us at fair London town."

"Now horses and serving men thou shalt have,
With sumptuous array most gallant and brave,
With crozier and mitre, and rochet and cope,
Fit to appear 'fore our father the pope."

"Now welcome, sir abbot," the king he did say,
" 'Tis well thou'rt come back to keep thy day;
For and if thou canst answer my questions three,
Thy life and thy living both savèd shall be.

"And first, when thou seest me here in this stead,
With my crown of gold so fair on my head,
Among my liege-men so noble of birth,
Tell me to one penny what I am worth."

"For thirty pence our Saviour was sold
Among the false Jews, as I have been told:
And twenty-nine is the worth of thee,
For I think thou art one penny worser than he!"

The king laughed, and swore by St. Bittel,
"I did not think I had been worth so little!—
Now secondly, tell me, without any doubt,
How soon I may ride this whole world about."

"You must rise with the sun, and ride with the same
Until the next morning he rises again;
And then your grace need not make any doubt
But in twenty-four hours you'll ride it about."

The king he laughed, and swore by St. John,
"I did not think it could be done so soon!
Now from the third question thou must not shrink,
But tell me here truly what I do think."

"Yes, that shall I do, and make your grace merrie;
You think I'm the abbot of Canterbury;
But I'm his poor shepherd, as plain you may see,
That am come to beg pardon for him and for me."

The king he laughed, and swore by the mass,
"I'll make you lord abbot this day in his place!"
"Now nay, my liege, be not in such speed,
For alack, I can neither write nor read."

"Four nobles a week then I will give thee,
For this merrie jest thou has shown to me;
And tell the old abbot when thou comest home,
Thou hast brought him a pardon from good King John."

Try Again

King Bruce of Scotland flung himself down
    In a lonely mood to think;
'Tis true he was monarch, and wore a crown,
    But his heart was beginning to sink.

For he had been trying to do a great deed,
    To make his people glad;
He had tried and tried, but couldn't succeed
    And so he became quite sad.

He flung himself down in low despair,
    As grieved as man could be;
And after a while he pondered there,
    "I'll give it all up," said he.

Now just at that moment a spider dropped,
    With its silken, filmy clue;
And the King, in the midst of his thinking, stopped
    To see what the spider would do.

'Twas a long way up to the ceiling dome,
    And it hung by a rope so fine;
That how it would get to its cobweb home,
    King Bruce could not divine.

It soon began to cling and crawl
    Straight up with strong endeavour;
But down it came with a slippery sprawl,
    As near to the ground as ever.

Up, up it ran, not a second to stay,
    To utter the least complaint;
Till it fell still lower, and there it lay,
    A little dizzy and faint.

Its head grew steady—again it went,
    And travelled a half-yard higher;
'Twas a delicate thread it had to tread,
    And a road where its feet would tire.

Again it fell and swung below,
    But again it quickly mounted;
Till up and down, now fast, now slow,
    Nine brave attempts were counted.

"Sure," cried the King, "that foolish thing
    Will strive no more to climb;
When it toils so hard to reach and cling,
    And tumbles every time."

But up the insect went once more,
    Ah me! 'tis an anxious minute;
He's only a foot from his cobweb door,
    Oh say, will he lose or win it?

Steadily, steadily, inch by inch,
    Higher and higher he got;
And a bold little run at the very last pinch
    Put him into his native cot.

"Bravo, bravo! the King cried out,
    "All honour to those who try;
The spider up there defied despair;
    He conquered, and why shouldn't I?"

And Bruce of Scotland braced his mind,
    And gossips tell the tale,
That he tried once more as he tried before,
    And that time did not fail.

From The Forsaken Merman

Children dear, was it yesterday
We heard the sweet bells over the bay?
In the caverns where we lay,
Through the surf and through the swell,
The far off sound of a silver bell?
Sand-strewn caverns, cool and deep,
Where the winds are all asleep;
Where the spent lights quiver and gleam,
Where the salt weed sways in the stream,
Where the sea-beasts, ranged all round,
Feed in the ooze of their pasture-ground;
Where the sea-snakes coil and twine,
Dry their mail and bask in the brine;
Where great whales come sailing by,
Sail and sail, with unshut eye,
Round the world for ever and aye?
When did music come this way?
Children dear, was it yesterday?

Children dear, was it yesterday
(Call yet once) that she went away?
Once she sate with you and me,
On a red gold throne in the heart of the sea,
And the youngest sate on her knee.

Children dear, was it yesterday?

Matthew Arnold
483

The Blind Men and the Elephant

It was six men of Hindostan,
　　To learning much inclined,
Who went to see the elephant,
　　(Though all of them were blind)
That each by observation
　　Might satisfy his mind.

The *first* approached the Elephant,
　　And happening to fall
Against his broad and sturdy side,
　　At once began to bawl:
"Bless me, it seems the Elephant
　　Is very like a wall."

The *second,* feeling of his tusk,
　　Cried, "Ho! what have we here
So very round and smooth and sharp?
　　To me 'tis mighty clear
This wonder of an Elephant
　　Is very like a spear."

The *third* approached the animal,
　　And happening to take
The squirming trunk within his hands,
　　Then boldly up and spake:
"I see," quoth he, "the Elephant
　　Is very like a snake."

The *fourth* stretched out his eager hand
　　And felt about the knee,
"What most this mighty beast is like
　　Is mighty plain; quoth he;
"'Tis clear enough the Elephant
　　Is very like a tree."

The *fifth* who chanced to touch the ear
   Said, "Even the blindest man
Can tell what this resembles most;
   Deny the fact who can,
This marvel of an Elephant
   Is very like a fan."

The *sixth* no sooner had begun
   About the beast to grope,
Than, seizing on the swinging tail
   That fell within his scope,
"I see," cried he, "the Elephant
   Is very like a rope."

And so these men of Hindostan
   Disputed loud and long,
Each in his own opinion
   Exceeding stiff and strong,
Though *each* was *partly* in the right
   And all were in the wrong.

John Godfrey Saxe

The Beggar Maid

Her arms across her breast she laid;
   She was more fair than words can say:
Bare-footed came the beggar maid
   Before the King Cophetua.
In robe and crown the king stept down,
   To meet and greet her on her way;
"It is no wonder," said the lords,
   "She is more beautiful than day."

As shines the moon in clouded skies,
   She in her poor attire was seen:
One praised her ankles, one her eyes,
   One her dark hair and lovesome mien.
So sweet a face, such angel grace,
   In all that land had never been:
Cophetua sware a royal oath:
   "This beggar maid shall be my queen!"

Lord Tennyson

The Tale of a Dog and a Bee

Great big dog,
Head upon his toes;
Tiny little bee
Settles on his noes.

Great big dog
Thinks it is a fly.
Never says a word,
Winks very sly.

Tiny little bee,
Tickles dog's nose —
Thinks like as not
'Tis a pretty rose.

Dog smiles a smile,
Winks his other eye,
Chuckles to himself
How he'll catch a fly.

Then he makes a snap,
Very quick and spry,
Does his level best,
But doesn't catch the fly.

Tiny little bee,
Alive and looking well;
Great big dog,
Mostly gone to swell.

MORAL:

Dear friends and brothers all,
Don't be too fast and free,
And when you catch a fly,
Be sure it's not a bee.

From Goblin Market

Morning and evening
Maids heard the goblins cry:
"Come buy our orchard fruits,
Come buy, come buy:
Apples and quinces,
Lemons and oranges,
Plump unpecked cherries,
Melons and raspberries,
Bloom-down-cheeked peaches,
Swart-headed mulberries,
Wild free-born cranberries,
Crab-apples, dewberries,
Pine-apples, blackberries,
Apricots, strawberries; —
All ripe together
In summer weather —
Morns that pass by,
Fair eaves that fly;
Come buy, come buy:
Our grapes fresh from the vine,
Pomegranates full and fine,
Dates and sharp bullaces,
Rare peaches and greengages,
Damsons and bilberries,
Taste them and try:
Currants and gooseberries,
Bright fire-like barberries,
Figs to fill your mouth,
Citrons from the South,
Sweet to tongue and sound to eye;
Come buy, come buy."

Christina Rossetti

National and Love of Country

I vow to thee, my country—all earthly things above—
Entire and whole and perfect, the service of my love

The Gates to England

The great sea-roads to England
    Have many little gates—
You saw some once—those bustling ports,
    And winding ribbon straits;

And little foreign harbours
    Tucked safely in from blasts;
And lighted dockyards, swaying ships,
    And forests of straight masts.

And somewhere ever waiting
    A slim grey Man of War,
To keep the peace for England,
    Is never very far.

Marjorie Wilson

Home Thoughts from Abroad

Oh! to be in England
Now that April's there,
And whoever wakes in England
Sees, some morning, unaware,
That the lowest boughs and the brushwood sheaf
Round the elm-tree bole are in tiny leaf,
While the chaffinch sings on the orchard bough
In England—now!

And after April, when May follows,
And the whitethroat builds, and all the swallows—
Hark! where my blossomed pear-tree in the hedge
Leans to the field and scatters on the clover
Blossoms and dewdrops—at the bent spray's edge—
That's the wise thrush; he sings each song twice over,
Lest you should think he never could recapture
The first fine careless rapture!
And though the fields look rough with hoary dew
All will be gay when noon-tide wakes anew
The buttercups, the little children's dower—
Far brighter than this gaudy melon flower.

Robert Browning

490

This is England

And this is England! June's undarkened green
Gleams on far woods; and in the vales between
Gray hamlets, older than the trees that shade
Their ripening meadows, are in quiet laid,
Themselves a part of the warm, fruitful ground.
The little hills of England rise around;
The little streams that wander from them shine
And with their names remembered names entwine
Of old renown and honour, fields of blood
High causes fought on, stubborn hardihood
For freedom spent, and songs, our noblest pride
That in the heart of England never died,
And burning still make splendour of our tongue.

Laurence Binyon

O England, Country of my Heart's Desire

O England, country of my heart's desire,
Land of the hedgerow and the village spire,
Land of thatched cottages and murmuring bees,
And wayside inns where one may take one's ease.
Of village green where cricket may be played
And fat old spaniels sleeping in the shade —
O homeland, far away across the main,
How would I love to see your face again! —
Your daisied meadows and your grassy hills,
Your primrose banks, your parks, your tinkling rills,
Your copses where the purple bluebells grow
Your quiet lanes where lovers loiter so,
Your cottage-gardens with their wallflowers' scent,
Your swallows 'neath the eaves, your sweet content!
And 'mid the fleecy clouds that o'er you spread.
Listen, the skylark singing overhead —
    That's the old country, that's the old home!
    You never forget it wherever you roam.

E. V. Lucas

This Native Land

She is a rich and rare land;
O! she's a fresh and fair land;
She is a dear and rare land—
    This native land of mine.

No men than hers are braver,
Her women's hearts ne'er waver;
I'd freely die to save her
    And think my lot divine.

Thomas Davis

Jerusalem

And did those feet in ancient time
Walk upon England's mountains green?
And was the holy Lamb of God
On England's pleasant pastures seen?

And did the countenance divine
Shine forth upon our clouded hills?
And was Jerusalem builded here
Among these dark Satanic mills?

Bring me my bow of burning gold,
Bring me my arrows of desire,
Bring me my spear, O clouds, unfold!
Bring me my chariot of fire!

I will not cease from mental fight,
Nor shall my sword sleep in my hand,
Till we have built Jerusalem
In England's green and pleasant land.

William Blake

This England

This England never did, nor never shall,
Lie at the proud foot of a conqueror,
But when it first did help to wound itself.
Now these her princes are come home again,
Come the three corners of the world in arms,
And we shall shock them: Naught shall make us rue,
If England to itself do rest but true.

Shakespeare

Land of our Birth

Land of our Birth, we pledge to thee
Our love and toil in the years to be:
When we are grown and take our place,
As men and women with our race.

Father in Heaven who lovest all,
O help Thy children when they call;
That they may build from age to age
An undefilèd heritage.

Teach us to rule ourselves alway,
Controlled and cleanly night and day;
That we may bring, if need arise,
No maimed or worthless sacrifice.

Teach us the strength that cannot seek,
By deed or thought, to hurt the weak:
That, under Thee, we may possess
Man's Strength to comfort man's distress.

Teach us delight in simple things,
And Mirth that has no bitter springs;
Forgiveness free of evil done,
And Love to all men 'neath the sun!

Land of our Birth, our faith, our pride,
For whose dear sake our fathers died;
O Motherland, we pledge to thee
Head, heart and hand through the years to be.

Rudyard Kipling

The Best of All

I sometimes think I'd like to be
  A little Eskimo,
And drive a team of dogs before
  My sleigh upon the snow.

Or walk the streets of China, where
  Gay lanterns glow at night,
And have a pair of chopsticks and
  A pigtail and a kite.

Or if I lived in India
  A potter I would be,
And make a row of pots with clay
  For everyone to see.

And if I went to Africa
  Wild animals I'd track,
Or ride the desert mile on mile
  Upon the camel's back.

And Susan says, in blossom-time,
  She'd go to far Japan,
And wear a gay-hued kimono
  And always use a fan.

But all the same we're very sure,
  Although our island's small,
To be an English boy or girl
  Is much the best of all.

Margaret G. Rhodes

I Vow to thee, my Country

I vow to thee, my country—all earthly things above—
Entire and whole and perfect, the service of my love,
The love that asks no question: the love that stands the test,
That lays upon the altar the dearest and the best:
The love that never falters, the love that pays the price,
The love that makes undaunted the final sacrifice.

And there's another country, I've heard of long ago—
Most dear to them that love her, most great to them that
    know—
We may not count her armies; we may not see her King—
Her fortress is a faithful heart, her pride is suffering—
And soul by soul and silently her shining bounds increase,
And her ways are ways of gentleness and all her paths are
    Peace.

Sir Cecil Spring Rice

A Princely Ditty in Praise of the English Rose

Amongst the princely paragons,
Bedeckt with dainty diamonds,
Within mine eye, none doth come nigh
The sweet red rose of England.
    The lilies pass in bravery,
    In Flanders, Spain and Italy,
    And yet the famous flower of France
    Doth honour the Rose of England.

As I abroad was walking,
I heard the small birds talking;
And every one did frame her song
In praise of the Rose of England.
    The lilies, etc.

The bravest lute bring hither,
And let us sing together,
While I do ring, on every string,
The praise of the Rose of England.
    The lilies, etc.

Then fair and princely flower,
That over my heart doth tower,
None may be compared to thee,
Which art the fair Rose of England.
    The lilies, etc.

Thomas Deloney

The Toy Band

Dreary lay the long road, dreary lay the town,
    Lights out and never a glint o' moon:
Weary lay the stragglers, half a thousand down,
    Sad sighed the weary big Dragoon.
"Oh! if I'd a drum here to make them take the road again,
    Oh! if I'd a fife to wheedle—come, boys, come!
You that mean to fight it out, wake and take your load again,
    Fall in! Fall in! Follow the fife and drum!

"Hey, but here's a toy shop, here's a drum for me,
    Penny whistles too to play the tune!
Half a thousand dead men soon shall hear and see
    We're a band!" said the weary big Dragoon.
"Rubadub! Rubadub! Wake and take the road again,
    Wheedle-deedle-deedle-dee, come, boys, come!
You that mean to fight it out, wake and take your load again,
    Fall in! Fall in! Follow the fife and drum!"

Cheerly goes the dark road, cheerly goes the night,
    Cheerly goes the blood to keep the beat:
Half a thousand dead men marching on to fight
    With a little penny drum to lift their feet.
"Rubadub! Rubadub! Wake and take the road again,
    Wheedle-deedle-deedle-dee, come, boys, come!
You that mean to fight it out, wake and take your load again,
    Fall in! Fall in! Follow the fife and drum!"

As long as there's an Englishman to ask a tale of me,
    As long as I can tell the tale aright,
We'll not forget the penny whistle's wheedle-deedle-dee
    And the big Dragoon a-beating down the night,
"Rubadub! Rubadub! Wake and take the road again,
    Wheedle-deedle-deedle-dee, come, boys, come!
You that mean to fight it out, wake and take your load again,
    Fall in! Fall in! Follow the fife and drum!"

Henry Newbolt

The Union Jack

This little flag to us so dear,
　　The Union Jack of Fame,
Come, sit by me, and you shall hear
　　The way it got its name.

We first must look at other three,
　　Please hold them up quite tight,
They all have crosses, you can see,
　　Two red ones and one white.

St. Patrick's Cross, to Ireland dear,
　　Like letter X it lies;
St. George's Cross, so bright and clear,
　　Led England's battle cries.

St. Andrew's Cross is white, you see,
　　Upon a bed of blue,
The Scottish flag it used to be,
　　To it the folks were true.

In Course of time, the three combin'd,
　　It was a famous tack:
We'll do the same, and you will find,
　　Great Britain's Union Jack.

Jeannie Kirby

The Thames

The Thames will take us to London town,
"Of wonderful beauty and great renown."
The dew goes up and the rain comes down,
To carry us safely to London town.

We'll meet the ships from every sea,
With cocoa and cotton, with sugar and tea,
From fair lands and fertile, wherever they be,
All faring, all wearing, for you and for me.

M. M. Hutchinson

497

A Ship Sails up to Bideford

A ship sails up to Bideford;
  Upon a western breeze,
Mast by mast, sail over sail,
  She rises from the seas,
And sights the hills of Devon
  And the misty English trees.

She comes from Eastern islands
  The sun is on her hold;
She bears the fruit of Jaffa,
  Dates, oranges and gold.

She brings the silk of China,
  And bales of Persian dyes,
And birds with sparkling feathers,
  And snakes with diamond eyes.

She's gliding in the starlight
  As white as any gull;
The East is gliding with her
  In the shadows of her hull.

A ship sails up to Bideford;
  Upon a western breeze,
With fruits of Eastern summers
  She rises from the seas,
And sights the hills of Devon
  And the misty English trees.

Herbert Asquith

Sea Song

A wet sheet and a flowing sea,
  A wind that follows fast,
And fills the white and rustling sail
  And bends the gallant mast—
And bends the gallant mast, my boys,
  While, like the eagle free,
Away the good ship flies, and leaves
  Old England on the lee.

"Oh for a soft and gentle wind,"
  I heard a fair one cry;
But give to me the snoring breeze,
  And white waves heaving high—
And white waves heaving high, my boys,
  The good ship tight and free;
The world of waters is our home,
  And merry men are we.

There's tempest in yon horned moon,
  And lightning in yon cloud;
But hark the music, mariners!
  The wind is piping loud—
The wind is piping loud, my boys,
  The lightning flashing free,—
While the hollow oak our palace is,
  Our heritage the sea.

A. Cunningham

Prayers, Graces and Thanksgivings, Lullabies and Cradle Songs

He prayeth well, who loveth well
Both man and bird and beast

Evening Song

Soft falls the night,
The day grows dim,
To Thee I lift my evening hymn,
O Lord of dark and light.

My hands I raise,
A little spire,
And send my voice up high and higher
To Thee in happy praise.

For home and friend,
For books and toys,
For all the countless loves and joys
That Thou dost daily send.

Close Thou mine eyes,
That when the day
Returns once more from far away,
I may rejoicing rise.

Edith King

Grace and Thanksgiving

We thank Thee, Lord, for quiet upland lawns,
For misty loveliness of autumn dawns,
For gold and russet of the ripened fruit,
For yet another year's fulfilment, Lord,
We thank Thee now.

For joy of glowing colour, flash of wings,
We thank Thee, Lord; for all the little things
That make the love and laughter of our days,
For home and happiness and friends, we praise
And thank Thee now.

Elizabeth Gould

502

A Child's Prayer

O god

Father, we thank Thee for the night
And for the pleasant morning light,
For rest and food and loving care,
And all that makes the world so fair.
Help us to do the thing we should.
To be to others kind and good,
In all we do, in all we say,
To grow more loving every day.

Prayers

God who created me
Nimble and light of limb,
In three elements free,
To run, to ride, to swim,
Not when the sense is dim,
But now from the heart of joy,
I would remember Him:
Take the thanks of a boy.

Jesu, King and Lord,
Whose army goes to fight,
Gird me with Thy sword,
Swift and sharp and bright.
Thee would I serve if I might
And conquer if I can,
From day-dawn till night,
Take the strength of a man.

Spirit of Love and Truth,
Breathing in grosser clay,
The light and flame of youth,
Delight of men in the fray,
Wisdom in strength's decay;
From pain, strife, wrong to be free,
This best gift I pray,
Take my spirit to Thee.

Henry Charles Beeching

Lovely Things

Bread is a lovely thing to eat—
God bless the barley and the wheat!

A lovely thing to breathe is air—
God bless the sunshine everywhere!

The earth's a lovely place to know—
God bless the folks that come and go!

Alive's a lovely thing to be—
Giver of life—we say—bless Thee!

H. M. Sarson

Morning Thanksgiving

Thank God for sleep in the long quiet night,
   For the clear day calling through the little leaded panes,
For the shining well-water and the warm golden light,
   And the paths washed white by singing rains.

For the treasure of the garden, the gilly-flowers of gold,
   The prouder petalled tulips, the primrose full of spring,
For the crowded orchard boughs, and the swelling buds that
     hold
   A yet unwoven wonder, to Thee our praise we bring.

Thank God for good bread, for the honey in the comb,
   For the brown-shelled eggs, for the clustered blossom set
Beyond the open window in a pink and cloudy foam,
   For the laughing loves among the branches set.

For earth's little secret and innumerable ways,
   For the carol and the colour, Lord, we bring
What things may be of thanks, and that Thou hast lent
     our days
   Eyes to see and ears to hear and lips to sing.

John Drinkwater

The Knight's Prayer

God be in my head
And in my understanding;

God be in mine eyes
And in my looking;

God be in my mouth
And in my speaking;

God be in my heart,
And in my thinking;

God be at my end,
And at my departing.

The Robin's Song

God bless the field and bless the furrow,
Stream and branch and rabbit burrow,
Hill and stone and flower and tree,
From Bristol town to Wetherby—
Bless the sun and bless the sleet,
Bless the lane and bless the street,
Bless the night and bless the day,
From Somerset and all the way
To the meadows of Cathay;
Bless the minnow, bless the whale,
Bless the rainbow and the hail,
Bless the nest and bless the leaf,
Bless the righteous and the thief,
Bless the wing and bless the fin,
Bless the air I travel in,
Bless the mill and bless the mouse,
Bless the miller's bricken house,
Bless the earth and bless the sea,
God bless you and God bless me!

Old English Rhyme

505

A Child's Prayer

Thro' the night Thy angels kept
Watch above me while I slept,
Now the dark has passed away,
Thank Thee, Lord, for this new day.

North and south and east and west
May Thy holy name be blest;
Everywhere beneath the sun,
As in Heaven, Thy will be done.

Give me food that I may live;
Every naughtiness forgive;
Keep all evil things away
From Thy little child this day.

William Canton

The Elixir

Teach me, my God and King,
    In all things Thee to see,
And what I do in anything,
    To do it as for Thee.

A man that looks on glass
    On it may stay his eye:
Or, if he pleaseth, through it pass
    And then the heaven espy.

A servant with this clause
    Makes drudgery divine:
Who sweeps a room, as for Thy laws,
    Makes that and th' action fine.

This is the famous stone
    That turneth all to gold:
For that which God doth touch and own
    Cannot for less be told.

George Herbert

He Prayeth Well

From *The Rime of the Ancient Mariner*
He prayeth well, who loveth well
  Both man and bird and beast,
He prayeth best, who loveth best
  All things both great and small;
For the dear God who loveth us,
  He made and loveth all.

Samuel Taylor Coleridge

Praise

Praise the Lord for all the seasons,
  Praise Him for the gentle spring,
Praise the Lord for glorious summer,
  Birds and beasts and everything.
Praise the Lord Who sends the harvest,
  Praise Him for the winter snows;
Praise the Lord, all ye who love Him,
  Praise Him, for all things He knows.

Mary Anderson

The Willow-boughs

Lads and lasses gathering,
Willow-boughs and tapers bring,
  That they homeward bear.

Warmly do the flamelets glow,
Wayfarers cross them as they go;
  Spring-tide scents the air.

Little breeze from far away,
Rain, O rain, with tiny spray,
  Quench ye not the flame.

For Palm Sunday earliest,
I to-morrow stir from rest,
  Holy-day to acclaim.

Alexander Block

507

Good Night

Good night! Good night!
Far flies the light;
But still God's love
Shall shine above,
Making all bright,
Good night! Good night!

Victor Hugo

The Pilgrim

Who would true valour see,
    Let him come hither!
One here will constant be,
    Come wind, come weather;
There's no discouragement
Shall make him once relent
His first-avow'd intent
    To be a Pilgrim.

Whoso beset him round
    With dismal stories,
Do but themselves confound
    His strength the more is.
No lion can him fright;
He'll with a giant fight;
But he will have a right
    To be a Pilgrim.

Nor enemy, nor friend,
    Can daunt his spirit;
He knows he at the end
    Shall Life inherit:—
Then, fancies, fly away;
He'll fear not what men say;
He'll labour, night and day,
    To be a Pilgrim.

John Bunyan

A Child's Grace

Here a little child I stand
Heaving up my either hand;
Cold as paddocks though they be,
Here I lift them up to Thee,
For a benison to fall
On our meat and on us all.   Amen.

R. Herrick

A Child's Morning Prayer

Look down on me, a little one,
Whose life on earth is but begun:
    Dear Saviour, smile on me.

Watch over me from day to day,
And when I work, or when I play,
    Dear Saviour, smile on me.

Help me to do Thy holy will,
With lovely thoughts my mind to fill:
    Dear Saviour, smile on me.

J. Kirby

A Child's Prayer

For Morn, my dome of blue,
For Meadows green and gay,
And Buds who love the twilight of the leaves,
Let Jesus keep me joyful when I pray.

For the big Bees that hum
And hide in bells of flowers;
For the winding roads that come
To Evening's holy door
May Jesus bring me grateful to His arms,
And guard my innocence for evermore.

Siegfried Sassoon

509

Thanks to Spring

We thank Thee, Heavenly Father,
For all the lovely spring,
For primroses and bluebells,
And little birds that sing.

For woods and fields to play in,
For bright blue sky and sea,
For everything we thank Thee.
All beauty comes from Thee.

Mary Anderson

School Creed

This is our school,
Let peace dwell here,
Let the room be full of contentment.
Let love abide here.
Love of one another,
Love of mankind,
Love of life itself,
And love of God.
Let us remember
That as many hands build a house,
So many hearts make a school.

From "The School Creed" of a School in Canada

Go, Pretty Child

Go, pretty Child, and bear this flower
Unto thy little Saviour:
And tell Him, by that bud now blown,
He is the Rose of Sharon known.
When thou hast said so, stick it there
Upon His bib or stomacher.
And tell Him, for good handsel too,
That thou hast brought a whistle new,
Made of a clean straight oaten reed,
To charm His cries at time of need.
Tell Him for coral, thou hast none,
But if thou hadst, He should have one;
And poor thou art, and known to be
Even as moneyless as He.

Robert Herrick

510

The Shepherd Boy's Song

He that is down needs fear no fall,
   He that is low, no pride;
He that is humble ever shall
   Have God to be his guide.

I am content with what I have,
   Little be it or much:
And, Lord, contentment still I crave,
   Because Thou savest such.

Fullness to such a burden is
   That go on pilgrimage:
Here little, and hereafter bliss,
   Is best from age to age.

J. Bunyan

The Divine Image

To Mercy, Pity, Peace and Love
   All pray in their distress:
And to these virtues of delight
   Return their thankfulness.

For Mercy, Pity, Peace and Love
   Is God, our Father dear,
And Mercy, Pity, Peace and Love
   Is man, His child and care.

For Mercy has a human heart,
   Pity a human face,
And Love, the human form divine,
   And Peace, the human dress.

Then every man of every clime,
   That prays in his distress,
Prays to the human form divine,
   Love, Mercy, Pity, Peace.

William Blake

A Thank You for Friends

There are all kinds of men
   Who have done me good turns,
That I still never think about,
   Not for a minute;
Yet if I were making up
   That sort of grace,
They would all of them have
   To be in it.

One man made up stories,
   Another wrote verses
I found, and I liked,
   And I read till I knew them.
Another one saw
   All the things they had written,
Then, being an artist,
   He drew them.

Another took wood
   And a saw and some glue,
And put each of them just
   In the place that would need it—
So that is the chair
   Where I sit with my book
And am so much at ease
   As I read it.

I'm forgetting the one
   Who read tale after tale
When I was too young
   To know letter from letter,
And the other who taught me them,
   Till in the end
I could read for myself—
   Which was better.

Rodney Bennett

The Country Faith

Here in the country's heart,
  Where the grass is green,
Life is the same sweet life
  As it e'er hath been.

Trust in a God still lives,
  And the bell at morn
Flouts with a thought of God
  O'er the rising corn.

God comes down in the rain,
  And the crop grows tall—
This is the country faith,
  And the best of all!

Norman Gale

Ex Ore Infantium

Little Jesus wast Thou shy
Once, and just as small as I?
And what did it feel like to be
Out of Heaven and just like me?
Didst Thou sometimes think of there,
And ask where all the angels were?
I should think that I would cry
For my house all made of sky;
I would look about the air,
And wonder where my angels were;
And at waking 'twould distress me—
Not an angel there to dress me
Hadst Thou ever any toys,
Like us little girls and boys?
And didst Thou play in Heaven with all
The angels that were not too tall,
With stars for marbles? Did the things
Play "can you see me?" through their wings?
And did Thy mother let Thee spoil
Thy robes with playing on our soil?
How nice to have them always new
In Heaven, because 'twas quite clean blue!

Didst Thou kneel at night to pray,
And didst Thou join Thy hands this way?
And did they tire sometimes, being young,
And make the prayers seem very long?
And dost Thou like it best that we
Should join our hands to pray to Thee?
I used to think before I knew,
The prayer not said unless we do.
And did Thy mother at the night
Kiss Thee and fold the clothes in right?
And didst Thou feel quite good in bed,
Kissed, and sweet, and Thy prayers said?

Thou canst not have forgotten all
That it feels like to be small:
And Thou knowest I cannot pray
To Thee in my father's way—
When Thou wast so little, say,
Couldst Thou talk Thy Father's way?
So, a little child, come down
And hear a child's tongue like Thy own;
Take me by the hand and walk,
And listen to my baby talk;
To Thy Father show my prayer
(He will look, Thou art so fair)
And say: O Father, I, Thy Son,
Bring the prayer of a little one;
And He will smile, the children's tongue
Hast not changed since Thou wast young.

Francis Thompson

The Vision Clear

Child's eyes to see,
  Child's ears to hear—
God grant to me
  That vision clear.

Grant me the sight
  Of heaven and earth—
Quiet rest at night,
  Day's glorious mirth.
Help me to hear
  Those little things,
Faint, far and clear,
  Rememberings.
So I may learn
  Fully to praise
Thee for my life
  Of happy days.

J. M. Westrup

A Prayer

Teach me, Father, how to go
Softly as the grasses grow;
Hush my soul to meet the shock
Of the wild world as a rock;
But my spirit, prompt with power,
Make as simple as a flower.
Let the dry heart fill its cup,
Like a poppy looking up;
Let life lightly wear her crown,
Like a poppy looking down,
When its heart is filled with dew
And its life begins anew.

Teach me, Father, how to be
Kind and patient as a tree.
Joyfully the crickets croon
Under shady oak at noon;
Beetle, on his mission bent,
Tarries in that cooling tent.
Let me, also, cheer a spot,
Hidden field or garden grot,
Place where passing souls can rest
On the way and be their best.

Edwin Markham

Lines from Invocation of Peace

Deep peace, pure white of the moon to you;
Deep peace, pure green of the grass to you;
Deep peace, pure brown of the earth to you;
Deep peace, pure grey of the dew to you,
Deep peace, pure blue of the sky to you!
Deep peace of the running wave to you,
Deep peace of the flowing air to you,
Deep peace of the quiet earth to you.

"Fiona Macleod"

Hindu Cradle Song

From groves of spice,
O'er fields of rice,
Athwart the lotus-stream,
 I bring for you,
 Aglint with dew,
A little lovely dream.

Sweet, shut your eyes,
The wild fireflies
Dance through the fairy neem,*
 From the poppy bole
 For you I stole
A little lovely dream.

A Danish Cradle Song

Lullaby, sweet baby mine!
Mother spins the thread so fine;
Father o'er the long bridge is gone,
Shoes he'll buy for little John.
Pretty shoes with buckles bright.
Sleep, baby mine, now sleep all night!

*Neem is a lilac tree (Hindustani).

516

Sweet and Low

Sweet and low, sweet and low,
    Wind of the western sea,
Low, low, breathe and blow,
    Wind of the western sea!
Over the rolling waters go,
Come from the dying moon, and blow,
    Blow him again to me;
While my little one, while my pretty one, sleeps.
Sleep and rest, sleep and rest,
    Father will come to thee soon;
Rest, rest, on mother's breast,
    Father will come to thee soon;
Father will come to his babe in the nest,
Silver sails all out of the west
    Under the silver moon:
Sleep, my little one, sleep, my pretty one, sleep.

Lord Tennyson

The Dustman

When the shades of night are falling, and the sun goes down,
O! the Dustman comes a-creeping in from Shut-eye Town.
And he throws dust in the eyes of all the babies that he meets,
No matter where he finds them, in the house or in the streets.
Then the babies' eyes grow heavy and the lids drop down,
When the Dustman comes a-creeping in from Shut-eye Town.

When mother lights the lamp and draws the curtains down,
O! the Dustman comes a-creeping in from Shut-eye Town,
And the babies think the Dustman is as mean as he can be,
For he shuts their eyes at nightfall, just when they want to see.
But their little limbs are weary, for all they fret and frown,
When the Dustman comes a-creeping in from Shut-eye Town.

Nod

Softly along the road of evening,
  In a twilight dim with rose,
Wrinkled with age, and drenched with dew,
  Old Nod, the shepherd, goes.

His drowsy flocks stream on before him,
  Their fleeces charged with gold,
To where the sun's last beam leans low
  On Nod the shepherd's fold.

The hedge is quick and green with briar,
  From their sand the conies creep;
And all the birds that fly in heaven
  Flock singing home to sleep.

His lambs outnumber a noon's roses,
  Yet, when night's shadows fall,
His blind old sheep-dog, Slumber-soon,
  Misses not one of all.

His are the quiet steeps of dreamland,
  The waters of no-more-pain,
His ram's bell rings 'neath an arch of stars,
  "Rest, rest, and rest again."

Walter de la Mare

Cradle Hymn

Away in a manger, no crib for a bed,
The little Lord Jesus laid down His sweet head.
The stars in the bright sky looked down where He lay—
The little Lord Jesus asleep in the hay.

The cattle are lowing, the Baby awakes,
But little Lord Jesus, no crying He makes.
I love Thee, Lord Jesus! look down from the sky,
And stay by my cradle till morning is nigh.

Martin Luther

Evening

Hush, hush, little baby,
   The sun's in the west;
The lamb in the meadow
   Has laid down to rest.

The bough rocks the bird now,
   The flower rocks the bee,
The wave rocks the lily,
   The wind rocks the tree;

And I rock the baby
   So softly to sleep—
It must not awaken
   Till daisy-buds peep.

Bed-time

The evening is coming,
   The sun sinks to rest;
The rooks are all flying
   Straight home to the nest.
"Caw!" says the rook, as he flies overhead;
"It's time little people were going to bed!"

The flowers are closing;
   The daisy's asleep;
The primrose is buried
   In slumber so deep.
Shut up for the night is the pimpernel red;
It's time little people were going to bed!

The butterfly, drowsy,
   Has folded its wing;
The bees are returning,
   No more the birds sing.
Their labour is over, their nestlings are fed;
It's time little people were going to bed!

Here comes the pony,
    His work all done;
Down through the meadow
    He takes a good run;
Up goes his heels and down goes his head;
It's time little people were going to bed!

Good night, little people,
    Good night and good night;
Sweet dreams to your eyelids
    Till dawning of light;
The evening has come, there's no more to be said,
It's time little people were going to bed!

Thomas Hood

Norse Lullaby

The sky is dark, and the hills are white,
The Storm King speeds from the North to-night,
And this is the song the Storm King sings,
As over the earth his cloak he flings—
    "Sleep, sleep, little one, sleep!"
He rustles his wings, and gruffly sings,
    "Sleep, little one, sleep!"

On yonder mountain side, a vine
Clings at the foot of a mother pine.
The tree bends over the trembling thing,
And only the vine can hear her sing—
    "Sleep, sleep, little one, sleep!
What can you fear when I am near?
    Sleep, little one, sleep!"

The King may sing in his bitter flight,
The tree may croon to the vine to-night,
But the little snowflake at my breast
Liketh the song I sing the best—
    "Sleep, sleep, little one, sleep!
Weary thou art, a-next my heart,
    Sleep, little one, sleep!"

Eugene Field

Cradle Song

What does little birdie say
In her nest at peep of day?
Let me fly, says little birdie,
Mother, let me fly away.

Birdie, rest a little longer,
Till the little wings are stronger,
So she rests a little longer,
Then she flies away.

What does little baby say,
In her bed at peep of day?
Baby says, like little birdie,
Let me rise and fly away.

Baby, sleep a little longer,
Till the little limbs are stronger,
If she sleeps a little longer,
Baby too shall fly away.

Lord Tennyson

A Summer Lullaby

The sun has gone from the shining skies,
 Bye, baby, bye.
The dandelions have closed their eyes,
 Bye, baby, bye,
And the stars are lighting their lamps to see
If the babies and squirrels and birds, all three,
Are sound asleep as they ought to be —
 Bye, baby, bye.

The squirrel is dressed in a coat of grey,
 Bye, baby, bye.
He wears it by night as well as by day,
 Bye, baby, bye.
The robin sleeps in his feathers of down
With a warm red breast and wings of brown,
But the baby wears a little white gown,
 Bye, baby, bye.

The squirrel's nest is a hole in a tree,
     Bye, baby, bye.
And there he sleeps as snug as can be,
     Bye, baby, bye.
The robin's nest is high overhead
Where the leafy boughs of the maple spread,
But the baby's nest is a little white bed,
     Bye, baby, bye.

Eudora S. Bumstead

A Cradle Song

Sleep, baby, sleep!
Thy father watches the sheep,
Thy mother is shaking the dreamland tree,
And softly a little dream falls on thee!
Sleep, baby, sleep!

Sleep, baby, sleep!
The large stars are the sheep,
The little stars are the lambs, I guess,
The fair moon is the shepherdess;
Sleep, baby, sleep!

Sleep, baby, sleep!
I'll buy for thee a sheep,
With a golden bell so fine to see,
And it shall frisk and play with thee;
Sleep, baby, sleep!

Sleep, baby, sleep!
Thy father watches the sheep,
The wind is blowing fierce and wild,
It must not wake my little child;
Sleep, baby, sleep!

Sleep, baby, sleep!
Our Saviour loves His sheep:
He is the Lamb of God on high,
Who for our sakes came down to die.
Sleep, baby, sleep!

Lullaby

Lullaby, Lullaby,
Shadows creep across the sky.
See, the sun has gone to rest,
    Lullaby.

Lullaby, Lullaby,
Little one to Dreamland fly,
Till the morning sun awakes,
    Lullaby.

Phyllis Garlick

At Sunset

In the evening
    The sun goes down,
And the lamps are lit
    In the little town.

The bats fly low
    Round the grey church dome,
The thrush and the blackbird
    Are safely home —

Are safely home
    In their quiet nest —
The thrush and the blackbird
    Are both at rest!

Ivy O. Eastwick

Good Night

No more work and no more play,
Every toy is put away,
Ended is the lovely day,
    Then—good night!

Drink the milk all white and creamy,
Have your bath all warm and steamy
Close your eyes all tired and dreamy,
    Then—good night!

Through the window stars are peeping,
From their holes the mice are creeping,
Your white bed is soft for sleeping,
    Then—good night!

Ruth Ainsworth

At Night in the Wood

When night comes down on the children's eyes
    And all in the house is still,
For busy folk it is time to rise
    In the Wood Land over the hill.
There are those who wake when the moon is high;
    They have slept for the whole long day.
With a silent shake or a call or cry,
    They are off on the trail away.
The Owl, who hides from the sunlight's beam,
    Hark!—there is his "Too-hoo-hoo!"
The Vole who lives by the gurgling stream
    Steals out in the darkness too.

The Stoat, the Rat,
And the squeaking Bat
All open their keen little eyes
And rise.
And the Hedgehog peeps from his cosy nest
And hurries out with the rest.
And the bark of the Fox shows he's astir,
And the Rabbit shivers within his fur,
And the sleepy old Dormouse wakes at last—
There's none in the wood can move so fast.
Each one on his trail is off away
And never comes back till the dawn of day.
Oh, when in the night the moon is high
And the stars look down from the dusky sky,
If we crept out—if we only could!—
What wonderful things we should see in the wood!

Nancy M. Hayes

Wynken, Blynken, and Nod

Wynken, Blynken, and Nod one night
  Sailed off in a wooden shoe—
Sailed on a river of crystal light,
  Into a sea of dew.
"Where are you going and what do you wish?"
  The old moon asked the three.
"We have come to fish for the herring-fish
  That live in this beautiful sea;
Nets of silver and gold have we,"
  Said Wynken, Blynken, and Nod.

The old moon laughed and sang a song,
  As they rocked in the wooden shoe,
And the wind that sped them all night long
  Ruffled the waves of dew.
The little stars were the herring-fish
  That lived in that beautiful sea—
"Now cast your nets wherever you wish—
  But never afeared are we";
So cried the stars to the fishermen three:
  Wynken, Blynken, and Nod.

All night long their nets they threw
  To the stars in the twinkling foam—
Then down from the skies came the wooden shoe,
  Bringing the fishermen home;
'Twas all so pretty a sail, it seemed
  As if it could not be,
And some folks thought 'twas a dream they'd dreamed
  Of sailing that beautiful sea—
But I shall name you the fishermen three:
  Wynken, Blynken, and Nod.

Wynken and Blynken are two little eyes,
  And Nod is a little head,
And the wooden shoe that sailed the skies
  Is a wee one's trundle-bed.

So shut your eyes while mother sings
  Of wonderful sights that be,
And you shall see the beautiful things
  As you rock on the misty sea,
Where the old shoe rocked the fishermen three:
  Wynken, Blynken, and Nod.

Eugene Field

The Unwritten Song

Now where's a song for our small dear,
With her quaint voice and her quick ear,
To sing—for gnats and bats to hear—
  At twilight in her bed?
A song of tiny elfin things
With shiny, silky, silvery wings,
Footing it in fairy rings,
  And kissing overhead.

A song of starry glow-worms' lights
In the long grass of shadowy nights,
And flitting showers of firefly flights,
  Where summer woods hang deep;
Of hovering, noiseless owls that find
Their way at dark; and of a kind
And drowsy, drowsy ocean wind
  That puts the sea to sleep.

But where's the song for our small dear,
With her quaint voice and her quick ear,
To sing—for dreamland things to hear—
  And hush herself to sleep?

Ford Madox Ford

Lullaby

The wind whistled loud at the window-pane—
  Go away, wind, and let me sleep!
Ruffle the green grass billowy plain,
  Ruffle the billowy deep!
"Hush-a-bye, hush! the wind is fled,
The wind cannot ruffle the soft, smooth bed,—
  Hush thee, darling, sleep!"

The ivy tapped at the window-pane,—
  Silence, ivy! and let me sleep!
Why do you patter like drops of rain,
  And then play creepity-creep?
"Hush-a-bye, hush! the leaves shall lie still,
The moon is walking over the hill,—
  Hush thee, darling, sleep!"

A dream-show rode in on a moonbeam white,—
  Go away, dreams, and let me sleep!
The show may be gay and golden bright,
  But I do not care to peep.
"Hush-a-bye, hush! the dream is fled,
A shining angel guards thy bed,
  Hush thee, darling, sleep!"

W. B. Rands

527

Christmas and Easter Poems

Why do the bells of Christmas ring?
Why do little children sing?

I Will Keep Christmas

I will keep Christmas in the cold hedgerow,
With red, shining holly and winter snow.
I will keep Christmas far from any town
On the frosted side of the windswept down.

Stars will be candles of sweet silver fire,
Swinging at midnight over tree and spire,
Waves will be booming bells and break the air,
With glory and greeting and wingèd prayer.

I will keep Christmas alone and away,
Praising the Lord of all on Christmas Day.

P. A. Ropes

The Oxen

Christmas Eve, and twelve of the clock.
  "Now they are all on their knees,"
An elder said as we sat in a flock
  By the embers in fireside ease.

We pictured the meek mild creatures where
  They dwelt in their strawy pen,
Nor did it occur to one of us there
  To doubt they were kneeling then.

So fair a fancy few would weave
  In these years! Yet, I feel,
If someone said on Christmas Eve,
  "Come; see the oxen kneel

"In the lonely barton by yonder coomb
  Our childhood used to know,"
I should go with him in the gloom,
  Hoping it might be so.

Thomas Hardy

Silver Bells

Across the snow the silver bells
    Come near and yet more near;
Each day and night, each night and day
    They tinkle soft and clear.

'Tis Father Christmas on his way
    Across the winter snows;
While on his sleigh the silver bells
    Keep chiming as he goes.

I listen for them in the night,
    I listen all the day;
I think these merry silver bells
    Are long, long on the way!

Hamish Hendry

The Carol Singers

Last night the carol-singers came
    When I had gone to bed,
Upon the crisp white path outside
    I heard them softly tread.

I sat upright to listen, for
    I knew they came to tell,
Of all the things that happened on
    The very first Noel.

Upon my ceiling flickering
    I saw their lantern glow,
And then they sang their carols sweet
    Of Christmas long ago.

And when at last they went away,
    Their carol-singing done,
There was a little boy who wished
    They'd only just begun.

Margaret G. Rhodes

Christmas

An azure sky,
All star bestrewn.
A lowly crib,
A hushèd room.
An open door,
A hill afar,
Where little lambs
And shepherds are.
To such a world,
On such a night,
Came Jesus—
Little Lord of Light.

Mary I.

A Christmas Carol

The Christ-child lay on Mary's lap,
His hair was like a light.
(O weary, weary was the world,
But here is all aright.)

The Christ-Child lay on Mary's breast,
His hair was like a star.
(O stern and cunning are the kings,
But here the true hearts are.)

The Christ-child lay on Mary's heart,
His hair was like a fire.
(O weary, weary is the world,
But here the world's desire.)

The Christ-child stood at Mary's knee.
His hair was like a crown,
And all the flowers looked up at Him,
And all the stars looked down.

G. K. C

A Child's Christmas Carol

There was a little Baby once
    Born upon Christmas Day;
The oxen lowed His lullabye
    As in His crib He lay:
His tree, it was a lonely tree
    That stood upon a hill,
Its candles were the mighty stars
    That shine upon us still;
His toys were flocks of little lambs,
    He loved to see them play:
It is for Him we are so glad,
    Now upon Christmas Day.

Christine Chaundler

Cradle Song at Bethlehem

Oh! hush Thee, oh! hush Thee, my Baby so small,
The ass hath her crib and the ox hath his stall,
They shelter Thee, Baby, from Heaven above,
Oh! hush Thee, oh! hush Thee, my Baby, my love.

Oh! hush Thee, oh! hush Thee, my Baby so small,
Dim is the light from the lamp on the wall,
Bright in the night sky shineth a star,
Leading the Kings who come from afar.

Oh! hush Thee, oh! hush Thee, my Baby so small,
Joseph is spreading the straw in the stall,
Soon wilt Thou sleep in the nook of my arm
Safe from all trouble and danger and harm.

E. J. Falconer

533

Christmas Eve

On Christmas Eve my mother read
   The story once again,
Of how the little Child was born,
   And of the Three Wise Men.

And how by following the Star
   They found Him where He lay,
And brought Him gifts; and that is why
   We keep our Christmas Day.

And when she read it all, I went
   And looked across the snow,
And thought of Jesus coming
   As He did so long ago.

I looked into the East, and saw
   A great star blazing bright;
There were three men upon the road
   All black against the light.

I thought I heard the angels sing,
   Away upon the hill . . .
I held my breath . . . it seemed as if
   The whole great world were still.

It seemed to me the little Child
   Was being born again . . .
And very near . . . and Then somehow
   Was Now . . . or Now was Then!

Edna Kingsley Walla

Bethlehem

When the herd were watching
   In the midnight chill,
Came a spotless lambkin
   From the heavenly hill.

Snow was on the mountains,
   And the wind was cold,
When from God's own garden
   Dropped a rose of gold.

When 'twas bitter winter,
    Houseless and forlorn,
In a star-lit stable
    Christ the Babe was born.

Welcome, heavenly lambkin;
    Welcome, golden rose;
Alleluia, Baby,
    In the swaddling clothes.

William Canton

As Joseph Was A-Walking

As Joseph was a-walking
    He heard an angel sing:
"This night shall be born
    Our heavenly king.

"He neither shall be born
    In housen nor in hall,
Nor in the place of Paradise,
    But in an ox's stall.

"He neither shall be clothèd
    In purple nor in pall,
But all in fair linen,
    As were babies all.

"He neither shall be rockèd
    In silver nor in gold,
But in a wooden cradle
    That rocks on the mould.

"He neither shall be christened
    In white wine or red,
But with fair spring water,
    With which we were christenèd."

The Christmas Party

We're going to have a party
   And a lovely Christmas tea,
And flags and lighted candles
   Upon the Christmas Tree!

And silver balls and lanterns,
   Tied on with golden string,
Will hide among the branches
   By little bells that ring.

And then there will be crackers
   And caps and hats and toys,
A Christmas cake and presents
   For all the girls and boys.

With dancing, games and laughter,
   With music, songs and fun,
We'll make our Christmas Party
   A joy for everyone!

Adeline White

Santa Claus

He comes in the night! He comes in the night!
   He softly, silently comes;
While the little brown heads on the pillows so white
   Are dreaming of bugles and drums.
He cuts through the snow like a ship through the foam,
   While the white flakes around him whirl;
Who tells him I know not, but he findeth the home
   Of each good little boy and girl.

His sleigh it is long, and deep, and wide;
   It will carry a host of things
While dozens of drums hang over the side,
   With the sticks sticking under the strings.
And yet not the sound of a drum is heard,
   Not a bugle blast is blown,
As he mounts to the chimney-top like a bird,
   And drops to the hearth like a stone.

The little red stockings he silently fills,
    Till the stockings will hold no more;
The bright little sleds for the great snow hills
    Are quickly set down on the floor.
Then Santa Claus mounts to the roof like a bird,
    And glides to his seat in the sleigh;
Not the sound of a bugle or drum is heard
    As he noiselessly gallops away.

He rides to the East, and he rides to the West,
    Of his goodies he touches not one;
He eateth the crumbs of the Christmas feast
    When the dear little folks are done.
Old Santa Claus doeth all that he can;
    This beautiful mission is his;
Then, children, be good to the little old man,
    When you find who the little man is.

The Waits

Frost in the air and music in the air,
And the singing is sweet in the street.
She wakes from a dream to a dream—O hark!
    The singing so faint in the dark.

The musicians come and stand at the door,
A fiddler and singers three,
And one with a bright lamp thrusts at the dark,
    And the music comes sudden—O hark!

She hears the singing as sweet as a dream
And the fiddle that climbs to the sky,
With head 'neath the curtain she stares out—O hark!
    The music so strange in the dark.

She listens and looks and sees but the sky,
While the fiddle is sweet in the porch,
And she sings back into the singing dark
    Hark, herald angels, hark!

John Freeman

537

Carol

He came all so still
　There His mother was,
As dew in April
　That falleth on the grass.

He came all so still
　To His mother's bower,
As dew in April
　That falleth on the flower.

He came all so still
　There His mother lay,
As dew in April
　That falleth on the spray.

Mother and maiden
　Was never done but she!
Well may such a lady
　Goddès mother be.

Christmas Carols

I hear along our street
Pass the minstrel throngs;
Hark! they play so sweet,
On their hautboys, Christmas songs!
Let us by the fire
Ever higher
Sing them till the night expire!

In December ring
Every day the chimes;
Loud the gleemen sing
In the street their merry rhymes.
Let us by the fire
Ever higher
Sing them till the night expire.

Shepherds at the grange,
Where the Babe was born,
Sang, with many a change,
Christmas carols until morn.
Let us by the fire
Ever higher
Sing them till the night expire!

H. W. Longfellow

The Little Fir Tree

1. At Christmas time so long ago,
   The winds were blowing high and low;
   A little green fir tree grew by the Inn,
   A little fir tree straight and slim.

   "Noel, Noel!" the angels sang,
   "Noel, Noel! Goodwill to man,"
   A little green fir tree grew by the Inn,
   A little green fir tree straight and slim.

2. And, looking up, across the night
   The fir tree saw the Star so bright.
   The little fir tree wondered why
   The star was moving in the sky.

   "Noel, Noel!" etc.

3. The star shone over Bethlehem
   Over the stable inn, and then
   The little green fir tree shone with light,
   Lit by the star that wintry night.

   "Noel, Noel!" etc.

4. The fir tree shone so long ago;
   And still in winter's frost and snow,
   The little green fir tree comes each year
   To bring us joy and Christmas cheer.

   "Noel, Noel!" etc.

Margaret Rose
539

A Christmas Song

Winds through the Olive trees softly did blow
Round little Bethlehem long, long ago.
Sheep on the hill-sides lay white as the snow;
Shepherds were watching them long, long ago.
Shepherds were watching them long, long ago.

Then from the happy skies Angels bent low,
Singing their songs of joy, long, long ago.
For, in His manger bed, cradled, we know,
Christ came to Bethlehem long, long ago,
Christ came to Bethlehem long, long ago.

A Christmas-Tree Song

The Chestnut's a fine tree
    In sunshine of May,
With blossoms like candles
    In shining array;
But they're not half so pretty
    Or so welcome to me
As the little wax candles,
Red-and-white candles,
Lighted four-a-penny candles
    On a little Christmas tree.

The Apple's a gay tree
    With fruit shining red
Like glossy round lanterns
    Alight overhead;
But they're not half so pretty
    Or so welcome to me
As the gay paper lanterns,
Small crinkled lanterns,
Pretty red-and-white lanterns
    On a little Christmas Tree.

The Peach is a rare tree,
   The Plum tree is, too,
With fruit from green turning
   To golden and blue;
But they're not half so pretty
   Or so welcome to me
As the shining round peaches,
Pretty glass peaches,
Mellow plums and golden peaches
   On a little Christmas Tree.

All trees in their season
   Bear fruits that are good,
In hedgerow or garden,
   In orchard or wood;
But they cannot show anything
   So delightful to see
As the brown-paper parcels,
Plump paper parcels,
Jolly ribbon-tied parcels
   On a little Christmas Tree.

Rodney Bennett

Song

Why do the bells of Christmas ring?
Why do little children sing?

Once a lovely shining star,
Seen by shepherds from afar,
Gently moved until its light
Made a manger's cradle bright.

There a darling baby lay,
Pillowed soft upon the hay.
And its Mother sung and smiled:
"This is Christ, the holy Child!"

Therefore bells for Christmas ring,
Therefore little children sing.

Eugene Field

541

A Christmas Wish

To every hearth a little fire,
To every board a little feast,
To every heart a joy,
To every child a toy,
Shelter for bird and beast.

Rose Fyleman

A Child's Song of Christmas

My counterpane is soft as silk,
My blankets white as creamy milk.
   The hay was soft to Him, I know,
   Our little Lord of long ago.

Above the roof the pigeons fly
In silver wheels across the sky.
   The stable doves they cooed to them,
   Mary and Christ in Bethlehem.

Bright shines the sun across the drifts,
And bright upon my Christmas gifts.
   They brought Him incense, myrrh, and gold,
   Our little Lord who lived of old.

O, soft and clear our mother sings
Of Christmas joys and Christmas things.
   God's holy angels sang to them,
   Mary and Christ in Bethlehem.

Our hearts they hold all Christmas dear,
And earth seems sweet and heaven seems near.
   O, heaven was in His sight, I know,
   That little Child of long ago.

Marjorie L. C. Pickthall

The Christmas Tree

With spangles gay and candle light
And many toys, our tree is bright.
And gold and silver birds are there:
While over all there hangs a star.

The toys are given first of all.
For me a doll, for Hugh a ball.
The spangle stuff is pulled about.
The candles are then all put out.

The tree now strip't is dark and bare,
But still the star is shining there
As shone the star the shepherds saw,
Who heard the angels' song of yore.

The star that was a guiding light,
To kings and shepherds, through the night,
Where patient oxen calm and mild,
Shared their bed with Mary's child.

Christmas night is our Saviour's birth.
Joy in heaven, and peace on earth.
This was the story Mummy told me,
As she hung the star in our Christmas tree.

Isabel de Savitzky

Pudding Charms

Our Christmas pudding was made in November,
All they put in it, I quite well remember:
Currants and raisins, and sugar and spice,
Orange peel, lemon peel—everything nice
Mixed up together, and put in a pan.
"When you've stirred it," said Mother, "as much as you
    can,
We'll cover it over, that nothing may spoil it,
And then, in the copper, to-morrow we'll boil it."
That night, when we children were all fast asleep,
A real fairy godmother came crip-a-creep!

543

She wore a red cloak, and a tall steeple hat
(Though nobody saw her but Tinker, the cat!)
And out of her pocket a thimble she drew,
A button of silver, a silver horse-shoe,
And, whisp'ring a charm, in the pudding pan popped
    them,
Then flew up the chimney directly she dropped them;
And even old Tinker pretended he slept
(With Tinker a secret is sure to be kept!),
So nobody knew, until Christmas came round,
And there, in the pudding, these treasures we found.

Charlotte Druitt Cole

A Christmas Verse

He had no royal palace,
    Only a stable bare.
He had no watchful servants,
    An ox and ass stood there.
But light shone forth from where He lay;
The King of Love upon the hay!

"Kay"

Christmas Night

Softly, softly, through the darkness
    Snow is falling.
Sharply, sharply, in the meadows
    Lambs are calling.
Coldly, coldly, all around me
    Winds are blowing.
Brightly, brightly, up above me
    Stars are glowing.

B. E. Milner

Christmas Carol

God bless the master of this house,
  Likewise the mistress too:
And all the little children
  That round the table go.
Love and joy come to you,
  And to your wassail too,
And God bless you and send you
  A happy New Year.

Christmas Eve

On Christmas Eve the little stars
  Sparkle and glisten with delight,
Like strings of glitt'ring diamonds,
  Across the darkness of the night.

On Christmas Eve the little stars
  Dance in their places in the sky;
Ah! I would go and trip with them
  If I could only climb as high.

On Christmas Eve the little stars
  Sing merry carols all night long;
But O! I am so far away
  I cannot even hear their song.

On Christmas Eve the little stars
  Sparkle and dance, and sing till dawn;
And I am singing too, because
  To-morrow will be Christmas Morn.

Charlotte Druitt Cole

Ten Little Christmas Trees

Ten little Christmas Trees a-growing in a line.
　　The first went to Bedfordshire,
　　And that left only nine.

Nine little Christmas Trees all found it long to wait,
　　The second went to Monmouthshire,
　　And that left only eight.

Eight little Christmas Trees said, "Christmas will be
　　　　heaven."
　　The third went to London Town,
　　And that left only seven.

Seven little Christmas Trees, and all as straight as sticks!
　　The fourth went to Oxfordshire,
　　And that left only six.

Six little Christmas Trees, all growing and alive!
　　The fifth went to Lancashire,
　　And that left only five.

Five little Christmas Trees said, "Will they want some
　　　　more?"
　　The sixth went to Devonshire,
　　And that left only four.

Four little Christmas Trees, as sturdy as could be!
　　The seventh went to Scilly Isles,
　　And that left only three.

Three little Christmas Trees all grew and grew and grew,
　　The eighth went to Middlesex,
　　And that left only two.

Two little Christmas Trees, December almost done!
　　The ninth went to Timbuctoo,
　　And that left only one.

One little Christmas Tree, feeling very small!
　　She came to our school,
　　And that was best of all.

Ten little Christmas Trees, with Christmas drawing near,
  Wish you love and gladness
  And a Happy New Year.

Rodney Bennett

All in Red

Red for Santa's fur-lined cloak
  And his scarlet hood.
Red for the holly berries
  Gleaming in the wood.
Red for the breast
Of the bravest little bird,
R-E-D for the brightest Christmas word.

Red for the glow of the yule-log light
And the little crimson slippers
That Santa left last night.
Red for the paper lanterns
  Hanging from the wall.
Of the many Christmas colours
  Red's the best of all.

Eileen Mathias

"How Far is it to Bethlehem?"

How far is it to Bethlehem?
  Not very far.
Shall we find the stable-room
  Lit by a star?

Can we see the little Child?
  Is He within?
If we lift the wooden latch,
  May we go in?

547

May we stroke the creatures there—
    Ox, ass, or sheep?
May we peep like them and see
    Jesus asleep?

If we touch His tiny hand,
    Will He awake?
Will He know we've come so far
    Just for His sake?

Great kings have precious gifts,
    And we have naught;
Little smiles and little tears
    Are all we brought.

For all weary children
    Mary must weep;
Here, on His bed of straw,
    Sleep, children, sleep.

God, in His mother's arms,
    Babes in the byre,
Sleep, as they sleep who find
    Their heart's desire.

                                    F. Chesterton

The New Year

I am the little New Year, ho, ho!
Here I come tripping it over the snow.
Shaking my bells with a merry din—
So open your doors and let me in!

Presents I bring for each and all—
Big folks, little folks, short and tall;
Each one from me a treasure may win—
So open your doors and let me in!

Some shall have silver and some shall have gold,
Some shall have new clothes and some shall have old;
Some shall have brass and some shall have tin—
So open your doors and let me in!

Some shall have water and some shall have milk,
Some shall have satin and some shall have silk!
But each from me a present may win—
So open your doors and let me in!

A New Year Carol

Here we bring new water
    from the well so clear,
For to worship God with,
    this happy New Year.
Sing, levy dew, sing levy dew,
    the water and the wine;
The seven bright gold wires
    and the bugles that do shine.

Sing reign of Fair Maid,
    with gold upon her toe—
Open you the West Door,
    and turn the Old Year go.

Sing reign of Fair Maid
    with gold upon her chin—
Open you the East Door,
    and let the New Year in.
Sing levy dew, sing levy dew,
    the water and the wine;
The seven bright gold wires
    and the bugles that do shine.

The New Year

Oh! I'm the New Year,
  Come, look at my wares;
I've wishes all good
  And just a few cares.

Oh! what will you have?
  Come, buy, cheap or dear,
Oh! what will you have,
  A hope or a fear?

Oh! what will you have?
  Come, buy, young and old;
I've work and I've play,
  I've days warm and cold.

Oh! what will you have?
  There's no time to lose,
Bright days or dull weather,
  I know which you'll choose.

And for little children
  I've seasons so gay,
And each has a portion
  Of work and of play.

So come, young and old,
  And buy from my pack,
And be sure with each purchase
  Good luck you'll ne'er lack.

Easter Praise

Welcome, happy Easter day!
Winter now is far away.
Through the wide-world children sing
Praises to their Lord and King.

Through the woodlands, buds now doff
Their brown coats, and, throwing off
Winter slumber, bush and tree
Wear an April livery.

Now the wind more softly breathes,
Flowerets cast their sober sheaths,
And, to honour Easter Day,
Strew their petals on His way.

Birds that yesterday were dumb
Find their voices newly come,
And from branches all day long
Pour their joyous Easter Song.

Though but little I can sing,
I my Easter song would bring,
And for joy, as best I may,
In my singing I would pray:

Gentle Jesus, King of kings,
Yet the Lord of little things,
Though but small and young I be,
From Thy glory smile on me.

Keep it ever in my mind
To be kind, as Thou wert kind,
So I may be trusted by
Small things not so strong as I.

Then shall birds and flowers bless
My small hands for gentleness,
And in one thing I shall be
In my living liker Thee.

Help me every hour to make
Something happier for Thy sake,
So through all the year I may
Make each day Thy Easter Day.

Rodney Bennett

Easter

I got me flowers to strew Thy way,
   I got me boughs off many a tree;
But Thou wast up by break of day,
   And brought'st Thy sweets along with Thee.

Yet though my flowers be lost, they say
   A heart can never come too late;
Teach it to sing Thy praise this day,
   And then this day my life shall date.

George Herbert

An Easter Chick

"What a lovely world," said the baby chick,
"I've stepped from my egg to see!"

"What a lovely chick!" said the happy world,
"The spring has brought to me."

The children said, "God sent her to us,"
And fed her joyfully.

Thirza Wakley

Song

From *The Husband of Poverty*

There was a Knight of Bethlehem,
Whose wealth was tears and sorrows;
His men-at-arms were little lambs,
His trumpeters were sparrows;
His castle was a wooden cross,
Whereon He hung so high;
His helmet was a crown of thorns
Whose crest did touch the sky.

Henry Neville Maughan

552

When Mary Thro' the Garden Went

When Mary thro' the garden went,
   There was no sound of any bird,
And yet, because the night was spent,
   The little grasses lightly stirred,
   The flowers awoke, the lilies heard.

When Mary thro' the garden went,
   The dew lay still on flower and grass,
The waving palms above her sent
   Their fragrance out as she did pass,
   No light upon the branches was.

When Mary thro' the garden went,
   Her eyes, for weeping long, were dim,
The grass beneath her footsteps bent,
   The solemn lilies, white and slim,
   These also stood and wept for Him.

When Mary thro' the garden went,
   She sought, within the garden ground,
One for Whom her heart was rent,
   One Who for her sake was bound,
   One Who sought and she was found.

Mary E. Coleridge

Envoi

Earth puts her colours by,
And veils her in one whispering cloak of shadow;
Green goes from the meadow,
Red leaves and flowers and shining pools are shrouded;
A' few stars sail upon a windy sky,
And the moon is clouded.

The delicate music, traced
In and out of the soft lights and the laughter,
Is hushed, round ledge and rafter
The last faint echoes into silence creeping;
The harp is mute, the violins encased,
And the singers sleeping:

So, now my songs are done,
Leave me to-night awhile and the starlight gleaming,
To silence and sweet dreaming,
Here where no music calls, no beauty shakes me;
Till in my heart the birds sing to the sun
And the new dawn wakes me.

P. H. B. Lyon

Complete Index

Index of Titles

Index of Titles

557

Index of Titles

Index of Titles

Index of Titles

Index of Titles

Index of Titles

Index of Titles

Index of Titles

Index of Titles

Index of Titles

Index of Titles

567

Index of Titles

568

Classified Subject Index

Action Rhymes

Animals, Fish, and Insects

569

Classified Subject Index

Classified Subject Index

572

Classified Subject Index

The Moon

Morning

Narrative Verse

Out of Doors

People and Places

Classified Subject Index

Poems for the Very Young

580

Classified Subject Index

Classified Subject Index

Rain

Sea, Seaside, and Ships

Seasons

General

Spring

Classified Subject Index

Classified Subject Index

Index of First Lines

587

Index of First Lines

Index of First Lines

589

Index of First Lines

Index of First Lines

591

Index of First Lines

592

Index of First Lines

Index of First Lines

Index of First Lines

595

Index of First Lines

596

Index of First Lines

Index of First Lines

Index of First Lines

Index of First Lines

600

Index of First Lines

601

Index of First Lines

602

Index of First Lines

603

Index of First Lines

INDEX OF AUTHORS

605

Index of Authors

Index of Authors

Index of Authors

Index of Authors

Index of Authors

Index of Authors

Index of Authors

612

Index of Authors

Index of Authors

614

615

Index of Authors

616

Index of Authors

617

Index of Authors

618

Index of Authors

Index of Authors

Index of Authors

Acknowledgments

For permission to use copyright material we are indebted to
the following authors, literary executors and publishers:
The D. Appleton Century Co. for *A Summer Lullaby* by
Eudora Bumstead; Mr. Martin Armstrong for *Gold*; Mr.
H. W. Allingham for *Wishing* by W. Allingham; Mr. Herbert
Asquith for *The Elephant* and *A Ship sails up to Bideford*;
Mr. Norman Ault for *The Pig's Tail* and *Ducks* from
"Dreamland Shores" (Oxford Univ. Press); Miss Jean Ayer
and The Macmillan Co., New York, for *Everyday Things*; Mr.
Laurence Binyon for *The Little Dancers, Song* and the extract
This is England; Miss Enid Blyton for *What Piggy-Wiggy
Found* and *Winter* and Messrs. Methuen and Miss Blyton for
The Field Mouse; Mr. J. K. Bangs Jr. for *The Little Elf Man*;
Messrs. Ernest Benn Ltd. for *The Blackbird* by Humbert
Wolfe; Mr. Rodney Bennett for *Christmas Tree Song, Easter
Praise, Fluttering Leaves. The Growing River, Little Brown
Seed, The Little Old Lady, Merry Birds, Mrs. Jenny Wren,
My Dog Spot, The Pigeons, Postman's Knock, Robin's Song,
Ten Little Christmas Trees, A Thank You for Friends, There
—and Back, Three Little Men in a Boat*, and Mr. Bennett
and the University of London Press for *Snail*; Messrs.
A. & C. Black for *Five Little Brothers* by Ella Wheeler
Wilcox. Messrs. Blackie & Sons Ltd. for *The Big Arm
Chair* by E. H. R., *The Frog and the Bird* by Vera Hessey,
Mr. Scarecrow by Sheila Braine, *The Old Brown Horse*
by W. K. Holmes, *Promise* by Florence Lacey, *The Shy
Little House* by Nancy M. Hayes, *The Silver House* by John
Lea, *Skippets the Bad One* by Christine F. Bradley, *Strange
Talk* by L. E. Yates, *A Summer Day* and *The Faerie Fair* by
Florence Harrison, *Trains* by Hope Shepherd, *When we are
Men* by E. Stella Mead, *The Silver Road, The Upside-Down
World* and *Silver Bells* by Hamish Hendry and *Three Dogs* by
E. C. Brereton. Messrs. Basil Blackwell & Mott Ltd. and the
authors for *The Apple Rhyme, The Caravan*, and *The Scissor-
Man* by Madeleine Nightingale; *The Duck, Evening Song,
Cobwebs, Pebbles, The Rabbit, The Hedgehog* and *To the Bat*
by Edith King; *From the Train, Gates to England, The Light-
house, The Little Things that Happen, Jungle Trees* and *Through
the Porthole* by Marjorie Wilson, *The Blacksmith* by B. K. Pyke,

Acknowledgments

The King of China's Daughter by Edith Sitwell, *Whale* by Geoffrey Dearmer and *The Wind* by Elizabeth Rendall. The Bobs-Merrill Co. for *Sea Song from the Shore* from "Poems Here at Home" by James Whitcomb Riley; Miss Joyce Brisley for *The Two Families*; Messrs. Jonathan Cape for *Evening* and *The Moon* by Emily Dickinson, and *Secret Joy* and *Foxgloves* by Mary Webb from "Poems and the Spring of Joy," *Goldenhair* by James Joyce, and *Leisure, The Rain, Rich Days* and *White Sheep* by W. H. Davies. Messrs. Chappell & Co. Ltd. for *The Fairy Cobbler* by A. Neil Lyons. Miss Christine Chaundler for *The Tree in the Garden*; Messrs. Charles & Son Ltd. for *A Day at the Farm* by L.J.; Mr. Hugh Chesterman for *Outside, A Rhyme Sheet of Other Lands, Sir Nicketty Nox* and *Yesterday*. The Clarendon Press for *The Cliff-top, Gay Robin is Seen No More, I Love all Beauteous Things, Spring Goeth all in White, The Upper Skies* and *First Spring Morning* from "The Shorter Poems of Robert Bridges." Mr. Aidan Clarke for *The Journey* from "Song and Poems of Richmond Hill"; Messrs. Chatto & Windus and Lady Kilbracken for *Ragged Robin* by Elizabeth Godley; Messrs. Chatto & Windus for *The Far-Farers* and *Song of a Traveller* by R. L. Stevenson; Miss C. Druitt Cole for *Christmas Eve, The Clothes Line* and *Green Lady*. Messrs. Wm. Collins Sons & Co. and the authors for *Amy Elizabeth Ermyntrude Annie* by Queenie Scott-Hopper, *Banbury Fair* by Edith G. Millard, *Billy Boy* by Dorothy King, *The Carol Singers* by Margaret Rhodes, *London Trees* by Beryl Netherclift, *Snowdrops* by Ruth M. Arthur, *Three Mice* by C. Druitt Cole, *Water* by John R. Crossland, and the following poems from "Underneath a Mushroom" (Laurel and Gold Series), *The Fiddle* by Neil Munro, *Jenny and Johnny* by Dorothy King, *Little Betty Blue* by Agnes Grozier Herbertson, *The Yellow Fairy* and *Sun and Moon* by C. Druitt Cole, *My Party* by Queenie Scott-Hopper, *The Little Men* by Flora Fearne, *The King's Wood* by C. S. Holder, *Merry Little Men* by Kathleen M. Chaplin, *The Lace Pedlar* by Catherine A. Morin, *June* by Jane G. Stewart, *All in Red* by Eileen Mathias, *Sowing Seeds* by Ursula Cornwall, *The Christmas Tree* by Isabel de Savitzsky, *The Best of All* by Margaret Rhodes and *The Kite* and *My Little Dog* by Pearl

Acknowledgments

Forbes MacEwan. Padraic Colum for *The Old Woman of the Roads*; Messrs. Constable & Co. Ltd. and the authors for *Dawn* by Gordon Bottomly, *The Lamp Flower* from "The Gift" by Margaret Cecilia Furse and *Envoi* by P. H. B. Lyon. Miss Frances Cornford for *Spring Morning*; Messrs. Coward McCann Inc. for *The Mouse* from "Compass Rose" by Elizabeth Coatsworth; Messrs. Curwen & Sons Ltd. for *Pedlar Jim* by Florence Hoare and *Three Little Pigs* by A. Scott-Gatty. Messrs. J. M. Dent & Sons Ltd. and authors for *Song of Summer Days* by J. W. Foley, *The Witch* by Percy Ilott, *A Rune of Riches* (from "A Masque of Sybils") by Florence Converse, *Bethlehem* and *A Child's Prayer* by William Canton and *Christmas Carol* by G. K. Chesterton. Messrs. Doubleday Doran & Co. Inc. and Miss Rachel Field for *The Playhouse Key*; Messrs. Noel Douglas Ltd. for *Jack Tar, Wandering Jack* and *Who's that a-Knocking* from "Nursery Verseries" by Émile Jacot. Messrs. Gerald Duckworth & Co. Ltd. and the author for *The Elephant* and *The Early Morning* by Hilaire Belloc; Messrs. E. A. Dutton & Co. Inc. for *Christmas Eve* from "Feelings and Things" by Edna Kingsley Wallace; Miss F. Ann Elliott for *Pictures* and *The Snow*; Lady Erskine-Crum for *Goodnight, says the Owl*; Miss Eleanor Farjeon for *The Flower Seller, The Night will never stay, There are big waves, The Children's Bells*, and *There isn't time*; Miss Elizabeth Fleming for *The Balloon-Seller, Fires, The Hedgehog and his Coat, The Hurdy-Gurdy Man, If I were a pig, In the Mirror, The Patchwork Quilt, Old Mrs. Jarvis, The Secret, Toadstools, The Window-Cleaner*, and *Who's In*; the executors of the late Ford Madox Ford for *The Unwritten Song*; Mr. Michael A. E. Franklin for *The Scarecrow*; Miss Rose Fyleman for *A Christmas Wish* from "Small Cruse" (Methuen), *Conversation, The Donkey, The Frog, Good Morning, Mice, Primrose Hill* and *The Weathercock* from "Fifty-One New Nursery Rhymes" (Methuen), *Mrs. Brown* from "The Fairy Green" (Methuen), *The Goblin*, from "Widdy-Widdy-Wurkey" (also by permission of Messrs. Basil Blackwell & Mott), *Jock o' Dreams* and *Pretty Lady*; Miss Elizabeth Gould for *Midsummer Night*; Mr. Robert Graves for *I'd Love to be a Fairy's Child*; Miss Marjorie Greenfield for *Things I'd*

626

Acknowledgments

Like; Messrs. Harper & Bros. for *Familiar Friends* from "I Spend the Summer" by James S. Tippett. Messrs. Harrap & Co., Ltd. and the authors for *Dicky-Birds* and *The Kind Mousie* by Natalie Joan, *At Night in the Wood* by Nancy M. Hayes, *Autumn, The Bird Bath* and *Who?* by Florence Hoatson, and *What the Thrush Says* by Queenie Scott-Hopper. Messrs. Heinemann & Co. and the author's executors for *Prayer for Gentleness to all Creatures* from "Collected Poems" by John Galsworthy; *A Ship Sails up to Bideford* and *The Elephant* by Herbert Asquith. Miss Pamela Hinkson and Messrs. Macmillan for *Sheep and Lambs, Leaves,* and *Pink Almond* from "Collected Poems of Katharine Tynan" and to Miss Hinkson for *The Nightingale* and *Slow Spring*; Messrs. Hodder & Stoughton Ltd. and Mrs. Adcock for *Travellers* by St. John Adcock; Miss Ruth Holmes for *No Thoroughfare.* The Houghton Mifflin Co. for *Sea Shell* by Amy Lowell and *Christmas Carols* by H. W. Longfellow. Messrs. John Lane, The Bodley Head, for *Child's Song in Spring* by E. Nesbitt, *Gipsy Jane, Stalky Jack, The Pedlar's Caravan, Lullaby* and *The World* by W. B. Rands; *Jack Frost* and *Romance* by Gabriel Setoun, *The Rock-a-by Lady* and *Wynken, Blynken, and Nod* by Eugene Field. The Little Gem Poetry Books, Bk. 1 (G. Bell & Sons Ltd.) for *Winds through the Olive Trees softly did blow* and *Hindu Cradle Song*; Messrs. Longmans, Green & Co. Ltd. for *Pray, where are the little Bluebells gone* by Jean Ingelow, *Day* and *I Vow to Thee, my Country* from "Poems" by Sir Cecil Spring-Rice; Mr. Louis Loveman for *April Rain* by Robert Loveman; the Lutterworth Press for *Haytime* by C. M. Lowe. Messrs. Macmillan & Co. and the author's representatives for poems by Christina Rossetti, the author or executors and Messrs. Macmillan for *Danny Murphy, Day and Night, The Fifteen Acres, The Night, The Rivals, The Shell, The Snare, White Fields* and *The Wood of Flowers* from "Collected Poems" by James Stephens, *A Frolic* from "Collected Poems by A.E.," *Jack o' the Inkpot* from "The Education of Uncle Paul" by Algernon Blackwood, *Michael's Song* from "Collected Poems 1905–1935" by Wilfrid Gibson, *The Oxen* and *Weathers* by Thomas Hardy (by permission of the Hardy Estate), *Time, you old Gipsy Man*

627

Acknowledgments

and *The Bells of Heaven* from "Poems" by Ralph Hodgson, *Street Scene* by W. E. Henley, *Vespers* from "Collected Poems" by T. E. Brown, *Land of Our Birth* by Rudyard Kipling (also by permission of Mrs. Bambridge). The Macmillan Co., New York, and the author for *Gypsies* by Rachel Field. Mr. Walter de la Mare for *Mrs. Macqueen, Nicholas Nye, Nod, Old Shellover, Silver, Someone, Sooeep* and *Tired Tim.* The executors of the late Mr. W. E. Martyn for *The Little Herd Boy's Song* by Robert Buchanan. Mr. John Masefield for *Roadways* and *Tewkesbury Road* from "Collected Poems of John Masefield" (Wm. Heinemann Ltd.); Miss Stella Mead for *The Last Gate*; Messrs. Meiklejohn for *Haymaking* by A. P. Graves; Messrs Methuen and the executors of E. V. Lucas for *Mr. Coggs,* and *O. England, country of my Heart's Desire* by E. V. Lucas and *Snow in Town* by Rickman Mark, the authors concerned and Messrs. Methuen for *Duck's Ditty* by Kenneth Grahame, *Gypsy Man* by Dorothy King, *Johnny's Farm* by H. M. Adams, *Hay-Harvest, The Puk-Wudjies* and *When Mary Goes Walking* by Patrick R. Chalmers, *Michael Met a White Duck* by J. Dupuy, *Muffin Man* by A. Coasdell, *Puppy and I* by A. A. Milne and *A Sussex Legend* by Charles Dalmon. Mr. Wilfred Meynell for *Chimes* by Alice Meynell and *Ex Ore Infantium* by Francis Thompson. Mr. T. Sturge Moore for *Beautiful Meals.* Mrs. Harold Monro for *Bird at Dawn, Milk for the Cat, One Blackbird* and *Overheard on a Saltmarsh* by Harold Monro. Mr. Christopher Morley and Messrs. J. B. Lippincott Co. for *Song for a Little House.* Messrs. John Murray for *Pensioners* and *Spring the Travelling Man* by W. M. Letts; the National Sunday School Union for *Jack Frost* by Cecily E. Pike. Capt. Francis Newbolt for *The Toy Band* from "Poems New and Old" by Sir Henry Newbolt and *The Deserted House, Street Lanterns, Chillingham, The Train, L'Oiseau Bleu* and *When Mary thro' the Garden Went* from "Poems" by Mary E. Coleridge. Mr. Alfred Noyes and Messrs. Blackwood for *The Barrel Organ, The New Duckling* and *Sherwood* from "The Collected Poems of Alfred Noyes"; Mr. Lloyd Osbourne for *The Wind, A Child's Thought, Farewell to the Farm, Foreign Lands, From a Railway Carriage,*

628

Acknowledgments

Happy Thought, Marching Song, and *Windy Nights* from "A Child's Garden of Verse" by Robert Louis Stevenson. Mr. Seumas O'Sullivan for *A Piper* and *The Trains.* The Oxford University Press for *From a Walking Song* from "Windows of Night" by Charles Williams. Messrs. A. D. Peters for *The Idlers* by Edmund Blunden; Sir Isaac Pitman & Sons Ltd. for *Little Tommy Tidler* from "Songs and Marching Tunes for Children" by Paul Edmonds; "The Poetry Review" for *Apple Blossoms* by Helen Adams Parker and *The Scarecrow* by Michael Franklin; the Proprietors of "Punch" for *Four-Paws* by Helen Eden Parry, *The Aconite* by A. M. Graham, *The Elfin People Fill the Tubes* by W. M. Letts, *Picnics* and *The Watchmaker's Shop* by Elizabeth Fleming, and to the Proprietors of "Punch" and Miss Rose Fyleman for *A Fairy Went a-Marketing* and *The Fairy Flute.* Miss Dorothy Una Ratcliffe and Messrs. John Lane for *February* and *The Pirates' Tea-Party.* Mrs. Roberts for *Old Morgan* by G. D. Roberts; Miss Margaret Rose for *November, The Little Fir Tree, Little Bird's Song, The Magic Whistle* and *The Butterfly*; Mrs. F. Rogers for *Wishes*; Mr. Clive Sansom and Messrs. A. & C. Black Ltd. for *The Dustman, The Milkman* and *The Postman* from "Speech Rhymes"; Mr. Siegfried Sassoon for *A Child's Prayer, South Wind* and *Daybreak in a Garden* from "Selected Poems" (Heinemann); Messrs. J. Saville & Co. Ltd. for *Fairy Music* by Enid Blyton; Messrs. Charles Scribners Sons Ltd. for *Foreign Children* by R. L. Stevenson; Messrs. Martin Secker & Warburg Ltd. for *Afternoon on a Hill* by Edna St. Vincent Millay, and *The Badgers* by Eden Phillpotts; Mr. R. Farquarson Sharp for *The Wasp* by William Sharp, *Bells of Youth, Invocation of Peace* and *The Unknown Wind* by "Fiona Macleod". Messrs. Silver Burdett Co. for *The Five-Fingered Maple, The Little Plant* and *Lady Moon* by Kate L. Brown; The Society for Promoting Christian Knowledge for *Every Day* by Mary Osborn and *Christmas*; Messrs. Sidgwick & Jackson Ltd. for *Child's Song* from "Poems" by Gerald Gould, *Four and Eight* from "The Very Thing" and *The Poppies in the Garden* by ffrida Wolfe, *Moonlit Apples, Morning Thanksgiving* and *A Town Window* by John Drinkwater and extract from *Ducks* by F. W. Harvey.

629

Acknowledgments

Mrs. Thomas and Messrs. Faber & Faber Ltd. for *Tall Nettles* by Edward Thomas; Miss A. Alma Tadema for *Bed-Time, A Blessing for the Blessed, Playgrounds, The Robin* and *Snowdrops*; Mr. Wilfrid Thorley for *Fan the Filly* and *Song for a Ball Game*. The University of London Press for *The Squirrel, Cradle Song, Here we come a-Piping, Harvest Song* and *Shell Secrets* from "The London Treasury of Nursery Rhymes"; The University Tutorial Press Ltd. for *A Bit of Colour* by Horace Smith; Messrs. A. P. Watt & Sons and the executrix of the late Frances Chesterton for *How Far Is It to Bethlehem?*; Messrs. Frederick Warne & Co., Ltd. for *Five Sisters* and *A Happy Child*, from "Under the Window" by Kate Greenaway, and *The Owl and the Pussy Cat* from "Nonsense Songs" by Edward Lear. The executors of Sir William Watson and Messrs. Harrap & Co. Ltd. for *April*; Messrs. Wells, Gardner & Darton Ltd. for *The Windmill* by E. V. Lucas and T. Werner Laurie Ltd. for *Song* by Eugene Field.

Whilst every effort has been made to trace the owners of copyrights, in a few cases this has proved impossible, and we take this opportunity of tendering our apologies to any owners whose rights may have been unwittingly infringed.

630

jacket, aimed wide, and with a single, careless glance, fired in the general direction of the staircase. The ringing silence following her shot swung the attention of the room toward them. Pistols, knives, and the odd sword rang out and clattered as they were drawn. And with that small explosion of powder and spark, the fight Sophia had been looking for, the one she'd tried a dozen times to get from him, from the serving girl, from whoever so much as looked at her the wrong way, broke out in earnest.

One man, limbs clumsy with rum, elbowed another man in the back of the neck while trying to pull his own weapon out. With a strangled cry, *that* sailor swung his fist around, knocking the first clear across the nearest table, scattering cards, dice, food, and ale in every direction. The card players rose and charged into the nearest throng of gawking men, who were forced, of course, to push back lest they be trampled.

A sailor emerged from the fray, swinging a chair up from the floor, aiming at Sophia, who stood where she was, smirking.

Blind to it, he thought in horror, in that short instant before he bellowed, "On your left!"

Sophia's hat flew off as she jerked around. Her foot rose instinctively, her aim true: the powerful kick landed directly on his bawbles. As the sailor crashed to the floor with a shriek, she relieved him of the chair and smashed it over his head.

The fiddle shrieked as the bow jumped off the strings. The fiddler himself dove to the floor, just in time to avoid a chair hurtling toward his head from a whiskey-soaked doxy trying to hit her rival across her rouge-smeared face.

One lone drunk seaman stood in the center of the chaos, eyes shut as he swayed around in some odd reel, holding out his rum bottle as if it were his dancing partner.

"Damn your eyes!" Nicholas hollered.

conversation along. He could understand the necessity of secrecy, but each second that passed without searching for the astrolabe was a second too long. "Are you to take us to this lady, then?"

The man took a deep drink of his pint, coughing as he shook his head. With one more furtive glance around, his hand disappeared into his cloak. Nicholas's own fingers jabbed inside his jacket again, curling around the hilt of his blade.

But instead of a pistol or knife, the man pulled out a folded sheet of parchment and set it on the table. Nicholas glanced down at the red wax seal, the sigil of the Linden family stamped into it, then back up at the man. Sophia snatched it up, turning it over and shaking the folded parchment as if expecting poison to trickle out.

"Our . . . *flower,*" the man said, emphasizing the word, "had other business to attend to. And now I've repaid her favor, and I'll be off to see to my own—"

"Favor?" Sophia repeated, the ale making her even more brazen than usual. "Aren't you supposed to be a guardian?"

The man pushed himself back from the table. "Used to be, before another family killed nearly the whole lot of them. Now I do as I please. Which, in this moment, is leaving."

Nicholas stood at the moment the Linden guardian did, dogging him through the thick crowds until he was close enough to grab his arm. "What other business did she have? We've been waiting for her—"

The guardian wrenched his arm out of Nicholas's grip, bumping into the back of another tavern patron. Ale sloshed over the edge of the pint and onto Nicholas's shoes. "Do I look like the sort Rose Linden would tell her bleeding secrets to?"

Actually, given his rumpled state and the rather impressive scarring around his neck, which could only have come from surviving a hanging, he seemed like the *exact* sort.

"Did she give you *any* other information?" Nicholas pressed, annoyed he had to raise his voice to be heard over the squealing fiddle and the boisterous laughter of the men and women around him. "Is she still on the island?"

"Are we not speaking English, lad?" the guardian continued. "Do I need to be giving it to you in French, or—?"

A feminine shriek broke through the loud roll of deeper male voices. Nicholas spun, searching out the table he'd just left, only to find a serving girl frantically trying to pick up the pieces of several broken glasses that had smashed across their table. Another small figure in a navy coat helped mop up the liquid as it rushed over the edge onto the floor.

"You—you *cow*!" Sophia shouted, snatching a rag out of the flustered serving girl's hand to mop down her front.

"An accident—so sorry—stumbled—" The poor girl could barely get a word out.

"Are you *blind*?" Sophia continued. "I'm the one with one eye!"

"Best of luck with that one," he heard the guardian say, but by the time Nicholas turned back, the man was on the other side of the tavern, and a sea of bodies had filled the space between them. The wind caught the door and slammed it open as the guardian disappeared into the night. The Three Crowns proprietor was forced to abandon a tray of drinks to bolt it shut before the rain flooded in.

"What's this about?" Nicholas asked, moving toward the table. Sophia dropped back into her seat, glowering as the serving girl swept up the last of the glass into her apron.

"*Someone,*" Sophia emphasized, as if that someone weren't standing directly beside them, "decided to be a right and proper fool and waste perfectly good rum by making me bathe in it—"

Truthfully, the liquor had improved her smell.

"I'm not a fool!" The serving girl's face reddened. "I was watching where I was going, sir, but something caught my foot!"

She stormed off before he could tell her it was all right. And, of course, Sophia only seemed further infuriated by her absence.

"What? She can't take a hint of criticism?" she snapped, then yelled after her, "Stand up for yourself, you sodding—"

"*Enough,*" Nicholas said. "Let us have a look at the letter."

Sophia crossed her arms over her chest, slumping back against her chair. "Hilarious. You couldn't even let me hold on to it for a moment before you took it."

"I don't have time for your games," he said. "Just give it to me."

She returned his sharp look with a blank one. A cold prickling of unease raced down his spine.

"The *letter,*" he insisted, holding out his hand.

"I. Do. Not. Have. It."

They stared at each other a moment more; Nicholas felt as though her gaze was slicing him to pieces as his mind raced. He stooped, searching the floor, the chairs, the area around them. The serving girl—no, he saw her kneeling, and surely she wouldn't have hovered by the table if she'd just stolen something. She hadn't swept it into her apron, either. He would have seen that. Which left—

The other man. The one who had wiped down the table.

"Where did the man go?" he said, spinning on his heel.

"What are you on about?" Sophia grumbled, pushing herself ba up to her feet. As she spoke, he caught sight of the deep blue jac he'd seen before, but the wide-brimmed hat did nothing to disguise slight man's distinct features. The Chinese man stood, watching th from the landing of the staircase leading to the private rooms ab Nicholas squinted through the tavern's dim lighting and took a si cautious step in his direction. A flicker of a movement, really, bu man bolted with all the ease and speed of a hare.

"Hell and damnation," he groused. "You wait—"

Sophia slid a pistol he had never seen before out from und

"I think you mean *eye*," Sophia said, reloading the last of their powder into the pistol, pausing only to steal the half-empty rum bottle from the next table over when its occupant turned to the sprawling fight.

Nicholas shoved his way through the thrashing tangle of limbs, dodging to avoid a sword winging its way through the air. The proprietor climbed to the top of his counter, and, instead of stopping the fight with a well-timed shot into the room, leaped onto the back of the nearest man, tackling him to the floor with a loud cry.

Nicholas had seen more civilized tar-and-featherings than this.

He arrived at the stairs in time to see a man, while fleeing the fight, shove a doxy out of his way and send her tumbling in a mass of skirts down the stairs. He managed to catch her, narrowly preventing her from breaking her neck.

"*Christ!*" he gasped, coughing as he waved away a cloud of her wig powder.

"Thank ye—thank ye—!" The woman kissed whatever patch of skin she could find, moving to block his path up the stairs, even as he tried to gently push her away.

"Ma'am, please—"

"Move, wench!" Sophia stood at the bottom of the stairs, pistol aimed at the doxy's face. "He doesn't have two coins to rub together, let alone any to waste on you!"

At that the girl ceased her assault, turned in a huff, and marched down the stairs to join the fray.

"Did she kiss you senseless?" Sophia snarled. "*Go!* He's getting away!"

Nicholas took the steps two at a time. He burst onto the second floor, his chest burning as he drew each heavy, uneven breath. Down the hall, at the very end of a length of worn rug, a bedroom door had been thrown wide open, and Nicholas strode toward it. Just inside, a dark-haired girl, wrapped in a knit blanket, leaned onto the shoulder of another girl who patted her back now and then as she spoke in rapid, almost nonsensical English.

"On me—the door—a mite—funny little man—waving his knife—out the window—"

"A funny little man?" Nicholas asked, just as Sophia repeated, "Out the window?"

The girl blinked at their sudden appearance. "Why—short, yes, very small, almost like a child. And he's one of them—he's, how do you say—"

"From the Far East? Chinese?" the other offered. The first nodded, then turned to him, clearly thinking she should be rewarded. But Sophia was right—he didn't have two coins in his pocket. After their drinks and supper, he no longer had even one.

Sophia pushed past him into the room, Nicholas following at her heel. The room was choked with the scents of smoke from the blown-out candles and perfume reeking of flowers. Rain had blown in from the open window and soaked the carpet in dark splotches.

Sophia retrieved a torn piece of fabric stuck to the frame, and inspected it as Nicholas stuck his head out, searching the flooded streets for any sign of movement. He swung a leg over the window frame and climbed out through it, jumping from the ledge to the porch's roof and, finally, dropping to the ground. A heavy thud and curse followed as Sophia landed behind him.

Nicholas ran forward, shielding his eyes against the tropical torrent. Water rushed along the dirt and cobblestone paths, carrying away, just for the night, the grime and filth of the island.

But the thief was gone, and Rose's letter along with him.

"Carter!" Sophia stood a short distance away, at the edge of the tavern, rooted in place. A large dark lump leaning against the brightly painted wall suddenly took the shape of a man.

"What's the . . ." The words shriveled in Nicholas's throat as he took a step back.

The Linden man sat slumped, his eyes open and unseeing. His skin had taken on a white, waxy quality, as if the blood had been drained from it. Between the rain and the near complete dark, Nicholas could see no obvious mortal wound—no gunshot, cuts, marks of strangulation.

"What happened?" he asked Sophia as she knelt beside the body. She turned the dead man's head to the side, where a rivulet of blood was working its way down from his ear and along his jawline.

"There they are!"

Nicholas looked up to where one of the doxies was leaning out of the window, pointing directly at them. Several men at her shoulder turned to run back down the stairs, through the tavern, at the sight of them.

"We need to run," he told Sophia.

"No argument from me," she said, and sprang forward, leading them deeper into the night's storm.

SAN FRANCISCO
1906

THREE

ETTA FELT HER WAY ALONG THE EDGE OF HER DREAMS, carried by the soft rocking of memory.

The waves thrashing beneath her suddenly steadied to a gentle pulse that mimicked her own. Faces ringed around her in the dim candlelight, whispering, their rough hands tugging at her bruised skin. She pulled back to the cool silk and shadows of her mind, searching for that bit of light she'd seen: the moon on water stained with midnight.

He found her first, as he always did, from across the length of a ship. The parts of her that had dimmed with loss flared again, flooding the aches and fears until nothing but the sight of him remained. The tide kept the same pace, dipping, rising, with each step they took toward one another.

Then, suddenly, he was there, she was in the circle of his arms, and her face was pressed to the folds of his rough linen shirt. She breathed in his sea scent, her hands sliding along the strong planes of his back, seeking the familiar warmth of his skin. *Here, here, here—* not without, not anymore. The simplicity of it took root in her chest, blossomed into all of the possibilities she had dreamt about. A rough cheek brushed her smooth one and his lips moved against her ear, but

Etta couldn't hear a word, no matter how hard she gripped him, drawing him closer.

The world beneath her eyelids shifted again; the shadows pulled back, just enough to see the others around her, the curve of the Underground tunnel. A violin's notes slanted against the air, and she realized they were swaying to its sound, moving in a slow, endless circle of two. She thought of the way she had taken his arm, stroked the strong veins and ligaments, created a masterpiece of his pulse and muscles and bones. The walls shook and banged and roared, and Etta thought as she looked up, as she tried to see his face, *Let them roar; let it all fall apart.*

He ducked his head down and drifted back, receding. She tried to catch him, his sleeve, his fingers, but he disappeared like a warm breeze, and left her overturned and alone.

Don't leave me, she thought, as the heaviness in her body subsided and she resurfaced in her skin, flushed with panic, *not now, not now—*

Nicholas called back, laughing, *And now, good-morrow to our waking souls. . . .*

Etta opened her eyes.

The fire that had singed her veins in the desert was gone, at least. But she felt as insubstantial as the specks of dust dancing around the flickering lamp on the nearby bedside table. She stayed still, keeping her breathing even, and surveyed the room beneath her lashes.

And there, right at the foot of the bed, slumped in a high-backed chair, was a man.

Etta caught her gasp and swallowed it back. All she could see from the bed was the crown of his head, his thick, dark hair. Candlelight caught the few silver strands mixed into it. He wore a simple shirt and dark slacks, both crumpled from the position he had slept in. One hand rested on the open book in his lap, a loose bow tie woven between his fingers; the other arm had fallen over the side of the chair. His chest rose and fell slowly with each deep, sleep-drugged breath.

Her discomfort at the thought of being watched while she slept, unable to do anything about it, was defused by how weak of an effort this guard had put into the task.

A breeze caught the tears and sweat on her face and ruffled his open shirt collar. The window, framed by long crimson velvet curtains, had been left open.

Slowly, so as not to make a sound, Etta shifted up, biting her lip against the pain that lanced from her scalp down to her toes. Her eyes skimmed quickly around the room, searching for anyone else, but saw no one. A handsome little writing desk was nestled up against the floral wallpaper, a short distance from a bureau that looked so large, Etta had a feeling the room must have been built around it. Both had been carved from the same gleaming wood as the bed; leaves and vines arced along their edges, the pattern weaving in and out of itself.

It was a pretty little gilded prison, she had to admit. But it was already past the time when she needed to be searching for a way out of it.

Several candles were burning in the room: on a side table, on the desk, in a sconce near the door. It was the only reason she could make out her own reflection in the dusty mirror hanging over the bureau, though the image was split by an enormous crack across its center, and distorted from hanging at a crooked angle.

Oh God.

Etta rubbed at her eyes and examined herself again with growing disbelief. She knew her time in Damascus had given her pale skin some color, but now her face, ears, and neck were sunburned to the point of peeling. Her greasy hair had been braided away from her bruised face and hollow cheekbones. She looked ill—worse than that. If someone hadn't cleaned the dirt from her face and arms, she would have guessed she'd been dragged beneath a taxi through Times Square. Repeatedly.

Yet, somehow, the worst thing about it all was that someone had taken her clothes from Damascus off her—while she *slept*—and replaced them with a long, ankle-length nightgown, tied high and prim at the throat with a hideous mauve ribbon. She hoped it was the same person who'd taken the care to wrap and bind her shoulder—the same person who had cleaned her up the best they could. Still, she shuddered, both at how vulnerable she'd been and how badly it could have gone for her.

Unable to ignore the stinging pain a second longer, Etta turned her attention to her left shoulder, peeling the fabric back to inspect the itchy bandage that covered it and her upper arm. Biting her lip, she fought the unhelpful rush of tears that came as she pulled the fabric away from the sticky, healing wound.

It was a hideous, grim shade of pink—not the sheen of new skin, but the furious color of a burn. The splotch was still swollen with an uneven blister. The tightness in her throat became unbearable; Etta heaved in a breath, her gaze darting back over to the sleeping guard.

Let's go, Spencer. Run first; think later.

As soon as she could manage without feeling as though she would vomit from the motion, Etta swung her legs around and pressed her toes into the dusty Oriental rug. Just as she began to test whether her legs could bear her weight, a fast clip of steps drummed out beyond the closed door at the opposite end of the room.

In a rush of motion that smeared black across her vision and made her head feel like it was collapsing, Etta dropped to her hands and knees, ducking down until the bed blocked her from the view of anyone who might come barreling through the door.

"... *have to get* ..."

"... *try telling that to him* ..."

The voices trailed past, disappearing as quickly as they'd appeared, but the faint buzzing in her ears had subsided long enough for her to detect the strains of garbled music rising up through the floorboards. The clinking of glasses cut into the rising voices that bubbled like champagne froth.

"—*three cheers*—!"

"A toast!"

Fear woke inside Etta all at once, blazing through her confusion.

It seems like this Ironwood does have some luck left to his name, after all.

Both Nicholas and Sophia had warned her that Cyrus Ironwood had guardians watching each of the passages. She hadn't recognized the man who'd spoken to her, but it didn't matter, seeing as that single word, that single name, was enough for her to know she was in serious trouble.

But even that thought was devoured by another fear.

Where is Nicholas?

Those last few seconds in the tomb were splintered in her memory. She remembered the pain, the blood, Nicholas's horrified face, and then—

The only way to describe the sensation she had felt next was as if some invisible rope had knotted around her center and yanked her through a veil of imploding darkness. Etta pressed her fists against her eyes, unknotting the idea inch by inch.

I've been orphaned by my time.

The timeline has changed.

My future is gone.

Panic swelled in her chest, hot and suffocating. It fit—all of these pieces fit with what Sophia and Nicholas had explained to her. Time had reached out and snatched her, tossing her through a series of passages before spitting her back out at whatever the last common point was between the old timeline she had known and the new one they had inadvertently created.

Because the Thorns took the astrolabe? Etta knew carelessness could change the timeline, but not severely enough to cause travelers to be orphaned. That required *intent*. Focus and strategy. Taking the astrolabe from her, preventing her from destroying it—that hadn't been enough to orphan her, but something else had. *They must have used it.* That was the only explanation she could think of. The Thorns had used the astrolabe and irrevocably changed—broken—some event or moment in history.

And now she was here, with the Ironwoods, and Nicholas was not.

Colors burned beneath her eyelids, blood beat between her ears, a crescendo that broke over her in a frenzy of pain and grief.

Mom.

She couldn't think about her right now. Ironwood had sworn to kill Rose if Etta didn't return with the astrolabe by his deadline. *But . . .* She took in a deep breath. Knowing what she did about her mother now, Etta had to believe—she had to hope—that Rose was alive, that she'd already escaped from wherever the Ironwoods had been holding her.

Now it was her turn to do the same.

She forced herself to relax the muscles bunching up her shoulders, to breathe the way Alice had taught her to when her stage fright was at its most crippling. The anxiety, the terror, they were useless to her; she breathed in, out, in, out, until they were chased out of her mind, replaced by a floating, graceful measure of notes. The music was soft, serene, filling the shadows in her thoughts with light. Vaughan Williams's *The Lark Ascending.* Of course. Alice's favorite, the one Etta had played at her instructor's birthday, a few months before . . . before the Met concert. Before she'd been shot just outside the mouth of the passage.

Stop thinking. Just go.

Her guard shifted in his chair as she slowly rose, and adjusted his own position with a soft sigh. The book was on the verge of slipping out of his hands, onto his feet. She didn't let herself wonder at how strange that was, that the guard had felt comfortable enough to take off his shoes and curl up with a book.

It doesn't matter. There was a literal window of opportunity, and she needed to take it now.

Its frame creaked in quiet protest as Etta pushed it open further. She leaned out to assess her options, quickly recoiling back into the room.

The moon was high overhead, illuminating the bruised remains of a city. There were no streetlights, save for a few distant lanterns, but Etta had a clear view of the hills that rolled down beneath her window, of slanted, winding streets that disappeared beneath heaping mounds of brick and wood, only to reappear again, scorched.

The air held a hint of smoke and salt. An insistent wind carried thick fog up from a distant body of water, as if the city was breathing in the clean, cool mist. Skyscrapers had whole sections of themselves scooped out, their windows knocked loose like teeth. But here and there, Etta saw buildings and structures that looked freshly built—all framework and unfinished brick faces. While many streets and patches of ground had been cleared, the sheer scale of the destruction reminded her of what she had seen in wartime London with Nicholas.

She had the ghost of an idea where she was, but it fled before she could grab onto it. The *when* seemed more obvious. The furniture, the expensive draperies and bedding, the hideous Victorian-doll-like night-gown someone had stuffed her into, the destruction . . . late nineteenth century? Early twentieth?

Well, she thought, hoping to prop up her spirits a bit, *the only way out is through.*

She was on the second or third story of a house, though it was difficult to tell by the steep angle of the road below. This side of the house was covered in an intricate puzzle of wood scaffolding that extended from the roof above her to where the long beams were anchored on the ground.

She stuck an arm out, testing the distance between her and the nearest support. Her fingers easily folded around the rough wood, and before she could question the decision, before she could consider all the reasons it was a very, very terrible idea, Etta climbed up onto the window frame and swung her legs around first to its ledge, then toward the nearest horizontal plank of scaffolding.

"This is insane," she muttered, waiting to make sure the wood could at least hold some of her weight. How many times growing up had she seen news reports of scaffolding collapsing in New York City?

Eight. Exactly eight.

The blood drained from her head all at once, and she was forced to wait, heart beating an impatient rhythm, until her balance steadied again. Etta held her breath, arms trembling from the strain, as she scooted off the window ledge and onto the wood plank in front of her.

It didn't so much as groan.

There, she thought, *good job. Keep going.*

In some ways it was like heading down a strangely constructed ladder. Every now and then, Etta felt the structure tremble with her added weight, and some gaps between the planks and beams were almost too wide to reach across. But she gained confidence with each step, even as the wind plucked at her back, even as she realized she had no idea where to go once she reached the ground.

The bay windows on the floor below were longer and jutted out from the house. More dangerous yet, the glass was glowing, light spilling out onto the scaffolding. Etta crawled forward to peer through her cover of darkness; if the room was occupied, she'd have to move closer to the edge of the scaffolding to avoid being seen by its occupants. But first she wanted to know who, exactly, was in the building—the enormous house—and why they'd taken her in.

The room was larger than the one she'd just climbed out of, and lined with stately, dark wood shelves that contained row upon row of books. There was a desk stationed in front of the window and a large broad-backed chair turned away from her, but the room was otherwise empty.

"Come on," she whispered. "Move it, Spencer."

Her lip began to bleed as she dug her teeth into it, trying to keep from crying out in pain each time she dropped down and overextended her hurt shoulder. Gripping the beam she'd been sitting on, as if she were on the monkey bars, she stretched her toes out and felt a tremor of panic deep in her gut as they barely scraped the beam below.

Too far. Her arms strained under her weight as she looked to her right, her left, trying to judge how far she'd have to shift and scoot over to reach the nearest vertical support and slide down it. No—she wasn't going to make it, not with her shoulder on fire and her entire body shaking.

Not going to make it. She looked down again, this time to the ground below, the slant of the street, and tried not to picture what she'd look like lying there in a broken heap of gauzy white fabric and blood. If she could drop softly enough, she might be able to balance, catch herself—

A sudden movement at the window in front of her snapped her attention forward again. A bemused face stared at her through the glass. She blinked rapidly, her breath locked inside of her throat. The window creaked open, out toward her.

"Well, that's a bit of trouble you've gotten yourself into, old girl—"

Arms reached for her, and Etta didn't think, didn't speak, just *kicked.* Her heel connected with something hard, and she took some satisfaction in the surprised *"Cripes!"* laced with pain in response.

"That was uncalled for!" came the same voice, now muffled as he clutched his nose.

The pain in her shoulder and left arm stabbed straight through her fear, and her fingers spasmed and relaxed their grip on the beam. A gasp tore out of her as she dangled there by one arm. Her jagged fingernails dug into the wood as she frantically tried to line up her footing below before she lost what grip she had.

"Take my hands—come on, don't be a fool about this," the young man was saying. Etta leaned back out of his reach, struggling to pull far enough away, as he climbed onto the frame. "Really? You think the better option is breaking your neck? I'm hurt."

The wind picked up, tossing her loose hair into her eyes, lifting the hem of her nightgown.

"I can admire the intent here, but you should know that all it would take is one shout from me and you'll be swarmed by unhappy Thorns having to climb down to fetch you. I doubt you want to die, either, so let's have it, then—I'll help you back inside, as easy as pie."

"Thorns?" Etta's brows knitted together. *Not Ironwoods?*

She didn't recognize the sounds at first, the odd rumbles and creaks, but the vibrations under her hand—those, she understood. The whole structure of scaffolding was being shoved to the left by the wind, leaning, until she heard a snap and felt something clip her bad shoulder as it fell behind her.

Then she was falling, too.

FOUR

IT HAPPENED TOO FAST FOR ETTA TO EVEN SCREAM. ONE moment she was falling; the next, her arm was caught and yanked in its socket as two hands closed around her wrist and dragged her toward the pale exterior of the house. Her cheek slammed against the rough stone, and she squeezed her eyes shut as the scaffolding began to shudder, folding in on itself and collapsing down onto the old-fashioned cars parked on the street below.

"Reach up, will you?" the young man said, the words strained. Etta shook her head. Her wounded shoulder was too stiff, and the whole length of it, from neck to fingertip, felt like it was filled with scorching, sunbaked sand.

Instead, he released her wrist with one hand and reached down to grab her nightgown. There was a loud grunt overhead as he heaved her up. Etta's feet scrabbled against the wall. She didn't breathe again until her elbows were braced on the windowsill. Then she was spilling through it, onto the young man and the carpet below.

She rolled off him and onto her back as soon as she landed. Her whole body sang with pain and adrenaline, and it was several long moments before her heart steadied enough for Etta to hear anything over its frantic rhythm.

45

"Well, that was exciting. I've always wanted to rescue a damsel in distress, and you've given me twice the fun on that front."

Etta cracked open an eye, turning her head toward the voice. Next to her, propped up on his elbow, the young man was making an appraising, appreciative study of her. She pushed herself upright and scooted back against the desk to put some much-needed distance between them.

He was young—her age, or a few years older, with short, chestnut-colored dark hair brightened by streaks of red. It was mussed to the point of standing on end, and Etta had the horrifying realization that she really *had* gripped it for leverage when she'd tumbled back into the house. His shirt was open at the collar and inside out, as if he'd picked it up and thrown it on without a second look. He scratched at the shadow of scruff along his jaw, studying her with piercing light blue eyes that warmed with some unspoken joke.

His voice . . . those eyes.

Ironwood.

Etta pulled herself to her feet, but her path was blocked by the desk. He'd claimed they were with the Thorns, which could only be true if he'd defected from Cyrus Ironwood's ranks and joined theirs. Or if he was a prisoner, same as her.

Or it would make him a liar. But if this was the truth, then . . . Etta was exactly where she needed to be.

With the people who had stolen the astrolabe from her.

"I suppose you gave me a bit of a fright, I can be man enough to admit that—"

"Where am I?" she asked, interrupting him.

He seemed startled by her ability to speak, but he stood and retrieved a glass of some amber liquid from a corner table for her. "You sound as terrible as you look, kiddo. Have a sip."

She stared at it.

46

"Oh, you're no fun," he said with a little pout. "I suppose you'll want water instead. Wait here and be quiet—can't raise the alarm just yet, can we?"

Etta wasn't sure what that meant, but she complied all the same, watching as the young man walked to the door and stuck his head out into the hall.

"You, there—yes, you—bring me a glass of water. And don't bloody well spit in it this time—you honestly think I'm not well versed enough in that fine art to notice?"

The response was immediate and irritated. "I'm not your damned servant."

So there are guards after all. The only question was whether they were protecting him, or protecting themselves from him.

"I do believe the official decree from your master and commander was, 'Give the dear boy what he wants.' This dear boy wants water. And make it snappy. Pep in your step and all that. Thanks, old chum."

Etta's lip curled back. Definitely an Ironwood. And, by the sound of it, definitely working *with* the Thorns.

"I'm not your—" The young man shut the door on the response and leaned back against it with a pleased little smirk.

"They're such a serious bunch that it's all too easy to rile them up," he whispered to her with a wink. "You and I will have the best fun together now that you're here."

She glared back. *Unlikely.*

After a moment the door popped open and a hand thrust itself in with a glass of cloudy-looking water. The instant the young man took it, the door slammed shut. This time, Etta heard the lock click from the outside.

"You use your old bathwater?" the young man shouted through the wood.

"You'd be so lucky!" came the reply.

He was still muttering as he crossed the room again and handed it to her. It was tinged a putrid brown, with a few suspicious particles floating in it.

Seeing her face, he said, "Sorry, the water situation is none too good after the earthquake, as you can imagine. No one's gotten sick from it." And then, after she'd already taken a sip, he added, "Yet."

The water did have an odd taste—a little metallic, maybe, a little dirty too—but she downed it in two quick gulps. Her hands and arms were still trembling as they tried to recover from the strain.

"Where am I?" she demanded. "When?"

"San Francisco," he said. "October 12, 1906. You've been out a number of days. . . ."

Etta's heels seemed to sink further into the rug as the weight of his words slammed into her. Thirteen days. She'd lost *thirteen days*. Nicholas could be anywhere. Sophia could be anywhere. And the astrolabe . . .

"We were briefly acquainted in the middle of the Texas desert, just after you were spat out by a passage. You might remember?"

"Are you looking for a thank-you?" Etta asked.

"Don't I deserve one? You are damn lucky we were orphaned through the same passage. I saved you from both the nearby guardian *and* the coyotes circling nearby, waiting for you to croak. In fact, I'd like to think that if it weren't for *me*, the boss man would be lowering your tattered remains into the ground."

That confirmed her suspicion, at least. Some change must have been made to the timeline that orphaned all the travelers born after that time. Etta closed her eyes. Took a steadying breath through her nose.

"What changed?"

"What changed—oh, you mean the timeline? Judging by the party they neglected to invite me to, the timeline's shifted the way they were hoping it would. The dimwits running this joint said something about

Russia losing but winning. Drunken nonsense. Why we're still in scenic post-earthquake San Francisco is anyone's guess, though. Stay with these people long enough and, believe me, they'll show you the armpit of every century."

"You haven't even tried asking them, have you?" Etta asked, unimpressed. "What year?"

His look was lightly scolding. "I told you. 1906."

She swallowed her noise of irritation. "No, I mean, what year was it in Texas?"

"I'm not entirely sure I should say—"

Etta lunged forward, barely catching the words burning the tip of her tongue before they had the chance to singe him. He wasn't going to keep the last common year from her—that was the only way she could figure out how to retrace her steps to Damascus, and to Palmyra.

"Oh ho—!" He stood and backed away from her. "You've got that wild look in your eyes like you did just before you bopped me on the nose. Believe me, they've removed everything that can be used as a weapon."

Etta looked down at the glass in her hand, then back at him, one brow arching. "I've gotten pretty creative over the past few weeks. I think I can handle one minor Ironwood."

"Minor?" he shot back, his voice wavering between incredulity and outrage. "Don't you know who I am?"

"No. You were so busy congratulating yourself, you never got around to making introductions," Etta said. "Though I take it you know who I am?"

"Everyone knows who you are," he muttered, sounding annoyed. "How far I've fallen that I actually have to *introduce* myself."

He placed one arm behind his back and the other across his waist, giving her a mocking little bow. "Julian Ironwood, at your service."

HER DISBELIEF MUST HAVE BEEN SPLASHED ACROSS HER FACE, because his smile shifted, becoming sardonic. Clearly not the reaction he had been expecting.

Julian Ironwood? Etta let out a small, lifeless laugh. Time travel had already presented a number of brain-bending possibilities—meeting an eighteen-year-old version of the violin instructor she'd known from the moment she was born, to name only one. But, surprise, experiences like that didn't make it any easier to come face-to-face with the dead. Etta tried to keep her expression neutral, knowing that staring at him in horror was going to raise some flags in his mind.

Nicholas had warned her repeatedly about the dangers of telling anyone their fate, that knowing how and when they would die could affect the choices a person made, and potentially, the timeline. Alice had given her an out, had specifically asked her not to say, but now . . .

The guilt felt familiar as it pooled in her heart. Etta bit her lip. It was just . . . what were the chances of meeting Nicholas's brother, and here, of all places? And why hadn't Nicholas mentioned that Julian had been held at some point by the Thorns?

"Either my adorably sadistic grandfather has done something terrible to you, or you're about to inform me that I've died by—rather stupidly, if I say so myself—falling off a mountain," he said. "Those seem to be the only two reactions I get these days."

"You—" Etta sputtered, whirling back around. "I didn't mean to—it's just—"

"Calm down, will you? You're going to give yourself the vapors for no good reason," he said. "As you can see, I am *not* dead."

"Wait . . ." she began, coming closer to better study his face. His eyes were the same icy shade of blue as Cyrus's, and she could detect, under the scruff and grin, the same high cheekbones and long, straight nose that age had tempered on the old man's face. Julian *also* seemed to have the Ironwood affinity for grappling for control of every conversation, no matter how short.

"You're *alive*," Etta finally managed to get out. "You . . . you didn't die after all?"

He grinned, enjoying the conversation, and motioned down to his body. "Still in one piece. The luck of the devil, as old Grandpops used to say. Rather odd, that, considering he *is* the devil—"

"What happened?" she interrupted.

He gave her an infuriating grin. "Tell me what you think happened."

Etta, with patience she had no idea she possessed, managed to tamp down her temper long enough to say, "There was a storm. . . . You slipped on the path leading up to the monastery, Taktsang Palphug—"

"Did Grandpops really give the world that much detail?" Julian asked, flattening his hair with his hand. "He's usually so quick to defend the family's honor, but I guess even he couldn't resist making me sound like a right idiot."

There was a sharp undercurrent to the words that seemed at odds with his jocular tone. Etta studied him again—the slouching posture, the unkempt clothes, the glint in his eyes she'd originally taken as mischief—and wondered which side of him was the truth, and which he'd simply made a home in.

"I thought he would have . . ." He kept pacing, but this time turned his eyes to the floor. "Did he . . . I never heard anything about a memorial or the like . . . ?"

Etta's brows rose. "I don't know. I'm assuming."

"It's not that it matters to me," he said quickly, shaping the words in the air with his hands, "but it's sort of . . . anticlimactic to disappear into a puff of snow and mist. A chap wants to know that—you know, actually, it doesn't matter. None of it really matters."

"Stop—*stop* pacing, you're making me nervous," Etta said. "Can you stand still for one second and actually explain this to me?"

He popped himself up onto the corner of the grand desk, folding his hands in his lap. Within seconds, his bare feet were swinging, drumming against the leg of it, and Etta realized she'd asked for the impossible. Not only did he not shut up, he couldn't seem to burn off enough energy to stop moving.

"In that instance, the Thorns were *also* responsible for orphaning me," Julian said. "Three years ago, they used a passage to New York in 1940 to set a fire at the New York World's Fair, hitting at Grandfather's business interests in that period. At the same time, I happened to be stupidly falling down a mountainside in Bhutan. Since I was born in 1941, I was kicked through the passages to 1939, which was, at that point—"

"The last common year between the old timeline and the new one," Etta finished. Between tracking the timeline, the collection of years at the mercy of the travelers' actions, and each traveler's personal life that they lived straight through, even when they were jumping between centuries, she thought her brain might explode. "But I was born after 1940, too, and I wasn't orphaned when that change occurred."

"Then the change must have been confined to that year, and not rippled past 1941. I'm sure you've heard this a thousand times by now, but you know how the timeline is about inconsistency."

Etta did know. It had self-corrected as if passing over a speed bump, instead of the road completely diverging. Interesting.

"At least that time I got spat out in the Maldives. Made for quite the vacation. But by the time I located the necessary passages and resurfaced, I caught news of my supposed death and decided I might as well make the most of it."

"And it never occurred to you once—*once*—over the past few years that you might, you know, *tell* someone that you were alive?"

Not Nicholas? Not Sophia? Not any other member of his family?

Julian pushed away from the desk. He moved to the bookshelves, dragging his fingers along the beveled spines of the books as he made his way around the room. It was like watching a cat pace in front of a window, restless and watchful.

If she hadn't heard the words leave Nicholas's mouth, she would never have believed they were related at all. It went beyond their looks. Where Nicholas moved in assured, long strides, even when he was uncertain of where he was going, Julian had a kind of agitated undercurrent to his movements. He didn't have Nicholas's height, either, and his body hadn't been honed and chafed by the hard work of life on a ship. Julian's words fell over each other, as if fighting over which got to escape first, while Nicholas took careful measure of each and every word he said, knowing how they might be used against him. Julian seemed to be bursting at his seams, and Nicholas had been so careful, so steady, in holding his feelings in check.

Because he had to.

Because he'd had none of the privileges Julian had, born into a family that never wanted him and a society that scorned and disrespected him.

Anger bloomed, vivid as the crooked portraits on the wall. If this really was Julian Ironwood, then it was the very same person who had taken advantage of Nicholas's love for him, the one who'd turned around and treated him like little more than a servant, rather than genuinely teach him the ways of travelers.

I'm the fool, Nicholas had told her, *because in spite of everything, he was my brother. I never saw him as anything else. And it clearly wasn't the same for him.*

Julian hadn't even had the common decency to find a way to tell his half brother he was still alive. Instead, he'd let Nicholas drown in his guilt. He had let him spend years questioning his honor and decency. He had let Nicholas take the exile and rage-fueled beating from Ironwood.

All of this time, Nicholas had been suffering—and for what?

Nothing.

"Well, kiddo, to continue this tale, I floated around for a while, living life as one does—without much money to speak of, which got me into more than a few scrapes. It all became rather tedious and boring. Enter: the Thorns. I thought it might be best to sell some knowledge about Grandfather, try to exchange it for steady meals and a safe place to sleep at night."

He glanced at her, as if expecting Etta to coo with sympathy. She kept her gaze on the unlit brass chandelier overhead, fingers curled so tightly around the lip of the desk that her hands prickled with pain. *Don't do it. He's not worth it.*

"Speaking of," Julian said, swinging around toward her, "I'd like to get back to you—*holy God!*"

Etta relished the throbbing pain in her knuckles as her fist made contact with his cheek and he stumbled back over his own feet, landing in an ungraceful heap on his bottom. He stared up at her with huge eyes, one hand still cupping the red mark on his face as she shook out her hand.

"What the bloody hell was that for?" he howled.

"Do you have *any* idea," she said, voice rising with each word, "what your 'death' did to your brother? Do you have *any* idea what he went through—what your jackass of a grandfather put him through?"

"Brother?" Julian repeated, rather stupidly. Her instinct to give him another kick, this time beneath the belt, must have registered on her face, because Julian scrambled back on the rug.

Then, to her surprise, he said, "But . . . how do you know Nick?"

Etta studied him. He looked genuinely shocked, either from her hit, Nicholas's name, or both. Unsure of how much information to trust him with, she answered, "I traveled with him for a little bit."

His brow creased. "On behalf of Grandfather?"

She shook her head, but before she could elaborate, a key scraped in the door's lock. It should have been enough to send Etta diving behind the desk, out of sight. Instead she stood there, towering over Julian, the door letting out a tortured groan as it was thrown open. Two men barreled in with guns in hand, both dressed in trousers and plain white shirts, coming up short at the sight of her. The one out in front, a dark, bushy mustache disguising half of his face, actually took a generous step back, crossing himself.

"Christ," said the other, glancing at the first. He was somewhat shorter, his pale hair cut close to the scalp and almost gone from balding. "The others were right. It's the bleeding ghost of Rose Linden."

The other one merely crossed himself.

"Aren't you supposed to be protecting me?" Julian complained. "This girl is clearly deranged—"

"*Deranged* is one word for it," the dark-haired man said. Now Etta recognized his voice as that of the man who had sparred with Julian over the water. "How in the hell did you get in here, miss?"

"I think the better question is, why did it take you almost a half hour to realize I was gone?" Etta said, reaching back for the water glass she'd left on the desk. Before either man could answer, she slammed it down on the edge of the desk, shattering its top half and leaving a jagged edge on what was left. For one insane instant, Sophia's lesson on where to cut them, how to slit their throats, floated to the front of her mind.

Get a grip, Etta. She needed to stay here and find the astrolabe, and she wouldn't be able to do that if she was locked away. But part of her hated that these people had seen her at her weakest, her most helpless, and she couldn't ignore it. They needed to know she would fight back if they pushed her.

"Easy there!" Julian cried. He craned his neck up to look at the men. "Aren't you going to do something?"

The pale-haired man raised his small black pistol, then swore, tucking it back into the waistband of his trousers. "Come along, girlie, it's time for you to go back up to your room."

Etta swung her makeshift weapon toward him, ignoring the small, warm pool of blood collecting in her palm from where she'd cut herself. "I don't think so."

Dull footsteps grew to a pounding storm out in the hallway, and the music she'd heard before cut off with a loud scratch. She caught snatches of voices shouting, *"She's gone!" "Find her!"* and a variety of swearing that would have made even the men in Nicholas's crew blush.

"She's here!" the dark-haired man called. "The office!"

The rush of panicked activity ceased, but one voice rang out. "Thank you; that'll be all the excitement for this evening, God willing."

The two guards straightened—the smaller of the two even reached up to fix the limp cloth hanging around his neck into something resembling a bow tie. A man strode into the darkened corner of the room, hands tucked into his trouser pockets.

"We were handling the situation, sir," the dark-haired one said quickly. "I was about to return the girl to her quarters."

"I see," came the amused response. "But it seems to me that she's the one who has this situation well in hand."

The man stepped into the shallow firelight, giving Etta her first real glimpse of him. It was the guard from her room. Dark eyes swept around the room, studying each of them in turn, but his gaze lingered on her, so unflinching that it seemed to wipe everyone else away, leaving just the two of them.

The man's presence made her blood slow, and finally still in her veins, but the trickle of uneasiness she'd felt at his appearance was nothing compared to the torrent of uneasiness that came in the moment where her memory met recognition. Etta wasn't aware that the glass had slipped from between her fingers until it fell, striking the top of her bare foot, and rolled away.

The black hair, cut through with silver strands . . . his rough-hewn features . . . she wasn't seeing him in the high-waisted pants or loose white shirt he currently wore. She saw him in a classic black-and-white tuxedo, wearing silver-rimmed glasses, in the Grand Hall of the Metropolitan Museum of Art. In the twenty-first century.

"You recognize me," he said, with a small, approving note in his voice—like he'd expected she wouldn't?

Not only had she bumped into him, he'd come running when she and Sophia had found Alice dying in a pool of her own blood. Almost as if he'd known it might happen.

Or as if he'd been the one to pull the trigger.

The two guards immediately stepped closer to the man's side, as though they'd been drawn into his orbit.

He looked to Julian and said, this time with a slight edge, "How did I know to check this room first?"

"She dropped in on *me*," Julian protested, pointing to the window. "I was minding my own business. For once."

The man flicked his dark gaze to Etta, and this time she forced herself to meet it. The corners of his mouth tipped up again. "I don't need to ask how you got in here, for I suspect the mountain of scaffolding piled up outside is likely my answer. Tell me, did it ever occur to you that you could have broken your neck?"

He was so calm, his voice so measured, that he made the rest of them sound manic. Even his posture, the way he hadn't once tensed up, made her want to ruffle his composure, just to see how far he could be pushed. To see where the boundaries of his anger began. It would be useful later, she thought, in trying to trick him into saying something about the astrolabe, and where the Thorns might be keeping it.

"You know," Etta said, "you're making me wish I had."

She wiped her slick palms against the horrible nightgown, wary of the man's warm laughter, the spark of enjoyment in his voice. He turned to the bald guard, knocking the back of his hand against the other man's chest. "I told you she had some spirit, didn't I?"

"You did," the guard confirmed. "Sir, I take full responsibility for all of this—"

"Sir" waved his hand before placing it on the guard's shoulder. "I

FIVE

THE STORM HAD BROKEN AT DAWN, BRINGING A BIT OF MERCY to what had been a night that redefined misery. Nicholas and Sophia trudged and waded through still-flooded streets, following the path of the runoff toward the beach. Servants were waking, appearing on the balconies of bright, two-story wooden buildings to beat rugs and toss out the waste, and the smell was rank enough to leave him feeling as if the small town had become one large chamber pot. After a rather unfortunate splash of something he didn't care to inspect, Sophia's mood had gone from sour to curdled.

They'd spent hours hiding from the tavern owner; the whoreson had sent out a veritable gang of men and Redcoats to find someone to hold accountable for the damage the fight had wrought, and had settled on them. This, despite his own gleeful participation. The dodging and hiding had considerably hampered their search for the man who'd stolen Rose's letter. As it turned out, even a rare Chinese man in the Indies didn't attract the necessary attention to leave a trail of witnesses behind. Nicholas had caught himself wondering more than once if he'd had more to drink than he thought, and made a man out of a shadow.

But the doxies and their customers upstairs had seen him, so surely . . .

He stilled, turning back toward the harbor. Would he make for a ship? If he was an Ironwood, not just some enterprising opportunist looking for possible targets for theft, he'd try to catch the first ship out. The more Nicholas turned over the thought of investigating that area, the sounder it seemed. Information traveled like flies between sailors, and surely someone of the man's ethnicity wouldn't have evaded their notice. Someone might know where he was staying, and if he had any plans of sailing out of port within the next few days.

Damn your eyes, Rose, he thought, not for the first time. *You couldn't have come yourself and saved us the trouble?*

Sophia had charged forward as his steps slowed; a good three lengths ahead, she turned back. "Did your mind suddenly go on holiday? Let's *move.* I'm ready for this hellish cat and mouse game to be over."

"You continue on," he told her. "I'm going to follow another lead—"

No sooner were the words out of his mouth than she came stomping back toward him, sending muddy water shooting up around her already-soaking shoes and splattering him in the face. "What lead is this?" she pressed. "Or have we started redefining 'lead' as 'wild guess'?"

He took a deep breath for patience, and parceled out his words carefully, so as not to reveal anything she might be able to use herself. It would be like handing her the knife she'd later jam into his spine. "I'm headed to the bay, to see if anyone might have information on our thief."

"Fine," she grumbled, turning in that direction. "We'll make it quick."

He shook his head. "You go back to the beach, get some rest—"

"I have to say," she interrupted, her small, pale hands curling at her sides as her stare burned into the side of his face, "I have no idea how Linden tolerated traveling with you. A few hours into our special partnership and I wanted to push you out a window."

Nicholas was surprised by how hard, how fast, fury gripped him. Exhaustion, hunger, frustration—he could make any excuse he liked, but the truth was, she'd touched the one sore on his heart that was still raw. "Utter her name again. Test my resolve, ma'am, please."

Sophia glowered. "I *meant,* I don't know how she could stand this game of evasion and stupid, masculine pride you seem so fond of: *stay here, go back, don't move, go on ahead.* You're not my governess, and I'm not one of the men on your stupid bloody ship, so stop ordering me around. Try to leave me out of this—try to leave me behind—one more time, and I *will* actually shoot you. In a delicate area."

"Do I need to remind you," he said, hating how quickly she seemed to be able to get his temper rolling on stormy waves, "that *you* got so deep into your cups last evening that instead of being reasonable and maintaining our disguise, you *fired a pistol,* and fired it badly, inside of a crowded tavern? That just yesterday, you harassed and abused a British regular because you 'disliked the way he looked at you' and nearly got us thrown into a rank gaol?"

"Would have been an improvement over where we've been sleeping," she grumbled.

She will never respect me, he thought, sick with hate. *She will always see me as nothing.*

"One day they will name a plague for you," he said.

"Hopefully a particularly nasty one," she answered. "A girl can dream."

"From the beginning, you treated me no better than a rat," he continued, ignoring her smirk. "Do you want to know how Etta *tolerated* me? Because we were partners, because we trusted each other, and because she was capable of taking care of herself. You seem to have appointed yourself to the task of getting us both killed. And while you might consider yourself to be expendable, I need to confirm she survived *your* treachery."

Nicholas braced himself for her inevitable snide comment, the smirking condescension she seemed to favor.

Instead, Sophia busied herself by removing her hat, unknotting the

63

small scrap of leather she'd used to secure her short braid. Her hands worked through her hair, mussing the weave in silence. They fell in line with the men stumbling bleary- and beady-eyed out of the inns and taverns, the wreckage of the previous night's frivolities. Some at least were making an attempt to tuck their shirts back into their breeches. Still, Nicholas shook his head. Captain Hall would have knocked each of them in turn off his ship if they'd reported back in such a state.

Hall. He'd sent word that he was alive and mostly well, but had yet to receive a response. And he likely would not until they returned to port. Nicholas didn't resist the small echo of longing for the thought of boarding a ship and disappearing into the horizon—for the simplicity of that life, and how quickly it would welcome him back.

Someone began to whistle, a high, bawdy tavern tune that made the men around him chuckle. All at once, seemingly without him knowing, the port city had shaken off the night. Crimson coats dotted the streets, the prim uniforms and gleaming buttons only looking primmer in contrast to their surroundings. Wagons moaned and rattled with the weight of cargo being drawn up and down the path, coming or going, just like the residents of the island. The green palms and underbrush looked as if they had been painted by the sun, glowing with pleasure in the heat, the way they only did after a hearty storm. The old fort stood above it all like a four-pointed star to the west, high walls winking as the light glanced off its wet gray stones.

"Just go," Sophia said, nodding toward the ships in the bay. "You want an out, you've got—two—three—*four* chances out there."

"What are you on about?" he asked, batting away how bloody unnerving it was that she'd traced his line of thought. "Are you still drunk?"

"Only observant," she sang.

"Whatever you think you know, I assure you, you do not."

"I know you've wasted our time here. I know you don't truly care about the astrolabe, just the first girl who turned her big blue doe eyes on you."

"That's not true," he insisted. "And can a deer even have blue eyes?"

"Then what are we still doing here?" Sophia challenged, hands planted on her hips. "Are you hoping that if we wait long enough, the woman might find her daughter and bring her here to you? We don't *need* information about the last common year. It's irrelevant. If the Thorns have the astrolabe, they're traveling with it, and finding them is our best bet for finding it. But you haven't even considered that, have you?"

He was tired; so tired of the Ironwoods, of travelers, of all the meddling in the lives of innocent people and the hardship they suffered over the greed and demands of his kind. He was inclined to say Ironwood could take the blasted astrolabe to hell with him, if it weren't for the damage he knew Ironwood could do to Nicholas's own time.

"I made a promise," was all he said.

"Promises are for saints and losers. Most of the time we can't even keep the ones we make to ourselves."

He gave her a sour look from beneath the brim of his hat. "You and I are *entirely* different people."

"You don't say!" Sophia scoffed. "At least be man enough to admit that what you really, truly want is to find Etta."

More than my next heartbeat. But it was like swimming out to sea in the rain; no matter where he went, he could not avoid the cold drench of truth. Etta would want him to finish what they'd begun by finding the astrolabe.

And leave her to die?

His right hand curled at his side, and he could almost catch the memory of what it had felt like to have her hand tucked there.

And that was it. That calm certainty in knowing her as he knew himself. There was no point to any of this if Etta didn't survive; the future didn't belong to him, it had belonged to *her*, and had always been tied to her dreams. He wanted that success and celebration for her, the chance for her to resolve the unfinished yearnings in her heart. Everything good in this life was her or meant for her.

At the time, it had felt like an inevitability that they would collide, even in the face of such insurmountable odds. Each time something had blocked their path, it had only served to feed that necessity of staying together. Now and then, though, when he stared into the fire at night, or stole a moment to himself, a passing doubt caught him in its snare. They were both so very, very stubborn. So determined to strike back at the rules of life, the way their situation had confined him, that he worried they had only come together purely as an act of rebellion.

But then her face would find him, as fierce as the moment he'd first clapped eyes on her. When his hands were dry and chapped, he recalled the softness of her skin. When the world shivered at the approaching winter, he recalled the warmth of being beside her. When he felt the sneering judgment of the eyes around him, he recalled the invincibility she'd instilled in him with her belief.

And the doubts, they would recede as quietly as they came, leaving a peace as vast as the deep, dark ocean. Nicholas believed they could find that place she had spoken of, the time that was meant for the two of them. He had to believe that.

It was weeks since she'd been orphaned. If she had survived her wound and found help, as he hoped she had, Etta was strong enough to keep surviving and begin finding her way back to Damascus. Perhaps they'd meet each other halfway and continue what they'd begun, rewrite the rules of this life.

Sophia pressed on. "Go find her, sail off into your sunset, and leave me to . . ."

"To . . . ?" he prompted when she did not continue, already knowing the answer. *Leave me to find the astrolabe alone.* Oh; he stifled the bitter laugh before it could emerge. She would cherish the opportunity to remove him from the playing field; to not have any obstruction between her and whatever she was planning.

Instead of answering, Sophia turned her gaze back out to the tents and stalls and argued, "What about Rose Linden's promise to meet you here? Aren't you sick of sitting here and twiddling your thumbs, waiting for Mummy to tell us what to do? If you want us to find Etta, if *that* will perk you up and get you back on the trail of finding the astrolabe, then we'll start by looking for her. It'll be a risk, knowing Grandfather could get to those Thorns first, but I guess we'll have to take it. The price we pay for you being so revoltingly lovesick."

He studied her carefully, frowning. Being compassionate was at odds with her natural disposition, and she was so entirely resistant to niceties that he couldn't stop the trickle of suspicion inside him—that she was arguing this point for more than what she was letting him see.

"He doesn't necessarily know what happened—" Nicholas started.

"Don't be ridiculous. By now, he knows what's happened. We have the small advantage of him being more interested in finding those Thorns than finding us, and we need to use it. So, ticktock. Let's *go*."

As loath as he was to concede it, she did have a point. Over the last few days, it had become clear to him that he was the only one willing to play this game with any decency, and he'd begun to wonder if decency was merely the trade of fools.

"Where do we begin to look for her?" Nicholas heard himself ask. "How do we go about ascertaining the last common year without turning to another traveler?"

Any Ironwood or Ironwood ally would immediately report them to the old man for the reward. Without Rose's information, searching for Etta would feel like a dead reckoning. He did not enjoy navigating a ship blindly, and the same could be said of his life.

"We go find Remus and Fitzhugh Jacaranda, like I've been telling you," Sophia said. "Grandfather gave them the worst posting imaginable when they came crawling back into the fold after they betrayed him and joined the Thorns. I would bet anything there's no love lost between them and Grandfather, and they might be willing to share what they know for a price. Or you can just tell them your tragic tale, let slip a manly, heroic tear."

Pity. Wonderful. His patience finally slipped its leash. "If they have such a terrible, remote posting, who's to say they'll even have heard about the shift in the timeline?"

"If they haven't heard anything, they'll be able to point us to someone who might know. It won't be a wasted trip either way."

Nicholas released a harsh breath through his nose, considering this.

Sophia, possibly for the first time in her life, was being reasonable. They *were* losing time. He *was* bloody well tired of Rose's games. If the Jacarandas could aid in making quick work of finding Etta, then that was the way forward. If they couldn't help him, at least he could console himself with the knowledge that he was actually moving forward, that he'd broken out of the gaol of inaction in which Rose had locked him.

"All right," he said, relenting. "We will try it your way, then. If nothing comes of searching for Etta, then . . . we'll proceed with finding the astrolabe on our own. I promise you."

Sophia rolled her eyes, moving ahead of him again. "Saints and losers, remember?"

And if Sophia truly was after the astrolabe for her own gain, as he was now doubly certain, then their weak truce would conclude and he would do anything in his power to keep it from her. *Anything* necessary.

"Being good on your word is a core tenet of honor," he called.

"Honor." She looked disgusted. "Good thing I don't have much of the stuff left."

NOON ARRIVED, BRINGING WITH IT A MISERABLE HEAT THAT sagged against him, and seemed unjust for October. They passed their walk back to the camp in blessed silence, Sophia stalking forward,

Nicholas staying several steps behind, not just because he didn't want to encourage any words between them, but because he knew that the white men and women they passed would expect it of a servant, a slave—Nicholas shook his head, rolled his shoulders back, as if he could fling it off. The charade sapped what little good mood he'd managed to eke out of the day. And an hour later, when they finally reached the deserted stretch of beach where they'd set up camp, the last lingering traces of goodwill between them evaporated altogether.

"Bloody *hell!*" Sophia snarled, and would have charged forward had Nicholas not gripped her by the collar of her tattered coat.

Their blankets had been carelessly thrown around, and the hammocks they'd stretched between palm trees had been dug up and left in tangled heaps. Their single cooking pot, the one he'd disguised among the lush greenery to collect rainwater, had been overturned, thereby catching nothing that they could boil and drink.

But it hadn't been the storm that had turned the earth over and washed up what was left of their possessions for anyone to steal: it was a small figure sitting cross-legged in front of the rain-filled fire pit, eating the last few pieces of their jerky, playing with a light Sophia had insisted on bringing, despite the fact that it wouldn't be invented until the next century.

"Drop that at once, sir!" Nicholas demanded.

The small man looked up, a piece of jerky dangling from his lips. His dark eyes were strikingly distinct. Two thick, dark brows were angled over them, as if someone had taken ink and thumbed the shapes across. A surprisingly delicate nose and high cheekbones were sunburned—the only flaw in otherwise clear, fair skin.

His mouth stretched into a shameless smile around the jerky clenched between his teeth. A weathered navy coat rustled as he brought a gloved hand up, fingers dancing in a little wave.

Thief.

SIX

IT WAS SEVERAL OUTRAGED MOMENTS BEFORE NICHOLAS was able to collect himself enough to speak. "What is your name, sir? And what business do you have with us?"

The man cocked his head to the side, studying him. After a moment he answered, his voice higher than Nicholas might have expected, speaking a language he'd never heard before. The grating laughter, however, did not need translation.

Sophia answered, barking out a string of words in that same language, wiping the gleaming humor from the thief's face. Nicholas released the grip he'd maintained on her coat, and watched as Sophia lunged toward the small man. He rolled back off the fallen palm tree he'd been perched on, dancing away from her reach again and again.

After everything she'd imbibed last night, he suspected Sophia had a headache pounding like the drums of hell, so frankly, he didn't blame her for reaching into her coat for her pistol and taking aim.

The small man froze. Nicholas caught a hint of gold tucked into his belt—a knife, perhaps? The ceasefire, at least, gave him a moment to assess the risk: the man wore the attire of an Englishman, but the loose fabric of his shirtsleeves and breeches had been rolled and tucked at the ends to account for his diminutive stature.

"Put the flintlock down, *nǚ shén*," the man said.

Sophia lunged toward him, snarling. In two fluid moves, the man had Sophia disarmed and on her knees on the ground, looking stunned.

She growled and, undeterred, rose just enough to try to knock the man's feet out from under him. He simply leaped back out of the way.

Something in the man's face shifted, a feminine softening that arrived with a flurry of delighted, girlish laughter. Sophia seemed to realize their mistake the precise moment Nicholas did, and cut off her next attack, stiffening.

Not a man.

A *woman*.

Nicholas cocked his head to the side, studying the thief again. He could see it now, of course; how blind and presumptuous he'd been, but the Three Crowns had been dark and his glimpse fleeting. The binding of linen wrapped around her chest peeked out from beneath the loose collar of her shirt.

Her focus shifted off Sophia's face to meet his. "Remove your gaze, *gǒu*, or I will remove your eyes."

"I know better than that," he said, holding his own pistol steady. "I want the letter you stole."

"Neither of your weapons are loaded," the young woman said, flicking her fingers in their direction. "They are too light in your hands. Neither of you carry a powder flask. And . . ." She spared a glance around their pitiful campsite. "Could you afford such?"

"More than one way to use a gun," Nicholas noted. "Would you like to discover how many?"

At that, a small smile curled her rosebud lips. "I suspect I know far more than you, *bèn dàn*."

He tried to quell the tightening in his guts at the knifelike edge to her words.

"Who. Are. You," Sophia managed to get out from between her gritted teeth.

The young woman removed her hat, dropping it to the sand with a look of disgust. She lifted her long black braid from where she had tucked it under her cloak, and then a heavy jade pendant, the length of one of Nicholas's fingers. The image of the tree carved into it looked like an evergreen; it stood tall, arrow-like in shape. Its branches were not as full as several of the other family sigils, but still robust and proud.

Damn it all, he thought, feeling a weariness creep into him. And here he'd been hoping, however in vain, that the culprit would be a random thief, one without ties to their hidden world. Nicholas supposed he would never be so lucky.

"Hemlock . . ." he began.

"Did my grandfather send you?" Sophia interrupted.

The girl scowled. "I will never work for him. Not even if he were to offer a fair price for my services."

A mercenary, then. He'd heard stories about them from Hall—members of the Jacaranda and Hemlock families who had refused to bow to Ironwood once he seized control of their travelers and guardians and absorbed them into his own clan. They offered their services to any traveler or guardian who could pay them. He'd always wondered about the kinds of jobs they took, assuming they were mostly occupied with tracking down wayward family members or lost possessions, or maybe even quietly making small changes to history that wouldn't result in the timeline shifting.

"Call me Li Min," she said.

"I'll call you Jackass if it suits me," Sophia snapped. "Tell me what the hell you're doing here before I take this knife and slice you from gullet to gut."

Nicholas wondered briefly if it was his destiny to be surrounded by women possessing varying degrees of murderous intent.

The girl smiled. "This is no way to speak to one with whom you wish to do business."

Sophia sucked in a sharp breath, filling the bellows of her chest to explode, but Nicholas was quicker on the draw. "We have no business with you beyond retrieving our letter. I don't suppose you'll be so kind as to offer any sort of explanation for why you took it? Who hired you to steal it?"

And why you are here, dangling it in front of us, if someone paid you to take it? Unless, of course, she was angling to dip into two different pots of profit, hoping he and Sophia would bribe her for a look.

"I never said I was hired," Li Min said. "It is in my interest to know the business of the travelers I come across. Work is hard to find, you see, and occasionally I must look for it, rather than wait for it to come to me. Many Ironwoods have traveled here in recent months. But imagine my surprise to see a Linden guardian scuttling around the beaches like a little crab. And then you appeared to conduct your business. . . ."

Unsure of whether or not he'd live to regret it, Nicholas lowered his pistol and returned it to its place at his side. Feeling steadier, he began to consider their situation in this new light.

"If you stole it to ransom it back to us, then you already know we have nothing with which to pay you," he said, sweeping his arms out to indicate their sorry state of affairs.

"I wish to know what the letter says," the girl said. "It is written in a peculiar way. I will give it back to you on two conditions."

"I'll take it from your dead body!" Sophia swung an arm out, her fist barreling through the air. Nicholas saw it happening, felt that wrench of dismay, as Sophia misjudged the distance between her and the other girl by nearly a foot. Li Min easily dodged, her face passive, as Sophia lost her balance and slammed into the sand, sending up a spray of it.

Sophia raised a hand to her eye patch, nearly howling in frustration. It wasn't the first time Nicholas had seen her struggle with her altered vision, and it wasn't the first time his heart had given an unwelcome, involuntary clench at the sight, either.

Li Min forced her dark gaze up from the girl, back to him. "I will give you this letter, and you will show me how to read it."

Nicholas shook his head. "Unacceptable."

If the writing was "peculiar," he had a feeling it was written in the way Rose had coded the other letters to Etta—a calculated risk on Rose's part, because what if Etta *hadn't* shown Nicholas how to decode them?—and he was loath to reveal that secret to anyone outside the family.

The envelope emerged from inside of Li Min's shirt, stained brown by the ale, rumpled and worn, but in one piece. That is, until the girl ripped it in half. Nicholas and Sophia both lurched toward her, crying out.

"If I do not read it, you will not read it," Li Min warned, her voice shifting from its airy tone to flint. And to make her point, she turned the halves to the side and began to rip them into quarters.

Sophia turned to look up at Nicholas. "It's not worth it. Let her have the damn letter. We already have our plan."

But it would save us time . . . tracking Etta would be a simpler thing if we could have the last common year now, without delay, Nicholas thought.

"Don't do it, Carter," Sophia warned, voice low.

"I will not show you how to read it—" Nicholas held up his hand, stilling Li Min. "But I will read to you what it says."

"Unacceptable," Li Min said, mimicking his tone. "You might deceive me."

"You accuse me of being dishonorable?" Nicholas said.

"What does an Ironwood know of honor?" Li Min wondered aloud, waving the pieces of the letter at him.

"My name is Nicholas Carter," he said. "I am an Ironwood by only half my blood, and never in character. If nothing else, I am honor-bound to the Linden family not to show a stranger the sole way they have of communicating with each other without Ironwood being able to discover their secrets. You can understand that, I think, given your line of work."

"The Linden family is dead," Li Min said, eyes lighting up with obvious curiosity. "Only a few guardians remain."

"Their methods work, then," Nicholas said, "if you have not discovered that some of their travelers are still very much alive."

Li Min inclined her head toward him, giving him that much, at least. "I will accept this condition, then. But I have one other."

The girl was smiling again, and within the span of less than an hour, he'd already learned to fear the implications of that expression. His mind began to take tally of what little they had, and he braced himself for the loss of any of it. "Go on, then."

"As my payment, I would like a kiss," she said, glancing between the two of them. "A proper one."

Nicholas paused.

Of all of the things he'd suspected she would ask for—flintlock pistols, shoes, a favor, a signed confirmation of debt—a *kiss*? He stared at her a good long while, waiting for her to give the true price, but she simply gazed back, her dark eyes unwavering.

Nicholas had kissed a number of women in his twenty years of life; not as many as Chase, but then, even Lothario could not top that tally. He was far—*far*—from being a saint, but at some point over the past few weeks, his heart had resolved that it only wanted to kiss one girl ever again, and his whole spirit seemed to retreat at the thought of kissing another.

I could kiss her forehead, her cheek, he thought quickly. She hadn't specified where, or how.

Do it, Carter. He pressed his hands to his thighs, trying to steady the rioting dismay. Get the matter over with, read the letter, and go. That was all that mattered now. He would not think of Etta, the way she'd tasted of rain when she'd kissed him in the jungle. How he could have sworn there were stars in her hair that night in Damascus. The way she made him feel solid, and terribly brave.

Well, *his* mind was unhelpful.

"All right," he said, resigned. "Let's have it, then."

Li Min took a step back, dark brows rising over her forehead in both amusement and disdain. "I was speaking to *her.*"

It was physically painful to exist inside the long stretch of silence that followed. *Oh.* The wheels of his mind began to turn again. *Her.*

"Oh. Well, that's . . . it's certainly . . ."

Sophia had begun to collect their scattered belongings, grumbling every curse and oath known to mankind none too quietly. At Li Min's words, she slowly began to straighten.

"Ma'am, I apologize," Nicholas said sincerely, inclining his head. "Forgive my presumption."

Li Min flicked her fingers dismissively in his direction. "It can be hard for men to believe they are not all gods walking the earth, as so many women are forced to fall at their feet."

He lifted a shoulder in a faint shrug. Where was the lie in that?

"And you expect me to fall at your feet now?" Sophia asked, her expression surprisingly even.

"No one expects that," Nicholas said. "It's your choice. As you said before, we have other avenues of inquiry to pursue. She can take the letter and be damned."

"Oh? I have your permission to refuse, then?" Sophia rolled her eye.

"I only meant to make it clear—" He closed his mouth, knowing he'd botched this moment beyond repair.

"Fine," Sophia said, cutting him off. She squared her shoulders, glancing back at him as she stepped toward the other girl. "We could go on without the bloody letter, but if it helps us find the men who— I just want this to be over with."

Nicholas didn't miss the catch in her voice when she said "the men."

"Have at it," Sophia said, removing her hat. She stood straight in front of Li Min, who mirrored her stoic expression. Nicholas had

76

the peculiar sense that he was watching a duel, with neither of the aggrieved parties willing to fire into the air.

He kept a hand on the unloaded pistol at his side, and was startled to find that Sophia was not doing the same. Rather, she was holding her ground, waiting for the other young woman to approach.

Sophia's throat worked as she swallowed with some difficulty. Li Min brought a hand to her face and curled a loose strand of dark hair behind the other girl's ear. With a tenderness that made Nicholas want to avert his gaze, Li Min leaned forward.

"I'll wait," she said, her lips a breath from Sophia's. "One day you may be willing to pay, and I will delight in collecting."

Sophia's face, already flushed from the sun, deepened to crimson as Li Min offered the halves of Rose's letter to her. She snatched the parchment away and thrust it in Nicholas's direction, never once taking her eyes off the mercenary. "Read it."

Nicholas felt the knots around his lungs ease, and briny air filled them, tempered with the scent of the rotting green flesh of the jungle. He moved a short distance away from the young women and sat down on the bowed body of a fallen palm tree. With great care, he lined up the raw, torn edges.

Dear Little Heart, the center of my being . . . It went on to discuss the weather, King George III, and so on, like tiny riots of nonsense across the page.

Nicholas felt his brows rise as he reached up and swiped the sweat from his forehead. The endearment would read as a bit much to the casual reader, but Etta had explained to him that, in the absence of a key to read it, the way to decode the letter was embedded within the salutation. She'd used "star" before, and "heart" was easy enough— though, what to make of "little," and the curious inclusion of "the center of my being"?

Unless . . .

He curled his index fingers and thumbs together, forming a heart, and positioned it at the center of the parchment. The message it revealed was still padded with gibberish, and he couldn't make sense of it until he imagined the shape of a small heart laid over the words at the center of the letter.

Cannot meet you. Will lead the shadows away from you as long as I can. For year, seek belladonna.

Another blasted riddle. The paper wrinkled under the force of his grip as he read the message aloud to the young women. *Bloody Rose Linden.*

"Iiiinteresting," Sophia said, something sparking in her eyes. "Dare I say it, but the woman might have actually come through for us. I hadn't considered it as an option, but she's onto something."

"Foolish," Li Min shot back. "And you were right *not* to consider it."

"I would prefer to know what it is the two of you are referring to, rather than watch you argue the point," Nicholas said with a patience he did not know he still possessed.

Sophia ignored Li Min's look of disbelief, saying, "There are two people in all of time that know the workings of our world—who make it a point to know everything everyone is doing. One of them is Grand— is Ironwood himself, and the other is the Belladonna."

"Belladonna is a she, not a thing?" he confirmed, trying to extinguish the eagerness in his voice.

"Julian never spoke of her?" Sophia asked him, at his look of confusion. "She's . . . I'm not quite sure how to put this. She seeks out treasures lost to time and holds auctions for them; only, instead of paying in gold, you pay for them in favors and secrets. Ironwood has allowed it because, generally speaking, these treasures must stay 'lost' to preserve his timeline."

"What is it that you hope to accomplish with this visit?" Li Min asked. The sunlight gleamed off her coal-black hair as she cocked her head to the side. "Perhaps you might purchase the information from me, instead?"

"What business is it of yours?" Nicholas asked. In truth, he was mildly concerned about what she might ask for next, and whether or not he could trust her answer.

"I told you, it's my business to know others' business."

"We are attempting to uncover the last common year with this most recent major shift in the timeline," Nicholas said. "Is that information you possess?"

There was a single beat in which his hopes shot into the air like a firework, only to crash back down a moment later. Li Min glanced off toward the turquoise water. "No. I could . . . I might seek the answer for you, however."

"For a handsome fee," Sophia burst in. "Trying to poach some business from the Belladonna, are you? No, thank you. We'll go to someone who will actually know, not a second-rate mercenary who can't even decode a message." Sophia ignored Li Min's light laugh and turned back to Nicholas. "The Belladonna knows *everything*. Julian told me that on his last visit accompanying the old man, she rattled off the full scale of *all* of Ironwood's comings and goings, and the supposedly secret changes he'd enacted."

"And your quarrel with her is . . . ?" Nicholas asked, turning back to Li Min. He did not entirely like the sound of this, aside from potentially having a more direct, guaranteed route to Etta.

Li Min lifted a shoulder, but her gaze darted over to Sophia, just for a moment, as she pressed her lips into a tight line.

"She's bought into the rumors that the woman is a witch," Sophia said with obvious ridicule. "That she'll ensnare your soul. Ridiculous!"

Nicholas did balk at that. *Witch* was a strong accusation in his native time, and flung around far too quickly when it came to ladies with unusual interests or predispositions.

Li Min's lips parted, but after a moment, she only smiled. Tossing her long braid over her shoulder again, she bent to retrieve her cape and hat. "You seem to have your path charted, then. Be well."

She was several feet away and retreating into the palms before Nicholas's mind took note that she was leaving.

"That's it?" Sophia called after her. "After all that, that's *it*?"

Li Min didn't miss a stride as she called back, "For now. Until we meet again."

When it looked as though she might try to follow the other girl, to haul her back for further interrogation, Nicholas caught Sophia's shoulder with one hand and used the other to tuck Rose's correspondence back in his jacket pocket.

"Can you *believe* the nerve of that girl—"

"Sophia," he interrupted, "a *witch*? Is there anything else I should know?"

"Oh, we'll be fine," Sophia said, turning from the trail of broken underbrush Li Min had left behind.

"Are you personally acquainted with her?" he pressed.

"Well, no; but she is a legend, and between Julian's stories and the old man's absolute loathing of her, I feel as though I've a handle on her," Sophia said quickly. "I can't believe I didn't think of this. The only thing we have to worry about now is finding a passage to Prague. She operates in the fifteenth century—I think there should be a passage to Spain if we can reach Florida, and from there—"

"Not to interrupt your planning, but how do you propose we buy passage off this island?"

Sophia cocked her head to the side, her lips curling up at the edges as she lifted a fist-size leather bag from inside of her jacket and tossed it to him. "Some thief she is. Didn't even notice when I cut this from her belt."

Nicholas actually laughed, unknotting the laces to reveal enough gold coins to momentarily stop his heart. "She'll be back for this."

Sophia glanced back at the path Li Min had taken. "Good."

SAN FRANCISCO
1906

SEVEN

THEY RETURNED TO THE SAME ROOM ETTA HAD CLIMBED out of, accompanied by a different pair of guards, as well as a maid who her father—she shook her head, clearing the impossible word from it—who the *man* had practically flung at her. Also joining them was a tall, silver-haired woman with posture so severe, Etta wondered if it'd be possible to break a wooden chair against her spine. No one had introduced them, but Etta was reasonably sure this was the Winifred the man had spoken of.

"You may proceed," the older woman told the maid. Etta would have been shocked if the girl was even seventeen; she peered out from beneath a heavy mop of dark curls escaping from a loose braid. The girl was curious, but not at all frightened or overawed, which made Etta think she was likely a guardian, someone connected to the Thorns. The lantern in her hands made fragments of light jump around them on the thick carpets and gilded wallpaper, fluttering like newly disturbed ghosts.

"A little privacy would be nice," Etta told the older woman.

The old blade reached behind her to lock the door. Etta raised a brow, taking in the dark violet of her dress. It looked painfully cinched at the waist, with a trail of small pearl buttons that ran up the bodice to the place her tight collar ended, just beneath her chin. The silk skirt was draped with all the elegant ease of a waterfall, collecting in a slight bustle at the small of her back.

After rummaging through the wardrobe, the maid pulled out a plain white blouse with a little dark embroidery around the collar, and a long gray skirt that looked to be made of wool. It was cut narrowly at the waist and along the thighs, but flared as it got closer to the knees and brushed the floor. The poor girl seemed to realize at the exact moment Etta did that there was an icicle's chance in summer that the tiny waist would fit her.

"I'll let it out, it won't be but a moment," the girl swore, her gaze darting to Winifred.

A moment too long, apparently. With an irritated look, Winifred turned back to Etta and ordered, "Strip."

"Can I get a *please*?" Etta grumbled, eyeing the very familiar garment in the woman's hands. "I'm not wearing the corset. Absolutely not—"

Winifred seized the scruff of Etta's nightgown and yanked it hard over her head. Momentarily blinded by the fabric, Etta reached up, trying to loosen the ribbon before it strangled her or tore off an ear. She crossed her arms over her chest, shielding her body as the woman threw her a thin chemise.

It occurred to Etta that the woman was literally and figuratively stripping her, trying to make her feel as vulnerable as possible, and that she shouldn't simply let her do it without a fight. When she tried to twist away from her, Winifred shoved her off-balance, dropped the corset over her head, and began to lace it up before Etta caught her next breath. The woman handed her another thin, sleeveless top to pull over the corset. Etta resented the little cheerful pink ribbons on it almost as much as the woman's smirk.

"You poor creature. You've your mother's sorry figure."

"Touch me again and I'll show you how alike we are," Etta spat out.

Winifred had already turned away, retrieving the blouse and newly let-out skirt from the maid. She threw them at Etta's feet.

"With *haste*, you stupid child," she said, when Etta did not immediately do as she was told. "The Grand Master won't be pleased if he's kept waiting."

Etta's temper flared at the word *child*, singeing whatever restraint she might have had left. That was the only explanation she had for why she said, "Cyrus Ironwood is the Grand Master."

The slap came so suddenly that Etta could not have dodged it if she had enough time to try. She careened back onto the bed, pressing her hand to the burning skin on her face.

"Look what you made me do," the woman growled. "Such insolence! And after I cared for you! Washed you! Tended to your courses! And with nary a complaint. If he hadn't asked it of me, I would have smothered you from the start."

"You are insane," Etta informed her, fists already clenched. "Hit me again and your friends will be picking pieces of you out of the rug!"

The maid blanched, but Etta didn't care, she didn't—she was shaking now with the full force of her fury, embarrassment, and resentment. She tried to quell the hurricane of emotions swirling in her chest as she finished dressing and was forced to sit at the vanity and have her hair braided. She avoided looking in the mirror, unwilling to see the throbbing red mark across her cheek.

"Hardly acceptable," Winifred said, once the ordeal was over, "but follow me."

Etta knew she needed to go with her if she wanted to confirm the Thorns had the astrolabe, but obeying this woman felt like swallowing seawater: it incinerated her throat, choking her.

"I think I'll stay," Etta said, crossing her arms over her chest.

The woman's hand reached out, and Etta instinctively struck her arm out to block the hit—only, the woman wasn't aiming for another slap. Her other hand came up and fisted into Etta's braid, twisting so tightly that Etta yelped in pain. "Let me go!"

Instead, the woman dragged her across the room, never once breaking her stride as Etta kicked and scratched at her to release her grip. The door opened to the other guard's wide-eyed shock, and, as he fumbled for his words, the woman continued on her path, letting Etta's bare feet drag and burn across the carpet, down the stairs.

There really was some sort of party happening on the first floor. As Winifred hauled her across a gallery hallway, Etta could hear the excited chatter and laughter, even as a man poured himself into playing a jaunty tune on a piano. The smell of liquor and perfume permeated the air as they passed the door to the library, with Julian's amused face peering out.

"Attagirl," he called after them. "Keep fighting, kiddo!"

"Stop calling me that!" she snarled back, gritting her teeth as his laugher chased them down the hall.

And, finally, to another door, this one guarded by three men in fine suits. Winifred released her grip on Etta's hair, and Etta righted herself. Two of the men blanched at the sight of her. The other twitched a heavy brow in her direction, struggling to swallow his laugh as he gave Etta a pitying look.

"Come now, Winnie. She's just a girl. Have a care."

"*Her* girl," Winifred said, pounding on the door. "Never forget this."

"Come in," came the immediate reply.

Not an invitation, of course, but a command. Etta had arrived ready to fight, her pulse raging as she huffed. *Calm down, calm down, remember the plan*—she had to find out if they had the astrolabe, and try to figure out how to get it away from them to destroy it once and for all.

The guards fell back as Etta was pushed inside by the older woman, her hand twisted in the loose fabric of Etta's blouse to ensure, she guessed, that she didn't try to make one last run for it. Instead, she passed through the threshold at her full height, trying not to glare.

This office had been decorated in a similar style to the library—all masculine dark wood and jewel tones. It aimed to be impressive, and hit the mark. The window captured much the same view of the crippled landscape, along with the first hint of dawn brightening the sky.

There were already four people in the room, seated around the stately desk at its center. Etta's eyes landed on the woman first, taking in her tailored skirt suit and the dark hair she'd curled and twisted into victory rolls. The older man beside her wore plain linen trousers and a tunic, both almost entirely hidden beneath his leather chest plate and sword belt. His long gray hair was slicked back from his bearded face, with small silver beads braided into several of the strands that grazed the fur pelt draped over his shoulders. To his right was a young Asian man, wearing a kimono in a shade of blue usually found only in the deepest heart of the ocean.

An incredulous laugh bubbled up inside of her at the sight of them.

Etta inhaled a deep breath through her nose, letting the smell of wax and wood polish settle her. Henry Hemlock sat behind the desk, his feet crossed and propped up on it.

The others turned to look at Etta and Winifred, and then back at Henry, shifting uncomfortably in their seats. Henry Hemlock, however, continued on with what he was saying. "I hear you, Elizabeth. I do. The last thing I want is for your children to go to sleep worrying you won't be there in the morning. So many of us lived through that time and suffered for it. I'll take another look at the postings and see if anyone is amenable to a switch."

The woman's shoulders slumped in relief. "Thank you. *Thank you.*"

"We shouldn't delay in meeting them, sir, if the situation is as dire as the message seems to convey," said the man with long silver hair. "We must help them and secure our advantage before making any changes to our personnel. In fact, I think I should go round up John and Abraham before meeting the rest of you there."

Henry grinned. "Perhaps leaving the fur behind."

The man laughed, stroking the tufts of it. "I think I'd make quite a statement stomping down the Seine."

"And cause a disastrous change for a laugh, I suppose," Winifred said, with ice in her voice.

Etta counted more than one set of eyes rolling in that room.

"You'd try to shoot a star down from the sky for shining too brightly," the man groused back.

"All right," Henry said, taking his feet off the desk and standing. Everyone in the room, except Etta, pivoted to follow his path back and forth as he began to pace. "That's enough. You know how I feel about this sort of sniping. Remember there's a true enemy out there to aim at."

"Yes, of course," Winifred breathed, the very essence of sweetness, even as her grip on Etta tightened.

"I don't think we've considered the fact that he, too, could be dead, and that Ironwood might already have the astrolabe," the Japanese man interjected, leaning over to poke at an open letter. "Who else could they mean by 'shadows'? Who else has the resources to hunt the brothers the way he describes?"

What? Etta felt the moment tilt sharply beneath her feet, the realization its own earthquake.

"If it were so easy, we would have done so decades past," Henry said, turning his gaze onto Etta. "You seem surprised. Almost as if, perhaps, you'd expected to find the astrolabe with us?"

Etta said nothing, only turned her face away, to stare at the place where the wood floors met the carpets. There was a kind of lure in his dark gaze; his focus tracked her every shift and breath. The weight of it registered so strongly, it felt as if he'd put his hands on her shoulders and was stubbornly trying to turn her back toward him. She didn't want him to have easy access to her thoughts, not when her mind was racing like this, trying to keep pace with her thundering heart.

It had been two weeks since the two Thorns, along with Sophia, had wrested the astrolabe from her in Damascus. They should have been able to create a passage directly back to the rest of the Thorns here in San Francisco; but from what she'd understood of their conversation, not only had they not brought the astrolabe, they'd disappeared altogether. And there had been no word at all from Sophia, who'd gone with them.

"All we've seen are the Ironwoods he's sent out to try to rewrite our changes in small ways," Henry said. "Were it in his possession, Cyrus wouldn't have hesitated to use it, to reset the timeline back to his own. It's greed and greed alone that compels his family."

"Let's not forget," the silver-haired man said with a chuckle, "we both have Ironwood on our mothers' side."

"No," Henry said with a quick smile, "*let's*. But my point stands. We must trust in Kadir's ability to get to safety, and in our own to ensure we can get to him in time and retrieve the astrolabe from where he's hidden it. I'm sorry to cut the celebrations short, but tell the others to make ready to travel in the morning. And we'll need to leave at least some travelers to support the guardians staying here to watch the children."

"A wise decision," Winifred gushed.

Etta tried not to gag.

The others nodded, and, sensing they'd reached the end of the conversation, rose as one. They brushed past Etta, one at a time, each stealing a last look at her. For a second, she could have sworn the man with silver hair gave a little shudder.

"Please have a seat, Henrietta. Winifred, thank you; that will be all. Ensure we're not disturbed."

The older woman bobbed a slight curtsey, giving Etta's back a parting pinch, hard enough to make her jump forward a step. Etta waited until the woman had vanished through the door in a swirl of dark skirts before turning to Henry and spitting out, "She doesn't travel through passages, does she? She sacrifices a puppy and flies through the centuries on her broom."

He gave a sharp cough into his hand.

"I assure you, your great-aunt is quite loving," Henry said, only to stop and reconsider. "That is, she's quite loving in her own way . . . every other Sunday. In May. Won't you sit?"

Great-aunt. No way in hell.

Etta didn't sit; her hands curled around the back of the chair so tightly, its joints creaked.

"The first thing I want you to know is that you are safe here," he said, not breaking his gaze. "You have nothing to fear from myself or anyone here. I've taken measures to ensure your safety from Ironwood, as well. Unless you choose to go looking for him, he will no longer concern himself with you."

That seemed unlikely. Before she could press the point, Henry turned his attention to shuffling through the unruly stack of opened correspondence and parchment piled into small, unsteady mountains on his desk. He seemed to find what he was looking for; he pulled a black velvet sack out from under the mess and dumped something into his palm—a gold earring. A hoop decorated with a pearl, blue beads, and tiny gold leaves.

Mom's earring. Etta's whole self seemed to tense in belated panic. One hand rose to touch her ears, only to find both of them free of jewelry.

"Winifred found this in the folds of your clothing when you were brought to us," he said, offering it to her. "I thought you might like it back."

Just one? The question hung in her mind, quiet with devastation. In the grand scheme of everything that had happened, losing an earring was hardly the worst failure she'd endured, but it was another betrayal of trust, another way she had let her mother down.

She couldn't add yet another notch to that tally by falling prey to this man's lies. "You keep it. I found it in some junky old thrift shop."

Henry's lips compressed at that, and, when he did speak, there was a new edge to the words. "I realize you are out of your depth, and I am quite sympathetic to all that you've been through. But one thing I cannot tolerate is lying, and another is disrespecting your family. You did not find these earrings in a thrift store. I imagine they were a gift from your mother, as I know they were a cherished gift from her beloved uncle's wife."

He knows about Hasan.

That didn't prove anything. He and the others had talked about having many sources out there; he could have easily learned about Hasan that way.

Even that his wife was the one who gave her the earrings?

Etta began to bite her lip, but forced herself to stop. She would not give in to the temptation to fill the uneasy silence between them with chatter. Not when Henry seemed so comfortable in it, and was watching her so closely.

"Who did you bribe for that information?" she asked, taking the earring from him.

One corner of his mouth kicked up, and he opened the same drawer, retrieving a long velvet case. Resting inside was a strand of glistening pearls, each slightly irregular in shape. Every third pearl was nestled between breathtaking sapphires. "Samarah made them to match this necklace I commissioned upon our engagement. Is that proof enough for you?"

At that, Etta did sit down. Henry placed the jewelry case between them.

Engagement. *Engagement.*

Memory clouded her mind, dulling all of the certainties with which she had walked into the office.

But, darling, who's your father? Alice had asked her in London. *Henrietta . . . is it . . . is it possibly Henry?*

"I'll have another earring made to match," he told her. "Or we might adjust it to be worn as a necklace. Whichever you'd prefer."

Etta felt like she was barreling down a road at night without a brake pedal. This wasn't right—it wasn't him. This man couldn't be her father.

"I don't want anything from you," she said.

"And yet, it's my duty to provide for you," Henry said. "At least grant me that much. I'm nearly eighteen years behind on the matter."

"I can take care of things myself," Etta said.

"Yes," he said with a faint laugh. "That seems likely, given your mother. It's rather remarkable, you know, the resemblance between the two of you. Uncanny, even."

"Yeah, I didn't miss the folks in the hall who crossed themselves when they saw me," Etta said dryly.

Henry didn't seem to hear her. He was carefully studying her face, his hand absently ruffling his dark hair. "But she gave you my name. . . ."

Is it possibly Henry?

There seemed to be a question buried in the words, but his voice trailed off; he looked away, focusing on the empty bookshelves on the other side of the room. It gave Etta the opportunity to study him again—to prove to herself, and that small, chiming part of her heart, that there was no resemblance there to be found.

"I don't know what to tell you," she admitted.

"'He who dares not grasp the thorn should never crave the rose,' as Brontë said." There was a wry expression on Henry's face as he continued. "She has always been fiercely intelligent and determined, but she held herself apart from most others, for her own protection, to give herself distance if she ever needed to run. Capturing her heart was like wrestling a bear. I still have the scars to show for it."

Etta, not for the first time, or even the twentieth, wished she had a better grip on the timeline of her mother's life—when she had left the Thorns, when she had gone to infiltrate the Ironwoods, and when she had ultimately betrayed both by hiding the astrolabe and disappearing into the future. But it fit. All of this fit.

Is it possibly Henry?

More than possible. Etta brought her hand to her face, pressing her fingers hard to her temples, as if that could ease the pounding there. Her shoulder complained each time she shifted, but the pain only chiseled down her thoughts to their bare truths. Each small argument, each scrap of evidence, was beginning to form an undeniable picture.

She wanted Nicholas—she wanted to see his face, and measure his thoughts against her own until they made sense. Etta hadn't understood how she'd used his steady resolve as a shelter until it was gone, and she was raw and exposed and trapped. When she'd been orphaned, she'd left the braver parts of herself with him, and what was left of her now was too cowardly to admit what she already knew to be true.

"It was for her as it was for me," Henry said, eyes back on hers. "Truthfully . . . I don't know that she named you for me, so much as for a moment in time. I suppose you are a tribute, a kind of memory to who we were. It's—well, it's unexpected, given the way she left us."

Etta didn't trust her voice enough to speak.

Her whole life, all eighteen years of it, her father had lingered as a kind of question mark in the background. A ghost that came around haunting now and then in her thoughts to remind her of the loss—to expand that gap in her family portraits. But there had been *many* ghosts, and *many* gaps, on both sides of her family, and Etta had never let herself dwell on any of them in particular, because it seemed ungrateful in the face of everything and everyone she did have.

Father. A word from a vocabulary of love she'd never learned. Etta couldn't make any more sense of it than she could of the way she felt. An involuntary, panicked elation that left her feeling like she needed to run to him or *away* from him.

"What am I doing here?" Etta asked finally.

"At first, we only wanted to protect and heal you—you were almost dead when Julian Ironwood brought you back to us. From here on out . . . well," he said, "I should like to hope you will aid us against Ironwood, considering all he's done to you. And if I'm lucky, you might tell me a little about yourself, beyond what I know."

"Which is what?" she asked, shocked by the eagerness in his voice.

"That you were born and raised in Manhattan. That you enjoy reading, and were homeschooled from a young age. I know that you have performed across the world in many competitions, and that you feel very strongly about Bach over Beethoven."

"You read the *Times* article," she said quietly.

"I read everything I could find from this . . . *Internet* . . . creation," he admitted. He said *Internet* like he was testing the word in his mouth for the first time. "Not nearly enough. There's one question in particular I've had for weeks now, and I desperately wish you'd consider answering it—but only if you are comfortable."

The way he framed it satisfied her pride and appealed to her curiosity, but there was one weight she needed to remove before she could continue.

"I need you to answer a question for me first," Etta said. "But I don't know if I can even trust your answer. . . ."

"Ask and see."

She took a pacifying breath, waiting until the pain in her throat eased enough to speak normally. "The night of the concert . . . were you or any of your Thorns involved in a shooting?"

There. A flicker of something in his face. Henry's lips compressed and she heard the harsh breath leave his nose. "Do you mean Alice?"

Etta had expected a quick dismissal, an annoyed defense. But that softness in his expression rubbed at the fragile shield she'd constructed around her heart, and the heaviness in his words nearly cracked it altogether.

She swallowed again. Nodded.

It was a long while before he spoke again, and the whole time, he never broke his gaze away from her. Etta could see his mind working, as if deciding how best to continue—or was he deciding what she could handle?

"Never," he told her. "I would never harm Alice, though I'm not sure she felt the same about me. I believed her when she said she tried to stop you from traveling. To protect you."

"She told you that?"

A rebellious thought rose in her. *Alice trusted him.*

"After you disappeared, I stayed with her," he said. The words slammed through Etta's heart, making it throb in her chest with a mess of relief and gratitude and envy.

"Her last thoughts were only of you."

She wasn't alone. Alice didn't die alone.

Etta pressed a hand to her face, drawing in breath after breath to stave off the crush of tears. "She wasn't alone."

"She wasn't alone," he said softly. "She shouldn't have suffered that at all, but at least . . . there was that one small bit of mercy."

Etta heard him shift, his feet moving against the carpet, but he didn't reach for her, didn't feed her comforting lies. He remained nearby, silent, ready, until the metronome of her heart slowed enough for her to find her center again.

"Thank you," Etta managed. "For staying with her until the end."

He nodded. "The honor was mine. Are you satisfied with your answer?"

"Yes," she said. "What was your question?"

"Did your mother give you any sort of traveling education and training?" Henry asked. "The fact that you so willingly followed the Ironwood girl made me think not, and yet it's so unlike your mother not to have thought through something five steps past everyone else, and there should have been any number of precautions to protect you against this."

Etta gritted her teeth at the humiliation that itched inside of her. The embarrassment at being so unprepared for a traveler's life was familiar, but feeling it now meant that she cared what this man thought of her. She didn't want him to somehow think less of her.

"I didn't know I could travel until the night of the performance."

His hand rasped over the faint stubble along his chin and jaw, eyes softening in a way that made her hate herself, just a little bit, for how much she appreciated it. "None of us are born speaking a half-dozen languages or feeling at ease in the Roman Empire. You'll pick it up quickly enough, and there are many here, myself included, who would be happy to help you in any way we can."

Etta raised her eyebrows at that—from her unscientific survey, less than half of the Thorns she'd met had been willing to look her in the eye.

"She did what she had to do," Etta said. "Mom, I mean."

"She did what she was *told* to do," Henry said, rising again to his feet. He was tall, but not imposingly so. Yet, when he moved, he took command over every inch of the space around him. "How can you not be angry with her? How can you defend her after everything she's subjected you to?"

There were so many ways she would have answered that, even a few days ago, but now Etta felt all of her explanations crumbling, slipping through her fingers like the hot dust of Palmyra.

"She didn't come for you when you needed her most." His face was strained as he spoke. "She let you fall into Ironwood's trap."

She had . . . Etta had taken care of herself the best she could, tried to wrest some control from the situation, but it didn't change that simple fact.

"He's holding her prisoner," Etta explained. "There was nothing she could do. He might have . . ." *Already killed her.*

Henry made a noise of disgust, waving the thought away. "Your mother was free of Ironwood's men within days. I had numerous reports of her scampering about, staying well clear of you."

"She's *alive*?" Etta breathed out. The fear released like a sigh, blowing hot, then icy as what he didn't say finally set in. *She's alive and she didn't come to help me.*

"I can forgive her for what she did to us. She betrayed the trust of this group by lying and saying her family no longer had the astrolabe. The Thorns loved her, cared for her, and she took the key to everything we hoped to accomplish." He raked his hand back through his hair again, mussing it further. "We've known each other since we were children, Rose and I. For a time, I truly believed I understood her better than I knew myself. I'm not proud to admit it, but I did not see just how ruthless and hopelessly misguided she had become. She is no stranger to using people, Thorns or Ironwoods, but for *you* to bear the brunt of it is cruel, even by her standards."

Etta didn't like that line of thought, the way it worked her stomach into disarray. She wanted to argue in her mother's defense, to call his own bias into question, but when she reached into her memories, she found she'd already run through what little evidence to the contrary she had.

Making his way to the window, Henry looked out, keeping his face from her. "There's so much darkness to this story, there are times I feel suffocated by it. Our lives became a tapestry of family and revenge and devastation, and it wove around us all so tightly, none of us escaped its knots, not even you. I should have seen the signs, but I wanted to believe she was beyond it. You have to know that if I had known she was with child when she left, I never would have stopped looking for you. I would have gone to the very edges of time to save you from this."

"What are you talking about?" Etta pressed. Her fingers twisted around each other in her lap. She could almost hear the way her thoughts were swelling, racing through the beats of lies and secrets to one final, crashing crescendo. She didn't want to hear.

She had to.

His gaze met hers over his shoulder. "All of this—this journey she's sent you on—is rooted in nothing more than delusion and lies."

EIGHT

RATHER THAN STAY SEATED AND SPEAK TO HIS BACK, ETTA pushed the chair from the desk and padded over to him. Sunrise edged ever closer with each second, adding to the unrelenting pressing of time's swift march away from her. The sky near the horizon had lightened to a soft violet and, in the gentle light, she saw what wasn't there: the footprints of the decimated buildings and streets hidden by rubble, streetlights that had been twisted and snapped like dry long grass.

"I—" she began. But the story wasn't about her, not yet.

"I don't know what you know of the Thorns, of us," he said, giving her a sidelong glance as he clasped his hands behind his back. "I cannot claim we are without fault and failures. Many of us lost everything in the war against Ironwood. Families, fortunes, homes, a sense of safety and independence. But the people here are good and decent, and want do something meaningful. We want to protect each other. It was your mother, you know, who came up with the name. It was something she used to say, that she could no longer be a rose without thorns. She nearly destroyed every hope we had of succeeding when she disappeared. Rose turned our castle to glass and left us exposed and one strike away from shattering."

"I know about all of that," Etta said. Rose had infiltrated the

Ironwoods for a time to keep them from finding the astrolabe. She knew now she'd come back to the Thorns briefly before leaving for the future, with child. "I want to know what you meant by *delusion*. That's a strong word."

"I've never told anyone this, the more fool I," he murmured. The reluctance in his tone made Etta step forward, as if to seize the secret he was offering. "After her parents were murdered, Rose claimed she was visited by a traveler, one who warned that if Ironwood were to possess the astrolabe, it would result in some sort of endless, vicious war, which could destroy everything and everyone."

Etta made a sharp noise of surprise. Henry glanced over at her again, and seemed to be measuring her response. "You have to understand that she was deeply, deeply unwell after their deaths. She witnessed them herself as a young child, and they were so gruesome I feel I must spare you the details."

Etta's gaze sharpened on him. "So you just dismissed it? Because she was an *unwell* little girl?"

He held up his hands. "I would never use that term lightly. She described this traveler as shining like 'the sun itself,' golden, his skin and form flawless. She told me once that when he spoke, it was as if she heard his words in her mind, and that he could plant images in her thoughts. That even our shadows served him—*shadows*."

Etta was at a compete loss for words, trying to reconcile this image of her mother with the stiff, immaculately put-together woman she'd grown up with.

So . . . all of this was . . . not a fantasy, but . . . Her mind stumbled over the words. Hallucinations and delusions. If she was following Henry's thinking on this, Rose's parents' deaths had been so deeply traumatic, the psychological aftershocks so damaging, it had eventually ruined not only Rose's life, but compelled her to ruin her daughter's as well.

All of this was a lie.

Her blood was pounding wildly inside of her, like the flapping of a bird's wings struggling against a fierce wind. A tiny figure at the edge of her memory tiptoed forward, hesitating, curling the ends of her bright blond hair with her small fingers. Quiet, as always, so as not to disturb. Perfect, as always, so as not to disappoint. Only watching the careful, meticulous strokes of her mother's paintbrush against canvas from the doorway of her bedroom.

Wondering if the reason her mother seemed to rarely speak to her was because her language was color and form, when Etta's was sound and vibration.

Henry reached out a hand for hers, but jerked it back when Etta flinched.

After a moment, he continued, "As a child, her grandfather helped put her off the notion, but years later, after she'd joined me in trying to restore the original timeline, she had a dream about that meeting with the 'golden man,' as she called him. Her fixation was renewed. The fierce, lively person I knew withered away, and in her place grew someone who was paranoid, erratic. Rose would go for days without sleep, then disappear for weeks, only to return more levelheaded, folding away more and more secrets inside of her. I wanted to help her, but she didn't believe she needed help; not even as her delusions worsened, and she claimed she could feel people watching her from the darkness."

Each word pulled at a new thread in Etta, slowly unmaking her.

"I should have fought her on her plans to spy on the Ironwoods by ingratiating herself to them, but it was like trying to bend steel with my hands. And then she vanished, and for years, I was afraid . . . I thought for certain she had . . . ended her own life."

Her mother would never have surrendered. Forfeited her life that way.

"Are you all right?" he asked, his brow creased.

Who would be? she wondered.

"Why did she hide it, then, instead of just destroying it?" Etta asked instead. "That's the only way to truly keep it out of Ironwood's hands, right?"

"It gets at a struggle we've felt for years, the debate we've been locked in." He reached down to the satchel near his feet, removing a dark leather journal. "This came into our possession almost twenty years ago, when your great-grandfather Linden died. It's one of his ancestors' journals, one of the old record-keepers who compiled information from old traveler journals and tracked changes to the timeline. From her understanding of her old ancestor's legends, destroying the astrolabe would have a nullifying effect on any alternations to the original timeline."

"Meaning," Etta said, "it would revert to the exact thing you and this group are after—the original version of the timeline?"

"Yes, but at a steep *cost*," Henry said, placing the journal back on the desk. "Do you know that passages collapse when a traveler nearby dies outside of their natural time?"

Etta nodded.

"Imagine losing the one thing that could reopen them in the event of someone becoming trapped—being forced to wait out years or decades in an unwelcoming time, separated from your family," he said. "There used to be thousands of passages, and now, there are only a few hundred. Many would argue that, as more of us die than are born, our way of life will vanish as the last passages close."

"But not you."

"Not me," he said. "I understand that not everyone uses the passages for their own selfish ends, the way Ironwood does. Many simply need them to visit members of their family and friends who can't travel, or to conduct studies and research. Even your mother felt that way— unwilling to potentially risk losing her family in other centuries. But recent events have proven to me that this has become a necessity if we're to restore what's rightfully meant to be."

The buzzing static in Etta's ears finally exploded, swallowing his words. Some part of her strained against what he was asking of her;

she didn't want this information, didn't want to know this, or put the pieces together.

"This doesn't make sense," she said, hating the desperation in her voice, as she reached for logic to protect her heart, "none of it. She wanted me to destroy it. She told me that herself."

Unless *he* was lying about wanting to destroy the astrolabe, or what destroying it would do—but then, what was the point? He would be trying to convince her of all the reasons it needed to exist, and what they intended to do with it. But none of her usual red flags were being raised. If anything, he just sounded tired and angry—there was nothing calculating in his eyes or tone. He *believed* what he was telling her.

"Then she should have returned to us the moment she was able, but she didn't," Henry said. "Instead, she concocted a scheme to force *you* to do the work for her. She endangered your life every step of the way, and somehow, worst of all, she kept you in perfect ignorance. Because—my God, because she needed events to play out the way this *special destiny* required. She knew that Ironwood would eventually learn of you and try to use you, and she *allowed it.*"

Etta leaned heavily against the desk, and used her very last defense. "She did it to save my future."

"Ironwood's future," he corrected gently. "I see you struggling with the lack of logic. There's simply none to be found. Instead of destroying the astrolabe, she created this game to justify—to reinforce—what she believes she saw as a girl. It is the only explanation for this charade."

"Because if she had wanted to save my future," Etta said around the knot in her throat, "she would have told me to protect the astrolabe, not destroy it."

Her mother would have had her be the means of her own future's destruction, all the while lying about that being the only way to save it. The pain of it stole her breath.

When Etta was young, she had come to understand that loneliness had a pitch—that high whine of static that coated silence. Sometimes, she'd sit at her bedroom door and watch her mother paint in the living room, quiet and lovely. Cool and sharp. Etta would count the *wish, wish, wish* of the brushstrokes.

She stood in the silence, asking, *Do you see me?*

She played concert after concert to the empty seat beside Alice's, asking, *Can you hear me?*

As a child she went to her bed at night, leaving the covers near her feet, her light on, until her mother's bedroom door would squeak shut. Etta would cry the question into her pillow. *Do you care?*

All of her life, Etta had been quiet, and determined, and gifted, and caring, and patient, and so hopeful, even in the unbearable loneliness of her own home. Now she could barely breathe. She could not hear Alice, she could not find her way back to those memories, because then she'd have to see, she'd have to accept, that the one person who'd cared for her, about her, with her, was gone. She would have to see her life not as a seed sprouting into bloom after years of work, but like an orchid her mother had precisely clipped and watered just enough to survive.

"It's not true," she said.

But Henry only watched her, a hand rubbing his mouth and jaw. He looked as if there were something else he wanted to say, something that could possibly be worse, but he held it back.

It's not true, she whispered.

She knew she was crying too late to stop it.

"I don't—" Henry began, forcing his arms down to his side. His fists clenched, curling with each agonized word. "*Please*—I don't even . . . I don't even know how to comfort you." He repeated it, in wrenching disbelief. "I don't know how to comfort you. She did not even let me have that."

Etta felt herself dissolve into her own pain, pressing a fist against her throat to lock in her sob. The cruelty of this—the *viciousness*. How much her mother must have hated her to try to trick her into destroying her own life.

"As it turns out," she managed to say, "nothing about her has ever been real, except her indifference."

"Oh, Etta, *Etta*—" He shook his head, and whatever had held him back before was gone. The warmth of his fingers as they curled around her own reached her, even as she shook. "Etta, you're wanted, you're everything, don't you see? My God, it breaks my heart to see you like this. Tell me what I can do."

Henry's anger was *real*, and it was palpable, building a charge with each word he spoke, until Etta wasn't sure which of them would explode first. In some strange way, Etta was grateful he was there, that his fury was flaring, mirroring and building upon her own. It validated every doubt. It spoke to all of those times she'd cried herself to sleep, wondering if that would be the night her mother finally heard her, or if the silence would swallow that, too. Etta wasn't stupid, but like Henry had said, she'd been blinded by her own love, and the pointless pursuit of her mother's love.

And somehow the worst part of it wasn't how Etta had been used, but how Rose's plan for her had created collateral damage. *Nicholas.* What would he say to this—would he hate her, knowing that her family, not his, had ultimately been the cause of so much of his pain?

She was shaking, and tried to hide it by moving to the other side of the desk, sucking in enough air, smearing the tears from her face, until she found some calm undercurrent in herself to grasp.

"Can you tell me what's going on? I need to understand what happened. The last I knew, *your* men had nearly killed me and N—" She caught herself, because her feelings for Nicholas weren't something she wanted to share, not with this virtual stranger.

"And your . . . companion?" he supplied carefully, well aware of those feelings regardless.

"Partner," Etta continued. "And they stole the astrolabe and rode off into the sunset with it. The next thing I knew, I was waking up in another desert and another century. If these men aren't with you, where are they? And what happened?"

Henry sighed, rising back onto his feet. "I kept your identity and my interest in you secret from the others, and I regret it more than I can say. As for the rest, I realize you've been through a trial, but would you consider taking a walk outside with me? It's far easier to show you."

WINIFRED—WHO, IT SEEMED, HAD BEEN LISTENING AT THE door—handed her a pair of shoes as soon as Etta emerged from the office. By the time Henry appeared at her side, a light coat over his suit jacket, the woman had faded back down the shadows of the hallway like the ghoul she was.

"No coat?" he asked, eyeing her up and down.

"Darling Winifred didn't think I needed one, apparently," she said. One of the guards chuckled into his fist, earning him a swat across the chest from the other.

Henry looked mildly startled. "Your mother called her that as well."

"My mother met that woman and they both survived it?"

One corner of his mouth twitched, and the parts of her that were still raw, and awkward—and, worse—unsure, eased. "I never said they emerged unscathed."

"I always wondered how she got the scar on her chin," Etta said, trying to squeeze the smallest traces of humor from this.

"That was me, I'm afraid," Henry said. "We were rather ruthless fencing partners when we were much younger. It was another scar in her extensive collection, but, once she returned the favor"—he pointed to the pale, thin mark above his left brow—"the matter was settled."

Etta tried not to grimace at that. Blood for blood. How very Rose Linden.

The thought was drawn away by Henry placing his overcoat around her shoulders.

"Is that all right?" he asked. "The Octobers here are mild, it likely won't be too cold—"

It was the anxious look he gave her that made Etta keep the coat around her, clutching it closed between her hands. "Thanks."

"We'll be taking a quick walk down the street, Jenkins," Henry said, turning to the guard who'd laughed. The other man gave a curt nod, and when Etta and Henry started down the hallway, he and the other guard fell into step behind them. Etta turned, confused, only to be drawn back around by the offer of Henry's arm.

Rather than take the grand stairway down, he led her to a smaller staircase, one so thoroughly plain and serviceable that Etta assumed it was meant for staff. They made their way down two levels, emerging in a large, echoing entryway.

A portrait of a beautiful young woman, as regal as any queen in her velvet gown and diamonds, kept watch over the comings and goings of the foyer, lit by an enormous crystal chandelier that had somehow survived the quake by only molting a few of its feather-shaped ornaments.

Jenkins stood off to the side, next to the massive front door, and was soon joined by two other men, all roughly the same height, all with the same dark hair, some dusted with gray, others not. Etta stopped to examine the portrait for a moment, rubbing her sore shoulder.

"Are you in pain, Miss Hemlock? Would you like something for it?" Jenkins asked.

"Oh—um, no, thank you," Etta said, letting her hand fall. It did hurt, but she wasn't sure she wanted to be under the influence of any medication—she needed to be as focused as possible. "And it's actually Spencer, not Hemlock."

"You're a Hemlock through and through," Henry said with a faint chuckle. "Suffering in silence because of indomitable pride. Get her the medicine, Jenkins."

"That does sound familiar," Jenkins said with a wink. The friendliness of it, like a shared private joke, startled her all over again.

Henry offered her his arm again, but Etta breezed past him, still preoccupied with those six words. *You're a Hemlock through and through.* That would be easy, wouldn't it? To accept that, to give in to the comfort of fitting into those qualities, to have that place offered to her?

He removed two white tablets from a silver pillbox in his coat pocket.

"Aspirin," Jenkins reassured her with a small smile.

"I'm all right," she said, trying to keep the wariness out of her voice. "Really. Thank you."

Henry looked like he wanted to push the matter, but when he saw her face—which Etta was sure must have looked swollen and red after her crying jag—he decided against it.

"Shall we, gentlemen?"

Standing next to them, the resemblance between Henry and the others was overwhelming, so much so that Etta wondered if they were all related. All Hemlocks.

If they were security, were they also decoys? The thought moved through her mind like a lance. The four men, including Jenkins, stepped into a tight unit around her and Henry, cocooning them on all sides before they even stepped outside. Etta waited for them to step farther away, to break up the human shield as they stepped into the crisp night air, but they never did, even as they began down the steep path. Their movements had the practiced precision of a military maneuver, and she had to wonder what Henry was being shielded from.

But she already knew. *Ironwoods.* This man, just as much as her mother, was the sworn enemy of Cyrus Ironwood, and had been working to undermine him for decades.

They came to a turn in the road and stopped short. It was only then that Henry gave a small signal with his hands to send the other men back a few feet. They went with reluctant, shuffling feet.

"Now," he said, turning his attention back to her. "Tell me what you see."

Etta caught herself looking up at him again, studying the crooked bridge of his nose, the gruesome scar at the base of his left ear where it looked like someone had begun to forcibly cut it off. He'd attempted to tame his hair beneath his hat, but it was already rebelling, curling up to greet the moisture in the air.

She turned back to face the hills and streets that rolled out below her, easing down into the bay. "I see . . . suffering. Pockets of homes. Twisted buildings."

But on the whole, the damage—what her history texts had painted in broad, catastrophic strokes—was terrible, but not crushing. Frightening, but not terrifying.

"What you're seeing is a city which has taken a severe knocking with the quake, but has been spared from fire damage, which is what ultimately caused the bulk of the damage and deaths in the timeline you know," Henry explained, tucking his hands into his pockets. "But if you had come to this moment in Ironwood's timeline, there would have been almost nothing to see. That was how devastated it was, by one small change that rippled out to a much larger one."

This isn't Ironwood's timeline. Etta whirled back toward him. "What was it?"

"When Ironwood was pursuing his interests, or rather, the interests of his family's ancestral territory in the Americas, he altered the outcome of a war. The Russo-Japanese War. Are you familiar with it?"

Etta shook her head. "No—wait, that was before World War One, wasn't it? Over land disputes?"

"Over rival interests in Manchuria and Korea," he said. "When it was clear the Russians were beaten and riots at home were breaking out, Ironwood convinced Theodore Roosevelt to mediate the peace talks, rather than let the war proceed a few more months as it had in the original timeline. It cost far more Russian and Japanese lives, but it resulted in sweeping reforms in the former, and spared the lives of millions of Russians in World War One."

That was . . . impossible.

Like time travel, she thought grimly. And so was standing there, in an alternate version of the history she had grown up with. A passing breeze kicked a loose strand of Etta's hair up, forcing her to smooth it back. Instead of smoke and ash, the breeze brought with it the briny scent of the sea, the metallic breath of exhaust, and the simple stenches of humanity.

"But what does that have to do with an earthquake in San Francisco?" she asked.

Henry turned to face her more fully. "This is what I want you to understand, Etta. I sympathize with you, knowing that your future is no longer what you remember. I know that pain, feeling your life and friends and dreams are gone. All of us have had to come to terms with the fact that our loyalty is to time itself. It's our inheritance, our nation, our history. But the future you know is filled with strife and war; it is nothing like the world of peace that existed before Cyrus Ironwood decided to remake it."

Etta recognized that she was as much in mourning over her dreams of being a concert violinist as she was for Alice. She had slowly come around to the idea that there was something more for her in life, and that she could still play without the validation of crowds and success. But the idea of an entirely unfamiliar future would always remain overwhelming.

"Each change we make, big or small, ripples out in ways we cannot always predict, that we can almost never control," Henry continued. "A war in Russia spreads its vines throughout the years, touching individual lives, nudging them to different locations, shifting their choices, until one man, Dennis T. Sullivan, San Francisco's fire chief, is in the wrong place when the earthquake strikes, and he dies of his injuries, leaving inexperienced firemen to wield dynamite to create firebreaks. A woman wakes up a few hours earlier than she would have and decides to make breakfast for her family, causing one of the most devastating fires of the entire century."

"So . . . we're in . . ." Etta began, trying to wrap her mind around the words. "We're in the original timeline now? The men who took the astrolabe managed to change it back?"

Henry nodded, and, with that, changed her life as she had known it.

"We've been identifying potential linchpin moments in history for years—moments and people and decisions that have a huge impact when it comes to these ripples," he explained. "They tested our theory that the Russo-Japanese War was one, and altered the future from 1905 onward. Ironwood's focus was on the nineteenth and twentieth centuries, and, thank God, most of his changes prior to then were minor. There wasn't enough wealth at stake for him to care or make a major play before then."

"But, unfortunately . . . ?" Etta prompted, detecting the anxiety underscoring his words.

He gave a faint smile. "Unfortunately, we've heard reports that he's already dispatched his men to see about altering events back. If we don't move quickly, we'll lose this advantage."

"Move quickly to destroy the astrolabe, you mean," Etta clarified.

"My men who took it from you were immediately followed by Ironwood's men. One of them was, from the note we received, killed. The survivor is in hiding in Russia, still in possession of the astrolabe, waiting for us to rescue him," he said. "Tonight, I need to inform the others that the only way forward is with its destruction. The complete reversion of the timeline to what was meant to be. We cannot leave the astrolabe in play; if Ironwood ever got his hands on it, he'd open up passages to new years, inflict more crippling changes on humanity. He does not care how many people die, or suffer, so long as he and his line survive. He wants more and more and more, and yet all of these years have proven nothing will ever be enough."

Until he saved his beloved first wife from death. Until he had *everything.*

Etta drew his coat around her shoulders more tightly, trapping in the warmth.

Meant to be. He kept using that same phrase. "Do you believe in destiny, then? That something deserves to exist, just because it once was?"

"I believe in humanity, in peace, and the natural order of things," he said. "I believe that the only way to balance the power of what we can do is with sacrifice. Accepting that we cannot possess the things and people not meant for us, we cannot control every outcome; we cannot cheat death. Otherwise there's no meaning to any of it."

"There's one more thing I don't really understand," Etta said. "If my future changed, if my life isn't what it was, then wouldn't I have been prevented from going back in the first place? Wouldn't it have invalidated finding the astrolabe and losing it?"

The information was offered freely, patiently. Etta was so grateful, she almost smiled.

"We live outside time's natural laws; that's why you remember your old life, even as it no longer exists. But time has its own sentience in a way, and it despises inconsistencies. To avoid them, it maintains or restores as many of our actions as possible, even in the face of great change. So, in your future, you still travel back from when you did, but perhaps you weren't performing at a concert; perhaps you were only at the museum visiting."

And perhaps Alice might still be alive, her mind whispered.

That sweet spark of hope lit her from her scalp to her toes.

The astrolabe *had* to be destroyed. That was nonnegotiable to her. It was more power than any one person should have, by far, and she could sacrifice her future knowing that at least any future damage could be somewhat contained. But she liked this, what Henry claimed. That they thought not just about themselves, but of how their actions would affect the true victims of Ironwood's meddling: the regular people who were at the mercy of his whims and wants.

Her time, the future she'd grown up in, had come at the cost of untold lives and damage: not just to the travelers, but to the world. Returning the timeline to its original state spoke to the part of her that had struggled so badly with the notion that travelers *could* inflict positive change, but chose not to. It could be a return to a moral center, a new beginning to build stronger rules for the travelers to adhere to.

She needed to finish what she'd begun, and soon.

But . . . Nicholas.

Nicholas, who was waiting for her; who rose in her memory like the lavender sunrise stretched out before them. She let the thought of both wash over her, steady, brightening, beautiful.

I can spare him this. He never should have been involved in this mess to begin with. If she could keep him safely out of it, until the astrolabe was destroyed, maybe then she could begin to make up for the havoc her family had wrought on his life.

"Can I come with you?" she asked. The wind picked up around them, tugging at the coat, her hair, as if trying to move her more firmly onto this path. "To Russia?"

Henry looked as if he couldn't quite believe it. "You're sure? If you need a few days more of rest—"

"No, I need to see this for myself," she said. "Don't think about leaving me behind for 'my own good,' either."

"I wouldn't dream of it," he said, and it took Etta a moment to process that the unfamiliar tone in his voice was pride. She became just a tiny bit hungry to hear it again. "Let's go back, shall we?"

The guards formed their protective shell around them again, and they walked in companionable silence back up to the magnificent home that overlooked the city that had been spared by time. Inside, Etta started toward the stairs, but Henry nudged her to the left, into what looked to be a large, formal dining room. Piano music no longer sang out, but there was chatter and the heavy steps of people milling around.

Packing up, as it turned out. Several people attacked the last of the drinks and food left out on the tables. Others swept up any and all messes as men rolled up the sleeping pads and bedding at their feet; even more were laying out the contents of their packs, counting supplies or trading what they had with others.

Although many people were dressed in the severe style of the era, there were equally as many in a rainbow of silk or chiffon ball gowns and stately military uniforms. Women in the corner were helping one another arrange their hair in artful piles, every now and then reaching out to snag the few small children running loops around everyone's legs. Their laughter struck a chord in her, resonated even in her battered heart.

It was a liminal space, where dawn met night, and the past met the present. These people had gathered here to conduct their work in hiding, but, more than that, it was a secret, special place that created its own warmth and light, even as the fire was smothered and the candles were doused.

Etta tried to step back, but Henry led her forward. He did not have to say a word for silence to fall like a curtain.

Even the children turned to him, eyes wide, small pearly teeth flashing as they grinned. One held out an open palm, to the obvious, fond embarrassment of his mother. Beside her, Henry dug into his pockets, screwing his face up as if struggling to dig through all of the imaginary things there. A small wrapped piece of candy finally emerged, and the boy snatched it and ran back behind his mother's skirts with a shriek of giggles.

But not even that could distract the others from their fixation on Etta's face. The way panic gripped her entire chest made her feel like that little girl performing under the bright stage lights for the first time. *I'm not that girl anymore.* Not after everything she'd faced.

"The similarities end with the face and hair," she managed to say, vaguely gesturing there with her hand.

There was a moment where the expressions of bald hostility turned to confusion. And then the woman, the same mother, began to laugh. The others around her caught the sound, relaxing into their own rueful chuckles. And like the timeline changes Henry had spoken of, the laughter rippled out, until the entire room settled into it.

"We have much to discuss tonight about our path forward," Henry said, placing a hand on her shoulder, "but would you all allow me the pleasure of introducing my daughter, Etta, to you?"

"Well, hey!" a man shouted from the back, cutting through the quiet din of surprise. "Another Hemlock to add to the ranks—it's high time for us to finally outnumber you Jacarandas for once! Congrats, old boy! And welcome, doll!"

Henry rolled his eyes but was smiling so hard he was nearly pink with it.

Once their surprise melted away, all that was left were the whistles and shouts that left Etta stunned in turn. The wave of women washed up to her, and warm hands clasped her own, touched her shoulder beneath Henry's coat, where the bandage was just visible. They were talking over each other, so fast Etta couldn't keep up with them.

"—kept you up there—"

"—was wondering where he'd gotten off to—"

"—aren't you a sight—"

But there was one cool voice that seemed to unfailingly climb over the others. Winifred came up behind them, touching Henry's shoulder. He turned away from the men who were slapping his back and giving him handshake after handshake.

"That creature you insist on working with is here to make her report," she informed him. "Would you like me to tell her to wait?"

Henry's brows rose. Interested. "No—no, I've been waiting for her report for days. Is she in the hall?"

The women were urging Etta deeper into the throng of Thorns, eagerly absorbing her, peppering the air with questions. She turned, searching for Henry's dark hair, and found him passing through the door, back into the hall.

With the morning light coming through the high windows, she could see the small figure waiting there in the entryway. Julian was out there as well, chattering away beside her. He gave her a playful punch to the shoulder, and whoever it was returned it in earnest, socking him hard enough in the solar plexus to send him staggering back, choking on his laughter.

As Henry approached, she pushed Julian aside altogether and straightened, flicking her long, jet-black braid back over her shoulder. She wore a cornflower-blue silk tunic buttoned at the throat, its wide sleeves embroidered with an intricate pattern. She tucked up her hands inside of the sleeves as Henry began to speak. Her loose matching trousers shone as she moved, heading toward the stairs. Just before she took the first step, the girl looked around Henry's shoulder into the room and caught Etta's gaze. Her lips parted, as if in disbelief. Etta wondered what the woman had that Henry wanted.

Julian hesitated at the door, watching the others, until one of the guards—Jenkins—shooed him away. Only the Ironwoods, it seemed, were unwelcome where the Thorns were concerned.

Etta turned back to the men and women around her and, for once, silenced the questions, the doubt that had chased her through the centuries. She fell deeper into the hands that reached out to greet her, and let herself find relief in their elation.

A family.

Meant to be, she thought. *This is what was meant to be.*

But in the back of her mind, there was a face: Nicholas.

Nicholas alone, the desert blowing hot and blinding around him.

I'm coming, she thought. *Stay alive. I'll find you.*

But not yet.

116

PRAGUE
1430

NINE

JULIAN HAD ONCE SAID SOMETHING TO HIM THAT STRUCK Nicholas now, as he breathed in the fog and cold mist: *All cities are jealous of Paris, but Prague is the envy of Paris.*

Tucked into the alcove of the building where the passage had released them, he had only been able to see the busy market in the open courtyard before him. As the weather turned and night crept in, the stalls rapidly emptied. Footsteps and cart wheels clattered over the cobblestones as all manner of people, in all manner of simple, colorful dress, fled the rain, carried off by surprised laughter and shouts.

Though he'd hoped his breeches and shirtsleeves would be unremarkable enough for him to pass among the century's occupants unnoticed, Nicholas was rather dismayed to find that it was not the case, unless he wanted to commit to the part of a peasant and rend his clothing. The men of this time wore doublets and jerkins, in the sort of style that made them appear to be strutting around with their chests puffed out like pigeons. Or, in the case of the paler fabrics, enormous eggs with limbs.

He turned to Sophia, only to find that she had shed her jacket, pulled the shirt out of the waist of her breeches, and affixed her belt over both, in a close approximation of a tunic. Perhaps not exactly correct, but perhaps not quite so *incorrect*, either. At least they'd both managed to keep their hose from ripping. Whatever small consolation that was.

Although he felt less aware of the color of his skin than he had in the eras they had passed through to arrive here, Nicholas now was struck by the first stirrings of doubt that the residents of the city might explain his presence away as a Moor or Turkish merchant. It was a blessing, then, to have the soaked, darkened city streets to themselves for a short time, and he meant to make the most of it.

Of course, that was before he stepped out from under their shelter and truly took stock of the place.

He understood what Julian had meant now. Rather than charge forward, Nicholas's feet came to a sudden, halting rebellion. Rain ran down his face in rivulets, soaking him as he studied the twin spires of a Gothic church. Around him, the sweet faces of the buildings stretched up into the low-slung clouds, the precise curves and angles of the gables and finials glowing in the odd light. At first look, it had all seemed rather simplistic in design, but he was almost delighted to find that the city defied him, that it refused to be absorbed in a single glance. The roads and paths away from the market curved into shadows, inviting mysteries. There was an unreal quality to the place, one that made it seem as though it had been someone's dream, imagined into stone and timber.

Sophia smacked the back of his head, knocking him out of his reverie.

"'We must make haste! We cannot delay!'" she said, in a mocking version of his voice. "So let's stand around and gawk where anyone can see us!"

Despite having sworn to himself that he wouldn't keep rising to her taunts, Nicholas felt himself bristle. "I was—"

"Good evening, sweet lady and kind sir."

Nicholas spun around, searching through the sheets of rain for the source of the small voice. A young blond boy dressed in a gold-and-ivory

120

doublet and jerkin, his hose dampened by mud and rain, stood a few feet away, glowering at them. The feather on his jaunty little cap was wilted, and flopped as he tilted his head. "My mistress has invited you to take tea with her."

A hot cup of tea sounded like heaven itself, actually. But Sophia answered before Nicholas could accept. "We take wine, not tea."

He could have argued against that, very strongly, but the boy pouted in response and executed a smart little bow. Sophia smirked at Nicholas, just as he'd begun to suspect he'd missed something—some sort of code.

"If you and your . . . guest . . . would please follow me?"

Their golden child led them around the tower the passage had emptied into, and Nicholas was arrested by the sight of a large clock on its side layered with symbols, arms, charts. At first glance, the intricate layers of its face reminded him of nothing so much as the astrolabe.

Sophia retraced her steps back to him, her eye squinting at it. "Will you please take that ridiculous look off your face? It's an astronomical clock."

Which told him nothing other than that this, perhaps, was like a great geared astrolabe that also served the useful function of telling time, rather than corrupting it.

The boy continued on through the streets of Prague with the ease of a native, ignoring the architecture, the art embedded in the city's skin. Behind him, Nicholas was so absorbed in the wonders of the city that it took him longer than it might have otherwise to notice the peculiar thing unfolding around him.

He slowed his pace, wondering if it was his eyes, or . . . Nicholas *was* exhausted, practically dragging himself forward. But, still, he'd felt the sting of invisibility and dismissal far too many times to let this stand.

The next small cluster of men and women approached quickly, giving him another opportunity to investigate. But—*again*. He sucked in a breath, watching as the soldiers, the young woman, an elderly man, all stopped despite the rain, and turned their backs as he, Sophia, and the boy passed them.

"What are you huffing and puffing about?" Sophia asked. "You sound like a teakettle about to go off."

"We're being shunned," he said in a low voice, so the child wouldn't hear. "Or at least, our guide is."

Sophia's bewildered expression turned to one of muted surprise when he pointed it out to her, splashing through the puddles of the next narrow street. What confused him, truthfully, was that, despite their firm action, these people bore no signs of disgust, or even scorn. No obvious markers, such as sneers, or hateful, distrusting eyes. In fact, their expressions were as serene as marble statues, and once their party had passed, the men and women would turn back around and continue on their way. It made his skin prickle and tighten around his bones.

The boy glanced over his shoulder and must have caught his expression, for he said, "Don't be troubled, sir. They cannot help it."

Which meant . . . what, precisely? They were somehow being compelled? And in such perfect uniformity?

"Oh, I'd forgotten about this," Sophia said, waving away his attempts to engage her on this. "Some trickery to ensure there are no real witnesses. Grandfather—Ironwood—believes the Belladonna loaded everyone in this city with so much gold they don't dare breathe her name, let alone acknowledge her or her guests."

While money could buy a great deal, no matter the century, this seemed a step beyond mere coordinated cooperation. Nicholas crossed the short distance between himself and the nearest woman. She looked to be a servant, perhaps, as she was older and wore unadorned clothing. On closer inspection, the basket over her arm carried a small heap of vegetables, covered with a piece of burlap. She went impossibly still as Nicholas stepped closer to study her impassive face, and risked a faint tap between her shoulder blades.

The woman did not move, except to breathe. Not so much as a blink.

"You said she was not a witch," Nicholas whispered as he caught up to Sophia and the boy again. "You swore it!"

"She *isn't*," Sophia insisted, glancing back over her shoulder just as the woman shook herself, as if coming out of a deep sleep, and turned to continue on her way. Nicholas did not miss the rare flicker of uncertainty on her face as she admitted, "At least . . . I am reasonably certain she is not."

THE BOY BROUGHT THEM AT LAST TO A STREET OF STORIED mansions. Perhaps "small palaces" was a more apt description, each marrying different shades of colors and styles of stonemasonry. The homes announced themselves to passersby with doors that looked as though they could withstand battering rams if necessary, and windows from which candlelight and the gazes of servants fell softly over the three of them.

At the very end of the street, past the splendor of Prague's wealthy, lived a narrow little shop, which leaned so severely to the right on its haunches that the windows and door had been installed on a slant. Its front window was covered with a curtain, blocking the interior, and it bore no sign.

Nicholas reached up to touch Etta's earring on its leather cord and took a steadying breath. As he followed Sophia inside, the shop coughed up warm dust and the smell of rotting earth. Dozens of candles were scattered around the room like guiding stars. The dingy light, however, only served to make the shelves of bottles and jars, many cracked and half-full, seem filthier than the lace of spiderwebs connecting them.

Half of these same shelves had buckled and snapped, spilling their contents onto the floor, where they had been promptly forgotten. Wax from the candles was dripping onto the glass cases and chairs, many of which were torn or broken altogether. As much as he had longed to be in a place warm enough to begin drying out his clothes and thawing his blood, Nicholas's skin only felt an overwhelming itchiness amid the decay.

"Madam!" the boy called.

A crimson curtain behind the far counter rustled, and out from under the portrait of a doll-faced child came a young woman. Her hair was like a raven's wing: black, with a natural sheen that caught the candlelight, even without the gold-and-pearl netting that had been pinned to it. A heavy gold cross hung around her neck, dipping into the low bodice of her strawberry-pink silk gown—at odds with the filth that seemed to be steaming around her. Her face, with its too-large eyes and lips, was oddly arresting, so much so that Nicholas took a step toward her without meaning to. The thoughts that had been trying to sort themselves out went soft at the edges.

The woman received the boy warmly, leaning down to ghost a finger along the bridge of his nose, her smile as sweet as pure honey. He nodded at something she whispered in his ear and happily skipped off to a stool a short distance away, reclaiming a thin leather volume.

The woman glimmered in the candlelight as she smiled at them. Her skin, the gold, the beading and metallic thread shot through her gown—all called to him, shining and bold. The light caught her like flame on glass.

Nicholas leaned back against the pull of her, cocking his head to the side to better study her. There was something in the way she didn't move so much as flicker around, like the candles burning on the counter near her hands—something that made him question his eyes.

"See?" Sophia scoffed. "I told you you'd forget Linden soon enough."

He whirled on her, grasping for the words that only a moment before had been poised on the tip of his tongue. It wasn't that. Nicholas didn't feel a rush of attraction that set him back on his heels, the way he had with Etta, but . . . this was . . . it seemed closer to the flush that came with too much whiskey on a too-empty stomach. A sickness.

"Welcome," the woman said, in such a soft voice that Nicholas and Sophia took another step forward to hear her. The candles mimicked their movement, and, for just a moment, he was able to tear his eyes off the woman—the Belladonna—and notice that, in the middle of the stack of reeking, swollen tallow candles was one burning a sullen blood red.

"Welcome, weary travelers," she said again, this time with a smile that revealed beautifully white teeth, like seed pearls—something unheard-of for anyone in this era. "How may I assist you?"

This woman? This was the woman who had dueled with Cyrus Ironwood and won her independence from him? Perhaps this . . . beguiling charm . . . worked even on the stone-hearted.

"We've come to trade for information," Sophia said, leaning an arm and hip against the counter.

Nicholas glanced up at the slight vault of the ceiling, not quite a dome. Much of it was covered with a damp cloak of dust and mildew, browned by time, but here and there he could make out the strange, mystical symbols that bordered its edges. At the peak was a large silver crescent moon, half masked by the dark clouds painted around it.

"I possess many remarkable objects," the woman hedged. "And know of many more."

"Can we cut through this nonsense and get to the heart of this?" Sophia said. "I was made to believe that you know everything and everyone. If that isn't the case, we'll take our business somewhere else."

"Perhaps if you were to be more specific about what it is you're searching for?" The Belladonna's voice sounded as though it were being coaxed out of a violin.

"We're looking for information pertaining to, ah," Nicholas said, "travelers of a particular nature."

"Perhaps you could be a little less specific and a bit more cagey," Sophia muttered, shaking her head. "I'd *love* to be here to greet the next century."

A sound shuddered up from beneath the floorboards—a heaving, stomping sound that seemed to rattle even the timber beams overhead. A portrait of a benign, pale man tumbled from the nearby wall behind where the boy sat. It smashed out of its frame when its gilded corner struck the ground. The steps passed beneath them—Sophia straightened, tracking the sound with her eye. Nicholas kept a hand on the knife at his side.

"Who the devil is that?" he asked.

The woman smiled serenely. "I sell the finest of elixirs, sir. Perhaps I might interest you in a set for your pretty little wife at home?"

"That's not what he asked, you stupid cow—"

Sophia's words were cut short by the tremendous bang of the door behind her as it struck the wall, and the sudden appearance of a bundle of black-and-silver silk and netting. All of which didn't appear, so much as roll toward them with the force and menace of a thundercloud.

A woman nearly as tall as Nicholas strode forward. The bottom half of her face was hidden beneath a veil of black lace, but her eyes were a gleaming, almost feline yellow. Somehow, either by piercing or some art, three small pearls trailed down from the corner of each eye like tears. Her décolletage was modestly covered by a sheer panel of white fabric, but what Nicholas initially took for lace was anything but. The markings were the climbing, swirling lines of what appeared to be a tattoo. When she spun toward Sophia, Nicholas saw that her snow-white hair had been braided, intricately looped and knotted together.

"Who—?" The woman leaned toward Sophia, sniffing the air around her.

Sophia let out a small cry of surprise, swatting at her, but the woman had already moved on. Nicholas leaped back instinctively as she swung her attention toward him, subjecting him to the same sniffing. Truly, she sounded like a pig searching out a truffle, her teeth clattering behind the veil. He was dosed with her scent—that earthy undertone he had detected when they'd first entered the shop.

"Ma'am," he began, with as much composure as he could gather, "if you would be so good as to—"

She spun, carrying the same hint of damp soil and lavender away with her.

"Sir, please let me show you our latest arrivals," the woman behind the counter said, her smile never once faltering. The other woman glanced back, first at her, then the boy.

"Put her out." If the first woman sang her words, this one crushed them between her teeth.

The golden boy marked his place in his book and went over to the counter. He planted two hands on its dusty surface and jumped up, just high enough to blow out the bloodred candle Nicholas had noted before.

The Belladonna vanished, disappearing into the candle smoke that trailed up toward the groaning rafters.

That settled, the boy returned to his stool, picked up his book, and resumed his place in the story.

Sophia jumped forward, a wild expression on her face as she looked behind the counter for the woman—she met Nicholas's gaze when she looked up again and shook her head.

Disappeared. Gone.

Impossible.

He might have to accept that they were edging toward the shadows of the unnatural. Nicholas knew he would need to be on guard, and despite his shaky faith in a higher power, found himself thinking those words he'd heard Captain Hall say throughout his childhood: *God defend us.*

"How . . . ? Are . . . ?" Nicholas was not quite sure what he meant to ask.

The woman in black stormed back toward Sophia, who lifted a leather-bound volume off the floor and sent it flying toward the older woman's head, coming within inches of striking her.

The sniffing intensified, until finally the woman held out an arm, silvery black lace dripping from the end of the sleeve. "Come here to me, beastie."

Sophia took a rather large step back.

Before Nicholas could leap forward, the woman snatched Sophia by the arm and whirled her around, as if to swat her bottom. In one smooth movement, the woman pulled up the back of Sophia's shirt and pulled something out that had been tucked into the belt around the girl's waist.

For a moment Nicholas thought it might have been another trick of his eyes, because when her hand emerged it was holding a long, thin blade, but the end of it had been snapped off, leaving it a jagged claw. The base was adorned with a large ring, thin bands of silver weaving in and out of each other.

"Good God!" The words burst out of him as the woman held the pointed end up to her nose with one last, satisfied sniff. "You've been carrying *that* around this whole time?" he asked Sophia. "Where did you come across such a thing?"

Even as the words left his mouth, he knew. The body of the Linden guardian in Nassau, the one with the peculiarly small wound through his ear. She had reached the body first, and had somehow taken up the blade in the darkness of night. Without him ever noticing.

And she had held on to it for . . . what purpose, exactly? His guts clenched, picturing her expression of joy as she drove it through him while he slept.

Sophia refused to look in his direction. "How did you know I had it?"

The question was directed to the other woman—the true Belladonna, Nicholas suspected.

"The blood smells like the rotting intestines of a goat," the woman growled at her. "This will be payment enough for entry."

Holding it up to the candlelight, she studied something on the ring that Nicholas couldn't quite make out—it might have been the etching of a sun. Her breath made the veil over her mouth flutter.

"Payment?" Nicholas heard the disbelief in his voice.

"Yes, beastie. *Payment.* This is a place of business. Or did you expect me to offer you refreshments and the moon?"

"Is information part of the deal?" Sophia asked, eyeing her with her usual look of mistrust.

"It depends, of course, on what it is you wish to purchase," the Belladonna said. "I have been known to barter. From time to time. Boy, lock up the shop."

"Yes, madam," the boy said, brave enough to give her a petulant look for interrupting his reading again, but not brave enough to ignore the order.

"Children," the Belladonna huffed as she led Nicholas and Sophia to the door behind the counter. "The only thing they're good for is eating."

Sophia barked out a surprised laugh, but Nicholas wasn't quite convinced she was joking, given the casual way the woman had begun to twirl the blade with a shocking disregard for her fingers.

"She can follow me," the Belladonna said, gesturing to Sophia as she began down the dark stairs, "and to hell with you, you humorless sop. Oh—you'll want to hold your breath as you take the last few steps. If you faint, you roll down at your own peril."

"I beg your pardon?" Nicholas caught a hint of something vaguely putrid and found himself doing as asked.

The lower level seemed to be two flights down, lit only by the faint orange haze crawling up the steps from fires below. Nicholas had a vague memory of something Julian had told him—that there was a kind of underground city in parts of Prague where they'd been forced to build the streets and buildings up to avoid flooding. The overall impression he had was of climbing through a dark vein to reach the city's pale bones.

The light was coming from a fire in the corner of what looked to be some sort of workshop. The first small section they moved through contained mostly plants and herbs left to dry, as well as what looked to Nicholas like an area for blowing glass. They continued down the narrow, rough stone artery that connected that room to the next. At the very center of the room was a sort of circular stove, each layer stacked upon the next like the tiers of a dingy stone cake. Glass bottles ringed it like ornaments, many with long, hollow stems for pouring the liquids inside into another, simpler bottle below. As she passed by it, the Belladonna stooped to fan the small fire burning inside its base. Once past it, they were confronted with the sight of what looked to be a bell-shaped oven with small openings, as well as barrels, and mice scampering around them.

"Are you an alchemist?" Sophia asked, understanding the odd sight.

"Well spotted," the Belladonna deadpanned. "I dabble. You might consider the use of my youth elixir, beastie. You look old beyond your age."

Nicholas grabbed Sophia's shoulder before she could make good on the murder in her expression.

One last jaunt down another hall brought them to their destination: an even smaller, darker room. Its only occupant, save for them, was a painting that stood taller than himself, and wide enough to cover the entirety of the wall. Nicholas's eye was caught first by the glowing moon depicted in the dark, cloudy sky, and next, by the waves washing up onto a deserted, unknown shore.

"Now," the Belladonna said, "do not touch anything, do not look into any of the mirrors, do not sit on my chairs, and most of all, know that thieves will be dealt with in the manner of ancient justice."

Sophia gave a sarcastic salute, but Nicholas put a hand on the knife at his side.

With no further instructions or warnings, the Belladonna turned and stepped inside the painting.

UNKNOWN
Unknown

TEN

IT WAS A PASSAGE, OF COURSE—AN ODDLY QUIET CREATURE of a passage that sat just in front of the painted sky. The air shimmered and distorted the peaceful image as the Belladonna passed through it, and the usual drumming sounded off.

Both Nicholas and Sophia turned to look at one another expectantly.

"Oh, no, we're here for you and your beautiful beloved, not me," she said. "You test the waters!"

"I only wished to ask if you knew where it led," Nicholas said brusquely. "I always intended to go first."

She made a strangled sound of frustration, throwing her hands up. "And subject me to a lifetime of shame and guilt because that witch turns you into a pig and roasts you, before I can get through the passage to save your hide?" Sophia sniffed. "You'd like that, wouldn't you, with all of your miserable, obnoxious honor."

"I would have to say most men wouldn't enjoy being transfigured into a pig and eaten," he said. "But if something were to happen, it might as well be to me. You have the better knowledge of where passages are located, and could continue on—"

Sophia rolled her eye and stuck out her hand. Nicholas stared at it, until Sophia let out a huff and grabbed his wrist, dragging them forward. The whole experience was so bewildering that Nicholas hardly took notice of the passage's usual stormy assault against his senses.

They were launched out of the passage at a run, their steps slowed only by the presence of a heavy Oriental rug and the ragged growl of a large white wolf, curled around the base of an imposing structure of iron that looked like it would better serve as a drawbridge than a desk.

Nicholas backed up as far as he could without brushing the passage, eyes skimming the space around them.

The room was small and without windows, but here and there were drapes slung down over the walls, and rows of glass bookshelves and cases, as red and rich as tides of blood. More alarming, however, was the lack of a door—at least a visible one. There was no indication of where or when they were. No telling sights or sounds. Beyond the dust and smell of age, the only scent he could detect was that same earthy one as before, heightened greatly.

Nicholas sent a wondering look up at the rows of dried herbs and flowers hanging low over their heads, pushing the bundles out of his way to better see the Belladonna. Before she sat behind her desk, she retrieved a jar of foul, bitter-smelling liquid from her shelf and dropped the dagger into it. The mixture bubbled over like a hellbroth.

Sophia took a step closer to the nearest case, where a heavy sword was displayed. The long, heavy blade was chipped and dull along its killing edge, but the gold hilt was pristine, embellished by two golden chimeras. While he marveled, Sophia's first instinct, naturally, was to lift the glass and make as though to take it out.

"If you touch that sword, I will use it to slice off your fingers, roast them, and feed them to Selene," the Belladonna informed her, not looking up from the glass she had dropped the blade into. Beside her on the floor, the wolf looked up from the bone it had been gnawing and gave a snort of confirmation. Nicholas looked away quickly, attempting to not identify it as a human femur.

"What sword is that?" Sophia asked, still eyeing it.

"Arthur's Caliburn," the Belladonna said.

"Excalibur?" Nicholas couldn't stop his brows from rising. A legendary sword—one that didn't exist. So far as he knew.

"How has someone not bought this off you?" Sophia asked. "Ironwood would probably love to use it to behead his most hated enemies. His murders could use a little poetry."

The Belladonna's veil rustled and crimped, as if she'd smiled at the word *Ironwood*.

She knows who we are, Nicholas thought with a growing sense of unease.

"One of my scavengers fished it out of a filthy lake for me," the Belladonna said. "However, I've never been able to prove the provenance of the object to your Grand Master's standards, and so it remains. Until it one day needs to be found. No, beastie, take that thought of stealing it from your mind—" Sophia's hand immediately lowered. "I'd hate for you to join my cadre of thieves."

Without lifting her eyes from Sophia, the Belladonna pointed to a large, drooping net hanging from the ceiling. It was filled with human skulls, all boiled and polished as smoothly as pearls from the sea. At the sight of it, Sophia scowled and moved on to examine the next case, which contained a line of eight bejeweled and gold-trimmed eggs of various sizes.

"Imperial Fabergé eggs, lately of Russia," the Belladonna said, pulling a grape from a nearby plate of them and popping it into her mouth. "I'm willing to bargain, if they're of interest. It's become damned difficult to auction them with the instability of that period."

Instability. Nicholas seized upon the word, storing the information away. Where there was instability, there were likely changes to the timeline.

"Maybe I should have let you go first," Sophia muttered to Nicholas, greedily eyeing a bowl of pristine apples that seemed oddly out of place. "I could be eating a fresh pork dinner right now."

"That does sound rather appealing, I must say," the Belladonna said, tossing a grape to the wolf, who snapped it out of the air. The animal gave a curious sniff in Sophia's direction, but lowered its head and resumed its watch over them. "There's King John's treasure in the corner over there, next to Cromwell's head, and a panel of the Bayeux Tapestry, if you've yet to finish wasting my time."

At her interested hum, Nicholas grabbed the scruff of Sophia's shirt, cutting off her path. "We've business here, mind you."

"Oliver Cromwell's head, though," Sophia said pitifully, as if this might convince him.

He stepped forward, winding through the rows of shelves that separated them from the desk. Sophia followed reluctantly, shaking off Nicholas's grip. To his complete and utter lack of surprise, there were no chairs for them to sit in. They presented themselves to the Belladonna like a mustering militia.

"Now," the woman said. "Tell me what it is Ironwood seeks, and I shall tell you my fee."

Sophia made a noise of disgust. "We're not here on the old man's business."

The woman settled back in her chair. "Are you not Sophia Elizabeth Ironwood, born in July of 1904, *lovingly*"—the word was impaled with sarcasm—"pulled from St. Mary's Orphanage in 1910 after you were caught pickpocketing for the third time—"

Sophia put her hands on her hips and said, "Well, they didn't catch me the other hundreds of times. Three is hardly a bad score."

Nicholas couldn't be sure why the other woman had said it, other than to awe them with her knowledge, or disarm Sophia.

Rescued, orphanage, pickpocketing.

Christ. Julian had vaguely mentioned to him in passing that Sophia had not had a lady's upbringing until Ironwood brought her into the family. But this . . . it went beyond humble origins. And as he himself knew, when you were forced to learn survival as a child, the instinct became etched into your soul.

The Belladonna smirked and her attention fell over him so heavily that Nicholas felt as though he'd gained another shadow.

"Everyone present knows of my origins; it's not necessary to reiterate them to prove some mysterious point. We've come because we wish for information," Nicholas said finally.

"Is that so?"

"We're looking for what the last common year is," Sophia explained. "To find someone orphaned by the shift, which I'm sure you are well aware of."

The Belladonna leaned forward, resting her arms against the desk. A quill fluttered in its cup, and two grapes escaped their plate to find freedom on the floor. She stroked the veil covering her mouth, the way a man would stroke a beard. "Indeed? That is certainly within my knowledge. Who is this person you seek?"

"It's Hen—" Sophia began, but Nicholas gave a curt shake of the head. He would rather not have the woman turn her eye onto Etta; the darkness of this place, the way it seemed alive with its own curiosity, made him want to protect her from this stranger's interest for as long as possible.

The older woman turned her gaze back toward Nicholas. The small silver bells sewn into her mass of hair tinkled.

"Well," the Belladonna continued, "your desperation reeks worse than your intriguing stench. You are clearly without earthly possessions, and neither of you was close enough to Ironwood to have new, useful secrets to trade. So perhaps our business has concluded before it began."

Sophia took a furious step forward, reaching for whatever sharp weapon she had strapped to her belt. The wolf jumped to its feet, baring its teeth as the girl came toward her, but Sophia growled back, glaring at the animal until its lips relaxed and its ears rose to their usual position.

Nicholas's heart began to beat back against the thoughts of *no* running through his mind. They had not traveled through centuries of swamps and storms to arrive at a denial. This search could be simple; they wouldn't have to chase down every passage in every century for a lead on Etta's whereabouts.

"Is there nothing else you want in exchange from us?"

In the silence, an idea seemed to shape itself from candlelight and shadow. Nicholas noted the moment it struck the Belladonna, how her hands laced together and her veil shifted, as if masking a smile.

"Many of my auctions are for items that are priceless. They defy valuation. As you may know, I select winning bids based on what they can offer me. A secret, or a favor they're willing to do. Here, we can negotiate—in exchange for the information you seek, I'll ask for a favor," the Belladonna said, her chair creaking as she leaned back. "It will be of my choosing, to be completed sometime in the future."

"I won't do anything . . ."—Nicholas struggled to find the right words—". . . scandalous. Immoral."

One eyebrow rose. "Goodness. What an imagination you have. By favor, I mean a task. Perhaps to find and retrieve something for me. Carry a message. Assist in my own travel. And so on."

That . . . did not sound entirely intolerable to him.

"So he has to serve you?" Sophia demanded. "No questions asked?"

"For a time, only insofar as it pertains to the task," the Belladonna said, flicking her long nails at the girl.

"Slavery," he said, the dull burn inside of his chest growing. *Intolerable.* He should have guessed this underhanded "business" of hers would strive to bind the wings of his soul.

"Nothing so foul," the Belladonna said, her voice sharp with offense. "It's indentured servitude, and only a day or two's worth. Your task pays off your debt to me. Once our business is concluded, that bond will be broken."

Sophia grabbed his collar, yanking him down to her height and startling him out of his tangle of thoughts. "Forget this. We'll try the Jacarandas instead, like we planned."

And risk them not knowing? Risk running in circles long enough for this starting point to disappear? They'd failed to master time on this search, and now it was threatening to best them. Etta was hurt and alone, and the thought of taking a moment longer to debate this was intolerable. If anything, it was Sophia's infernal pride speaking for her again, her entitlement. Nicholas hadn't expected the answers to be handed to them. This was a business deal, and he had to believe that Rose Linden wouldn't send him into the jaws of a literal and figurative wolf. The woman's methods were patently ridiculous, but she was still his ally.

"Everyone has a master, whether you realize this or not," the Belladonna said. "Luckily, I am a benevolent one. Mostly."

How very bitter that truth was when swallowed. Some were bound by loyalty and vows, others by an obsession with wealth, and others were owned by other men through no fault of their own.

There was something else that Hall used to say—that life itself was uncertainty, and the only remedy to its madness was to act boldly. This was a risk, yes, but it was tied to a tantalizing reward. At least this was presented as a choice; at least he was retaining some measure of free will. Nicholas could tolerate this debt, so long as he felt the information he would be receiving was proportional to the work.

"There's no *we*," Nicholas told Sophia, detangling her fingers. "This is the answer."

Find Etta. Salvage her future. Fix those things he'd ruined.

And to one day live a life of his own making, be left to his own ends, whatever shape that might take now.

"You won't say what the task will be before we agree?"

The Belladonna's eyes narrowed, glancing toward a grandfather clock behind him. "I haven't yet decided. But you've thirty seconds to agree before the offer is rescinded and Selene escorts you out." She reached over and used one of her grotesque nails to tap the lip of the jar containing the thin silver weapon, marking the seconds.

Nicholas's instincts were murmuring in displeasure about the lack of time to weigh the costs of this. Perhaps if he could make the deal more tolerable, sweeter, he could find that boldness that good faith required . . .

"I have a single condition," he said, meeting the Belladonna's feline gaze. "Before I agree, I would like you to answer a different question first."

Are you in league with the devil? He shoved the thought aside. *Will you devour my soul like a tart?*

The Belladonna snorted, puncturing the silence that followed. "Yes. All right."

"Are the Thorns still in possession of the much-sought-after astrolabe, the one that used to belong to the Lindens?" Nicholas tried to be as specific as possible, so she could not twist her answer, or tell him the fate of a different astrolabe.

After a moment, with obvious reluctance, she said, "In the last report I received, yes, a Thorn was still in possession of the astrolabe." Her veil ruffled as she took in a breath, sucking it against her lips. "Earlier, you mentioned the Jacarandas—I do not suppose you mean Remus and Fitzhugh, the traitors?"

Sophia glanced over at Nicholas before asking, "So what if I did?"

"If you are hoping to find the Thorns, the group's last known location was in San Francisco, in 1906. They appear to be on the move, however," she added, "and I'm not entirely certain of where they'll settle next. And if *I* am not certain, those two toadstools have no hope of knowing, either."

Nicholas's brows rose. That was more information than he ever could have prayed for. He dared to test the limits of his luck by asking, "Do the Thorns have other times they frequent?"

"They do, but I'm certain they are investigating the changes to the timeline and will not be returning to any of those periods at present."

Nicholas felt the knotted muscles in his shoulder ease. He gave her a curt nod of thanks, feeling more secure in his decision to proceed now.

The metal desk creaked as the Belladonna leaned her weight onto it, but before she could speak, Selene let out a sharp whine.

A warning.

Through the wall to his right, Nicholas could have sworn he heard voices shouting the word *Revolyutzia!* in the instant before the room blurred like fogged-over glass and began shaking violently.

Thunder stole through the air, deafening and absolute. The jars and display cases rattled, heaps of glass smashing into each other as whole shelves collapsed. Sophia stumbled hard into the edge of the desk with a startled cry. Nicholas jerked backward, but caught himself in time to avoid the section of ceiling plaster that smashed near his feet.

"What the devil was that?" he demanded. A mortar strike?

More voices now: *"Za Revolyutzia!"*

The Belladonna shook the dust from her hair and gown not unlike Selene, and began to sniff inquisitively at the air. Satisfied with whatever she'd discovered, she glanced at the small silver watch pinned to her hip. "Calm yourself, beastie. This room has withstood any number of revolutions and riots. The only entrance is the passage. We are quite secure."

There were only a few moments of silence before the sound of heavy footfalls seeped through the walls, slashed through by the steady, racing sounds of shouts and gunfire. Voices were muddied, in a language he couldn't speak—*"Ochistite dvorets!"*

The Belladonna rose, her gaze sweeping around her room, breath hissing from her. She stooped to pick a small silver bell and rang it.

The longer it went without answer, the harder she rang it, until finally she heaved it at the passage. The young boy ducked as he entered, just missing a dead-on strike to the head.

"Clean up this mess," she told him. "And take an account of anything beyond repair."

The boy was sensible enough to wait until the woman looked away before sticking out his tongue.

"That's *another* year you owe me," she told him without taking her eyes off her desk. "Such ingratitude. And after I rescued you from my brother."

The already-pale child turned the shade of chalk. With a nod, he went back through the passage, setting off its usual thunderous roar, and returned a moment later with a broom and pan.

"Now, where were we?" the Belladonna said pleasantly, ignoring the irritated sweeps of the boy. "Oh, dear—"

She picked up one of the skulls that had fallen from the netting, stroking the curve of its empty eye sockets lovingly. "I was rather fond of her. She used to bring me daffodils."

"That was the timeline," Sophia interrupted, her voice hollow. "It shifted again."

Because someone used the astrolabe, or—? Nicholas had never experienced the sensation of time aligning from one version to a new one; by the time he'd begun to travel with Julian, it had settled into some stability under Ironwood's rule.

But the woman had mentioned revolutions, riots, implying that one might very well be happening outside of these walls. Could it be that the explosion they'd felt had been the actual cause of the change, and not someone acting in an earlier year?

Which meant . . . what, exactly, for Etta?

"We weren't orphaned," he said slowly, trying to reason this out on his own. "Are we in the last common year, then? Was that the change itself, and not just a ripple?"

"Yes. But if that's your attempt to get me to reveal our year and location, you will be sadly disappointed," the Belladonna said, "I shall neither confirm nor deny we are in a year after both of your birth years."

Meaning, by her sad attempt at a wink, they were.

"A change this large would impact the information we've discussed as part of the deal," Nicholas said. "To locate the person in question, we'd need to know this year as well as the prior change. To ascertain if she's been orphaned again, to this very year."

The Belladonna's jaw worked back and forth beneath her veil, eyes flashing. "All right, beastie. I suppose it's time to move this shop again, anyway. But know, my dear child, that you have asked and received far more of me than any man. I will not be pressed further."

"Understood. The transaction, then," Nicholas said, trying to clear the dust from his mouth and throat before he swallowed it. "How do we complete it?"

Nicholas had noticed in passing that she wore an abundance of gold and silver rings on each of her fingers. They stacked up past her knuckles, some as thin as veins, some seemingly as thick as the finger itself.

Now the Belladonna drew one off her ring finger and rose on creaking bones, shuffling through the fallen plaster and glass to the other side of the desk, carrying the whole room forward with her. Nicholas took the small gold band from her, surprised to find it so cold after being on her finger.

Under her gaze, he slid it onto the ring finger of his right hand, and waited. Not a permanent mark on his flesh, thank God, for he'd enough scars for a dozen men. But a sign of ownership all the same, however temporary.

Something inside of his heart began to sound in warning, like a ship's bell at the edge of a storm.

No. I have come this far, and there is still too much ahead to stop now.

"Our agreement is thus: a favor of my choosing for information on the last common year and the Thorns," the Belladonna said. "'I swear to abide by our agreement, or my life will be forfeit. That is my vow.' Repeat it."

He did, and no sooner did the word *vow* leave his lips than the ring seemed to flare with heat, tightening around his skin. Nicholas took a generous step back as he pulled away from the woman's clawlike grip. Not wanting to alarm Sophia, he clasped his hands behind his back and attempted to pull the damned thing off, or at least twist it to relieve the sudden pressure.

It did not move.

Selene retrieved her bone once more, her teeth clacking against its battered form. The Belladonna returned to her seat, sinking slowly into it.

Sophia leaned both hands onto the desk and said, "Let's have it, then."

The Belladonna's veil rustled again. How someone so old could have the laugh of a young girl, he would never know.

Horror was a beast of a thing. It devoured everything it encountered. Hope. Faith. Expectation. Nicholas felt a chill stinging along his spine.

"Ma'am . . . ?" he began, forcing his voice steady.

"Sweet beastie," she said, "for all of your talk, for all of your thinking you were clever enough to weight this deal in your favor, it never once occurred to you to specify that I needed to provide the information *before* you completed my favor. 'The future,' of course, can mean centuries or seconds, minutes or hours."

Nicholas gripped the edge of the desk so tightly he heard his own knuckles crack. "That is dishonorable—unconscionable!"

Sophia was more plainspoken. "You deceitful *witch!*"

The Belladonna's eyes were so harrowing, they nearly sent Nicholas's soul retreating from his body. "Such a thing to say."

"That is outrageous!" Sophia hissed. "They stole it from *me*! They beat me to take it—they left me with—"

She pressed the heel of her hand against her eye patch and swore again, spinning away, stalking back toward the passage.

"Hardly a tragic tale," the Belladonna called after her, "when it has created the woman you are now. You'll be of great help to him in this task. One eye will be enough."

Sophia stopped just for a moment, her posture rigid. "I don't need any eyes to tear you to shreds."

"You made it sound as though you weren't entirely certain what you would ask of me," Nicholas managed to get out between gritted teeth. *A deal is a deal.* He never, not for one solitary moment, would have agreed to this *favor* had he known it would eat up the one currency he didn't have: time.

"I've only just decided you were right for this particular one. It should not take you long, provided you are as industrious as I've heard."

Another faint stirring at his core. He squared his shoulders, meeting her delighted gaze.

"It's quite simple, really," the Belladonna said. "I would like for you to kill Cyrus Ironwood."

RUSSIA
1919

ELEVEN

IT OCCURRED TO ETTA THAT PERHAPS THE PASSAGE ITSELF wasn't cold; it was simply breathing out the frosty air of what lay on the other side of it.

She opened one eye slowly, half-amazed by the fact that she was still vertical. The passage had tossed them out at alarming speed after seeming to spin them head over heels, but . . . she'd *landed*. Landed solidly, as if she'd taken the jump out of it herself.

"There are you are," a voice said over the rattling moan of the passage. There was a slight pressure on her wrist, and the shallow daze ripped away, jolting her back into the moment. Etta forced herself to take smaller breaths, sipping at the freezing air, cooling her lungs and pounding temples. At their backs, a wave of pressure burst from the passage, and she didn't need to turn to know that the last two guards had finally come through it.

Etta swung her gaze around; when she'd traveled with Nicholas, she'd learned quickly enough that survival meant assessing her surroundings, determining the year, and figuring out how best to blend into the scenery. The lance of panic that went through her dissipated as her mind caught up to her instincts.

They had taken a passage on Russian Hill in San Francisco to

149

Russia itself, which struck her as too big of a coincidence to be an actual coincidence. Her mind would never truly accept this, how her heels could be crunching through loose gravel one moment, then sinking into the soft earth of a forest in the next. But trees sheltered them from all sides, their leaves shot through with fiery shades of red and gold, and the silence of this place made it feel more like a memory she rediscovered than a moment.

To her left, jutting out of the glassy surface of the crawling river, was a rock formation that looked like something out of a dark kingdom, its jagged height like the remnant of a small watchtower.

That same dark stone had been used to construct the breathtaking bridge that rose high over the water in an almost perfect arc. Its spine looked as thin as a finger from her vantage point. The way it was settled into the earth, becoming part of the mass of life around it, made her wonder if it wasn't just old, but ancient.

But what struck her most, what held her there in disbelief of its beauty, as the Thorns milled around, was the way the late-afternoon light reflected the image of the bridge into the water below.

"A perfect circle," Henry said from beside her. "Two halves meeting, for a time, as a whole."

Etta's brows furrowed at that show of romanticism, but Henry had already directed his attention to a pinched-faced Winifred, who was working her way through the mass of assembled guards. She'd changed into a fur coat, and a hat that looked like some sort of enormous, exotic flower was about to eat her face.

"Sir, all of the preparations have been made," she said. "He's expecting you for dinner this evening."

"He?" Etta asked, though she knew it was useless.

Winifred's eyes flicked over at Etta, at Henry's coat still wrapped around her shoulders. "I've procured a gown for her, if you'd like her to dine with you."

"Excellent," Henry said. "We'll stop by the others' hotel so that we can both change. I'm assuming you found an appropriate suit for me as well?"

"Of course," Winifred said. "It was the very first thing we did after we confirmed the alterations had taken hold."

"Any word from Kadir?"

The missing Thorn. Etta's focus sharpened on the woman's face, searching.

But Winifred shook her head, clearly troubled. "It's likely he's safe in the palace, and waiting for us to arrive."

"Why, Aunt, that almost sounded optimistic," Henry said with a knowing look to Etta.

"Otherwise," the woman finished, "he's dead and we'll only be in time to collect his remains."

"There it is," Jenkins murmured nearby. "Can always count on her to douse the light of hope."

Henry held out his arm to Etta, and once she'd taken it, they made their way toward the rough path that edged out from below the overgrowth of trees and bushes. Two of the guards jumped into place in front of him, leading the way. Etta found her feet naturally sinking into the footprints that already marked up the trail.

While not all of the Thorns had left San Francisco, an even dozen had gone ahead to make preparations for Henry's arrival. Julian, to her surprise, had been escorted out with them. She'd caught sight of him being half dragged onto the street, trying to hide the decanter of brandy inside of his coat.

"Where are we going?" she asked.

He glanced at her. "I hope you don't mind, but it's a surprise—oh, no, I promise, it's a welcome one. I simply want to see . . . I'd like to introduce you to a friend of mine, and an important place to my side of the family."

A parent who shared with their child. What a novel concept. "As long as it doesn't involve tigers. Or cobras."

"Pardon?" he said, startled.

Winifred swept into the conversation with her usual awareness and tact. "Far be it from me to tell you what to do, Henry, but I worry—the girl has hardly been trained, and the stakes of this dinner will be so high—let me at least work with her for a few days."

"There are no stakes. It is simply dinner with a friend," Henry said. "I need you to take charge of searching the various rooms for Kadir and the astrolabe."

The world darkened around them as the trees closed ranks over their heads and the sun continued its downward slide.

"What happens if he and the astrolabe aren't here?" Etta asked, her boots squelching loudly through the mud. "What then?"

"I haven't gotten past the prayer that he is here," Henry said. "I'm curious, though, what would you do in my position?"

"Do you care what I think?" Etta asked.

He seemed confused by the question. "Would I have asked otherwise? I want to know your thoughts."

Etta wanted to bask for a moment in the small, trembling warmth of that idea, but quickly stomped it down.

"The thoughts of a seventeen-year-old child," Winifred said. "Really, Henry."

But he wanted to know, and was plainly waiting. It made her feel . . .

Trusted.

When in her life had her mother ever stopped to ask her about her thoughts or feelings on something, without having already made the decision herself?

Even Nicholas. Even Nicholas had tried to take advantage of her trust, however halfhearted the attempt had been. He was overburdened with a guilty conscience, and was honorable in a way only the heroes of history and fiction seemed to be.

"Immediately start sniffing around any Ironwoods you can find," Etta said. "Set off more alterations—as many as you can manage at once."

Henry inclined his head toward her, considering this. "Ah. To lure Cyrus out with the astrolabe to fix them?"

Etta nodded. "Even if he didn't bring it out into the open, you'd still split the Ironwoods' attention. Meaning more chances to follow one of the Ironwoods back to wherever he's taken up and find the astrolabe there."

"Fortunately, we already have that information. He's bought back his old home in Manhattan, eighteenth century. We're having a damned time getting near to it with the British occupation, though." He let out a thoughtful hum. "I had considered using the Ironwood yearling to lure him out to more open ground. We simply don't have the manpower for what you're describing, though it's an excellent strategy otherwise."

"An excellent thought," Winifred said, picking up her pace to keep up with their long strides. "He has never brought anything to us to merit the kindness we've shown him. He's a leech."

"That's not entirely true," Henry said, with a fond look at Etta.

"That was pure luck," Winifred groused.

"Well, it was certainly fortunate," he agreed. "What did you make of him, Etta?"

"Julian?" she clarified, brushing a leaf from her hair. "He's . . ." *A brat, obnoxious, high on himself, rude.* ". . . an Ironwood."

"Was he untoward to you at all?" Henry asked carefully. "He's a shameless flirt, but I judged him to be fairly toothless. Many of the Thorns feel he's outstayed his welcome, and if it wasn't for the happy serendipity of finding you, I daresay I might agree."

"What do you mean, Julian's outstayed his welcome?" she asked.

"You've more questions than sense, child," Winifred muttered.

"He's no longer able to provide information about Ironwood that we don't already know," Henry said. "Ironwood has taken a few of our travelers prisoner over the years, and I had considered trading Julian for them."

"That's probably the thing he's most afraid of," Etta told Henry. "Ironwood might actually kill him."

A road emerged beyond the trees ahead of them. Within an instant of its appearance, streams of headlights swept over it, and two old-fashioned black cars rolled into place in front of the trees.

"You really think so?" Henry asked. "Everything is such a joke to him, I half expected his dalliance with us to be for amusement alone. Ironwood wouldn't kill his heir, not when he needs him."

"The astrolabe could be used to create new heirs, if he uses it to save his wife," she pointed out.

"That was your mother's theory, yes," Henry said. "And a likely one."

"Julian could have gone back to Ironwood at any point, especially when it became difficult to survive in hiding," she continued, working out her own thoughts on the matter. "Instead, he came to his grandfather's most hated enemy and betrayed him to you. He needed help, but he clearly felt like he needed protection, too. So I don't know if you should send him back to Ironwood, but you could at least use that same fear to get some last important details out of him that he might not give you otherwise."

He nearly beamed at her. Etta, again, had to fight the ridiculous glow her heart gave in response.

"Second most hated," Henry said. "I daresay that honor belongs to your mother, and she'd skin me for taking that from her."

Winifred let out a loud *harrumph* and released her hold on her nephew's arm, charging forward to the first of the cars. The driver barely had time to jump out and open the door for her.

"I might have a better use for him, if tonight turns out the way I imagine," Henry said as he wisely steered them toward the second car. He nodded to that driver. "Paul, how are the boys?"

Etta missed the man's answer as she ducked inside the car and slid across the seat. Henry joined her after a moment, removing his hat and gloves.

"All the logic of the Hemlocks, without the ruthlessness of the Lindens," he said, as he set both on the stretch of leather between them. The car dipped as one of the guards sat in the front beside the driver. "You'll do very well indeed."

As she settled into the warmth of the car and let it thaw her stiff skin, she passed his coat back to him. Henry folded it in his lap and turned his gaze out his window. Etta watched his face in its reflection, how the easy humor and brightness vanished like a flame blown out. He seemed to retreat into himself, leaving a look of severe contemplation as he touched the rose she hadn't noticed he'd tucked into his lapel.

And Etta could picture it so clearly then, how the reflection of the bridge had disappeared in the water, leaving one half to wait to see its other self again.

THE CITY DWELT IN DARKNESS. THE ROAR OF THE ENGINE swallowed every other sound from the world outside her window, those streets cloaked in the gray evening haze. Etta felt she was watching a kind of silent movie. As the car rolled down a huge main thoroughfare—"Nvesky Prospeckt," Henry explained—Etta had the sense they were slipping into St. Petersburg on the edge of someone's shadow: uninvited, unwanted.

The light slush covering the ground was nearly indistinguishable from the sludge of garbage that lined the street's gutters. The car jumped as it rolled over something—Etta craned her neck back, but saw only the tattered remains of a banner and two poles that were being dragged away by men in stark military uniforms. Her gaze followed their path to a courtyard where a bonfire raged. The cloth and wood were fed into it behind a wall of soldiers standing shoulder to shoulder, backlit by the flames. A few men and women lingered at the fringes of its glow, but the car sped by too quickly for Etta to see what they were trying to do besides stay warm.

The beautiful façades of the buildings that rolled by, with all of their glorious arches and domes, looked as though they'd been painted with jewels. It made the contrast of what was happening on the streets that much bleaker.

Etta leaned back against her seat, resenting the thick white fur coat Winifred had stuffed her into. The truth was, she burned with the desire to be herself, to see more clearly the points at which she and Henry might intersect. But dressed so grandly, wearing another creature's skin, and still feeling the burn of Winifred's crash course on period etiquette, she felt the pressure to let Etta slip away. To disappear into this false image of a lady.

Her dress was a thin, rose-pink silk sheath, cut straight and falling just above her ankles. The topmost layer was sheer, draping over her in scalloped tiers, each edged with the smallest bit of shimmering fringe.

Before they'd left the venue, Henry had handed her a pair of white gloves that stopped just above her elbow and a long strand of pearls, and had given Winifred some sort of diamond—hopefully crystal— barrette to affix in Etta's hair. After an hour-long struggle, the woman, with the help of two other maids, had managed to wrestle Etta's hair into something resembling finger waves, pinning the length of it up and under like a false bob. She'd be lucky not to find bald patches later that night when she finally got to take the pins out.

Etta wrung her hands in her lap, glancing around—at the driver, at Jenkins in the front passenger seat, at Henry. He had his gold pocket watch open again, but quickly snapped it shut. Etta caught a glimpse of the time: seven something. Way too early for there to be no other cars or carriages out on the street besides the ones that were parked, or those that looked more like tanks—clearly military. Here and there, a few scattered people moved by, ducking into shops or making their way home. It reminded her of the short time that she and Nicholas had spent in London during the Blitz; this scene had all the uneasiness of the last dying leaf on a branch, waiting to fall.

"Are we in the 1920s?" Etta asked, turning to look at Henry again. It was an obvious guess based on the cars, style of dress, and small touches of décor in the hotel.

He, however, had turned his head to look up at something the car was racing past—flagpoles?

"1919," Jenkins offered, turning to speak to her through the partition. "It's—"

"I thought the reforms had been passed," Henry said, with an edge of anger. Jenkins and the other guard seemed equally startled by it. "Why does the city look this way?"

They've already broken from the original timeline, Etta realized. In some way, big or small, the timeline had altered enough that Henry no longer fully recognized some of the parts in the century's great machine.

"Some socialist leader was imprisoned, caught red-handed in an assassination attempt on the minister of the interior," Jenkins explained. "A small alteration, not nearly enough to cause a ripple, only a headache for our preparations. Rumor has it there are some of the old Bolsheviks out working people up about it, hence the military presence. Give it a day and it'll pass."

"Bolsheviks," Henry muttered, pressing a hand to his forehead, "or Ironwoods?"

A single drop of sweat worked its way down the ridges of Etta's spine.

"This isn't the St. Petersburg you knew?" she pressed. "You seemed surprised by the state of the city."

"It's called Petrograd in this era," he corrected, with his usual gentleness. "I *am* surprised to see the state of it, knowing the reforms to improve lives across the country had passed. Whatever messes have been made, we'll clean them up while we're here."

The first tap against her window sounded like a rock kicked up from the road—it was the second hit that made her turn, just as a man launched himself out of the darkness of an alley and leaped over the sidewalk.

His arm craned back like a pitcher's, and Etta gasped, instinctively cringing as a bottle hurtled toward the car, smashing against her window. Another man, a woman, more, surged out from the city's cracks and crevices.

"Faster!" Henry barked, reaching into his jacket for a pistol.

"Trying!" the driver barked right back.

Another stone flew toward the web of cracks on her window, but she refused to be pulled down, to have her face pressed against the seat until she was nearly smothered by leather and flickering fear. Clattering, shattering, smashing. The whole car rocked with each hit.

Etta searched the buildings around them for more protestors. Up high, on top of a bakery, two cloaked shadows moved. As impossible as it was with the distance between the buildings, they seemed to easily make the flying leaps to keep pace with the car. There was a flash of silver, like a blade—

Or a gun.

This time, she yanked Henry back down with her as a gunshot—two—shattered her window, blowing shards of glass inside, over her head, along her back. Etta's whole body jumped at each blast, one hand pinned beneath her, the other rising to cover her right ear.

The men up front were slinging words and orders to each other over her head. Etta fought to breathe, to sit up again, but the heavy weight of Henry's arm kept her down until, finally, the shouting outside became muffled. The car wheezed and shuddered, but began to cruise faster.

She stayed in that same awkward position for the next ten minutes, until she felt the wheels of the car begin to slow. Henry released her, still swearing beneath his breath. Etta sat straight up, her vision black and spotty. She brushed small, sparkling pieces of glass from her coat and hair, watching, stunned, as they collected in her hand and lap like ice.

"Are you all right?"

Etta hadn't realized Henry was speaking to her until he gripped her shoulder, almost to the point of pain, and turned her toward him to begin inspecting her. There was a small cut above his left brow, but he seemed otherwise fine.

"My God," he was saying, "I'll kill them myself."

"I'm fine, I'm fine," Etta insisted. A cold wind blew up the back of her exposed neck through the opening in her window. "What was that all about?"

"Protestors," Jenkins said. "Damn it all! We should never have taken Nvesky Prospeckt. But the palace assured us it would be safe. Sir, believe me—"

"The people on the roof—" she tried to say.

Henry held up his hand, still breathing hard as the car rolled through a gate and came to a slow, shuddering stop.

Several figures in suits and nondescript uniforms flowed out of a nearby building's arched entryway. With a start, Etta opened the door and let herself out on unsteady feet, the glass spilling out around her feet, disappearing into the light smattering of snow. Her breath heated the air milk-white as she slowly tipped her face up.

They'd arrived at a building that was beyond imposing—*ornate* couldn't begin to capture its presence. It was almost Baroque, the way the pale green façade was trimmed with gold. The building itself was massive, stretching on as far as her eyes could see in both directions. Statues of women and saints watched from the roof above, dusted with the same sooty snow. It had to be the palace.

The second car with Winifred, Julian, and another guard zipped up behind them a moment later, skidding to a stop in a similar state of disarray. Winifred all but rode out of the automobile on a wave of her own fury, bellowing, "Those *beasts!*"

Julian was close behind, looking far less angry and far grayer in the face. He raised his brows in Etta's direction. *Bumpy ride?* he mouthed.

Etta's brow creased as she looked away, back toward Henry, who had deigned to let Jenkins brush the remaining pieces of glass from his coat. Then an elderly man was at her side, clucking and cooing at her, bowing in a way that made Etta take a startled step back. The Russian came too fast and furious for her to find the three words in the language she actually knew.

The whirling activity seemed to still somewhat as Henry stepped up behind her and followed her gaze upward. His face softened, the stern line of his mouth relaxing, as if seeing an old friend.

"Welcome," he said, "to the Winter Palace."

UNKNOWN
Unknown

TWELVE

NICHOLAS COULD NOT FIND THE WORDS TO ASK THE WOMAN to repeat herself, but she did it regardless, that same girlish laughter riding the ends of her words.

"Dare I ask the obvious question," Sophia said, oddly calm, "of why?"

"It's not your place to ask questions," the Belladonna said, never taking her eyes off Nicholas. "Only to obey. If you value your life, that is."

Nicholas's feet were rooted to the floor, but he felt his soul release and swing about the room, banging at the walls. In his life, he'd been made to feel the burn of humiliation and impotent rage many times, in many ways, by the world. But this—*this*. Unyielding anger choked him now. If he could have compelled himself to move, he would have slammed his fists against her great metal desk until he cracked it.

Around his neck, the thin leather cord that held Etta's earring felt like a wreath of bricks.

"What do you mean by that?" Sophia demanded. "Stop talking in riddles!"

She stormed forward, only to be brought up short by Selene.

And still, the Belladonna was watching him. Waiting for him.

"You . . ." he began, when his mind began to work again. "You expect me to kill my own kin? Can you begin to fathom what you're asking of me?"

He couldn't kill Ironwood. Desire and rational thought were at odds. Of course, he'd dreamt of it a thousand times, by a thousand different means, and woken less satisfied than he might have imagined, considering the tortures to which the man had subjected every person Nicholas loved. But when it was all distilled down—the torment, the fury, the desperation—the truth of the matter was laid bare: killing the old man would stain his soul and irrevocably bind them together, until Nicholas met his own reward and was forced to answer for it.

It was one thing to do violence in self-defense, but this was *murder.* Assassination. The thought alone left a taste like rust in his mouth.

"It's him or yourself," the Belladonna said. She snapped her fingers and the boy stopped pretending to sweep the same pile of glass and dried-out insects while eavesdropping. Nicholas turned just as he scampered back through the passage. "You'll come to find that I am the only one who can remove that ring, and the longer it stays on your finger, the more the poison inlaid in it will sap at your strength."

"I'll cut it off, then—cut the whole bloody hand off if I have to," he told her, reaching for the knife at his belt.

"Do it," she encouraged. "In fact, you may as well cut your wrists. Your weakened body will only absorb the poison more quickly. But of course, you're welcome to test the theory. It just strikes me that there's *someone* you wish to find first?"

She knows of Etta's existence. His blood seemed to turn to bile. The wave of nausea stole over him so quickly he was sure he was not going to be able to stay upright. *She knows of Etta.*

Witch. *Witch.* The illusions, the deceit, the cunning, and now . . . poison.

"Come now," she said, "would it be so terrible? Have you forgotten that he kept you as property? That you are the issue of a vile man who forced himself upon a helpless woman? That he sold your mother to a man in Georgia who used her, who beat her, until the sickness finally freed her?"

Nicholas pressed a fist against his mouth, and would have turned his back to her to collect himself, had he trusted her not to stick a dagger through his back.

"He resides in the old house of your childhood," she said. "You haven't much time. He travels soon. I imagine I will see you back here soon as well."

"Madam," he said, "I will see you in hell."

There was a tugging on his arm, and he did not realize he was moving toward the passage until Sophia dug her nails through his shirt, into his skin. "Don't look back at her," she muttered, "don't give her that."

He did not. He held his breath as they stepped through the passage, and then released his scream into its thunder. The smell of the air changed as they emerged on the other side. That same stench of wet earth her clothing seemed to breathe out as she moved.

"Carter—wait—damn—!" She had to catch his arm to stop his path, swing him around to prompt his gaze. Nicholas had the oddest feeling that he was back on his deathbed, a fever wracking his brain. There was a haze about her, an unreal quality.

Fool—bloody fool! Christ!

Rose Linden had led him like a lamb to the slaughter, but he'd only himself to blame. He'd been rash, hadn't thought his calculations through, and now he was—

A slap across the face snapped his head to the left. Sophia raised her hand again, prepared to issue another blow.

"You looked like you were going to pass out," she explained. "And you're too bloody big for me to drag you."

"Thank you . . . my apologies . . . my . . . thanks . . ." He had no idea what he meant to say. But the hit had blown the dust off an old thought, one he hadn't dared to court in years.

Kill the old man and be free.

Of vows. Of guilt. Of this unbearable heaviness anchoring his heart to his guts— *No.* He'd sold his soul, but he wasn't about to damn it.

He held his hands to his face, trying to smother the bellow that tore out of him. The gold ring pressed a hot kiss to his cheek. Nicholas tried to yank it off again, with no luck.

He needed to find Etta, he wanted to find Etta, there was only Etta—

"Forget what the old bat said," Sophia said fiercely, her voice ringing like steel. "She doesn't have a hold on you. She only wants you to think she does. Show her you're above it! Show her you aren't afraid, damn it!"

"Are you saying that because you believe it," he asked bitterly, "or because you need Ironwood alive, so you can bring the astrolabe back to him?"

Sophia recoiled. It had been some time since he was on the receiving end of her murderous glare, and he was almost comforted by its familiarity. "You think I won't gut that man the first chance I get?"

"I think you're in this for your own ends," he told her. "I think a rather large part of you, the very same part that prevented you for years from lowering yourself into even conversation with me, loves seeing me bested by circumstances."

"*Of course* I'm in it to serve myself, you fool, and so are you!" she hissed. "We've derailed our search for the one thing that matters to find someone who ultimately really doesn't. But if you think I'd go back to the same family that wanted me just about as much as they wanted you, then you need to pull your head out of your ass before I do it for you!"

Orphanage. Pickpocketing. The past she'd kept hidden beneath the layers of silk and lace. She had worked hard to polish herself into something shining, gleaming, and what had it gotten her? Not the heir, or even being named it once the heir was gone.

As if he would ever let either of us truly forget our origins, he thought with a pang.

Anger, however, was easier to live inside than unwelcome sympathy. "Isn't that why you kept that blade hidden? Because you intended to use it?"

Her eyebrows flew up. "Is that what this is about? Yes, I picked that blade up when we were in Nassau. I might have told you about it, except I knew you wouldn't believe I hadn't had it on me the entire time. I just wanted to be able to study it without you snatching it away like I'm a child."

"You should have told me," he insisted.

"Because you've shown *me* so much trust? You've listened to me so well, such as ten bloody minutes ago, when I told you not to take that deal?" she said, throwing a finger in his face. "But you did take it, and now we have to live with it. So stop making that pitiful face and *buck up.* We'll go to Carthage, all right? Ironwood sends out notices about major changes to the timeline to all of the guardians and travelers posted throughout the centuries. By the time we arrive, the two Jacarandas will likely have the answer we need, or they can point us to someone who *can* tell us. Rose Linden can go take a long walk off a cliff and drag the Belladonna to hell with her!"

She'd mauled him with the truth—he had not, in fact, trusted her. Not even for a moment, because he'd been so certain she hadn't given him a reason to. They could not continue this way, but they could not seem to break out of this cycle of loathing, either.

"She said it'd be useless to talk to the Jacarandas—"

"And you *believe* her? After the trick she pulled?" Sophia pressed. "She told us all that nonsense about the Thorns to get us to trust her enough not to question the terms of the deal. Forget her. I'd rather travel to Carthage on a chance than believe *her* ever again."

She was right. If nothing else, they needed to leave this infernal place. Nicholas straightened, cracking his knuckles at his side to try to release the pressure that seemed ready to shoot from his hands.

This is shameful. I'm falling apart like a boy during his first boarding. Pull yourself together, man.

Nicholas passed through the alchemy workshop at a near run, and took the stairs two at a time. Sophia kept pace with him, plundering the depths of her extensive knowledge of profanities as she misjudged the distance of a step and fell forward, catching herself on her hands. She sprang up the last few steps, nearly spitting on Nicholas's offered hand. "I don't need your bloody help!"

"Then you won't have it," he shot back.

The golden-haired boy didn't look up from his book as they passed. With a chill that sank into his bones, Nicholas realized the woman was behind the counter again, the bloodred candle glowing beside her.

"Come again, your business is appreciated!" she sang out.

He and Sophia made matching rude gestures.

"Tell your mistress I'm coming back to skin that overgrown dog of hers," Sophia said to the boy, "and turn it into my next coat!"

He looked up, pale eyes shining with tears at the mere thought. "Selene?"

"All right, no, I won't," Sophia called back. "But tell her I said it!"

Nicholas chased his anger as he left the store, trying to master it before it mastered him. Rain rushed down the back of his neck, soaking him through in moments. He would have welcomed a bitter wind, anything to cool the monster of grief sweltering inside of him. Instead, the heat that started in his right hand, the ring finger, seemed to throb like a second heartbeat in his body. When he finally looked up, the city was lost to the fog, disappearing like the beautiful dream it was.

"Which way?" he asked Sophia. "How do we get to Carthage?"

"Follow me," she said, turning north.

And with no other choice obvious to him, he did.

RATHER THAN WASTE WEEKS TRAVELING BY SEA, SOPHIA charted a journey for them across the years and continents that involved a considerable amount of danger, but—blessedly—less vomit from her seasickness.

First, a journey back, yet again, to the swamps of Florida, and several hours of navigating murky waters and wasting coins to bribe the pitiful guardian punished with watching the passage there. That deposited them in Portugal, in what Sophia claimed was the thirteenth century. From there, they walked to yet another passage, this one leading to Germany in the tenth, and finally, after stealing a pair of horses and nearly bringing the wrath of a whole village down upon them, they found themselves in 1700, this time in Tarragona, in the region of Catalonia.

Of course, as seemed to be their lot, Nicholas and Sophia spent hours following the shoddy dirt roads on foot in the hope that her memory would serve them better than his own judgment. To pass the time, he tried to muster up what details he could about Carthage after years of the memories collecting dust. Perhaps the facts that remained would offer some protection against what might lie ahead.

Much of said knowledge had come from Hall, whose retention of maritime history remained relatively sharp, if slightly rusted by age and exposure to too much sun. The ancient city of Carthage, once Rome's great rival, lay in a supreme position on the northeast coast of Africa, with sea inlets to the north and south. Its immense wealth, without the flash of Rome's opulence, was owed to the fact that all ships passing in and out of the Mediterranean sailed through the gap between it and Sicily.

There had been three separate Punic Wars between Rome and Carthage; the one Hall recalled best, the second, had produced Hannibal, who had been a great favorite of Chase and Nicholas during the captain's post-supper tales. The ingenious general had sailed with an army of nearly a hundred thousand men and dozens of elephants, and together they'd torn open Spain and marched through the Alps to Italy. As boys, he and Chase had even attempted to re-create the crossing of the Rhône River by Hannibal's army, using discarded siding from Hall's ship as rafts, and rats in the place of elephants.

He tried to take some refuge in those lantern-lit memories, but the longer they walked, the easier it became to slip inside his darker thoughts and dwell there. Save for a few hares, they'd yet to encounter another living soul; while he'd taken careful count of the weapons Sophia had strapped to her body, he could no longer be sure there wasn't yet another knife hidden somewhere on her person—or that she wouldn't use it to strand him here and continue on without him. Or worse.

She cannot kill me without the nearby passage closing, he thought. How comforting.

The deception from the Belladonna had rattled him, but now he found himself regretting how easily he had trusted Sophia when she'd argued in favor of traveling to Carthage; he'd followed her to this spot, which might not lead them to Carthage at all, but a grisly death or yet another ruse.

Nicholas's hands curled into fists at his sides, bunching the already-tight muscles of his shoulders. He was useless as a traveler. Why couldn't he have pushed harder to learn the locations of the passages? Why did he have to place his trust back in an Ironwood, especially one who hated him with a force that could grind whole mountains to dust?

He was an able seaman, skilled in his trade, but here, he might as well have been one of those rats clinging to a poorly made raft.

"Who are these travelers?" he asked. "You said they were Jacarandas, and that they were being punished by the old man for something?"

"Remus and Fitzhugh Jacaranda," Sophia said. "They were both close friends of Ironwood's for decades, some of his most trusted advisors. Julian said the day he discovered they had defected to the Thorns, he went into such a rage that he burned all of their belongings, landholdings, and records. When they realized the Thorns weren't all they were cracked up to be, they tried to come crawling back to ask for forgiveness. Rather than kill them, he sent them to Carthage during the Roman siege as punishment to prove their loyalty. They're assigned to watch the passages there."

Roman siege. The Third Punic War, then.

"I'm sure it gave them plenty of time to consider their crimes," Nicholas said. "I can't imagine this is, or ever was, a popular destination for travel. What is there to observe?"

"Don't be ridiculous. The guardians and travelers assigned to watch passages aren't just there to track comings and goings in and out of them," Sophia said, to his surprise. "They ensure the passages remain stable and aren't in danger of collapsing."

Nicholas nodded. Julian had told him a passage became unstable—or collapsed—under two circumstances: with the death of a nearby traveler who was outside of their natural time, or, Ironwood believed, simply from overuse and age. As if they became worn-out and flimsy, like old fabric that had been turned too many times.

"More passages than ever have been collapsing and closing altogether," Sophia said, her profile outlined by the rough sea below. "That's why I believed him, you know. That he wanted the astrolabe to examine newly discovered passages, for their destinations and stability. I'm not *gullible*. I didn't believe everything he told me, and I didn't want everything he wanted."

Once the words were out, he saw her shoulders slump, as if relieved of the weight of them. He recalled his accusation in Prague, and wondered at how long she had let her temper simmer without exploding.

I know, he wanted to say. *No one who believed Ironwood so fully would have survived this long.*

He tried to picture her then, in her native time, in that orphanage. Small, filthy, and hungry enough to risk being caught stealing. That, at least, he understood. A child faced with the raw desperation of survival had it imprinted on their soul. They were never able to shake the sense that one day, everything good in their life might again vanish—not fully.

"Maybe that's the real reason he never made me heir." Her mouth twisted in a cruel little smile.

"He didn't make you heir because you're a woman and he's a bloody fool," Nicholas said. "And because there was Julian, in all of his shining glory."

Sophia glanced up, brows raised ever so slightly as she let out a *tsk*. "Speaking ill of the dead now, Carter?"

"He didn't—" Nicholas caught the word before it could escape.

"He didn't *what*?"

Damn it all.

He hadn't told her yet about the conversation he'd had with Rose about Julian likely surviving . . . not because she didn't deserve to know, but because Nicholas couldn't tell how she might react. While it might improve her view of him, it might just as easily throw off the uneasy balance between them they'd managed to obtain. No need to rock a boat already struggling in stormy waters.

Sophia seemed to be careening from unpredictable highs to surly lows, her moods like errant breezes, and he needed her steady and focused on finding Etta, not changing her mind and disappearing to search out Julian—it was callous of him, he knew this, and hideously selfish. It took him buffeting his heart with years of memories of her vile insults and cutting dismissals before the notion sat well with him.

The end here justified the deceitful means. He could lie, if Etta was there to later absolve him of the guilt of it. There could be no side trips to find Julian or learn where he might have been all of these years, or even what might have become of him in the meantime. If he knew his half brother at all, he had commandeered some palatial island retreat to hide away in. Julian always landed right side up.

"'Shining glory,'" she muttered. "How can you not see it? He never liked Julian. Hated everything Julian loved. Gambling and drinking and painting. Wasn't shy about telling him how worthless he was on any given day. He was a resounding disappointment, no matter what he did."

Nicholas's brow furrowed. He'd known the old man hadn't outwardly mourned the "loss" of his heir, but he'd assumed that was because any sign of weakness, any crack in his veneer, would have been taken as an invitation to his enemies to try and seize his throne. That, and his heart had calcified long ago. "Was it truly as bad as all that?"

"Worse, probably. Ironwood was ashamed and plagued by him. He was *convinced* Julian would ruin his empire. If Julian hadn't died . . ."

"What?"

"He probably would have done it himself," she finished slowly, eyes forward.

"And yet, you didn't believe us when we told you in Palmyra he desired new heirs," Nicholas said coolly.

For once, Sophia had no response to that.

"Was he a disappointment to you?" he countered. He'd always wondered about this: Julian chased every skirt he saw, knowing Sophia was at home, waiting for their wedding day. He'd spoken of his intended with a kind of affection that, having met and known Etta, Nicholas saw now wasn't the sweet fire of love so much as the cool balm of friendship. But Sophia had mourned him—genuinely mourned, with all the black crepe and seclusion it required.

"His *death* was the disappointment," she said. "You letting him *fall off the side of a mountain* was a disappointment."

"So now you believe it was an accident after all?" Nicholas challenged. "I didn't push him?"

She cast him a pitying look that made his soul heat and itch. "I can see now that you don't have what it takes to pull off a murder. There's no iron in you. If you *had* done it, you'd still be on that mountain, weeping about it."

173

Nicholas opened his mouth and barely caught the words. *I'm more Ironwood than you are.*

An icy current swept through his blood, and he let out a low, bitter laugh at himself. Did he really have so much pride that he'd use his hated heritage to argue that he wasn't as soft as she believed?

"He was my best friend," she said. "My *only* friend. I'm not going to apologize for being furious with you for what happened, because his life mattered to me. But . . . it wasn't what you had with Linden. If I'd had a choice, if there'd been any other way to get a modicum of respect in that family, I wouldn't have . . ."

"Become betrothed to Julian?" he finished.

"Nor any man." Her eye bored into him in the beat of silence that followed, daring him to say something about it. "I have always preferred the company of women, regardless of history's views of it. The rare exception being your idiot beloved, who can eat rocks and choke for all I care."

Nicholas, as it stood, did not have an opinion or prejudice about any of this, other than to think the feeling she'd described was likely mutual on Etta's part.

"Have a care," he said, with a light warning in his voice. "My beloved is not by any means an idiot, but she has been known to have a rather vicious backhand."

"I'm not . . . I'm not without a heart," he heard Sophia say, her chin raised, eyes straight ahead. "I'm *not*. I just don't have the luxury of being soft. I am trying to survive."

The same as you, his mind finished for her. Life had offered them both poison—different, bitter variations of it, but poison all the same. He reached up, rubbing a hand over the curve of his scalp.

"You don't have to trust me," she told him, eyes shifting away. "Just trust my anger. I would rather die than let that old man have everything he wants. He needs to know what it feels like to want something forever out of his reach."

Nicholas nodded. He could manage that much. She'd made excuses about needing his help to disappear once the astrolabe was found in their initial bargain, but he had a far easier time trusting revenge as her motivation. But there was something about the way she held herself, tugging at her ear, that made him wonder what was being left unsaid.

Sophia walked faster, moving ahead of him on the path, dodging his questioning look entirely.

Their destination rose into view on the cliffside. The crumbling remains of the Roman amphitheater, stacks of stone slabs left to manage the weather and world the best they could, looked ghostly under the bone-white touch of the moon. Beyond them was the sea, its endless glistening, thrashing darkness. He wondered, given the strategic position, if the Romans had held this land to watch for, and ward off, the Carthaginians in ancient times.

"I think it's just this way," Sophia said. "Remind me to nick a harmonica if we ever find ourselves past the eighteenth century again. Finding the passage by resonance would make this bloody mess a great deal easier."

They ventured down the steps, the seats, toward the main stage at the center of it all. Dust flew up around Nicholas's feet, staining his damp shoes, filling his lungs. He squinted into the dark, but the only indication the passage was nearby was a faint tremor that crawled along his skin.

"I'll check this way," he called to Sophia, who was walking the perimeter of the amphitheater above him.

Nicholas turned to make his way down the next set of steps, which seemed to lead into some sort of partly collapsed pathway or room beneath the section of seats.

"I'll take the lower level, if you search—"

He walked into a shivering patch of air—and walked face-first into a cold, crushing pressure that stole the breath from his lungs and seemed to wrench his heart clear out of his chest.

Before his mind made sense of what had happened, before his body seemed to wake to the fact that he'd stumbled onto the passage, he was drowning—salt water rushed into his lungs as he gasped in alarm, choking him. Water—water—he was caught in a rolling current, feet over head, feet over head, tumbling—

Nicholas kicked his legs to break out of the riptide, his mind so disordered his vision blackened like tar. He couldn't find the surface of the water—it was all darkness, darkness and the moaning drum of the passage, which made the water around him beat with a frantic rhythm.

Do not panic, get ahold of yourself—bloody hell—bloody passage—

And bloody Sophia, as well, for not so much as alerting him to the fact that some madman had hidden the passage underwater.

Salt water turned his eyes raw, but he kept them open against the burn. His entire chest ached with the need for air. He wasn't going to drown, damn it all. But it was night, and without a good glow from the moon or fire, it was nearly impossible to tell up from down. He forced himself to stay still, feeling for the current. Just as he was about to start swimming in the natural direction his body wanted to float, there was a burst of movement beneath him, almost like an undertow, as the passage exploded back to life and Sophia shot out of it. He reached down, gripped whatever part of her he could, and began to kick wildly in a direction he hoped was *up.*

Nicholas broke through the surface of the dark water with a rattling gasp, one hand clawing at the sky, as if he could haul himself up into the cool air. Sophia made a sound like a furious bird of prey as she followed, and Nicholas realized after the fact that he had drawn her up by her hair.

"Terribly—terribly sorry," he managed to get out, his voice ragged from the water he'd choked down. "Forgive—"

"Quiet!" she snapped back. "Do you want them to find us? *Swim!*"

"Where?"

"Anywhere!"

Nicholas blinked, willing his eyes to adjust to the darkness. The water around them shook and waved in a peculiar, unnatural way. The *clang-clang-clang* he'd merely assigned to the passage was louder now and far more varied in speed and intensity, to the point where, at last, he knew more than one person was hammering and banging along.

Recognition sliced through him, a searing blade of alarm. It was the sound of something being built, of blades being hammered. It was a sound of war.

Above even that persistent clanging was a creaking sound, the moans of wood being strained and pestered by waves—a sound as familiar to him as his own skin. *Ships.*

Nicholas turned. A large circular arcade, almost coliseum-like, stretched around them, interspersed with columns that reached up high into the night sky, giving it the unified look of a portico. The sight was made all the more impressive by the ships berthed between them, waiting to be launched.

They were of a design unlike any he'd ever seen outside of etchings, with a smaller draft and almost flat across the deck like a barge.

He swam forward a bit toward the closest one, docked between the nearest two pillars of the arcade, his eyes roving over the openings for dozens upon dozens of oars. At the front, glaring back at him like a fiend, were two brightly painted eyes, and an enormous bronze piece at the bow, which, he imagined, would tear another ship apart when it was rammed—

He was yanked back by his collar before he could swim closer.

"Would you stop making eyes at that bloody ship? It's a *siege*," Sophia grated at him. "If they catch us, they won't just kill us; they'll make a whole show of it. Use our decapitated bodies to boost morale."

Right. Yes. Siege. According to Hall, Rome had laid siege to its great rival Carthage for years, ultimately pillaging and razing the city to the ground and killing hundreds of thousands of its occupants. Depending on the timing of their trip, they might very well be eyewitnesses, if they did not get on with their business.

Wonderful.

Adrenaline flooded into Nicholas, warming his cold limbs, lighting up his mind and sharpening his thoughts. Behind them, at the very center of the arcade, was a mountain of a structure, a kind of watchtower constructed in four layers that grew smaller as it reached the top. The lowest layer, with all of its arches and columns breaking up the ship sheds, also seemed to serve as a dry dock—there were several skeletal frames of ships waiting to be completed.

But it was the highest level that intrigued Nicholas, that turned his heart cold in his chest. There, he could see torches—the shadowy outlines of men standing guard.

"Follow me," Sophia said, taking a long, confident stroke toward a bridge that connected the watchtower to the entrance of the city. This time, he was the one to snatch her back, pressing a finger to his lips at her look of outrage and splashing.

This wasn't a mere harbor—it was a *military* harbor, likely making it one of the best-protected and most -watched locations in the whole city. As a preventative measure, there would be few places they could use to slip inside of the city, and all would be defended.

He swiveled his head in the opposite direction. If Hall's stories had been true . . . Nicholas's eyes finally began to see through the veil of darkness, and—there it was. There wasn't just one harbor in ancient Carthage, but *two*. One military, one merchant.

Nicholas had no doubt that the Romans had it well blockaded by now, but what mattered was that the merchant harbor would be far more open to the city. Merchants would need a way to bring their goods into the markets and conduct their trade.

Without wasting breath on explanations, he dropped beneath the cold waves and began to swim, his body taking to the water in long strokes. Nicholas came up for air only when necessary, and only slowly, to avoid splashing. Every few strokes, Sophia's hand would brush his leg or foot, reassuring him she was still there. He kicked his way beneath the iron chain gate, the moonlight just strong enough to give him a glance of it as he swam beneath.

He hadn't realized, until his stomach cramped and his limbs went as hollow as straw with effort, how long it had been since he'd last eaten, since he'd given them any sort of rest. How long he *and* Sophia had gone without more than a few bites of bread. The next time he broke through the surface for a breath, he made it a point to curb his nerves and stop to ensure Sophia was still keeping pace.

He waited.

The water in the harbor shoved at his back, rocking him, splashing into his eyes and nose as he kept low to the surface and waited for Sophia's dark head to pop up again. Unlike its military counterpart, this harbor kept to a long, rectangular shape, allowing a few scattered ships to dock along it lengthwise, like fingers. Several shadowy figures moved steadily along the water's edge, occasionally crossing paths as they moved in opposite directions.

A light patrol, then; the harbor was large enough that he felt confident all they needed to do was wait a few more moments, until the closest soldier moved out of sight. As he'd suspected, there were several low limestone buildings constructed along the harbor, their faces darkened by night. Those would be the warehouses used for storing goods. Some things never changed with time.

What he *hadn't* expected was to find Sophia ahead, already climbing up from the water onto the docks. He watched in growing disbelief and, frankly, mild outrage, as she snaked her way toward the entrance of one of the warehouses, up behind one of the guards posted there with his back turned. She leaped onto his back, smothering him with one hand against his mouth and an arm banded over his throat. When another man emerged from the nearby warehouse, she pounced on him and did the same.

By the time Nicholas had climbed out of the water and ducked over to her, she'd already stripped the men of their tunics and shoes, as well as their swords. Nicholas accepted his with a pointed look of disapproval.

"Can you attempt to keep up?" she groused, turning her back to allow him to change.

"I will endeavor to do my best," he said dryly, quickly tugging off his wet clothes and pulling on the soldier's uniform with expediency as Sophia did the same. He bundled everything, including his soaking shoes, into his travel satchel. "Now where—"

A shadow melted away from the wall of the warehouse behind her, tucked into that very same pocket of blindness that had bedeviled her before.

"Move," he breathed. *"Move!"*

But Sophia had, it seemed, already read the fear in his features, and she threw herself to the ground, just as a sword blade sang through the air, coming within a hair of scalping her. The sword instead slammed into the building, embedding itself so deeply, the attacker abandoned it in favor of another.

A curved dagger that stretched from the man's finger like a claw.

THIRTEEN

A LANCE OF PAIN SLASHED ACROSS HIS SHOULDER BLADES. Nicholas was thrown forward by the force of the unseen hit, his breath exploding out of him. He whirled to see the last glimpse of a long spear disappear into the nearby water. Blackness threatened to swallow his vision as he rolled closer to the nearest building's wall, trying to find cover from above.

Sophia— He searched her out, fuming and fearful. A hard gust of air and a grunt had him flying back, narrowly avoiding a new hooded figure as he slammed his sword down hard enough onto the stones for the blade to spark. It was close enough for him to see his own startled reflection in its surface.

Hell and damnation.

Nicholas ripped his own knife from his belt, parrying the swipe the first attacker took with the clawlike dagger. His forearm throbbed as it absorbed the shock of the blow, and he couldn't pull back far or fast enough to avoid the bite of its tip at his chin. The cloak the man wore smelled of salt and sweat, and looked to have been cut from the night sky. It was only because the moon shone from so high above them that he could make out the embroidery stitched along its edges, the swirling pattern of what looked to be vines, or the powerful rays of a hundred small suns.

His attacker's foot lashed out, hooking behind his knee, taking advantage of Nicholas's unsteady balance and exhaustion. He crashed to the ground hard enough to see the lights of heaven behind his eyelids. As he tried to push himself off the ground, his right arm seemed to fill with white-hot needles and collapsed beneath him, aching.

A sickening thump struck the ground to his right, but Nicholas didn't dare take his eyes off his attacker except to throw himself back onto his feet. His mind locked into the elaborate dance of death—strike, block, swipe, jab—the heat beneath his skin growing as he leaned into the fight. He allowed the towering man to back him up closer to Sophia, where she was now bending to retrieve her own knife from the neck of the shuddering body on the ground.

These attackers were all the same: black in the cloak, silver in the claw.

What the devil is this?

The attacker missed slicing the tip of Nicholas's nose off, but clobbered him with a blow under the chin. Hard enough to knock that thought, and his brain, loose. Seeing double now, he couldn't tell which of the split forms was the man, so he took a broad swipe at both. The claw lashed out, slicing up his arm, nearly puncturing his wrist. Closer, he saw the paleness of the man's skin, the waxy quality of it, as if he had known nothing but night itself.

The attacker stumbled suddenly with a lurch and a gasp. Behind him, Sophia wrenched her knife out from where she'd jabbed it between his shoulder blades. Nicholas raised his wrist, but his arm still felt peculiar, heavier than it ought to have been, so slow that his next slash was blocked by heavy dark leather gauntlets. The attacker righted himself, keeping his claw on Nicholas and his blade on Sophia.

"You must be joking," she said, eye white as a pearl in the dark.

He was not. If the man had split himself down his center and become two, he couldn't have been any more effective than he was then, with his attention divided between them. Nicholas struck, Sophia struck, and he threw them back again and again. Nicholas felt every ounce of pent-up fury crest over his final bit of restraint. A last gasp of strength surged into his body, and, beneath it all, a single, cool thought.

Lure him in.

He feinted left, letting the man's next hit knock the knife from his hand, letting him crowd closer. Sensing easy prey, the attacker moved in for the kill. The claw ripped the air in two, skimming over his throat as he leaned back.

Sophia slammed her blade into the base of his skull. The attacker's hood was thrown back as he fell to the ground, his long, pale hair stained with bubbling blood.

The air heaved in and out of Nicholas, his lungs screaming for mercy as the red haze disappeared from his vision and that most basic instinct—to kill or be killed—abandoned him. He wiped his face with his sleeve, ignoring the way his hands shook.

"That was . . ." he began at the same time that Sophia said, "It's the same weapon, isn't it?"

Trying to rub away the prickling pain from his right arm, he glanced down, searching for a wound that might explain the slash of hot pain that stretched across the back of his hand. But there was nothing, not even a cut.

A word hissed through his mind, unbidden. *Poison.*

Impossible. If anything, he'd strained a muscle or given himself a sprain. This would resolve itself, with nothing so nefarious to blame.

But the sensation did not disappear. It worsened. There'd been longer and harder battles fought for his life that had left him feeling nowhere near the level of exhaustion overtaking him now, like a sudden illness. Nicholas coughed up dust he'd inhaled and spat out a wad of blood, retrieving the satchel from where it had fallen some distance away. The hollowness at his core spread as he checked to make sure the string with Etta's earring was still around his neck, still safe. He clutched it in his left fist, as his right felt nearly too numb now to move.

Not good. Nicholas glanced down at the ring again, and forced himself to look away before his thoughts sank him any deeper into worry.

"Come on, we need to get rid of the bodies before—" Sophia interrupted herself midsentence, her gaze shooting up toward the warehouse above.

But Nicholas had seen the shadows first—five of them, fluttering around like ravens, jumping between the buildings with animalistic ease. Nicholas took her arm and forced himself into a run, moments before the first arrow cleaved through the air over their heads.

He looked up in time to see another shadow on a nearby roof. With the lingering traces of his composure, he hefted a large stone and threw it as hard as he could. It startled their attacker long enough for Nicholas to drag them under the cover of the nearby building's overhang. But the pounding steps behind them didn't cease, nor did the realization that they were running without any particular destination in mind.

Better to be like rats, he thought, and try to confuse a pursuing cat by taking as labyrinthine a path as possible. It was just a matter of finding the right hole to disappear into.

"Who are they?" Sophia gasped out.

The Belladonna's men? The rogue idea cut up through the rest. She had taken particular interest in getting the claw back, hadn't she? She might have overheard where they were going and taken action after his refusal to serve her.

"I'm reasonably sure we should not stay to find out," he told her, craning his neck just far enough to check for the shadowy figures on the roof. Seeing nothing but the clouds and stars, he motioned for her to follow, and picked up his punishing pace again.

The whole of the city reeked as though it had been boiling in its own waste for a month. It felt like climbing into a festering wound. Unwashed bodies, living and near-dead, blocked their path no matter which street they turned onto, sleeping scant inches away from rotting garbage—or, in a few sorry instances, using the rotting garbage as a kind of pillow against the unforgiving stone streets.

Sparks flew up, scattering across the night, as they passed a blacksmith busy beating a sword into submission despite the late hour. Feeling the unwanted prickling in his right hand again, he switched his knife to his left, and he kept his head down as they passed, only glancing at the pile of metal goods waiting to be melted down and re-formed, and the pile of finished, somewhat crude weapons waiting to be picked up and taken to battle.

There was a sliver of space between his workshop and the next building, an alleyway that curved around. He led Sophia into it, giving them a moment's reprieve to catch their breaths.

"I think we've lost them—"

Sophia had cursed them with that. A darkly cloaked woman burst out of the streams of fabric that had been draped over lines to dry, like a wraith.

Without a second thought, Sophia tossed Nicholas the soldier's blade she'd been carrying and, catching it, he whirled back, smashing the hilt against the attacker's throat, stunning her. While she gasped, Sophia seemed to flow in, cutting the woman across her face with her knife. The moment the attacker hit the ground, pressing her hands against the flowing blood with a howl, they were running again.

The city curved before them like a question mark, laid out like a maze within a puzzle. Pale, sturdy limestone buildings leaned against their close neighbors, and lines of them stretched as far and wide as Nicholas's eyes could see, culminating on a hill at the city's heart. The homes rose not just two stories, but usually six or seven, as if the city had one day decided the best course was to grow up, rather than out. Much like, he thought with a sad sort of smile, the way Etta had described her Manhattan.

At the next small lane they approached, Sophia stopped, blocking him.

"Let's go a different way," she whispered quickly.

Nicholas held his ground as he felt Sophia pull at his shoulder, searching for what had upset her—and, with a shudder, located it. Stretched across the stone, curled up on his side as still and pale as a seashell, was a child. On closer inspection Nicholas saw that his eyes remained open, unblinking, that his skin was dotted with scabbed-over sores. He followed the line of the boy's desperately thin arm. His fingers were still hooked around a slender hand hanging out of the bottom of a pile of bodies, already at the mercy of flies and vermin.

He kicked a rat away before it could reach the boy, his stomach rioting. The only reason he didn't cast up his accounts was because there was nothing left in his stomach to lose. Sophia heaved once, twice, pressing the back of her hand against her mouth, and looked away.

"There's disease here," he said unnecessarily. "We'd better make quick work of this. Try not to touch anything or anyone."

Sophia nodded, wiping her hands against the tunic she'd taken from the unconscious soldier.

As they approached a low hill and the stately structures atop it, the stench of the city was tempered by smoke. But rather than masking the excrement and sickness, it drew out a different flavor of it. History, as it was, stank of disease and desperation, fire and ash. The slightly damp quality of the air made Nicholas feel as though it were seeping inside of his skin, as though he would carry the proof of his visit here forever. And in the distance, the infernal clanging carried on unseen out in the dark water.

Where the Romans are lying in wait . . . Building something? Manufacturing the tools of Carthage's destruction? The sound was incessant, without beginning or end, and Nicholas wondered how long it had been carrying on for. If the people of this city had been forced to listen to it each day and night, like the heavy steps of a predator edging ever closer.

A rattling up ahead drew his feet up short; both he and Sophia pressed themselves against the nearest wall, their backs flush against it.

He had only just closed his dry eyes, rubbing at the crust forming on them, trying not to dwell on the hopelessness of it all, when a familiar scent hit his nose. Swinging around, Nicholas cast about for the direction the breeze was blowing from. And there it was, just to the east of where they stood. Warm, fresh animal excrement.

"I think there's a stable near enough," he told Sophia, already picking up his steps, trying to fight the urge to run when his suspicions were confirmed. A long, two-level building was up ahead, with piles of dried grass tucked up against the back wall. There, stalls had been formed from arches, not unlike the ship sheds in the harbor, which opened to a kind of courtyard. Nicholas crouched low, trying to massage the burning sensation in his right arm away as he crept forward, using the tents and draped fabric for cover.

A lone soldier stood guard at what looked to be a side entrance, leaning back against the heavy iron door. Nicholas glanced at Sophia, who had caught up and crouched beside him. At her nod, he slipped out into the night's shadows, casting one last glance around to ensure there was no one else watching.

He decided he liked these soft sandals the men of Carthage wore—they made sneaking up on a soul far easier than the leather shoes of his own era. By the time the soldier startled fully out of his light doze, Nicholas already had his arm hooked around the man's throat.

The soldier smelled of sweat and sweet wine, and his breath exploded out of him with a spray of spittle. He thrashed, kicking his legs out and around, clawing so deeply into Nicholas's arm that he wondered if the marks would scar. With the slightest bit more pressure, the man passed out. Despite being nearly a full foot taller, Nicholas struggled to get a grip on his weight—it was like holding an unwieldy sack of warm water, limbs spilling and flopping around as he dragged him.

Sophia rushed forward, feeling for the ring of iron keys hooked to the man's armor. Her hands shook, either from exhaustion or excitement, as she tried each of the six in turn.

"Hurry!" he whispered.

"Hah!" she breathed out when the right key slid into the crude lock. She shoved the door open with her shoulder, and showed an enviable amount of patience in holding it open long enough to allow him to drag the soldier inside the stable's warm darkness.

Nicholas dropped him behind several barrels, stopping only long enough to use the sword to crack the wood and see if there was water or wine inside.

Wine. Sophia doubled back to help herself to a mouthful of it and would have tried to gulp another if Nicholas hadn't taken his turn. The sourness exploded across his tongue, but it wet his dry mouth and aching throat.

A few candles held on to their faint glow, casting shallow pools of light along the path leading to the front of the animal stalls. Nicholas balked a moment at their size, wondering how many horses they were keeping in each to require them to be that large. The walls were covered with bright paint—in the low light, he could just make out the soldiers, the scenes of ferocious battle. Nicholas felt his feet slow to a stop, and was leaning in to study the legions of soldiers depicted, when the sudden sound of heavy steps rained down over them.

There was something awake up there. Dust drifted from the ceiling with the movement, marking a path.

Sophia's gaze shot toward the other end of the stalls, where another door, this one likely leading upstairs, stood closed. He waited a beat of silence more, his body drumming with adrenaline, but no one emerged. He waved Sophia forward.

"Let's find the storeroom," he whispered. "If it looks like oats or barley, take it, even if it's from the horses' feed bins."

Sophia nodded and took off at a fast clip. She swung her attention up toward a stall in the middle of the long line. The candlelight caught the angle of her face as she looked up, then up again—first in surprise, and then in pure wonder.

Nicholas doubled his pace, catching up to her in a few short strides. "What's the matter—?"

He stumbled back against the wall in alarm.

A long, leathery gray trunk snaked out from between the stall bars, coming within inches of Sophia's face. The elephant watched them, interest flickering in its dark eyes. Its ears flapped against its neck like butterfly wings as it made a small trumpeting sound. Nicholas had never seen an elephant before—only etchings and sailors' descriptions—and he found it almost impossible to look away. He leaned forward, only to fall back again when its ivory tusks banged loudly against the stall door.

"They use elephants in war," Sophia muttered, her voice as soft as he'd ever heard it, her fingers brushing the trunk. It seemed to tickle the loose pieces of her hair. "Sorry about this, my handsome fellow."

She reached between the bars and carefully, with a touch as soft as a flower petal, unlatched the door.

"Sophia!" Nicholas whispered. Scraping up the remains of her trampled body from under an eight-foot-tall beast hadn't been included in his plans for the evening. "Stop this!"

Sophia held out a hand and eased her body into the stall. The elephant shuffled its heavy body back a step, giving her enough room to slip inside the stall and crouch in front of the large food trough, half-full of what looked to Nicholas to be grain and grass. Sophia took up her small bag and began to stuff handfuls of the raw food in it, before motioning for him to pass his bag over.

"Here." She filled it, then threw his bag back to him. "Let's get moving."

He caught it easily, turning back toward the door. Sophia gave the beast's flank one last pat before she shut its stall. Eyes scanning the ground, the walls, for anything that might be of use, Nicholas had nearly missed the one thing that *wasn't* present.

The guard.

He gripped Sophia's arm and brought a hand to her mouth, muffling her protests. Nicholas nodded to the spot where they'd left the unconscious man and felt her suck in a small gasp of surprise. Pulling away, he moved back to the entrance and put his eye back to the door's lock, peering out into the darkness.

There was movement outside—shadows gliding against one another, fading in and out of the night. Sweat broke out at the base of Nicholas's skull, his mouth shaping into a silent warning as a nearby guard was knocked out in an instant, crumpling to the ground; shadows swept in around him, covering him, dragging him away.

Hiding the evidence.

Not killing him, so as to avoid changing the timeline? He and Sophia had played a dangerous game in how careless they'd become, risking change after change to ensure their own survival. These . . . travelers? These *warriors*, men and women, were decidedly *not* careless.

Nicholas strained his ears to catch the murmuring on the other side. Once his eyes adjusted well enough to the darkness, he was able to count four figures of varying stature, all sweeping toward the door like a high tide. It might have been the thrumming fear in his mind playing an unwelcome trick, but he could have sworn the ring on his finger grew warmer with each step closer they took.

Sophia pointed up, but Nicholas shook his head, competing thoughts racing to best one another. There might be more soldiers on the second level, and to get out of the stables, their ultimate goal, they would need to jump onto a nearby building—but none were near enough, and all were taller. He didn't fancy breaking his neck after nearly being drowned and stabbed already in one night.

In battle, you could fight a foe head-on until both of your ships were in splinters around you. But, when outmaneuvered, there was always the potent combination of creating a distraction of some sort and escaping at full speed, hopefully with the wind on your side.

His idea was almost absurd. In spite of everything that had occurred, or perhaps because of it, Nicholas felt a grim smile touch his lips. It hadn't made sense to him why they would store wine here in the stables, other than to hide it from the people outside who desperately needed it. But what if the wine wasn't for men at all, but for the elephants?

They'd pour it down the elephant's throats, see, Hall had told him and Chase, miming the gulping. *Get them good and primed. The wine would send them into a rage, enough to trample any men who stood in their way.*

Nicholas ducked down, peering one last time through the lock to see if the men had moved. As if they'd somehow heard him, one of the men—the one nearest to the door—shouted something. Sophia clucked her tongue, likely at the viciousness that coated the nonsensical words.

"I have a thought," Nicholas told her. "About what to do—"

"Is this a thought that's going to get us murdered, our heads smashed under an elephant's foot, poisoned, et cetera?"

He gave her an exasperated look that Sophia shrugged off as she took his place at the door. "Keep watch for a moment—make sure they aren't planning to storm their way in."

She gave a sloppy salute and leaned down to peer through the lock. "What are you on about, Carter—?"

He took the sword and swung down, cracking open each of the wine barrels in turn.

"Are you *deranged*?" Sophia whispered, jumping to her feet.

191

He took her by the arm again and launched them at a run back toward the nearest elephant's stall. Before Sophia had time to question him, Nicholas unlatched the door and dragged it open.

The elephant didn't move.

There was a sliver of a second in which he was furious with himself for wasting good drink. Then, as the air thickened with the smell of the wine, the elephant let out a deafening trumpet, as if alerting the others, and all but charged out of the stall. Sophia leaped back with a cry of alarm, even as Nicholas attempted to shield them with the stall door. The animal must have weighed well over a thousand pounds. The whole building quaked as it galloped toward the pooling wine.

"My God," Sophia said. "That's an animal with his priorities straight."

"Come *along*," Nicholas insisted, waving her after him.

There were two more elephants stamping and hollering to be let out, their enormous ears flapping like a ship's colors. Nicholas leaned back, away from one of the trunks that was feeling down his front, as if trying to hurry him along, as he worked the door open.

The third elephant, larger than even the first had been, had no patience at all—he rammed his way out of the stall, his tusks tossing the barrier to the side. Sophia dove out of the way, narrowly missing the door as it smashed back onto the stone floor.

Somewhere, beyond the gray mountains of their leathery hides, the main door burst open and the shadowy attackers attempted to rush inside—attempted, because the nearest elephant lifted its head from the wine and trumpeted a warning that would have made the dead turn in their graves. The two in front had a moment to fall back before the elephant reared up, scraping the ceiling with its tusks, and forced its way out through the door, stampeding into the night.

"What now?" Sophia asked, righting her eye patch.

Nicholas pointed to the side of the nearest stall, which led into an open-air exercise or training courtyard. Hopefully there would be a way back into the city through it as well. He hoisted his full bag, switching shoulders, as he entered the stall. The soft grass padding it seemed to eat his footsteps, but it didn't matter—three drunk elephants were enough of a distraction for their pursuers.

Nicholas edged around the nearest wall, tucking himself between two tall structures, out of sight from the street. A moment later, Sophia followed. He leaned his head back against the stone, looking down at her, brows raised. She returned the look. "Elephants. That was a first. Not bad, Carter."

He inclined his head, accepting the rare compliment. He wasn't such a fool to think it would be the first of many; fighting had a way of bringing even the unlikeliest of allies together. Once the haze of excitement wore off, they'd be back to circling one another like half-starved sharks.

And their brief alliance would devour itself.

"We need to find the Jacarandas," Sophia whispered. "Now. I don't want them to catch wind of anything strange and guess there might be travelers here before we have a chance to come forward."

"All right," he said. "How do you propose we—?"

The clawlike blade caught the light of a nearby torch from above, casting a glow on Sophia's dark hair. Nicholas shoved her as hard as he could, but not nearly soon enough to prevent her from taking a kick to the face as a cloaked attacker leaped down from the roof of the building behind them.

"You just can't take no for an answer, can you?" Sophia growled, clutching her cheek.

The fall should have broken his legs, but the man rose, pushing his hood back just enough for Nicholas to see the gleam of his bald head, his pointed features. It was a man well within the prime of his life—a life that had sliced his face into a quilt of scars.

"Give it to me," he rasped out. "I will spare the woman. Give it to me—"

The tip of an arrow sprouted from the center of the man's throat. The spill of blood from the wound left him sucking at the air, his claw clicking against the arrow's crude metal tip. The fear that had coiled so thickly around Nicholas's chest did not release—not when Sophia staggered up to her feet; not when the frail old man in a homespun tunic stepped out of the night, his bow still in hand.

"Come now," he said, his voice frayed with fear. "The Shadows feed on the night, and they will not stop until they consume us all."

PETROGRAD
1919

FOURTEEN

IT WAS A STRANGE KIND OF PROCESSION THAT WOUND ITS way through the entrance of the Winter Palace. Henry led the small flock of them, talking quietly with an elderly man with a bowed back—some sort of courier. Etta studied the two of them from under her lashes, listening to their muted Russian. A long, seemingly unending red carpet stretched out before them, running along the tile and stonework like an invitation into the palace's hidden heart.

The cold and shock finally began to thaw out of her. Etta was surprised to find that the palace was well heated despite its immense size, to the point where she shrugged out of her absurd coat and let one of the men in suits take it off her hands.

Behind her, Julian was whistling a faint tune just loudly enough to be annoying. Winifred remained behind him, complaining to the Thorn guards about their "shocking lack of foresight" in the route they'd had the party take. Those men, behind even her, kept slowing their pace, as if trying to build more distance between themselves and the mouth spewing venom at them.

"Is there a way to shut her off? Some hidden switch?"

Etta didn't turn back or even acknowledge Julian. He was forced to lengthen his strides to keep pace with her. When the sleeve of his formal dinner jacket brushed her arm and she took a generous step away, he gave her an amused look.

"The last girl I chased at least gave me a kiss for my trouble," he said in a low voice, sparing a quick look at Henry's back.

"Do you often accept kisses from *deranged* girls?" Etta asked.

His mouth twisted. "Don't be sore about that, kiddo. For a second it really looked like you were ready to engage in mortal combat. It was just self-preservation."

More like wounded pride, she thought. He hadn't expected her to try to fight her way out of that room in San Francisco, never mind back him into a corner.

"So what do you make of all this?" he asked. "The changes, I mean. I've only ever known the world Grandfather created, which I'm guessing is the same for you?"

She looked ahead, breathing in the faintly perfumed air, drinking in the sights around her. It didn't feel real—she knew that this wasn't her timeline—but she had expected *something* about it to register as different to her senses, like seeing the world in a mirror's reflection. This was a glimpse of what Henry and the others had lost. What the world itself had lost.

But instead of appreciating it, all Etta could think of was the last time she had been in Russia, for the International Tchaikovsky Competition. With Alice. Competing. Winning it all. The *Times* article. "Classical Music's Best-Kept Secret."

All of it had melted away from her life like the snow in the palace's courtyard, leaving her nothing but pockets of glistening memories that felt like they could disappear completely at any time.

My future isn't the real future, she reminded herself. *It only existed because of one man's greed.*

Etta shook off the thought, reaching up to smooth back a loose strand of hair. Julian walked with the easy nonchalance of someone who had no idea he was being led into the mouth of a wolf. And that soft part of her she had hated so much, the one that now set her apart from her mother, ached a little at the thought. Standing in Ironwood's presence for less than an hour had been a triumph of courage. She could only imagine what growing up with the man had been like.

"You know . . ." she began, "you'll be able to pay him some compliments about it directly. Soon, if I had to guess."

"Pay him some . . ." Julian's words trailed off at the exact moment his eyes widened slightly. He turned away from her, coughing into his fist. "Please. You think . . . that is, I'm sure you think you're warning me, but I already know. Of course I do. My best skill is knowing when to leave a party before the fun's gone."

"I'm sure that's been incredibly useful—"

"Etta?" She looked up to find Henry had stopped and was extending his arm to her. "May I escort you in?"

With one last glance at Julian, she crossed that last bit of distance and took Henry's arm. The courier moved ahead, signaling to the two guards posted at an imposing set of doors to open them. As they stepped into the next room, Etta felt unsteady on her small heels.

"Have they found your man yet?" she asked. "Kadir?"

Henry shook his head, but gave her hand a reassuring pat. "He mentioned in his note that if he did not feel it safe to stay, he would hide the astrolabe somewhere in the palace. It may take days of searching yet, but I haven't any doubt we'll find it here as he promised. The others will begin their search immediately, but I'd like you to meet an old friend of mine first. There are a few things I need to discuss with him to secure this timeline."

The ceiling stretched high above, a dome beautifully painted in the colors of sky and earth, framed—of course—with gold. The black-and-white-checked tile was a quiet design touch compared to the stone figurines of women and angels carved into the arches where the gray granite columns met the roof. Around them, two layers of windows brought in a flood of moonlight to aid the glowing golden sconces. The walls were a pristine white where they weren't covered with panels of silk or art or gold, most of those embellished to within an inch of their lives with meticulously crafted vines, leaves, and flowers.

The party went up one staircase; on the next landing, steps led left and right, winding up to the same high point overlooking the room.

"This is the Jordan Staircase," Henry said by way of explanation. "Impressive, isn't it?"

"I don't know," Etta said. "I think it could do with a touch more gold."

"More gold—" He turned toward her, brows furrowed, before his face broke into a wide smile. "Oh. Sarcasm. That's a *most* unattractive trait in a young lady, you know."

"Yes, sarcasm; one of the many services I have to offer," Etta said, her voice even more dry, "along with driving Winifred insane."

He gave her a knowing look. "She'll soften, given time."

"The way a fruit softens as it rots away?" she guessed.

He struggled to summon a stern look. "That was unkind."

But not untrue.

They walked for seemingly forever, until Etta, an experienced city walker, felt like she might want to sit down and take her shoes off, just to spare her toes the agony of being pinched for a few minutes. The rooms blurred together in a rainbow stream—edged, of course, with gold. Blue rooms. Green rooms. Red rooms. Great halls with chandeliers the size of modern trucks. Ballrooms waiting to be filled with flowers and dancers. Parquet floors whose swirling designs were made up of a dozen types of wood. Marble floors so very glossy Etta could see her reflection as she moved over them.

And still, it took another ten minutes before a crisply dressed servant met them at the base of another grand staircase and said, in accented English, "He'll see you in his study before dinner. Shall I show your guests into a drawing room?"

"I think we all shall wait—" Winifred began.

"I'll be bringing this young lady with me," Henry said. "The rest are to have free range of the rooms to conduct their search."

Etta's gaze slid over to Julian's, just as Winifred drew herself to her full height with a huff and curled a thin hand over his shoulder.

Don't leave me, he mouthed as the woman dragged him away, following another servant back down the hall. Jenkins moved to follow Henry and Etta, but was waved off.

"Sir—" he began.

"We're safe here," Henry reassured him. "Lock the Ironwood child in a room and go see to the search. Inform Julian that if he throws a temper tantrum or breaks anything, we'll certainly break something of his."

Jenkins nodded, but didn't look especially pleased as he retreated.

The servant opened the door and went inside, but Henry held Etta back a moment.

"This friend of mine is neither a guardian nor a traveler, though he knows of our existence," Henry said, his voice barely above a whisper. "I ask that you not share the details of the timeline you grew up with, as it might frighten him into acting rashly."

Etta nodded and reached up again, pushing a rogue strand of hair back out of her face. Sophia had told her, in no uncertain terms, that to reveal what they could do to any non-traveler brought layers upon layers of consequences. She was surprised Henry was taking the risk at all.

Dark wood paneling surrounded them on all sides, making the awkwardly shaped room seem almost coffinlike. It was so aggressively masculine in its bold lines, the air drenched in wood polish and tobacco, that Etta wondered if the room ever received female visitors. Bookcases, most with glass doors, ran along the edge of the room, broken up in places by small oval portraits of men in military uniform. Around a corner, Etta saw a grand piano peeking out. At the center stood an impressive desk covered with picture frames of all shapes and sizes. She didn't notice the man sitting behind it, a book open under the glow of a brass desk lamp, until he lifted a tumbler of alcohol to his lips.

"Your Imperial Majesty, Mister Henry Hemlock and Miss Henrietta Hemlock."

Imperial Majesty.

The words dripped through her mind, slow as syrup.

As in . . . the tsar.

All at once she understood the warning that Henry had given her, not to speak of the timeline she'd grown up in. Because this man, who stood only an inch taller than her, with neatly combed brown hair and piercing blue eyes, should have been dead a year ago, along with his whole family.

"Thank you, that will be all," Tsar Nicholas II said, dismissing the servant, who gave one last swift bow on his way out.

"Nicky," Henry said simply, and it was Etta's turn to be stunned as he favored the other man with a true, warm smile.

His friend. A friend he hadn't saved, or hadn't been able to; one who'd been murdered, along with his family, as a new regime had risen to power in his country. Etta's hands felt cold and damp inside of her gloves.

This was what it meant to form attachments to people outside of their small, insular world of travelers, Etta realized. They were at the mercy of the timeline. Saving them was no guarantee that events wouldn't change for the worse, but to live with the knowledge of their deaths . . .

Etta glanced at Henry again, took in the way he rubbed a hand over his face, fought to keep his expression from slipping. A sharp jolt of pain went straight through her heart. She knew this feeling. She knew this exact brand of painful elation. Seeing a younger Alice had changed her perception of death entirely, forced her to recognize that time wasn't a straight line. As long as she—as long as any of them— could travel, they wouldn't be constrained by the natural boundaries of life and death.

And this was what truly set the Thorns apart from the Ironwoods; the old man only saw humanity as tools to carve and hone his vision of what the world should be. But here, in the way Henry had to press a hand to his face to mask his relief, was a kind of love; a compassion for messy, flawed humanity. A wish to spare this life, just as they had struggled to spare the lives of San Francisco's many fortunate strangers.

The thought made Etta eager to leave, to join the other Thorns combing the rooms for the astrolabe.

All of this could be over in a night. *Less* than that.

"Oh, dear," the tsar said with a faint laugh, extending a hand toward him. "I can't imagine what's about to happen to me to provoke that sort of reaction from you."

His English was better than hers, somehow crisp and smooth all at once, with a refined edge.

"No, it's only—" Henry cleared his throat and laughed. He took the tsar's hand, releasing Etta to clasp it with his other one. "I was only thinking it's been so very long. Will you do me the honor of allowing me to introduce my daughter, Henrietta?"

"Daughter!" The tsar came around the desk, grinning. "You never said! What a charming beauty she is."

Henry nodded. "And wit to match."

The tsar smiled. "Of course. Intellect and charm."

"It's . . ." Etta realized she should be doing something—something like curtseying—and did an awkward sort of bob at the knees. "It's incredible to meet you."

Because, honestly, what else could she say? It was incredible, absurd, and more than a little alarming.

"The pleasure is, of course, all mine." The tsar turned his attention back toward Henry, repeating that same stunned exclamation, "*Daughter!* I wish you had sent word. I would have brought my own with me from Tsarkoye Selo. As it was, I hardly had time to travel into the city myself."

"Please forgive my abhorrent rudeness on the matter. We made an unexpected trip here, as you might have gathered. And, regretfully, I only recently became reacquainted with Henrietta after a number of years apart," Henry explained. "We've been making up for lost time."

The tsar's lips twisted into an ironic smile. "It seems odd to me that your kind can 'lose' time when you stand to gain so much from it. Please—sit, sit, and tell me, how have you been, my old friend? What news from your own war?"

Oh my God. The knowledge that he was well aware of their world, and had directly benefited from his association with it, made Etta shift uncomfortably. This was the very first lesson of their world Sophia had given her. How chillingly serious the other girl had been when she'd said, if nothing else, they couldn't reveal themselves or what they could do. They couldn't share news of the future with the past, save the dead from their fates, or even break character.

The passivity of it had infuriated her, but to see the effects of breaking those rules now, even in the service of something good, was a little frightening.

Etta found herself in a stiff-backed chair without ever remembering sitting down. Henry settled into the chair beside hers. The tsar reclaimed his own.

"It continues," Henry said. "I take it you became acquainted with two of my men?"

The tsar sat back in his seat, his hands folded over his chest, his initial pleasure dimmed. "I think perhaps you already know the answer to that."

Henry tried for a smile. "Are you furious with me, then, Nicky?"

"I was many things," the tsar said. "Defeated soundly by the once-inferior Japan. Humiliated in the eyes of my cousins and peers the world over. Chastised by the poorest of this country for the conditions they were subjected to. Sickened by the Duma taking more and more power, mine by birthright."

Etta tried to fight her cringe as the man's voice grew hoarse. "Betrayed by former allies. Humbled by the notion that I have failed to maintain the power of my father and his father before him. But *alive*. The tsar. My country struggles, as all do in the face of great change, but the reforms you encouraged have been a boon, including the cessation of pogroms against the Jews, which I would never have believed."

"The recent disturbances . . ." Henry began, looking troubled.

"Already tidied up," the tsar finished. "I will find a way to soothe the ruffled feathers."

"I'm certain of it. But what of the treaties?"

"Breaking them came more easily than I might have imagined, with France aiding the revolutionaries, who were misguided in thinking one less monarchy would better the world. It was a simple thing to stand against political assassinations, given the history of my family. Serbia was a sacrifice, but one that kept us from the war."

The First World War, Etta thought, straightening. Russia had lost millions of soldiers; the badly managed effort, the poor conditions at home, and the machinations of other governments had all led to the ousting of the tsar, and his own eventual assassination.

"I hated you. Bitterly, I'm afraid, for countless years," the tsar said. "I cursed you with every breath. But I trusted you and prayed on each decision. Your family has been the steward of mine for many generations, the caretaker of this land for longer than even the Romanovs."

As in . . . guiding their choices? Etta wondered. *Advising them on the right ones to make?*

How was that any different than what the Ironwoods were doing?

"I thought you were against interfering in the timeline?" Etta asked Henry, however rude they might think her for interrupting.

"Oh, no, Etta, it's not quite like that," he said, quickly. "We worked very diligently to protect the timeline from the changes other families were making, especially as they pertained to ruining the fortunes of this part of the world."

"That is true," the tsar said. "They have never bowed to the demands of my family for more information, for ways to overcome our enemies. They have been protectors, not puppeteers."

Settled somewhat, Etta nodded. Henry turned back to the tsar.

"The Germans no longer had quite as much interest in your rule, did they," Henry said knowingly, "once they considered you humiliated after the war with Japan. Did they even bother with Lenin?"

The tsar shook his head. "And now they are quite busy, as is the rest of the world, with pulling themselves back together after their own humiliation. Your traveler war seems to be the only one which cannot find its end."

Henry smiled. "We might surprise you yet. Did one of my men indicate they would be hiding something in the palace during their visit in 1905? Do you recall?"

The tsar stroked his mustache. "I'm afraid not. They were harried and bloodied, in no state to do anything but hand off your letter. The guards were reluctant to let them in to see me. They were given food and rooms to rest, but by dinner they had fled again. I'll have one of the maids show you to their rooms after dinner—you'll stay and dine with me, won't you? Your men will be busy searching. There are fifteen hundred rooms here, you'll recall."

And how many hundreds of hiding places in each? Impatience stirred in her. *We'll be searching for days.*

"Where is your foe now? I'm not sure I've ever seen you look quite so relaxed."

"My spies have Ironwood safely ensconced in an earlier century, in Manhattan. His men are far too distracted by the changes in America to focus on you and your country."

"I'm glad to hear it," the tsar said, showing what Etta thought was admirable restraint in not pushing for more details. The man took only what was offered, though he probably had ways and means of demanding more. He reached back for his glass and held it up in Henry's direction.

"Yes, thank you," Henry said as the tsar crossed the room to a small cabinet, where a crystal decanter was stored.

"I'll take one, too," Etta said before she could stop herself. The tsar laughed as he poured out the liquor into the two glasses, but Etta wasn't joking. She could have used the liquid courage to prop her nerves up. Her back only straightened as the tsar passed the glass to Henry and resumed his former position.

"Tell me about yourself, my dear," he said. "I'm afraid you've got me at a disadvantage, as you likely know more about me than even I do."

Etta swallowed again, feeling Henry's gaze bore into the side of her head.

"Well," she began, "I grew up with my mother in New York City some time past, ah, now."

The tsar raised his glass to Henry. "For your own protection, I'm sure. A wise choice, my friend. There are times I wish I had done it myself. But continue, child."

"I'm not sure there's anything else all that interesting," Etta said, then added, "beyond the obvious, I mean. I've recently begun to travel. I do play the violin, too."

"A fine pursuit!"

"The tsar is a great lover of music," Henry explained, visibly relaxing. "You should know, Your Imperial Majesty, that Henrietta has quite undersold herself. She's exceedingly talented and has won numerous international competitions for her skill."

Etta turned toward him, her heart in an absolute riot—because, for a minute, he'd sounded like he was *bragging* about her.

To the last tsar of Russia.

"Brilliant," the tsar said. "You'll play for me, won't you?"

"I—yes—what?" Etta blinked.

"She's got Tchaikovsky in her repertoire," Henry continued.

"I do, but—"

"The violin concerto, no doubt," the tsar said, crossing the room in several quick strides. He retrieved a small case from where it was tucked beneath the piano.

That looks like—

A violin case.

"Oh," Etta said, feeling rather stupid. "You meant right now."

The tsar's smile fell somewhat as he set the case down on his desk. "I shouldn't have presumed you'd feel comfortable—"

"No, I'm happy to," she said. The usual tingle of stage fright was gone, swept off by an overpowering sense of longing—for the instrument, for the music. Weeks had passed since the concert at the Met, and Etta hadn't gone longer than two days without playing since she was five years old. The anticipation hit her like a drug, and she was shaking with it.

"Wonderful. It will send us to dinner on a pleasing note. Henry, you'll accompany her, won't you?"

Henry stood, too, ignoring Etta's look of surprise. Accompany her—the violin concerto was generally played with a full orchestra, but there was, of course, a reduction for a simple violin and piano duet. Sure enough, Henry was moving toward the piano, trailed by the tsar. He took a seat at its bench.

"Perhaps just the first movement," he suggested. "Unless you'd prefer the second?"

"Yes—I mean, of course. The first movement is fine." Etta realized that she was still standing by the tsar's desk, stunned and trembling with nerves, and quickly moved to join them. She accepted the violin, taking a moment to simply feel the slight weight of it in her hands, to let her palm run down the graceful neck, along the striped grain of the wood.

There was a single moment when she debated the propriety of taking off her gloves, but went for it regardless, needing to feel the instrument against her fingertips. She tossed the long lengths of silk over the back of the nearest chair. If the tsar was scandalized, he didn't show it, merely wetting his mustache as he took another deep sip of his drink.

Henry pushed back his sleeves, giving himself more freedom of movement. Etta wondered if he was truly planning to play without any sheet music, and felt a swell of admiration despite herself.

"When you're ready," he said.

She drew the instrument up, tucking it beneath her chin. She'd played this piece any number of times, the last of which being the competition in Moscow; Alice had never favored it all that much, despite its dominance in their world, and loved to repeat an early review of the concerto that claimed to play it was to "beat the violin black-and-blue." She only hoped she remembered it well enough to do it justice, and not humiliate herself in front of her . . . in front of her father again, like she had at the Met concert.

Her left shoulder stung with the effort of keeping the instrument up, but Etta pushed past the strain, forced her hands to stop shaking, and drew the bow against the strings. She nodded to Henry, who made his gentle entrance into the piece on the piano, launching them into the music.

And that was how Etta found herself playing Tchaikovsky's Violin Concerto in the early twentieth century for Tsar Nicholas II.

The piece wasn't just hard, it was devilishly difficult, to the point that Etta wondered if Henry hadn't suggested it because of Tchaikovsky's obvious ties to Russia, but because he wanted to showcase her skills in the flashiest way possible.

But from the first note, it was like learning to breathe again—the simple relief of hearing the music, using that part of her mind and heart. The tactile presence of the violin swept her away as she began, gliding into the gorgeous framework Henry established, announcing the piece's main theme.

The first movement of the concerto built and built, adding a theme, repeating the main theme, creating variations that grew more athletic. The runs became faster, reaching an amazing cadenza that made Etta's heart feel like it would burst from the joy of it.

Her eyes flicked over to Henry, watching his own eyes slide shut, as if imagining each phrase as he carved it out on the keys. An expression of pure, unself-conscious joy.

This is where it came from, she thought in wonder. *I inherited it.*

And that was what she would still have, now that she had altered the course of her life. No concerts, or competitions, or debuts—simple joy. And, much like seeing how Henry had nudged the timeline to reveal its secrets, it wasn't bad; it was *different.* It was a new, sweeter future to match the world's.

When it was over, Etta reluctantly lowered the violin, and let the world back in.

The tsar clapped, rising to his feet. "Wonderful! Absolutely wonderful, the two of you. Perhaps we won't discuss business after, but will simply play—"

There was a faint knock at the door, and the same servant that had escorted them in stepped back inside at the tsar's command to enter.

"Ah, of course. Every dream ends. That will be dinner, then," he said, retrieving the violin from Etta.

As they walked to dinner, trailing the tsar, Henry whispered, "You've got an odd look on your face. Is something the matter?"

"No, I just . . ." Etta lifted her gaze off the plush carpet and looked at the man ahead of them. "It surprised me—that he's just a normal person. That he's a *real* person, I mean, not just words on paper or a photograph. And *nice.*"

Even with the infinite possibilities of time travel, Etta hadn't truly considered that she might *meet* someone famous or noteworthy. She and Nicholas had kept to themselves, avoiding the people around them as much as possible, and she'd assumed it was the same with other travelers, too. All her life, she'd thought of these historical figures as still lifes, to be studied through a layer of distance and glass like precious objects in a museum.

Henry snorted. "He's real, all right. And as fallible as any of us uncrowned mortals. He is rather nice to his friends, but of course, there have been many versions of his life that have seen him oppressive, cruel to those of other beliefs, foolish, and even blind to the needs of his most vulnerable subjects. You could say it was because he came to power too soon, before he was ready; because he picked poor advisors; or that it was a collision of unfortunate events. But I've seen it, time and time again: he cannot stop the march of a future that no longer has a place for him and his family."

"He's killed in this original timeline, too?" Etta whispered.

Henry rubbed a gloved hand over his forehead, considering his answer. "His death . . . it's inevitable. The events leading up to it grew worse and worse with Ironwood's interferences and alterations, but it has happened, and it will happen; only this time, it must play out the way it was intended a year from now."

He took a deep breath. "You remember what I told you before, that we must accept it, we must be ready to sacrifice what we have in order to see to the well-being of the whole? When I was younger, I came up with so many scenarios, so many different plans of how to save him, this one life, and still keep the timeline intact. But the pattern is undeniable. He is taken again and again; we are separated again and again. That is why I believe that certain things are destined; I can see the patterns, and cannot deny the repetition and the greater purpose they are trying to serve. At least in this timeline, I can be content in knowing the rest of his family will only go into exile."

A tremor of sadness in the words, but also resignation. "Etta . . . I wish I could spare you this, but it is inevitable that you, too, will be asked to relinquish something. You will see the pattern, too."

Etta tightened her grip on his arm, giving him a reassuring squeeze. In truth, she didn't know how to comfort him, or what to say, but she was grateful beyond words that he could see his friend again, even if it was for the last time. She would have shattered every rule the travelers had ever imposed if it meant being able to throw herself into Nicholas's arms and feel his steady heartbeat murmuring beneath her cheek.

As much as he presented himself to the world with a grin and an infectious laugh, every now and then Etta caught a glimpse of the part of himself that Henry tried to hide. It complicated her perception of him, made her want to study him that much more closely. She'd had a hard time seeing how her mother, who was so cold and sharp at times that she could cut without a single word, had ever found herself entangled with someone who acted as though laughing and smiling were as necessary to him as oxygen. But now Etta had seen the embattled parts of him; she'd witnessed that irresistible quality he had that made him a friend of tsars and Thorns alike.

"Henrietta . . . *Etta*," he corrected himself. Her heart gave a twist at his gentle tone. "You play exceptionally well. My compliments to Alice. I don't think she'd mind my saying that you surpass even her skill."

He'd heard Alice play at some point. She smiled sadly. It helped, somehow, to know that someone else remembered the way Alice had made her violin sing.

"Thank you," Etta said. "How long have you played the piano?"

"Nearly my whole life," Henry said. "From before I was tall enough to reach the pedals."

Etta nodded, her fingers pressing against his sleeve. "It must be hard to find time to play. What with all the traveling. Hiding. Scheming."

"Not as hard as you might think," he said. "I *make* time. It's true that altering timelines or events is a kind of creation, but there are always consequences, good or bad. Music is something I can create that is neither. It simply is the meeting of the composer's mind with my heart. Oh, dear—" He laughed. "Don't tell anyone I said that. It's rather maudlin, even for me."

Etta smiled. It had made perfect sense to her.

"Why do you play?" he asked her. "Not just play—why would you want to make it your life?"

Etta had been asked this question so many times over the years— by Alice, by reporters, by other performers—and had asked it of herself even more often. Every answer had been a reprise of the same practiced refrain. And yet here, with Henry, she felt safe enough to admit the other truths, the ones she had pushed so far back in her heart they'd begun to rust. The ones she hadn't even shared with Nicholas.

"I wanted to find something that would make Mom proud of me. Something I could excel at," she told him. "But some part of me thought that if I was out there performing, if everyone knew my name, I might reach my father or his family. They might recognize me. They'd hear my music and want to come find me. Know me." She let out a deep breath. "It's stupid, I know."

Up ahead, the tsar had slowed to greet Winifred and Jenkins near yet another of the palace's elaborate doors. Their voices carried down the hall, punctuated by polite laughter.

Just as Winifred turned to make her way over to them, Henry looked away, thumbing at his eye. When he looked back at her, nearly stricken, she wasn't sure what to do, other than tighten her hold on his arm.

They were still feeling around each other's edges. Trying to learn the same étude, each trial bringing them closer and closer to learning the skills of caring for the other.

"I heard you, Etta," he said softly. "I heard you."

CARTHAGE
148 B.C.

FIFTEEN

THE MAN IN THE DARKNESS STEPPED CLOSER, HIS FOOTSTEPS muffled by nearby insects and a cloud of disturbed birds launching into the night sky.

"That's quite far enough," Nicholas said, raising the sword so that its tip rested at the man's throat.

His eyes bulged at the implicit threat, but he did as he was told. Nicholas took careful stock of him. He was stooped at the shoulders, like a man who'd spent his life out in the fields, toiling over a plow. His red tunic was threadbare, nearly as weathered as the deep-set wrinkles in his ragged, dark skin. All of this was offset by a shock of white hair; his thick beard and brows looked as though they'd been left out to gather frost.

"What business do you have here, travelers?" the man demanded. "How did you find us?"

What Nicholas could see of the man's legs looked thin, almost knobby-kneed, and that general unsteadiness likely accounted for his slight limp and his reliance on a tall walking stick.

"My name is Nicholas Carter," he said. "We've come to trade information, nothing more."

"No, child, all you've done is bring the Shadows, disturb our peace," he said hoarsely, his gaze darting around the courtyard, as if expecting to find someone else there.

There was that word again, *Shadows*, and always whispered, as if to avoid summoning them.

Sophia snorted at the word *peace*. "It's not about Ironwood. We want a true trade—we have information we could share, but we've also got *food*"—she held up her sack of elephant feed—"food we'd be willing to part with for answers to a few questions that would stay between us. Which one are you, Remus or Fitzhugh?"

"Remus." The old man muttered something else to himself, one hand rubbing the other as he looped the bow over his shoulder. His gaze drifted away, his breath coming in quick, urgent bursts.

"Sir? Time is of the essence in this matter," Nicholas tried. The man leaped back as if struck.

"All right, yes, come with me," he said, voice strained. "Yes, follow me. Quickly now. It will be all right."

"We'll see about that," Sophia said, and her words leeched the rest of the color from the man's face.

His senses were piqued, his attention snared and drawn back toward the stables. Voices were rising, and the sound of the elephants' cries had ceased altogether. It seemed their diversion had run its course.

"It is lucky you survived," the man told them as they moved through the night, "but far luckier indeed that you did not cause a change to the timeline with that elephant stunt."

Fair point. Nicholas knew that his luck was bound to run out, but having received so little of it in his life, he was willing to push on to find its limits. Still, he couldn't release the last few tremors of doubt as he followed the man's unsteady steps any more than he could take his eyes from him. It was unfair, perhaps, given that the man had saved them when he could just as easily have left them to die on the attacker's blade, but he couldn't change his nature in a night.

"Ease up and unclench, will you?" Sophia muttered, taking notice.

"He's ancient. And he'll have a pot to boil whatever it is we just stole from the elephants."

"You're thinking with your stomach, not with your head," he sniped back quietly.

"Didn't you catch what he said about the *Shadows*?" she whispered. "He knows who they are—"

Remus spun around, his voice low. "For the love of Christ, do you want someone to hear you speaking another language and assume you've snuck in? I won't be saving you then, believe you me!"

Nicholas and Sophia kept their mouths shut. A good thing, because as they rounded onto the next street, Nicholas had to take a generous step back to avoid crossing into the path of several women heading the opposite way, toward the homes they had passed, where candles were lit and waiting for them. The ladies' dresses were longer and somehow more elegantly draped than the simple tunics of the men, their gauzy hems swirling around their sandaled feet. One nodded as Nicholas passed her, with dark hair shorn shorter than even Sophia's.

"Lice?" Sophia asked Remus cautiously, once they were clear of the street and onto a far smaller and quieter one.

He shook his head. "They cut their hair to give to the soldiers for their bows. Do you know nothing, child?"

Sophia made an insolent face behind his back.

"Why would they need to?" Nicholas asked. "I thought they were renowned for their military?"

"They are a fierce people," Remus said, his voice sounding steadier the farther they walked from the city's center, away from anyone who might overhear them. "Every man, woman, and child is or will be armed and expected to fight. Each home is a fortress in and of itself. They are rebuilding their arsenal."

"What happened to their original weapons?" Nicholas asked.

"When the Romans landed on these shores, they demanded hostages and the whole of the city's arms, which they were given. But that was not enough—they wished for the complete surrender of the city. The Carthaginians defied them, taunted them, even tortured Roman prisoners in full sight of the Roman army. And so it goes."

"The Romans are building something out in the harbor, aren't they?"

Remus gave him an exasperated look. "A mole, yes."

As he'd suspected—moles were massive structures, built from rock, stone, or wood, to be used as a kind of pier or breakwater. In this instance, it would seal up all of the warships he'd seen in the military harbor.

As the sun started to climb, they began their ascent up the hill toward the citadel that overlooked the harbor—Byrsa, the old man called it.

Nicholas kept his head down as they moved; the men and women here wouldn't be alarmed or find his dark skin particularly noteworthy, but he knew from long experience that men were unlikely to remember someone who didn't meet their gaze. His sandals shuffled along the worn stone, his thoughts dwindling to merely *left, right, left, right,* to order himself to keep going. He didn't look up until he was met with the sight of feet less than half the size of his own, bare and covered in cuts and sores.

The dark-skinned boy stepped aside quickly, allowing Remus, who was building speed like a churning storm, to hobble past. Sophia slid around Nicholas, shooting him an irritated look as she continued on ahead.

The boy couldn't have been more than eight or nine, Nicholas decided—too small, and wasted to the very bone. His tunic hung off his shoulders in tatters, knotted here and there in awkward lumps to keep it on him. The boy met his gaze from beneath his mass of matted hair. His dark eyes were bold with pride, in absolute defiance of his dismal state.

Nicholas knew that look well; the pride meant going hungry in silence, rather than lowering oneself to asking for charity, to begging. He'd been the same way, even as a slave, even once he was freed by the kindness of the Halls. If the captain hadn't force-fed him the first few nights, Nicholas wouldn't have eaten at all.

You've the pride of Lucifer, Hall had informed him. *It's the only thing that family gave you, and believe me, you don't need that inheritance.* Unbidden, his mind drew up the image of the child he and Sophia had seen earlier in the night, dead and wasted away from disease and hunger, left in the street like a common animal.

Nicholas gave the boy a tentative smile and lifted his bag from his shoulder, carefully removing the few things he might need from it, leaving only the food. The leather bag's design was simple enough to pass for something created in this time—and he doubted the boy would take care to notice it much at all. Careful not to say anything, he held it out toward him.

The boy stared at him, and Nicholas knew the moment he'd understood the gift. He snatched the strap of the bag from Nicholas's hands. Nicholas let out a faint laugh, but as he turned away, a small hand caught his wrist, forcing him to turn back around. The boy's fingers disappeared inside of his shirt, and he tugged off a thin strand of leather Nicholas hadn't noticed before. Dangling from it was a small pendant, just smaller than Nicholas's little finger. The boy held it up, gazing at him with fierce, dark eyes until Nicholas took it.

A trade, then. Nicholas nodded in thanks, and the boy turned and ran, never once looking back. He studied the unexpected gift, holding it up to the light. It was a face—glass that had been painted or colored somehow, and shaped to resemble a man with a curling row of hair, dark brows, large eyes, and a rather magnificent beard that extended from his chin in ringlets. An amulet, perhaps?

He shifted the objects he'd retrieved from his bag in his arms, and, with enough care that his hands shook from it, slid the glass bead onto the leather cord around his neck, next to Etta's earring.

"Carter!" Sophia barked.

Nicholas's long legs devoured the distance between him and Sophia and Remus, who had watched the exchange with suspicious eyes. He didn't look back—didn't want to give the boy the opportunity to refuse his gift.

Stay alive, he thought. *Stay alive. Escape.*

"You are *ridiculous*," Sophia said in a low voice. "How *will* you continue to play the hero if you don't eat?"

"I'll find something else," he said. *I've gone longer without.*

Hunger was tolerable. The alternative was to be haunted by those eyes, by the bitterest sort of regret that wouldn't ever dissolve, no matter how much sweetness the years brought. It wasn't a weakness to have those thoughts, to feel that need to help another, to save lives. It made one *human.* He couldn't help but think that the travelers had fallen too deep into the practice of being silent witnesses. It drained the empathy from them, allowed them to build a wall of glass between themselves and suffering.

Sophia looked at him, making a strained sound. "All you're doing is prolonging the inevitable. Isn't it better to go this way than suffer what the Romans have in store for him?"

I'm not heartless, she'd said. And so she wasn't. Their hearts were made of different fibers, and perhaps her heart was more durable for that sort of decision than his own.

He was too exhausted to argue with her. Sophia's feet, much like his own, were dragging across the stones. Even her words lacked their usual venom and conviction.

"Is Fitzhugh at home now?" Nicholas asked the old man instead.

Remus shook his head. "No. My husband's a physician, you see. He is out making his rounds to visit the ill. It was left to me to investigate who came through the passage."

"You heard it from all the way up here?" Nicholas asked, glancing back over his shoulder at the city spread out below. The pale hue of the limestone was all the more breathtaking in the early morning with the tint of violet spread over it.

He'd lost the sound of the passage as they'd slipped further into the city. All he could hear now was the distant banging of the blacksmiths, who had woken with the dawn.

"We're near the other passage," Remus said. "It resonates with its brother in the water. Dreadful noise, but useful in knowing when to expect company."

Nicholas nodded.

"Satisfied, detective?" Sophia asked. "Might we try for a bit of shutting up now? Tonight's given me a crashing headache."

Remus's pace slowed as they reached the next door. He turned one last time to press his fingers against his lips before pushing it open. It creaked painfully, scraping the uneven stone. Nicholas ducked beneath the low arch and stepped into a small, shady courtyard, one hand on the hilt of his sword.

"This way," Remus whispered. Nicholas cast one last look around, searching for any potential entrances. Piles of bows, swords, shields, and spears rested beside brooms and other simple household tools, waiting. A prickle of anxiety fizzed in his blood; there was one way in, yes, which meant it would be easier to keep watch for trouble, but it also meant there was only one way out if trouble did actually arrive.

The three of them went up a steep stack of steps to the second level, where a second door waited. Remus cast one last nervous glance around before opening it and ushering them inside.

The smell of earth and greens had bled into the dry air, giving the open room a musty, medicinal smell that instantly put Nicholas back in a place of unease. Physicians in his time were often no better than butchers, their tools as dull as their skills.

On the left side of the room was a bed pressed against the wall, with strands of greens left to dry over it. The opposite wall was dedicated to Fitzhugh's work—more drying herbs and plants, along with small vials and ceramic pots, a grinding stone, and a rudimentary scale. Across the room, below the windows, was a carefully arranged living area; there was a low table, a rug to cover the polished stone floor, a chair, and pillows on which to sit. At the center of it all was a hearth, with a pot boiling over, spitting bubbling water into the hissing fire below.

It was a comfortable home, but nothing like he would have expected for two travelers. To their credit, at least there were no outward hints that they weren't native to this era—most travelers, as he'd seen even with Etta's great-grandfather, couldn't resist the temptation to cobble together small stashes of trinkets and souvenirs. Instead, there were just a few small statues and stone figurines of foreign, ancient gods.

"We can eat and discuss whatever it is you're here for after I finish my rest, and you've had some yourself," Remus said, sitting on the bed and removing his battered shoes. "At a decent hour."

"Time is not on our side," Nicholas began, even as Sophia made herself a small bed from the pillows near the hearth and table.

"When is it ever, my lad," the man said, as the feather mattress and rope frame settled beneath him. "When is it ever?"

"How can you be sure the attackers will not bother us?" Nicholas asked. "That they haven't tracked us here?"

"They move in darkness," the man said, blowing out the candle on the table beside the bed. "We are safe. For now."

Nicholas released his frustration in a harsh breath, but found a place to stretch out on the rug. The uneven ground beneath him was as unforgiving as it was in every other century he'd recently visited. He took the opportunity to assess his aches and cuts, as well as the new, hot spikes of pain in his right hand. Holding it up, he examined the pattern etched into the ring in the soft morning light.

He tried tugging it off again.

Failed.

With another snort, he crossed his arms and turned his back to the wall, closing his dry eyes. But he did not sleep. His mind did not relent in trying to chase the ghost of Etta's face, remembering how sweetly her body had curved against his own. Nor did it allow him to ignore the familiar pressure of someone's gaze taking the measure of him.

But hours later, when Nicholas finally turned over to confirm his suspicions of being observed, Remus had dipped deeply into his dreams, and the only thing that moved beyond the door was the lonely wind.

HOURS LATER, AS THE SUN SWEPT INTO THE ROOM AND THE fire warmed its confines, Nicholas propped himself up against the table on the floor and attempted to stay awake. Or at least alert. Sophia, who had slept without a second thought, drummed her fingers on the low table, impatient for the man to finish brewing his tea and cooking the oats.

"Here you are," Remus said, offering a cup of the former to Sophia, wincing as the hot tea splashed out of the small wooden cup and onto his trembling hands. Without any sort of prompting, he pressed another cup into Nicholas's hands, turning back to fill one of his own.

"We need to agree to secrecy, before we begin," Nicholas said. "What we discuss here cannot leave this room."

Remus's brows rose. "Who do you think I would tell, beyond Fitzhugh? We don't exactly receive guests, and even if we wanted to, Cyrus has forbidden contact. I cannot contact my Jacaranda family any more than Fitz could his immediate Ironwood family. He would have us killed for disobeying his explicit orders."

Nicholas should have known that—he himself had been exiled, confined to his natural time. But the man's words did not sound promising for the information they needed.

"Let's get on with this business, then, my new friends," Remus said. "Ask me your questions. I have a few of my own."

Sophia blew on her cup of tea, then took a deep gulp. Her face screwed up, lips puckering. "Why does it taste like I'm drinking dirt?"

"It's *green tea*," Remus said indignantly. "It tastes of the pure earth. It's not readily available in this era and continent, so have some respect for my hospitality."

"Whatever you say."

Nicholas had always been one for coffee over tea, the bitterest, darkest coffee available, but he was willing to try any sort of stimulant to keep his thoughts sharp.

He raised his own cup to his mouth, letting it wet his lips. It smelled of wet grass, and what taste he got was sour, not at all fortifying or refreshing. Setting it on the ground beside him, he leaned forward against the table. "We're hoping to discover the last common years of the two most recent timeline shifts. Have you received any notices about them?"

The man looked stunned. "Oh, I'm afraid you've gravely overestimated how much contact we have with the outside world. In case it wasn't clear: none. We don't receive notices from the messengers anymore because we are not allowed to travel, and therefore any dangers the shifts present don't affect us. We've been trapped in this era for *years*, with no communication—no food, no assurances we'll ever be allowed to leave."

Damn it all, Nicholas thought, weary and frustrated down to his soul. But of course.

"You were stupid enough to think he'd forgive you if you came back groveling," Sophia said, one brow arched.

"I wished he'd just gone and executed us then, with all the others. The bastard put us here because he knew it would be our tomb, and that we'd think every day of what we did to spite him, and regret it," Remus said. "Now, Fitz and I only regret the cowardice of leaving the Thorns. It was rough living, especially when it seemed as if Ironwood had massacred half their ranks. But tell me—with everything going on, is he sufficiently distracted now for Fitz and I to make our leave to another era undetected? He told us there were men posted at the entrances to both passages to ensure we could not leave."

"There was no one at the one we came through," Sophia admitted. "Did you really not even check? Ever?"

"No. His rage is absolute, and we were foolish enough to think we might earn our forgiveness eventually, with good service to him." Remus laughed darkly. "What a fool I've been. Well, no more. Fitz and I will accompany you to the other passage out of the city when he returns. We'll disappear this time."

Nicholas approved of the manner in which the old man's words vibrated with fuming resentment. Rubbing his tingling hand, he watched Remus for any signs of deceit, and found only the portrait of a man hardened by the bitter taste of disappointment.

"I thought for sure you came because of the work I'd done on the Shadows—the research Cyrus had me conduct," Remus said, rising to stir the oats. Testing their consistency, he scooped out two steaming bowls to serve to his guests. "Ancient traveler lore, yes, I can assist you with. It's very likely the only thing I'm good for these days. The rest is beyond my sight and knowledge."

Nicholas was momentarily distracted by how hard he had to grip the wooden spoon in his hand to feel it. Batting down the fear pawing at his heart, he turned the whole of his attention to the food. The oats were plain and burned his tongue, but Nicholas was sure neither he nor Sophia had ever consumed a meal with more speed.

"Is there anyone who might be willing to help us discover the last common year without it getting back to Ironwood?" Nicholas asked, setting his empty bowl aside.

Remus considered this. "Most of his large alterations were made in the nineteenth and twentieth centuries. You might try asking a guardian named Isabella Moore, in Boston. Ironwood had her son killed around the same time Fitzhugh and I left to join the Thorns, and I know her to be well connected, but with no love of the man. Try her any time after 1916 and before 1940."

Another lead. Which might go just as far as this one did in answering their question: nowhere. He forced his good hand to release the edge of the table he'd been gripping.

"What did you mean when you said you thought we were coming because of the . . . Shadows?" Sophia asked, blowing on the surface of her tea before taking a deep gulp of it. "What do you know of them?"

Remus looked offended when she let out what was either a small hiccup, belch, or some charming combination of the two.

"First, I think you ought to be honest about what you're truly searching for," he said, "for I've only ever known them to hunt one thing: the astrolabe."

Nicholas felt the skin on the back of his neck start to crawl. Even Sophia choked on the last sip of her tea.

"Surprised?" Remus said. "Cyrus never changes, not even in the most dangerous of times. But then of course, knowledge is power—all the more reason for him to hoard the truth about its history and nature."

That, Nicholas could not dispute. "And you know of it how?"

"Before Ironwood did away with the position, I was a record-keeper for the families for longer than you've been alive," Remus explained. "I know things that would slow the blood in your veins. It's one of the reasons he was so irate that we left, you see. He did not want anyone else to have that knowledge, least of all Henry Hemlock. But he cannot execute me, either, for the old records were burned and I might have one last detail or piece of knowledge he needs. I know that, to create a passage, legend holds that you must have the astrolabe, but you must also have something from the time and year you wish to go. I know the songs all others have forgotten."

Sophia gave Nicholas a nod, confirming all of these things.

"What do you know of alchemy?" Remus began. "Of its principles?"

"I know it's a load of garbage," Sophia said. "Outdated hogwash that has spurred on countless pitiful idiots to waste their time trying to turn lead to gold, look for a cure for all ailments, and find a way toward immortality."

"Sophia," Nicholas said, his tone warning. He didn't want to scold her, but he wanted to get what information they could and leave this place as quickly as possible.

"You've covered some of it, yes, but the principles of alchemy extend far beyond the tangible. You might say that it is the search for understanding about the true nature of life, and how energy can be manipulated: a careful study of the beautiful mysteries of life, death, and perhaps resurrection. 'As above, so below, as within, so without, as the universe, so the soul.'"

That might explain some of the odd symbols he had seen in the Belladonna's store and workshop, then. It was as much a belief system as a craft or profession.

"There once lived a man who achieved this perfect knowledge by broadening his understanding of how *immortality* might be accomplished—what better way to conquer life than to destroy that which limits it?"

"Time," Nicholas finished. "You mean to say . . ."

"This man, the originator of our line," Remus continued, "harnessed these energies, transmuted them into something new, something tied to the earthly influence of his own blood. It was contained within a device, a key that allowed him to control it. Three copies of this master key were made for his three children, but each copy was weaker than the next. His children fought viciously for control of the original version, each with what they thought was the true path for it, until one day, two of the children turned on the youngest, who they felt was the alchemist's favorite. When the alchemist attempted to intervene, both he and the youngest child were killed in the fray."

"There's the Ironwood in them," Sophia muttered.

"In the chaos, the master key was stolen by a fourth child, an illegitimate bastard, a by-blow of some poor wench."

Sophia straightened at that, her top lip peeling back in a snarl at the word *bastard*. And, for the first time in a long while, Nicholas realized he had never quite considered her own parentage in this context—the same context as his own.

"Having lived and worked in the shadows of his legitimate brothers and sister, having been the alchemist's apprentice, he knew how to harness the power of the master key—the master astrolabe—and he knew well that the others would never let him possess it. And so the apprentice ran for centuries, weaving in and out of time until his trail became too muddied for the others to follow with the lesser astrolabes," Remus said. "Years passed, and he began to release his fears, fathering families across the continents. But the continued use of the astrolabe had altered the composition of his body, with curious results. His life was extended a century beyond what was natural, and the children he sired inherited the ability to travel through the passages he had created without needing to be in possession of the astrolabe. Almost as if, by using it, he had absorbed some of its essence into himself, and had become an extension of it. The same proved true of his remaining half siblings, and the eldest finally succeeded in finding his bastard brother, by then old and decrepit, and killing him."

"How, if their lives were prolonged?" Sophia asked.

"Their lives were prolonged and they aged and aged and aged, but only so long as they were not unnaturally interrupted by, say, foul murder," Remus said. "Though our bloodlines have been diluted, and we no longer live beyond the normal years of men, some small spark of the astrolabe remains, allowing us to travel."

Nicholas shook his head. The talk of alchemy, this kind of immortality outside of heaven, was almost too heathen to believe.

And yet . . . he thought again grimly.

There was a kernel of pure, primal truth in Remus's tale—fear, even more so than greed, was a powerful motivator, especially when coupled with the determination to survive. However the story may have been embellished, there was some validity to it.

"The daughter fell to history's mercy, and no record of her remains, other than that her elder brother stole her astrolabe and used it in some unnatural way. The record is unclear, only that the copies disappeared. There is only one left now—the master astrolabe—and, if Cyrus's wild beliefs are true, the eldest son still hunts for it."

"I thought each of the four families had their own astrolabe?" Nicholas said. The Lindens, then, had held the master copy in their family for generations.

"Perhaps they possessed them for a time, but all were stolen back. The eldest son has quite the force behind him—travelers taken from their families, who have had their lives stolen and shaped to serve only him. For lack of a better, proper term, they were noted only as Shadows in our histories." Nicholas's mouth tightened at that, a small flinch that Remus caught. The old man chuckled before he continued. "I can sense the disbelief in you both. I realize how it all sounds, of course."

"Like bullshit you're trying to sell us," Sophia snarled.

"There are things in our forgotten history that are so ancient, one must search for the few clues embedded in our lore, our shared nightmares. Generations ago, the old records vault was burned in what was said to be the fault of a single candle, and now, so little proof remains of the alchemist and the Shadows that many travelers simply refuse to believe in their existence. Missing children are explained away as having been orphaned by the timeline, or that they simply wandered off into passages, never to be seen again. The mind can dream up any number of explanations for dark things, of course."

Nicholas shook his head, rubbing at his eyes once more. "What is the role these Shadows play, then?"

"It is said they work on behalf of the alchemist's surviving son, carrying out his wishes and stealing traveler children to continue a cycle of service to him and his mission to find the master astrolabe," Remus said, as if this were not absurd. "Though their story itself has been lost, and fewer and fewer children are lost, the fear is still taught to traveler children to this very day, however unwittingly. Tell me, girl, that you don't recall the old song: *From the shadows they come, to give you a fright . . .*"

Sophia surprised Nicholas by easily finishing the rhyme. *"From the shadows they come, to steal you this night."* She looked unimpressed, to say the least. "You don't need to shill bad poetry."

"Finish it, girl," Remus said. "How does the rhyme end?"

She gazed at the man in defiance, but softly sang, *"Mind the hour, mind the date . . . and find that path which does not run straight."*

"These Shadows are the ones who hunt you now," Remus said. "The shadows of his glorious sun. They will stop at nothing to prevent you from taking possession of the astrolabe, should you find it. Your paths have crossed, unfortunately, and now there is no way to disentangle them."

"Is there really nothing to be done about it?" Nicholas asked. "You read nothing else about their methods in your time as a record-keeper?"

The old man shrugged the question away as he stood and went back to the hearth, this time for his own meal. In the silence that followed, he was absorbed in the simple, hypnotic task of stirring, and stirring, and stirring. A spark of instinct began to tug at Nicholas's ear, begging an audience.

Sophia, in deep contemplation of this information, pressed her face into her hands, breathing deeply. But Nicholas felt too anxious to remain seated, too full of absurd stories to sit idly by. He began to do laps around the cramped room, stopping occasionally to study a small piece of decorative tile, a bust, small wooden boxes. One of which yielded a solid, rectangular object wrapped in burlap: a harmonica.

It was one of those painful moments when need was at odds with morality. His fingers ran over the cool, shining surface, and he leaned over, far enough to see the reflection of his haggard face. He'd stolen as a child—scraps of food, affection, his own freedom for a time—and the thought of doing so now stirred a poisonous self-loathing inside of him. Nicholas shut the box and turned to the spot where Fitzhugh Jacaranda ground his medicines and did whatever it was physicians or ship surgeons or healers did when they weren't pulling rotten teeth or sawing off limbs.

Below the wooden bench, tucked nearly out of sight, was a stiff, cylindrical leather bag with a long strap, its drawstring opening just wide enough to look into. Glancing back to ensure the man was busy with the pot on the hearth, he nudged it open the rest of the way with his toe. It was filled to the brim, nearly spilling over with sachets, neatly wound bandages, and those same small vials he saw on the table. Beneath that was a layer of tools, primed and ready for use.

That nagging feeling was back, until realization lit Nicholas's mind like a blast of gunpowder, blowing him back off his feet. Studying the man out of the corner of his eye, he forced his voice to remain even, and took a deep breath before asking, "Why, if Fitzhugh is making his rounds as a healer, has he left his bag here?"

Remus stopped stirring, his shoulders bunching up as he froze in place. Nicholas's heart made the dive from his chest to the very pit of his stomach, and his hand came to rest on the hilt of his sword.

In the breath of silence that passed between them, Remus reached for one of the nearby knives, his hand shaking as it closed around the hilt and he brandished it.

"Don't run. You'll only make it worse for yourself," Remus said. "And you won't get far at all."

PETROGRAD
1919

SIXTEEN

ETTA WAS MISTAKEN IN ASSUMING THE "SMALL DINING Room" would bear some sort of resemblance to the simple dining room you'd find in any house—slightly worn furniture, a floor scuffed by chairs and feet, a few personal touches here and there. Instead, it was a miniature version of the grander rooms they'd passed on the way in, with one chandelier instead of five, six, or seven.

There was almost too much to absorb at once—Etta saw her stunned reflection in the mirror that hung over the small fireplace, just past the gold clock and candelabras artfully arranged on the mantel.

Etta was led to a seat two over from the tsar, beside Henry, who sat at his right. Winifred, preening, sat to the tsar's left, and beside her was Jenkins, who seemed as much at a loss as Etta over what to do with himself. Missing were the other Thorn bodyguard and Julian, who, despite being invited to the palace, was not welcome in the tsar's company. She thought that wise, given the havoc his grandfather had brought to this side of the world in the other timeline.

A footman pulled out her yellow-silk-covered chair for her, guiding it back in once she'd settled into place. Now that she was sitting, the arrangement of the table seemed egalitarian—the tsar could easily look at and speak to everyone around him. It did have the trappings of some kind of a family dinner in that way, at least.

And then, the elaborate dance that was their meal began. Soup was spooned into Etta's bowl, and small meat pies were placed on one of the plates. Etta's eyes slid over to Henry, watching him watch the tsar. Once he began eating, so did Henry, and, for that matter, so did Etta. With gusto. She'd had a bit of bread in San Francisco, and a little fruit at the hotel where they'd changed, but nothing as filling as the rich, creamy soup, or as warm as the meat pies.

"Tell me," Henry said into the silence, "how does your wife fare, Your Imperial Majesty? She was unwell during my last visit, and I regret I wasn't able to see her."

"She's much improved, thank you," the tsar said. "She is enjoying life outside of Petrograd, and it gives me pleasure to see her so content."

"Indeed," Henry said. "I'm glad to hear it."

As he finished his course, Henry set his cutlery on the plate and his hands in his lap. Within seconds, one of the waiters was there to clear. Winifred did the same, and like magic—or at least a well-rehearsed stage production—another waiter swept in.

Etta did the same, and was still surprised by the speed at which her bowl and small plate were taken, and by the sudden realization that each diner had his or her own waiter to serve them. The tsar's, even more surprisingly, was an older gentleman, who seemed to bow beneath the weight of his heavy tray. Etta watched in sympathy as the tsar subtly helped steady the waiter's trembling arm when he refilled his wineglass.

Winifred's and Jenkins's waiters exchanged a glance over the table at the sight, young and robust compared to Etta's own waiter, who looked as if he was on the verge of being ill. He was pale-faced and sweating profusely at the brow as he carried another tray out.

The next course was fish, *Dviena sterlet* in champagne sauce, for which Winifred went into such overblown raptures that Etta felt embarrassed to be sitting at the same table as her. Next came chicken in a richly flavored sauce she couldn't identify, and, because that wasn't enough meat, a course of ham. Each was served with a different kind of wine; there was so much of it that Winifred looked ready for a nap, and Etta herself had to switch to mineral water to keep from sliding out of her chair.

Some pirate, she thought. *Can't even handle a few glasses of wine.*

Etta was still picking at her ham when the tsar finished his plate. Another apparent rule: when the tsar was finished, so were you, regardless of whether or not you were still eating. Etta lost her plate with the fork still in her mouth.

"Peach compote, my favorite!" Winifred crooned as the next batch of small plates was brought out. Jellies, ice cream, compotes—Etta was afraid that if she ate even one more bite she might be sick. Her waiter might *actually* have been sick. His hands shook as he set the last of the plates down in front of her, shook so badly that the porcelain clattered against the table. Etta could have sworn she felt a drop of sweat hit her bare neck. She turned toward Henry, to find his narrowed eyes already tracking the progress of Etta's waiter as he made his way back around the table. Etta felt a jump in her pulse like a staccato note.

"I remembered as much," the tsar said. "I'm sure they had quite the time finding peaches during this season, but it's worth it to see the smile on your face."

Etta's waiter had left the room at last, and a new waiter swept in, moving to the sideboard. He lifted a wine bottle out of an ice bucket. It looked no different than any of the others, with the tsar's monogram and the imperial insignia, but as he turned back to the table, he held it by its neck, not its base.

"You are too kind," Winifred said. "I'm sure it was—"

Jenkins lurched up out of his seat. *"Iron—"*

One minute Etta was seated; the next she was falling back, knocked over by the force of Henry's arm as it smashed across her chest. In the sliver of an instant before she hit the ground, she saw the waiter raise the bottle of wine and send it sailing down onto the table, between the tsar and Winifred. Just before the glass shattered, two words tore from the man's throat.

"Za Revolyutziu!"

The whole of Henry's weight drove into her, knocking the breath from her as he covered her. The walls and ceiling above her seemed to run with colors, as if washed with rain. Time trembled, thundering with the force of the oncoming change. And with an eardrum-piercing roar, the air exploded into a tidal wave of fire, and the floor disappeared beneath them.

CARTHAGE
148 B.C.

SEVENTEEN

THE FIRELIGHT CAUGHT THE LONG BLADE OF REMUS Jacaranda's knife as he held it between them, but the man's face was in shadow. The only sound in the room beyond the popping fire was Nicholas's harsh breathing.

Finally Remus said, his voice small and quaking, "You have to understand. . . . There is nowhere we can go. . . . This is the only way."

"The only way to *what*?" Nicholas demanded. His eyes slid over to Sophia, who was still sitting at the table, her head in her hands. He hissed at her, "Get up, will you?"

"To survive. None of us can survive without Cyrus's protection, without kin or kindness. There is nowhere we can go that he will not find us, that the Thorns will not try to kill us for betraying them, too. We need him. I need him to *trust* me again—"

"*Sophia,*" Nicholas hissed. "We're leaving."

"It's a sign of how much he wants you," Remus said, trying to straighten his hunched shoulders, "that a runner came even to *us* to promise a bounty. This is our way back to his good graces."

"All of those things you said before, about being free, escaping him—why can't that be true? Why not leave with us now?"

"It will not work, it will not work. . . ." The weakness, that pathetic quality to the old man, had made Nicholas dismiss the threat of him so easily, knowing he could be overpowered with ease. Twice now, he'd been tricked. Hatred scorched his heart. There truly was no end to the villainy travelers possessed. Each was more self-serving than the next.

"So Fitzhugh has gone to bring back the cavalry, has he?"

Damn his eyes. He and Sophia wouldn't make it back to the passage in the water, but he might be able to find the other one the man had spoken of, if she would just—

Nicholas turned toward her at the sound of the first, retching gasp. Sophia jerked back from the table with a rattling cough, her hands seeming to spasm against the wood.

"What's the matter?" Nicholas asked her. "Sophia?"

"Can't—" she gasped out, "can't feel—legs—"

Nicholas spun toward the man, drawing his sword so quickly, it sang as it sliced the air. "What have you done?"

Remus smiled, backlit by the hearth.

"Did you know," he began, his voice brittle, "that the clans of the families united under the names of trees because they thought it was a clever way of symbolizing their reach into the future, and their roots winding deep into the past? Ironwood, Jacaranda, Linden . . . I've always thought that the Hemlocks picked their name not for the tree, however, but for the flowering plant."

"You—" Sophia choked out.

Nicholas stilled, hollowed by his words. The flowering plant. But then, that was . . .

Holy God.

"That's right," Remus said, smiling. "The Hemlocks are poison itself, and they inflict their terror in the same manner as the *tea* you drank. They identify what it is you desire, lure you in with promises of trust and respect, only to trick you into doing their bidding, into believing their lies about the timeline."

Sophia turned to Nicholas, her face etched with naked terror. That alone set his blood to boiling. For someone so unacquainted with fear to have that expression—he was sure it would be seared on his memory forever. Both hands were clawing at the muscles of her legs, as if trying to work the feeling back into them by force.

"You won't be able to return now, will you?" Remus sneered at her. "I've put myself beyond your reach, and you matter so little to this world that the timeline has not even shifted to account for your impending death."

Nicholas came down on the man like a thunderbolt, forcing him up against the hearth, close enough for his tunic to smolder and for the stench of burned hair to pierce the air. Remus's smile faltered, his eyes flaring.

"You didn't . . ."

"Drink your nasty concoction?" Nicholas sneered. "No, I did not, sir."

Remus slashed wildly with his knife, catching Nicholas across the back of his sword hand and nicking his jaw. He slammed the man against the wall, hard enough this time to knock the breath from his lungs and the knife from his fingers. It clattered to the ground, and Nicholas kicked it into the hearth.

The old man's face scrunched up mockingly, as if daring Nicholas to push him into the flames as well. Nicholas's hand knotted in the front of the man's tunic, giving him a warning shake. "Is there an antidote? Tell me, damn you!"

The bulk of his fury wasn't even directed at Remus Jacaranda— Nicholas could have punched himself for missing the signals, the clues. Even when he'd noticed the other man stalling, he hadn't pinned any sort of purpose to it.

"You'll find out soon enough," Remus said, eyes sliding over to Sophia, who was twisting around on the ground, struggling to rise onto her feet. "You were fools to come here—"

Nicholas smashed the hilt of the sword against the man's temple, knocking him clear into unconsciousness. He barely managed to keep his grip on him, yanking him forward out of the flames and letting his prone form slam to the ground.

The fool you *are,* Nicholas thought, *if you think for one second that Ironwood will ever show you mercy.*

"Nic—Cart—"

He spun back toward Sophia, kneeling beside her. Her hand lashed out; he caught it, giving what he hoped was a reassuring squeeze. What did he know about hemlock, other than that it had killed Socrates? "Do you know any sort of antidote?"

Her face was distorted by pain and panic, but she still managed to give him an incredulous look.

Damn. Who would know how to help her? They couldn't stay here in Carthage; they didn't speak the language, they didn't know how to find another physician, and it would be too easy for them to be tracked.

A crack of thunder cut through the clear morning sky; Nicholas jerked at the drumming beat that muffled the crackling pops of the fire, rivaling the sound of the Romans hammering out in the harbor. The other passage.

No time, he thought, *no time—*

He dove toward the ground, scooping up his possessions and stuffing them into Sophia's bag, looping it over his shoulder. He turned back to see her struggling to compose her face and failing.

"Pardon me," he said, bending down to scoop her up off the ground. One of her hands came up, smacking him in the face in protest. "I wasn't aware you walking out of here on your own was still an option, but if you think you can fly out on pride alone, by all means . . ."

She went very still.

"I thought not."

He rose onto unsteady feet, his vision blacking out as the blood left his head. He wasted precious seconds waiting for his exhausted body to steady before carrying her to the door. Her skin had gone the sickly shade of a fish left too long out of water, and her trembling hands . . .

Medicine. Surely they wouldn't have made the poison without an antidote? Surely there was something here if Fitzhugh Jacaranda truly was a healer? Surely?

Nicholas carried her over to the worktable, setting her down only long enough to pick up the man's bag and cinch the opening closed. He had them to the door in two quick strides when he doubled back to the chest, where he'd seen the small wooden box. With a huff, he plucked the harmonica out of its bindings and slid it into Sophia's bag. They wouldn't need it now, not with the passage bellowing loud enough for all of creation to hear, but he couldn't trust the future to bring the next one to him so easily.

He kicked the door open, shifting Sophia from his arms to over his shoulder. She hit him weakly in protest.

"Be easier to run—" The words died in his throat. From his vantage point on the second story of the building, he could see over the courtyard's wall into the street below.

Four figures were shouldering quickly through the milling crowds—four men, in a sea of women and children. The one leading the way at the front wore a faded blue tunic, his head ringed with blond, strawlike hair, clearly older than the rest. He looked to be in danger of being trampled by the men charging up behind him. Their "tunics" were poor imitations of togas, with sheets likely stripped off a nearby bed in a hurry—worse, their hair was still parted and slicked down in the style of the nineteenth or twentieth century. One even had a dark, neatly trimmed mustache like a slug above his upper lip.

It was a surprising lack of planning by a group of Ironwoods, who usually prided themselves on prudence and an overabundance of caution to avoid tampering with the Grand Master's timeline.

Not for the first time, Nicholas wondered what price Ironwood had put on his life. Most travelers wouldn't risk the old man's wrath, or throw away decades of conditioning and training, for anything less than a tidy sum. He felt a foolish swell of pride at that.

"It's just up here," he heard the old man in front—Fitzhugh?—say.

"Your tip better be good, old man—" groused the traveler behind him. Miles Ironwood, of course. The last time he'd seen the man, Miles had been ordered by Ironwood to pummel him with his fists for Julian's death. What a charming reunion this would be.

No time.

"Who . . . ?" Sophia asked.

"Miles Ironwood," he said.

"Always . . . wanted to . . . stab him."

"Well, here's your opportunity," he said. "Don't die before you give me the pleasure of watching you do it."

The house had the same problem the city did: if the Ironwoods were coming through the courtyard, then he and Sophia had run out of exits. Unless . . .

Nicholas made for the stairs that led up to the next level, and the next one after that. Sophia went alarmingly slack against his shoulder. "Sophia? *Sophia!*"

"Hey!" The shout rose from the street, cutting through the din of voices. *"Carter!"*

His legs burned as he raced up the uneven stairs, Sophia bouncing against his shoulder, his whole body quaking with the effort of keeping them upright. Third story, fourth, fifth—he nearly lost his footing as they reached the roof, momentarily distracted by the heavy pounding of steps behind him. He swung them both around, scanning the roofs around him for the nearest one to jump to.

His breathing was so labored, tearing in and out of him, that he didn't hear the whistle of the arrow at all—only felt the pain of it slamming into his shoulder. Nicholas staggered forward, knocked off-balance by the force of the blow.

"Carter, stop!" one of the men shouted. "You'll only make it worse for yourself!"

Make it worse how? As far as he was concerned, these men would only be taking him back to Ironwood one way: dead. And he still had too much to accomplish before he'd ever let that happen.

He still had to find Etta.

Nicholas dug deep into the well of his strength, moving to the far end of the roof, trying to judge whether or not the distance would be too great to throw Sophia, when he heard a sharp whistle.

It took him a moment to locate the source: a small, dark-robed figure, crouched on the roof just beyond the one he'd been studying, waving him forward. His heart surged with the hope that it was Rose, that he might finally achieve the dream of strangling her for this mess she'd tossed them all into—but he wasn't, to his surprise, disappointed to realize that the mystery figure was Li Min. If the choice was between Ironwood's men and a thief who was at least clever enough to find them a way out of Carthage . . . well, the choice was rather simple.

"Apologies," he told Sophia as he slid her down off his shoulder.

"—what—"

He tossed her like a basket, wincing as she struck the solid roof. He reached back, gritting his teeth, and snapped off the long end of the arrow, ignoring the warmth soaking through his tunic. There was only about a yard of distance between the two buildings, and he crossed it without trouble. Li Min met him there, kneeling to help him pick Sophia back up.

"Ma'am, are you here to help for your own mysterious reasons, or are you here to kill her for stealing your money?" he asked, his face serious. "Because I haven't the time for the latter, and your competition is arriving shortly."

Li Min looked up from her study of Sophia's ashen face. "What has she been given?"

"Hemlock." Saying the word aloud made the immense danger of it tangible, gave the threat new life.

"Quickly, then," Li Min said. "We haven't much time."

Out of other options, his body fast approaching that murky line of uselessness, Nicholas followed her over to the next roof.

"Drop," she told him, eyes flickering to something just over his shoulder.

He barely had time to take a knee before she flung a small knife from the depths of her hooded cloak, striking the first man at the dead center of his heart. The weight of his body sent the others tumbling back down the stairs. The one who managed to remain on his feet found another knife lodged directly in his throat.

Nicholas turned back to Li Min, only to find her already making her way down the stairs winding around the back of the building.

"This way, this way," she called. "Keep up!"

"Keep up, she says," he muttered, trying to pick up his pace without sending both himself and Sophia into a tragic tumble.

Li Min was incredibly light on her feet, not difficult for her diminutive size; still, he felt like an inelegant beast lurching along behind her. He was beginning to lose feeling in his left arm, where he felt the tip of the arrow scraping against the bone. Nicholas couldn't focus on that thought without feeling like he was about to retch; instead, he turned what remained of his drifting attention to maintaining his grip on Sophia. The voices shouting in English were still so close, tearing through the unpleasant stillness of the besieged city.

He was grateful when his feet were back on solid ground, but there was no time to stop and clear the darkness edging into his vision. His eyes tracked Li Min as she wove in and out of the startled crowds around her like a dolphin leaping through waves. Someone—a woman—put a concerned hand on his arm as he passed, but Nicholas brushed it off and kept going, his stomach tightening as they continued up the hill to the buildings crowning the Byrsa.

Just before they reached the apex of the hill, Li Min took a sharp turn and ducked between the last two homes, kicking open a gate that stood in her way. There, just beyond a shaft of light pouring into the narrow alley, was the shimmering entrance to the passage.

As if sensing them, the pitch of its voice grew higher. Nicholas felt himself faltering, choking on dust and the metallic tang of blood, but he gave himself one last shove forward and felt himself vanish like a passing breeze.

PETROGRAD
1919

EIGHTEEN

ALICE HAD TOLD ETTA ONCE THAT IN ORDER TO BECOME A concert violinist, she would need to protect four things above all else: her heart, from criticism; her mind, from dullness; her hands, so she would never falter in eking out the notes; and her ears, so that she could always judge the quality of the sound she was producing.

But in that moment, Etta couldn't hear anything over the sharp, painful ringing that jabbed like knives into her head. The weight of the world pressed down on her chest and shoulders, smothering her next few breaths.

She forced her eyes open, gagging on the thick air.

The cloud of smoke masked everything, creating a dreamlike haze, even as fire raced up the silk panels hanging from the wall, scorching the plaster. The chandelier above the table had shattered, glass raining down like ice on the wreckage below. And the table . . . the table and a section of the floor beneath it had caved in, leaving a jagged, gaping hole. Etta's eyes stung as she blinked, searching for the others through the embers rising up.

They were gone—the tsar, Winifred, Jenkins. The waiter. They'd gotten out, then—rescuers had already taken them to get help—

No.

A chill of sudden certainty crept over her, stifling the scream in her throat.

No.

They hadn't gotten out. There would have been no time to move away from the blast. Which meant that . . .

They fell through the floor. Or they . . . their bodies had . . . the blast . . .

Etta gagged again, her chest too tight to breathe. There was a stabbing in her side that seemed to drive deeper and deeper each time she shifted, trying to push the crushing weight off her chest and bring air into her lungs. One hand was pinned beneath her back, the other between her chest and the warm mass on top of her.

Henry.

"Henry . . ." Etta felt the word leave her throat, but couldn't hear it above the ringing in her ears. "*Henry! Henry!*"

He'd managed to throw himself over her, covering her almost completely. Her heart began to ricochet around her rib cage, beating so fast, so hard, she was terrified it might burst.

His face was turned away from her, one arm drawn up over it protectively. But he wasn't moving. *He wasn't moving.*

Etta dragged her hand out from where it was trapped between them, her still-healing shoulder screaming in protest. Without the benefit of her hearing, with the smoke still churning around them like waves, Etta felt like she was moving underwater, watching the distorted images of life beyond the surface. Her hand flopped around, touching the exposed, raw skin of Henry's back; he'd been burned by the blast. She began to tremble as she felt up his neck, searching for a pulse.

Don't die, don't die, please—

It took her a moment to sort her own shaking from the faint murmur beneath his skin, but it was there. He was alive, if just barely.

With as much care and strength as she could muster, she rolled his weight off her, just enough to slide out from beneath him, but not enough to flip him onto his scalded back. The stench of burned flesh and hair made the bile rise again in her throat. She had to press a fist against her mouth to keep from retching when she looked over and saw what remained of Winifred. *Oh my God, oh my God—*

Iron—Jenkins had shouted *Iron*, unable to finish the word, to fully name the assassin. *Ironwood.* The waiter, the *assassin*, had shouted a word she hadn't been able to make out, but she'd recognized the moment when the timeline had shifted again.

Henry had been right—Cyrus Ironwood *had* sent agents out to push the timeline back to his version . . . but this wasn't what had happened in the timeline she had grown up in. This couldn't be Ironwood's timeline. Which would make it . . . a new one?

Her hatred made it feel as though her whole soul had caught fire.

The floor beneath her feet was still crumbling; she felt a section of it collapse and realized she'd lost both shoes in the explosion. It wasn't safe—Etta felt a wave of panic swelling, threatening to wash away whatever rational thoughts she had left as she surveyed the room. Its bright, glorious colors and shining gold had been replaced by shards of glass, splashes of blood and cinders.

She was alive. She had to stay alive. She had to—just breathe—just get out—

The ringing was so piercing that she could think of nothing else. She reached down on unsteady legs and got her arms under Henry's, circling around his chest. The open wounds on his back oozed blood onto her dress, and the mere touch was enough to make him groan; Etta felt the vibration move through his body.

The jagged mouth of the floor revealed the smoldering room below. The fragments of metal and wood that had flown like shrapnel sliced through her stockings, lacerating her heels and ankles. She winced as Henry's long legs butted and bobbed helplessly against the ground. The only way she could move him was through sharp, short surges of strength, and she could already feel herself fading when a door appeared through the smoke. It had been left open, a tray of food overturned nearby.

The smoke had already drifted into the hall, but Etta felt herself take her first real breath as she put Henry down, carefully laying him out on the plush carpet. She knelt, searching his face again for signs of life. He'd cracked his forehead against something—a knot had formed on his right temple, and blood continued to trickle down his cheek.

She should have surged up onto her feet and started to run back the way they had come through the palace, but Etta found herself rooted there, unable to move when parts of her felt like they were fading.

She'd only just found him, and now . . .

Etta choked on an unwelcome sob, unwilling to release that last bit of control she had over herself until she could *think*.

What would it have been like, she wondered, to stay with the Thorns? Her mind played scene after scene, waltzing through the possibilities. To be with a father who wouldn't use her, who appreciated her talent, who explained their way of life, who showed some sliver of interest in her beyond some task he was saving her for in the future. To strike back against Ironwood until his grip on their kind dissolved into memory. To find Nicholas, and bring him to a group that might appreciate and respect him the way he deserved. To see the whole of time, the scale of everything her beautiful world could offer. . . .

"Etta."

With the piercing whine in her ears from the explosion, Etta would never be certain if she'd actually heard her mother, or imagined her voice the instant she felt the deadening weight of Rose's presence. She turned slowly, and a moment later her mother took shape in the smoke.

When she'd been taken by Ironwood, drawn into his net of deception, Etta would have done anything to see her mother and have her explain what was truly happening. But now she knew, and it had come only through loss and the most devastating of betrayals. Staring at

Rose now, truly seeing her, Etta wondered how she had ever missed the tremor just below the surface of cold calculation Rose projected. As if the wild delusions skimmed just beneath her skin.

She would be here now for a reason. Rose *always* had a reason.

"Did you do this?" she demanded, shouting to hear herself.

Her mother wore man's pants tucked into tall boots and a loose white shirt. Her long blond hair was braided back away from her bruised left eye and right cheek. Etta's heart gave an involuntary clench at the sight, before she let the anger back in to harden it. At Etta's question she flinched.

That's right, Etta thought, *I know what you're capable of. What you want.*

Her gaze lowered from Etta's face to Henry's and she took a step back, as if only seeing him now. When she came closer, making as if to kneel, Etta felt the last of her self-control snap. "Do *not* touch him!"

"All right, all right, darling." Rose's face looked strained as she spoke loudly, holding out her hand. The other strayed to the gun at her side. "You need to come with me now."

God, how Etta had prayed for this exact moment—how desperate she had been for any sign that her mother was alive and coming for her.

A sign that she wanted me.

"Henrietta," Rose said, her voice scalding. "You don't know what's coming, what's been chasing me for years! I've kept them off your trail for weeks, from the moment you were taken, but the Shadows—!"

Shadows. Etta let her lip curl back in disgust. That last, small hope in her that Henry had been wrong, that they'd jumped to the wrong conclusion, turned to dust.

Beneath her hands, Henry shifted, and Etta grabbed him by his lapel as if she could hold him there, conscious. As a child, she had always hidden her tears from her mother, too aware of how little patience Rose had for them, but she didn't care now—not when Henry's eyes opened. They moved from her face to Rose's.

259

Her mother's hands went slack at her side. Neither moved, but Etta felt his heartbeat as it began to drum harder and harder against his ribs. She leaned down, straining to hear him. "Come . . . to finish me off, Rosie?"

Her mother's face was stone. She stood, unflinching, even as her voice iced over.

"You never understood. You never believed me—"

"I understood . . . me . . ." he rasped out. "But Rosie . . . *Alice?* Why . . . *why* did she have to die?"

Alice.

"Etta, she'll protect you . . . go now—" He clutched her hand, trying to get her to look at him.

Alice.

Rose's face appeared in front of her own, still speaking loudly, urgently, "I can explain as we go, but—"

Alice.

Etta stepped back, out of her mother's reach.

She'd been taken and manipulated and shot and nearly lost her hearing for *Rose.* Everything Etta had ever done had been to earn a smile, squeeze a measure of respect, from *her.* She'd made excuses for her mother time and time again, even as the material she was using to build those protests dwindled down.

Etta turned, gripping her elbows, trying to fold in on herself. Disappear.

She killed Alice.

Had she watched Etta go through the passage with Sophia? Had she *smiled*, knowing she'd won that round, too? All Rose had to do was pretend to believe in her, just one time, and Etta had let her shape her future.

She left Alice to die alone.

Her eyes pricked with shame and a humiliation that would not quiet. She'd been so proud of herself, so defiant, so ready to *show* everyone in this hidden world that Rose's daughter could be just as strong and sharp and cunning as the woman herself. But she wasn't Rose's daughter—she was her tool. Years spent fighting for her love, her praise, for some kind of acknowledgment . . .

"You—" she choked out. She pressed a hand to her eyes, felt the fat, hot tears spill over her fingers. *Look up,* Etta ordered herself. *Look and see who she is. Who she's always been.* "It was you—"

Rose met her gaze. Defiant.

Denying nothing.

It was Alice's face now that she saw, freckled and young, in the uniform that brought her so much pride; in her apartment on the Upper East Side, smiling as Etta learned her first scales; upturned in the audience, as she watched Etta perform from the front row. Her *life.*

I was raised by a stranger. The words roared through her mind, barbed and scalding. *I never meant anything more than what I could do for her.*

Maybe this was the reason her mother hadn't told her about their hidden world, about her father—because she knew Etta's soft heart would twine her together with the Thorns, and she would lose the best hope she had of seeing this fantasy through.

No more.

Alice, the woman who had raised her, who had given her love, attention, focus, everything of herself—Alice had been her true mother, and *this* was the woman who had taken her from Etta. *Murdered her.*

She straightened at the sound of pounding feet, and looked up in time to see two figures in black cloaks race down the edges of the hallway, long, curved daggers in their hands. Rose spun, swore viciously, and without a second's hesitation raised her gun and fired. The attacker on the right dove into a marble table to avoid it, but Rose fired again, and this time did not miss. Her aim, as always, was perfect.

Until she ran out of bullets. She fired again at the other attacker, but the gun clicked in her hand, the chamber empty.

Henry watched, riveted, still trying to summon his strength to rise. His mouth was moving, he was saying something, but Etta couldn't hear anything over the sound of her own furious heartbeat, the static of the blast.

Rose threw the gun aside and charged the remaining attacker, slamming him to the ground. When she rose to her feet again, the man sprang up as well, his blade arcing up as if to pierce beneath her chin.

Etta kept her focus on the soldiers charging down the hall, the footmen that rushed in behind them. By the time they were within reach of the dining room, Rose had already run past her, shoving her aside as the attacker leaped forward to follow.

The impact of slamming into the wall jarred the grief from Etta's mind, leaving nothing but pristine, pure hate. Fury would have to be enough to carry her for now.

"Etta—" Henry was trying to sit up, choking on his own breath. She could barely hear him over the ringing in her ears, as he was surrounded and lifted by four of the soldiers. One tried to grab her, but she slipped away again and again, pulling out of their reach. "Listen—listen to me—!"

This has to end. If her mother had started this, then Etta, the only other living Linden, would take the responsibility of righting it. Any doubt she'd had was gone now, blasted away. The original timeline had to be restored. It was the only hope she had of salvaging everything, possibly even the lives that had been taken.

The choice was offered to her. It should have been frightening, the weight of it, but as Etta shook off the past, the unbearable questions and the uncertainty, it freed her instead.

She looked at Henry and made a promise. "I'm going to finish this."

"No—*no!*"

She tore herself away from Henry, from the soldiers, and bolted down the wide hall, until only a trail of bloody footsteps on the carpet was proof she had ever been there at all.

Reaching down, Etta gripped where the hem of her dress was torn, ripping it further to give her legs a better range of movement. She made a sharp left around the next corner. Her ears had begun to pop and crackle in a way that frightened her, but the ringing was fading enough to give her a warning.

Her feet slid to such a sudden stop that the Oriental runner bunched beneath them. Dozens, maybe even hundreds of people were charging down the narrow hall toward her, chanting, shouting in fragmented Russian—*"Ochistite dvorets!"*—over and over and over. The man in front held a bloodred flag in one hand and a gun in the other. Behind him, a variety of tools and weapons were waving in the air.

They're taking the palace, clearing it out. Etta struggled for her next breath, limping heavily. Ironwood's plan here went beyond mere assassination. No doubt his men had been here all along, sowing the seeds of discontent, greasing the revolutionaries' wheels before setting them on a path toward violence. Had he known Henry would come with the other Thorns? Had he ordered them to wait for his arrival?

She turned and doubled back the way she had come, taking a left rather than a right. Etta couldn't stop herself from looking back over her shoulder one last time. But she could not make anything out through the heavy cover of smoke.

A hand reached out, snatching her arm. Etta felt a shriek tear out of her throat as she was yanked off-balance and dragged through a doorway. She kicked, clawing at whoever had grabbed her. The door slammed shut and she was slammed up against it, knocking the breath out of her again and smearing black over her vision.

"—ta, what's happening? *Etta!*"

She jerked away from the hands holding her in place, rubbing at her eyes.

"What . . . that . . . can . . . me . . . ?" The words were broken up by the pulsing in her eardrums. Etta looked up, surprised to find Julian's face tight with worry as he touched the side of her cheek, his fingers pulling away red with blood.

"Explosion!" She had to shout the word to hear it herself. Julian cringed, nodding.

"Thought as much."

Etta pulled away from him, going for the door again. *"Attackers!"*

He said something that might have been "revolt" or "revolting."

"Run," she told him.

"Where are you going?" he shouted back, finally loud enough for her to understand.

"Search the palace—find astrolabe—"

"It's not here!" He grabbed her shoulders, turning her back toward him. "They found his body—stuffed in a bloody wardrobe, no astrolabe in sight. They were going to tell your father after dinner—"

If Etta had taken a knife and stabbed it deep into her belly, it would have been less painful than this. He'd killed his enemy; he'd taken what he wanted most. Her mind shaved down each of her wild thoughts, until only facts remained: *Ironwood has it. Need to find Ironwood. Need to finish this.*

Julian opened his mouth to say something else, but Etta pressed her finger to her lips and opened the door a crack, peering out of it. There was a dull roar coming from down the hall, but she couldn't pick out any one word. Satisfied that the men and women who'd flooded the palace were heading toward the dining room, Etta grabbed Julian's arm and pulled them both back outside.

Even before she began to run, she felt him dig in his heels, resisting. Etta sent him an incredulous look over her shoulder, which was met, to her surprise, with genuine fear. Julian seemed flummoxed by what was happening—at least until a man at the edge of the crowd turned and shouted something at them that made the others turn as well. Then survival instincts kicked in, and suddenly he was the one running, the one dragging her.

Etta wasn't sure it mattered whether or not he knew where he was going. The palace was large enough for anyone to get lost on a good day, with countless halls and rooms and closets to duck into. But that didn't seem to be the plan. Etta looked back again, just in time to see a man raise a gun. The bullet slammed into the face of a golden angel statue, splintering off the cap of its skull.

"*Cripes!*" Julian yelped.

How did anyone ever find their way out of this place without help? She blew the loose hair out of her face, trying to assess her options. They needed an exit, any sort of exit—a door, a window that could be smashed, a sewage pipe, she didn't care, as long as it was in the opposite direction from the mob. Neither did Julian, who had taken to running blindly forward, his arm thrown up over his head like that could somehow protect him.

There were hallways that served as large arteries to the palace, but those seemed to be clogged with soldiers, staff trying to flee, and the plainclothes people who'd come storming in from the outside. Right now, the only thing guiding Etta's steps was silence; she found herself searching for it beneath the throbbing and whistling in her ears, reaching for some part of the palace that was still, that hadn't been engulfed by the fury pouring through its gilded veins like acid.

Revolution. Her mind spun the word out, with all of the disaster and destruction and promise it encompassed. In a different year, in a different form, but revolution all the same, this time stirred up by the Ironwoods.

She drew them around a corner and, in the next instant, felt a blow to her chin, a knee to her leg. The breath wheezed out of her, and when she finally inhaled, dazed and on the floor, there was the smell of laundry and starch. A young girl, a maid, was sprawled out on the floor in front of them, her uniform ripped at the skirt and slightly askew from where she'd slammed into Etta.

Julian had managed to stay upright and say something to the maid in halting Russian. The maid pointed, her whole arm shaking, toward a door at the end of the hallway.

The maid took the opportunity to scamper off, picking up her small valise and all but running down the hall in the opposite direction, her blond braid streaming out behind her. It was the last clear sight Etta had before the electric lamps around them surged with brightness, and, with a hiss, flashed out completely, leaving a few scattered candles in sconces to light a hall bigger than Etta's whole apartment building in Manhattan.

"Well, that was bloody ominous. She said to go this way," Julian told her, jerking a thumb up ahead, to where the small hall dead-ended at the nondescript door Etta had seen before.

"You speak Russian?" Etta asked as they began to run again.

"Er, just barely. She either said this was some sort of inner servant hall, or their quarters, so I guess we'll be in for a surprise, won't we?" Excitement bubbled out of him, giving him a slightly breathless quality.

The door flew open then; the sudden light momentarily blinded Etta, who threw up an arm to shield her eyes. The silhouette of a man appeared in the doorway, a box-shaped flashlight in his hands—it wasn't until he made a noise of surprise and turned the light away that Etta saw it was one of the men who had met them outside, still wearing the palace's ornate livery. He adjusted his grip on the light so they could see him press a finger to his lips and wave them forward.

Etta and Julian exchanged a look.

"What are the chances . . ." he began.

". . . we're about to be murdered?" Etta finished as they made their way forward. "The better question is, what do you have on you to defend yourself?"

"Um . . . besides you? Did I need something else?" he whispered. "You won't let them take us alive, will you, kiddo?"

At any other moment Etta might have laughed, but the truth of it landed hard: there was only so much Julian could do to contribute to their survival. If it came down to it, she *would* be the one fighting. And she had no doubt that if things went badly, he'd leave her to deal with the mess.

But she *also* knew that if anyone was going to help them get back to the passage in the woods, it would be him.

In exchange for something else, I'm sure, she thought grimly. Not for the first time, she felt her heart crimp at the thought of how much easier this would be, how much safer she would feel, if it were Nicholas at her back. Even if neither of them knew where to go or how to find the passages, there would have been an equality between them. The thought of putting herself in the hands of a born-*and*-raised Ironwood again, even temporarily, made her feel sick to her stomach.

"Come, come, this way—" the man said in heavily accented English. "This way—"

Julian's pace eased off long before Etta's; she reached the man first, her fingers curled into fists at her side, trying to read his face in the darkness. The man studied her with open horror. "Is he dead?"

Etta hesitated before nodding. The man closed his eyes, turned his face upward to steal a calming breath. Then he stood at his full height and pressed the handle of the flashlight into her hands.

"Follow this hall to the end," he said haltingly. "There is a window left open. Go *now*."

"Wait a tick—" Julian started, but the man pushed past them both, and went the opposite way.

"All right," Julian said after a beat of silence. "Have to admit, I'm still waiting for the firing squad to spring up and take us out, Romanov-style."

"That is *not* funny," Etta said sharply, stalking down the hall.

"Lighten up, Linden-Hemlock-Spencer," he whispered back, jogging to catch up to her. The inner hall muffled the chaos outside of it, but only just. The gunfire was endless, blurring into thunder. "Maybe we should just hide—stay here until the trouble passes?"

"Until someone finds us and finishes us off?" Etta said, catching the first hint of the open window's freezing draft curling toward them. *The way they probably grabbed Henry.* Every time she blinked, the explosion seemed to set off again behind her eyes, blinding, disorienting, incinerating her from the inside out.

Did I really leave him?

With a start, she realized she was crying.

Did I leave him there to die?

"Come now, old girl, it's not as bad as all that," Julian said. "We'll be fine. I can get us out of here in a jiff. There's a passage at the Imperial Academy of Arts, just across the Neva River. How do you feel about sunlight and warmth and a charming lack of Gatling guns?"

NINETEEN

FROST COVERED THE WINDOW; AT SOME POINT, THE DARK
sky had begun spitting down snow. Some of it had blown inside through
a small crack, leaving a mess on the floor. A few different sets of
footprints were already pressed into the slush, leading away from the
window—clearly, others had taken the chance to leave.

Outside, she heard that same phrase being chanted in the distance:
"Ochistite dvorets!"

Etta got her hands under the window and tugged it up high enough
to slip through. The chill cut straight through her flimsy dress and the
silk slip beneath, but it was a good sort of cold—it lifted the mental fog,
sharpening her thoughts.

"Up you go," Julian said, offering his hands to hoist her up. Etta
ignored him and pulled herself through, despite the pain that lanced
through her shoulder and bare feet at the impact on the hard stone path
below. Julian landed just as roughly behind her.

The palace sat close to the river, separated only by a small street
and embankment. There was no one around them that she could see,
but Julian heard something. He reached over, switching off her flash-
light, and held out an arm to keep her in place as a car raced down the

road, slinging mud and slush up into the air. Julian let out a noise of protest as it splattered onto the front of his otherwise pristine trousers.

Etta scanned the street and river for any way across both. There seemed to be a bridge in the distance, but between it and them was a mass of humanity making its way down the street. She wasn't about to stick around and see if the marchers were soldiers or more of St. Petersburg's—Petrograd's—unhappy population.

Julian darted across the street to the embankment, leaning over the wall. He shouted something down—Etta saw his mouth moving, even if she couldn't make out his words. The fact that her hearing hadn't fully come back, that she was still drowning beneath that same piercing whine, threatened to sink her with fear.

Etta limped over to him, peering through the darkness to see what was below—a boatman, as it turned out, in one of three rowboats tied up to the small dock, smoking as if he didn't have a care in the world. The trail of smoke curled up toward them, a wriggling wisp of white.

Julian's face was outraged when he looked at her. "He wants over seven thousand rubles to use one of his damned boats. Said the other servants were willing to pay for him to ferry them. I don't have that kind of money, do you?"

After everything that had happened over the course of the last hour, Etta felt a strange, unnatural calm settle over her. Improvised explosives were a problem. Fleeing a furious mob was a problem. Greedy boatmen were not.

"May I have the flashlight?" she asked, holding out her hand.

He passed it to her, but tried to tug it back at the last second. "What are you planning? You've got that deranged look in your eye—"

Etta yanked it out of his hand and sidled up over the wall, then down the short hill that brought her to the wooden dock.

"English?" she called out.

The boatman stood up, stepping out of the boat, a leering smile on his face. His eyes skimmed over the place where the strap of her dress had ripped, exposing one shoulder. "Little English for little lady."

Etta mentally gagged as she returned his smile with one of her own and said, in what she hoped was a sweet tone, "Yes, little lady in desperate need of help. Will you be a hero and help a girl out?"

"You're *flirting* with him?" Julian called down in disbelief.

"Where?" the man asked, smirking.

Etta glanced across the wide stretch of the river, to where another imperial-looking building loomed. She pointed, and the man turned his head to follow the line of her arm, her finger—

Etta slammed the flashlight into his skull, blowing him back into the boat, where he collapsed, unmoving. Stunned, but still breathing.

"Good God, Linden-Hemlock-whoever-you-are!" Julian called, stumbling down the hill.

Etta threw the broken remains of the flashlight into the nearest boat, and reached down to untie the boat the man had fallen into, letting it drift into the patches of ice on the Neva. She thought about apologizing, but then decided that moment that she just didn't care.

A pirate wouldn't apologize or thank him. A pirate would just *take*. And if she had to shut off some crucial, feeling part of herself to survive this and find her way back to the real pirate in her life, she would.

She heard Nicholas's voice whisper in her ear, a protesting, *Legal pirate, thank you,* and for an instant allowed the small, sad laugh to bubble up in her chest.

Julian gave her a look that told her exactly what he thought about that laugh.

"Spencer," she told him. "My last name is *Spencer.*"

Etta quickly stepped down into the boat, feeling it wobble beneath her feet. It steadied with the added weight of Julian, allowing her to easily reach up and unknot the line anchoring it to the dock. They drifted out toward the clumps of ice forming in the river's slow waters, and for a moment they both looked at each other expectantly.

"I would row," Etta told him, "except my shoulder is killing me and I can barely move my arm—so maybe you could try contributing to this escape?"

"Of course," he said quickly, not meeting her gaze. "I was just waiting to see if you'd be stubborn enough to attempt it yourself."

Julian picked up the oars, got them on either side of the boat, and then lifted them up and down in the water, doing little more than splashing. Etta stared at him; she was freezing, tired, shaken, and on the verge of reaching over to strangle him for even trying to make a joke at a time like this. But he kept doing it, his brow wrinkled, as if confounded about why the boat was slowly turning in a circle and not moving across the water as expected.

"Are you serious?" she asked him in disbelief. "You don't know how to *row a boat?*"

His shoulders set against her words. "I'll have you know, Nick was always there to do it when the situation called for it."

Etta felt her jaw tighten to the point of pain as she held out her hands. He hesitated a moment before passing the heavy oars over. With a movement that made her shoulder protest pitifully, she got the boat turned around, her back to the other bank, and made the first long stroke. Those days with Alice rowing by the Loeb Boathouse in Central Park had been for something more than enjoyment after all.

Julian released a relieved sigh, leaning back to look up at the snow falling on them. No matter what he did, he always seemed to be posing and waiting for someone to compliment him on it.

"You're rather handy, Linden-Hemlock-Spencer," he said. "That was some brilliant teamwork, if I do say so myself."

"I'm not sure you know what that word means," Etta managed, her teeth clenched. She tried to mine the small bit of gold out of this situation—she was alive, and the rowing was at least warming her stiff muscles—but she could already feel the rising urge to take one of the oars and whack Julian into the freezing water.

"You're the brawn, I'm the brains, kiddo," he told her. "You don't need my help with this."

Etta was beginning to think that the real reason he'd gone to the Thorns was that he was at least self-aware enough to know he wouldn't be able to survive on his own.

"Call me kiddo again . . ." She felt the words growl out of her throat, too low for her to even hear over the splash of water and the painful ringing.

"Your ears still giving you a spot of trouble?" he asked. "It's a good sign you can hear at all—it means it might heal completely. Lesser explosions have destroyed people's eardrums, from what I understand."

Etta grunted, putting the full force of her anxiety into the next pull of the oars. Beethoven could compose and play instruments when he was mostly deaf. But she wasn't Beethoven, and the thought of never hearing music again left her feeling as if her chest had been hollowed out.

Stop thinking, just row.

"What happened at dinner, exactly?" Julian asked. "One minute I was being berated by the Thorn guard for innocently inquiring about his mother's species, and the next, the whole place started rocking on its bones."

Etta looked down at her lap, avoiding his gaze. She might as well tell him—though it seemed unlikely, Julian might have the answer to the question that had been nagging at her since she'd been jolted back into consciousness.

"We had . . . we had just started the last course, when one of the waiters brought out a wine bottle to serve the tsar. He shouted something and slammed it down onto the table. The next thing I knew, I was on the ground and half the floor was gone. Henry was hurt badly, and the others . . ."

Julian's brows shot up. "Was there liquid in the bottle?"

She nodded, pulling the next stroke.

"Based on the year, it was probably nitroglycerine. It explodes on impact. Very volatile. Even Grandfather didn't like using the stuff." His expression turned thoughtful. "How on God's green earth did you manage to survive that?"

A good question. "Jenkins—the other guard, I mean—he jumped on it, I think, just before it hit the table. And Henry, he . . ."

I left him there to die.

I left him.

Etta wiped the sweat from her forehead with her tattered sleeve. "It was an Ironwood—both Jenkins and Henry recognized him. But he shouted something before he threw down the explosive—" She tried to repeat it the best she could.

"*Revolyutzia*, maybe? That's *revolution*," Julian said, his voice oddly quiet. "Pretending to play the part of a revolutionary for the assassination. Evil, Grandpops, but rather elegant. There is a rather unfortunate tradition of tsars being assassinated, so no one would question it."

Etta took a breath, trying to wipe the blood from her face against her shoulder. Her stiff knees ached as she tried to stretch them out in the cramped boat. "So we're back to your grandfather's timeline?"

"Hell if I know, kid," Julian said, briskly rubbing his arms to try to bring some warmth back into them. "I don't intend to find out, and neither should you. Your opportunity to escape has presented itself, and you are hereby invited to join me in Bora Bora for as long as it takes them to sort this out."

Etta dragged the oars through the dark water again. "I'm not going to Bora Bora."

"Oh? I wasn't aware that this escape involved a real plan, but do share."

"If the Thorn, Kadir, was found dead, it means your grandfather got to the astrolabe, which means I need to find him," Etta said, explaining it to him slowly, as if he were a small child. His mouth twitched, trying to hide a smile. "As far as I know, he's still in 1776, in New York. How do I get back there from this point?"

"No," Julian said, throwing his hands up in the air. "*No*. Because this is absurd. You should just come with me. This doesn't have to be on your shoulders. You don't need the weight of it—it'll just smother you. Come with me to Bora Bora and let the devils have their hell."

"It's always that easy for you, isn't it?" Etta said, shaking her head. "Let everyone else risk their lives to try to fix what your grandfather has done. Don't take any responsibility for your family."

He gave her a pitying look that set her teeth on edge. "Christ, you sound like Nick, with all of this talk of *responsibility*. Morality is a bore, kiddo. And if you think any one person can stop Grandfather, you're mistaken. He was born out of a cloud of sulfur and his bones are brimstone."

"Imagine what you could accomplish with your life," she said, "if you weren't so damn afraid all the time."

The gentle thud of the broken ice against their boat and the splash of the oars in the water was the only conversation for several moments.

Julian let out a dramatic sigh and dipped a hand into his jacket, pulling out a small leather notebook.

"I suppose I'm going to have to be the lesser person in this situation and allow you to take the title of bigger," he said, thumbing through the pages. It must have been his traveler's journal, with notations of where and when he'd been, so he didn't cross paths with an older or younger version of himself.

"Here we are," he said. "There are three passages in this year and city. The one we're headed to will take us to Alexandria, 203 A.D. From there, there's a passage through the Vatican, and from there, you can connect to New York in . . . 1939. Little Italy, on Mulberry and Grand."

Etta's grip on the oars tightened. "How does that help me?"

"You'll just need to get to where Whitehall Dock used to be. There's a passage to 1776, in Boston," he said. "That's the most direct route to that year."

She could find a way from Boston to Manhattan. If nothing else, she could turn herself over to the Ironwood guardian who would inevitably be watching the passage, and let him or her bring her to Ironwood for her punishment.

"Why is everyone still banging on about that damn astrolabe?" Julian complained. "It's always been more trouble than it's worth. No one is ever satisfied with life, are they? What more does he have to sacrifice at this point? He's gone and killed his entire family over it."

"I had it. . . ." She could hear the pain in her voice. "But it was taken by the Thorns—the ones who went missing. It's my responsibility to find it and finish what I started."

"Why? The timeline's already changed again, and it'll only get worse from here."

Etta leaned forward. "You're sure it changed?"

"You didn't feel it?" Julian shook his head. "I suppose not. It's not that different from the pressure of an explosion. The whole world blurs for a moment, and the sound is deafening. It's unmistakable. Whatever this new timeline is, it's bound to be bad."

"More reason to find the astrolabe," Etta said, through gritted teeth. "And destroy it in order to reset it back to its original state."

Julian wore a strange expression. "Is Grandpops's timeline really that bad? I wasn't around to see the original one, and neither were you. Who's to say he didn't improve on a few things?"

Etta shook her head. This was the trouble with meddling at all—who decided what was considered more peaceful, or improved? A benefit to one part of the world might be a detriment to the other. You could stop a war, and it might inadvertently cause another. You could change the outcome of a battle, and it would just be the other side who experienced the losses.

"It doesn't matter. No one should have tampered with it in the first place, least of all Cyrus Ironwood." And even though she already knew what his answer would be, she tried anyway: "You could help me . . . find Nicholas and Sophia and the rest of your family. Apologize for tricking them into grieving for you."

"Appealing to a sense of honor only works if a person *has* one," Julian informed her. "I'll go with you as far as the Vatican, but—"

She heard the crack of the gunshot and its echo as the bullet slammed into the water, sending up a spray of freezing water at them and rocking the boat. Both Etta and Julian ducked instinctively.

The next bullet splashed down on the other side of the boat.

"Can't you row any faster?" Julian complained.

"Can you try *helping*?" she fired back, but Julian had already turned around to shout something at them in Russian.

The next shot from the embankment hit the rim of the boat, splintering it so close to his hand that Julian yelped in alarm, and made as if to dive into the freezing river. Through the curtain of snow, Etta could just barely make out the men gathered there, one of whom was climbing down toward the other boat.

"Why are they chasing us?" he complained.

"*Thorn!*" one of them bellowed in an American accent. *An Ironwood.* "Come back at once and you will be shown a measure of mercy!"

Julian groaned, sinking back against the boat in dismay. Etta's arms worked faster, the oars beating at the water as the other embankment finally came within a few dozen yards.

"It's just not fair. How did you get us into this mess? What kind of bad-luck charm are you?"

"Can you *please shut up*?" she snapped. "Reach for the embankment when you can and pull us in—"

The next two gunshots splintered the floating ice, spraying water across her face. Etta's heart felt like it was about to unhook from her chest and pass up her throat. Rather than wait for Julian, she used one of the oars to catch the lip of the embankment and pull them over to it.

She felt the slice of a bullet across the back of her exposed neck before she heard it explode through the air. Etta gasped in shock more than pain.

Don't think about it don't think about it don't think—hard to ignore a literal brush with death, but Etta slithered up onto the snow-dusted embankment, trying to get her bearings. She clung to her last shreds of focus, swinging her gaze around. Most of the embankment's walls were high—too high to climb up from the water. But just in front of the building—which she hoped was the Imperial Academy of Arts that Julian had mentioned—were steps that led down to the water's edge, guarded by two enormous stone sphinxes facing inward, as if squaring off against each other.

"Don't leave me!" Julian called after her, still crouched in the boat. A shot zinged off the stone embankment, forcing Etta's attention up toward the group of rowboats moving toward them, shining flashlights across the dark ice and water.

"They'll kill me," he told her in a rush, struggling to reach the embankment again. "That's why I never came back—Grandfather didn't want me for his heir, and he would have killed me—"

She wasn't surprised by Julian's admission, but she also didn't have time for it.

"Come on," she said, stretching a hand out toward him. Her shoulder was on fire, her ears felt like fireworks had been set off inside them, and her whole body was trembling from the cold; but, digging deeper, she found the last burst of strength she needed to grip his hand and draw the boat forward again. Julian scrambled up onto the embankment, lying as flat as he could across from her—so close that Etta could smell the alcohol on his breath.

"What do we do?" he asked.

"You said you were the brains!" she snapped. "Where's the passage?"

"The statues—do you see them? The right sphinx, just at the base."

The air around its enormous stand did seem to be shimmering, but

Etta had chalked that up to shock and exhaustion—and had chalked up the faint drumming buzz in the air, as if it were electrified, to her ears coming back around.

"Then we run," she told him. It was a short distance, maybe five feet. Granted, that would be five feet of opportunity to be shot dead, but she liked those odds. Before Julian could launch his newest protest, and before she could give herself time to think about where in the world the passage might open up, Etta pushed onto her feet and ran as hard as she could. She brought her hands up just in case he was wrong, and she was about to slam headfirst into immoveable stone.

"Stop! This is your last warning—!"

Etta didn't hear the rest. She dove into the wild heartbeat of the passage and felt the pressure of its touch tear at her skin and tattered dress. The dark chaos made her feel like she was spinning head over feet, until it shoved her out with a final, shuddering gasp.

Inertia carried her forward into a skidding stop. Her feet slid against rough stone, and she swung her gaze back over her shoulder. A small sphinx, identical to the one that had brought her here, gazed out over a glistening white city and an enormous bay that had turned pink with the sunset.

Julian shot out through the passage behind her, snatching her arm and forcing them both back into a run.

They dashed around the statue and made their way down a broad avenue. The moon-bright limestone columns and steps led up to buildings that looked more like temples than homes or places of business. Etta dragged in air that was completely void of gasoline, but brimmed with hints of life—just animal sweat, human waste, and a touch of brine that could only come from being close to the sea. As they kept to the darkness, she caught sight of a distant lighthouse between the next two buildings she passed, its bright, watchful eye sweeping over the harbor below it.

"How much farther?" Etta gasped out.

"We're following this big avenue down until we find a rather handsome temple called the Caesareum. We're looking for two enormous red marble obelisks."

They found them. Her heart felt like it was about to tear out of her chest by the time they reached the passage, and they sped through it into further darkness.

Julian slid to a stop on the stone floor, nearly crashing into a row of prayer candles that had carelessly been left to illuminate what appeared to be a church nave. Etta turned, her eyes sweeping over the altar's shadowed cross, then back out at the rows of pews that spread like ribs between the confines of the walls. They were alone, finally.

"Come on," he said. "I'll get you to your passage."

She nodded, rubbing her hands over her face. *The Vatican.*

But this wasn't the Vatican she remembered visiting with Alice. It lacked the heartrending works of art and the sweeping grandeur that conspired to make the visitor feel as insignificant in the face of God as the dust on their shoes. It was almost humble. "What year?"

"Fourteen ninety-something," he said with a vague gesture as they reached the doors. Pressing an ear against them, he was satisfied by whatever he did or didn't hear, and dragged the heavy doors open just enough for them to slip into the hall.

The torchlights blazed on the walls alongside them. Etta tried, failed, to calculate the hour. She reached back to rub her neck, but only felt what wasn't there. *Where—?*

The chain she had used to carry her mother's earring had slipped down the front of her dress and caught on the beadwork, but the earring itself was gone.

Etta couldn't stop the panic that writhed in her as she looked around the floor for it. *Why do I care?* She'd used the earrings as proof of her mom's belief in her, to steady her when she was afraid. The mere thought of what it represented should have sickened her.

And yet . . . it didn't. Not entirely.

Alice, she reminded herself, *she killed Alice—*

"What's the matter?" Julian whispered, doubling back when he realized she wasn't behind him.

She looked up. "Nothing. Where to now?"

He opened his mouth, eyes narrowing, but thought better of it. They walked in silence, Etta trailing a step behind him as she tried to pull the pieces of herself back together, to forge them into new armor.

Julian stopped, backing up a few steps. "Wait—" He looked at his journal, checking something. "Ah. This is my stop. Yours is three doors down, just at the entrance to the apartments."

He pushed the door to the small chapel open.

"Are you not coming with me?" Etta asked. "You could do real good."

He threw her one last smirk over his shoulder. "Where's the fun in that, when I could go to Florence instead?"

She blew out a harsh breath from her nose and let her expression tell him what she thought of that. The idea of him slipping away from facing the consequences of his actions sparked that same helpless anger she'd felt while listening to Nicholas confess his pain and shame and doubt over what had happened on the mountain.

"Godspeed, Linden-Hemlock-Spencer," he said, stepping into the small chapel. "Here is my final benediction: wherever your road takes you, may it never cross with Grandfather's."

She heard the passage's tempestuous language bang on through the wall.

"A-hole," Etta muttered, blowing her hair out of her eyes. She had turned to continue down the hall when a sound like a gunshot bit the silence. Something heavy smacked into the door with a grunt of pain.

She fumbled with the latch and opened it. Julian spilled out at her feet, blinking up at her. After a moment, he pressed his hands against his face and let out a frustrated holler.

"What . . . just happened?" Etta asked, alarmed.

He pushed himself upright and began the impossible work of patting down his unruly hair. "I got *bounced* out of the passage. Crossed paths with myself. Some version of me is already there."

Whoa. "Didn't you check your notebook?"

"I *did*," Julian said, smacking a hand against the stone. "Which means it's the future me, and I haven't gone yet. Damn!"

Etta stared. "Does this . . . happen a lot?"

"To me more than others, apparently. Once or twice it's kept me out of a bad scrape, but I cannot even begin to explain how obnoxious it is to be babysat and scolded by your future conscience. I can't believe Future Me is such a . . . a *wurp*. A chuffing bluenose!"

What he was saying seemed possible and impossible all at once—but it was time travel, and the usual rules never did apply.

"You're sure you didn't just get completely drunk and forget to note your visit?" Etta asked, leaning over him.

"I love that you know me so well, Linden-Hemlock-Spencer, but I assure you, no. Say what you will about changing the timeline, but my whole life has been a lesson in self-fulfillment. I can't know what's ahead, but Future Me knows what's behind, and he's a humorless fool about letting me have my fun."

To her, it sounded like Julian's future self was pretty skilled in keeping himself alive, but Etta kept her mouth shut and moved away, so he could stand up and brush himself off.

"Maybe Future Julian wants you to be a better person?" she suggested.

He pulled a horrified face.

"All right, kid, let's go to the Big Apple, then. We'll split up in Little Italy. I've a hankering for good pasta, anyway," he whispered as he stood. "Oh boy, 1939 means that my old nanny will be there—she retired to her natural time once she was finished with me and Soph. I like to think we were the ultimate cosmic test, and she didn't dare risk getting worse little demons—"

"Shhh," Etta begged, her head pounding, as they walked. "Shh . . ."

"I wonder what the old bird is up to? I could give her the fright of her life and drop in," Julian said, his voice low. "You know, I think I'll do just that. She can keep a secret, especially now that Grandfather no longer controls her purse strings. Or I'll just play it off as past Julian, rather than present Julian. . . . Hmm . . ."

Etta gave up and let him talk, let him fill her head with his memories until they pushed away her own painful ones for a time. She tried to bring up Nicholas's face, to imagine finding him after she saw this mess through to its end, but seeing its bold lines, the curve of his contemplative smile, brought no relief—it only made her feel desperately alone.

THE PASSAGE SHOVED THEM OUT TOGETHER, SENDING JULIAN to his knees and throwing Etta on top of him. Black ringed her vision at the jarring impact, and it took her longer than she would have liked to recover enough to stand.

"That was a definite *ouch*," Julian said, staggering up. "You sure your head isn't made out of marble?"

Etta held her throbbing arm close to her chest, waiting until the pain passed before saying, "Sorry."

They'd landed in the middle of a rocky, fog-smothered path. Etta could hardly see a few inches in front of her, let alone take in what was supposed to have been the city's skyline.

"Manhattan, huh?" she said, turning to Julian with an arched brow. "What was that about having excellent records?"

But Julian was rooted to the spot, one hand twisting the front of his shirt.

"No, Etta," he said. "This *is* New York City."

"In prehistoric times?"

The terrain was wild—craggy hills shadowed by thick, silky fog. Etta could just make out the shape of other mounds in the distance. Someone nearby had lit a fire; the smell of charred wood bloomed in the air.

The silence breathed thickly around them, as if trying to get her attention. To tell her something. *Listen.*

"Maybe we took the wrong passage out of the Vatican?" she suggested.

"No," Julian said, the word harsher now. He still hadn't moved. *"This is New York."*

Etta was about to shake him when a breeze stirred the fog, swirled it. The muddied shapes, which had clearly been hills and rough terrain, were now sloping piles of brick and stone, the warped frames of buildings and burned-out bodies of cars. The frost near her feet wasn't frost at all, but shattered glass. Flecks of white flurried around her, and for one stupid, insane second, Etta thought, *Snow. It's snowing.*

But the only thing falling around them was ash.

VATICAN CITY
1499

TWENTY

THE DARKNESS NEVER LIFTED.

For a single terrifying moment, Nicholas was certain he, too, had somehow lost vision in one or both of his eyes. The blackness was absolute; the air breathed around him, thick enough to slice into ribbons. Already unsteady from exhaustion and—*Christ*—blood loss, he landed hard enough on his knees to nearly bite off his own tongue. Sophia almost slipped out of his arms. He gripped the back of her tunic for purchase, avoiding her cold, slick skin.

"Sophia?" he said, his voice echoing back to him threefold. "Sophia? Can you hear me?"

Silence.

Stillness.

The touch of death, he thought.

The hairs on his body prickled to attention as panic surged through him, and he shook her gently, trying to provoke any sort of cutting word. "Sophia!"

"Give her to me," Li Min said, forcing the matter. He should have fought her, he should have argued with her for propriety's sake, but there wasn't the time, and he hadn't the strength. Sophia was inches taller than her, but the other young woman easily arranged her on her back and carried her forward quickly, her steps light. Nicholas was horrified that, even with the additional weight gone, his limbs dragged as if he were deep in his cups.

Pounding steps . . . or perhaps his own heart. No—there was another sound underscoring it, one that pierced his awareness. Someone was dragging a blade against stone, and he felt it, he felt it as if the sword or knife were scraping at his own bones.

"There's nowhere you can hide that we won't find you!" Miles Ironwood. "Come out now, Carter, and I'll let you choose how you'd like to die."

The other men laughed in response to Miles's threat. Nicholas barely managed to catch his tongue before he shouted something back.

"Blade or barrel, blade or barrel," Miles sang out. "I don't think you want the old man to choose for you. Blade or barrel, what'll it be, Carter? My knife or gun at your throat?"

Li Min muttered something he was sure was an oath.

"This way!" Her voice floated to him through the darkness, bounced between whatever walls were around them, cutting through even the passage's groaning.

"Where—?" He coughed, trying to clear the tightness in his throat. "Where are you?"

It was so dark—so very, very dark and still. There wasn't a hint of starlight or moonlight to warm the air with their glow, and there was no wind stirring against his skin. The utter stillness of this place was devastating. Terrifying. There did not seem to be a beginning or end to it.

"Get *up!*" Li Min sounded nearly breathless.

Where are we? A cellar of some sort? Holy Christ, why hadn't he even thought to ask before he'd gone charging through the passage?

Get ahold of yourself. Nicholas was nearly frenzied with the need to seize some sort of control, some understanding, over what was happening.

Over the scraping and footfalls, there was a snick of sound, and a small spark of light floated like a firefly a few yards in front of him. His mind reached through its tangled mass of chaos for the word. *Match.*

Li Min had lit a match. She drew it close to her face, illuminating the stark lines of concern etched there.

"She's not . . ." he tried to tell her. "I can't . . ."

"We haven't much time—stand *up,* Nicholas Carter. If you cannot, then I will carry you both."

His legs bobbed like a newborn calf's, but Nicholas, seemingly by the grace of God alone, got his feet under him. His eyes had adjusted to the darkness well enough to see the stark lines of the narrow walkway, the walls that opened here and there in doorless entryways.

In this state, he couldn't think and walk at the same time, so he shut off the valve to his thoughts and followed each prick of light that the girl lit, until finally they veered off the main walkway, and into what looked like . . .

A mausoleum.

It was one in a string of three that shared walls. Li Min had stepped through the nearest, her hand brushing a small engraving of a leaf, nearly hidden by the fading fresco of men. Nicholas stepped down into the structure, carefully balancing as loose stones bit into the thin soles of his sandals.

"Is she alive?" he whispered, but Li Min ignored the question. Sophia hadn't said a word since they'd made their way through the passage, and he could no longer feel to ensure her chest was rising and falling. He could barely see her in this impenetrable darkness.

You cannot die, he thought, the words searing and unyielding. *You owe me a debt.*

Etta's terrified face, the moment before she disappeared, cut through his mind. What would happen if Sophia died? The passage they'd come through would likely collapse—but would she disappear, the way Etta and Julian had when they'd been caught in a wrinkle and tossed through time?

I need your help. Desperation turned his stomach hollow. *I cannot do this without your assistance. Do not die, do not die, do not die—*

Li Min blew out her match just as the passage began to make itself known again, beating out a warning against the stale air.

Reinforcements. Nicholas clenched his jaw, struggling with the pain in his shoulder, the way it leeched at his strength.

Li Min grunted in the darkness, adjusting Sophia's weight. "This way."

From what he'd seen before the light went out, there was nowhere else to go. Nothing to do but hide and hope and pray.

"Must be up in the Basilica by now—"

"—split up, see if we can find a light—"

The voices were thrown between the walls, allowed to volley back and forth, to meet the passage's calls blow for blow.

"This way!" Li Min's voice became more urgent.

She struck one last match. Nicholas felt himself balk—first at the sight of the open sarcophagus at the center of the mausoleum, and again as Li Min all but shouldered him toward the stairs that had been hidden beneath its lid and silently urged him down into a darkness deeper than sleep.

The quick steps of the Ironwoods were pounding down like rain, growing in speed and strength. Nicholas couldn't question it. He had to *move*.

The sensation of descending into a tomb, into a maze of graves and stones, made him feel as if Death himself had one hand around his throat, his bony fingers bruising. Nicholas stopped, poised at the edge of the steps. What small sliver of light Li Min's match had provided disappeared as the girl set Sophia down and pulled the lid shut over them.

For the first time in a long, long while—since he'd been a child, since his mother had told him to climb into that cupboard and *stay hidden* until it was safe to come out—Nicholas felt his throat tighten to the point of choking. His mouth had gone so dry, it felt as if he were breathing ash in and out of his lungs. Every sense was dampened; what innate sense of direction he possessed was stripped away, leaving him with only touch to feel his way down the last of the steps.

"'Through me you enter into a city of woes,'" he muttered, half-delirious. "'Through me you enter into eternal pain . . . through me you enter the population of loss. . . .'"

"'Abandon all hope, you who enter here,'" Li Min whispered, just above his ear. "Dante. How original."

Nicholas grunted back, his feet finding flat ground, and his forehead the disastrously low ceiling. His forehead cracked against some sort of stone support, igniting the aches and agony he'd managed to push aside. That was it for him—his body simply ran out of whatever means it had of continuing on. He drooped like a slack sail.

Distantly, he heard Li Min set Sophia down and race back up the steps to pull the cover back over them.

Nicholas fell onto his knees, his strength draining as quickly as the blood from the arrow wound. His limbs shook from the strain of their run, from carrying Sophia's slight weight for as long as he had, and he fought to stay conscious. Inching forward, even just a foot, felt like a Herculean task. A beast that would not be slaughtered.

And then . . . there was light. It spilled out from a gas lantern in Li Min's hands, illuminating the mosaics on the floor and the peeling frescos dancing on the walls around them. She was rummaging through a small bundle of wares in the corner: blankets, pots, a ruthless-looking dagger, and a leather sack of something he hoped was food.

This was her hiding place, her stash—or someone else's stash that she'd taken advantage of. He watched as Li Min spread the blanket out over the ground, snapping it to shake the dust free.

Nicholas felt himself take his first deep breath in hours.

Li Min drew her lantern closer and unknotted the laces of her hooded cloak to drape over Sophia's shivering form. She wore an approximation of the longer draped dresses he'd seen on the women of Carthage, her hair braided into a crown around her head. She worked silently, her fingers pressing along a point on Sophia's neck. Then she leaned forward, an ear to Sophia's chest.

"Is . . . is she dead?" Nicholas asked, voice hoarse.

Li Min sat back. Shook her head. "She lives. Barely."

"I brought—" Nicholas fumbled with the physician's bag, yanking it over his head and passing it to her. "I brought this—do you know anything of medicine? Of poison?"

She snatched the leather bag and began sorting through its contents, lining up each sachet, small bottle, and pressed herb on the ground beside her. She stopped now and then to sniff one or dab a drop of liquid on her tongue.

"Sit her up," Li Min commanded at last, seizing one of the small bottles and uncorking it. "Hold her jaw open with care, or else you'll break it."

He rolled his stiffening shoulder back, trying to loosen it into use, and felt a trickle of fresh blood race down the curve of his spine. His thoughts took on a flickering quality that set off a clanging bell inside of his skull.

Still, he did as Li Min asked, sitting Sophia's slack body up and tilting her head back. He used his index finger and thumb to nudge her jaw open wide enough for Li Min to pour whatever was in the bottle down Sophia's throat. She measured it out, sip by sip, her free hand stroking Sophia's face sweetly, like a delicate spring rain.

"What—what is that?" he demanded. "Won't she choke—?"

Sophia had been nothing but deadweight from the moment he'd carried her out of the house in Carthage, but she'd at least had her usual barbed edges and venom. Over the course of ten, fifteen minutes, it had all bled away, leaving nothing but a husk of bones and skin. But now she returned to life, seemingly all at once: retching, gagging, and then casting up her accounts all over him with a wet, putrid splatter.

Her eyes remained closed, but he could feel her breathing more steadily now, the puffs of it warming the air between them.

"Dear *God*—" he said in alarm, pounding on her back to help her clear her throat. The smell—the *smell*—

"Something to help her get the vile poison out of her," Li Min said, finally answering his earlier questions.

"Thank you," he said, wiping his chin against the shoulder of his tunic, "for that timely warning."

"Lay her back," Li Min said, sitting back on her heels. "She needs to rest now. Some of the poison has been absorbed by her body, but we may have luck on our side yet. The Thorn's intention wasn't to kill her. Ironwood's bounty specifies he wants you both alive, or else the payment will be forfeit."

Nicholas didn't realize his sword hadn't made the journey with them until he tried reaching for it. His fingers had to settle for a broken shard of stone, some crumbled section of the statue behind them. "Is that the reason you've come, then? You caught wind of the bounty and knew where to find us?"

Li Min snorted, smoothing Sophia's hair out of her face. "I came to ensure I might be able to claim my end of our bargain. The bounty is a handsome windfall from the gods, but the Ironwoods can rot."

"I warn you—" Nicholas blinked, trying to clear the spots floating in his vision. "I warn you that we won't . . . we won't be taken."

Li Min ignored him, taking Sophia's hand. She spoke to the other young woman firmly, leaning over her as if to drag her spirit back, should it try to escape. And with time, those same words became embroidered with soft pleading, though their meaning couldn't penetrate the fog growing in his mind.

"That's not—" Nicholas tried to push up onto his feet, but the world swung wild and unhinged around him, knocking him back into place. "Won't be . . . taken . . ."

The ring on his hand burned as he felt his body betray him.

Nicholas slumped back to the ground, fighting the way the light faded around him, gently receding in waves until there was nothing left of the world but blissful emptiness.

NICHOLAS WOKE TO A SHARP COMPLAINT FROM HIS LEFT shoulder, a badgering, insistent sting that dragged him forward again each time he tried to slip back into the darkness.

He was flat on his stomach, the side of his face pressed against the ridges of the mosaic beneath him. By the time his vision cleared and the cotton stuffing inside his skull was plucked out, Nicholas had the very disturbing realization that someone was stabbing him repeatedly and quite literally in the back.

"You—" His attempt to surge off the ground was met with firm resistance; a hand easily pushed him back down.

"Be still while I finish," the voice growled back. "Unless you'd like me to accidentally sew your neck to your shoulder? It might improve your looks."

Li Min. His gaze pivoted; from his vantage point, he could just see Sophia, still stretched out on the ground. The tiny bottles, herbs, and medicines had been stowed in the bag again, but now Li Min was rummaging through it for something else, muttering to herself. When she returned, her touch was as rough and uncaring as it had been before.

"Did you . . . give me something . . . to make me pass out?" he asked, teeth gritted. He'd had at least a dozen slashes stitched up in his career at sea, and the feeling of being sewn back together like a doll never improved.

Li Min leaned forward, so he had a clear view of her face as she raised a dark brow. "No. You are weak and faltering—not only in body, it would appear, but in judgment."

He followed her gaze to where his hand was splayed out against the dirt. The ring looked like a tattoo in the darkness.

"Nonsense," he said, even as the band burned, tightened. The wave of nausea that passed through him momentarily stole the feeling from his lower half. Nicholas jerked, bucking like a horse.

"Settle yourself," Li Min ordered. "Activity will only make her poison work faster. I might ask what you traded this favor for, but I already know. You were a fool, but you are even more foolish to avoid the terms of your contract. What was her task?"

"Murder," he muttered.

"Ah," was her reply. "A life for a life, then."

"You might have . . . warned us," he said, letting the bitterness bleed into his voice.

"I never thought you foolish enough to go through with it," she said simply.

"Foolish," he agreed, "and desperate. Where are we?"

She continued her work. "The Necropolis of the Vatican. 1499."

He rubbed at his eyes, clearing the dust and grime. He'd been right, then, to feel as though they were descending through the levels of hell to the dark heart of the earth.

There was another sarcophagus flush against the far wall, and he wondered idly if they'd moved the poor occupant from his rest upstairs to this . . . chamber. More importantly, he wondered who "they" were.

"Is this . . . your hiding place?" he asked. If nothing else, talking was a distraction.

"Yes. It belongs to a particular line of my family—the Hemlock clan, I should say." Li Min pressed a hand flat against his bare back, holding him steady. The last surge of pain was short, at least—she knotted the thread she'd used to patch the wound in his shoulder and gave him a pitying pat on the head.

He wasn't feeling up to it, but he forced himself to sit up regardless, hating the disadvantage the prostrate position had put him in. The Ironwoods and Lindens had secret homes and hoards—he shouldn't have been surprised to find the same of the Hemlock family.

Li Min made another of her disapproving noises, pushing him back down. "This was used as a place to amass treasure and documents until it was forgotten. Someone sold me its secrets for a price."

"Seems a rather inconvenient hiding place for you," he noted, rubbing the back of his neck. To have to go through the hassle of Carthage to arrive here . . .

"It's abandoned in every era, up until the twentieth century. And there are many, many passages in the Papal City, as you know. Three in this year alone."

He didn't, but Nicholas nodded nonetheless. "What is your plan, if not to bring us back to Ironwood?"

"She's unconscious, and you're as weak as a lamb," Li Min reminded him. "You've trusted me thus far. I do wish to receive recompense for the gold that was stolen from me, but I am curious about this mission of yours. How it ties to the many threads that are reverberating throughout time."

"We've already spent it. Your gold. There's nothing left, and we've nothing else to trade you."

"You've that gold." She pointed to the leather string tied around his neck—Etta's earring. "That is not *nothing*."

His hand closed over the earring and the glass pendant. "If you think about touching this, you will lose more than a hand."

Li Min looked doubtful at that, her dark brows lifting in pity.

"You can have this," he said hopefully, holding up the hand with the ring. Sensation had fully returned to it; his arm felt unusually stiff, but cooperated as he tested its range of movement. Perhaps he had simply torn a muscle, as he'd originally believed.

"I'd have to cut it off, which would only kill you faster," she informed him.

Hell and damnation. That confirmed the Belladonna's warning.

"Where did you come by that amulet?" she asked after a moment, pointing to the large bead he'd been given.

"A boy gave it to me," he said.

"A stranger?"

"Yes, what of it?"

She shrugged. "Nothing. Everything. He wished you protection and good fortune. It has value. Do not part with it for anything less than your life."

"If it's so valuable, then why don't you take it to cancel our debt?"

"It is not the object that holds power, but the intention behind it. The wish made when it changed hands. I could no more steal that than I could take the light from the stars."

Something in her words rattled him to his core. *I shouldn't have accepted it.* Who needed protection more than that child?

"I suppose you see yourself as 'protection and good fortune,'" he said, wiping the sweat from his face.

"How you wish to see me is your choice," she said. "For now, you should know that I am your only chance of survival."

Neither friend nor foe, it seemed. More a temporary ally, the way Sophia had ultimately come to fit into his life. Nicholas looked around again, drawing his knees to his chest. "As long as we don't run out of air, this will be a suitable hiding place."

"It is convenient, too," she said idly. "If you die, I can leave you down here."

"If Sophia dies, you mean," he said, surprised at the tightening in his throat.

Li Min shook her head. "She will not die. Too stubborn. Too much left unfinished. It's *you* I fear for. Huffing and puffing like a locomotive over a minor flesh wound."

"A *minor*—" Nicholas fought his wince. To knot the tattered remains of his pride, he added, "I've seen myself through far worse than this."

Li Min made a disbelieving sound at the back of her throat. "Running from Ironwoods?"

"Ship boardings," he said. "My—" Nicholas paused, then continued. "My adoptive . . . father, he is a captain."

How strange that he'd never referred to Hall that way aloud. It was always "the captain" or "the man who raised me." But for all his hesitance to put that label to it in his own era, Nicholas had always known the truth in his heart. As a grown man and an officer on Hall's ship, he hadn't wanted the others to feel he was receiving preferential treatment, or that he hadn't earned his position there. As a child, some part of him had feared that Hall might face judgment if Nicholas went around telling that to other, less . . . *forward-thinking* people of their century.

What a poisonous thing it was, to distance himself from a man he loved, a man who had cared for him, for fear of what others might think.

He craned his neck back to find Li Min's dark eyes studying him. When she didn't break her gaze, he realized he hadn't finished his thought. "Fought off pirates for years on voyages, and then became a legal one at the outbreak of the war. Sorry, the American War for Independence. There's been quite a number of them, hasn't there?"

"Pirate?" Li Min said with disbelief. "No chance."

"And what do you know of it?" Nicholas said, trying to straighten his shoulders.

He felt her shrug. "It's not an insult. I only mean to say you'd hesitate before cutting off a man's head to steal his gold teeth. It's not a qualm you're allowed in that line of work."

Fair point. "Spent a lot of time with pirates, have you?"

To his surprise, she said, "Yes. I served under Ching Shih for ten years, from . . . the time I was a child."

"Who the devil is that?" Nicholas asked curiously.

"A pirate unrivaled," Li Min said. "There is no greater one in all of history."

"When did he live? Or she?"

She seemed appeased by this, her gaze softening slightly.

"Ching Shih bridged the eighteenth and nineteenth centuries. She was born in 1775. Tens of thousands came under her command, and she beat back whole empires."

That partly explained why he hadn't recognized her name; that and the biases of the West had likely prevented her legend from spreading past the Pacific. "What became of her?"

"She successfully negotiated her retirement."

"Impressive," he said, because it *was*. More than glory or infamy, successful pirates were those who survived the endeavor and didn't drown, hang, or rot in prison. He stored the story away, to save for Etta.

"Have you always known you were a traveler?" he asked. "How did you get mixed up in all of this?"

"I have always known. I inherited the skill from my mother, who had once been captive under Ching Shih. When I . . . when the time came, I sought Ching Shih out to learn from her. To manifest my strength." Li Min shifted, rising onto her knees and then her feet. "And now I answer only to myself."

"That's something," he said, hoping he didn't sound as bitter as he feared. "I've spent my whole life trying and failing to reach that place."

For the first time since crossing paths with her, Li Min's expression softened. "It's not so easy for some. I should know—I've felt the grinding of the world as it has worked against me. The worth is in the fight, not the conquest. Do not give up."

"I don't intend to," he said.

"But something stands in your way . . . ?"

"Things are . . . rather complicated at the moment."

"Complicated how?" she asked.

"My life has taken me down a path I did not expect," he said, dodging the root of her question. "I have come so far. But the path ahead of me, the one I know I should take, is at odds with the one my heart believes is right. What's the value of my life if I sacrifice my soul?" How much easier it was to admit such things to a stranger, and how well she listened as he continued on, his story flowing from him as simply as if he'd cut a vein and let it bleed out.

Nicholas would carve a path through hell itself to find Etta and finish answering the question of what their life would be together. That was the only certainty on which he could hang his hope. But there were too many factors beyond his control now, and he felt himself drifting further and further from all of those shining possibilities which had been a safe harbor for his heart.

In his life, he had been a slave to man, and now he grew more and more certain that he had allowed himself to become a slave to death. There was no way to break this chain that bound him to the Belladonna without staining his soul; in killing a man, he would murder his own honor and decency.

Li Min considered his story carefully, as if turning over each word to examine it and see what might be hidden beneath it.

"I understand. There is the journey you make through the world— the one that aches and sings. We come together with others to make our way and survive its trials," she said. "But we are, all of us, also way-farers on a greater journey, this one without end, each of us searching for the answers to the unspoken questions of our hearts. Take comfort, as I have, in knowing that, while we must travel it alone, this journey rewards goodness, and will prove that the things which are denied to us in life will never create a cage for our souls."

Nicholas closed his eyes, drawing the damp, cool air into his chest, easing the fire there.

"I will return shortly with food and clothing," she said. "If you leave this spot, you will be lost forever to the darkness of this place. I will not find you, not even to bury your rotting carcass. Do we have an understanding?"

"We do, ma'am," he said.

"Keep watch over her," Li Min said. "Her color is returning, but it will be some time before she regains use of her legs. She will be frightened upon waking."

"And you think I'm the best one to comfort her?" Nicholas scoffed. Sophia would rather accept the tender ministrations of a rabid dog over him.

Li Min seemed genuinely confused by this. "But . . . you don't care for her? Why, then, did you fight so hard to save her?"

Is that what he had done—fight for her? Nicholas had felt himself stumbling again and again. Half of his rage had been aimed at Remus Jacaranda; the other half had been reserved for himself. Not just for ignoring his own instincts, but because . . . because . . .

I nearly let someone die under my protection.

"I require her assistance," he said. "She owes a debt to me."

Sophia made a faint sound, a whistle of a breath between her teeth. Nicholas dragged himself closer, his hand straying down to her wrist to feel for her pulse. It felt steadier than before, and her breathing was no longer labored. The yellow light of the lantern warmed her skin from its former pallid, marblelike state, and he was surprised to find it reassuring.

I'm glad, he thought, the words jolting him to the core. *I'm glad she's not dead.*

He'd wished for nothing so much as that in the moments after Etta had disappeared, after Sophia's betrayal. If she'd been standing before him then, he would have reached out and strangled her.

Nicholas tore his gaze away, studying the shape of his shadow on the opposite wall.

"I wasn't going with them. . . ."

The voice was so faint, he might have marked it as another unnatural breeze. Sophia's eyes were closed, but he could see her lips moving.

"Don't speak," he told her, gently laying a hand on her shoulder. "Save your strength. You'll be well again soon."

"I wasn't . . . going with them . . . wouldn't have . . ." Sophia swallowed hard. "Wouldn't have gone to the Thorns."

"When?" he asked. "In Palmyra?"

Her eyes cracked open and she winced at the light. "I heard . . . what Etta was saying. What you were saying. About Grandfather. The timeline. I went to steal it back from the Thorns. I would have . . . I would have come back with it. Instead . . . *humiliated.*"

"Just rest," he told her. "We are safe here."

"That's why . . . it's my fault . . . my eye—"

Nicholas straightened. "You mean to tell me you went with the Thorns to steal the astrolabe back from them? *That's* why they beat you?"

"And because . . . I'm an Ironwood . . . They thought I was . . . *his.*" She looked at him from under her dark lashes, her eye patch flipped up to reveal the hollow socket beneath. After a moment, Sophia nodded. "Kill them. Will . . . kill them both . . . kill them . . . all. . . ."

It had never made sense to him that she had been so savagely beaten when she'd been a willing participant in the betrayal, riding off with the Thorns. But because of her nature, it had been easy to brush aside and dismiss. Sophia had an unusually potent talent for bringing out the absolute worst in the people around her, and it had drawn out his own ugly, heartless suspicions. He'd dismissed his doubts with the cruel assumption that she'd said something, done something, to provoke their ire—as if *anyone* could deserve that fate.

Li Min had been so quiet on the stairs that it wasn't until she released a low, pained sigh that he noticed her again. She was at the edge of the lantern's light, but the bleakness of her expression lent itself to the darkness.

But she said nothing as she continued climbing. Nicholas reached for the handle of the old, rusted lantern. "Don't you need this?"

Her voice floated back down to him, soft as a memory. "I have always found my way in the dark."

Li Min shouldered the weight of the heavy stone cover, pushing it aside. A small chill raced down the steps and made a home inside of the tomb in those few moments before the lid was shut again.

He took hold of Etta's earring between his fingers again and worried the metal hoop between his fingers, rolling it back and forth.

"If I . . . die . . . *sorry.*" Sophia's voice wasn't even a shadow of a whisper, but he heard her well. He understood.

"Don't be ridiculous," he told her, mimicking her prim tone. "It's as I told you before, in Damascus. You are not allowed to die."

Her answer was silence.

We are, all of us, on our own journeys. . . .

Sophia would never be privy to the journey he had undertaken since childhood, to find that freedom denied to him. But as much as Etta was his heart's helpmate, Sophia was the sword at his side on the expedition he undertook now. From this moment on, for as long as their paths were aligned, she would have his trust and his blade to rely on.

Nicholas leaned back against the nearest wall, the stone cold against his overheated, sore skin, and closed his eyes. For a moment, he merely breathed in. Out. Believed, didn't. Trusted, didn't. Doubted, didn't. Rode the tides of his emotions, the way he and Chase used to float on their backs in open water, watching the sky. And in that way, in a city of the dead, he finally slept as the dead did: undreaming, and unburdened.

TWENTY-ONE

There were certain kinds of exhaustion that lingered like a drug in the body, making even the simplest tasks, like lifting one's head from the ground, feel impossible. Nicholas's mind seemed to be in combat with the needs of his body. He startled awake, and felt as though he were locked inside a drunken stupor. Soft voices drifted over to where he remained on the ground, curled around his throbbing right hand. The lantern had been dimmed and his eyesight was blurred, but he made out Li Min's shape leaning against the wall, Sophia's head in her lap.

". . . is this quite necessary?"

"Very," he heard Sophia say. "I am very delicate at the moment, you see."

"I do see," Li Min said dryly. "*Delicate* is most certainly a word I would use to describe you, what with how you flee from weapons and faint upon seeing a drop of blood."

"I haven't the slightest idea as to what you're implying," Sophia said primly. "I might die yet."

"Oh, dear," Li Min whispered. "However can I prevent this?"

Sophia seemed to consider it, then lifted her hand from where it had been draped across her chest. "You ought to check my pulse again. Make sure you count it for . . . a few minutes."

He drifted away again to the sound of Li Min softly counting *one, two, three, four* . . .

The next time he woke, it was to screams.

They came to him from a great distance, muffled but ripe with agony. In the moment it took his mind to shake off sleep, the voices seemed to transform into a living, breathing thing. Nicholas surged up off the floor, knocking his head against the low ceiling and sending a spray of plaster dust down over his body.

"*Shh!*"

Sophia was awake and sitting upright, having positioned herself against the wall. Her dark eye fixed on him as she struggled to hold up a half-eaten loaf of bread. Nicholas accepted it with ravenous relief, tearing off a chunk for himself. He chewed and swallowed absently, his attention shifting from the much-needed food to the small figure at the base of the stairs.

With the sword Nicholas had taken in Carthage in one hand, a dagger in the other, Li Min kept one foot braced on the bottom step and her eyes fixed upward, toward the entrance.

"What is that?" he whispered, coming to stand beside her. The screams tore at his nerves; his hands curled at his sides, slick with sweat. "*Who* is that?"

Surely not . . . the Ironwoods?

"We are being hunted," Li Min said. Her eyes looked black in the low light. "Eat and put on the clothing I've brought you. We will not be leaving in the near future, but when we do move, it will be quickly."

Nicholas ignored her, taking two steps up to better hear the fighting outside—the wet sound of flesh and the piercing yelps somehow permeated even the thickest of stone tombs. "What—*who*—is out there? You know, don't you?"

Li Min wiped the sweat from her brow, glancing back at Sophia.

With a start, Nicholas saw that Sophia had already changed into a plain white shirt and fawn-colored breeches, and had busied herself with trying to lace up a leather waistcoat. Two pairs of scuffed black boots had been tossed onto another pile of clothing at the center of the room—his, he assumed. The Chinese girl wore a billowy white shirt as well, only she had found thin hose for herself, and a red pleated doublet to be layered over both and secured in place with a heavy leather belt. They would all be traveling as men, then.

"For the love of God, tell us whatever you know," he said. *"Please."*

"You wouldn't believe it," she murmured. "If it is what I think . . ."

"I *believe* we are possibly about to be savagely killed, so the time for thoughtful hesitance has sadly passed," Nicholas said. "Do you know who they are?"

"I do. They have been hunting you for as long as I've tracked you. They left a trail of bodies behind them—guardians and travelers alike—all dead, the same as that Linden man in Nassau."

Nicholas's whole body stilled.

"There is an evil here that reeks of age and decay," Li Min said, turning to look at him. "They will not stop until they have what they're looking for."

"And how do you know that?" Sophia demanded. "Did you use your nose for that as well?"

"I know," Li Min said quietly, cradling each word as if afraid to release them, "because I used to be one of them."

"Pardon?" Sophia said mildly.

"There is not enough time to explain," Li Min said. "They are the Shadows nurtured by the Ancient One. Stolen from their families as children, their humanity ripped from them with bloody training and manipulation. They are here for one purpose alone: to serve him. To find what he seeks above all else."

Sophia scrabbled along the ground until she found the knife she usually kept tucked into her low boots. She swung it out toward Li Min.

"No," Li Min said, kneeling before her again, letting the tip of the blade press against her heart. "I escaped as a child. My mother was a guardian, as was my sister. I was born able to travel, so the Shadows took me to fill their ranks and murdered my family. Witnesses to their existence dig their own graves, you see."

"Then how did you escape?" Sophia asked, still not lowering the blade.

"I was always the smallest, the weakest," Li Min said quietly. "The Ancient One felt I was undeserving of the privilege of serving him. One night, when the elder Shadows were teaching night stalking, I was chosen to serve as prey. As bait. Whoever killed me would receive his radiant blessings."

Nicholas reeled back in horror.

"But it was a moonless night," Li Min said, the words tumbling out of her. "I slipped away. They never found me again. They have not, at least, until now."

I sought Ching Shih out to learn from her, she had said. *To manifest my strength.*

"It's all true, then," Nicholas said, fighting not to touch the ring on his hand, to ignore the way it scalded him deep down, at the seat of his soul. "*From the shadows they come, to give you a fright. . . .* Why does this . . . why does this . . . Ancient One, you said? Why does he want the astrolabe?"

"Because he believes that he will be granted complete immortality if he consumes its power; he will be impervious to harm and time's ravages," she said. "He has prolonged his life by taking the power of the copies, but they were not nearly enough to sate him. He fills the heads of the Shadows with promises that they, too, will live forever and inherit the world. They are acolytes as much as they are his servants."

Sophia shook her head, as if she could fling the story away. "No. *No.*

307

That Jacaranda was full of it. Alchemists? Hogwash and horsefeathers!"

But Nicholas was nodding, rubbing his face. Forcing himself to accept this, the way Etta would, in order to move on.

"You believe me?" Li Min asked. "Truly?"

He met her gaze in the low light. It was the first time he had detected true vulnerability in her voice. A hopefulness threaded with disbelief. "It aligns with what we already knew, and you've no reason to lie to us. But I imagine few would believe it without this evidence in front of them. Have you never spoken of this before, then?"

She tossed her braid back over her shoulder again, the corners of her mouth slanting down. "I did not think—as you said, the story is impossible to believe for anyone who has not lived it. One cannot go about prattling on about Shadows and immortality and such and be hired for delicate jobs, you see."

"I do see," Nicholas said, understanding better now why she worked as a mercenary, rather than inside the fold of the Thorns and Ironwoods. A secret was easiest kept by one, or none.

"It's all true," Li Min said. "And if we cannot escape, then we will never leave this place."

The tortured cries died to whimpers. Li Min placed a finger to her lips. Nicholas held his breath, reaching for a weapon on his tunic's belt that was no longer there. He looked to Li Min, who blatantly ignored him, keeping both weapons in her hands and lowering into a defensive stance. But then his attention was drawn upward again, toward the entrance to the tomb.

They sounded as any man's footsteps would in a careful approach. It was only when that same scratching began, that long, continuous drag of sound, that Nicholas realized they weren't hearing anything at all—not through so many layers of old stone. They were *feeling* the vibrations of the movements. Plaster shook loose from the ceiling, and he wondered, with a sickening twist of his stomach, what could be so heavy as to have caused that.

"Li Min," he whispered. "Do they use a peculiar kind of weapon—a long, thin blade like a claw?"

"Yes," she breathed out. "They receive it upon their initiation. So you *have* seen them for yourselves."

They had. They'd struggled blow for blow against them in Carthage, without ever realizing it. His hand reached up and closed around the small amulet and Etta's earring. The shaking worsened, thunder crackling through the walls, making it sound as though whoever these travelers—these Shadows—were, they were in the tomb beside them.

This is hell, he thought, *or all the devils have escaped.*

The light around him dampened as Sophia reached over and dimmed the lantern.

If they died down here, who would be the last of them to bear witness to the others' screams?

Cease this at once! he barked at himself. My God, he was becoming prone to theatrics in a way that would have made Chase weep with pride. A heap of good that would do him. He'd fight, as he always had. He'd give Sophia and Li Min the opportunity to escape, and then he would follow. He would not die down here in the dark when there was a future to claim.

Nicholas could not say how much time passed before muffled voices began to bleed through the walls. He spoke French and Spanish, as well as passable Italian, owing to his time mixing with other sailors in ports. He could speak and read Latin and a touch of Greek, thanks to the patience of Mrs. Hall, but this was simply too low to make out.

Li Min cocked her head toward the door, her face twisting in concentration. For the first time in their short acquaintance, he saw a tremor of helplessness run through her expression, and a lingering flare of hope he didn't know had died out.

There was a moment of silence before another sound began to drift through the air, curling against his skin, making his every hair stand at attention. It seemed so out of place that his mind had trouble placing it:

Laughter.

Sophia pressed a hand against her mouth. Nicholas's skin felt as though it might actually retreat from his bones.

The steps grew softer. The vibrations settled from quakes to shivers to nothing at all. He and Li Min exchanged one last look before he released the tension that had wound up his system. He took a deep breath, expanding his lungs and chest until both ached.

"Change," Li Min told him. "Quickly. We will need to leave before they think to return."

Nicholas nodded, moving back to the pile of clothes. "Do you require assistance with your boots?" he asked Sophia. Her arms and hands were moving again, but he had yet to see the same of her legs and feet.

She drew in a sharp breath and, with great effort and an enormous swallowing of pride, nodded.

"I will do it," Li Min said, brushing his hands away. He glanced at Sophia, ensuring she was comfortable with this, before picking up the breeches and sliding them on. They were undersized, which might have been a comment on how Li Min viewed him, but was more likely a matter of what was available—what she could steal or purchase without incurring any notice.

She herself wore a heavy cloak that served to blot her out of sight. He hadn't considered before how strange it was to have a slight advantage over someone else, in spite of the disadvantages the world had foisted upon him. A dark-skinned man in the Papal City, especially one in simple clothing, would not be nearly as remarkable as a young Chinese woman.

The boots were also small, but tolerable. He turned his back to the others for a moment, changed out of the soiled tunic, and slipped the soft linen shirt on, tucking it into the breeches. He left his own doublet unlaced, ignoring how short it was on his frame. No one would be allowed to see him long enough to question it; and, well, the world had a way of ignoring its poor and simple.

He ran a hand over his face, the rasp of whiskers growing in. "If we should need to fight . . ."

"Aim for their skulls, throats, or along their sides just below the rib cage where the seams of their chest plates can be cut," Li Min said. "We are safer disappearing."

"Is there a passage nearby?"

"Two upstairs," Sophia said. "I can guide us. Help me up, will you?" She reached an arm out. Nicholas and Li Min both moved to her side, but he arrived first, gripping her by the wrist and pulling her upright— and, as it turned out, forward. Her legs gave out and she gasped in alarm.

Nicholas caught her easily enough. "Do you have any sensation in them yet?"

Sophia nodded, clearing her throat and blinking, until finally her gaze hardened again. "I might . . . need help. Just for a little while longer."

"I'm amenable to that," he told her. His shoulder was aching from the stitches Li Min had put in, but he felt stronger just having rested. His right arm, the one that had plagued him in Carthage, protested in pain as it absorbed some of Sophia's weight, but he tossed that concern aside.

"You won't tell a soul of this, not even Linden," Sophia said. "And you'll carry me on your back, not as some sort of damsel, otherwise I'll cast up my accounts in disgust."

"Naturally," Nicholas said.

"Not a *word*," she grumbled.

"Not on my life," he promised.

Behind them, Li Min was gathering up their bags, pushing her dark cloak back to loop them over her shoulders.

"You're actually coming?" Sophia asked. "And helping us? It would be so easy to leave us as bait and escape."

"I may be a mercenary, but I'm not a beast, nor am I an imbecile. I cannot fight them alone. He cannot protect either of you that way, or quickly escape," she said, "not without dropping you first. And you are incapable of running or fighting should it happen."

"I wouldn't drop her," he said, just as Sophia snarled, "I've never run from a fight in my life!"

"If we are *leaving*," Li Min said, talking over both of them, "then let us *leave* this place. I know the way up into St. Peter's Basilica."

"The lantern—" Nicholas began.

"No; we move in darkness, as they do," Li Min said, taking the first few steps up. "Quickly; quickly."

As it turned out, he did have to set Sophia down to help Li Min lift the cover off the sarcophagus. Almost immediately, the stink of fresh, hot blood assaulted his senses. He heard Sophia gag behind him, her arms tightening around his neck as he bent to pick her up again.

"Do you hear that?" she whispered. When he didn't respond, she put his head between her hands and turned it to the right.

Drip . . . drip . . . drip . . .

The air was cool down here, too dry for condensation. A shudder rolled through him, prickling at his scalp, cutting down his spine. Li Min stood off to the side of the grave, her weapons raised, looking up—up to where Miles Ironwood's body had been stuffed into one of the tomb's alcoves, his unblinking eyes glowing in the dark. Rivulets of blood raced down the wall to the body of a second man, his body contorted as if his back was broken.

"Holy God . . ." Sophia breathed out. Nicholas swung back toward Li Min just in time to see the glint of silver, the dark shape that swung down toward the girl's face.

"Li—!" he began, but the girl was already moving, the shorter of her two swords spinning out, catching the arm with a sickening *thwack*. A gasp split the air as the Shadow flew back and Li Min stooped for something on the ground. When she stood up again, she threw the longer blade his way, only to have Sophia grab it out of the air and slice at the Shadows behind them; he felt the reverberations as she struck something solid.

"Who's there?" she bellowed near his ear. "Show yourselves! Show yourselves, you bloody cowards!"

He could see it now—see *them*. They were a shade darker than the air, until one, a young man with a startlingly pale face, looked up at him from beneath his hood. Nicholas felt himself dissected by the piercing gaze, cut down to his marrow. He took an involuntary step back as ice flooded his system, the backs of his knees bumping into the sarcophagus.

In one smooth movement, he pulled the sword out of Sophia's hand and lunged forward, stabbing into the Shadow's throat as Li Min had instructed. A hand lashed out, and he had to jump and twist onto the sarcophagus's lid to avoid being skewered by the claw.

Sophia released her grip on his shoulders, slamming back against the edge of the sarcophagus. She reached over and pulled the knife off his belt, bracing herself as if to take a blow. Li Min let out a ferocious cry and dove toward the other Shadow, a woman with a shock of red hair. She swung her blade around, swirling the disturbed dust as she spun with it, swinging down to try to take off the Shadow's head. The other woman was too fast, parrying with a kick hard enough to throw Li Min back a step, but not hard enough to stop her. Rage steamed off the Chinese woman, searing the air, hollowing her cheeks as she opened her mouth and let out another roar.

The furious clanging of their blades should have woken the dead.

A blade lanced down through the darkness, forcing him to drop to the ground to prevent it biting into the juncture of his neck and shoulder. Nicholas lashed a leg out, trying to upend the Shadow, but the man jumped to a nearly inhuman height, flipping back down to catch Nicholas in the face with the full force of his body.

A thousand stars burst behind his eyelids and he was momentarily blinded by the flashing of them. Sophia's shout made him turn just as the Shadow's claw would have pierced the inner part of his ear. It caught him over his cheek instead. Nicholas slipped in the pools of blood on the floor, unable to get his feet beneath him.

Damn it all, get up, get up—

He had fought a hundred battles at sea, fended off pirates and boardings. He'd avoided knives to his belly and axes to his neck and he had *survived*; even the fighters hardened by the sea, he'd survived. But the best-trained of those men were raging, dumb animals compared to this Shadow, who seemed to anticipate his blows before Nicholas decided to try for them.

Etta— He took a vicious punch to his chest, and felt ribs crack. *Etta*—

He tried to imagine her the way she had been on the *Ardent*, when she'd appeared in the haze of battle; he tried to use that image, like a prayer for strength, to drive his next hit. Yet, when his mind's eye drew the memory forward, the scene was cracked between the jaws of darkness. Her screams suddenly silenced, the blood running in rivulets over her face. The clean slice of a claw through her ear.

Her body as pale and still as the marble angels that surrounded them.

He surged up from the ground, knocking the Shadow back. The attacker made as if to lunge forward, but halted, dropping to a knee and howling in pain. Behind him, Sophia had slipped to the ground and cut the tendon of his ankle. Nicholas seized the opportunity at the same moment she did, each of them slicing toward the Shadow's neck.

The body fell to the ground.

Another screech of metal on metal brought Nicholas back around to where Li Min was using her arms, every trembling ounce of strength in her body, to turn the Shadow's long claw back onto the woman's body, piercing the soft flesh of her neck.

"I am . . . forever . . ." the woman gasped out.

"You are dead," Li Min corrected, and finished her.

"As are you," came another voice. Nicholas whirled back toward the entrance of the tomb, his sword following the path of another Shadow as he stepped inside. Two more fell in line behind him. "Little lost one. Do you remember me, as I remember you?"

He knew she didn't mean to, that it was likely the way the man's voice licked at the air like a snake's tongue, but she stepped back, just that small bit. Her hands gripped her dagger hard enough for him to hear her knuckles crack.

Though he knew she would likely despise it, Nicholas felt a fierce surge of protectiveness for the young girl stolen from her family and brought into their darkness, and the young woman who stood before him now, having survived it.

The entirety of his right hand lost sensation, and then the rest of his arm. Nicholas barely caught the sword with his weaker left hand, his gaze narrowing on them, as his heart beat a vicious tattoo of fear.

"Li Min," Nicholas said quietly. "Take her and go. I'll catch up to you."

"No—" Sophia began as Li Min knelt beside her. "Wait, are you—"

"I have the astrolabe," Nicholas told the Shadows. "Who will fight me for it?"

The flash of Sophia's white shirt at the edge of his vision told him, if nothing else, that they had gotten out of the cramped space. One of the Shadows broke off to pursue them, only to be summoned back by the flick of the first man's hand.

Nicholas raised his sword, swallowing the blood in his mouth. *I will live.* It was not a question, but a necessity. He only needed to create a path to the entrance of the mausoleum, and then he could lose them in the darkness.

The Shadow in front matched his stance, letting the hood fall away from his face.

A voice in the darkness began to whisper, to pulse, to growl. The Shadows recoiled at the sound of it. Two ducked back through the entrance, vanishing with a soft patter of footsteps.

"Liar," the Shadow said, lingering just a moment more before pulling his hood up and following their path. Nicholas staggered forward, using the walls to support himself as he moved. If the Shadows had gone left, he would go right, and hope it might lead him to Li Min and Sophia. To the Basilica.

But from the depths of the city of the dead, a voice rang out, as brittle and airy as the plaster dust that swirled around him. *"Child of time."*

The words scored down his heart, tugged his attention back. He turned, clutching his numb arm to his chest. And though his tired mind was prone to tricks, and his heart weary of them, he could have sworn he saw another figure standing there. The long, pale cloak clasped around his neck flowed down the line of his back, curling at his feet like a cat. It gave his bearing a forceful regality that made Nicholas wish he could summon the strength to turn away again. The distance seemed to close between them, though neither of them moved, and Nicholas saw that his profile was as faultless as if it had been painted by a master's hand. All at once, the ring on his finger began to sing its song of pain, flaring as the man turned his head more fully, his gaze dropping to it. It was only then, when he caught the whole of the man's countenance, that Nicholas saw that his features were like that of a demon—like that of Death himself.

He turned and ran as if hell burned behind him.

TWENTY-
TWO

IT SURPRISED HIM SOMEHOW THAT A CITY OF THE DEAD would be arranged like an actual city, but here he was, running down dark, winding streets that split the rows of tombs and structures into a grid. When, at last, his feet found the edge of a set of stairs, he realized he'd begun to climb toward the surface. He was grateful for the challenge of the steps, the warmth that crept into the air as he rose up through the layers of earth and carved stone, and nearly wept at the first sighting of fat candles perched along the wall of a narrow hallway. It meant he was near the end.

He was even more grateful to find that Sophia and Li Min were already there, waiting for him.

"What took you so long?" Sophia demanded from where she sat on the ground. "Damn you for sending us away!"

Nicholas looked at her as though she'd declared herself recently hatched from an egg. He wiped the stinging line of blood from his cheek, only to find that he was still clutching the sword. His right arm hung uselessly at his side, and he forced himself to quell his fear at the realization, so as not to frighten them. "I worried for you, too, Sophia."

"Ugh," she said, crossing her arms and turning away. "I knew you'd be revoltingly sentimental about this."

"Forgive the presumptions I made about your character on our first meeting," Li Min said. "I see the sort of person you are now."

"Yeah, a bleeding *idiot*," Sophia muttered.

"Are you hurt?" Li Min asked. "Beyond what we can see?"

The smell of warm wax coated the air, clearing the lingering touch of decay in his throat and lungs. Nicholas turned back to see if there was a way of barring the door behind them—there was. He slid the latch into place, fully ignoring the voice that told him it wouldn't be enough.

"I saw something," he told them, instead of answering her. "I need to know . . . I need to understand what it was."

"You saw *him*. The Ancient One," Li Min said, as if his face alone had revealed it. "He allowed you to live?"

In that moment, when he'd met the man's gaze . . . there was no other way to describe it, save to say that Nicholas had felt acutely aware of his own years, how they might fit inside the man's palm.

"He called them—the Shadows—away," Nicholas said. "I haven't the faintest notion as to why."

"I did not know he was capable of mercy." He did not, for one moment, enjoy the flash of fear he saw trespass on Li Min's face. She continued in a hurry. "Something more is at play here. Where is it that you hope to go? Are you still hoping to find the last common year?" She swiped the back of her hand against her forehead, smudging the blood and dust there. Her hands were covered in liquid so dark, it almost looked black.

Blood, he realized. That was the travelers' blood. In the rush of their fight and flight, he'd neglected to spare more than one horrified second thinking of the Ironwood travelers who had been killed and left for them to find. Their lives had been reduced to splatters of gore, and they'd become nothing more than a way to taunt the next victims. These Shadows could have done the same to any of them, and that put their odds of surviving this in rather stark terms.

"Yes," he told her. "Did you learn what it was?"

"1905," she said, with a look that hinted that she had known the whole time. He was too ravaged by pain and apprehension to care much in that moment. "We can take the passage upstairs, the one that leads to Florence. From there, it will be a voyage, but it should not take more than a few days—"

"What the hell is wrong with your arm?" Sophia interrupted. Without preamble, she reached up, gripping his right wrist and using it to haul herself, at last, to her feet.

Nicholas looked away. "It is only sore—"

"You haven't moved it once!" He could see that Sophia had dug her nails into his hand, but could not feel it. "What—you mean it's the ring?"

Her voice was rising in pitch, and she looked as if she wanted nothing more than to pull the arm out of its socket and beat him senseless with it.

"The Belladonna's poison," Li Min said, taking a turn at lifting his arm and turning it to and fro, as if reading a map. "If you do not complete her task, it will eventually travel to your heart and cause it to seize in the same way. What did she ask of you?"

"To kill Ironwood," Sophia said, before he could.

"But why?" Li Min asked, her tone hushed.

"Have you *met* him?"

"Enough," Nicholas said. "We can discuss it along the way to 1905."

"Yes, please," Sophia said.

Li Min drew the hood up over her ears, obscuring most of her face from view. "Niceties don't suit you."

They suit almost the entirety of the world, Nicholas managed to think, not say.

"This way, then." Li Min urged them forward again, her cape fluttering down the hall.

"You need to do this," Sophia ordered him as they followed. "You can't trade your life for the old man's. It's not worth it. Half the world would throw you a parade for it."

"Like you'll kill the men who harmed you?" he asked.

She turned, staring straight ahead, her jaw set. "That's different. *I* won't die if I never find those roaches. If you won't do it, I will. The day Cyrus Ironwood gets what he wants is the day my corpse is lowered into its grave."

Ironwoods, he thought, shaking his head. Always so eager to shed their own blood.

"What happens when the old man is gone?" he asked. "Will you step up as heir? Expect the other families to fall in line behind you?"

"All I care about is wiping that smear of shite off the face of this earth, and salting the ground that grew him," she snapped. "Whatever becomes of the families when he's gone is up for someone else to decide. I want no part of any of this anymore."

She wants to be free of this. The one person he saw as being an emblem of everything the family stood for wanted nothing more to do with it. Remarkable.

Li Min slowed as they reached the next imposing door, pressing her ear against the rough, dark wood. She glanced back, nodding to Nicholas, then pushed the door open, revealing a set of steps that spiraled up out of sight.

Nicholas started forward, only to stop again at the sound of a voice floating down to them. He drew Sophia back into the shadows of the nearest wall, his mind trying to spin up possible explanations for what they were doing down there—to be caught now, and in their bloodied appearance—

A light moved along the stone wall of the stairwell, marking the man's progress. He appeared sooner than expected, an older gentleman in robes whose pleasant face went slack with surprise.

"We are—" Sophia shifted smoothly into Latin. *"We have come to pay our respects—"*

Li Min's arm lashed out, thumping the priest on the head with the flat of her sword. Nicholas barely managed to step forward to catch him in time as he wilted to the ground.

"Too slow," she said to Nicholas's incredulous look. "Time to move."

"She was right about one thing," Sophia said as she passed him. "You're no pirate, Saint Nicholas. Where's that ruthless edge that lets you hack sailors apart on ships?"

"Affronted by this lack of honor," he told her.

She must have rolled her eye. "Hang honor before it hangs you."

Li Min, at least, seemed to know where they were going. It took Nicholas some time, however, to even realize that they'd entered St. Peter's Basilica and were walking its quiet halls. Sophia had referred to it as the "old" St. Peter's, and he saw the truth of that immediately. This structure had none of the grandeur he'd witnessed when he and Julian had visited it in search of the astrolabe—but that had been, what, the twentieth century? He'd been struck mute by the masters of art who graced its ceilings and walls; it had collected treasures and grandeur over time, the way a traveler family would. This iteration was simple, with stark lines and angles that lacked both a sense of gravity and permanence. Still, it was by no means as humble as the Anglican churches in the colonies, which seemed to pride themselves on being as plain and grim as possible.

He glanced up as they passed by a large chapel, its door open just enough to catch the glimmer of rows of candlelight. Beside him, Sophia kept her gaze down, her pace as labored as his own. Nicholas was so deep in his own thoughts that he did not notice when she drifted a few steps behind him, stopping.

"Good *lord*, Carter," Sophia whispered. "You've been mooning over this damned thing for a bloody month, and *now* you just drop it willy-nilly?"

Sophia held up a familiar gold earring, its small leaves and blue stone shivering with the breeze. Nicholas's hand flew to the leather cord around his neck, his heart slamming up from his chest into his throat.

Hell and damnation—

But the talisman and the earring were still there, secure. He felt the slight weight in his hand. So how . . . ?

A drumming began in his chest, spreading out and out and out through his blood until he couldn't quite feel his fingers.

"Surely it's not the same," Li Min said, taking it from Sophia. "Look—"

But when placed side by side in his hand, they were almost identical, to the best of an artist's skill and capability. They were a pair. They were . . .

Etta.

Nicholas tore away from the others, stumbling back toward the chapel, running down the length of it, finding nothing and no one. He returned to the hall, wild with disbelief and hope, searching for any other hint of her—anything that might tell him where she had gone. Dust stung his eyes, blurring his vision. It choked him, filling his lungs, wringing the last gasps of air out of him. The desperation was intolerable, but he couldn't let it go, not yet—

"Etta?" he called, his voice as loud as he dared. "Etta, where are you?"

"Oh God," he heard Sophia say. "This is painful to watch. Make him stop. Please."

It was Li Min's face that brought his frantic searching to a halt. The carefully constructed cipher cracked as she bit her lip, her eyes darting to the side. "Surely you are not referring to Henrietta Hemlock?"

"Hemlock?" Sophia said, holding up a hand. "Wait—"

"Henrietta, the daughter of Henry Hemlock—"

"Etta Spencer," Nicholas said impatiently. "Her mother is Rose Linden, and, yes, Rose told me Hemlock is Etta's father."

"Why didn't you tell *me* that?" Sophia asked. "You didn't think it was relevant that the leader of *the Thorns* procreated with the beast that is Rose Linden? My God, this explains so much. *So* much."

Li Min could not look at him. Her jaw worked silently, her hands clenching at her sides. Nicholas felt his stomach roll in revolt, and he'd stepped into a trap, and there was no way to free himself from the painful, searing cage of hope. "Do you know where she is? That's who we've been trying to find. She was orphaned, to the last common year—"

She closed her eyes, releasing the breath trapped inside of her. "I do. I am . . . truly sorry. Your search ends here, for she is dead."

NEW YORK CITY
1939

TWENTY-THREE

ETTA WAS NOT SURE HOW LONG SHE STOOD ROOTED TO THAT same spot. Terror had such a firm grip on her that it could have pulled the skin off her bones. Julian ventured forward a few steps, waving the soot and ash out of the way as best he could. Revealing only more soot and ash.

"There's . . . there's *nothing*," he said, turning back to her. "How is that possible? The buildings, the people . . ."

He wasn't wrong; as far as the eye could see through the smoke—which turned out to be very far, without the hindrance of buildings crowding the park's boundaries—there was nothing beyond the husks of what had once been. If the air cleared, Etta knew she'd at least be able to see the East River. She had thought the destruction of the San Francisco earthquake had been absolute, but this . . . this was . . .

"Oh my God," she said, pressing a hand against her mouth.

She'd been right. This was a third, alternate timeline—it hadn't reverted back to Ironwood's timeline like he must have intended with the assassination. He'd grasped burning, dangerous threads of history and knotted them into something far more sinister. Something unrecognizable.

There's nothing left.

327

She lowered herself to her knees, suddenly unable to support her own weight.

"What could cause this?" Julian asked. "Shelling? Aerial bombings?"

"I don't know," she said. "I don't know—we need to—we need to go—"

If it was something worse, like a nuclear weapon, then they'd already exposed themselves to harmful radiation. The thought pushed Etta back off the ground, dried the tears that were beginning to form in her eyes.

But when she turned to tell Julian, something else caught her eye— the sweep of headlights cutting through the thick smoke, brushing over them.

"Survivors, call out," a voice crackled over a speaker, broken up by either emotion or the technology. *"Help is on the way. Survivors . . . call out if you can. . . ."*

"Come on," Etta said, turning back to the passage. "We need to go!"

Julian shook his head. "No—Nan—I'm going to find her—"

Etta's words caught in her throat. If she'd been in the city, there was very likely nothing left to find. But before they could protest, the headlights found them again, and an engine revved as it raced toward them. Before the vehicle had fully stopped, a man in a full black jump-suit and gas mask—something that closely resembled what Etta knew as a hazmat suit—leaped out of the back of a Jeep and rushed toward them.

"My *God*! My God, what are you doing here?" The man's voice was muffled by his oxygen mask. "How did you survive?"

"That, chap," Julian managed to get out, "is an excellent question."

ETTA KNEW THAT SHE SHOULD HAVE STEERED THEM BACK through the passage, but some part of her wanted to know—wanted to see for herself—what had become of her city.

She should have considered what that would do to her heart. After a while, she stopped looking out at the devastation as the military-issue Jeep bounced through the smoldering wreckage, and cupped her hands over her eyes.

This isn't right, this isn't right. . . . None of this was right. This timeline . . .

A medic riding with them had given them both oxygen masks, which cleared her head somewhat. Etta winced as he swiped antiseptic over the cut on her arm again, and then turned to the slash across her forehead.

"Say . . ." Julian said, his voice trembling slightly as he leaned forward to speak to the driver. "They figure out who to pin this on yet? We've been a bit, uh, out of it. Trapped in that basement, you know?"

Julian Ironwood: worthless at paddling a boat, but quick with a lie.

"I'll say," the driver called back. "The Central Powers proudly took credit for their handiwork. Made sure to hit Los Angeles and Washington, too, just to drive the message home."

Etta had to close her eyes and breathe deeply, just to keep from vomiting.

"Never seen anything like the flash when this hit. Millions, just—" The man trailed off.

Gone, Etta's mind finished.

It was light enough outside that once they approached the Hudson, heading toward what the men had described as a medical camp and survivor meeting point in New Jersey, Etta could see the dark outline of a bicycle and a man against one of the last standing walls. Almost as if they had disappeared and left their shadows behind.

"Paris and London are still standing, but it's only a matter of time," the medic said bitterly. "This was to warn us off joining them in their fight, I bet. They knew Roosevelt was thinking about sending aid or troops over to the Brits—that they've been gearing up for a fight. So the Central Powers declared war on us."

"This isn't war," the driver said. "This is hell. They knew we'd jump in first chance we got, and so they crippled us. They showed us who's boss."

Etta didn't ask about the government, about the other cities. And she didn't ask Julian about how they would get back to that passage, or what other ones they could reach in this year. Exhaustion swept over her. It stole whatever spark of fight she had left. She closed her eyes on her ruined city.

"Almost done, honey," the medic said. Under any other circumstances she would have hated the endearment, but she was feeling battered, and the man had a grandfatherly quality that reminded her of Oskar, Alice's husband. "You'll need to find a doctor to stitch up your arm when we get there, you hear me?"

Etta couldn't muster the strength to nod.

Where would she even start? How could anyone fix *this*?

Anywhere, she thought, and *with everything I have.*

THE MEDICAL CAMP WAS SET UP IN ELIZABETH, NEW JERSEY. Far enough from the blast site in the center of Manhattan to be out of immediate danger, but still close enough to be shrouded in toxic clouds of fumes and dust. To get there, they'd had to drive by cleared fields where the bodies of victims had been brought, some covered with tarps, others not. Etta's breath was harsh in her ears, and she couldn't seem to let go of the image of their twisted shapes, the way the charring had left them looking almost hollow. As much as she felt like she had to be a witness to these atrocities, that she owed it to them to form a memory of their wasted lives, Etta didn't protest when the medic leaned over and covered her eyes.

"You don't have to see this," he said. "It's all right."

But she did.

I did this, she thought. By letting the astrolabe slip away, she was responsible; the thought left her trembling so hard that the same medic had her lie down across the seat to administer an IV.

330

By listening to the radio in the Jeep, Etta learned the following: the attacks had happened five days ago; the secretary of labor was now the president of the United States, as he'd had the good fortune to be on vacation outside of the District when the bombs struck; and there'd been no decision on whether or not to make peace or declare war.

"Is there a registry?" Julian asked. "A list of survivors from the city?"

"Not yet," was all they were told. "You'll see."

And they did see. The old warehouse that had been converted into an emergency medical facility was wrapped around twice with a line of people waiting to get inside. Many of them—in fact, most—were African American. They, too, made up the bulk of those coming in and out of the tents that had been set up along the nearby streets. Their rudimentary bandages looked like basic first aid, not actual treatment.

"Why are there two lines?" Julian asked, sounding as dazed as Etta felt. She turned to see what he was staring at. Two separate booths, both with the Red Cross's symbol, both handing out the same parcels of food. But there were two very distinct lines: one for white people, the other for blacks.

Etta fought the scream that tore up through her. The whole city was in ruins, millions of people were likely dead, and they still followed this hollow, cruel tradition, as if it accomplished *anything* other than humiliation.

"You know why," she told him. Julian was an Ironwood; he traveled extensively; he had been educated about the history his father had created; and he was acting like none of that was true. Somehow, it only infuriated her more.

"But *why*?" he repeated, his voice hollow.

"Come on, you two," one of the soldiers said.

"What about the rest of them?" Julian asked as they were walked right past the line waiting to get into the warehouse.

"Waiting for blood from one of the black blood banks in Philadelphia," the soldier said, as if it weren't a completely insane statement. *Blood is blood is blood is blood.* The only thing that mattered was type. This was an emergency, an utter disaster, and still—*this.*

Calm down, she told herself. *Calm down.* . . . She crossed her arms over her chest to keep from tearing the world apart around them in a rage of devastation. *My city. These people* . . . Etta choked on the bile that rose, and it was only by pressing the back of her hand against her mouth that she kept from throwing up until she was truly as hollow and empty as she felt.

"What are we doing here?" Etta whispered as the men led her and Julian toward the warehouse. "We can't stay, you know that."

He shook his head, turning back to look at the faces of the people at the door, waiting to get in. "There are open beds. Why are they outside if there are open beds?"

"They'll be treated when the rest of the staff from Kenney Hospital arrive," the medic said, speaking slowly, as if Julian were a child. "This way."

The medic relinquished them to a bleary-eyed doctor, who ushered them over to sit on a cot. The man began to examine the cuts and burns on Etta's arms and hands without so much as a word. A nurse with strawberry-blond hair eventually wandered over with a pail of water and a rag.

Julian stared at a man two cots over, quietly weeping into his hat.

"Let me help you there, sugar," the nurse said, and cleaned away the grime and blood Etta had been carrying with her since St. Petersburg. "It's all right to cry. It's better if you do."

I can't. Something cold had locked around her core, so that she didn't even register the doctor stitching a particularly bad cut without anesthesia. She didn't register Julian scooting to the edge of the cot so that the nurse could lift Etta's legs up, laying her out on the cot.

Etta watched, in some strange state between sleeping and wakefulness, as the doctors, nurses, servicemen, and families of the injured moved between the cots and curtains that divided the enormous space into makeshift rooms.

"Will you stop with this—" A nearby voice was rising, flustered. "I don't need to be examined."

"Madam, you do if you'll let me continue, I won't be but a moment—"

"Can you not understand me?" the woman said, her voice dripping with a venomous mix of fear and tension. "I don't *want* you to touch me."

Etta opened her eyes, craning her neck to see what was happening. The doctor who had stitched her up went right to the other, badgered doctor's side. A black doctor.

"I'll finish here, Stevens," the other man said. "The next shift will start soon. I'm sure they need your assistance more outside."

"*Why*—" Julian had been so quiet, she'd assumed he'd gone and wandered off. "Why are there empty beds, when there are people outside?"

He wasn't speaking to the doctors; he wasn't speaking to the nurses, or the patients, or any one person in particular. There was a manic edge to his tone that drew eyes, nervous glances.

"I want you to tell me *why*—"

"The same reason," Etta murmured, "you never truly trained your half brother. The same reason he had to sign a contract just to travel. The same reason," she continued, "no one ever acknowledged him as being a member of your family."

Julian turned on her. "That's not true! That's not! You have no idea—"

She wondered if his privilege had made him blind to others' suffering in his travels, or if maybe it took something of this magnitude to shatter that shield of self-righteousness that being white and male and wealthy had always provided him with. Etta didn't doubt for a second that, as the heir, he might have been protected from harsher years so as to keep him alive, but she also didn't doubt that Julian had never been able to see further than a foot in front of him when it came to other people.

Or maybe he'd treated traveling as all of the other Ironwoods seemed to; they disconnected themselves from decency time and time again to play the parts each era demanded of them. They had seen so much, they must have become desensitized to it—the way she could watch a film, see characters suffer, but never fully invest in their lives because of the emotional distance. Because it never truly felt real; not in a visceral way.

This kind of destruction was what traveling did to people—not the travelers themselves, but their victims, the common people who could not feel the sands of history shifting around them before they were smothered.

Julian's hands were limp at his side, turned slightly toward the room, as if he could weigh the odds of life or death for each person stretched out on a cot. He had closed his eyes; his breathing was shallow, his face screwed up. *Powerless.*

"Remember this," she told him. "How you feel right now."

What it felt like to move through the world without power, at the mercy of things bigger than you. Unable, even if just for an hour, to control one's life. How Nicholas had felt for years, before he'd taken all of that strength she loved so much about him and pulled himself up, out, back to the sea.

Etta turned her face against the rough fabric of the cot and focused on nothing beyond her own breathing, fighting back the sweep of shame and anger.

I have to finish this. A single man, on Ironwood's orders, had set this disaster in motion. The blast from the explosion hadn't just killed the tsar; its effects had rippled out, exactly as Henry had said, cutting through millions upon millions of innocent lives. For the first time in her life, Etta felt *lethal.*

"We need to leave," she told Julian. "We have to find your grandfather. He has the astrolabe. We can still fix this."

Julian shook his head, rubbing his hands over his face. "I can't go back—I *can't.*"

"The survivor rosters have gone up," she heard a soft voice say. "I'll take you to them, if you'd like. They only account for this field hospital. We should have others by the evening."

Out of the corner of her eye she saw a nurse leading Julian toward the entrance, where a man was hammering up handwritten lists on large sheets of butcher paper. Those who could rise from their cots did so, swarming that small space. The line outside began to push forward as well, surging toward the sheets in a tangle of arms and legs, until everyone was nearly climbing over each other to get a better look.

By the time she saw Julian again, almost twenty minutes later, the same nurse was by his side again, leading him toward an area in the far back of the warehouse that had been sectioned off by sterile white curtains.

Etta pushed herself up and followed, bracing herself for this next hit. Either his old nanny was alive, or he was being drawn back to identify a body. She caught the tail end of the nurse's instructions as she came up behind Julian.

". . . need to wear a mask and try not to touch her—the burns are exceedingly painful."

"I understand," Julian said, accepting both gloves and a face mask from the young woman. Her tidy uniform seemed at odds with the barely managed chaos of the place; she cast them both a sympathetic look before falling back.

Etta accepted her own set and pulled them on. *She survived.* What a small, precious miracle.

"They say she doesn't have long," Julian told her, with an odd, forced lightness. Etta knew this feeling, too, of overcompensating to rise above the pain in order to function. "The air way out in Brooklyn was so hot it damaged her lungs."

Etta put a hand on his arm. "I'm so sorry."

He lifted a shoulder in a shrug. "I'd like to ask her a few things, if she can answer. But mostly . . . I think I . . ."

Julian never finished his thought. He took a deep breath, smoothed his hair back, and stepped through the curtain.

Inside, about a dozen or so beds were arranged in a U shape around a central station, where two nurses were cutting bandages and measuring out medicine. The lights from the lanterns were kept dim, but the shadows didn't hide the heavily bandaged figures on each of the beds, the blistered patches of exposed, unnaturally gleaming skin.

Julian paced toward the far right end, counting under his breath. Finally, he found the one he was looking for, and Etta saw him straighten to his full height as he moved to the small wooden stool beside the cot. He moved the basin of water onto the floor and reached for the hand of the woman on the bed.

Etta hung back, unsure whether or not she was meant to be listening or watching. The woman seemed less bandaged than the others, but wore a bulky oxygen mask. Her face was as pink as the inside of a seashell, and her eyebrows were entirely gone, as were patches of her gray hair.

With utmost care, Julian stroked the back of her hand, careful to avoid the IV line. Within a moment, the woman turned her head toward him, her eyelids inching open. Etta knew the precise moment she saw him and made the connection, because her free hand floated up to pull down her oxygen mask, and those same blue eyes went wide.

"You're . . ."

"Hullo, Nan," Julian said, his voice painfully light. "Gave me a bit of hell trying to track you down in this mess."

Her mouth moved, but it was a long while before words emerged. "I thought I might be . . . I thought I might have passed. But . . . you're not you, not from before—?"

Etta wasn't sure what she was asking, exactly. Julian just responded with one of his infuriating shrugs.

"Before I supposedly plummeted to my untimely death? It's all right. It was only a bit of play. I never did go splat. You know how I love my games."

Even in her condition, the woman, a guardian, knew to be wary of revealing his fate to a traveler—however false a fate it might have been. She blinked almost owlishly at him.

"I thought . . . I thought so. You've the look of a man now. You've grown so well." As if the whole scene wasn't awful enough, the woman began to cry. Etta began the slow process of backing away without being noticed. "I'd always hoped to see you . . . one last time . . . that you'd come to visit me when I was older, so I could see you . . . smile again."

Etta's heart stretched to the point of ripping at the unbridled emotion in the old woman's voice.

"A fair bet, that. You've always known, Nan, there's no getting rid of me," Julian told her. "What did you say? Luck of the devil, lives of a cat? I'm only sorry I didn't come sooner."

The eyebrows had been singed from her face, but Etta imagined them lifting at that, just by the way her eyes took on a sudden glint. "Thank the good Lord you didn't. Or else you'd . . . be . . . ."

Dead. Dying. Incinerated.

Gone.

Etta's stomach turned, and she looked away, toward the heavy, dark curtain covering the shattered window. The movement must have finally caught the old woman's attention, because Etta felt the pressure of her gaze like a chain jerking her head back up.

"My God—*Rose*—"

Etta jumped at the viciousness of the woman's tone, less amused now to see yet another person all but cross themselves at a reminder of her mother.

"No, Nan," Julian said, pressing her gently down onto the bed. "This is her daughter. Etta, this is the great Octavia Ironwood."

This didn't seem to improve the woman's opinion in the slightest. Her breathing had become labored, to the point where even Julian shot a panicked look at a nearby oxygen tank. Etta took another step back, wondering if she should leave—Julian's old nanny was so fragile right now, any sort of disturbance seemed capable of shattering what strength she had left.

"I never thought . . . I'd see you with the likes of a Linden, and *her* daughter, no less," the woman coughed, hacking up something wet from her lungs. Julian's face softened; he reached for a rag and a bowl of warm water from the nearby stand and dabbed the blood from the corner of her lips.

"Don't . . . bother yourself. . . ."

"It's no bother at all," he told her. "Just returning the favor for all the times you did it for me as a little prat."

"You were never a prat," Octavia told him, her voice severe despite the whistle of air in and out of her chest. "You were *trying.* You tested. But you were never"—she cut her eyes at Etta—"stupid."

That one stung, Etta had to admit. Initially, hearing things like that had made Etta think of her mother like one of the paintings Rose restored at the Met—its true image obscured by layers of age and grime. Now, she wore the truth like a badge of shame. "You tried your best raising me," Julian was saying, "but you know me—all style, no sense. I was bound to run with a rougher set sooner or later."

The burned half of the woman's face pulled into an agonizing smile. Etta couldn't tell the difference between her choking and laughter.

"You're a little love," she informed him. "I might like you . . . even better . . . if you could find me a drink of the good stuff."

"I'll bring you a whole bottle of Scotch," he vowed, "if I have to go to Scotland and bring it back, still cold from the distillery."

"Tell me what's . . . what's happened," she said. "This wasn't what was meant to be."

Julian began to explain what had happened, quietly, quickly.

"There's a lot to be said about Cyrus Ironwood," Octavia began. "There's . . . much to be ashamed of. How he treats—how he treats his own family, for one. He was so hard on you . . . for not being what he meant you to be. For not fixing . . . your father."

Etta's hands curled around her biceps, squeezing the muscles. Nicholas and Julian's father, Augustus, had been a vile piece of work; Etta had to wonder if *he* was what Cyrus had "meant for" Julian to be.

The shadow that passed over Julian's face lifted again as the woman's eyes flickered over to him, then to the room's other sleeping occupants. She spoke so softly, Etta had to move closer to her bed to hear. "There is . . . madness in him. Oh, don't look so surprised. Those of us . . . those of us closest to him have watched him step closer . . . closer . . . to the fire. But he did create a world better than what had . . . come before. None of this . . . none of this should have happened. But Rose Linden—she and her outcasts could never accept it."

"This wasn't part of the original timeline?" Julian clarified, just as softly. "I didn't think so, but I couldn't be sure. There were so many changes when Grandfather went to war with the families."

"No," Octavia said. "I wouldn't have stayed. I wouldn't have . . . let children . . . let anyone die . . . I wouldn't have let this happen."

Etta's heart froze in her chest, seizing painfully. If Octavia thought—*believed*—that she could have prevented this, or at least saved herself, then that meant . . .

She'd had it wrong. Etta had assumed that guardians, unlike travelers, wouldn't be able to recognize when the timeline shifted—that they would simply be carried forward, their lives and memories adjusted, blissfully unaware that their lives had ever been different. But that wasn't the case at all. The Ironwood guardians, in service to the old man, would know how things were meant to play out. If they survived the changes, they would *know* the timeline had been altered, and live out its consequences. Etta was almost breathless with the unspeakable cruelty of it. These people were born into this hidden world, yet were as much at its mercy as a normal man or woman. Only, they would know when something was lost, and when there was a reason to be afraid.

"I know, Nan," Julian said, cupping her hand between his. "You would have saved the whole damn city if you knew."

"You didn't know, either . . . so why . . . why come?" Octavia asked, turning her head to better look at him.

"Because I needed to find out a few things," Julian said, lying just a little, "and you're the only person I trust."

Another painful smile as her burned skin pulled beneath her bandages. "Tell me. But—*she* goes."

"Nan," Julian cajoled. "Etta's not like her mother. She wasn't even told she was one of us until last month. If you hold her mother against her, you'll have to hold my father against me."

"Her mother *was* the reason for your father's change . . . for his cruelty. She created it in him—"

"Let's not—" Julian cut her off, then cringed. "She didn't make him who he was, she only released what was already inside of him, waiting to be let out. Let's just . . . I only meant that we're trying to find out what's been happening with the family. Grandfather has been trying to track down his old obsession again, and now we need to find him."

The candlelight drew deep shadows across Julian's face as he leaned forward, searching Octavia's face. He shifted uncomfortably, and the creaking of the chair cut through the murmur of life and death in the makeshift ward.

She won't talk until I leave, Etta realized. But she wasn't about to step outside and rely solely on Julian relaying the complete picture to her.

"Easy, Nan," Julian said. "This one's all right. Vetted her myself, otherwise I wouldn't have brought her to you."

She clearly had some doubts about his judgment, but let this pass.

"Be careful . . . won't you? He's been . . . traveling again. Came here only days ago . . . called a family meeting. Don't let him . . . find you," Octavia said, fixing her gaze back on Julian.

"Him?" Julian repeated. "Grandpops? Why? The old man moves once every two decades at best."

"If I tell you . . ." Octavia blew out a long, wheezing sigh. "What trouble . . . will you find yourself in?"

"The good kind," Julian promised her. "The kind that makes you proud of me, even as you put me in the naughty corner."

The sound that came out of her must have been a laugh, though it was painful to hear. "There's . . . an auction. Came through . . . the family lines. He came to take . . . the gold from his vault here. Buy-in."

"An auction?" Julian repeated, glancing at Etta. "Did he say what for?"

"Is there anything else . . . he could want . . . so desperately?"

The astrolabe.

"He doesn't already have it?" Etta asked. Who had taken it from Kadir in the palace, then?

Julian must have had a similar thought, but arrived at an actual guess. "The Belladonna. I should have known the blasted thing would turn up with her. She must have sent one of her minions to steal it, or one of Grandpop's men went rogue and brought it to her for a fee. Do you know the location of the auction? The year?"

Octavia shook her head, and Etta felt herself deflate. The old woman grabbed Julian's hand, holding him in place. "Leave . . . go back. As far . . . back as you can."

"I've got a few things to do first," he told her, "but I will. In time."

"No—Julian, the Shadows—even guardians hear whispers of such—of such things—*murders*—"

341

"Shadows?" Julian's brow creased. "Are you trying to be funny with me, Nan?"

Despite her condition, she leveled him with a look perfected by years as a nanny.

"You also told me my hair was going to fall out if I didn't stop eating sweets, so forgive me if I doubt the story about the creatures who snatch naughty traveler children in the night."

"What are you talking about?" Etta asked, looking between them.

"You know, the one your mother gently traumatized you with from a young age—about people who live in shadows and steal little traveler children who don't follow the rules?" He rubbed at the stubble on his chin, and Etta wondered why everything he ever did made it seem like he was posing. "Huh. You don't know. Oh! Right. Your terror of a mother kept everything secret, et cetera. Have to say, this is the first time I've been jealous of you. *From the shadows they come . . .*"

It was only because he had mentioned her mother. It was only because the memory of the Winter Palace was still so close to the surface, blooming with renewed pain every few minutes. It was only because of those things that Rose's words circled back to her then, and tentatively linked with what Julian said.

"You can say if I'm telling it wrong," he told Octavia. "But there's this old story, about a group that lives in the shadows and takes traveler children who stray from their families. I always thought it was made up to explain how kids got left behind in time periods or were orphaned. Is that not the case?"

"Killers—" Octavia let out a brutal cough, bringing blood to her lips. Julian leaned forward, gently dabbing them with the wet cloth.

"Easy now," he told her.

"Murderers . . . the whole lot of them," Octavia said. "We knew of them . . . Cyrus—he wants the same thing that—that they do. Destroyed all records of them. Never wanted . . . anyone to know about them . . . otherwise, they'd be too frightened . . . to help him search for it."

It. The astrolabe.

You don't know what's coming, what's been chasing me for years, her mother had said. *I've kept them off your trail for weeks, from the moment you were taken, but the Shadows—*

But the Shadows . . .

What had Henry told her about Rose's delusions? That she'd become afraid of the darkness, that the delusion of the radiant man who'd haunted her had sent Shadows out after her?

"What do they look like?" she asked. Rose's attention in the palace had been drawn away by attackers in black. She'd assumed they were Ironwoods, even palace guards, but—her mind was moving too quickly, strumming through possibilities. There was one more piece to this, something that would weave the truth together. It couldn't be as simple as . . . no, it wasn't.

Henry wasn't wrong. Her mother needed help. She was a *murderer* who'd killed a member of her own family—her best and only friend.

"Don't . . . know," Octavia said. "I don't—just stay *away*—"

"All right, it's all right," Julian said, glancing at Etta.

But the Shadows . . .

What's been chasing me for years . . .

Octavia's chest began to rise and fall, fluttering shallowly. When the old woman turned to him again, it was with a wide-eyed desperation, with wretched, gasping breaths. Julian stood from his stool, and Etta thought for one infuriating second that he was about to bolt for the exit—but he only slipped that same tattered notebook out of the fold of his clothing. He retrieved the stubby pencil secured to the back cover with string. The leather was so soft, the journal fell open on the bed, revealing an unfinished sketch of a street.

He's an artist. Etta had forgotten that, somehow. Or maybe she'd just never been willing to see him as anything other than a coward and a flirt, because it would have been another complication when her entire world had become a series of them. If he had been one of her mother's paintings, one of those at the Met she had worked so hard to restore, peeling back layers of age and patches, Etta wondered how bright his colors might be beneath.

"Do you remember the old house, Nan? The one we lived in just off the park, up on Sixtieth?" he asked her. His right hand held hers, but his left was already sketching on a blank page.

"With the . . . with the . . ."

"The columns and marble and carriage entry," he continued softly. "Our little palace. Remember how I slid down the banister and cracked my head on the ground?"

She nodded. "Blood. Amelia . . . fainting. Butler moaning about . . . the damned vase . . ."

"That's what you remember," he told her. "What I remember is this."

He held up the rough sketch for her to see, but the cover blocked it from Etta's sight. It wasn't meant for her, anyway.

"I remember you scooping me up, holding me, telling me that it would be all right, and that you were there and always would be, to take care of me," Julian whispered.

Octavia touched the page with her finger. "Beautiful . . ."

"That's right. I had a proper, beautiful life, thanks to you." He kissed her bandaged hand. "And now I'll do the same for you."

"Don't do . . . anything . . . foolish. . . ."

"Nan," he said, fighting for his smile. "You can bet on it."

THE WOMAN SLIPPED INTO SLEEP AND ETTA MOVED AWAY, leaving Julian to keep vigil. Her head felt empty of real thought, even as her heart was clogged with everything threatening to burst out of it. What surprised her most, though, was the jealousy, burning just beneath the pity and fear.

He gets to be with her.

Julian would be there for Octavia when she died. Etta didn't think she had much time left at all, but she knew with certainty that Julian would not leave her. It was more than she'd been able to give to Alice.

Henry had stayed with Alice.

And who had stayed with Henry?

Etta lost track of time, walking between the rows of cots, trying not to notice the new openings in the beds. It didn't feel like nearly enough hours before Julian emerged and came straight toward her, shooting through the rows of the dead and dying like a fiery arrow. He took her arm and drew her forward, stopping only long enough to lift a pile of plain gray trousers and white shirts—the same thing the nurses had changed most of the wounded into.

"Here," he said, motioning her toward a screen. "Change here."

Etta slipped behind it, watching his silhouette move against the white fabric, pacing. "What happened . . . ?"

She let her dress fall to the ground and tugged on the soft, oversize clothing.

"Nan's finally at peace," he told her quietly, coming closer. "I was waiting for it . . . for the timeline to shift. To be flung out of here. But it never came. And then I tried to remember—I tried to remember if any change had ever been caused by a guardian dying, or if time just sees them the way Grandfather does: disposable."

"And?"

"And I couldn't. I couldn't. It feels like it should have shifted the whole world. A traveler can do one thing outside of his time and the whole of it can shift. I don't like that—that it makes it seem like she wasn't important." He was talking quickly, almost too quickly for Etta's tired mind to keep up with. "All done?"

Etta stepped out from behind the screen and let him pass her to start changing.

"Julian," she said gently. "Are you all right? Take a minute if you have to. . . ."

"I don't think we have a minute, do you?" he said. "There's an

Ironwood message drop in this year just a ways upstate. The Belladonna will have flooded the drops with invitations to the auction, just to get as many bidders as possible. We can start looking there."

"Who is the Belladonna?" Etta asked.

"She's a collector and an agent of sale for rare artifacts," he said, pulling his new shirt over his head. "There's going to be a buy-in amount in gold we'll need to provide, but the bidding is done by submitting offers of secrets and favors. We just need to get inside, and then we can do whatever it is you think we're supposed to be doing."

"Destroying the astrolabe," Etta said.

Julian leaned out from behind the screen. "Destroying it—what good is that going to accomplish? Shouldn't we use it to try to save these people?"

One of the first things she'd learned about life as a traveler was that you couldn't save the dead, not without consequences. But whatever fate the original timeline had intended for these people, this wasn't it.

"It'll reset everything," she explained. "Bring it back to the original timeline. The one we knew . . . it'll be gone."

Julian turned away from surveying the cots, the weeping men and women by the survivor boards, and glanced back at her over his shoulder. "Then let's go."

VATICAN CITY
1499

TWENTY-FOUR

NICHOLAS FELT HIMSELF NOD.

Nod as if to say, *Yes, I expected this. I accept this.* Because in truth, some part of him had. This was fate's delight. To give him what he desired, or what he had not known he desired, only to viciously snatch it back again, just when it seemed as if he might seize it.

"What?" he heard Sophia say. *"How?"*

"A notice went out to all of the travelers and guardians," Li Min said, struggling with each word, like her throat threatened to choke on them. She dug into her bag, retrieving a small slip of paper, and passed it to Sophia.

"'Henry Hemlock demands satisfaction from Cyrus Ironwood for the unspeakably cruel murder of his daughter, Henrietta, who has lately passed into eternity from wounds sustained from an attack by his guardians, while she was already weakened'—oh my God. Date and place of death is listed as October 2, 1905, Texas."

Something like bile or fire was rising in his throat. He couldn't speak. Nicholas felt parts of himself begin to close off, as if to deny entry again to that now-familiar pain.

I wasn't fast enough.

I couldn't reach you.

I only wanted to save you.

The cathedral of hope in his heart, which he'd carefully crafted each day since he and Etta had been torn apart, burned down to its foundations of desperation and despair.

Oh God. *Oh God.*

"Carter," Li Min said. "I think perhaps we should continue through the passage, find a place to sit, and take some water, yes?"

He shook his head, straining to get away from her. He began to stalk down the hall again, reaching for doors, tearing them open. It couldn't be right. Her earring was *here*. Hemlock must have been mistaken. He would have felt it, wouldn't he? He would have felt the world crash down upon itself if she'd passed on. The bell of his spirit would have been silenced. "She's—"

She had been dead, nearly the whole time he'd been searching for her.

He had been chasing a ghost. A memory. No.

No.

Sophia stood there watching him, letting the death notice slip from her fingers. Li Min finally caught his arm, and this time she didn't let him shake her off. "I know what it is you think, but consider the possibilities."

"They said she died in Texas, two days after she disappeared, but then—then, how is her earring here?" he demanded.

Li Min's response was as infuriatingly calm as always. "Someone might have taken the earring from her, or traded her for it. Or this earring, this version of it, might be from a past time in her mother's life, before she ever gave them to her daughter. It might have been you, in the future, who returned here."

Her words dripped through him one by one, poisoning that last small hope moving beneath his skin. He did not know Etta's father from Adam, but he knew Li Min now. He trusted Li Min.

His stomach rioted. He raised his hand, pressing his fist against his mouth. Time travel. Bloody impossible, bloody unmerciful, bloody befuddling time travel.

Why had he ever accepted Ironwood's job? Why hadn't he just *listened* to Hall when he'd advised Nicholas to steer as far away from the family as he was able? Why hadn't the sea been enough for him? He never should have allowed himself to be drawn back into this web. It was only ever going to catch him, wrap around his throat until it strangled him.

But it wouldn't have stopped Ironwood.

He still would have stolen Etta out of her time. She would have been sent on the search alone. Nothing, and no one, was ever going to stop Ironwood until he had the astrolabe, and everything he'd ever desired.

"She's not here," he rasped out, trying to grasp the meaning of those words.

Li Min nodded.

"She . . ." Nicholas forced himself to say, ". . . was most likely never here at all."

Sophia looked away. Pride warred with humiliation in him, before both were sunk by a devastation that left him breathless. It stole the years of experience he'd collected in steeling himself to the world, took even that small measure of dignity he'd eked out from his existence. And what was left inside him was that same pain he'd felt as a child, alone in the dark cupboard of the Ironwood house in New York, waiting for some signal of when he was allowed to step outside of it.

"Thank you," he told Li Min. "I apologize . . . I am . . . not myself . . . I do believe . . ."

"Will you find her mother, then, to tell her?" Li Min asked. "This Rose Linden?"

"No. I'm almost certain she already knows," Nicholas said. Perhaps that was, in the end, why she had never come.

"If she'd taken her revenge we'd know by now," Sophia said. "That bit of news would travel quickly in our circle."

A light shone from down the hallway, marking the path of someone coming toward them. Sophia took his limp arm and pulled him toward the door they had stopped outside of. On instinct, he tried to drag his feet, as if another search might turn up a different result. Li Min lifted a candle from the wall and opened the door, then latched it behind them.

Nicholas knew the *Pietà* the moment he saw it, though it caught him off guard to find it in such a small side chapel. The Carrara marble was flawless, glowing like warm moonlight. The Virgin Mary, her face too young to be holding the body of an adult son, was a mysterious contradiction of sweetness and grief.

Love. Sacrifice. Release. An endless, eternal story—no, this traveler war wasn't anything so pure. This was a story of revenge. Of families who'd warred so long that no one could remember who'd instigated the fights in the first place. An Ironwood had killed Lindens, and a Linden had caused the death of Ironwood heirs, and so the Ironwoods claimed the life of the Linden heir. The awful symmetry of it all did not stop with only those two families. There must have been hundreds, thousands of stories like it over the years. It was a cycle that he himself had been caught in.

Staring at the woman's serene stone face, with Sophia and Li Min whispering behind him, Nicholas felt as still and quiet as if he'd become the eye of a hurricane. In the candlelight, it was so very easy to imagine Mrs. Hall's face, warmed by the fireplace as she read to him and Chase from the Bible, as she did every night. *Never take your own revenge, beloved, but leave room for the wrath of God. . . .*

But God had had His chance to pass judgment on the evil that lived in Cyrus Ironwood's heart, and had failed to act. Nicholas, for the first time in his life, questioned His judgment, because it was neither true, nor righteous, nor acceptable.

It's left to me.

"I require a path," he said. "Back to 1776."

Li Min and Sophia ceased their conversation.

"Look, Carter," Sophia began. "I know how you feel—"

"Do you now?" he said coldly. "How would you feel, then, to know that Julian survived his fall and wasn't ever lost to you or any of us?"

He was surprised how easily the words flowed out of him after being held inside for so long. Some part of him recognized how unfeeling it was to drop it on Sophia's head like an anchor, but Nicholas found himself beyond caring. If anything, he felt his hurt should be catching. There was more than enough to be shared by the parties present.

Sophia turned toward him, her lips parting.

"I was mistaken in how I interpreted that moment on the cliff. Rose Linden was the one to correct my misunderstanding. He was orphaned by a timeline shift, and never returned to us. I apologize for not telling you sooner," he said, his bloody guilt getting the better of him, her single dark eye burning with the intensity of its gaze. "Initially, before you told me the truth of your heart, I thought if you knew he might be alive, you'd want to find him and restore your engagement. Find forgiveness with Ironwood. And then it was only a matter of not wanting you to be distracted."

That earned him a hard fist to the cheek, blowing him sideways.

"What I always *wanted* was respect!" she growled out. "Shame on me for thinking I might have found some of that in your regard. Shame on me for ever being so *stupid*."

"You're not—"

"I nearly got myself killed helping you—not because I owe it to you, but because I want to find the men who attacked me. I want to take from them what they took from me, and even our score. I want Grandfather's rule to crumble, I want to watch it pulverized to dust, and see everything he loves ripped away from him," Sophia seethed. "Why would I ever search out someone who abandoned me? Someone who had no regard for *any* of us, who ran because he's too much of a damn coward to stand up to his family!"

"I know that now," he said. "I'm sorry. But it felt like too much of a risk—I—"

"Needed to use me?" Sophia said. "To go after *your* person, to achieve your ends? My *desire* was to be heir, which might have gotten me treated like a whole person, not fodder for marriage. Julian was my friend. I cared—*care*—about him. But I decided in that desert, before you ever found me, that what I really wanted was the freedom to do as I pleased, with whomever I pleased. I wanted to move as freely as the wind, and not be called back into port against my will. *That* is power. Do you understand?"

He nodded, his throat tight. "Beyond measure."

Their conversation had drawn the attention of someone outside the chapel. There was a pounding on the door, a muffled voice that called out a question. Li Min whirled back toward Nicholas.

"If you mean to complete the Belladonna's task," she said, "then I will be your guide."

"No." It was a terrible thing, and he wanted them far from it. "I need to see this through myself."

She shook her head. "You will need someone to dig your grave, for even if you finish with the old man, the journey to that moment will end you."

Sophia let out a harsh breath, crossing her arms.

"This is my path now," he told her, using his left hand to lift his right, to show her the ring. "I am dead regardless. If I don't kill him, the poison will take me; if I'm not quick enough arriving there, the poison will take me. If I succeed, at least there will be one fewer evil in the world."

At least this way, I might yet live long enough to return to Hall and die at sea.

The pounding on the door grew louder, as if someone was throwing their weight against it.

"You're not leaving us behind to sweep up your mess after you,"

Sophia snarled, pulling him toward the shivering air of the passage. "You'd just better pray I don't kill you first myself."

THEY PASSED THROUGH A SERIES OF PASSAGES COBBLED together from their combined memories, leading, at various points, to a rather treacherous section of the Australian outback, a pristine glacier, and the most dire year of the Middle Ages that Austria had to offer, with countless small insignificant connections between each. When they encountered anyone, he and Li Min shrouded themselves, letting Sophia speak in the rare instances speaking was necessary.

Nicholas wondered several times over the course of this journey if a man could feel so hollow as to become invisible, or if people only saw what they expected to see—which, in the case of their situation, was not a Chinese woman or a black man. In any case, the silence suited him well enough. It was easier to keep his mind still and focused on the days ticking down.

On the night of the sixteenth, a few miles from the last passage on the outskirts of Mexico City, Nicholas began to sense Li Min and Sophia slowing, eating away at his own pace. Out of the corner of his eye, he saw the young women exchange a look; not wanting to confront it, he dug his heels into his horse's side to urge it forward. Before the mare could work herself back up to a gallop, a small hand lashed out and ripped the reins from his hands.

"What the *devil*—?"

"You will do what you have now attempted three times—you will ride that animal until it collapses and dies beneath you," Li Min told him sternly, pulling the reins further out of his reach. "I do not intend to share my horse. Do you, Sophia?"

"Certainly not."

"I have not—" he began.

"We haven't slept in two days, Carter," Sophia interrupted.

Surely not. "We stopped a night ago."

"*No*. That was Austria. That scenic little spot you picked by the rancid moat. I'm sure one of us picked up the Black Death as a parting gift."

Christ. She was right.

"Let's move off the road. Camp for a few hours," Li Min suggested.

Revolt surged inside of him, and must have been clear from his expression, because Sophia turned her horse and led them off the worn road and onto the lush, green earth. Somehow, Nicholas had always pictured this part of the world as entirely desert. But even this late in the year, there was life and vegetation sweeping up from their valley to the peaks of the mountains around them.

He counted the paces under his breath, from the road to where Sophia decided was far enough to drop her saddlebags, and decided it was two hundred paces too far.

He could go ahead. Let them rest and catch up to him later.

Before he could devise a course of action, Li Min led his horse forward toward the others and began to unhook its harness.

He breathed sharply out of his nose, but finally dismounted. "I'll hunt."

Shooting something sounded marvelous, now that he had gunpowder again. He could not shoot with his right arm, useless as it was, but he wasn't a terrible shot with his left.

"Li Min is already going," Sophia said, from where she was laying out the bedding. He turned, then turned again, surprised to find Li Min's small form retreating into the distance. "You can find the firewood and kindling."

"All right. But I'll cook."

Sophia made a face he didn't understand.

"And water?"

"We're fine for now," she said, tossing away the wide-brimmed hat she'd found abandoned on the road. "*Go*. Before your expression finally does *me* in. For someone out for cold-blooded revenge, you've got the look of a sad, sorry bastard about you."

Somehow, he didn't doubt it. Nicholas gave her an ironic little bow before setting about the task in front of him. Li Min had not returned by the time they had started the fire and brought the little pot they'd acquired to boil. Rather than try to talk to a stone-faced Sophia, Nicholas slid his right arm from the sling Li Min had knotted for him and lay down with his back to the fire.

His eyes felt too gritty to shut, but he tried. He tried relaxing his body against the unyielding dirt, and he tried to clear the swirl of dark thoughts rising up inside of him before they pulled him under. One hand dipped inside his loose tunic and closed around the string of leather. When he felt brave enough, he opened his eyes to study the bead in the image of a man and Etta's earring.

He was seized by a compulsion he didn't understand. He yanked hard on the cord, trying to rip it off by force, then reached back to fumble with the knot.

"By doing that, you'll only feed the fire of regret that burns in you," Li Min said from nearby, having returned from her hunt. "Not extinguish it."

His hand relaxed, but didn't fall away. Nicholas shoved himself up off the ground, intent on cooking now that she had returned.

"This reminds me of a tale," Li Min said casually, before he could fully stand. She sat between him and the fire, casting a long shadow over him. "Would you care to hear it?"

Not precisely, but he grunted, knowing she would tell it regardless.

"It goes as follows. Many, many years ago, Emperor Yan had a daughter, Nüwa. She was as lovely and elegant as a crane, but stubborn as an ox. More than anything, she loved to swim, and often chose the East Sea for its wild beauty. I think you understand the impulse, no?"

He only seemed to be capable of grunting. His chest was too tight to manage actual words.

"But tragedy struck. One day while swimming, she drowned. Her will, however, was strong, and she would not give in, not completely.

She broke the surface of the water and transformed into a Jingwei bird—have you seen one? They are quite striking. A gray beak, red claws? Well, regardless, she sought out her vengeance for drowning. Every day she flew to gather stones and sticks from the Western Mountains and dropped them into the East Sea. Her desire was to fill it, to prevent others from drowning. She never rested in her task. She continues to this day."

He turned over fully, when it was clear her story was at an end. "Then it was an impossible task. What meaning am I supposed to derive from this?"

Li Min shrugged. "You may make anything of it you wish, Carter. The purpose of that tale was to distract you long enough for dinner to be served, and that has not been an impossible task after all."

Nicholas sat up straight, outrage burning through the gray haze around his mind. "I told you I would do it!" What good was he if he couldn't contribute his share of work?

"This may come as a surprise to you, but I don't actually prefer my meat shriveled and charred so far beyond recognition I mistake it for old firewood," Sophia told him, turning the skinned rabbits over on the spit.

"That's how you know it's cooked!"

Both women gave him their variations of a pitying look. His stomach rumbling, he took his share of the meat with a reluctance that could only come from pride. When he finished, he accepted Li Min's suggestion that he rest first, and take the later watch. On his bedding once more, he turned his back to the fire, resting his head on his arm and staring out at the dark mountains. He drifted to sleep, ignoring the warm grip of the gold band around his small finger.

A *clang* cut through the darkness, followed quickly by another.

"—better, better, but do not lean in so much as you thrust—no! To your left! Yes!"

Nicholas fumbled his way back to awareness, unsure whether he was hearing Li Min's voice or dreaming it. Turning onto his back, he looked toward the fire, watching as two slight, shadowy figures sparred with swords.

"It's *useless*," Sophia said. "I'll never get it right, not really."

"You've done it perfectly, as well as you have everything else I've shown you tonight," Li Min said, a smile in her voice. "You move through the world like a cat, all silk and sinew. Soon you'll be better than me, and then I'll really need to watch my gold."

"No chance of that," Sophia said after a moment. Frustration edged into the words.

"You are a superb fighter," Li Min said, settling on the ground and resting her sword across her legs.

After a moment, Sophia lowered herself to her knees, placing her weapon down on a nearby blanket. "It's just . . . I used to be better, before this."

She gestured absently to her eye patch.

"Ah," Li Min said.

"The world looks different," Sophia said. "At first I thought it was only my imagination, self-pity, what have you. But the truth is, the shadows and highlights have peeled back. Colors seem flat. And my perception of how near or far something is from me is occasionally a little off. But the biggest problem is the blind spot."

He closed his eyes, sighing. He'd expected as much, and felt rightly worse for not trying to help her overcome it in any way he could. Whether or not she would have accepted his help was debatable, but he should have *tried*, dammit.

"Stand up, I'll show you something," Li Min said. There was a shuffle of fabric and feet in the dirt as Sophia did. "Assume your usual stance."

When Sophia slid her left leg back, angling her right half forward, Li Min clucked her tongue and reversed it, her fingers gliding along

Sophia's skin, clasping, just for a moment, around her small wrist. "Fighting is all angles, yes? Altering your stance so your good eye is set back might help; however, I think you'd feel most comfortable switching back and forth quickly, like this—"

Li Min danced from side to side, quick and light on her feet as she circled Sophia, constantly adjusting her stance so her left eye, which she had shut to demonstrate this to Sophia, was never in front for long.

"It looks like you're dancing," Sophia said, voicing Nicholas's own awe. After a moment, she attempted to replicate the movement. Her face fell at her initial clumsiness, but soon she seemed to match Li Min step for step. And she was *smiling.*

"It feels a little ridiculous," Sophia admitted, as they returned to the blanket and relinquished her blade again.

"You've not had time to become used to it," Li Min said, placing a soft hand on Sophia's wrist. "It will get better with time. You should know that there are countless stories of warriors who've borne a similar injury and overcome it. One general from my land was said to have been shot in the eye with an arrow. Rather than crumble, he pulled the arrow out, and ate the eye off it."

"That's disgusting, even for me," Sophia said, laughing. "And you know it's far more likely he did crumble and scream like a child. But who can blame him?"

"There is no doubt in my mind about that," Li Min said, and for a while, they seemed content to play a game of trying to avoid the other catching their gaze. The slow drift of fingers across the blanket, easing closer and closer with each soft breath.

He was about to close his eyes and turn again to give them privacy when Li Min said, "There is still such a shadow on your face. What is troubling you?"

Rather than pull away, Sophia slid her hand lightly up along the other girl's arm, drawing her loose sleeve up to touch her pale skin.

She leaned forward, so close that, for a moment, Nicholas was sure she might rest her forehead against Li Min's shoulder. "Did you mean what you said, about seeking revenge? That there's no way to survive it?"

A deep sigh. "After I escaped the Shadows, I wanted nothing more than to grow strong enough to return and butcher them, as they had done my mother and my sister. It was enough to sustain me for years. I fed on the anger, bathed in fury, prayed with malice. But one morning, a woman on my ship asked me what I would make of my life after I had taken my revenge for their lives. I had not pictured anything beyond it. To me, it was a destination, and I had let it become a final chapter in my story. That realization made me decide the best revenge of all was to not willingly squander my gift of survival, but to live with the strength I had fought for and won."

"But—" Sophia began, struggling to master her voice. "How do you live with it—the anger? The shame?"

Shame. Nicholas felt something rise and lodge in his throat.

Li Min's hand stilled from where she had raised it, hovering just above Sophia's tangled dark hair.

"No matter how hard I try," Sophia continued, "I can't forget it. It never leaves me. Its hands are hot around my neck."

"Because one moment in life does not define a person," Li Min said. "Without mistakes and misjudgments we would stagnate. It is no shameful thing to be beaten when outnumbered, not when you were brave enough to try. Nor is a scar or injury something to despair over, for it is a mark that you were strong enough to survive."

"But it's beyond me. The mistake didn't end with me." Sophia turned her head in Nicholas's direction, as if trying to see whether he was still asleep. "I feel . . . we were in no way friends, but I feel sore about Linden. Responsible for what happened to her. His sad bastard face isn't helping matters, either."

"That's understandable," Li Min said, an odd quality to her voice.

Her free hand cupped around Sophia's, turning her palm up to rest in her own. She did not speak again until Sophia looked up and met her gaze. "But she had made her own decisions that brought her to that point."

Had she? As far as Nicholas saw, Etta had never had a true choice from the moment Sophia Ironwood had entered her life.

"I mostly just worry about what will happen to *him*," Sophia said. "Before, I wouldn't have believed him capable of taking his vengeance out on Ironwood. Now I'm not so sure."

Him.

Me.

Nicholas shifted on the ground, wishing he could use his right arm to brace himself.

Li Min nodded. "Earlier, I wanted to give him comfort, tell him that after the first death, there is no other. She has returned to the cradle of her ancestors, who shield her and protect her. But you can only say such things to people willing to hear them. He's not there yet."

It was like a hot blade sliding between his ribs. Nicholas pressed the back of his hand against his mouth.

"But what matters is what *he* believes, and he seems to be suffering not only a loss, but a questioning of faith and his path forward as well."

"That seems to be going around these days," Sophia said.

"It occurs to me that, while losing your eye has partially hindered your sight, the experience has allowed you to see through the lies you were raised to believe. You may go anywhere you like, so long as you take care, and you may be whoever you set your heart to be. There is true power in that, as you said to Carter before. Some of us are not so lucky—please do not take this for granted."

"I won't." Sophia shifted, turning so she could brace a hand against the ground, trapping Li Min's legs between her arm and the rest of Sophia's body. She leaned forward, studying Li Min's face as closely as Li Min examined her own. When she spoke again, the words were in that secret language between them, husky and low. The fire popped, devouring itself, and the small sound was enough of a distraction for Li Min to tear her gaze away, turning her head toward the distant city.

"You have been a good . . . *friend*," Sophia said, softly. "Thank you."

Li Min shook her head, rising out of the other young woman's grasp. "I am not your friend, *nǔ shén*, nor will I ever be in the way I want. I cannot be anything but what I am. Take care with your heart."

"You don't have to be alone, you know," Sophia said. "You don't have to keep making that choice. You talk about wearing the past with honor, but yours hounds you. You let it. You cannot let yourself accept that people would believe you. Help you."

"You know nothing," Li Min said, without a hint of anger. It was only frustration that wound itself through her words, an unmistakable ache.

It was a few moments later, as Li Min's steps came toward him, that they both heard Sophia say, "And you should know, I wouldn't go anywhere the two of you couldn't follow."

NEW YORK CITY
1776

TWENTY-FIVE

T̲HEY WATCHED THE WEALTHIEST OF THE CITY'S REMAINING gentlemen strutting like peacocks, and the ladies in all of their silk and pearls stepping off carriages and washing up the steps of the brick house before them, as if carried on a wave of high spirits and laughter.

Perched two roofs over, embracing the darkness of a new moon, Nicholas leaned forward as much as he dared, counting the latest batch of officers coming up the street. He might have thought them on patrol with the other regulars he'd seen, save for the inordinate number of decorations they'd lavished on themselves. It was a time of war, but the city had been occupied for months with little trouble, and the high polish of their boots, as if hardly used, seemed to prove that point. Their ceremonial swords caught the glow emanating from the three stories of windows. As the door opened for the guests, time and time again, it gave the effect of the sun rising over the streets.

"I can't believe the bastard is throwing a *ball*," Sophia snarled.

"He has to keep up appearances in this era, if only to maintain his timeline," Nicholas said. The hollow mouth at the center of his chest widened. It devoured the black mood in which he'd arrived in his natural era, devoured his anger, his pain, and now his heart. There was a

367

freedom in this, too, in relinquishing decorum and manners, and giving himself over to the chill spreading through his veins.

The people on the streets below were going about their merry little evening, untethered by worry or fear. Those who weren't entering the frivolities were making their way down the street, to one of the theaters putting on a production that evening.

I never took her to a play.

One more thought to feed the hollowness. He could not bear to think of her now, not on the cusp of doing something so vicious. Etta believed so doggedly in the good in him—that he was honorable, a man of merit and esteem. What would she see now, looking down at him? He was unrecognizable even to himself.

Li Min had been still for so long, wrapped in that impenetrably dark cloak of hers, that Nicholas might have forgotten she was there at all if she hadn't turned to look at him. He was beginning to suspect— and accept—that she was the sort who could measure, swallow, and digest a man and his mettle with a single look. Rather than feeling frustrated or startled by her merciless insight, he was almost relieved by not having to explain himself or attempt to put a name to the storm raging inside of him.

"Do not fight it," she told him. "It will help you. Anger is simple. Anger will move you, if you find yourself faltering. If you cannot avoid the darkness, you must force yourself through it."

Li Min held out something in front of him—a dagger, made of what looked like ivory. He took it from her gingerly, examining the dragon's head carved into its hilt. The curved blade smiled in his palm.

"I'm a better shot," he told her, trying to give it back.

"You can't use a flintlock," she said, pushing it back toward him. "Even with the music, someone is bound to hear."

Fair point. He accepted the dagger again, testing its weight and the feel of the hilt in his hand. The knife he'd been carrying was dull by most weapons' standards, and while it had accomplished what he'd demanded of it, a sharpened, well-made blade would make a better tool for . . .

Assassination. Nicholas rolled his shoulders back.

"Know a little something about this, do you?" he asked.

"After I escaped the darkness, before I was able to secure many types of jobs," Li Min told him, "I had just one."

He looked at her again, but her expression was blank.

"He is not a man, Carter, but a beast," she said. "Do not waste your time on his heart. Slit his throat before he can say a word."

It wasn't Nicholas's first time killing a man—the abhorrent pride in him wanted to inform of her of that. It was, however, his first time killing a man when not in defense of his own life, and that was a difficult thing to reconcile with his soul. Each second that passed seemed to grind him down to his raw, fraught essence. Now and then, he felt bewildered by the notion that he was here again, that it had come to this. This journey had begun here, in this very city, with a choice.

With a young woman.

He tucked the dagger into his belt, reaching up to touch the pendant and Etta's earring beneath his shirt. *Let the ends justify the means.*

"Thank you," he told Li Min. She had been a stranger mere days before. Now she was attempting to comfort him, when what he needed most was a voice of reason beyond the berating one in his mind. He would never forget it.

"That's the minuet," Sophia whispered, crawling back over the slight slant in the roof. "Do you want to wait until they're a few more dances in?"

Ironwood's balls always began with a minuet, during which he danced with a lady of his choosing. The focus of all of the attendees would be on the dancers congregated on the first floor of the old house, gliding around the card tables, trays of food, and hothouse flowers.

Even Ironwood's bevy of guards might be distracted long enough for Nicholas to make his entrance on the third floor.

He shook his head. The time was now, or he'd never muster the strength.

THE HOMES ALONG QUEEN STREET—SPARED BY THE FIRE TO the west of Broad Way—were tall, proud creatures that might have been transplanted from the streets of London's gentry. The old Ironwood house, by virtue of the man's ego, was a rose among daisies, his own palace from which to rule an empire of centuries. Its endless series of windows, and the natural attention it drew, of course, made it damned hard to creep up on if one made one's approach from the street.

Rope, tied to the chimney of the neighboring house, tossed with a hastily procured grappling hook onto Ironwood's roof, made the task easier—but only just. Without the use of his right hand, Nicholas had to hook his right arm and both legs over the rope, and inch forward with an agonizing, awkward slowness. Sophia followed at a determined pace, and he found his expectations disappointed when Li Min didn't walk across the rope like a cat, but deigned to cross it like a mere mortal.

The rope was cut free, a section falling slack against the neighboring house. The remaining length was tied to Ironwood's chimney. Li Min used it to walk down the back of the house and then along its walls, passing between the windows with practiced ease. Suddenly, Nicholas had no problem seeing her at home on a pirate ship.

She disappeared from their sight, but he heard her negotiating a window below them.

"Rather handy, isn't she?" Sophia said with clear appreciation, leaning over the edge of the roof to watch her at work. Nicholas gripped the back of her dark jacket to keep her from tumbling off the ledge.

A tug on the rope told him it was safe to descend, but Sophia, who was to keep watch, stopped him. She seemed to be struggling to speak; her mouth twisted as though she'd tasted something bitter.

"You'll be all right . . . won't you?" she asked after a long moment.

"I'll be quick, at least," he said.

"Seems unfair," she said as he began to edge down, gripping the rough rope. "He deserves a worse end than you'll be able to give him."

"If something happens—"

Sophia gripped him by the collar of his shirt. "Nothing is going to *happen*."

Nicholas nodded. "Understood, ma'am."

Sophia used the rope to ease him down just enough for Nicholas to swing his legs forward through the open window. Li Min reached out, pulling him the rest of the way through the frame.

His memory of the house's layout had served him well, after all. Li Min took a candle from the wall of the servants' staircase, leaning around the landing to ensure no one was coming. Though they were inside the house now, the staircase was so insulated, set so far apart from the house's grandeur, that even the lively music seemed muted.

It was remarkable, he thought, how swiftly memory could cut a man. It was the air, the way it seemed to sour in his lungs, the familiar creaks of the floor, that upset his stomach. This was a house in which all things were eventually extinguished, even hope. Whatever composure he'd summoned took a lashing as he stood there; for a moment, he was too tense to think about moving, too afraid that he might see his mother's ghost walking up the stairs toward him.

Nicholas felt Li Min's eyes on his face, trying to take the measure of his response. He didn't turn toward her. The bile in the back of his throat stung and burned, but he swallowed it, ashamed that standing within this house's walls was enough for his past to begin nipping and tearing at his resolve.

He had thought he'd known hatred, but he had not realized it lived in this place like a fine coat of dust. The familiarity of it was devastating; in all the many ways he had changed, the house hadn't. Even now, the shadows seemed to grasp at him, pulling at his skin, as if to remind him, *You belong to me. You will always belong to me.*

It would always claim a piece of him he would never have back.

I need to leave this place. Finish what he had come to do, and leave.

"Signal if you need assistance," Li Min said. "If his death causes any of us to be orphaned, find your way back to Nassau in this year. We will regroup."

He nodded, sliding the dagger she'd given him out of his belt. He couldn't think of the consequences of this just yet. The passage they'd come through, to the north of the city, would likely collapse—but what else might? For decades, time had revolved around Ironwood himself, and there was no way to predict what might happen once the center of that control collapsed.

He began to climb the stairs. They were shorter than he remembered, but spoke to him each time he put his weight on them, reminding him why he was there, what he needed to do. For the first time, he was glad he had a blade instead of a flintlock. Perhaps he'd give the old man a cut for every year he'd stolen from her life.

Etta.

Ironwood never liked to see his servants and slaves unless they were performing a specific task in a particular room. Each floor had a narrow servants' hallway built into it, connecting to the hidden staircase, and each bedroom of this floor had a door disguised as part of the wall.

Nicholas was careful, achingly careful, and waited at the top of the stairs for any sign of a servant. But the entire house was occupied with seeing to the needs of the men and women below; he would need to enter the old man's bedchambers and wait. If time had been an ally and not an enemy, he might have waited until the man was asleep and do it then, but the wasted hours would only provide more opportunity for his own body to fail him. Even now, he felt as if his head were stuffed with feathers; his vision was blurring at the corners. It had to be now. Once the task was completed, Sophia would drop a rope down from the roof for him to escape by.

It was simple, but even simple plans were prone to unexpected disasters.

Nicholas navigated forward, ignoring the squeaks and rough brushes of the mice scampering past his ankles. From the other side of the wall, he heard two men—guards—muttering to each other about the amount of food they'd eaten, and knew the next door would be the one he was looking for.

After a moment to ensure he couldn't hear anyone inside, he put his hand on the latch. Lifted it. The door swung open, surprisingly silent, given its weight. Nicholas took a steadying breath. His eyes were drawn to the crackling fire at the far end of the room, hidden by a large red velvet chair.

This room, too, had been resurrected to its previous life, when Ironwood had first owned it. Nicholas remembered the patterned rug, smugly imported from across the world. The forbidden leather-bound volumes that lined a small bookshelf had tormented him with their unknowable words. Even the bed seemed to have been carved out of his memory, with its plain white linens and tall posts strung with toile curtains.

He shut the door softly, still gripping the dagger in his hand as he moved across the room. The rhythmic pounding of feet and clapping from the dancers below broke up the silence, their voices dulled to a low rumble as they passed up through the cracks in the floors.

It seemed to him that the best, and possibly only, place to hide was behind the screen in the corner. Even the bed was too low to the ground to slip beneath and wait. Nicholas crossed the room, softening his steps, but was caught by the sudden, sweet smell of tobacco.

He stilled.

Nicholas had initially dismissed the smoke as escaping from the fireplace; as he stepped past the chair, he saw how deeply mistaken he was.

Ironwood's fine dress coat lay over his lap like a blanket, despite the old man's position directly in front of the fire. Under Nicholas's gaze, his grandfather relinquished the powdered wig he'd been toying with to the carpet, where it kicked up a small white cloud.

The man kept his attention on the small book in his lap, his hooded eyelids masking his expression. The way the firelight brightened his round face gave him unmerited warmth, and almost masked the way his cheeks seemed to hang like jowls. One of his fingers rubbed at the notched tip of his chin.

"'—But there's a tree, of many, one, / A single field which I have look'd upon, / Both of them speak of something that is gone,'" the old man read. "'The pansy at my feet / Doth the same tale repeat: / Whither is fled the visionary gleam? / Where is it now, the glory and the dream?'"

Nicholas remained as still as stonework, as if he'd been run through the heart with a blade. His every last thought fled.

"Wordsworth," he explained, setting the small volume aside. "I find I don't have the patience for merrymaking these days, but there is comfort in reading."

He rose to his feet and laid his coat over the chair. Nicholas took an instinctive step back, both at the suddenness of the movement and the weary tone of Ironwood's voice. The old man brushed past Nicholas as if he weren't holding a dagger in his hand, and moved toward the corner of the room where he kept his whiskey.

Move, Nicholas ordered himself as the man poured two glasses. *Move, damn you!*

Without a word, Ironwood offered one glass to Nicholas, and, when he didn't take it, drank it down himself in one swift gulp.

"How does this house speak to you, I wonder?"

That jostled Nicholas out of his stunned silence. It was impossible for the old man to know his thoughts—he recognized this—but the other implication seemed worse; their minds followed similar tracks. Their hearts spoke the same language.

"It speaks to me of regret," Ironwood said, pressing the rim of his glass to his temple. And this was the precise moment Nicholas began to feel the hair prickle on the back of his neck; for Cyrus Ironwood was a great many things, but none of them were maudlin or sentimental.

Drunk? Nicholas wondered, fingers tightening around the hilt of the dagger. He'd seen the man drink three bottles of wine himself and remain sober enough to take business meetings. In fact, Nicholas had always assumed it was a carefully cultivated skill, this tolerance for alcohol, meant to disarm rivals and potential business partners who hadn't a prayer of keeping up.

Every aim, every word, every action from this man was meant to disarm his opponent. This false sentimentality was surely the weapon he'd picked to rattle Nicholas, and, all at once, he was furious with himself for falling for it.

"I wasn't aware," he heard himself say, "that you were acquainted with a feeling like *regret*."

"Ah," Ironwood said, saluting him with his glass. "And yet, I've regrets enough to paper the walls of this house."

He finally looked at Nicholas, studying him in the room's relative darkness. "From the moment you entered, I wondered why—I have always known there would be a *when*, but the *why* of it, that was the mystery. Because of your status when you lived in this house? Because your mother received Augustus's unwanted attentions and was sold away? Because you felt slighted by the family? Because you broke our contract, and knew that this was the only way out of it? Or is it, Samuel, simply for the satisfaction?"

Nicholas knew by the gleam in the man's eye, by the use of his birth name, that he'd laid out all of these strikes the way a chef would lay out his knives, debating which one was best to use to make a cut.

"Or . . . is it because you've come to take revenge for *her*?"

Nicholas swung the dagger around, tracking the man's movements. Rather than go toward the chest of drawers or his bedside table, he went toward the trunk at the foot of his bed.

"No," Nicholas said, knowing full well that he could be hiding a flintlock or rifle in it. "Take a step back."

"Of course," the man said, with mocking graciousness. "If you'll retrieve the package inside. I have, after all, been keeping it for you."

Nicholas recognized this bait for what it was, but he was disarmed by the man's demeanor. Ironwood was never more truthful than when he was trying to inflict a mortal wound on another person's heart.

Keeping his eye on Ironwood, keeping his dagger out, Nicholas bent to retrieve a flat parcel, wrapped in parchment and tied with string. It looked as if it had come a great distance, whether that was miles or years.

"Go on, open it," Ironwood said, clasping his hands behind his back.

And, God help him, Nicholas did. He tore into the paper with one hand. Even before he saw the fabric—the sheer *gömlek*, the emerald *chirka*—he smelled jasmine; he smelled the soap-sweet scent of her skin.

And he smelled blood.

The feeling in his hands was gone. His pulse began to pound at his temples. So much blood, the fabric was stiff with it. It flaked off as he ran his fingers across the delicate embroidery, moving along the seams of the jacket until they snagged at the ragged hole at the shoulder, where she'd been shot.

"A guardian sent these to me weeks ago," Ironwood said. "As proof of Etta Spencer's death. Her father claimed her body, but I thought you might want the reminder of her personal effects."

This is what remains. . . .

Memory would fade from him, her footprints would be washed away—this was all he was to have of Etta Spencer now.

"You did this. . . ." He breathed out, his gaze snapping up. *"You—"*

"Yes," Ironwood said, his face drawn, as if—as if he *cared*. As if he felt *sorry* for this. Nicholas's fury overwhelmed him, and he slashed out with the dagger, catching the man across the chest. Ironwood leaned back in time to avoid being gutted, but a gash of red extending from his shoulder to his hip began to ooze. Nicholas felt frantic, sloppy, like he was damn near to clawing his own face off to try to release the boiling anger and grief. He did not want to collapse onto his knees. He did not want to scream himself hoarse.

"All because you want one blasted thing, when you already have *everything*! You aren't satisfied with the destruction you wrought; you need the tool that will make it complete," Nicholas seethed, knowing full well that the man's guards would be coming in, that they'd kill him where he stood. And yet, Ironwood didn't move, didn't taunt, didn't defend himself.

Kill him—just finish him! his mind was bellowing, but he couldn't move from that spot.

"What you feel now," Ironwood said, "I have felt every day of my life, for forty years."

"Don't say another word," Nicholas said. "You know *nothing* of me or what I feel. *Nothing.*"

"Don't I?" Ironwood said carefully, glancing over at the portrait by his bedside. Minerva. His first wife. "I can see how badly you wish to stick that dagger in my heart, and I cannot blame you."

"You don't have a heart," Nicholas snarled. "If you did, you never would have dragged Etta into any of this. She wouldn't be—"

He couldn't bring himself to finish, coward that he was.

"And if Rose Linden hadn't betrayed us and hidden the astrolabe, if her parents hadn't fought as hard as the rest of us to control the timeline, if our ancestors had never used the astrolabes to begin with—do you see how futile this line of reasoning is, Nicholas? We can live in the past, but we cannot dwell there," Ironwood said. "What you cannot seem to grasp is that the astrolabe isn't a tool of *destruction*, it is one of *healing*. It can right wrongs. Save lives."

Save her.

He had not even considered that. How was it possible he had never once considered that by waiting out a year, he might travel back to the spot where she was to die, and save her, before the Ironwood men had a chance to reach her? That he could find a way to prevent Etta from being taken?

"You would risk," Nicholas began, "orphaning countless travelers, shifting the timeline, for your own selfishness."

"For love," Ironwood corrected. "For *her*."

There was nothing ironic in his tone, or even condescending. Nicholas shook his head in disbelief, his chest bursting at its seams with dark, humorless laughter. As if this man had any inkling of what that word entailed, the scale of it.

But he hated the softer part of him, the one that whispered, over and over, *Forty years. Forty years. Forty years.*

Forty years of *this* feeling. This unbearable tightness, of being caught in a cage of helpless rage and grief.

Because some part of Nicholas was listening. Some part of him heard the truth in the old man's words, and was reaching, grasping for the solution presented to him. Nicholas had the oddest feeling that he was back on his deathbed, a fever wracking his brain. There was a haze about the man, an unreal quality.

"You seem to believe that I am blind to my own faults," Ironwood said. "But I *improved* the world. I did my part to fix it, after years of fighting between the families. I brought us stability and order, and brought the worst of the travelers to heel. As long as the astrolabe is in play, we will never have peace."

"Is that why you let your sons die?" Nicholas asked sardonically.

The man rasped a hand over his chin, his shoulders sagging. "I have been asked to sacrifice so much, and I have come so far, and still . . . still we die out, like an inferior species. I wonder from time to time what my life would have been like, had I not been tasked with this role. I think I might have been a merchant, a sailor. You've felt it, too, haven't you? How vast the world is, when you cannot see anything but water on the horizon?"

"Stop it," Nicholas said. "I know what it is you're doing—"

"The moment I knew you had that inclination, that you were a natural . . . I recognized myself in you," Ironwood said. "My father. *His* father. All forged in the same fire. And when you fought so hard to leave our family's service, I knew for certain; for a true Ironwood cannot bear stagnation, or to be held against his will. You made your brother seem like nothing more than a yearling. He never had the grit he needed to manage the family—that grit which has kept me searching for the astrolabe all these long years. That which brought you here tonight."

Nicholas startled at the word *brother.* As long as he had known the man, he had never heard him use that phrase, without qualifications.

"I am nothing like you," Nicholas said. The old man rose to his full height, looking him in the eye.

"You have not yet lived a full life," he said. "You have not accumulated the triumphs and the sorrows. When you are my age, you will look back and see a stranger, and then all you will have to your name will be your convictions."

He believes he has done right by us all, Nicholas realized. There was nothing false or scheming about his words. He had spent years as a child cowering in the servants' hall and shrinking back at the sight of the man as he strode through the house. Like a soldier, his swinging fists always seemed to enter the room first.

In his youth, when he traveled with Julian, he had seen a calculating emperor who demanded tribute from his followers and tribulation from his enemies. And now he saw . . . an inverse of himself. A warning of what might come from rationalizing the lapse of his own morals, compromising his deepest values with the false promises of *just this once* and *never again.*

"You are my true heir," Ironwood said. "You alone. I was a fool for squandering your potential for so many years. We can begin again. I am not as young as I once was, and there are so many now who would

379

betray me. I need your assistance in certain tasks, as a guard, as my eyes in places I cannot be."

I cannot kill him. Sophia and Li Min were right, but their reasoning was flawed. To give over to the baser instincts of revenge would hand the old man a victory; it would undo Nicholas utterly, splinter him more and more with each year. He could not damn himself with this. There was nothing so important as being free from this man, his poisonous words and bloody legacy. If that meant his own death, then at least he might escape this man's pull that way, and deny him an heir.

His grip on the dagger tightened, until he felt the dragon on its hilt imprinting its shape into his skin, lending its ferocity.

"You say these things like you know where to find the astrolabe," Nicholas said.

"I do. It's found its way into the Witch of Prague's hands," the old man said. "I received the invite to the Belladonna's auction only yesterday. We only need to bid now and it's ours—I have far more secrets to tempt her than anyone else who may come."

The words swept over Nicholas's skin like fire, blistering through the layers of muscle and bone. The Witch of Prague, indeed. What a fool he'd been. If he'd known at the beginning of their appointment that she was the original bad penny, he would have parsed her words more carefully. *In the last report I received, yes, a Thorn was still in possession of the astrolabe. . . .*

So precisely phrased. If he hadn't been blinded by his own desperation he might have been able to dissect what she didn't say. *In the last report.* Not *presently.*

The woman was a fearsome creature, choosing and evaluating her words with the mind a jeweler would pay to buying precious stones. Loathsome, of course, but there was no denying her cunning; if it hadn't been for the fact that she'd poisoned him, he might even respect her for it, just that small bit. No wonder she had survived Ironwood's rule. She was that rare, dark thing that thrived by tricking the light into passing over it, that fed only on shadows and deceit.

"You need time to think on this, I know," Ironwood said. "But we haven't any. You—I must tell you something, and it cannot be shared outside of this room. I will not have panic in our ranks, and I know logic prevails for you as it does for me."

Our. Our ranks. Of course, to Ironwood, Nicholas's acceptance was a given.

"I've had a great rival for the astrolabe these many years—"

"The Thorns," Nicholas said, interrupting him.

"No," the old man said. "He who has no name, but has lived generations. I believe him to be one of the original time travelers, for there has never been record of him apart from legend. He has found the other copies of the astrolabe, drained them of their power. He cannot have this one, too."

Nicholas, again, listened to the tale of the alchemist and his children, forcing his face to remain as stone. On his hand, the ring burned.

"Why does this . . . Ancient One seek it?" Nicholas asked at the end. "And why should it matter beyond your personal gain that he take it?"

Ironwood lowered himself onto his bed, staring into the fire. "There is an incantation, a spell of sorts, I'm sure of it, that bleeds the power of the astrolabes and feeds him, extending his life beyond its natural years. But it must destroy the astrolabe itself, leave it as an empty shell. And that cannot happen."

"Why is that?" This was in line with what Remus Jacaranda had explained to them, but there was a thread of worry in the old man's voice now that made him wonder if there was something more to this. Something worse.

"Because, if the legends passed down within our family hold true," he said, "destroying the astrolabe will not just revert the timeline back to its original state . . . but it will also return every traveler to their natural time, and seal the passages forever."

The dagger slipped from Nicholas's hand. His mind was adrift in the storm of possibilities that tore through it.

He lies. He lies with every breath. He wants you to help him. He will do anything to have it.

But the fear—the slick, sweaty coating of it over the old man's words—*that* painted a portrait of truth, because if there was one thing the old man had never been in Nicholas's eyes, it was afraid. Or vulnerable.

Late at night, while at sea, Hall would sometimes wake Chase and Nicholas and bring them up on deck to learn to read the stars and navigate by them. Once, while he'd been stretched on his back, the sails flapping sweetly above them, the sea rolling beneath them, he'd seen a star fall from the sky, scorching the air with its speed and brilliance.

His next thought occurred to him in much the same way. *He does not want the astrolabe destroyed, because it would dismantle the traveler life. It would ruin him. Break his rule.*

It wasn't enough to take this man's life. This was the problem with these traveler families, their history. Another cruel man or woman would step up their own savagery to fill the void he left behind, and they would all be thrown into further chaos. Better to end this, once and for all—to spare the families, the world, the kind of grief he felt now.

And then I can rest. He could die knowing that he had finally broken the last chain binding him to this man. But Etta . . .

Love. Sacrifice. Release.

He could not save her and still destroy Ironwood. Even if he had the time to steal the astrolabe and escape—the shallow flutter of his heart, the labor it took to stay on his feet, spoke the truth: if he did not kill Ironwood, he was not long for this world.

And he would not kill Ironwood.

This was all he could do, and still live as he chose. It would be a good death, an honorable one. And, in this way, he could tolerate the surrender.

He would see them again. His mother. Friends lost at sea. *Etta.*

Wait for me, wait for me, wait for me. He would follow, as he had before, into the unknown; into whatever adventure awaited them there.

The man began to pace, his hands clasped behind his back. His words ebbed and flowed, disappearing into nonsensical muttering as Ironwood worked through his plan. If he had stripped out of his attire, Nicholas was not sure he would have seen the man as naked as this. The veneer of steel was gone, and it was deeply, deeply unsettling to him to see Ironwood's desperation rise to a pitch of such barely restrained frenzy.

"Say yes, Nicholas," Ironwood said. "She's not lost to you. This is your inheritance. This is what you deserve."

A sureness took his heart, lightening it enough for him to breathe for the first time in days. With each thud of his pulse, he felt the poison inch through his system. He moved toward the window, looking down into the garden where the candlelight from the ball seeped out, highlighting where Sophia was hiding in the bushes. Her face was turned up like a stargazer's in the darkness, searching for his.

When their eyes met, he gave the slightest shake of his head and pulled the curtains shut on her confusion. *I'm sorry.*

"I accept your offer as given," he said, turning back. "But I would ask for ink and paper, so that I might write a letter to Captain Hall, and assure him I am well."

Cyrus Ironwood looked up, eyes gleaming. He moved to his own secretary desk, retrieving the necessities.

"Of course," he said. "Of course. You'll come to find you have a great deal of paper and ink now, as much as your heart desires. My man will search him out to deliver it. I'll have him bring a physician to repair whatever it is you've done to your arm. Better yet, you'll join me

383

in the twentieth century. Medicine is remarkably improved by then."

"No, it's not necessary," Nicholas said, his voice loud to his own ears. "I am already healing."

"Good," he said, "good. There's a bed for you down the hall. Rest. We'll discuss plans to retrieve the funds necessary to enter the auction in the morning."

"My God," he heard the old man say as he reached the door. "My God, my boy, this is almost at its end."

Indeed.

Nicholas wandered down the hall, past the startled guards. He walked along the carpet, not hidden in the walls like the unwelcome secret he'd been. But when he arrived at the staircase and heard the dancing, the airy melody of crystal and glass gently colliding, he turned toward the entrance to the servants' stairwell and wound his way down it.

He was unsurprised to feel Li Min's hands on his throat the instant the door shut behind him. Good. He could face her in the darkness.

"What is the meaning of this?" she hissed. "You'll serve him now?"

"You heard it all?" She nodded. "Good. I haven't much time to explain. I'll take on the role of his heir only long enough for him to find the astrolabe, and for me to then take it from him and destroy it."

It was an easier thing to tell Li Min, who, in her way, always seemed to see the path they undertook from several steps ahead. Sophia would have turned back and finished the old man herself.

"I did not expect you to choose artifice," she said. "Can you maintain the deception long enough to reach your end?"

He nodded. What else did he have now but this one goal?

"Do you despise me for this? It'll mean an end to your way of life. If you've accumulated wealth in other eras outside of your natural one, now is the time to collect it."

And to prepare for the worst of it.

"If this is my last—my only—opportunity to say so, I am grateful to call you my friend. No, please hear me on this," he said, seeing her begin to speak. "I generally consider those who save my life friends, and hope that doesn't offend your mercenary sensibilities. I'm grateful for all that you've done, and that I've known you, even if that bond is broken by what comes next."

"I believe that nothing breaks the bonds between people, not years or distance," she said. "But you seem to simply take his word for it? What if his claims about its destruction prove false? I have heard—" She caught her next words, taking a moment to reconsider them. "It's been a rumor for years that destroying it would revert the timeline back to the original. But the other points sound like fear tactics."

He was too tired to argue this with her. As it was, he could hardly keep himself upright, and had to lean against the corridor's wall to support his own weight. *Too quickly, all of this is coming too quickly—*

I need more time—please, God, more time—

"The man I saw in that room was afraid," he said finally. "I do not know what to believe now. The world is upside down and this is the only way I can think of to right it."

"All right, my friend," she said. "We will follow you and assist in any way we can. If we need to meet, unknot your sling."

Nicholas, in truth, had not expected this, and he was moved by the fact that she'd made the decision so easily.

"What if you need to speak with me?" he asked.

"We will find a way."

"As you always do," he said, with a ghost of a smile. "Until then."

She raised her hand, touching his shoulder just for a moment before pulling back. His vision had adjusted to the darkness enough to make out the pale moon of her face as she stared hard at the buttonless jacket she'd stolen for him only a few hours before. "What would you have done . . . if she had survived? If you had found her?"

He couldn't bear to say Etta's name; it was a thorn on the tongue, as much as it bloomed in his heart. "I think . . . it does not matter much now. If the chance doesn't present itself, tell Sophia I'm sorry it's come to this. That I hope she'll understand."

"She'll understand; she may yet even appreciate your cunning in destroying the old man," Li Min said, drifting further from him as she found her way back to the same window she'd entered by. "But she'll tear down the gates of hell and drag you back by the throat if you allow yourself to die."

That, at least, was absolute in his mind. But he felt pleased in knowing that Sophia would never allow herself to be constrained by the limits of her natural time in the twentieth century. She would carve a way toward the same independence that had eluded him for so long. He had been so very wrong to assume that their uneasy alliance would rest on nothing more than a mutual hatred.

He had been wrong about so many things.

Rather than continue down the stairs, past the glittering souls dancing into the morning hours, past the cooling kitchen, he began to climb. The steps bore his weight with quiet protest, and he drifted up to the attic that had been his home for the first years of his life.

The support beam came within a hairbreadth of cracking against his temple. Nicholas sucked in a surprised breath and ducked through the entryway, bent at the waist to avoid skinning his back against the rough roof.

The old man must have completed some sort of renovation—the rafters couldn't have been so low as this, suffocating the attic so it was little more than a crawl space. He tried to recall if his mother or any of the other five house slaves who had slept with them in this room had been forced to make themselves smaller to enter, to contract their bodies to fit inside what little space they'd been granted.

Now there was no bedding on the floor, only the bed jammed up against the wall below the window. Straw exploded out of the bare mattress through a hole some industrious rat had likely chewed in it. Dust carpeted the floor, undisturbed for many years.

The room coiled around him, nearly unrecognizable from the vantage point his height gave him; he knelt, trying to reclaim some semblance of memory, to understand why this room had once felt like a kingdom. There had been so many times he'd sat beside the room's low window and watched the wide, pale sky above the townhomes, tantalizingly endless beyond the glass. Nicholas wondered if that was the reason Ironwood had given them this room and not the cellar—to show them that everything in their lives would remain just as far out of reach.

The lacework of spiderwebs spread from corner to corner, catching the fragile moonlight. Time began to slip around him, peeling back the years, mending the cracks in the floor and the scuffing on the wall, filling the room with soft candlelight and whispers of life. The bed linen still smelled as he remembered it, of starch and leather and polish. Even in this small sanctuary, they hadn't been able to fully escape their work. They lived it.

He sat on the bed and, using his left hand, finally went about writing a short missive to Hall. But after the salutation he stopped, uncertain of what to say, beyond, *I am well. I will find you when I am able.* Both were lies, and he couldn't abide the thought. But if Ironwood himself didn't break the seal to read it, one of his men would, and report on its contents. So, instead, he gave Hall all that was left to him now: gratitude.

For all that you have done for me, I thank you. I have been warned of the regret of being too sentimental in the face of an uncertain outcome, but I would be remiss not to take this opportunity to say this to you, if nothing else. I have lived a life of vast fortune owing to the generosity of your heart. I will never cease fighting to be the sort of man who will honor those values which you have so graciously bestowed by example. If there is a way back, I will find the bearing and come posthaste. —N.

Nicholas folded the paper and stowed it inside of his coat.

How strange it was, to be near the end of one's journey, and to find oneself back at the place one began and see it as if for the first time. To remember that small rebellion that had lived inside him at the thought of the untraveled world that lay beyond these walls.

The name Carter had come from his mother's first master, and he had kept it, even as he'd chosen a new given name for himself at Mrs. Hall's suggestion. It had been the sweet lady's idea, a way to make him feel as though he had some mastery over his life. But he had kept the surname as a way to honor all that his mother had endured, and all that she had risked in hiding him. If Ironwood had sold him away down to Georgia with her and the others, he knew he likely would not have survived it.

This was the bed he'd slept on with his mother. Here she had cradled him in her arms, her scarred hands smoothing his hair, soothing his spirit. Here she had sung that song from her faraway home, thousands of miles from the cramped, dreary room. It had filled his ears like a fervent prayer, the only weapon she'd had to drive the darkness away from him. It had breathed life into his unconquerable soul.

He had lived so many lives, and yet the sum of his existence felt like so much more than any one part of his history. Even now—even *now*, in the face of the poison he felt inching through his veins, that same rebellion burned inside of him. That same demand for the distant horizons summoned him to fight.

Nicholas, he named himself on the deck of that ship, in the light of a sea of stars.

Bastard, the Ironwoods declared.

Partner, Etta swore.

Child of time, the stranger beckoned.

Heir, the old man vowed.

But here, in this hidden place, he had only ever been *Samuel,* the son of Africa, the legacy of Ruth.

REYNISFJALL MOUNTAIN
IIOO A.D.

TWENTY-SIX

Your presence is requested at the auction of a rare artifact of our history: one astrolabe, origin unknown. October 22, 1891, at the cusp of midnight. Kurama-dera Temple, north of Kyoto. The entry fee remains a hundred pounds of gold or jewels per bidding party.

Etta read the note again, ignoring the soft patter of freezing rain on her hair and face. They'd gone upstate, to a cabin that sat like an afterthought in the woods, and waited a day, watching its doors for any Ironwoods. Hungry and frustrated, she'd broken away from Julian and gone to where he said the key would be: buried beneath the root of a nearby tree.

By the time she'd gotten the door open, he'd been brave enough to join her in sorting through the endless piles of letters and notices that had been slipped inside of its mail slot. Some were torn, clearly battered by their delivery; others showed the era in which they were written by the quality of the paper and the ink. Most were sealed with the same wax seal, bearing the sigil of the Ironwoods, except for one: blank wax, marked with a *B* that rested inside the curve of a crescent moon. Julian had picked it up between two fingers and shaken it, as if afraid it might suddenly reveal a set of teeth.

He had gone through his travel journal to try to locate the nearest passage, but she'd found a small reference book of passages, left on the empty cabin's table for anyone who dropped in and needed help in navigating away. A passage in Brazil would take them directly to Mount Kurama, but one rather weighty problem remained.

A hundred pounds of gold or jewels—not just difficult to locate, but difficult to carry to the auction site.

"I don't want to alarm you," Julian began. He pulled back from the hulking outcropping they'd hidden behind, observing the black beach below. "But there seems to be a gaggle of Vikings rowing up to shore."

That startled her out of her thoughts. Etta pulled him back by his simple tunic and took his place, scanning the fog spreading its pale hands across the sea. A carved wooden face appeared ahead of the rest of the ship, slicing silently through the heavy cover of gloom.

The figurehead was a serpent, a dark specter, all teeth and long, curving neck. Etta sat back, flinching as it broke through the gloom, gliding forward like a knife through a veil. The rush of the tide and the birds circling overhead covered the sound of the oars splashing through the water.

"I thought you said he picked this place for his gold reserve because it was deserted—your exact words were 'untouched by time and man,'" she said, glancing back over her shoulder.

"All right, I've been known to embellish my tales with a touch of drama, but do you honestly believe I wouldn't pay special attention to where I could find my shiny inheritance?" Julian said, leaning over her shoulder. "This was the safest place to keep the loot because of how little play it got with the timeline. No one is supposed to actually like this place enough to come visit."

Several other caches they'd checked had already been emptied and moved to an unknown location, or the timeline had shifted so severely that they had faded out of existence entirely. "Except Vikings," Etta said.

"All right, except Vikings."

"And the Celts," Etta said. "And other Scandinavian peoples. Why didn't he go way back—beyond ancient times? Prehistoric. Actually, how far back do the passages go? Could you see, like, the dinosaurs? Cavemen?"

Julian leaned back against the rock, pressing a hand against his chest, his expression one of pure astonishment. "My God, Linden-Hemlock-Spencer. I believe you've just given me a new purpose in life."

Etta's brows drew together. "Finding new passages?"

"No, hunting for dinosaurs," he said. "Why did I never think of that—oh, right, the eating thing. Big teeth and all. Well, never mind."

"How quickly the dream dies," Etta said wryly, turning back toward the beach.

For an hour now, they'd kept watch on the cave, hidden just out of their line of sight by a curve in the mountain. All they could see of it through the mist and fog was the edge of the entrance: towering stacks of stone, some round like pipes, others as straight and narrow as bone, had seemingly splintered from a rough rock face. From a distance, Etta had thought they'd merely been piled closely together, like ancient offerings for whatever king had ruled the mountain and beach below.

The longship navigated between the narrow, towering black rocks jutting up from the water, before driving up onto the shore itself. The landing was quick work; the oars were tucked inside, the sails drawn up so as not to catch the whistling wind.

A half dozen men poured out of the belly of the ship, their feet striking the black sand, moving swiftly to catch the five empty leather sacks thrown by the others on the deck. The depressions their feet left in the black sand filled with rain, shining like scales from a distance.

Finally, a tall figure jumped down from the deck of the second ship, struggling for balance with one arm cradled against his chest. He was darker than the others, both in skin and dress, wearing none of the fur they did. The men around him gathered slowly, as if with reluctance, their heads bobbing up and down with whatever instructions he was giving them. Then he began his long strides toward the very cave Etta and Julian had come to clean out, his shoulders set back, chin raised, the way—

She was on her feet before she could think to rise. Etta choked out something between a gasp and a laugh. "Nicholas."

Julian reached for the back of her shirt, trying to pull her down, but Etta twisted away, frantic. He was too far away, *too far*—her whole body trembled in protest at being forced to remain where it was.

She edged as close to the line of the cliff as she dared, starving for a better look at him; her heart was thundering so hard, she was half worried it might suddenly give out on her.

How long his hair had grown, how thin and battered he was in the face. The distance between them was more than just air and sand and mountains; it manifested in all of those missing days between them, creating a deep valley of uncertainty. The sling for his arm—what had happened? Who were these men, and why—

One last man was lowered down from the first ship, with the assistance of two other men. He was hunched at the shoulders, adorned with leather armor and gray fur, and she knew him—not because her mind put the impossible pieces together, but because Julian did. He recoiled, going bone-white in the face.

Cyrus Ironwood looked like a different beast without the finery he'd wrapped himself in to give the impression of civility.

Oh God, she thought, pressing a fist against her mouth to keep from making another sound. *He's got Nicholas.*

She'd been so focused on finding the astrolabe, so sure in her belief that Nicholas was in Damascus still, that she had somehow never considered the possibility that Ironwood would have snared him again. But then—the men were going where Nicholas was pointing, hauling the sacks toward the hoard inside the cave at the end of the beach.

When Ironwood came up to him, when Ironwood put a hand on his shoulder, Nicholas did not run. He did not flinch. He nodded, pointing to the cave.

He . . . *smiled.*

"What in the name of *God?*" Julian began. He shook off the surprise first, pulling her back down to a crouch beside him. "He's—that's Nick, isn't it? But then, that's Grandfather, and they're . . . they're together."

Walking side by side to collect the reserve of Ironwood treasure.

For one terrible moment, Etta could not feel anything below her neck. The cold air seemed to ice over the inside of her lungs, making it painful to breathe.

"He must be—the old man must be forcing him," she managed to say. The Nicholas she knew could barely stand to be in the same breathing space as the man, let alone tolerate his touch.

The Nicholas you knew for a month?

No. No. *No.* Etta shoved the thought away. He'd handed her his heart in complete trust, and she knew the shape of it, how heavily it was weighted with hatred and shattering sadness toward this family. This wasn't a betrayal—the only betrayal would be hers, if she believed he was doing anything other than finding a way to survive.

She blew out a harsh breath, gathering up her small bag of supplies. The landscape of Iceland had a cool, reserved kind of beauty, but its terrain was unpredictable, roughly hewn, as if shaped by the travels of giants. They'd come down a worn path that would eventually lead to the beach below, and, if she continued down it just a bit more, she might be able to get close enough to somehow catch Nicholas's attention without any of the Ironwoods noticing.

"He's treating him like . . ." Julian began, still sitting on the ground where she had left him.

"Let's go," she said. "Come on."

He turned, and for once she couldn't read his expression. "He's treating him like the way he used to handle my father."

"Nicholas is?"

He shook his head. "Grandfather. That's not a prisoner on that beach. That's an *heir*."

The words flew at her like an arrow. Etta took off, continuing up the path, to avoid it landing. She wrapped the heavy, drab wool coat around her tightly, and looked up to find that the rain had turned to snow, and was catching on her shoulders and hair.

Etta took the bend in the trail at a run, scrambling on hands and feet to avoid slipping on the ice and moss. The waves broke below her, snapping against the earth, sounding more and more like the blood rushing through her ears. She kept her eyes on Nicholas below, trying to keep up with him and the others before they disappeared into the cave.

Two hands caught her by the shoulders and swung her back around, hard enough that her feet slipped out from beneath her. Etta slammed onto the uneven ground, the air exploding out of her in a cloud of white. She wheezed painfully, trying to fill her lungs, to rise back up, but she was pinned in place by the kiss of a blade against her exposed throat.

It pulled back suddenly, and the weight that had crashed down on her chest lifted with a gasp. By the time the burst of light cleared from Etta's eyes and she could lift a hand to clear the snow from her lashes, a familiar face was gazing down at her in horror, partially disguised by an impressive-looking leather eye patch.

Her mind understood what she was seeing—who she was seeing—but couldn't make sense of it: the short hair, the shirt and trousers, the boots. Etta scrambled back as best she could, trying to put distance between her and Sophia, until her hand closed around a shard of stone. She thrust it between them to ward the girl off.

"Soph . . . ia?" came the weak voice above them.

Julian stood on the path, a short distance from them. When Sophia turned toward him, rising to her feet, his face seemed to crumble. He didn't just look remorseful—he looked as if he wanted nothing more than for a bolt of lightning to blow him off the face of the hill.

"I guess the obvious question is, how the hell are you alive?" Sophia's voice sounded as if it had been rubbed raw.

Julian dared to take another step toward her, holding out a hand, as if he expected her to take it. Sophia stared at it the way a wolf would assess whether or not it was worth chasing a hare.

"Oh, that—well, old girl—Soph, light of my life—" Julian seemed unable to tear his eyes away from the eye patch. There was an unhealthy sheen to his face, almost feverish, when the attention of the group finally shifted to him.

"You," she interjected, "I know about. I'm speaking to *you*, Linden."

"Me?" Etta repeated. "I'll admit I had a couple close calls, but—wait, *what?"*

"You were dead. D-E-A-D. As in, finished, gone to meet your maker, et cetera," Sophia said. "Your father issued a challenge to Ironwood. He demanded satisfaction for your murder at his men's hands."

"My murder?" Etta repeated, hauling herself back up to her feet, only to have Sophia tug her and Julian back down to their knees.

"Oh," Julian said, turning to her. "Didn't you tell me that your father said he had a way of keeping Ironwood off your tail? How better to do that than to confuse Ironwood into thinking you were already dead?"

"That's a leap," Etta said, even as something squirmed in her stomach.

"He kept it secret from you?" Sophia asked, looking unimpressed. "It's true, though. The only reason Ironwood would ever leave you alone is if he thought you were already dead, and he'd missed out on the fun of killing you himself."

Etta's eyes narrowed. "Ironwood, huh? Not *Grandfather*?"

The other girl drew back, her visible eye narrowing. In Etta's experience, Sophia had defended herself by deflection, by attacking. This time, Etta was prepared for it.

"Aaaand I'm just going to stand over here," Julian said, inching away. Etta cast him an irritated look. He cocked a brow in reply. "You court the dragon, you get burned, kiddo."

"What are *you* doing here?" Etta asked. "Why are you in disguise?"

Sophia laughed then. An ugly, exhausted sound. She flicked her leather eye patch up, revealing a scarred, empty socket. Julian either coughed into his fist or tried to muffle his retch. In either case, it wasn't well received.

"Cute," Sophia said in a cold voice. "I would guess you'd want me even less now, except you already went so far as to fake your death to get away from me."

Julian startled. "What? No—Soph, believe me, it had nothing to do with you—"

"I don't want your excuses," she said. "I want to know why you're here now, and what you're doing with *her*."

"I went to the Thorns," he said quickly, "which was a rotten idea all around. They despised me and I slept every night with one eye open— oh God—I heard the words leave my mouth and I couldn't stop them, Soph—"

Something dark bobbed at the edge of her sight, just past Sophia's shoulder. Everything was in harsh relief here, from the icy sky and feathery clouds to the browning moss that covered the black mountains and cliffs like flaking skin.

But there was another person there with them. In her dark cloak, with her dark hair, the land seemed to claim her as its own. Etta might not have noticed her at all if she hadn't moved.

Recognition linked with memory.

"You."

She was dressed differently from the last time Etta had seen her, in San Francisco. Her soft silk suit had been replaced by a linen tunic and baggy trousers, both held in place by a tightly knotted leather belt weighed down with scabbards and pouches.

There were a number of things about her great-aunt Winifred that Etta had willed herself to forget. Her penchant for vile turns of phrase wasn't one of them.

That creature you insist on working with is here to make her report.

Sophia turned, looking between her and Li Min. "What are you doing? Get over here before they spot you from the beach."

The girl did not move.

"You were wrong after all," Sophia said. "This is Etta Linden; not so dead, it seems."

Li Min was watching Etta, her head already bowed in resignation. Guilt was its own beast, Etta had learned. It took up residence beneath your skin and moved you to things you never thought possible, all to try to appease the discomfort it caused. Etta saw how they had all converged on this place. Fury leaped through her like a bow skidding off the strings of a violin.

Etta understood now.

"Funny that you told her I was dead, considering I saw you less than a week ago in San Francisco," Etta said coldly. "Did you finish your job for my father, or have you been working for Sophia this whole time to undermine him?" Another thought, almost more terrible, arose. "Did he tell you to keep us all apart?"

"Working for me? You're not making sense, as usual, Linden," Sophia said. But Li Min remained impossibly still. She couldn't tell if the other girl was breathing.

"Oh, *cripes!*" Julian figured it out a moment later, his brows shooting up to his hairline. "Li Min, you are one naughty little dame. I was wondering how the two of you ever would have met."

"What is going on?" Sophia demanded, an edge to her voice.

"What job is this, exactly?" Etta continued. "Have you been reporting back to her on the Thorns? Or did my father send you to watch her, on the off chance she found the astrolabe first?"

To her credit, the girl didn't retreat into silence to protect herself, as a coward would.

"I was hired by Hemlock," Li Min said, "to take the astrolabe, if either she or Nicholas Carter reached it first. Report back any useful information." She turned, meeting Etta's gaze. "He did not give me explicit orders to keep you apart, only to use my judgment in what would keep you safest. In the end, that was keeping your paths separate."

"What?" The word was so faint as it escaped Sophia, Etta wasn't sure it could be considered a whisper.

"You have to understand," Li Min said to her, a small, pleading note in her voice. "The Hemlocks found me again, after I escaped the Shadows, after I finished my training with Ching Shih. Her father is the head of my own family's line, yes, but, more than that, he believed in me. He arranged for jobs that helped to build my reputation. He provided whatever resources I needed to live my life on my terms, and he has never once asked for anything in return. I could never be one of them, not the way he hoped for—I could not tell him the things I told you. I was . . . afraid. Set in my ways. But I owed him a debt that demanded to be repaid. I offered to do this job for him and would not have committed to it for anything less than that; you must believe me."

"You—" Sophia stood, her feet carrying her toward the girl. She reached for the long knife at her side, yanking it from the hilt strapped to her leg. "*Believe* you? After everything else you've said and done was a lie?"

Etta understood that Li Min had perpetuated her father's lie and inserted herself into Sophia's life under false pretenses, but . . . Sophia wasn't just furious. Etta had seen fury in her before. She was *shaking*.

"Not everything," Li Min swore. "Not everything was a lie."

"The Thorns—the ones who beat me and left me for dead in the middle of the desert?" Sophia continued, stopping just short of the other girl. "You must have had a laugh, telling me all of that mystical nonsense about revenge. All the while, you were going to stop me."

"Not stop you, join you," Li Min said, her serene expression finally breaking. "I only—it—it all got rather complicated, you see—"

"It's not complicated at all," Sophia said, drawing the freezing air to her, turning her words to ice. "You showed me exactly who you were from the moment we met: a thief and a con artist. You were right. You are not my friend. You are *nothing*. Get out of my sight. *Leave!* Otherwise this time I really will kill you."

There was a long moment where no one spoke at all, not even Julian, who looked like he had a few thoughts on the matter. Li Min turned, shifting the bag on her shoulder as she passed the three of them. Whatever she whispered to Sophia seemed to enrage her further. The breath was steaming in and out of her, her pale face blooming a vicious red. Her one visible eye was screwed shut.

"Well, this has been a day of, ah, fascinating revelations," Julian said, daring to approach his former fiancée. He put a gentle hand on her shoulder, which she immediately knocked away.

"She was watching both you and Nicholas separately?" Etta asked. The question seemed so ridiculous that she almost couldn't get it out. "Or were you . . . *are* you working together?"

Sophia crossed her arms over her chest, turning her gaze out over the water. Her face mirrored the rough, jagged lines of the mountain, rendering her unrecognizable to Etta.

"Should we be preparing to catch her?" Julian murmured out of the side of his mouth. "Grab for the shirt, I'll try for an arm—"

Etta thumped him across the chest. Hard.

In Etta's mind, Sophia was always burning, always straining toward something. Now she stood with her face toward the bitter wind and welcomed it. She tilted her chin up, the way only Ironwoods seemed able to, and a smirk slid into place.

"You're hilarious, Linden," she said. "Work with him? I wouldn't let Carter polish my shoes."

"Soph!" Julian said, his voice sharp.

"Do you really want to take issue with that, considering all those things you called him in the past?" Sophia said. "Whoreson, gold-digger, ratfink—"

"Enough." Julian took a step forward, his face pale, his hair ringed by snow. "Enough! I know what I said in the past, and I was wrong for it. It doesn't excuse you to say any of it now."

"Aw," she said, cooing at him in a repulsive way. "Have I upset you? Or are you struggling with the reality that your bastard brother is now enjoying all of your old spoils of being heir?"

This was a trick Etta was familiar with—Sophia's uncanny ability to zero in on a chink in a person's armor and slip a blade through it. If Etta had had anything remotely sharp on her, it would have been wedged in the girl's windpipe in return.

"Liar," Etta said simply.

"Am I? I've been following him for weeks, that's all. I've watched him drift back into the old man's arms happily. Willingly. He's oversee-ing all of Ironwood's business ventures, repairing the changes caused by the timeline shifts, *advising* him. It's absolutely precious how well they work together. The old man actually looks happy. He's leaving Carter in charge of things, while he goes off to the auction."

Julian swallowed hard, glancing over at Etta, as if to gauge how possible this might be. She shook her head.

"He certainly didn't come looking for *you*, did he?" Sophia said.

A thin, hot thread began to weave itself in and out of Etta's chest.

"He thought her dead," Julian cut in. "As you did."

"And yet he's working for the man who was supposedly responsible for her death. It shows you exactly who he is, doesn't it? You had it in your head he was so good, such a hero, but he's no better than the rest of us. Your whole 'relationship,' your *love*—your *infatuation*—was based

402

on deals and transactions. Payment to bring you to Ironwood. Payment to stop you from taking the astrolabe. Shall I go on?"

Etta's stomach turned so sharply that she tasted bile. Not true. *Not true.* Sophia didn't understand. She wasn't there to see his regret. She didn't know Nicholas *at all.*

"Do you want to know why I'm here? The same reason you are: I want that gold they're carrying out, in order to attend a little auction for something stolen from me."

Of course she was. It was all about her, always. And just like that, Etta reached the end of the frayed patience that she had been clinging to. She lunged forward, ripping the knife out of Sophia's hand, and slammed the girl back against the rock behind her. Etta braced one arm over Sophia's chest, and brought the blade up just beneath her chin.

"Good *lord!*" Julian said, half in appreciation, half in horror. "The two of you bring out the worst in each other."

They ignored him.

"Too high," Sophia said, the words curling around Etta like smoke. "Lower. Did you already forget what I taught you?"

Etta's grip didn't ease. "You still don't see it, do you? The astrolabe *has* to be destroyed."

Sophia laughed—actually *laughed.* "Would you still be saying that if you knew what would happen, I wonder?"

"I've accepted that my future can't exist," Etta said. "You're the only one who still thinks she can get everything she wants in life."

"If you destroy that astrolabe, you'll have *nothing* you want in life," Sophia said. "Of course you don't know. You're nothing but a sweet little sheep being led by the nose, bleating on about right and wrong— wake up, Linden! There is no right and wrong, only choices. And you've made a decision without even having all the facts."

"What are you on about?" Julian asked, ineffectually trying to separate the two. "Sophia, come on. We'll go together—between the two of us, we know enough about the Ironwood holdings to scrape together the entry fee. There *is* a wrong choice in this, and that's letting Grandfather get his hands on it. You haven't seen what we've seen of the future, what's at stake. I don't know what Nick is on about, but it can't be helping him. He's too obnoxiously good."

Nicholas can't be helping Ironwood, Etta thought, her hands curling at her side. But then—he had made that agreement with Ironwood behind her back, hadn't he? Nicholas was supposed to follow her, ensure that she returned with the astrolabe. In exchange, he'd receive Ironwood's holdings in the eighteenth century.

She straightened. No. He'd turned his back on that. He'd confessed, he'd told her that he loved her. *Loved* her.

The small, dark wisp of a voice in her mind returned. *Infatuation.*

"I don't need to hear another word from you, you bloody selfish coward," Sophia snapped. "You've lost the right to care about me. In fact, why don't you just walk off that cliff now, finish what you started? At least Grandfather will have a body to bury this time."

"You don't mean that," Julian said, and Etta was almost surprised by how calm he sounded, how he didn't retreat from any of the ugly looks Sophia sent his way, the hissing words. "Tell me what's the matter, what's hurt you so badly. We've been friends our whole lives—do you honestly believe I can't tell when you're just lashing out?"

"It doesn't matter," she said, finally pulling free of Etta's arm. Sophia stalked over to pick up the bags she'd dropped. "None of it matters. Jump now, or destroy the astrolabe—your life is over either way. Since you can't seem to do anything yourselves, allow me to paint the full portrait for you: the Ironwood timeline won't just disappear. We will all be returned to our own godforsaken times, and the passages will slam closed behind us forever."

"God," Etta said, "you're such a liar."

Sophia had begun up the path, ignoring how Julian's hand reached for her. At Etta's words, she turned. "Am I? I guess you'll see, won't you."

"Wait," Julian called, following Sophia along the trail. "Soph, please—"

The two of them disappeared around a bend in the rocky path, and took that last small need for control with them. Etta's breath left her like she'd taken a punch to the lungs, and she brought both fists to her eyes, pressing the freezing skin there to cool the thoughts racing behind them.

Infatuation.

Returned.

Closed.

Forever.

If what Sophia said was true, and Etta had every reason to doubt her, then Henry clearly had never got the full story. He never would have risked separating the Thorn families from one another. God, what if a child was born in a completely different century than his or her parents—what if one of those children running wild in the house in San Francisco found themselves locked inside a violent time, in a place where they had no friends, and couldn't speak the language, much less ask for help?

Etta remembered what it felt like to have Nicholas's hands on her face, the way his fingers had run along her skin as if he could paint his feelings onto it. She remembered the way Nicholas had trembled, just that small bit, when she'd lain down beside him in the darkness. The warmth of his lips on her cheeks, her eyelids, every part of her, and how he'd given her his secrets. She remembered the way her fear had broken and dissolved against him, how carefully he had held her together each time she came close to shattering.

How quickly his mind worked, how earnestly his heart believed, how desperately he'd fought for everything in his life, including the belief that they could be together. In her heart, Nicholas was a song in a major key, bold and beautiful.

But Etta remembered, too, the way it had felt when the Thorns had reached for her, embraced her, claimed her with a thousand smiles and questions, trying to defeat the lost time between them. She remembered hearing her father's music join her own. She remembered her city, how its occupants and streets and trees had been blown into the same shifting, swirling cloud of ash.

She needed to talk to Nicholas; she needed to touch him, and kiss him, and know how he had hurt himself, know how she could help him. But there were a hundred men between them on the beach, and now, even more dauntingly, a hundred questions between them that Etta couldn't begin to answer.

There's so much darkness to this story, there are times I feel suffocated by it, Henry had said. How these things came back around. How everything circled back to the astrolabe, again and again and again.

A pattern.

No— Etta shook the thought away as hard and as far as she could.

Julian jogged back to her, running his hands back over his hair, breathing hard. "She wouldn't listen. There's something else going on that she's not telling us, I'm sure of it."

Etta nodded, keeping her back to the rock as she circled back to watch what was happening on the beach below. She found Nicholas immediately—it would have been impossible to miss him standing beside the old man, a short distance from the cave's entrance. He stooped slightly, to better hear what Ironwood was saying. Nodding, he stepped forward, cupping his good hand around his mouth to relay the message to the others.

What are you doing? she wondered. *What can you possibly be planning?*

There had been so many moments on their search together when Etta had felt like she understood his mind better than her own. But for the life of her, she couldn't understand why he'd taken this role in a game he'd never wanted to play in the first place, unless something had forced his hand.

"What should we do?" Julian said. "If she's right, then we'll get the original timeline, but then . . . that's the end for us, isn't it? Without the astrolabe to create the passages again, we're stuck."

Nicholas looked up toward them suddenly, as if searching through the mist and snow. Etta ducked before she realized she was doing it, her heart slamming in her chest as she leaned into the hard, jagged ground. She squeezed her eyes shut.

The one thing she had never doubted, never once questioned, was the constancy of her feelings for Nicholas; it was the part of her heart that kept a steady beat, that drummed a song only she could hear. By leaving Nicholas behind so she could chase the astrolabe with the Thorns, had she damned him to this choice, to survive the only way he could—through twisted loyalty?

The snow built around them, flake by flake, blanketing the black rocks and their twisted formations, smoothing them over until their wrinkles and crevices disappeared. When the idea came, it wasn't new; it was repurposed.

"How long would it take us to get back to San Francisco from here?"

Julian felt around the pocket of his coat for his journal. "If we hurry, maybe three, four days? Why? You want to try to link back up with the Thorns?"

"From there, how long to get to the auction site?" Etta pressed.

"If we use the direct passage that's in Rio de Janeiro . . . maybe three more days?" He thumbed through the pages again, checking his math.

"Then there won't be enough time," she said, sitting back on her heels, rubbing her muddied hands against the rough wool of her coat. "Especially if we're going to find a hundred pounds of gold. You didn't happen to notice any Thorn stockpiles, did you?"

"They spent everything that came in on food and water," Julian said. "Your father might have a reserve or two somewhere, but I'm not sure how we'd locate them and still make the auction date."

Etta nodded, recalculating. "And there are no other Ironwood reserves?"

"He's already cleared out the others—"

There was a sharp whistle from below, from the longship, as the men climbed aboard with the overstuffed leather bags. Nicholas followed suit, cupping his hand around his mouth to call out some order that was lost to the wind. Ironwood, it seemed, had already climbed aboard.

"Look at that," Etta breathed out, her heart giving an excited kick. "Did that look like more than a hundred pounds of treasure to you?"

"No," Julian said. "A hundred and a bit extra, maybe. But there's definitely more than that in the cave. They're not moving this cache, then, or clearing it out, are they? They only took what they needed."

"Which means we can take whatever he's left for our entry fee," Etta finished.

If Sophia doesn't beat us to it.

"And then what?" Julian asked. "Etta . . . I know you don't want to believe her, but Soph is never more truthful than when she's aiming for the heart."

"I know," she said, unable to take her gaze off Nicholas as he walked beside Ironwood back toward the vessels. One hand was tucked behind his back, and it reminded her of the way he had walked the length of the *Ardent*'s deck, so completely in his element.

Henry and the others had only known that destroying the astrolabe would revert the timeline, and prevent any new passages from being created to replace those lost by age and collapse. They had no idea that it would close *all* the passages, and strand everyone back in their natural times. She had to think he wouldn't want that—that Henry would come up with another, middle way.

Until she was able to figure out what that could be, she would have to try to keep the astrolabe in one piece. Once they confirmed that what Sophia had said was true, then she and the Thorns could turn their attention back to using the astrolabe to reach history's many linchpin moments, and nudge the timeline back to its original state by influencing them. It would send the Ironwoods lurching into panic, destabilize the old man's rule, destroy him with the knowledge that the astrolabe would remain just out of his reach forever.

It would be slow, dangerous work that might take years, but they could do it. *She* could do it, if Henry could not. It was a stark, disorienting reversal of their original plan, but Etta took comfort in the stabilizing thought that this, *this* would help her make amends for everything her family had done to contribute to the world's suffering across history.

They could start again. They could be better.

"I know," Etta repeated. "We'll get the astrolabe and try to regroup with the Thorns again to decide what to do with it. We can't destroy it, though, not until we know for sure what the consequences will be."

They did not have to sacrifice their families for the good of history and the future. Those two things didn't have to be mutually exclusive. There was a way to have both, and she would find it.

"And what of Nick?" he asked. "I hate leaving him with Grandfather—not because of what Sophia said. Being the heir is a curse, not a blessing. It just feels like, as much as he can handle himself, he's standing in the open mouth of a crocodile."

Etta drew back from where she'd been watching over the edge of the cliff. She felt light all of a sudden, as if she'd left something crucial there. "He's safe for now. We'll find the astrolabe, and then we'll come back for him."

If there was a path back to him in all of this, she would find it, or she'd carve a path where none existed—meet him halfway, as she always seemed to. There was a place for them, for all of them, to live with their families, and love and care for one another, but it couldn't exist in the world they lived in now.

They waited only until the longships had disappeared into the swirl of fog and snow before continuing down to the beach. Etta tried to shake the feeling that Nicholas was still there, that she was somehow walking beside an imprint of him. There were too many footprints on the beach to tell which were his, and she didn't want to cover his tracks with her own; not if it cost her proof that he had been here. That he'd been alive, and so close.

The cave was darkness incarnate, the mouth of a thousand-toothed creature. Ice-coated stalagmites shot up from the ground, the freezing wind whistling between them. It was as if the steps had been intentionally carved into the cave, and she followed them down, stepping with intent, ignoring the splatter of freezing water dripping from above.

"All right, then," Julian said, stopping a short distance ahead of her. They were at the very edge of the natural light emanating from the entrance, but there was a crack of sorts in the mountain above them. Etta looked up at it in wonder, watching the snow drift lazily down to her. She imagined each flake was a note falling against her skin, and the music in her began to stir once again, coaxing out a tentative, sweet song of hope. Nicholas hadn't gotten to see this. She would bring him back here one day.

"It looks like we'll have enough, though it might be close," Julian said, tossing Etta one of the sacks he'd brought with him. "Come on, Linden-Hemlock-Spencer. Gawking is my job. Appreciate the beauty of the world later, will you?"

Etta shook herself out of that reverie, crossing the distance between them. It was obvious where the Ironwoods had hidden their barrels beneath false rock covers. They'd been in such a hurry, they had left the empty ones to slowly rot. Julian popped the lid off a barrel stowed beneath a pile of rocks, cooing at the bright gold inside.

"The lost treasure of Lima," he told her, as if this explained everything. "He's greedy as sin, but lord, does the man have taste."

"Let's just hurry," she said, her fingers digging into the cold metal. There were days ahead of them before the auction, and too many chances for her plan to fail. But here, in the darkness, in the midst of their silent work, it felt safe to think of Nicholas on the beach, to wish that she had been there to warm his hands while the cold air nipped at his skin. She could almost remember what his voice sounded like as it whispered secrets into her hair.

Etta could be grateful even as she felt longing rise in her like an unfinished crescendo. One look had been enough; one reassurance that he was alive would sustain her. And whatever would come in the temple on the mountain, in the darkness of midnight, she hoped that he, at least, would be spared.

RIO DE JANEIRO
1830

TWENTY-SEVEN

SEAMEN WERE A SUPERSTITIOUS LOT, AND IT DID NOT surprise him in the least to find that stories were being traded in the confines of the forecastle, trailing him like sharks now that death had its fingers on him.

A ship's bell, as Hall's old sailing master Grimes had once explained, was the soul of the vessel. It was why they were meant to make such an effort to retrieve a bell from a wreck; over the course of its tenure, it served much in the way a church bell might: it marked the time for watches, and its bold sound was, to many of the men, a ward against evil and storms. But when it rang on its own, or when that same sweet tone seemed to rise from the depths of the dark water, it was an omen— it was a signal that a man was bound for his eternal reward.

Nicholas lay awake in his rented room, listening as the storm that had blown in at supper battered the city. The violent winds made play-things of the shutters and signs and roofs; it should not have surprised him that they were strong enough to shake even the nearby church bell, but it did. He felt the sound move through him as if it were striking each of his bones in turn.

The rain lashed at the window as Nicholas tried to sit up. Every joint in his body felt inflamed, locked into place. He attempted to roll himself over and put his feet down on the carpet, only to realize his left hand and wrist could no longer support his full weight without collapsing. It was slow, hard work to edge over on the mattress, and harder still to quell the disorienting feeling of foam sloshing around inside his skull. He regretted lying down for the night. It was always more difficult to begin again when you'd ground yourself to a halt.

"It's worse now, isn't it?"

Nicholas jerked back, forgetting yet again he couldn't lunge for the flintlock he'd placed beneath his pillow.

But it was only Sophia. She sat in the far corner of the room, shadowed. The steady drip he'd been aware of for a few minutes now hadn't been coming from a hole in the roof, but from her drenched overcoat. Beneath her, a puddle of muddy water was gathering around her feet.

"I feel as if I've been keelhauled, but it is manageable." Nicholas coughed, trying to clear the sleep from his voice. "How did you get in?"

"The guards downstairs are drunk, and the ones outside the old man's door are asleep," she said, crossing her arms over her chest. "What's that face for? There's a tree outside your window I can use to climb down, if you're going to be a grump about this."

At least one of them felt in command of the situation. The past few days of gathering and moving obscene amounts of gold and treasure from all of the old man's various hidden hoards to more secure locations had reaffirmed for him that he would never have a solid grip on the extent of the resources Ironwood had at his disposal. It only further served to reinforce his belief that another man or woman would simply seize control of it in the event of Ironwood's death, and the cycle would perpetuate itself.

"Where's Li Min?" he asked, waiting for his eyes to adjust to the darkness. With the storm clouds knitting themselves together so thickly, he couldn't rely on the light of the moon.

Sophia glanced toward the rivers of rain pouring down his window. "Out . . . finding food."

Suspicion stirred, rising in him like the winds outside. Somewhere, at some point on this journey they had undertaken together, he'd begun to develop the ear to pick out the subtle tones of her voice. He recognized this one all too well. It was the one she used when she was lying.

"Did he get the gold he needed?" she asked faintly. "For the entry?"

"That and a bit more to pay off the men for their silence on the cache's location," Nicholas said. "The old man assumes the astrolabe is as good as won, and has had us moving various stores and supplies to different locations. He wants access to them when he changes the timeline again."

Sophia nodded, rubbing a finger over her top lip. "That makes sense . . . so it's on, is it? Have you finally convinced him to let you accompany him to the auction?"

The old man had wanted to go alone with a small group of men and women for his protection. He claimed to need Nicholas to keep an eye on things at home, to fend off any attacks the Thorns might launch. Nicholas thought it more likely that some part of the old man still was struggling to fully trust him after what had happened with Etta, and did not want the astrolabe within Nicholas's reach.

But it had been far easier than anticipated to prey on the old man's rampant fears of theft or assassination. "He's so suspicious of everyone that it wasn't difficult to plant the seeds of the idea that he might need me to watch the guards watching him. With the twelve-hour time difference, Ironwood wants us to leave here no later than ten o'clock in the morning." He added, "I would keep back at least ten minutes, in the event Ironwood tarries near the passage to see who his competition might be. I will find a way to move him along."

"What's the old man's mood like? How has he been treating you?"

In the most disgusting way of all: like a prodigal son. "It's as if the past few years never existed. He wants nothing more than to discuss his shipping fleet. He lies and dreams in the same breath—I hear all about how much wealth and power I'm to inherit and how best to manipulate those around me if I'm to keep it, and yet I know for certain he wishes to save his first wife. I am a placeholder in his mind."

In truth, the man's property was astounding, but his collections of rare books, ships, and artifacts from across the eras were breathtaking. And he could not deny how truly alarming it was to find himself seated at a candlelit, food-laden banquet table with the old man's closest advisors and inner circle, when before, he had only ever been allowed to wash their plates.

Sophia hummed in thought, still fixated on the window, the swaying of the tree branches as they scratched against the glass. With all of the agility and strength of a man three times his age, Nicholas rose from the bed, ignoring the jabbing aches in his back and the hot blood needling through his veins. He felt himself on the hazy cusp of a fever, but the longer he remained awake and upright, the sharper it became. Using the bedpost for support, he came to stand directly in front of her.

"Have you seen any Shadows about?"

"No," she said. "Now that everyone knows where the astrolabe is, I imagine they've finally turned their attention away from us. But if Ironwood could never find any of the witch's hiding places, I doubt they will."

Sophia still did not look at him, but he was seeing *her* now. The dark ring around her visible eye, the sunken quality of her skin. Either she had spent far too long in the cool rain and was shrinking, or there was a knot of something painful inside her, deep enough that her body was curling itself around it.

"Is that all?" he asked. "I'm glad to see you well, but . . . I thought we were in agreement that it was too much of a risk to meet unless there was some crucial bit of information to exchange."

Sophia said nothing, only stood and wrung out the ends of her oversize coat, as if preparing to go. "You're right. It was . . . it was very stupid to come. I think—well, I thought—that is, we should talk about what will happen in Japan. I'll stay as close to the Ironwood bidding party as possible. If you spot someone about my size, do whatever you can to draw them toward the back of the group. I'll try to pull him or her away from the others and take the robes that the Belladonna supposedly makes everyone wear to make the bidding anonymous."

I'll try to. Singular.

"That sounds simple enough," he said slowly, waiting for her to continue.

She looked down at the back of her hands, her bottom lip caught between her teeth. Stepping to the right, as if to begin her usual listless pacing, she was startled back into place by the loud *squeak* of the floorboard.

"Sophia," he began quietly. "Li Min is not out gathering supplies, is she?"

The girl swallowed. After a moment, she shook her head. His breath stilled in his chest. "Is she alive?"

The devastation on her face pierced even the numbest parts of him. She had gone a sickly shade of pale, one he associated with someone about to cast up their accounts or swoon. Nicholas took a stiff step forward as she swayed on her feet, and urged her to sit down in the chair again. Though it made his body speak in ten languages of agony, he knelt down in front of her, joints popping with the effort. Black spots swam in front of his vision at the movement, forcing him to shut his eyes tightly until they cleared.

When he opened them, a single tear had escaped down her cheek, dripping off her chin like rainwater.

"What's happened?" he asked, gutted. "Sophia, please; tell me what's happened."

"She's alive," Sophia managed to squeeze out. "But I wish—I wish I had killed her myself. She's been lying to us the whole bloody time. She was working for the Thorns."

Li Min was a mercenary, and he could not say that he was surprised to hear she'd been on a job when they'd first crossed paths. "What does that have to do with us?"

Sophia gave him one of her humorless smiles, the one that curved with self-loathing. "*We* were her job. She was supposed to—to follow us. Keep us from finding the astrolabe before them."

"What?" Nicholas took her by the shoulder, forcing her to turn toward him fully. "She told you this?"

Her lips pressed into a tight line, her breath harsh as it wove in and out of her. He put his hand over the place where her hands were curling, tearing at the fabric of her coat.

Sophia turned her face up toward the ceiling, but to her credit, she was looking him in the eye when she said, "Yes, while you were on the beach in Iceland. That's also when I found Julian. And Etta."

"What does—" Nicholas heard her, but it was only several moments later that her explanation landed. It exploded through him like a mortar round, and the damage it caused was mortal. He could not move. He could scarcely gather the wherewithal to remember to breathe.

"They were both with the Thorns this whole time," she whispered. "Julian must have been caught by them or gone willingly in the hope they'd hide him, maybe. And they found Etta first—her father put out the false death notice to protect her, I guess. Etta was the one who recognized Li Min. Because they *saw* each other, just a week ago. And she still lied to our faces, she kept up their ruse that Etta was dead, even though she saw how you suffered from it. If we had gone after the astrolabe, she would have taken it out of our hands before we could have ever decided what to do with it."

Etta was the one who recognized her.

Etta was . . . Etta is alive.

But how—how was Julian with her?

"Are you listening?" Sophia was saying. "Do you even *care*?"

She was seething, her anger holding her hostage. Her face blurred in his vision, but he was not crying. That would have required feeling something at all. This swift churning of expectations, of reality, left him hurtling toward the barbed edges of horror and fury. But he never landed. With nothing solid to grasp, he could not seem to break out of the free fall. He fell back, sitting on the ground in a bid to get the world to stop tearing around him in a blur of darkness and rain.

Alive. Impossibly, beautifully alive. If there was ever a moment he might have pulled Etta from thin air, it was this one, when he felt so illuminated, so bold with the knowledge of her, that he could have reached through the darkness of the centuries and fetched her to him.

"Why were they in Iceland?" Nicholas asked with urgency. So close, damn it all. They had been so close to him. "Were they all right?"

"They were there for the same reason you were," Sophia said, her voice flat. "Only, the Ironwoods beat them down to the cave."

If only the fog had delayed the longship even one hour . . . *No.*

He shook his head. It was too dangerous, too seductive a thought. Nicholas would have seen them for himself, yes, but Ironwood would have done so as well. They'd have been reunited under the worst of circumstances, and his plan to destroy Ironwood would have unraveled the instant he saw her.

"They wanted the entry fee for the auction?" To attend with the Thorns, he presumed. But the thought did not seem to follow through logically. Sophia would have met with a larger party than just the two of them. And given what Ironwood had said of Henry Hemlock's personal wealth, it did not seem like they'd need to skim from Ironwood's holdings.

Etta's father's wealth.

The man had clearly known what Nicholas had known from the very moment he and Etta had come to terms with needing to destroy the astrolabe: Ironwood would never cease hunting her if she took what he wanted from him. He would never stop until she was dead by his hand, or someone else's.

But did the old man believe she *was* dead, with the bloodied clothes as his only proof? His anxieties about double agents in his family ran deep, and with good reason. Perhaps some of his men were truly in Hemlock's pocket, and had claimed responsibility for the death to perpetuate the lie.

That, or the old man had known she was alive all along and had decided to use the pain of it to turn Nicholas to his side, dropping the hollow promises of wealth and respect as additional lures. He thought he knew his grandson's heart so very well, didn't he?

"That's the third time," he said softly to himself, shaking his head. Seeing her inquisitive look, he clarified, "That I've allowed myself to be deceived. It's remarkable we've made it this far, given what a fool I've been."

"If you're guilty of being a fool, it's only because you expect the rest of us to be as honorable as you are," Sophia said.

"I actually expect the world to be fairly miserable in its handling of me," he said. "Over the past week, I've allowed desperation to speak louder than my better judgment. It's had me on a leash this entire time."

He glanced down at the ring on his finger, avoiding her gaze. Nicholas had paid the price for it, certainly.

"Do Etta and Julian still intend to participate in the auction?" he asked carefully.

"I think I might have scared them off," Sophia said, sinking down onto the floor in front of him. "I did something—you're going to hate me for it."

He found his mind stilling again, fixating on her words. His gaze narrowed slightly. "What did you do?"

She pressed her lips tight together, as if she were drowning, trying to save that last bit of precious air.

"What did you do?" he repeated.

"You won't understand—I was *so* angry, so bloody furious, and I went to this place inside myself I don't like, that I can't help but

422

disappear into, and I could hear myself saying all of these things, all of these lies. I wanted to *kill* them for ruining everything, the two of them; I hated them for shattering Li Min's lie; but I was scared, too."

"Of what?" he asked. "*Sophia*. What did you tell them?"

She pressed her hands to her face. The panic in her voice gripped him and held him there, at her next words' mercy.

"That you were—that you were the heir now, and happily working for Ironwood. I told them that you never bothered looking for Etta, and that you were happily won over by the old man, because whatever was between you and her wasn't real to begin with."

Was that all? Nicholas shook his head with a dismayed laugh. "She didn't believe you."

The girl pulled her hands away from her face with a look of surprise.

"There is an understanding between us," he explained. "She knows the whole of my heart. But why would you say such a thing? Why try to send them away?"

"*Because,*" she said, struggling to keep her voice down, "because of a *hundred* reasons! Because you would have reconsidered following through with the plan to destroy the astrolabe, knowing there was a chance you could be with her now. Because she would have interrupted you, distracted you, and cost you precious time when that loathsome ring could steal you at any moment and leave me to finish this all alone. And because I will be *damned* before I let you lie down and die without at least trying to give us the time to break the ring's hold over you."

Nicholas sat back, silenced by the force of her words.

"You can bloody well hate me for it, too, but I can't be sorry," she said, wiping at her face in disgust. "And now you have me weeping like a child! If I liked you any less, I would beat you senseless for this."

"I'm not surrendering to the poison, Sophia," he said. "I fight it every single day. This has been our plan—"

"This was *your* plan. Yours and Li Min's. You told me I wasn't allowed to die," she said. "Do you remember? In the desert, in the hospital, over and over again. Each time I wanted to slip away you were there, with your annoying 'You owe me a debt, you are not finished with your life, this is not your end' nonsense. It made me want to die just to irritate you, but I didn't. So why should I sit here and watch you make the same slow farewell?"

Nicholas's left arm began to shake under the strain of holding his weight. He shifted, leaning forward with a grimace. "Then why did you agree to follow me to the auction?"

She looked at him as if he'd asked her why chickens lay eggs. "Because I'm going to find the witch and stick a bunch of knives in her until I find the one soft, fleshy spot that makes her take your blasted ring off!"

He did not want to tell her that she was in the deepest sort of denial if she truly believed she could convince the witch of anything. The stories Ironwood had told him about the woman made his skin crawl, and he had very little doubt that killing her or wounding her would only cause the poison to work faster. She was as merciless as they came, and the only way to truly get his revenge on her would be to take the astrolabe and ruin her chances of adding another secret or soul to her collection.

He wasn't surrendering the ship; he was going down with it, and on his own terms.

"You said they . . . that Julian and . . . Etta," Nicholas said, trying to stamp out the ember that began to glow dangerously inside him again, "that they were planning to attend the auction? Or at least apply for entry to it?"

"They *were*, though judging by Linden's expression, I think I put her off the idea," Sophia said, with one last confession. "I told them what's going to happen when the astrolabe's destroyed. Neither of them took it very well."

It was amazing that, for all of their similarities, neither Etta nor

Sophia could decipher each other or understand the other's minds. Nicholas translated Etta's reaction for her: "That only means she'll be there to try to steal it."

"There wasn't enough gold left in the cache for an entry fee, anyway," Sophia said. "I came back and checked about an hour after you'd left. And Ironwood's cleared out the other ones Julian would know about."

That would pose an actual problem, though he had little doubt that Etta could think her way through the situation. "Then you're likely right, and they won't be there. You've kept them safely away from any trouble we might cause."

"Stop trying to make me feel better," Sophia ordered. "It won't work. I'm determined to be angry and guilty about this for at least another two days, and then again when I'm punching your corpse."

He tried his best to smile. "Though I sincerely doubt they believed you, you attempted to keep my pretense to maintain our plan, even in the face of great emotional turmoil. Ma'am, I regret to inform you that you now have honor in spades."

She pulled a hideous face. "Ugh. Is that why I feel so terrible? Take it back, it's awful."

Nicholas shook his head ruefully. "Can you not see it, though? How your situation might align with—"

"I don't want to hear this—"

"How it might align with Li Min's?" he pressed on. "She kept up a pretense on behalf of another that only served to keep Etta safe and alive. This whole situation might have taken a different direction, certainly, but it wouldn't have changed the manner of the deal I made with the Belladonna. Nothing but Ironwood's death or her mercy will take the ring off, and neither will ever come to pass. At least now . . . at least now something good might come of it."

She rubbed at her forehead. "I don't really want logic right now, Carter. I mostly want murder."

"Will you settle for an end to this?" he asked. "It's all I can offer at the moment."

"How can this not change anything for you?" Sophia asked, that same pleading note bleeding back into her words. "Why can't you be selfish like the rest of us?"

Etta's alive.

Julian is safe.

Li Min is gone.

All of these facts should have tilted the earth itself, upended him. But it changed . . . nothing.

It was better if Etta did not know about the ring, about the bargain, about his choice. She would fight him every single step of the way, and he couldn't risk being taken off that path now, not when he was so close to seeing everything through.

But the weight of that, knowing he was intentionally keeping her in the dark yet again, felt as though it might crush his entire chest. He had to fight for his next breath.

"I'm . . ." He tried to give a name to the quiet storm inside of him, but the moment he grasped what it was, it slipped away again, and all that was left was weariness.

Resignation.

He felt now like he was taking on water, moving forward sluggishly, toward an inevitable end. The thought of Etta breathing, fighting, filled the dark sky of his thoughts with stars. If he stretched out on his back, closed his eyes, he could imagine himself back on the deck of that ship. He would be able to see those stars falling once more, arcing down in one last flare of brilliance. It was seared upon his memory as she was.

Whatever would come the next night, Etta was still in possession of her life. He was unspeakably grateful, even as he knew once more the fear of his heart lying vulnerable outside of himself. She would continue on without him, blazing through the darkness in her way. If he could not give her back her own future, he could make a life for her that was safe, free from the retribution and strife between their families. He would end this cycle, wash the blood away.

But, oh, he was a coward, because he found himself seizing on that thin hope that Sophia was right, and Etta had been turned away from this task. It was harder to die than he imagined it would be, and desperately humbling. He did not want her to see him like this, no more than he wanted her in harm's way should things come to blows.

He did not think he could survive a final farewell.

The single power that time travel truly held over them was regret. If he could simply move back through the weeks, sift through the days, to arrive at that moment in the Belladonna's shop, of course he would have steered as far away from it as he could. But hindsight had given him something undeniably precious: insight. Into Sophia, into himself, and into their bitter, beautiful world. All he had ever wanted to do was travel, seek out those horizons; and he had, hadn't he? He had gone farther in these weeks than the limits of his own imagination.

"If we must act quickly, and there is no time tomorrow," he told Sophia, "I would like to say that I am proud to have fought beside you. I would never again presume to tell you how you ought to live your life; I would only say, as your friend, that there's no pain more acute than words left unsaid, and business which can never be concluded—"

She reached forward, pressing her hand against his mouth to silence him. Nicholas started to tug it away, exasperated, but in the next moment he heard it, too. Footsteps. A curt knock on the door.

"Everything okay in there, Carter?"

The Ironwood men didn't defer to him so much as guard him. Watch him. Judge him. He had seen the looks flying around the table, after Ironwood's proclamation declaring him heir during their last— and, please, God, final—family meeting.

"Fine," Nicholas called back. "Reciting . . . my prayers."

"Whatever you say," the man—Owen—grumbled. "Just keep it down, will you? If you wake him up, it'll be the end of all of us."

Too right.

Nicholas waited until the footsteps receded before turning back to Sophia, but she was already at the window, unlatching it. A slap of wind and rain struck him across the temple.

Right. The damned tree.

"You'll break your neck," he said, trying to stand. "Wait for the rain to settle. I'd rather not have to explain the presence of your broken body in the morning."

Sophia's lips curled ever so slightly upward. "Don't be ridiculous."

She sat on the window ledge, swinging one leg over, then the next. Her gaze roved over the tree's shaking limbs, the rivers of rainwater washing the street below clean.

"She might yet return," he told her as he came to stand behind her.

Sophia turned to him one last time, the mist of the storm collecting on her face. "No. She won't."

OUR LADY OF CANDELARIA WAS A STATELY PAPIST— Catholic—church, with all the embellishments the Baroque style of architecture had to offer. Two towers sat proudly on either side of an unfinished dome, dark granite accents contrasting neatly with its white-washed walls. Inside, however, the design was neoclassical, its pillars and statues of angels, saints, and the Virgin Mother carefully carved with an eye for the size and beauty of the place of worship.

It was blessedly far, at least, from the all-too-prosperous slave market on Valongo Street, the fattening houses where weak and thin "merchandise" were cajoled into gaining weight to increase their value, and the dock itself, which had no doubt been built by the hands of slaves to welcome each subsequent shipment of innocents. Of course, that had not stopped Ironwood from walking their party of an even dozen men right through it, with all the care and sensitivity of a monster.

"What's the matter with you?" the old man asked.

Wonders abounded—the man had finally broken away from the narrow lane of focus that was the astrolabe. The last five days had proven that when the old man was not speaking of it, he was thinking of it; and when he was not thinking of it, it was only because he was asleep and dreaming of it. It was the first word out of his mouth in the morning, and the last one he spoke in place of his evening prayers. Conversation with Ironwood was already forced, but it had become so rote and tiresome, Nicholas actually found himself missing the man's vile threats and bitter oaths.

Nicholas shifted his eyes away from the church. "Nothing. Am I not allowed to admire beauty when I see it?"

Ironwood snorted at that. "A terrible liar, now and forever. It's how I know I can trust you. How's the arm? Back in fighting form, I see. Good, good."

Rather than risk being left behind as a liability, someone who wouldn't be able to protect the old man from any enemies who might appear, Nicholas had removed his sling and tucked his useless hand into his coat pocket.

"It is—"

"Wonderful, yes," Ironwood said, in a voice that practically sang with glee. Nicholas was instantly repulsed by the heavy hand that landed on his shoulder. The added weight of it might as well have been a mountain, for how quickly his knees threatened to buckle.

Owen—the short, stocky guard—emerged from the church, signaling it was clear to enter and take the passage to Japan.

"One more step," the man said, as he urged the two of them forward. "One more night. Imagine her face; the future you wish to create is within your reach."

Owen held the door for them, allowing Nicholas to duck inside without moving his paralyzed arm. And, whether he wished it or not, he did see Etta there. He saw her in the flickering of the candles. He saw her in the smooth, pale lines of the arches. He saw her in the singular way the light struck the stained glass behind the altar and colored the world.

A hymn to her. A requiem to a future that was no longer his to claim.

"Yes," he said finally. "The end is in sight."

MOUNT KURAMA
1891

TWENTY-EIGHT

THE CENTURIES AND CONTINENTS MOVED AROUND HER IN dark waves, and the passage's usual bellow was more of a long, continuous whistle. The difference, while pleasant to Etta's ears, was rather disconcerting. But before she had much time to consider this, her feet struck the ground, and the full weight of the gold she carried in her leather backpack brought her down to her knees.

Julian tumbled out behind her, rocketing into her and sending them both down in a heap of limbs and bags. The gold plates and chalices dug into her spine.

"Ow," she said.

"Ouch," came the weak response. "Not one of our better landings."

"Better than the last six," Etta said, rolling out from under him.

Julian lurched up to his feet, struggling to stay vertical under the weight of his pack. "Time?"

Etta squinted at the wind-up watch they'd found tossed in with Ironwood's other treasures, still breathing hard from the run. "Half past ten?"

Julian punched the air in triumph. "Told you we'd make it in time, didn't I?"

While there had been enough gold and precious stones left in the cave, Julian had previously mislabeled one of the entries in his journal, which had subsequently sent them on a hair-raising journey through Jerusalem during the First Crusade, with twentieth-century clothing and more gold than anyone had any right to.

The passage's whistling receded, but the drumming continued to pulse through the darkness. The vigor of the drums and chiming cymbals was breathtaking; as Etta stood, stumbling to maintain her balance on the soft incline, she was surprised to find the ancient music wasn't the heartbeat of the mountain itself.

The passage had deposited them behind a line of flames that snaked up the mountain's cleared path. Etta crawled through the damp, cool mud for a closer look.

"Sai-rei, sai-ryo!" That same phrase was being shouted, over and over, for all the wild, dark world to hear. She turned to Julian for a translation.

"I think . . . 'good festival'? Something like that?" Julian scratched at his mussed hair.

The smell of pine and smoke bled through the line of trees, carrying with it the voices of young and old alike. Stripped to their loincloths, men carried torches over their shoulders. Small ones, yes; carried by boys, really, who looked exceedingly proud to have the task. But as the torches increased in size, so did the men who carried them, until a few bore the staggering weight of torches the size of—motorcycles, and likely as heavy. The men staggered beneath their weight as they wound through the one-street village below, ascending up the dirt path. Cheers of encouragement followed from the villagers walking in their footsteps, their faces lit, glowing warmly in the face of an encroaching midnight.

Etta's brow furrowed. "What is this? Why would this Belladonna person pick a place where we'd be more likely to bump into the people of this time?"

"To your first question, a festival of some sort, clearly," Julian said, turning to the task of trying to pick the dirt out from under his nails. "In deference to whatever spirit or god is enshrined at the temple. To answer your second, it's best not to dwell on the dark, spider-infested maze of the Belladonna's mind, but I assume the festival will be ending soon."

She blinked. "That was . . . surprisingly useful."

"As I like to say, always aim to disappoint in life," Julian said. "That way you'll never fail to be a delightful surprise when you don't."

Etta snorted. "All right, let's go."

They began their climb through the trees, up and over the rocks, until at last they saw that more villagers were flowing down the mountain than up it. Soon that number sputtered to a few, and finally, none.

They moved onto the cleared trail without a word between them, shuffling through the black ash left behind by the fires. Etta caught a glimpse of Julian in a narrow pocket of moonlight—the smear of dirt across his cheek, the stains on his hands and knees, the way the waves of his hair seemed to stand on end. She already knew she looked like she'd been nearly trampled by horses in a street of melted manure and mud . . . because she had been.

"I'm worried you're not going to be enough of a distraction," Etta said quietly, "for me to get behind this Belladonna woman and grab the astrolabe. I might get out, but you won't."

"I am a *very* fast runner," he told her, "when sufficiently motivated."

"I was thinking . . . maybe I should just make a bid. Win it legitimately." She glanced over at him in the darkness.

"She only takes favors and secrets," Julian said, stopping to adjust the weight of his backpack. "Do you think you have something Grandfather doesn't?"

Etta had one thing none of the others did: she had grown up in a distant future, whereas no other traveler still alive had been born after 1945. But that future was gone, and any information from her future was worthless now. Which left one secret—one she wasn't sure the woman didn't already know. "We know the real reason why Ironwood wants the astrolabe. If the woman knows that, then she can use it against him. I think it's valuable, but it still doesn't feel like a concrete plan."

"I told you," he said. "You're not supposed to be able to plan anything at these things—no thefts, no murders, no business deals beyond purchasing the witch's wares. You'll be as much in the dark as Grandfather, if that's any reassurance."

Beyond the good work of irritating Cyrus Ironwood by forcing him to travel, the Belladonna was smart to pick a time and location where there might be witnesses, as a deterrent against bad or outlandish behavior from the travelers.

As they continued up the path, Etta began to take account of the stone markers, the lanterns, the small, open shrine-like structures with their slanting roofs and rich crimson paint. Their journey spent more and more minutes, their most precious currency, but it was a relief to see the lights were fading in the village below, like a hearth reduced to silent coals after burning through the last of its wood. In time, the only sound she could detect was the rustling of the forest's night-dwelling creatures.

She breathed in the smell of the damp greens around her, comforted by the familiarity of the traces of woodsmoke. Her body ached, but it was a good hurt, an earned one. Etta had fought through these last weeks and felt no small amount of pride for surviving.

"We're doing the right thing, aren't we?" Etta whispered. "I've wanted it gone for so long that the thought of keeping the astrolabe intact feels unnatural. Maybe it's cursed—it infects the lives of everyone who comes in contact with that same darkness."

Julian sighed. "I don't know. You're the moral compass, you're supposed to tell me that."

She elbowed him lightly. Inside her pack, the gold coins sounded like heavy rain as they rubbed against each other.

"I guess in my mind, it's like this, Linden-Hemlock-Spencer: the astrolabe itself has never been evil. For better or worse, it only answers to the heart of the person using it, but there isn't a person alive unselfish enough not to take advantage of it in some way. If destroying it destroys us, then we have to . . . I don't know, we have to hide it again once we straighten the timeline out."

What Mom did years ago.

Etta had been so quick to blame this journey on Rose's madness, her trauma, that she felt heartsick now just considering this. Rose might have known all along that destroying it would destroy the travelers' way of life, and that was initially why she had only hidden it.

But it didn't excuse her for keeping the truth from her daughter, it didn't forgive what she had done to Alice, and it didn't explain why she had become so bent on Etta destroying it.

Halfway up the mountain, her legs burning and her back aching from the weight of her pack, Etta saw a glimmer of light. The ring of it grew until she could make out the distinct shapes of lanterns twinkling in the trees above the path, and a young boy with golden hair sitting on a stool beside a large brass scale and several baskets. Behind him, a large white curtain had been hung to cover whatever lay beyond.

Julian slowed beside her.

The boy wore an oversize white robe, but had tugged it up when he'd crossed his legs, and she could see the fine stockings and velvet breeches underneath. At their approach, he merely flipped to the next page of the book in his lap.

Julian cleared his throat, but the boy held up a finger, still eyeing his book.

"Hello?" Etta tried.

Finally, the golden child lifted his gaze, and she almost laughed at the annoyance on his face. She knew what it was like to be interrupted in the middle of a particularly good page.

"It's just the two of us in the bidding party," Julian told him, finally sliding his backpack off his shoulders with a relieved sigh.

This only served to further irritate the boy, who slid from his stool and motioned to the scale. He stepped onto one side, leaving the other for them to pile their sacks on top of, and they began their prayers that they had not misjudged the weight.

"How do we know you weigh a hundred pounds?" Etta asked.

The boy glowered back, bobbing like a ship on a wave as the scale balanced. Etta caught herself holding her breath as their side dipped lower than the boy's, only to straighten in triumph. They'd brought more than enough.

"Oh, thank goodness." Julian rushed forward to remove some of the gold. "Would've been a shame to let all of this—"

"Welcome! Welcome, my young beasties."

A woman pushed through the pale curtain, careful to close it again behind her before Etta could see what was there. Her long legs devoured the distance between them in two quick gulps, stopping uncomfortably close to Etta. She fought every natural instinct to take a step back and reclaim some semblance of comfort.

Instead, Etta looked up and met the woman's dark gaze over the silver veil that covered the lower half of her face. Her full-figured body was dripping with black lace that looked as if its ornate floral patterns had been cut from the shadows themselves. And, as if she thought the occasion might call for it, she had added a silver-and-diamond diadem that sat on her head like a row of wolf's teeth.

She exchanged a look with the golden-haired boy, who nodded some sort of confirmation.

Julian wobbled a bit on his feet with what Etta believed might have been a bow that he thought better of halfway through. "Good evening, madam. We've brought the requested entry fee."

"And not much else," she said, her catlike eyes flitting from his face to Etta's.

"It doesn't matter," Etta said, with what she dearly hoped was something resembling confidence, "when we have the secret we do."

"Indeed." The veil fluttered, as if she'd given a silent laugh. "Only two of you, when others have tried to bring in nearly a dozen."

"I know your rules," Julian said. "Only eight per party."

She ignored him, her gaze still fixed on Etta. "How curious, beastie. Yours is a face I have seen before."

She waved the other woman off. "Yeah. Been getting that a lot recently."

"And such a pleasant temperament to match. Now, if you'll each please take a robe and a mask from the basket and don them—yes, you'll need to put the hood up as well. Safety in anonymity, as I always say."

"A jolly good policy if I've ever heard one," Julian said, placing the mask on his face and quickly knotting it behind his head. It covered the whole of his face, save for his eyes.

The woman cocked her head to the side. "Aren't you—"

"The previously-believed-to-be-dead Julian Ironwood?" he said, with the eagerness of someone who'd been longing to be recognized.

"—going to close your robe?" the Belladonna finished, and without any sort of preamble, took up the task of knotting the series of ties that ran down its side. Etta quickly laced her own, and tried not to laugh when the woman ran her spindly fingers down Julian's front.

"I believe you are our last bidding party. If you would follow me . . . You have set us back several precious moments. I cannot delay the start of the auction any further."

The woman cut in front of Etta and pulled the curtain aside.

If Etta had been asked to guess what was behind it, she would not have gone with two dozen other white-robed, golden-masked travelers and guardians, all of whom remained facing forward, packed together like cattle in a stall. The Belladonna reached up for one of the silver lanterns hanging in the trees and held it in front of her as she pushed her way up through the ranks.

Julian started to follow her, but Etta held out an arm, shaking her head. It was better if no one took particular notice of them, and moving to the front would give everyone ample time to guess who might be under the robe. As it was, no one dared to utter a single word as the pack began to follow the Belladonna and her lantern up the rest of the path, toward the temple several hundred yards away.

Only one figure, bringing up the rear of the first group, risked a look back at them. He or she was the only one who allowed themselves to break from the quick march of the others, moving slowly, with an almost labored gait. Hurt, or old, maybe. Etta narrowed her eyes, wishing it wasn't so dark. Because it looked like, it seemed like . . .

That person is slowing down. Drifting back intentionally. Etta felt for the small dagger she'd plucked off a knight in Jerusalem, dread combing its cold, clammy hands through her hair, down her neck. She was so wholly focused on the figure that she did not see the movement in the forest just to the left of Julian, until something lashed out, hooking a black-cloaked arm around his neck. His shout of alarm was smothered by the gloved hand smashing against his face.

Etta dove into the forest after them, the dagger in her hand. It was just like the attack in Russia. The attacker was shrouded in black, and the blade was pressed against Julian's throat, even as he struggled to disentangle himself from the powerful grip. She was a step behind the attacker, and drew her blade back to stab—

The weight hit Etta's back and brought her down before she could catch Julian's attacker, but it was the mountain itself, its sharp decline, that sent her rolling, spinning over the soft earth and ferns, until finally her back collided with a tree big enough to catch her weight. The blow knocked the dizziness from her mind, enough that she ignored the bruising she'd taken and climbed back onto her knees, searching for Julian in the darkness above her. A short distance away, tangled in the ferns and obscured by the small stone marker, were the twisted, white-robed legs of her own attacker.

Etta scrambled up the hill on hands and feet, the blade of her dagger clenched between her teeth until the ground flattened out enough for her to stand. She swung around the edge of the stone marker, her gasping breaths steaming the inside of her mask. At the very last second, rather than stab with her right hand, she threw her left fist forward, smashing into the attacker's mask and knocking them flat on their back just as they made to rise. She dropped to her knees on their chest, ripping their mask off and bringing the blade up to their jugular.

She knew this face.

She loved this face.

"Oh my God," Etta gasped, flying back, pulling her own mask up. "Oh my *God*—"

His eyes widened, equally stunned by the sight of her.

Her hands sank into the dirt, shaking. She pulled up leaves and roots, trying to ground herself in that moment, to make it feel real to her. That valley between them that had devastated her with his absence, the one she hadn't let herself fall into, opened up again.

One single, soft word reached her: "Hi."

Etta's heart broke open, and the relief was as painful as it was necessary. The way he looked at her now, like she was a pearl in the darkness; the way his hand reached for her, waiting for her hand, its twin—she crashed into him just as he sat up, her lips on his, stealing his breath, his surprised laughter. Stealing him back into herself.

"Hi," she managed, her hands cupping his face, kissing him, kissing him—

"Where . . . have you been?" he asked when he could.

"Where have *you* been?" she demanded back, feeling his hands sink into her braid, weaving sweetness into it.

"I've been quite occupied . . . with looking for you," he said. "Had a . . . damned time of it. I might have known you'd find me first."

"Saw you—the beach—" She tasted blood from his split lip, but she didn't care, she didn't care—

"I know, I know—thought you were—"

"I know, I'm sorry—why did you chase me now? Why are you here?" Etta forced herself to stop, to pull back and wrap her arms around him so he'd have the opportunity to answer. His arm came up to lock around her waist, and his forehead rested against her shoulder; he was breathing hard.

"Are we incapable of meeting under remotely typical circumstances?" Etta heard him wonder. The damp ground was soaking through her robe, straight to her skin, but she hardly felt it. Nicholas's pulse was fluttering against her cheek, nothing at all like the steady, driving beat she remembered from even their most desperate moments.

It was the darkness, she was sure of it—it was only the hunger, the exhaustion, and the shadows that made him look so frail. But when her hands skimmed over his back, she felt each knob of his spine. The ridges of his ribs. Etta leaned back so she could brush a half-open kiss against his lips, his labored breathing mingling with hers.

"I can't even hold you," he whispered. "It's too much, it's all too fast—I wasn't afraid before, but I find myself—I find myself just that slightest bit afraid now."

"What are you talking about?" she asked, trying to shift so she could study him, see his face. He only held her tighter, his arm shaking with the effort. Her hands came up to slide through his tufts of hair, and his scalp was warm against her palms. Nicholas strained to kiss her again, his mouth grazing the soft corner of her lips.

"—I was just going for whoever looked to be about my—" Sophia's voice said behind them.

"I am *not* your size!" That was Julian.

"Well, would you prefer I said I went for whoever looked easiest to take down?"

She heard Sophia and Julian approach, felt the moment they were seen. The silence that followed was its own century.

"What are you still doing here?" Sophia aimed the words at

Nicholas, coating them with anger. "He's going to notice you're gone if you don't hurry back."

"Thought she—that Etta was—someone who could—hurt you—"

It was difficult to piece together the soft fragments of his words. Her mind did the best it could: Sophia had unwittingly snared Julian to steal his robes for the auction, and, seeing a disguised Etta pursue them, Nicholas had panicked, worrying that Sophia wouldn't be able to fight two people at once.

"Why are you—?" Etta asked. "Tell me what's happening—*Nicholas!*"

The cold wash of fear as he sagged against her was nothing compared to the hurricane that came with Sophia's sharp oath. She leaped over the fallen tree that stood between them and seized Nicholas's shoulders, giving him a hard, jaw-snapping shake.

"Damn you, Carter," she said, "not *now*, damn you—"

"Nicholas?" Etta couldn't stop saying his name, as if that would be enough to pull him back to consciousness. "Tell me what's happening!"

"We're running out of time, that's what's bloody happening," Sophia said, and with no other warning, slapped him across the face.

TWENTY-NINE

Even as he came to again, the darkness in his vision remained like a halo around her face, as if to dash away the dream of her. But she was still there.

Etta was still there.

She knelt in front of him, smelling of fire smoke, warm, sweet bread, a home. The mud that was smeared across her face had caught a single strand of her hair, sticking it to her cheek. For the life of him, he could not say why he found this unbearably endearing.

"You're not okay, are you?" she whispered.

He knew it was Sophia behind him, propping him up so he could face them—*them*, because Julian was hovering a few short feet away, looking so uncertain he was nearly unrecognizable to Nicholas.

"Julian," he said, letting his relief bleed into the words. He hadn't realized it until now, how grateful he was that these two had found one another. Etta would protect Julian; and Julian would ensure Etta didn't have to be alone.

Hearing his name, his half brother drew closer to their small circle. "This is the part where I tell you I'm a fool and an ingrate, and you punch me."

Meeting his gaze, seeing Julian's face, Nicholas thought of the rage that he'd always imagined would pour through him, boiling with years' worth of resentment and ill-humored thoughts and words. But what he felt now was simply peace. That small part of him was resolved, and thankful, and above all, glad; this was his brother, and not even death had changed his love for him. "Perhaps another time?"

He gave Sophia a meaningful look, then glanced at Etta.

"Fine," Sophia said. And then, to Etta: "I'm sorry about the way I treated you. I'm also sorry your mother is a demon from hell."

"I'm sorry about what happened to you, and the things I said, except for when you deserved them," Etta said, her words wavering, even as she tried to steady them. "But why won't anyone answer my question? What's happening?"

His abominable pride did not let him ask for help to stand, but the others offered it regardless. Etta held both of his forearms, keeping his balance for him. The fear on her face tore at him. Nicholas turned to look at Sophia and Julian. "I need a moment."

"We don't have long," Sophia said. "I can explain it to them. Just *go!*"

He shook his head. *God grant me time enough for this.* "It'll only be a moment. *Please.*"

He was sure she would fight him until the breath left both of their bodies. But instead, Sophia let out a small huff and nodded. She drew Julian away, back up toward the edge of the trail.

Etta turned his face back toward her own.

"Tell me," she said. "*Please,* just tell me what's going on. Why were you with Ironwood? Are you all right? What happened to your arm?"

Of course she had noticed.

"I am not completely myself at the moment," Nicholas admitted. "There isn't time for it all, only what is necessary. If I could pluck this moment out of time and keep us here forever, I would. But we cannot stop time; we can only right it again."

"That's what I'm trying to do," Etta said. Her heart shone in her face, lit softly like a candle, as she brought it close to his, as if trying to give him her light. He burned with the regret of it, not trusting his body to hold her the way he wanted to, without collapsing again.

"But our plan," she continued, her lips close to his ear, "it has to change. We can't destroy it."

And he knew devastation. Pure, unadulterated pain. Etta saw it flash in his face, and knew from the way denial pooled in her eyes . . . on this, they could not be reconciled. He captured her mouth again, trying to soften the blow, to find the words he needed. The cool night bit at his skin, but her lips were hot, insistent, moving over his own as if to launch her own argument.

Nicholas tore himself away, trying to still her long enough to reintroduce her to reason.

"It has to be destroyed, you said as much yourself," he said. "I know the consequences, I know what might come of it, but Etta—do you see? Do you feel how much of this is outside our hands? If this is ever going to end, let it be now. Your mother—she came to me in the desert, just after you were orphaned. She spoke of a war to come."

"I know all about this," Etta interrupted.

"She wasn't wrong. *This* is the war which never ends. The one that exists between the families," he said. "There's a shape to this, a pattern."

Etta flinched at that word, already shaking her head, trying to capture his lips again, keep him from finishing. "No, no, no—don't say that, don't use that word—"

He deserved a bloody medal for having the will to stop her from kissing him.

"I cannot help but think there is no lasting peace between the families because there is something deeply unnatural about us, what we can do," he continued. "It must be time's revenge that we inherently repel one another. It feels to me as if these conflicts are trying to force us back to our natural times, where we're meant to be."

She lifted her pale eyes, hardened now like chips of ice. "There is nothing more *natural* than families. You haven't seen what I have.

These are people who love and need one another. We can still fix the timeline—it'll take longer, yes, but it's possible to do it one piece at a time."

"And then what?" he prompted. "The astrolabe is hidden again? We risk someone else resuming the search, finding it, unraveling everything we've done? This is the only way to hold Ironwood accountable, to make him answer for what he's done to us all. If not for that reason, then think of the millions upon millions of lives he's toyed with, the disregard and apathy he's shown them. He is not the exception, Etta, he is the *rule*. There is too much power in what we can do."

Nicholas knew it was unfair of him that he could make this decision with the callousness it required, knowing it would be one of his last. But only days before, he'd been running toward vengeance like a man on fire, burning up the last parts of his soul. Some part of her, at least, seemed to see the truth in his last argument. Her whole body tensed in frustration.

He was staring down another loss, and, though he had been so logical, though he knew her to be logical, he saw the stricken look of betrayal on her face, and all of those arguments threatened to fly away from him. What was history anyway but the lies of the winning few? Why was it worth protecting, when it forgot the starving child under siege, the slave woman on her deathbed, the man lost at sea? It was an imperfect record written by a biased hand, diluted to garner the most agreement from competing parties. He was tempted to see her point, to imagine that she could realign the past and present and future into something beautiful. God, if anyone was capable of it, it would be her.

But their history, the one forged by travelers, was one of violence, war, and revenge; they had not simply made it. They were made by it.

"And what about us?" she asked, running her small, lovely hands up to his shoulders, his neck, his face. Nicholas leaned into the callused tips of her fingers. "What if I love you, and I need you? What was the point of this? Why did we fight so hard, if you were only ever going to give up?"

"*Carter!*"

The man's voice echoed down to them, still a distance away. *Owen.*

Etta made as if to draw him behind her, and he wanted to kiss her then more than he wanted his next breath. The seconds unraveled around him, blistered his raw heart.

"Stay with me," she begged. "Stay with me. This isn't over yet."

"This is freedom—*this*, the freedom from fear, is what it means to rewrite the rules," he said. "A world in which the astrolabe exists is a world in which either of us could be taken at a moment's notice. If nothing else, I'll know you'll be safe."

"*Alone,*" she corrected sharply.

"Never alone," he promised. "Did you not feel me with you in all of our days apart?"

Can you not feel my heart beating for you?

"It's not the same," she said, her eyes flashing again. "And you know it."

"I only know this: our paths were separated by centuries, but we converged. No matter the outcome, my destiny has always been joined to yours."

"*Carter! Where the hell are you?*"

Etta leaned forward into him, her face against the curve of his neck. "Don't do this—please don't do this."

"Do you believe in that world you spoke of, the one made for us?" She swallowed, nodding. Her soft lips were against his bare skin, and he was a man, damn it all, and he was burning for her. The words that escaped him were choked with emotion. "If we aren't to have it in this life, then in the next. If not now, then we'll have forever."

She pulled back, only to surge up onto her toes and grip him fiercely by his robe. The kiss shot down his spine like lightning striking a mast, blowing him apart.

ALEXANDRA BRACKEN

It wasn't a retreat, and it was far from a surrender. She invaded his every sense at once, the way the sun first breaks in the morning and illuminates the horizon. The taste of her, the smell of her, those small sounds she made in her throat; all of these things were secrets entrusted to him, prizes he had fought so desperately to retake. Etta seized every part of him at once, and he pushed the deadening dread away, let the frantic joy of *her* rush through him, flooding the empty places, turning him inside out.

His skin felt drum-tight wherever her lips touched, and Nicholas wondered, in those spaces between the battering of his heart, how it was possible that she was so soft, when all of the days that had led them here had been so very hard. She did not cry, his brave girl, but he felt the rage beneath her skin, moving her to fit against his body, to disappear into him.

"*Nicholas!*" Sophia called softly. "He's coming!"

The blade hanging over them fell at last.

Nicholas eased back from her, wondering if this was what death would feel like—the painful release. He had envisioned it so many times as wading out into dark, cool water, letting it rise past his hips, his shoulders, his head. This was a breaking, a thunderclap of agony. How short a person's life was, but how very many times they were asked to die inside.

"I love you," he told her softly. "Time can never steal that."

And somehow, before she spoke, Nicholas knew what she was about to say. Her face was steeled, defiant.

"I'm not giving up," Etta said, the loose strands of her hair flying about her face. A shining storm of a girl. "I won't destroy it. This isn't the end."

Nicholas turned her hand over, pressing one last burning kiss into her palm. "Then may the best pirate win."

449

"HURRY IT UP, WILL YOU?" OWEN WASN'T A LARGE MAN BY any means, but his voice could absolutely thunder when the situation called for it. He had lifted his mask, and was scanning the dark line of the forest for Nicholas. Sophia was right, then. The old man had noticed he was gone, and more quickly than he would have expected.

"I managed to get turned around," Nicholas said, limping up to him.

The other man took in the sorry state of his stained robes. "What kind of fool falls while taking a piss?"

"You do." Sophia had moved so quickly, looping in a large circle back up to the trail behind Owen, that neither man noticed her until she brought the rock crashing down on his head.

The whites of his eyes flashed as he crumpled. Nicholas watched in appreciation as Sophia stripped the robe and mask off him and set about rolling Owen off the trail, into the forest, where the mountain did the rest of the work in carrying him away.

"Did you finish your business?" she asked innocently.

"Did you?" he pushed back. Julian had gone ahead with Etta, and while there was much he wished he could have said to his half brother, there was likely quite a bit more that needed to be spoken between the formerly betrothed pair.

A gong sounded from above, where the graceful temple sat at the top of the trail. Nicholas straightened his mask and accepted Sophia's offered shoulder as support for the last few yards of their climb. They passed through the structure with its airy, open foundations, the upward slant of its roof, to find an enormous white tent pitched in the center of its stone courtyard. So, then; they would not be trampling over a sacred place. Good. Perhaps the Belladonna still had some scraps of decency clinging to her tattered soul.

The scent of wine and spirits floated to him on the next autumn breeze, followed by the sweet notes of fruit. A short distance from the tent, a table was elegantly piled with food, though it had clearly already been ravaged by the others. The Belladonna stood beside it, waiting for them.

"Help yourselves, of course," the Belladonna said, turning to greet a man who, Nicholas thought, must have been a priest or a monk, based on his ceremonial robes, different from the ones the travelers donned. He seemed harried, hovering near the tent but not daring to enter. The woman shooed him away by blowing a kiss.

"Is he a guardian?" Nicholas asked.

"No. Return a few legendary national treasures and you'll be surprised by the favors people will do for you," the Belladonna said. "And the things they're willing to forget."

Sophia snorted, drawing the woman's eyes over to her. The Belladonna hummed thoughtfully but said nothing. "If you are ready, follow me. The rest of your party is already situated."

The tent was far larger than it had appeared on the outside, so much so that he wondered if it might be one of the Belladonna's illusions. The central aisle led up to a raised and gilded table, on which a dark wooden box had been placed. Two masked men stood on either side of it, swords in hand, as if prepared to slice any who dared to reach for it. If he hadn't felt it just then, that chill creeping over his skin, the tremor in the air, Nicholas might not have believed the astrolabe to be inside.

"Do you . . ." Sophia whispered, sounding almost faint. *Feel that?*

The Belladonna jerked her head around. "*Silence.* Here. Here is your place."

Lining the long aisle were stalls, divided by heavy white fabric that looked, to Nicholas's biased eye, like sailcloth. At least one dark shape of a man or woman appeared to be sitting in each, backlit by a lantern or an arrangement of candles. So that was it, then—how she had managed to further the anonymity of the bidders and, likely, the winner who would be taking any of her auctioned goods home.

Where is Etta?

"You," she said, brushing his shoulder with her long, curling nails, "are designated as a bidder. Present your offer when I call for the fourth bidder—should you survive that long." As she leaned in closer, he breathed in that same earthy scent, as if she were a dark forest wearing a woman's skin. "There's still time, of course."

Nicholas ignored the tremor in his heart as he said softly, "Good evening to you, ma'am."

The Belladonna stood to the side, lifting the entrance to their stall. Inside, the Ironwoods were lifting their masks to taste the proffered food and wine, but they instantly slid them back into place. Sophia stepped in beside him, edging around the room to avoid too much notice that she was not, in fact, Owen.

"There he is!" Ironwood said as the curtain shut behind them. Still mercifully in possession of his good mood. "Now it begins."

His footsteps were soft against the rugs and pillows provided; there was little else, beyond a few candles and a small wooden table. Nicholas surrendered himself heavily to the floor. The bruises and cuts he'd acquired were a low throb of pain, but they were nothing compared to the fire searing his veins. Instead of letting himself notice the twitching of his left hand, he focused on the foul smell of the pipe someone was smoking in the stall beside theirs. The Belladonna had placed them directly in the middle of the stalls, but save for that whiff of bad air and the murmur of the Ironwood men around him, he could not hear or see evidence of any of the other bidders. He could not even hear the wind outside.

The gong sounded again. With a kick of his heart, Nicholas turned back toward the curtain draped over their stall's entrance, and beyond that, the muted shapes of the Belladonna and her guards.

"Ladies and gentlemen, I would like to welcome you to tonight's auction. As always, your silence is mandatory. I have taken . . . liberties, shall we say . . . to ensure this. I will be able to hear you, but to protect the privacy of the winner, you will not be able to hear one another."

Ironwood drummed his fingers against his knees, nodding repeatedly in an eager, childlike manner. The man's entire world was winnowed down to this moment, as he stood on the edge of grasping the only thing that had ever been truly denied him.

"The winner of this item will be liable for its transportation and protection outside the barriers of this site. All sales, regardless of satisfaction, are final and binding. Upon the conclusion of the auction, the winner will be allowed to leave first, followed by the rest of you in the order of my choosing. Rather than conduct multiple rounds of bids, please submit your best offer as it stands. I will call each designated bidder forward to hand it to me."

Nicholas's fingers dug into the muscles of his thighs. He dropped his eyes to the floor. *Please, God, keep her safe, let this end—*

"I thank the consigners who entrusted me with this sale. Without further ado, I present lot 427, a purported astrolabe—"

Purported. Nicholas actually laughed.

"—of unknown, ancient origins. First bidder, please."

Nicholas leaned forward, trying to peer through the smallest of gaps where the side of the stall met the curtain. His breathing had taken on that uneven quality that made darkness dance in his vision. Etta—where was Etta?

"Second bidder, please."

Hell and damnation, he thought, wiping the sweat from his forehead, his eyes. He tasted rust in his mouth. *Not yet. Not yet, damn you—*

A dark splatter—deep enough to show through the thick fabric—whipped against the curtain directly across from theirs. Nicholas and Sophia jumped to their feet just as the bidder's lifeless body, still spilling blood, was thrown out of the stall, a darkness deeper than night exploding after him.

THIRTY

As she made her way up to the Belladonna, Etta squared her shoulders, the scrap of paper on which she'd written her offer, *A secret about Ironwood's desires*, soft and damp in her hand. The candles' flames shook in their stands, the dimly flickering light outlining each of the stalls as she passed them. It was the silence that was unleashing her anger, unbraiding the knot of fury she'd wrapped around herself. Her hands clenched by her side again, as if to keep the feel of Nicholas's rough skin trapped there a moment longer.

May the best pirate win.

It wasn't even that they were at odds; she understood his line of reasoning, even as she wanted to strangle him for simply accepting it. It was what he had so clearly withheld: the reason why the fire had left his heart. Why, when she kissed him that last time, had he shuddered, as if on the verge of shattering? *Something's wrong, something is so wrong,* her mind had screamed as her hands skimmed over him, searching for a wound, a bandage that might explain the exhaustion, the weakness.

Pattern. She hated that word now, the lack of control it implied. The way it had hooked into what Henry had told her in Russia, grown through her like a winding, barbed vine. *You will see the pattern, too.*

They were both wrong. Etta didn't have to accept that anything was *meant* to happen. She had been orphaned in Damascus, flung centuries away from Nicholas, but that was nothing compared to being trapped almost three hundred years ahead of him, locked away from her family, from the Thorns, from this hidden life. This wasn't a pattern unless she let it become one.

We cannot possess the things and people not meant for us, we cannot control every outcome; we cannot cheat death. Etta hardened herself, straining to listen to the sound of her feet so she wouldn't have to hear Henry's words rising in her mind again, to see his bloodied face.

Etta stepped up to the table, feeling the icy pressure of the Belladonna's gaze on her. When she was sure she'd released enough of her frustration in order to keep her expression neutral, Etta met her eyes and held out the offer. The woman plucked it out of her hand like a petal off a flower.

Standing near the table, Etta picked up the murmurs of the bidders, the debates they were having with themselves, as if all of their words had been funneled to that exact spot. But even those conversations were lost to the sound of the blood rushing in her ears.

If she reached out, she'd be able to brush the smooth, dark wood of the box that held the astrolabe. The candlelight caught all of the intricate detail, the etchings and marks of the device resting on the box's velvet interior. Etta had held it for only a moment, but she recognized it all the same.

The flames flickered with her next step forward, and the sight gripped her, made her hold the next breath she drew in—because when the flames danced, so did the image of the burly guards.

A projection? An impressive one. How—?

Don't do it, don't do it— But she couldn't help herself. She brushed her fingers against the edge of the astrolabe's box.

The lid snapped down. The Belladonna's long fingers, knotted at the joints, held it firmly in place.

"I see your heart," the woman said. "It cannot be you."

The scream set Etta's pulse stuttering long before she saw the splash of dark blood against the curtain. A piercing laugh followed, an attack on her eardrums, and her legs were suddenly weak beneath her.

Them.

The Belladonna merely took a step back, crossed her arms over her chest, and watched as the same bidder's body was tossed through the curtain, landing in a sickening, blood-soaked heap in the central aisle, his mask askew. The force of it blew out the candles at the table and the guards vanished like shadows meeting sunlight.

Etta barely swallowed her gasp of shock as she turned toward the Belladonna. But the woman's face was impassive as she watched a new figure emerge at the entrance to the tent. It must have been a man, for he was broad in the shoulders and seemed almost inhumanly tall. He was draped in a shimmering cloak of gold and silver threads that made him look like a flickering flame. He reached up and slowly lowered the hood, never breaking eye contact with the Belladonna.

His shock of white hair was combed back neatly over his skull, and though Etta recognized his face as human, all of his features seemed to be exaggerated by the desperate way his skin clung to his pointed chin and prominent cheekbones. The arch of his brow was severe, and several veins bulged across his forehead. He looked as if he'd been carved from wax—patches of his skin seemed to gleam as golden as his cloak, while others were gray and flaking.

But even in decay, he seemed . . .

Radiant.

The small boy, the Belladonna's servant, had been sitting to one side of the table, his book open in his lap. Now he stood, calmly shutting the cover, and left through the rear of the tent.

"It's been a lifetime," the Belladonna called to him. "And now we find ourselves here again."

"I might have known it was you. What an intriguing reinvention;

and more intriguing still that you did not consume this one, this time." The man walked with an eerie silence, the only sound was his long golden robe whispering against the stone ground.

"You know, I've been quite content with two lives, the second of which will keep me in comfort for many years yet." The Belladonna's eyes drifted down the length of the man, skimming over the worn edges of his form. "It seems the same cannot be said for you. I wonder, how long would you have without it? I could not have drawn you out if you were anything short of desperate. Unless, of course, you merely wished to see the flock. I admit, they are amusing. From time to time."

"I am as impervious to your words as I am to your blades," he said, the words chiming like a song.

"We shall see." Etta almost jumped clear out of her skin. It sounded as though the Belladonna were standing directly beside her, whispering the words loudly to her for the man to overhear. "Why . . . it looks as though a single spark would set you aflame."

A shadow passed over the man's face. That strike, at least, had landed. "I felt your mark upon that child, that young man, and spared his life only to amuse myself by killing him in front of you. This game is at its end, sister."

The Belladonna gazed back, as serene and still as the moon. "And so it is."

The man's eyes were like sunlight passing through glass, intensifying as they fixated on something. Etta felt the gaze burn through her skin, to her core, as his eyes flicked over to her. They narrowed, as if in recognition, and terror froze her in place.

She sucked in a sharp breath; at that moment, darkness broke loose from the closest stall and flooded the tent with night. Blood slapped the white canvas, the fabric rending, as a body was thrown through. It rolled over to them, limbs flapping, sucking wounds visible, until the stranger—a traveler Etta didn't recognize—gazed up at her, unseeing.

She was pinned by that moment, unable to get her feet under her again. The screams of the other travelers tore through her ears, but she couldn't work up one of her own, could barely breathe.

"Etta!"

Nicholas, Sophia, and Julian tore out of their stalls as she dove for the table, for the box, for the astrolabe. Her fingers closed around it, and she felt the familiar pulse of the astrolabe's power inside. The air pulled around her—her only warning before she was blown off her feet by the impact of someone slamming into her. The ground rushed up to greet her.

No, no, no! The box flew out of her hands as she fell, her vision blanking out with the force of her impact on the stone. She heard the wood splinter; her knife, her sole weapon, clattered as it danced away; but before she could reach for either, a torrent of black fell over her. Hot spittle flew in her eyes; the attacker's weight was oppressive, as if trying to force her deeper into the ground. Etta choked on her next breath as the man leaned low, coming close enough for her to smell the decay emanating from his rotting teeth. His clawlike dagger dug into her upper arm and twisted.

With a cry, Etta managed to unpin one hand long enough to catch his jaw, desperately reaching with the other for the knife she'd lost, muscles straining, fingers grasping—

A sword swung out, its dull edge catching the Shadow on the side of his head. The blow was enough to stun him, but not to knock him off her chest. Etta managed to wriggle that last inch to the left, latch on to her knife, and, without any thought but getting out from under his weight, slam the blade upward, into the only place she could find without armor: his neck. The spill of dark blood made her stomach riot as it bubbled from the man's wound. The Shadow was shoved away from her, and she sucked the smoky air into her already burning lungs.

Etta scrambled to her feet, assisted by a hand that gripped her beneath one shoulder. She whirled—

ALEXANDRA BRACKEN

"Are you hurt?"

Henry stood there, his white robe spattered with blood. A bruise covered his skin from his temple to his jaw, and he couldn't seem to fully straighten to his full, powerful height. But it was him. *Alive.*

Etta felt the burn of tears in her eyes, and choked on her words. His face was so unusually soft as he looked at her that she had to wonder if he'd mistaken her shock for fear. She stumbled forward, surprising both of them as her arms wrapped around his center, and she buried her face in his shoulder.

Alive.

"Are you—are you all right?" he asked, one tentative hand touching the back of her head.

Behind him, around him, men and women burst through the entrance of the tent, in clothing that ranged in style from the twentieth century to the first, weapons in hand. Leading the charge was Li Min, shrouded in black silk. The young woman shot forward, skimming through the carnage, seemingly searching. Nicholas and Sophia were locked in the middle of a blood-soaked circle, the bodies piling around them, choking them off from the rest of the room—from the attackers, the victims, the men and women who clutched their dead, screaming, until they too were silenced. With the smoke filling the space, it was nearly impossible to tell a shadow from a Shadow.

Nicholas stumbled, taking a blow to his back that brought him to his knees. Li Min drew herself back, just like an arrow notched on a bow, and then she was flying again, straight for him. She pulled a small dagger from her boot, launching it at the neck of the Shadow who'd cornered them at the table. The range of emotions that exploded across Sophia's face at the sight of the other girl was indescribable.

"You are not forgiven!" she shouted.

Li Min kicked a silver serving platter up off the wreckage of canvas and wood on the floor. A man—an Ironwood—had taken up a gun and aimed, but she used the heavy platter to deflect the shot away from Nicholas and Sophia, and then to knock the man clear off his feet. In her next move, she seemed to produce a sword out of thin air, driving it through the back of the Shadow who had recovered enough to swing her claw and sword at Sophia's face. Nicholas, his face fixed in determination, ripped the blade out from between her shoulders and proceeded to slash her with the cold dispassion of someone who'd fought, and thrived, in many more battles than his opponent could ever imagine.

Sophia gripped the front of Li Min's cloak, drew her in, and kissed her soundly as the flames from the nearby candles caught the tent and set it ablaze.

"Thorns!" someone shouted above the shrieks, the vibrations of the dark one's speech, the screams of agony and fear as the travelers tried to flee.

Another voice. *"Hemlock!"*

Henry spun Etta away; she heard, rather than saw, the explosion of a gunshot that ripped through the din of clanging metal. He jerked, but didn't fall—Etta reached up, trying to pull back to see where he'd been hit, only to find that a man in a trim suit behind him was already slumping to the ground, shot clean through the skull.

The smoke from the burning stall began to fill the air, but it lifted as her mother stepped forward without a mask, her rifle still raised— pointed now at Henry, who calmly brought up his sword, bringing it to rest at the spot where Rose's long, pale neck met her shoulder. She, too, was wearing the white auction robes, though now she had painted herself red and black with blood and smoke.

Etta pulled back from Henry with a jerk of alarm.

Rose's cool expression slipped at the sight of them, cracking enough for her relief to bleed through.

"Can you get her out of here?" Henry asked.

Rose said nothing, only nodded.

"No—!" Etta ripped herself out of his grip. "You don't understand, the astrolabe—you can't destroy it—"

A familiar cry had Etta spinning back around. Nicholas had taken cover behind the overturned table with Sophia and Li Min. As one, they lifted it and used it as a battering ram, charging into the two Shadows who'd begun taking turns driving their claws through the body of one of the Thorns on the ground, trying to crawl over to another wounded young man.

When she looked toward her mother, Rose was nearly unrecognizable in her bone-pale terror.

Etta turned slowly.

It was the quiet, the way he absorbed the sounds around him like a vacuum, that was so deeply disturbing. The walls seemed to kneel to him, leaning forward, as if with each step he quietly devoured more of the world. The man in gold glided forward through the wreckage. The fighting fell away from him, the shadowed attackers drawing their prey into the stalls like predators wanting to feast on their kills. The hem of his robe was soaked up to the knee with blood.

Henry reached for her, but it was her mother who seized her. Etta found herself tucked between her mother's back and the wall of the tent as the glittering man passed by. This close, his face had the consistency of rice paper. For a terrifying moment, Etta imagined she could see the dark blood throbbing through his rootlike veins.

But she wasn't shaking—her mother was. Rose Linden, who had hunted tigers, betrayed Ironwoods, conquered an unfamiliar future, was *shaking*. As if that same raw fear carried vibrations through the air, the radiant man stopped suddenly, turning toward them, his eyes seeking. Recognition flared as he found Rose, his lips curving into a horrifying imitation of a smile.

"Hello, child."

A whisper.

A curse.

Knowledge flooded Etta, filling the cracks in the picture she had begun to assemble of her mother's life. Henry stepped in front of them both, but the man had no interest in him. As the man passed by, her father recoiled, as if the man had brushed his soul. There was something about the way the air itself seemed to curl and vibrate around the man, bowing to him, that made Etta's stomach clench again.

"My God, my God, Rosie—" Henry said, turning toward her.

"You . . . believe me?" The vulnerability in her mother's words was shattering.

"I'm sorry," Henry said, so softly that Etta wasn't sure her mother could hear him over the swarm of fighting. It felt as if she were standing in the path of two hurricanes finally on the verge of collision, the winds of clashing blades and blood whipping around them.

"Etta!"

Etta pulled herself free from her mother at Sophia's bellow. Sophia was standing back to back with Li Min now, staving off two Thorns who had blades of their own. "Ironwood's got it!"

Etta searched through the blazing fire and darkness until she found the place where the flames had eaten a hole in the side of the tent. There she saw an older man, his mask still on, rushing out into the courtyard, dodging the Shinto priests as they attempted to throw buckets of water onto the flames to stifle the fire before it jumped to the temple.

Between her and that opening, however, was Nicholas, with a Shadow clinging to his back; one clawed hand was on the verge of raking across his throat, no matter how hard Nicholas tried to buck his attacker off. His palm came up to block the next swipe of the claws, and blood instantly pooled where they cut deep into his flesh. Etta rushed toward him, but then Julian seemed to materialize out of thin air, shooting the man with what she thought must have been Sophia's flintlock. The bullet wasn't enough to deter the Shadow for

462

long, but it was long enough for Nicholas to reclaim his sword from the ground.

The Shadow lunged again, but as Nicholas moved, the small leather cord he wore around his neck escaped his robe, and a large bead swung out from beneath his shirt. Etta might have imagined it—smoke was gathering heavily around them, masking them in silver—but when the Shadow stabbed at his heart, the bead caught the tip of the blade. The Shadow seemed almost enraptured by the unexpected sight, and, seizing his chance, Nicholas swung the blade back with as much strength as he had in him, bringing it down on the Shadow.

Astrolabe—Ironwood, she reminded herself.

The last sight Etta had before rushing out into the courtyard was of the Belladonna, standing where she had stood the entire night, watching the blood creep across the stones and absorb the ashes at Julian's and Nicholas's feet. She surveyed the fighting with the long-suffering look of a mother. Then she turned and left through a wall of fire and smoke, disappearing into the star-encrusted belly of the night.

THE MOON WAS HIGH AND BRIGHT ABOVE HER AS SHE RAN, searching for Ironwood's figure down the path, among the trees, in any crevice the snake could have slithered into. The passage at the base of the mountain would have closed up with the first traveler's death, but he had the astrolabe—he could create his own escape, and then seal the entrance and prevent anyone from following behind.

The air was clean and sweet in her lungs, but Etta couldn't stop coughing, hacking up the smoke and spit and bile from deep inside her chest as she ran, her feet struggling in the soft earth.

Damn it, she thought. He couldn't take the astrolabe now, not after everything—

"*Etta!* Etta, where are you?" Nicholas's frantic voice carried down from above, but she didn't stop—she had caught another voice on the wind.

"—face me! Face me once and for all! Let us end this!"

Etta stumbled down the weathered path, stopping just long enough to keep herself upright before picking up her pace again. Ironwood's shouts sent birds launching from the safety of their branches.

The man had torn away his mask and robe, revealing a fine suit beneath. He was pacing up and down the path, his breathing ragged; his hand clenched at what remained of his hair, twisting it. Rivulets of sweat poured off him, along with the stench of blood.

"I know you're out there!" he shouted—to the trees, to the darkness. "It's mine, do you hear me? Come for it again and I'll tear you apart, limb from limb!"

Etta had only had one real interaction with the man, but the frantic quality of his speech, the way he paced and screamed as if the words were being torn from him, made her feel like she was meeting him for the first time. His control over himself, his family, the machinations of the world, had been so tight and refined; she couldn't reconcile that man with the knotted mess of anxiety and desperation in front of her. This was the same person who had bent time to his will? Who had subjected whole families to his cruelty?

"Do you hear me, you devil?" he shouted.

She came up short, a few feet away, but Cyrus Ironwood didn't seem to notice. The empty box lay overturned nearby, and he was waving the astrolabe in the air, holding it up for the moon to witness, as if expecting something to swoop down and snatch it. A torch in his hand nestled him in the center of a shallow pool of light.

"Ironwood," Etta said, walking toward him slowly. She kept the knife in her hand pressed to her side.

He spun toward her, eyes flashing. It was like looking in the face of a child, one who'd been struck once and knew he was about to be hit again. His rage was nearly choking him, polluting the cool mountain air.

She had a knife on her. He had only the torch.

And the astrolabe.

"Give it to me," she said, holding out her hand. "It's over."

Ironwood swung around toward her, his gaze clouding. "Over? The Ancient One is dead?"

Ancient One?

Etta swallowed. Nodded. She reached out her free hand, repeating, "Give me the astrolabe. . . ."

"It's mine," he told her, the rough lines of his face painted with blood and soot. His mouth twisted up in glee. "Years . . . *years* . . . it's mine, finally, and mine alone—"

Her fingers curled more tightly around the knife.

She was close enough to smell his sweat now.

Without giving him a second to prepare, Etta lunged forward, grabbing for the astrolabe. With a speed she didn't expect, his arm flew out, backhanding her sharply across the face. And suddenly, his rage had a target—a focus. Etta stumbled back, swinging her knife between them to try and keep him back. The torch dropped from his hand, but didn't go out as it struck the path.

Ironwood swung the astrolabe toward her temple, heavy and unyielding, and it narrowly missed crushing her skull. But she was off-balance, and Ironwood seized the advantage and dropped his head, charging her with a rough yell, throwing her down onto her back. Etta's breath left her in a rush as she rolled to avoid his next blow, but not quickly enough. Ironwood caught her by the hair and yanked her back down, hard enough to tear a clump of it out at the roots. The knife was out of her hand and in his, the blade flashing in the moonlight.

"You want this?" he cried, holding the astrolabe in front of her face. Etta reached for it, but Ironwood drew it back so sharply, so suddenly, that it went flying from his sweat-slick fingers. With a cry, he dove for it, but Etta yanked his leg back and dragged herself forward, snatching it just long enough to throw it as hard as she could into the dark forest, out of his reach.

Etta couldn't hear the words he screamed at her over her thundering pulse, she only felt him slam her back to the ground, flipping her over again, his spittle flying in her face. She kicked, trying to claw at his face, but the knife was back in his hand and suddenly at her cheek, dragging the blade down against it. He closed his other hand over her throat.

"You did this, all of you, you did this—"

Etta reached up, trying to drive her fingers into his eyes, her broken nails clawing at his face.

"*Rose,*" he howled down at her, his eyes unfocused, "Rose Linden! Are you satisfied? Are you *satisfied?*"

The sound the blade made as it pierced him from behind, the sickeningly wet thump and the spray of blood across her face, would never leave Etta as long as she lived. Then the blade was torn back through his body, and she was forced to watch as he choked on his own hot blood, his hand pressed to the gaping wound in his chest. His head turned as he slumped to the side, his fingers finally becoming lax enough for Etta to scramble out from underneath him.

"No," Rose said, wiping her blade against the side of her tattered white robe. "*Now* I have my satisfaction."

Etta stared up at her from the ground, willing the feeling back into her limbs. Her mother stared down at her, her skin tight over delicate bones.

"*Rose!*"

Henry's voice echoed down from the top of the mountain path. Rose turned—not toward the sound, but behind her, just as the man in the golden robe slashed a clawlike blade over her throat.

THIRTY-ONE

Nicholas heard only Etta's scream.

It flew to him over the sounds of savage fighting and the moans and begging of the wounded.

"Oh God," Sophia said, swinging around, searching for its source. Li Min took her hand and led them both out of the tent at a full run. Nicholas tried to dash after them, but he stumbled, his entire right side limp. He cursed his body, the weakness that threatened to dissolve him at his joints, the Belladonna—

But then there was an arm around his side, and his arm was being thrown over a shoulder, and Julian was there, sweat-soaked and grim. He glanced over at Nicholas, and at his brother's nod of acquiescence, dragged them both forward.

The last of the travelers shoved themselves through the burning mouth of the tent, only to be pursued by the Shadows, who left the massacre inside to claim more lives. Nicholas turned to look back, taking stock—there were dozens of bodies on the floor, both travelers and Shadows alike. Nearly the whole of Ironwood's traveling force, and an equal number of Thorns. More dead than he had ever realized were alive.

How many of our kind survive now?

Near the entrance a woman was crawling, laboring through the gore and flames to an older man, crying, "Father—*Father?*" Beside her, another man rocked the unmoving body of a younger one, weeping.

Julian hurried by, and then they followed the path the silvery smoke was taking, along the mountain path. But no sooner had they taken a few long strides down it than the nightmare claimed them, too.

For there was their grandfather, choking on his last gasps of life, clawing at the ground beneath him.

There was Rose Linden in Henry Hemlock's arms, her hand pressed to the line of blood at her throat.

There was the man in gold, striding toward the dark line of the forest, searching.

There was Etta, illuminating them all with the single torch in her hands. There was Etta, throwing it as hard as she could. The fire spun end over end, striking the back of the ornate robe, right where a powerful sun had been embroidered.

The blaze took hold like a spark on brittle parchment. The sound, the *whoosh* of purifying, ravaging fire as it caught the ends of the man's hair and lit him like a fuse, would never leave Nicholas, however long he lived. Nor would the look of quiet disbelief as the alchemist's son looked back over at his shoulder at a sobbing Etta in the instant before he was fully engulfed.

Li Min and Sophia stood a few feet from them on the path, thunderstruck by the sight. He had to believe it was the stink of scorched flesh that made Julian gag. Voices shrieked from the forest, ragged and almost inhuman. Li Min staggered, clutching at her chest as if feeling something release there. Sophia caught her before she fell, but Li Min could not tear her eyes away from where the body of the man was still burning.

They approached slowly.

"—had to be her." Rose was struggling with each word, her hand clutching Henry's arm, her eyes locked on his stricken face. "My baby—Shadows—"

"Shhh," Henry said, trying to stanch the flow of blood from the cut with fabric torn from his robe. "Don't speak just yet—it will be all right—be still, darling, be still."

Li Min ran to him and the man glanced up, desperate. He shifted to allow her to inspect the wound with careful hands. She reached for the small leather bag draped from her belt, one of her own knives.

"I understand now . . . you led them away from us, didn't you?" he was saying to Rose, distracting her from Li Min's work. "Clever, clever darling. You won't go, now that you've only just arrived, will you? Won't you stay for just one more dance?"

Just beyond them, Etta was on her knees, heaving for air, trying to crawl toward her parents. Julian started toward her, but she waved her hands, trying to control her crying so she could speak. Nicholas thought he had never seen anything so brave in his life.

"The astrolabe—" Etta pointed toward the nearby patch of forest, squeezing the words out between her tears. "I can't, I can't do it, it's—"

Footsteps crashed through the forest; voices cried out, searching for the astrolabe. Shadows, undeterred. Finishing what their master had begun.

He pulled Julian away from her. They were nearly out of time and he loved her, he loved her, he loved her enough to not go through with it, to not leave her side. Which meant he had to go, and it needed to be now.

He and Julian broke apart to search with nothing more than a frantic look between them, Nicholas bracing himself against one tree, then the next, making his way through the darkness. In the distance, he saw two shadowed figures weaving through the trees. Branches and rocks mauled and battered him on all sides, but he kept his eyes on the ground, searching through the pockets of darkness, the shifting dirt, the patchwork of ferns and shrubs. The breath burned in and out of his lungs, and his side began to ache in a way that might have doubled him over if he were not so singularly terrified for the lives of everyone he had left behind on the path, of the way the Shadows around him were beginning to shift and gather.

But he felt it. He felt the vibration, the dread that broke out across his skin; slowly, he turned and retraced his steps to where a glimmer of ancient gold peered out of a small animal's burrow. His left hand was slick with his own blood, from the deep cut which he'd been a fool to get; it had been protesting each time he so much as twitched a finger. He hardly felt it now—hardly felt the cold, or took notice of the way his hot breath steamed out into the air, hardly heard Sophia and Julian calling out to him.

Time seemed to bend around him, encasing his body in amber. Even his movements felt distressingly forced, as if he were struggling to move forward against a great wind without a line to assist him.

But he knelt.

He crawled.

He took the considerable weight of the astrolabe in his hand, staining it with his blood as he removed his dagger from his boot with his other.

Touching it flooded his senses, shot his blood through him with dizzying heat. He felt the astrolabe pulse, as if with its own heartbeat, its pace increasing to match the slamming of his heart. Now that it was in his hand, his reason for taking it slipped out of his mind; he couldn't quite remember it, not with the images that suddenly flooded his field of vision like dreams borne on the wind.

Standing on the bow of his newly commissioned ship, the wind fair and the ocean tame, as he gave the order to change course.

Moving through a great house, chasing a small child across the soft Oriental rugs, beneath the portraits of ancestors and descendants yet to come, sunlight spilling in through the tall windows that overlooked the green lands below.

His mother, taking his arm as he led her away from the fields, from the plantation, from the illness that had killed her.

And Etta . . .

Etta in the silk dress he had seen her wear to dinner on the *Ardent,* the one that had suited her so well, guiding him forward to a passage, her smile dazzling—

All of this. He heard the sweet whisper of words as clearly as if someone were sitting beside him. *I can give you all of this.*

Nicholas did not want to pull back from these dreams. He wanted to live each moment through to its conclusion, to see what other sweet wonders might be offered to him. But the light, the mist hanging over his mind, it all pulled back.

It left him in the darkness again, with a choice.

A man made his own future. He chipped it from whatever hardships insinuated themselves into his life; he carved out the happy, glad moments to capture his gratitude for them. It came from the simple magic of merely living. Of surviving. Seeking.

Not this. *Not this.*

Using his wounded hand, he pinned the astrolabe to the ground and raised his dagger, driving it down hard against the metal surface. If he could just crack it—if he had just enough strength left in him to wedge it apart—

The astrolabe heated beneath his hand, scalding to the touch. Nicholas let out a cry, but held it fast, blinking as it began to glow. He drove the dagger down again, piercing its center; the hotter it became, the more malleable it was, until at last the bulk of the blade broke through its case and black blood burbled up from inside, spilling against his hand, searing it with a pain that whipped him down to the seat of his soul.

He fell back, his jaw working out a scream as the light around him flooded his senses, drowning out the image of Etta racing toward him, her mouth open, calling something to him, trying to tell him something. But the light swept over her, and she vanished, dissolving in front of his eyes.

No, he thought, trying to rise again. *No!*

The sound of thunder and fury bore down on him, drowning out her name. There was a tug at his back, a weight that wrapped around his core, and he felt himself lifted, pulled and tossed, the pressure crushing against his skin. The whole of the world tilted around him as time caught him in its torrential stream.

And, in an instant, Nicholas felt himself vanish.

NEW YORK CITY
Present Day

THIRTY-TWO

SOMEHOW ETTA KNEW EXACTLY WHERE SHE WAS, EVEN before she had the courage to open her eyes and see for herself.

This isn't happening . . . this can't be happening. . . .

The stone stairs were cold against her skin, smelling of nothing more than the museum's old air-conditioning system and the lemon-scented cleaning product the custodians used to wash the stairs down.

Get up, she ordered herself. *You have to get up.*

Did she?

Etta forced her eyes open. Forced the breath to come into her lungs, and then out again. With arms like wet clay she pushed herself up, biting her lip to keep back her grunt of pain as the aches and bruises made themselves known again. The fluorescent light was nearly blinding, after living with sunlight and candles for so long. She shielded her eyes as best she could, lifting her arms, curling her legs toward her as she slid over the last few inches to rest her back against the closest wall.

She was still wearing the white robe. If it hadn't been stained so thoroughly with gore and dirt and soot, Etta might have believed the whole thing to be some sort of desperate dream. That she'd tumbled down the stairs on the night of her performance and knocked herself out. But she wore the evidence of her struggle on every inch of her skin; the bruising and dried blood decorated her like war paint.

Alone, she thought. *Trapped.*

For once in his miserable life, it seemed Cyrus Ironwood had told the truth.

But the last thought lingered as a question. Slowly, she unknotted the hooded robe and used the relatively clean inner side to try to wipe her face and arms. Her clothes were from the last century, but this was New York, where there was always something or someone more interesting to look at.

She tried to swallow the taste of smoke and blood in her mouth, and forced her eyes up to take in the familiar empty stairwell.

This was the passage that had taken everything from her. The same passage that had opened up a link to the past and carried her over land, across oceans, through time. She had arrived at the place she had departed from, back in her native time. *This is home.*

What was left of it.

Etta rose to her feet slowly, struggling for balance. Memories swirled there, all floating colors and sparks; not of the life she had lived, but of the destruction, the devastation of what New York had become in the altered timeline.

Anger climbed in her as her feet took to the steps, blinding her with its intensity. So much so that she had to lean heavily against the rail to keep from falling back.

Nicholas had done it. He had done this to her, to them, to everyone. Her mother was bleeding to death somewhere that wasn't here—that, Etta was sure of. Her father was alone in his own time, wondering what had become of the two of them. Julian would be left to his own devices. Sophia and Li Min, separated. The remaining Thorns, blown apart and scattered to the winds. For a moment, just one, she thought she might actually hate him.

Why had this been worth it? *Why* had he done this to them?

476

She drew in one breath, then another, trying to control the shaking that wracked her entire body. She smoothed her hair back, wiping the drying tears from her face. As she reached the top, voices drifted to her from beyond the door. The muffled wailing of a child. The endless stream of footsteps squeaking against the floor. But there, inside the stairwell, was nothing. There was devastating quiet.

Etta's breath hitched in her throat as she turned, looking down the stairs again. She hugged the folded robe to her chest. There was no shimmering wall of air to call her back. No thundering drums to announce her arrival. There was no passage at all.

There was only Etta, alone.

AS IT TURNED OUT, THE INSIDE OF THE MET WAS THE SAME, with enough small exceptions that Etta felt as though she were moving through a kind of shadowland version of her city. Exhibits had been moved; the style of clothing she saw around her seemed sharper, shorter, brighter; even the cell phones people carried to snap photos of the artwork were unfamiliar, razor-thin and sliding open like the old mirror compact Alice had carried to check her lipstick. Etta kept her head down and moved steadily past the school groups and couples meandering through the halls, through the blessedly familiar Egyptian wing, down the grand staircase, and out into whatever waited for her beyond the doors.

It was disorienting, the way the skin of the city had changed, even if the bones had not. Etta recognized the older buildings—the old-houses-turned-museums—lining Fifth Avenue, but when she jogged around to the part of the museum that backed up to Central Park, she faced an almost unfamiliar crowded skyline on all sides. Historic landmarks like the Dakota were gone, replaced by ever-reaching skyscrapers that literally blotted out the sunlight and cast impossibly long shadows across the park. The trees had changed color and were burnished with all of their golden autumn glory. Strollers wove through the park's paths.

Men in suits passed men out for a jog in the crisp weather. Women sharing coffee and conversation on nearby benches glanced at others making business calls as they power-walked by. It was a variation on a theme Etta had known and loved, and now she would need to study it to understand the underlying notes that had changed.

She wondered if the city had always been this loud, this clean, this frenetic.

Henry had said the timeline tried to account for inconsistencies and restore as many traveler events as it could. Maybe Etta's life here was what it had been, at least mostly, even if the trappings had changed? She had lost everything and everyone else . . . maybe she could at least have the scraps of her old life?

She felt the pressure of eyes and turned to find a young girl staring up at her, sucking on her thumb as she held her mother's hand, waiting for the light to turn. Etta tried to smile, but she'd noticed others giving her a wide, silent berth, and could only imagine her smell and how out of place she looked, despite having lived the whole of her life on these streets, moving through the veins of the city.

When the little girl and her mother crossed Fifth Avenue, heading home, or to a shop, to some real, concrete destination, the wave of longing and uncertainty and desperation finally broke over her, and Etta began to cry.

You're overwhelmed, but it's all right, she told herself. *You are all right. Give yourself a minute. Give yourself time.*

But there was nowhere for her to go.

There was no one.

Unless . . .

Etta turned, crossing the street just as the signal began to flash. Her jog turning into a full-on sprint through this new, slightly changed version of the Upper East Side. She dodged sleek city cabs in their familiar shade of yellow, delivery bikes, and the parade of evening dog walkers.

The sun was setting at her back as she turned onto Alice's street, and she felt her heart jump at the sight of her brownstone, looking almost exactly as she remembered it, the pots of flowers still alive on her stoop. The front windows were dark, but she tried knocking anyway; she stepped back, and then knocked again, practically bouncing in anticipation.

When there was still no answer, when she was sure her heart would beat its way out of her chest, Etta dug down in the base of the pot of pansies, dumping the dirt out onto the stoop, well aware that Martha, Alice's snoop of a neighbor, was watching her through the window. Her hand had just closed around the spare key hidden at the bottom when Martha's front door opened.

"Etta, is that you?"

She straightened slowly, hoping she'd managed to clean the better part of the blood from her skin. "Yes. It's me."

The old woman, already in her paisley silk robe, pressed a hand to her chest. "My goodness, we were so worried about you and your mother when we didn't see you at the service. It's been months, doll; how have you been? Alice was so excited for you to come back to the city for a visit. And goodness, you look as if you've crawled out of the ground—"

Service.

Months.

Etta had to swallow the bile down, forcing a smile that was more of a grimace. "I've been . . . traveling."

Martha seemed to accept this, at least. "That house has been sitting empty for an age! If you'd like a referral to an agent to sell—"

Etta's hands were trembling so hard, she could barely fit the key into the lock. It was a difficult door no matter the timeline, apparently. She had to shoulder it open.

"Careful, there!"

She stumbled inside, her chest heaving, and slammed the door shut on the woman. Gasping, Etta dropped to her knees, bracing her hands against them until she had the courage to look up. The whole apartment smelled as she remembered it: the cinnamon-apple potpourri Alice favored, and Oskar's pipe smoke, which had lingered long after he'd passed away. Etta leaned forward, pressing her face to the old blue floral rug covering the hardwood, and let it muffle her scream of frustration.

She's dead.

She's still dead.

And her home was as buried as she was—every piece of furniture, every piece of art, every surface was covered with white sheets. Etta breathed in through her nose as she stood, leaving a trail of dirt across the pristine floor in the living room. The floorboards squeaked as she approached the couch and placed a knee on it, pulling the fabric away from the painting hanging there. The city sang its medley of horns and trucks and rattling garbage containers outside, and all the while Etta stared at the impressionist field of red poppies, raising a hand to touch the paint, to brush the dust from its frame.

She moved from room to room, uncovering pieces of Alice's life. Photos of herself smiling naively, unscarred in and out, with her mother; neat stacks of bills; an unfinished novel on the bedside table. Her violin, the one she'd gifted to Etta years ago in the old timeline, rested in its case on the bench at the foot of the bed. Etta sat beside it, flipping open its latches, and for a long while did nothing but stare at it. Brush the glossy surface, breathe in the wood and rosin with her filthy fingers.

"I'll be seeing you. . . ." The words emerged broken, battered. *In all the old familiar places.*

But there was one painting she had never seen before, resting just outside the floor of Alice's closet, as if she'd gone to hang it up and forgotten about it. Having grown up in the halls of the Met, Etta recognized the Renaissance style of the piece, from the pose of the young woman to the warm, vibrant tone of its colors.

It was so unlike the other pieces in the apartment that it drew Etta forward for closer inspection. The ivory dress with its square cut was detailed with gold thread, but otherwise simple in style. The subject's golden hair was plaited down her back, crowned by a circlet of lush red roses. In one hand, she held a map; in the other, a key.

The eyes staring back at her were her mother's.

Her fingers touched delicate brushstrokes, and the roses blurred in her vision like an open wound. *This* was Rose Linden's natural time. Alice had indicated it to her the only way she could, by keeping this relic of the past. Sensing, or knowing, that Rose would never get around to telling her daughter herself.

Etta couldn't push the chill out from beneath her skin, any more than she could stop the shaking that overtook her as the vicious reality set in. She did not think she could ever forgive her mother, not fully, for taking Alice's life, no matter the reason. But she pitied Rose deeply; she felt an unwanted empathy trying to imagine making that decision with the trauma of her past, and the promise of more death to come, ringing her neck like a noose. She understood now that Rose was as much the hero as she was the victim of her own story, blooming in blood.

Etta wanted to speak to her, to understand, to finally clear the air between them, even if it was only one last conversation.

And now it would never happen. At least five hundred years and a single deadly cut had stolen their last chance. If her mother had survived . . . somehow survived, there was no way of finding her.

Etta sat on the carpet for hours, considering her mother, considering the life they'd had together. The sun tracked around Alice's bedroom like the arm of a clock. *Alone.*

Finally, thirst won out. Etta rose, carrying the portrait back across the apartment with her to its new place in the living room. In the kitchen, she went straight for the refrigerator. She'd already noticed that the water was running when she'd stopped to wash her hands and face, and the electricity, too; but she was surprised, somehow, to find that the food stocked inside the fridge had already been cleared out, leaving only a few water bottles.

Who had done that for her? Who had cleaned this place and covered everything inside of it?

Her answer came in the form of a letter, resting on the kitchen table beside two heavy letter-size envelopes. One was labeled with her name, the other with Rose's.

Dear Spencer Family:
My name is Frederick Russell and I have been appointed by my firm
to handle Mrs. Hanski's estate. I was recently asked by Mrs. Hanski to
serve as the executor of her will. As you may already know, the bulk
of it has been left to your family in a trust, but I have been unable to
reach you by means of phone or Netgram to confirm this.

Netgram? Whatever passed for e-mail in this timeline, most likely.

I'm leaving these envelopes here per Mrs. Hanski's request, and
against my better judgment, as I believe they may contain personal
material both sensitive and valuable. Funds to maintain the utilities
and upkeep of this home, as well as its taxes, will be paid out of the
trust until you specify otherwise. Please notify me the moment you
arrive, so that I may explain these next steps to you.

"Still taking care of us," Etta murmured, folding up the letter and the man's contact information. She reached for the envelope bearing her name, and dumped the contents out onto the table, finally taking a seat.

Inside, as the lawyer had expected, were personal documents—a birth certificate, a passport, a Social Security card, and vaccination records. Real, copies, or forgeries, Etta wasn't sure. She turned her attention to the letter itself, hoping for some clue. It was dated July 3.

Dearest Etta,

I don't know where to begin. It has been only minutes since I last saw you. Both you, and to a lesser extent, your mother, have been appearing and disappearing almost at random throughout the years. There have been moments where we are sitting together at a meal, and I'll rise to refill my glass of water, only to return and find you both gone. I cannot tell what has become of the timeline, only that it must be very bad. Your great-grandfather tried to explain the idea of "imprinting" to me once—how the timeline adjusts around the travelers' actions, and when it can't, it leaves impressions of them behind to maintain consistency. I wish I had paid better attention. The great gears of time are shifting, and I am powerless to do anything other than watch.

I remember our encounter in London as if it were yesterday. I remember the look on your face when you saw me—when you spoke of what our life would be together. I believe I have lived it in pieces. Not the whole, perhaps, but I am grateful to have been your instructor, and your friend. I am grateful I saw you become that young lady with my own two eyes. But I am afraid for you now. I've seen the world shift around me in tremendous waves—destroyed one moment, healed the next. I know it must be tied to your search, and I know my own end, the one I saw so plainly in your face, must be near. And so I have taken precautions for you, should you return to an unfamiliar city. These documents should suffice in establishing a life here again, should you choose to.

"Should you choose to . . ." These words strike me as odd, because it seems as if there has always been a kind of inevitability to your and Rose's travels. Those of us left behind, perhaps, can see it

more clearly, the way it all eventually weaves together and connects. There are patterns; loops are opened that ultimately must be closed. The choice is whether or not to open new ones, I suspect.

    Duck, you are the pride of my life. I should very much like to hear you play again, and I hope to see you return to me soon; if not here, then in the past. I've tickets to a concert at the Met in September, a night of Bach, but the only question is whether or not this blasted timeline will straighten out again before then, and weave you back into my days in time for us to go together.

Oh God. Of course the timeline would restore that moment to the best of its ability—she clearly wasn't a part of the concert, but what were the chances that she and Alice had still gone—that she had heard the sounds of the passage—that she had bumped into Sophia and followed it . . . ? Fairly good, if she had to guess.

But if something should happen before then, or if you are reading this years and years from now and I've merely kicked it from age and whatever else life has decided to throw at me, I wish to tell you only this: I love you and your mother beyond time and space.

Etta read and reread the letter before returning it to its envelope. She arranged it at the center of the circle of documents she'd laid out and began to consider her options.

The passage was closed. Whether there was another one in this year, or any forthcoming year, remained to be seen.

If any still exist at all.

Her mother, as far as she knew, was not here. Nicholas was not here. The only name she had that might be able to help was a lawyer named Frederick Russell, and what news he had about this supposed trust, this apartment, might turn out to be bad. Alice and Oskar had done well for themselves, but neither was astronomically wealthy. This fund would not last forever.

But it might last long enough to get her through school. Until she found a job to support herself.

Don't be afraid, she told herself. *It will be okay.*

She would do what any traveler would in a foreign place and time. She would blend into the life around her, to the best of her ability. She would disappear into it, observing, learning, living.

Etta would wait.

The only question now was . . . for what?

NEW YORK CITY
1776

THIRTY-THREE

NICHOLAS AWOKE WITH A MOUTHFUL OF DIRT AND THE sounds of fife and drums battering out a march nearby. Despite the rawness, the crustiness of sleep, he cracked one eye open to take in the gray, hazy light. The dirt beneath him had soaked through his robe and his shirt, and created a freezing cast over his skin.

Cold, he thought.

Pain, his body relayed back.

It was as if that one word was enough to wake it in him, the agony. His left hand burned as he flexed it, bringing it up to wipe the dirt from his face. Looking directly at the wound, he discovered, only made it bloom hotter and quicker. He turned the palm of his left hand up, staring in horror at the slices that ran from the base of his fingers to the heel of his palm, and the mutilated flesh of the burns that covered the rest of it.

Nicholas drew it closer to his face because—yes, *there.* The swelling had yet to subside, and the tender pink of the raw flesh seemed to burn its way down to his bones, but he saw the pattern in it. He recognized the looping lines and nonsensical symbols, the mysterious secrets they held. He carried a nearly perfect brand of the astrolabe on his flesh, and, if his past history with scars was any indicator, likely would for the entirety of his life.

The white light—

All at once, the memory pierced him and he jerked up out of the mud with a desperate gasp. He ripped the white robe, or what remained of it, off his person and threw it as far as he could manage with an arm that felt like mortar. It fluttered like a great white bird, sailing over the edge of the land, into the familiar gaping mouth of the river.

His right arm swung freely, with a strength it hadn't had in weeks. "No," he breathed out. "It cannot be. . . ."

The ring was missing from his finger.

Nicholas turned and turned again, his gaze passing over the trees around him to the lively sounds of war emanating from the Royal Artillery Park just beyond. From where he stood, he could make out the lines of drilling soldiers, their red coats made more vibrant by the odd, stormy gray light. He searched out the passage, strained to pick up its usual rumble.

He could not hear a thing.

Holy God.

Gone, as if it had never been there at all.

He paced through the small spread of trees in circles, as if expecting it to pop up like a snake disturbed from its hole.

He'd done it. The pressure at the center of his chest sharpened, unbearable.

It is finished.

And Nicholas wasn't just alone now; he was *alive*. He was whole, as if the closing of the passages had burned the poison from his body, wiped the last weeks away like a stain on his life. He found himself instinctively reaching for his memories, to cradle them close on the off chance they might be taken. Carried off, the way the crimson and gold leaves falling around him were eased along by the wind.

Nicholas stood still, simply breathing, trying to grip the life around him. All of his decisions . . . they had all been based on hypotheticals, speculation. Knowing that death was walking two steps behind him, it had felt somewhat like trying to shape air. The actuality of what would come had never felt substantial until this moment.

He could not simply reach for Etta, or turn to Li Min or Sophia, or make certain Julian had come through it all unharmed. He could do nothing but stand there, his thoughts drifting through the growing void inside of him like clouds.

It had to be done. It had to end.

Perhaps Sophia was right, and he was a coward for giving up on his life, even to serve this end. He certainly was a coward for choosing this finality while he believed he wouldn't live to see it affect him.

"You there!"

Nicholas looked up, meeting the gaze of a regular patrolling the edge of the Artillery Park. The man was young, younger than himself, and while there was suspicion embedded in his expression, there was also genuine concern.

"What business do you have here, sir?"

Nicholas straightened, clearing his throat. "I . . . came to appreciate the view. My apologies."

"I see," the soldier said, but a new tone in his voice left Nicholas wondering what, precisely, he *saw.*

Likely thinks I've escaped to freedom. The state of his clothing, his wounds; they all spoke to that very notion. The thought sent a prickle of alarm from the base of his skull down his spine. He hadn't merely returned to this era, he had been swallowed by it, sent back to drown in all of its hypocrisies, its cruelty. To be . . . *muzzled* by it. What proof did he have to offer this man if he was pressed on the matter?

His freedom papers, which he had carried with him every moment of his life after Hall had procured them on his behalf, were gone. Unless the original timeline was severely altered to something beyond what he'd known, the only copies were with the captain, presumably out at sea or imprisoned, and in his former employer's office in New London, Connecticut.

The all-too-familiar bitterness rose in Nicholas's throat like bile, and he fought to keep his expression neutral. He had faced darkness, shifted the timeline, and traveled to the ends of the world, and yet—his word would never satisfy those who believed he should still be in chains.

But Nicholas did not cower. He did not turn and run, though his instincts begged him to reconsider. He was a freeman—here, now, and everywhere. Any man who dared to question the point would be met with equal malice.

"Move along, then," the soldier said, returning Nicholas's nod with one of his own.

And so he did. What spare gold Ironwood—*Ironwood!*—had insisted he carry on his person as heir bought him a clean shirt, a buttonless coat, a skin for water, and a bottle of whiskey—the latter both for courage and, moments later, to clean the searing wound on his hand. The fact that he remained standing long enough to bind it with a clean cloth and did not soil himself in front of the entirety of the Dove was a miracle in its own right. The Dove's innkeeper was none too pleased to see him reappear, and all too happy to send him on his way again with the small bag of belongings he had abandoned in his hurry to follow Etta through the passage to London.

"Here it is," the man said, tossing it to him. "Kept everything you and your party left behind. Wouldn't dare to cross that man."

Nicholas lifted a brow. It looked full, but he had no doubt what few valuables were inside had been carefully assessed and possibly taken. Still, he thanked the man profusely, shifting the bag to his left hand to dig in his pocket for one last gold coin.

The flash of color and sight and sound at that touch blew him back off his feet. A crack of thunder whipped through his skull. He saw the tanner in Charleston he'd purchased the bag from years ago, as if the old man were standing directly in front of him. The shop began to take form, as if dripping into place around him, smearing down over the tavern's tired walls. There was the pressure, the insistent tugging at his core. . . .

Holy God.

He dropped the bag to the floor, feeling as if his bones were on the verge of turning to sand. The Dove's owner leaped back at the moment Nicholas did, his eyes narrowing in suspicion.

"Thought I heard . . . a rat," he said, his voice sounding far away. "In the bag. Just now."

The man tilted his head toward the door. "Best be off, then."

Nicholas stooped, hesitating a moment before picking the bag up again, this time with his right hand. When he was sure the world wasn't about to shatter to pieces around him, he made quick strides toward the door and stepped out into the cold grip of the late-October air. His skin felt as if he had been sitting too close to flames, and rather than see his original plan through—wait and see if he might be able to convince a passing wagon to let him trade work for a ride in the direction of Connecticut—he wandered farther down the road, away from the Dove, from the Royal Artillery Park, until the only sounds were the birds in the old oak above him and his thrumming heart. He pressed his back against the tree, sliding down until he sat again, his palms turned up against his knees.

That was a passage.

Impossible.

With considerable care, he went about the work of unwrapping his burned hand again, laying it side by side with his right one. He looked at the mark of the astrolabe on his skin, the raw, blistered, and scabbed image of it. *I saw the past.*

More than that, there was no other way to describe it, except to say he had felt himself begin to *go*. The world had shifted around him, and if he had only reached out, held on, the darkness would have reached out and taken him.

"Don't be ridiculous," he said, because Sophia was not there to.

But . . . how to test this? He needed to prove himself wrong. Remus Jacaranda's explanation for the astrolabe rose in his memory, creating a quake of horror in him: *to create a passage, legend holds that you must have the astrolabe, but you must also have something from the time and year you wish to go.*

He sorted through his bag, searching for something he might have procured in Nassau over the past year. The weapons were gone; the buckle from his shoe, sold; everything—

Everything except the thin leather cord around his neck, the one that held Etta's earrings and a small, broken bead. He reached up with his aching hand and closed his fist around it, letting his eyes slip shut.

The first drip of color brought the turquoise of the clear, pristine water; the next, the ivory sands of the beach; the third, the unstoppable, vibrant green of the palms that had shaded him and Sophia on their spot at the beach. The air began to stir, pinching at each of his muscles, until, in the distance, that dark spot appeared, twisting, flying toward him. Nicholas forced himself to stay in place, to meet that darkness as it came alongside him, gripped him by the collar, and dragged him forward.

There was nothing to do save surrender himself to the sensation of being buried alive. The darkness was as oppressive as the nudging pressure that raced toward him from every direction, and the high whistle accompanying it trilled ceaselessly, even after he was launched forward into sunlight and sand, the briny scent of the ocean rising to greet him.

"Bloody *hell!*" he swore, staggering to his feet. The tide rushed in behind, crashing against the beach and sending up a spray of foam that whipped him back to his senses.

"Aye," said a familiar voice behind him. "I think that's about the right of it."

Nicholas spun around, half-desperate with hope. There, standing less than three yards away, surveying the spot where he and Sophia had made camp, was Captain Hall.

His unruly whiskers had grown in, a stark contrast to the neat queue of his hair. The afternoon sun drove nearly all traces of silver from it, creating a crimson halo around his skull. Nicholas found himself choking on his next, surprised laugh. The Red Devil, alive and well and stalking toward him.

"What are you doing here?" he managed to rasp out. His legs had not quite steadied enough to gallop the distance between them as he wished. It was left to Hall to come to him, to take careful, obvious stock of Nicholas as he approached.

"Correct me if I'm wrong, Nick, but we were to expect you in New London 'shortly,' or am I misremembering?" His voice, while not harsh, bore an edge beneath its cheerful note that Nicholas recognized all too well.

"Did you receive any of my letters?" Nicholas asked in a ragged voice. He thought his heart might blow like a grenade in his chest. "Everyone—Chase—are they all alive? Sound?"

Hall took a step back, startled possibly for the first time in his life. "There have been a number of shifts; I've felt them all pass like storms. But, Nick, nothing's happened to us. Not in this timeline, at least."

Nicholas pressed his face into his hands and laughed and laughed until he was so near to tears he practically choked on them.

"Nick, my God, come here, come—is it as bad as all that?" Hall said. "We were worried for *you*. Tell me what's happened!"

When he steadied himself, Nicholas said, "I ran into . . . unexpected circumstances."

"Unexpected circumstances?" Hall placed his hands on his heavy

belt, the flintlocks and flasks swaying as he began to pace. "All along, I'm hearing stories, terrible stories—the kind that put a guardian ill at ease. The winds of change over the later centuries were foul enough for word to reach me at sea. Imagine my surprise *again*, lad, as I arrived here to question Ironwood's guardians about whether or not they'd taken you into their custody, only to find them all a-fluster over that very same passage disappearing. *And then*, here you are, appearing right out of the air."

Nicholas fell back, shaking his head, staring down at his burned palm.

"God defend us!" Hall said, seizing his wrist, turning his palm up. "Lad—what is this? What's happened to you?"

Nicholas blinked fiercely, trying to reconcile the torrent of disbelief. Hall wrapped an arm over his shoulder. "It is over now. All of it. He's dead. The passages have closed."

His adoptive father took his meaning instantly. Shock coursed through him.

"You'll tell me on the way, then," Hall said. "And tonight you'll dine with Chase and the crew. They'll be beside themselves to see you well. Nicholas, *I* am beside myself to see you whole."

The emotion that wove through his heart at the thought made his chest impossibly tight. He had dreamt of that moment. But he had dreamt of many others as well.

"That is just it," Nicholas said, looking down the beach. "I'm not sure I can rightly say that I am."

THE STORY EMERGED IN FITS AND STARTS OVER THE COURSE of weeks, as the *Challenger* prowled the Atlantic for new prey. Nicholas supposed some part of him felt that, if he did not acknowledge what had happened, the past weeks would eventually be consigned to memory and stop haunting his waking hours.

Of course, he was never so lucky.

The Revolution continued as it had before; the men of the crew sang songs as familiar to him as the sky; his routine of work became the very plaster that kept him together. Everything had a rhythm, he realized; a recognizable ebb and flow. Love, separation. Work, rest. Pain, rum.

Hall granted him a wide berth, with a patience that somehow shamed Nicholas into feeling like a child. But even that had its limits. His questions—about what had happened, about what would happen—became more pointed. Nicholas found himself grateful for the ever-constant presence of the crew. It provided him with cover, a legitimate reason to not speak of it. As a guardian, Hall was the only one who had ever possessed a key to their hidden world. And now, he was the only one who knew the girl who'd emerged in the smoke and chaos on the *Ardent*, the very same one who had charmed her way into the hearts of men who no longer remembered her.

So he smiled with Chase; he allowed the gentle rocking of the sea to cradle him; he relished the feeling of warm sunshine spreading its fingers through his dark coat as he walked the length of the deck on watch. The sea, he knew, was his remedy. And time, no longer an enemy, simply existed in tandem with him, not to vex him. Only occasionally did he feel the tug of something else deep inside of him, the burn of the healed scars in his hand.

But sometimes, when he was tired after a day's work, or deep into his cups, or when he let the strict discipline of his heart lapse, he was clumsy with his words.

"Looks like a packet boat in the harbor port," Chase said, handing him the spyglass. "They might have news of the war for us, then."

The crew was restless for a night on shore in Port Royal, but Chase had grown hungry to track the progress of the war, and the growth—or lack thereof—of the Continental Navy. They'd narrowly escaped pursuit by a seventy-four-gun man-of-war only days prior, and Chase was still stewing in the disappointment of the missed fight. His fingers drummed now against the rail like a war summons. Impatient for something he'd yet to articulate.

"When did you become such a Whig?" Nicholas asked, glancing up at his friend's face. "Surely you're not that eager to hear about Washington's latest defeat."

Nicholas was, in fact, rather curious to see if anything had been altered in the course of the war, due to the timeline shifting to its original state. But he was equally as frightened to search out the answers.

"He wasn't *defeated* on Long Island." Chase's lower jaw, heavy with blond whiskers now, jutted out as his pale blue eyes narrowed on Nicholas. "It was a strategic relocation of his forces."

Nicholas laughed, his first true laugh in quite some time. "Now you sound like Etta, turning over manure and calling it soil."

Nicholas did not understand the rise of Chase's brows, the suggestion tucked into his smirk. *"Etta?"*

The spray of seawater against Nicholas's face did nothing to ease the rush of hot blood there, the clench of his heart. "That is—"

"Ehhhh-tah. *Etta, Etta, Etta.*" Chase toyed with the name, rolling it over his tongue. "Who is this lovely Etta? Oh, do not be cross with me about that—of course she's lovely, if she caught your eye. Where is she? In Charlestown? Is *that* who was keeping you from us?"

Nicholas pressed his hand to his throat, pulling the tie loose to bring more air into his chest. Hall was a guardian, but Chase and the rest of the crew were not. And now there was no recognition at all on Chase's face as he spoke, as he'd turned Etta into a stranger.

"I said to the others, a simple sickness would not have kept Nick from the fight, I did! Tell me, did she issue tender . . . ministrations?"

He closed his eyes, the feel of her smooth cheek against his own still so close to him. The gates were down now, and the flood of feeling and memory devastated him as any hurricane would. His mind had not let him dream of her, unless it was a nightmare—her mother slowly bleeding to death, her wrenching sobs, the future she returned to alone.

He was caught by those thoughts, hooked clean through his center, and he could no more escape being wrecked by them than he could avoid Chase's concerned gaze.

"Nick," Hall called from behind him. "A word, please."

Chase put a hand on his shoulder, but Nicholas dodged it neatly, his eyes fixed on the black ribbon that gathered the captain's faded red hair. He trailed several steps behind him to the cabin, and let the man shut and lock the door behind him. Without needing to be prompted, Nicholas took one of the seats in front of the imposing table that served both as a place to eat supper and a place to spread out the charts and maps.

The captain pressed a glass of amber liquid in his hand, and came around to lean against the desk. Nicholas sniffed at it, but was too wary of the knots lingering in his stomach to drink it just yet.

"You look worse than when I found you," the captain said at last. "I cannot bear to see you this way. If you won't tell me what's the matter, I'll keelhaul you until you're picking barnacles out of your teeth."

"I've healed," Nicholas said, his eyes on the map of the colonies, on the narrow harbor of Manhattan. "Even my hand."

"However, the bruising runs deep," Hall said. "You told me of your travels, the auction, Ironwood's death. But nothing of what you intend to do now with your . . . newly acquired gift."

"And I never shall," Nicholas said.

"My dear boy," Hall began, crossing his arms over his broad chest, "am I wrong to say that perhaps something unexpected has happened? That, if we were to take account of the night of the auction, we might discover that you walked away with . . ."

"*Don't,*" Nicholas begged, his voice cracking. "Don't put it into words. I cannot understand it any more than I can understand the stars. I cannot . . . It cannot be."

He could not hope for it. If his resolve cracked just once, he would scour the earth for the means to open a passage to Etta, to her future.

And that would defeat the very reason he had destroyed the astrolabe in the first place.

I cannot be selfish. No man is meant to have everything.

His life had merged with the very thing his family had hunted and killed for. This ancient thing—the astrolabe—born again. As stubbornly resistant to death, it would appear, as Nicholas.

Was Etta alive? Was she safe in her future? Sophia, Julian, Nicholas, Li Min . . . all of them flung across the centuries, forever out of one another's reach.

But not mine.

Nicholas batted the thought away, gripping the arms of the chair tight enough for the wood to creak.

"But you worry for the others, don't you?" Hall had read him flawlessly. "It weighs on you, not knowing their fates, when it is within your power to."

My power. When he considered the weight of that, his heart seemed to thunder as the passages had.

"It is not as easy as that," he managed to say. "The passages were the source of strife, the heart blood of it. I would need to open them again, to spend years searching out the others, and by then, anything might happen to the other travelers." The skin of his palm was still stiff, thicker than it had been before. He clenched his fist again, trying to hide the markings burned into it. "I understand so little of what's happened. The terms of it are beyond my fathoming. The ancient ones who toyed with us extended their natural years by consuming the other astrolabes. Is that what's to become of me?"

"Did they bear a mark like yours?" Hall asked. "Or did they consume the power of the astrolabes some other way?"

Nicholas could not recall any such markings on the ancient man, though he vaguely recalled markings of some kind on the Belladonna, who—he was sure of it—had drawn them all to that temple for some purpose other than an auction. The true picture eluded him, but he could guess. He wondered if, perhaps, the alchemist's daughter had survived in the same manner the son had.

He did not care. He didn't care a single whit about them. Nicholas had taken stock of himself and found, in the aftermath, he was a selfish sort after all. He wanted Etta beside him. On a ship, in a home, in a city, in the jungle—he didn't care, so long as her small hand had possession of his own, and he could lean down and kiss her whenever he damned well pleased, which would be often, and always.

He'd been quick to scorn the sickly poets and playwrights who wrote of dying from love, but he saw now that this was a form of grief. A loss that stole some small bit of gladness from him every day until what was left of his heart was as cold and hard as flint.

As cold and hard as Ironwood's.

One could survive without a heart, but a life like that was stunted, like an unopened flower, never receiving the necessary sunshine in order to bloom.

And it was not just Etta. There was Julian, there was Sophia, there was even Li Min, who now owed him two farewells. That was a family of sorts, wasn't it? Perhaps not the most graceful example, but it bore all the necessary ingredients of one: care, concern, friendship, guidance, love.

"I used to dream of traveling, of what it might mean to me—that I might master skills enough to find a place for myself in the world beyond what this time was willing to give me." Nicholas stopped, testing Hall's reaction, afraid of the disappointment or hurt he might see there.

Instead, the captain nodded.

"There is good in it, Nick," he said. "There is wonder. You can sit and ponder the nature of morality and corruption, like all the old, moldy philosophers. But it was never the passages themselves that were evil. It was the way they were used."

"But that's my point. The fact that they exist—that they *existed*—and that some of us have this ability . . . it does not mean we have to travel," Nicholas said. "We do not have to risk causing further instability."

"You're thinking aloud," Hall noted, "but you're dancing around the heart of the matter. You recognize that there is an inherent threat in their existence, that just by being used, they open the timeline up to change. And yet . . . ?"

"These are *families*," Nicholas said. Etta's words that night on the mountain had never left him; they'd only crystallized in his mind. "You did not see the massacre. I don't know how many of us survive now, but it seems a crueler thing to keep apart those of us who did. I never felt the Ironwoods were my own, but I have people now I consider near enough to be my own blood. If others are stranded in their natural times, trapped there . . . How do they go about living their lives, knowing they will never again see the ones they love?"

"I suppose Miss Spencer is included in these ponderings," Hall said, innocently enough. "Perhaps you might make one more passage, to her time? It would allow easy access to return when you feel the call of the sea, or wish to see this old man."

But as soon as that warm thought settled, guilt rose to dash it to pieces. "I cannot. It's . . . Isn't it self-serving? And in truth, I'm not sure I'd be able to reach her at all. To create a passage, I would need something from her time. She is not just from the future—she is from the *far* future."

There was nothing in his possession that had originated in that place, not even Etta's earring. The Lindens seemed to be collectors of the first order, if the home in Damascus had been any indication. There might be something there he could use. So there were two passages needed, at least. How quickly this could spiral beyond his control.

Hall's brows rose sharply as he stroked his beard, considering this.

"If there are as few travelers left as you say, then would it not be easy to establish rules and hold others accountable? It was always my understanding that the greater portion of traveling was done innocently, for the experience of it, or to see the guardians who had to remain in their natural times."

"What you're speaking of is a new system of order," Nicholas said. "Simply considering it is overwhelming. The judgment about where and when to open a passage would fall to me, time and time again."

"And I'm grateful for that," Hall said. "For there is no traveler alive who would torture himself and labor over each decision the way you will. There will be sacrifices, no matter what you decide. You may spend your days tunneling through the years to link travelers to their families, and never know the life of a captain. You may risk persecution for what they'll discover you can now accomplish for them. Or you may choose the dream of your youth, and one day, perhaps, learn to live with knowing your choice has affected more than just your life."

Nicholas took a sharp breath in. "I did not ask for this. I never desired it—I only wanted to live my life as any man would."

It was too much power for any one person to hold. Was this not the *exact* reason he had fought so hard to keep Ironwood from seizing control of the bloody thing? To make a decision to act in his own self-interest, to save only Etta—how was that different from the selfish ends Cyrus Ironwood would have used the astrolabe to pursue?

He would not simply be able to stop after searching for the other travelers. He knew his heart too well, and thanks to Hall's searching, he knew where his mother had been sent after she'd been sold from Ironwood's service. He knew where she was buried. He had been gone, traveling with Julian, the very year she wasted away and went to her reward.

I can save her.

No—*no*—not without risking the stability of the timeline. Bloody hell, he needed to get out of there. Hall was chipping away at his logic, and soon he'd have none left to counteract the greed in his soul. He started to rise, but was startled by a knock at the door.

One of the ship's boys slipped inside at Hall's "Enter!" with a bundle of letters clutched between his hands.

"From the packet boat, Captain," he explained, then dashed back out before Hall could utter a thank-you.

"Am I really as frightening as all that?" the man wondered aloud, cutting the string that bound the letters together. He sorted through them quickly.

"Positively ferocious," Nicholas said wryly, noticing for the first time that the man had spilled ink down his shirt again. "Is that the one who struck you with the spoon on the *Ardent*?"

"No, that wicked little imp refused service—" Hall's jaw clenched suddenly, the words falling away.

"What is it?" Nicholas asked, leaning forward.

"There's a missive in here for you," Hall said, holding up a small yellowed envelope, then turning it backward to show the black wax seal. A single *B*, surrounded by creeping vines and flowers. He felt himself shudder.

"Yes, that's the correct response," Hall said. "This is the Witch of Prague's mark."

Nicholas took it from him, hesitating only a moment before breaking the seal. The smell of earth and greens rose off the page; a look at the date told him the letter was over three hundred years old. The brittle, withered quality of the parchment seemed to confirm this. How it had found its way to Port Royal was anyone's guess.

Darling Beastie,

I told you before that everyone has a master. As you may have sensed the night of the auction, so had I. Not a man, nor a woman, but a

certain dark history which threatened to repeat itself once more,
cycling endlessly through generations, until at last none of our kind
would survive. It is a cunning businesswoman who plucks at the greed
in other hearts, and a wise woman who acknowledges it in herself. I
searched many years for the answer, only to find you. A mere boy. I
have enjoyed watching your progress from afar these many years.

Indeed, a boon has been granted to you. Rather than despair,
consider the fact that this was by my design; that you were tested,
your heart measured and found worthy to bring this ancient story
to an end. The copies of the master astrolabe, when consumed,
prolonged life by hundreds of years. However, my brother sought the
master for its raw power, the ability which you now possess. Had he
seized it, everything would be ash and cinders, with only his chosen
few left to survive his dreams of a total rebirth of the world. With
him, naturally, as its god. The ego, beastie; honestly.

"Honestly," Nicholas repeated, his pulse thrumming in his veins.
Hall's eyes never left him as he read, but he could not bring himself to
say the words aloud.

The only soul deserving of such an ability is one that refuses
everything it desires, in the face of death and great loss, to protect the
lives of the many from untold strife. I applaud your decency, which is
rare and formidable, and something to be prized in a world that has
struggled so terribly to make you aggrieved. Whatever you choose
to do with this gift, take comfort in knowing that it will die with
you. You will live long, but you will not be impervious to harm or
unnatural death. A fine limitation indeed, should you choose to open
the centuries. Or, perhaps, simply seek a single girl. To that end, I
have something useful in my collection. You may find me in a willing
mood to negotiate on it.

The short letter concluded with *As always, your business is greatly appreciated. Please visit again soon.*

Wordlessly, he passed the letter to Hall, who devoured its contents like a man knowingly swallowing sour milk. His brows seemed to inch up his face with every successive line.

Nicholas's mind was a whirlpool, one that threatened to draw him into its depths and drown him forever. This had all been a game between a man and a woman—between a family. No one, save the Belladonna and the Ancient One, held all of the cards, but the truth had been scattered across the generations, waiting for someone to fit it together. He saw a thousand points of light connecting one traveler's life to the next as if they were stretched out in the room before him.

He understood, too, the source of Rose's great plan, its mysteries and contradictions stripped away. She knew—she *must* have known— that whoever destroyed the astrolabe would take its ability into him- or herself. That was the reason she had allowed Etta to be taken into the past, why she hadn't destroyed it herself or merely hidden it for her to find. In Rose's heart, the only one worthy of the power was Etta, in all of her goodness.

Hall leaned back in his chair, a whistling breath escaping his teeth. For a long while, they merely stared at one another, ignoring the ship's bell as it rang for the next watch.

"I knew from the moment our lives crossed, Nicholas," Hall began softly, "that yours would eventually lead to a road I could not follow you down. You have been on it for many years, with you none the wiser. Tell me, aside from saving the others, if you knew that it would not alter the timeline beyond repair, if you released yourself from the prison of right and wrong, what would you do? No—don't argue it with yourself. Just tell me."

"I would save my mother, purchase her freedom, set her up with a comfortable life," he said without hesitation. "But it's impossible. I can't risk an alteration."

"Impossible," Hall agreed, reaching out to take his hand, his eyes lit from within. His words spilled out of him with the force of a river dammed for far too long. "But tomorrow you leave this ship. You travel five years into the past, where you found—will find—me in Norfolk, force me to swear to God to keep this infernal secret, and then, my boy, we do *precisely* that."

NEW YORK CITY
One Year Later

THIRTY-FOUR

ETTA'S DEBUT AS A CONCERT SOLOIST CAME MONTHS AFTER she'd released that dream to the wind and let it soar away for someone else to claim.

"You'll do great. Don't be nervous!"

Etta glanced over at Gabriela. They stood in the wings of the stage, listening to the intermediate orchestra sail through its rendition of Mendelssohn's Symphony no. 4—the "Italian Symphony," as it was also known. They were playing only the first two movements, giving Etta about fourteen minutes to mentally take stock of her nerves and decide whether or not she really did need to throw up or if it would pass, as it usually did, once she was actually onstage.

She forced herself to smile at her friend, giving her a weak thumbs-up before she turned back to listen to the symphony. She breathed in and out, as Alice had taught her, but inside she was a little girl all over again, the one who burst into tears from fright the moment she stepped out onto the stage. It had nothing to do with whether or not she would be able to remember nearly thirty minutes of music, and everything to do with the fact that it was the same piece she should have played six months before with the New York Philharmonic, in Avery Fisher

Hall in Lincoln Center, with Alice sitting directly in front of her in the audience.

"I'm more nervous about the interview for the tutoring gig on Tuesday," she whispered back, needing to bolster herself a bit. Whether Gabby actually believed her was up for debate.

The strings caught her attention again, with a vibrancy and joy that breathed life into the tiers of Carnegie Hall's audience. She felt them stir, responding to the triumphant call of the first movement. And in that moment, she let *herself* resonate with that tone; she let the piece lift her out of the quiet, small existence she led.

It was an odd thing, she'd discovered, to haunt your old life. A year before, Etta had waited until the fourth of November, her eighteenth birthday, before self-enrolling late in the fall semester at Eleanor Roosevelt High School using the meticulous, not entirely truthful homeschooling records Alice had kept on her behalf. For the first two weeks, she'd walked past the music room, daring herself to go in, to see if there could be a place for her in the orchestra.

There was. She very much liked the idea of playing as part of a group, of disappearing seamlessly into a whole, but the challenge wasn't there, and Etta had felt herself settling into a complacency that frightened her. The teacher, Mr. Mangrave, recommended her to the director of the New York Youth Symphony, who allowed her to gladly take a seat left open by some poor boy who'd managed to break both of his arms falling off a bike. After graduating high school and spending the summer teaching violin and waitressing, she had auditioned again for a second year with the program to fill the time that wasn't spent applying for college.

Only sometimes did she let herself go to the Met. On days when it rained, or she was caught in a black mood, or it somehow seemed that enough time had passed to check again. She would always pay the full suggested donation to enter, walk through the exhibits she did not recognize, and sit at the top of the stairwell, waiting.

Now Etta was finished waiting.

The intermediate orchestra moved flawlessly into the second movement. Next to her, Gabby began to shift from foot to foot, adjusting the collar on her black dress. Etta had pulled her own plain, floor-length gown from Alice's closet. She wondered what her old instructor would have made of all this. Sighing, Etta reached up to smooth a stray hair back into her low chignon, and glanced over at her friend.

Gabby was the only other member of the senior orchestra from her school. She seemed determined to befriend everyone, even the shell-shocked blond girl who would only be in school for about seven months, and she had dragged Etta through all of the introductions in the group. She'd walked her home the night after their first practice, just talking, filling her in on the intricate hierarchy of who was who in their school. And then she'd managed to draw Etta right into her family's life, where they had welcomed her like another child, and never once mentioned how odd it was that her mother was constantly traveling and never available to take calls.

It was the oddest thing, because the more time Etta spent with Gabby, the better she came to understand her mother. She caught herself managing that same careful distance Rose had cultivated, not only between herself and her daughter, but with everyone in her life save for Alice. Etta tried to fixate on the memories of the life she'd had with Rose before all of this, but inevitably the image of her on the ground, bleeding, *dying*, was close behind.

The finality of the realization that her father, Nicholas, all of the others, were not just lost to her, but dead, had left her unable to leave Alice's apartment for days. It was easier to think of time, of their lives, as the loop Alice had written of—that, although they were not with her now, they were still alive in the past.

As much as she understood why Nicholas had done it, understanding did nothing to beat back the piercing loneliness, or the devastation of its finality.

There were moments Etta felt suffocated by the secrets and scars, times she'd had to dig her nails into her palm to stop herself from telling Gabby the truth: that her frequent nightmares weren't about stage fright or even failing school, but about ancient cities long dead, deserts, and shadows in a dark forest.

There were nights Etta dreamt of drowning, of sinking further and further into the black heart of the sea. No one came to rescue her.

She'd had to rescue herself.

It was only that . . . now and then, she caught a fragment of a memory long enough to examine it, each a lesson in heartbreak. Nicholas's secret smile in the rain. Henry's eyes, watching her play for the tsar. Her mother's pale hand reaching for her, just as the timeline reset.

The sudden roll of applause startled Etta out of her thoughts. She straightened, shifting her violin out from under her arm, feeling something like a warm buzz move against her skin. The orchestra cleared out through the other stage wing, allowing the senior orchestra members to flood out to claim their seats.

Gabby flashed Etta a huge smile as she stepped out with the others to renewed applause, taking over Etta's post as the concertmaster. The rest of the students whispered words of good luck and encouragement to Etta as they passed by.

"All right, here we go," Mr. Davis said, coming up behind her. "I'm so grateful this worked out—I can't thank you enough for stepping up like this."

Sasha Chung, a celebrated violin virtuoso new to this version of the timeline, had been slated to perform Mendelssohn's Violin Concerto in E Minor for the concert; the idea being, Etta supposed, that Sasha would be an additional audience draw and help further raise the profile of the program. On the way to the airport in Paris, however, she'd been in a car accident that had sent her to the hospital, leaving them without a soloist.

"Thank you for the opportunity," Etta said sincerely.

She liked Mr. Davis; it was easy to return the smile he gave her, to chuckle as he nudged her and whispered conspiratorially, "I think you play it better anyway."

The orchestra fell silent, leaving only a few stray coughs from the audience to fill the darkness.

"That's our cue," Mr. Davis said, motioning her to step out first. Etta ducked around the curtain, half-blinded by the lights at the stage's edge as she approached her spot near to the conductor's stand. Because she knew it would make her laugh, Etta reached out and gravely shook Gabby's hand, the way she would greet any concertmaster, and her friend turned pink with the effort to hold her giggles in. Mr. Davis situated himself at the front of the orchestra, and glanced her way.

She looked out into the audience one last time, at the way the lights under each tier of seating looked like necklaces strung with stars.

In most concertos, there was some small slice of time before the solo violinist entered the piece. But Mendelssohn broke with convention, and the solo violinist was present from the beginning, playing the tune in E minor that he once told a friend gave him "no peace" until he finally situated it in a concerto. Etta had always loved that story. There was something beautifully human in trying to capture a feeling, a fragment of notes, and translating it all into the universal language of music before it fled.

Mendelssohn's Violin Concerto in E Minor fluidly shifted between three movements: *allegro molto appassionato* in E minor, *andante* in C major, and, finally, *allegretto non troppo—allegro molto vivace* in E major.

All right, Etta thought, lifting the violin to her shoulder, *I hope you're listening, Alice.* Because she was going to play the hell out of this piece. She was going to bleed every last ounce of emotion out of it that she could.

Mr. Davis raised his hands.

Etta took a deep breath into her belly.

Felt the ripple of excitement race along her bare arms.

They began.

It was hard to describe exactly what she felt when she played. The best she had ever come up with was a feeling of being whole, though she hadn't been aware something was lacking to begin with. She became a drop in a larger stream, driving steadily forward without hesitation. It was a voice of beauty when her own faltered.

Etta knew this concerto so well that she barely needed to think through the bravura of ascending notes, which led to the orchestra restating the opening theme back to her. By the time she reached the cadenza, moved through its rhythmic shifts from quavers to quaver triplets and semiquavers, her muscles were warm from the ricochet bowing, her blood thrumming. Etta moved with the music, twisting, dipping, eyes closed. Relief flooded her—that she could still feel Alice nearby when she played, that it was still possible to know the joy of it when Alice wasn't there to experience it with her. And she wondered again what had ever been the point of holding back when it felt so good to fly.

Out of the corner of her eye, she saw Mr. Davis relax and lose himself in the piece. When she hit her first brief rest, Etta risked a glance out to the audience. Something pale caught and drew her gaze to the right end of the front row.

Rose.

The word swung wildly through her mind. But she was impossible in every way, by every definition: impossible to tame, impossible to capture, impossible to stop.

Her mother wore a navy dress, the bandage around her throat half-hidden by a scarf, gazing up at Etta with a faint smile on her face. Etta sucked in her next breath as a quiet gasp, the sight of Rose working through her like a lightning bolt, stunning her so greatly she nearly missed her next entrance back into the piece. But once she'd seen her, Etta found she couldn't stop looking at her, at her mother's expression of pride. When Rose turned to look to the other end of the row, Etta nearly dropped her violin.

Henry sat on the edge of his seat, his elbows braced against his knees, his hands covering his mouth, as if trying to hold something—some word, some feeling—in by force. Etta's heart began to pound, and she felt as if she were rising off the stage as she coaxed the music from her violin. She wanted to shut it off, that swell of emotion in her chest, but the moment she saw the light catch the tears in his eyes, Etta had to look away to keep from crying herself.

How?

The tempo picked up again as they flowed into the second movement, and the question was lost to the flurry of notes—but then the rest came, and she looked again, searching for their faces to ensure that they were still there.

The key changed from the E minor opening to a slower C major movement as they moved into the *andante*. The tone shifted to A minor, becoming darker. Her accompaniment took on a tremulous quality that required the entirety of her attention before they shifted back to the C major theme and glided to a serene conclusion.

They're here.

How are they here?

After the second movement came a fourteen-bar transitional passage back into E minor for her and her fellow strings, and Etta braced herself for the fast passagework of *sonata rondo* form. When she looked up from her strings, her eyes drifted to the back of the auditorium, where a lone, shadowy figure leaned against the wall. Etta squinted, trying to make out the face. The set of his shoulders . . . the way he held his head—

As if sensing her gaze, he leaned closer to the dim light fixture on the wall behind him.

And suddenly, Etta knew joy. It passed through her like a thousand fluttering feathers.

She felt it explode inside of her as the orchestra moved as one through the effervescent finale, and the music became demanding again. Her mind could scarcely keep up with her fingers, and she had to tell herself, *Slow down*—she had to tell herself, *Don't rush*—

Nicholas.

Etta soared through the ascending and descending arpeggios, trying to keep herself rooted to the stage, to the music. By the time she reached the frenetic coda, she was smiling, near to bursting with the rapid way her world had colored itself back in. She was playing now for the world to hear, and it didn't matter that she might never have the opportunity again, it didn't matter that the still life she'd built for herself over the last few months was on the verge of collapse. Etta reached the final note and felt as if the roof had cracked open and finally let the starlight back into her world.

She couldn't hear the applause over her own heart. Some part of her remembered shaking Mr. Davis's hand, him saying something to her that was lost as she turned to thank the orchestra. Gabby had to point to the front of the stage to remind her to take her bow.

Etta was the first one off the stage, setting her violin down in its open case backstage and bolting to the green room, and then to the west gallery, which ran along the auditorium seating. The man working the concession stand looked up, startled by her sudden, frantic appearance as she moved past him, exiting at the back of the house and all but exploding through the doors into the lobby.

Nicholas stood a short distance away, hovering near the closed ticket counters. To anyone else, he might have been the portrait of nonchalance, but Etta read the uncertainty in his stance as he tried to take in the lights, the sounds of this world around him. He kept one hand tucked into the modern, relaxed black slacks he wore; he used the other to smooth down the front of his crisp white button-down.

"Hi," she managed.

"Hi," he said, sounding slightly out of breath himself. "That was . . . astonishing. *You* are astonishing."

She took another step toward him. Another. And another. Slowly, until he could no longer stand it, and met her halfway. Etta felt unbearably raw, as if her chest had been cut open and her swollen heart was there for all to see.

"And you're . . . here."

The smile that crept across his face was mirrored in full effect on her own. "I am."

"And . . . my parents?"

How?

Nicholas laughed softly. "We might have been here to greet you before the start of the concert, but neither could agree on how best to arrive, and by then, there were few seats left to be had."

Etta was almost dizzy with the sight of him after so long. "I don't understand—the passage closed."

He slipped his left hand out from behind his back and turned the palm up to face her. What she saw there was a scar, a whole network of them, that crisscrossed and wove through one another, creating what looked to her like . . .

"The astrolabe," she breathed, reaching out to grip his hand, to take a closer look. He'd been holding it when it was destroyed, keeping it in place.

"It took me some time, pirate," he said quietly, stepping close enough to her that she could see his pulse flutter in his throat. "To find your father in Moscow, and your mother in Verona, and wait for her to be strong enough to travel once more. Li Min did something to keep her breathing before we were all scattered across the years. I'll not pretend to understand, and while it's cost her the ability to speak, she

is whole, and well. Then there was the not-insignificant matter of find-
ing something from your time to create the passage here. A separate
journey unto itself entirely."

Etta was so close to him now that she had to crane her head back
to look up past the strong line of his jaw into his beautiful face. "What
did you use?"

He dug a hand into his pocket and pulled out a cheap plastic key
chain with the I ❤ NY logo, dangling it in front of her. Etta laughed,
taking it from him. "Okay, I need this story."

Nicholas's smile was so unguarded, so freely given, she nearly cried
at the sight of it. "The Belladonna had it in her vast collection. She was
attempting to fetch a king's ransom for it—or another favor. The result-
ing destruction to her shop as your parents dueled for who had the right
to take the favor caused her to throw it at me and banish us."

"You're joking."

"Sophia called it the most breathtaking display of stupidity she's
ever witnessed—and passes along her regards," he said.

"So you tracked down Sophia," Etta said, understanding. "And
Li Min?"

"We separated only so she could search for her on her own." His
hand hovered above her face for a moment, tracing the shape of it into
the air. His throat jumped as he swallowed hard, bringing the tips of his
fingers to brush the loose hairs back out of Etta's face.

Etta wanted to always remember the look on his face as she kissed
his smiling mouth, kissed his jaw, kissed his cheek, whatever part of
him she could reach, until she felt like she could dissolve into scattered,
incandescent light.

"It was my turn," she said at last. "To find you."

"I consider us remarkably even on that score," he said with a soft
laugh. "But I thought, perhaps, you might like to accompany me to find
the others who might be in need of rescue?"

Etta took a small step back, feeling hope shimmer around her like a trembling note.

"You're opening them all," she breathed out.

He nodded. "At least, trying to bridge those gaps between what was, what is, and what should be. I think we'll try again. The families. I think we ought to make a life of it, and if there's a better way, I think I should very much like for you to help me find it, Miss Spencer."

She stroked the scarred skin of his palm again, letting her fingers slide down to interlace with his. A thread of doubt wove through the swirling mass of joy. Nicholas ducked his head to meet her gaze, and she saw the question in his eyes.

"Miss Spencer," she said softly. "Is that who I am?"

Over the last year, she'd tried to piece together her old life, only to find that most of its pieces no longer existed, and the ones that did exist felt like they might choke her if she tried to wear them again.

"You could be a Hemlock, as I could be an Ironwood; or you could sign your name with Linden, as I might sign mine with Hall. Or perhaps you are Miss Spencer, and always will be," he told her, his thumb skating over her cheek. "Or you could choose, one day, to be a Carter. Or we might be nothing beyond *you* and *I*, and be done with this business of names once and for all, for they have never once had a true bearing on who we are or who we intend to be."

And with that, the tension bled from her limbs, and the knot of confusion in her heart finally loosened.

"Then, yes, I think I should like that very much, too," she said, mimicking the formality of his tone. "But first . . . there's someone we need to see."

He nodded, plainly curious. "Name the horizon, and it's ours."

By the time the auditorium doors opened, they were gone.

LONDON
1932

EPILOGUE

THERE WAS A MAN IN THE GARDEN, HIDDEN BEHIND MAMA'S rosebush. She noticed him only because the sun was setting, but the gold of his long robe caught the light and seemed to burn behind the branches and bramble like a sunrise. And because she, too, was hiding in the garden; only, she was the one smart enough to choose to crouch behind the hedge.

There were always travelers arriving without warning, and never dressed properly. Fewer now, and soon none, if Grandpapa had his way.

You're in the twentieth century, she wanted to whisper to him. But when he turned, she did not recognize the stranger's face—not from memory, and not from any of the books of photographs her parents had compiled of the Ironwoods, Jacarandas, and Hemlocks for her to memorize.

The only reason to hide was for fear of being discovered, and the only reason to fear being discovered was if you'd arrived with bad intentions.

Rose drew herself deeper into the hedge, but the man heard the subtle shift of the leaves. He slowly turned his head toward her, revealing himself through the flowers. Her Mama had declared her brave so many times, but Rose found she could not move, not with his eyes locked on her face, glimmering like gold coins.

It was painful to look anywhere else. She saw only pieces of him. A long, thin nose. The skin over the curve of his forehead; tight, the way a snake's might be. Neither handsome nor hideous. Something else entirely.

"Hello, child," he called softly. "Are you frightened? I have only come to help you."

Rose knew the response to this was to run back into the house and call for Grandpapa. But she could not look away from him, the way his skin glimmered with light as he came toward her. His footsteps made no sound as they passed over the stones and grass.

Rose crossed her arms over her chest, shrinking back against the high wall that separated their town house from the neighbor's.

"S-stay back!" she ordered, reaching down to pick up a stone to throw.

The man's gliding path came to a halt in front of her. He towered, taller than any man she had ever seen, but he cast no shadow over her. Standing there, staring into his eyes, Rose felt only . . . warm. The hungry parts of her were suddenly full, calm. For a moment, she could not remember the reason she had come into the garden at all.

"I would never harm you," he told her, his voice drifting between her ears, soothing like an ointment over a cut. "There is such sorrow in your heart. Tell me, have you lost someone?"

She hesitated, but felt herself nod. "Mama. Papa."

"Death is an enemy few defeat," he said, coming closer. "But there is a way to save them, child. They should never have died."

Rose felt her eyes sting with the truth of his words. Her voice wobbled as she asked, "How?"

"There is a special object your family possesses. It is the key to saving not only your dear Mama and Papa, but all those around you."

Rose shook her head, trying to bring her hands up to cover her ears. Her arms would not move, not while the man's words wove around her, coiling and coiling around her until her chest was too tight to breathe.

No matter how hard she squeezed her eyes shut, Rose could not shut out images of the things he spoke of. Each word painted the images inside of her mind. Smoke, not the smell of wet grass, filled her lungs. Something hot and metallic-tasting filled her mouth and nearly choked her.

A cool hand closed around her wrist softly, leading her. It was only when Rose heard the distant honk of a horn that she realized she was standing at the open gate, the edge of the darkened street. She tried to tug her hand free, but there was a fever in her, painful and cloudy. His face was blotted out in her vision, a smear of ivory and gold.

Grandpapa.

"All I need is that special gift your family was given. Only that, and you can save everyone. *You.*"

The images raged through her now, flickering like colored film. Mama, Papa, the blood, a great city shuddering with flames, an explosion, bodies charred to bone and piled as high as mountains, her hands spilling over with tar, a rising dark river of drowning animals, children, blades flashing, tearing through skin and bone—they burned their way through her, searing her mind. The pain slammed into her, plucking and pawing and tugging at her until blackness rose in her vision and she felt hands cupping her back, her legs—

The astrolabe. The golden disc. Grandpapa had drawn it for her to see, but she had never touched it, never seen it pass through the house.

She realized she had been saying all of these words aloud when the man, at the end of a long tunnel, nodded.

"Rose!"

That voice . . .

"Rose!"

That was . . . Rose tried to think of whom the voice belonged to, but nothing existed outside of the man's face, the long, elegant fingers that stroked her cheek.

"Rose! Where are you?"

Afraid.

There is a place where you will never feel hurt. Where you will become strong.

The words slithered through her, unstoppable. When she opened her eyes again, the street was gliding past her, streaked with night.

"Rosie! Rosie! Come out, Rosie, this isn't funny!"

Alice. Why did she sound so far away? Why did she sound so frightened? *Who is hurting Alice?*

The man's face came into focus, glowing against the darkening sky. It felt good. So easy. So very safe here. He would protect her. He would make her strong, like Mama.

But who would protect Alice?

Rose struggled, squirming to break from his grip. He did not put her down. If anything, his grip tightened and, all at once, the soft blanket of contentment he'd wrapped around her was stripped off. Rose, suddenly, was fighting. Kicking, clawing, slapping, screaming. The images of death and destruction slammed into her again, tearing through her mind, but she did not stop. Rose screamed until her throat turned raw and she fell to the ground on her hands and knees. The darkness swelled up around her, over her head, crashing down the way she'd seen the tides of fire break over an unfamiliar city.

"Rosie!"

"Rose!"

Alice. Grandpapa. Someone—anyone—please—

Help me.

W HEN R OSE WOKE, IT WAS TO SUNLIGHT AND JASMINE, ON A bed of cushions and silk, centuries and continents away. She remembered Grandpapa easing her up, carrying her through the passage, but her mind had been soft with sleep.

Her heart began to beat madly when she saw that neither Nanny nor Grandpapa were with her. This was a room she'd never seen before.

He took me. The words were like claws in her mind. Rose flew to the corner of the room, crouching down, her arms above her head. *He's come back for me.*

The breath whistled out between her chattering teeth. For a moment, Rose could not move at all, not even to swallow.

But then she remembered.

Grandpapa's worn face as he'd told her again and again, *Hush, darling, nothing happened, you gave yourself a fright.*

"It wasn't real," she told herself, the way Grandpapa had barked at her when she'd tried to describe the man. "Not. Real."

But then, why could she still feel the sharp press of the man's fingers on her wrist? Why, every time she shut her eyes, did she see that same burning world?

"Stop it," she ordered herself, hating the tremor in her voice. She scrubbed her fists over her eyes. She'd only upset Grandpapa; he'd been so angry at her for wandering away from the house. He'd thought she'd run intentionally, because . . . yes, they were leaving London. He had bought them a new home, far from her mama's garden. She wouldn't upset Grandpapa anymore by crying and hiding like a baby.

He was all she had left.

Rose stood, breathing in through her nose, and ventured outside of her room, exploring the house. She called for her grandfather, for her nanny, but the rainbow of tiles in the enclosed courtyard only echoed her voice back to her.

Safe.

But alone.

Rose returned to the room she had awakened in, searching through the trunks at the far end of the room for books. Instead, she found her small easel and a neat stack of canvases and paint. Nanny had remembered to pack them.

She set everything up, but before she could begin to think of what she would paint, she heard voices on the street below. Pulling back the bedroom shutters, she leaned out. Down the dust-filled alley, the other children were playing some sort of game with a ball, women in rainbow veils and tunics hovering over them, clucking like chickens. Rose scoffed at the sight.

She swung her legs out of the window so that they dangled, pale and long, over the world below. The street emptied and silence returned.

When the tears burned her cheeks, Rose knew they were because of the wind and the heavy dust it carried. It had nothing to do with the man, the dreams of fire and blood. That was all. Grandpapa had told her to be brave, and so she would be. Rose Linden was not afraid, not ever.

"Not real," she whispered again, squeezing her eyes shut.

A *crack* from behind her caught her attention, and Rose turned, searching for Grandpapa's face, or Nanny to call her to supper. She would have even accepted silly, stupid Henry, if he'd be nice just once and not pull her braid. But no . . . she was not supposed to play with the Hemlocks anymore. Rose needed to remember this now. Not with the Jacarandas, either. And never, ever with the Ironwoods.

Instead, there was a woman at the door, staring at her.

"Ma—"

The word was swallowed back down her throat. This girl—this young lady—wore a simple cornflower-blue tunic of sorts, with a short jacket over it. She hadn't thought to do her hair, or even wear a hat, which was most improper.

But she was not like the man in gold. She was nothing like him.

Now that the young woman was coming closer, Rose found herself swinging her legs back into the room. She saw the echoes of Mama's face in the girl's eyes and her mouth. Reaching down, she picked up the small letter opener Grandpapa had left on the room's table and held it up. "Who are you?"

The girl stopped where she was and let out a startled laugh. She held up her hands. "I'm . . . like you."

Her accent was American. Rose had not expected that, either.

"There's no one like me," she said.

The girl laughed. "That's very true. I meant that I'm—"

"*Don't* say it!" Rose hissed, shocked at her carelessness. Anyone might hear. "I know what you are. You're doing a terrible job of it. You didn't even buy the right kind of shoes!"

The girl looked down, then back up again, her face flushed. "Well, you've got me there."

Rose slowly lowered the letter opener. "What do you want? Grandpapa isn't home."

The girl took a step closer. Rose allowed this. She took another step closer. Rose allowed this as well.

"I came to talk to you, actually," the young lady said. "I wanted to see how you are—to talk to you about what happened."

Rose shook her head, slapping her hands over her ears. "No, no, no! We aren't supposed to tell, we aren't—"

"I know, I know," the girl said, crouching down in front of Rose. "But . . . I could use someone to talk to, too. And there's no one I trust more to help me, to keep my secrets."

Rose could not tell her what the man had said. It would be like pulling splinters out from under skin that had already healed over them. It hurt so very badly to think of it.

But this stranger—not her Grandpapa, not any of the other travelers—believed her to be someone to speak to, not speak down to. She liked this idea, that she was strong after all. It was a very sad, hard thing, her Papa had told her, to be a traveler, for there were so very few people who knew what they could do, and fewer still that they could talk to.

"I'll listen," Rose allowed, her voice trembling only a little.

The girl's face clouded, her pale brows drawing together as she knelt down on one of the cushions, watching Rose come toward her, almost in awe. "I'm sorry about your parents. That must have been beyond terrible for you, and you were so brave. I've lost someone I love, too. My heart still hurts, even though I understand why it happened."

Rose stood with her back straight, clasping her hands in front of her as she met the girl's blue-eyed gaze with her own. "I'm not afraid."

"I know you aren't," the young lady said, almost in a whisper, "but I heard that you had another visitor recently, and that some of the things he said might have been upsetting. I promise you, though, everything will be . . . okay in the end."

Rose swallowed hard. Whenever she closed her eyes, she saw that man, the one who'd visited her before they left London. He had told her about terrible things, *horrible* things. She dreamt of what he said, the burns, the suffering—the—the *blood*.

"Will it?" she whispered, even though she knew it was wrong to press about the future.

The young lady nodded. "I promise." She turned toward the corner of the room, where Grandpapa had set up a small easel. "Do you like to paint?"

Rose hesitated a moment, then nodded. She had not painted since Mama and Papa had . . .

She closed her eyes, scrubbed at her cheeks. The girl rose up off the ground and touched her hair gently, stroking it down. "Would you paint something for me? Maybe . . . maybe something from your memory?"

"Something . . . happy?" Rose asked, looking up at her.

"Yes," the girl said softly, taking her hand. "Something happy."

ACKNOWLEDGMENTS

SOME BOOKS ARE BORN MAGICAL AND SHINY FROM THE FIRST draft, but this one proved to be a true labor of love. I'm so grateful for the friendships I've made this year, both with my fellow authors and with my amazing readers, for keeping me going on the journey from first draft to the finished book you're holding in your hands.

First and foremost, I'd like to thank my agent, Merrilee Heifetz, who fights so hard for her clients every single day and is always there to pick me up, dust me off, and set me on the right path. I'm so grateful for your unfailingly good advice, kindness, and patience. Thanks also to Allie Levick for being so reliable and wonderful—I don't know how you stay so on top of things! I'd also like to send some major love to Cecilia de la Campa, Angharad Kowal, James Munro, and the many subrights coagents who have ensured that readers around the world can find my stories. Rock stars, all of you!

Emily Meehan, Hannah Allaman, Laura Schreiber . . . thank you for navigating the absolutely insane world of time travel with me. I'm so grateful for your help in shaping this story and helping me find its heart. Thank you to Andrew Sugerman, for being such an incredible champion (Go Tribe!). Mary Ann Naples, Seale Ballenger, Dina

Sherman, LaToya Maitland, Holly Nagel, Elke Villa, Andrew Sansone, Sara Liebling, Guy Cunningham, Dan Kaufman, Meredith Jones, Marci Senders, and the entire team at Hyperion: you are all so, so, so amazing. I could fill an entire book with thanks for you.

I would have been completely lost this past year without Erin Bowman and Susan Dennard. Thank you both so much for your invaluable thoughts, your support, and for not letting me give up on this story. I'd say more, but we're probably already on Gchat talking . . . and, well, I think you know (#cattleprod). Massive love to Victoria Aveyard for staying up until the wee hours of the morning brainstorming alternate history with me. To Anna Jarzab, I love ya, buddy—thanks for putting up with me and my neuroses all these years, and for being the kind of good friend I aspire to be.

I'd also like to thank Sabaa Tahir and Leigh Bardugo for their caring, much-appreciated check-ins, and for whatever psychic ability they possess that allowed them to know exactly when I needed moral support most. To Amie Kaufman: your guidance through rocky waters is always spot-on, and I'm honored to call you my friend.

A special thank-you to my two favorite Kevins: Kevin Shiau for your help with honing Li Min's character and checking my Mandarin, and Kevin Dua for being kind enough to give me your thoughts last year on Nicholas and his journey. Likewise, my eternal gratitude to Valia Lind for helping me nail the right Russian phrases and to Evelyn Skye for helping fact-check.

Thank you SO much to my family. I love you guys which, duh, you know, but I thought I'd put it in print. (And Mom, I promise Rose isn't based on you.)

Finally, to the readers who came on this journey with Nicholas and Etta: thank you, thank you, thank you. You are the reason I'm able to do what I love, and I'll never forget that. Now go out there and make history.